Cryptoassets

Cryptoassets

Legal, Regulatory, and Monetary Perspectives

Edited by

CHRIS BRUMMER

OXFORD
UNIVERSITY PRESS

OXFORD
UNIVERSITY PRESS

Oxford University Press is a department of the University of Oxford. It furthers the University's
objective of excellence in research, scholarship, and education by publishing worldwide. Oxford is
a registered trademark of Oxford University Press in the UK and certain other countries.

Published in the United States of America by Oxford University Press
198 Madison Avenue, New York, NY 10016, United States of America.

Library of Congress Cataloging-in-Publication Data
Names: Brummer, Chris, 1975– editor
Title: Cryptoassets : legal, regulatory, and monetary perspectives / Chris Brummer.
Description: First edition. | New York : 2019.
Identifiers: LCCN 2019017648 | ISBN 9780190077327 (paperback) | ISBN 9780190077310 (hardback) |
    ISBN 9780190077334 (pdf) | ISBN 9780190077341 (epub)
Subjects: LCSH: Cryptocurrencies—Law and legislation. | Cryptocurrencies.
Classification: LCC K4431 .C79 2019 | DDC 343/.032—dc23
LC record available at https://lccn.loc.gov/2019017648

1 3 5 7 9 8 6 4 2

Paperback printed by Marquis, Canada
Hardback printed by Bridgeport National Bindery, Inc., United States of America

Note to Readers
This publication is designed to provide accurate and authoritative information in regard to the subject
matter covered. It is based upon sources believed to be accurate and reliable and is intended to be
current as of the time it was written. It is sold with the understanding that the publisher is not engaged
in rendering legal, accounting, or other professional services. If legal advice or other expert assistance is
required, the services of a competent professional person should be sought. Also, to confirm that the
information has not been affected or changed by recent developments, traditional legal research
techniques should be used, including checking primary sources where appropriate.

*(Based on the Declaration of Principles jointly adopted by a Committee of the
American Bar Association and a Committee of Publishers and Associations.)*

Contents

Contributors   xiii

1. Introduction   1
   Chris Brummer
       I. Cryptoasset Controversies   3
      II. An Overview of This Volume   5

2. Cryptocurrencies and the Evolution of Banking, Money,
   and Payments   11
   Benjamin Geva
       I. Introduction   11
      II. Money, Payment and Payment Intermediation   12
     III. Deposit Banking, Payment Services, and Paper Money:
          Historical Perspective on Payments Intermediation   14
          A. Antiquity   15
          B. Middle Ages   18
          C. Post-Medieval Era   20
      IV. The Coming of the Cyber-Age: Electronic Payments, E-money,
          and Access to Central Bank Balances   24
          A. The Advent of Electronic Banking and E-money   24
          B. Availability of Central Bank Account Balances and Their
             Equivalents to the Public   27
       V. Cryptocurrencies: Heralding a New Form of Money and
          Payment Disintermediation?   30
      VI. Conclusion   36

3. Deconstructing "Decentralization": Exploring the Core
   Claim of Crypto Systems   39
   Angela Walch
       I. Mainstream Discourse around "Decentralized" Permissionless
          Blockchains   41
      II. The Complex Nature of "Decentralization"   47
     Notable Themes   47
          A. No One Knows What "Decentralization" Means   47
          B. Satoshi Didn't Invent Decentralization   48
          C. Decentralized Does Not Equal Distributed   49
          D. Decentralization Exists on a Spectrum   49

E. Decentralization Is Dynamic rather than Static 50
F. Decentralization Is Aspirational, Not Actual 50
G. Decentralization Can Be Used to Hide Power or Enable
Rule-Breaking 51
H. Calls to Action 51
III. Examples of Concentrations of Power in Permissionless
Blockchain Systems 52
A. Critical Bug Discovery and Fix in Bitcoin Software in Fall 2018 53
B. Bitcoin's March 2013 Hard Fork 54
C. Secret Meetings of Ethereum Core Developers in Fall 2018 55
D. Ethereum's July 2016 Hard Fork 56
E. Hashing Power Concentration and 51% Attacks 57
IV. Using "Decentralized" to Make Legal Decisions about Blockchains 58
A. Decentralization's Uncertain Meaning Makes It Ill-Suited
for a Legal Standard 58
B. Decentralization's Dynamic Nature Complicates Its Use as a
Legal Standard 60
C. If Actual Decentralization Is Now Just a Dream, Wait Till
It Comes True 61
D. Decentralization Veils and Malleable Tokens 61
1. Who Needs an Entity When You've Got a Veil of
Decentralization? 62
2. If People Wield Unnoticed Power, Tokens Are Unexpectedly
Malleable 65
V. Closing Reflections 67

4. Cryptoasset Valuation: Theory and Practice 69
Nic Carter

I. Introduction 69
II. Disaggregating Cryptoassets by Value Drivers 70
A. Unique Access to Network Services 71
B. Asset-Backed Cryptoassets 73
C. Cash Flows from an Underlying Network 74
D. Consumability 75
E. Governance Rights 75
III. Case Studies 77
A. Bitcoin and Its Peers 77
1. Valuation with the Equation of Exchange 78
2. Relative Network Usage Models 80
3. Competing Models of Price-Hashrate Dynamics 81
4. The Cost of Production Is a Determinant in the Value of the
Token 82
5. Hashrate Follows Price 82
6. Joint Determination 83

B. MakerDAO 84
C. Binance Coin 86
D. 0x 87
IV. Conclusion 87

5. Toward a Stable Tokenized Medium of Exchange 89
Alexander Lipton

I. Introduction 89
II. The Banking System 91
A. Overview 91
B. Money 91
C. Credit Money Creation and Annihilation 93
D. Bookkeeping and Transactions 94
E. Domestic and Foreign Payments 95
F. What Is Wrong with the Current Setup? 95
III. Distributed Ledgers 96
A. General Considerations 96
B. Types of Distributed Ledgers 98
C. Cryptocurrency Creation and Transactions 98
D. What Is Wrong with the Current Setup? 99
IV. Stablecoins and Their Taxonomy 100
A. Overview 100
B. Coins Fully Collateralized with Fiat 101
C. Coins Partially Collateralized with Fiat 102
D. Coins Overcollateralized with Cryptos 103
E. Dynamically Stabilized Coins 104
F. Coins Collateralized with Assets 105
G. Narrow Banks as Emitters of Digital Cash 107
H. Mixing and Tumbling 109
I. KYC and AML Considerations 110
J. Privacy 110
V. Conclusions 110
VI. Glossary 111
VII. References 112

6. The Law and Finance of Initial Coin Offerings 117
Aurelio Gurrea-Martínez and Nydia Remolina León

I. Concept, Features, and Structure of ICOs 118
A. Tokens 119
1. The Concept and Features of Tokens 119
2. The Presale of Tokens 121
3. The Crowdsale and Distribution of Tokens to the Public 122
B. Cryptocurrencies as ICO Proceeds 123
C. Blockchain: The Technology behind Initial Coin Offerings 124

D. The White Paper   124
E. Differences between ICOs and Other Methods to Raise Capital   125
II. Regulatory Approaches to Deal with ICOs   129
A. Existing Regulatory Approaches   129
1. Contractual Approach   129
2. Bans   130
3. Security Token Registration   132
4. Comprehensive Token Registration   134
B. Toward a Safe but Efficient System of ICO Oversight   135
III. Accounting and Finance Aspects of ICOs   136
IV. Corporate Governance Issues   139
A. The Concept and Nature of Tokenholders   139
B. Protecting Tokenholders from the Promoter's Opportunism   141
1. Agency Problems in a World of Tokenholders   141
2. Legal Strategies to Protect Tokenholders   143
3. Market Devices to Protect Tokenholders   145
V. Anti-money Laundering Implications of ICOs   146
VI. New Challenges for Privacy Law and Data Protection   148
VII. Insolvency   149
VIII. International Challenges and Cooperation in ICOs   151
IX. Future of Capital Markets, Finance, and Corporate
Governance in a World of Tokenized Securities   153
X. Conclusion   155

7. What Should Be Disclosed in an Initial Coin Offering?   157
Chris Brummer, Trevor I. Kiviat, and Jai Massari

I. Introduction   157
II. ICOs: The Shot-in-the-Dark Investment Decision   159
III. Crypto-Economics and Token Pricing   162
A. Demand-Side Factors   164
B. Supply-Side Factors   165
IV. White Papers as Disclosure Documents   167
V. ICO Disclosure Models: The Logic, Forms and Limitations   169
A. The "Full" Disclosure Model   170
1. Financial Statements   171
2. Description of Token   172
3. Blockchain Governance   174
4. Management and Technology Team   175
5. Secondary Trading   176
6. Risk Factors   177
B. Scaled Disclosure Regimes   179
1. Crowdfunding/Rule 4(a)(6)   179
2. Reg A+   182
3. Private Offerings   183

VI. Beyond Disclosure: "Plain English" Requirements
and Third-Party Validators   184
VII. Conclusion   187

8. Blockchains and Risk Management Infrastructure of
the Derivatives Industry   203
Petal P. Walker

    I. What's a Swap?—A Look at a Basic Transaction   203
      A. An Overview of Registration Obligations   204
   II. How Blockchain Technology Would Transform Derivatives
      Markets   206
  III. The Risks and Rewards of Blockchain Technology   208
      A. Newfound Transparency, Supervisory Potential for
        Regulators   208
      B. Common Risk Concerns Raised   209
        1. Language Gap Risk   209
        2. Technology Risk   211
        3. Permanency Risk   211
        4. Transparency Risk   212
  IV. The Risks and Rewards of Registration   212
      A. The Blockchain Network   212
      B. The Smart Contract Writer   214
      C. The Contract   216
      D. Oracles, Nodes, and Validators   217
   V. Conclusion   217

9. Difficulties in Achieving Neutrality and Other Challenges
in Taxing Cryptoassets   219
Christophe Waerzeggers and Irving Aw

    I. Introduction   219
   II. Challenges in Classification and the Problem of Hybridity   220
      A. Money or Property   221
      B. Securities Tokens   225
      C. Asset-Backed Tokens or Stable Coins   227
  III. Taxing Increases in Value of Cryptoassets and Other Specific
      Transactions   228
      A. Disposal Gains   228
      B. Mining and Forging   230
        1. Proof-of-Work   230
        2. Proof-of-Stake   233
      C. Token Airdrops   234
      D. Hard Forks   236
      E. Employment Remuneration   237
      F. Token Pre-financing   238

| | G. Token Burning | 239 |
| | IV. Conclusion | 241 |

10. Blockchain and Identity Persistence 243
   Alex Marthews and Catherine Tucker
   I. Introduction and Definitions 243
   II. Blockchain 243
      A. What Is Blockchain Technology? 243
      B. What Is the Current State of the Art of Protecting Privacy on
         Blockchain? 244
   III. Digital Identity 246
   IV. Legal Identity and Smart Contracts 247
   V. Narrative Identity 250
      A. Resolving Incompatibilities between Narrative Identity
         and Blockchain Records 251
   VI. Use-Cases 252
      A. Marriage on the Blockchain 253
      B. Money Laundering on the Blockchain 254
      C. Criminal Justice Records on the Blockchain 256
   VII. Decentralized Identifiers and Verified Claims 257
   VIII. Conclusions 258
   References 259

11. Policy and Regulatory Challenges of Distributed Ledger
   Technology and Digital Assets in Asia 263
   Douglas Arner, Ross P. Buckley, Dirk Zetzsche, Bo Zhao,
   Anton N. Didenko, Cyn-Young Park, and Emilija Pashoska
   1. Introduction 263
      A. DLT, Blockchain, and Cryptocurrencies in Asia 264
      B. Recent Developments and Policy Responses 267
   II. DLT and its Applications: Evolution and Typology 272
      A. Centralized and Distributed Ledgers 272
      B. Permissioned and Permissionless Systems 274
      C. Blockchain 274
      D. Technology-Based Trust Solutions 275
      E. Smart Contracts 276
      F. DLT Use Cases and Investment Trends 276
   III. Cryptocurrencies 278
      A. Non-Sovereign: Alternative Currencies and Payment Systems 278
      B. Alternative Currencies: Legal Status and Regulatory Implications 280
      C. Sovereign Digital Currencies and Cryptocurrencies 281
      D. Central Bank P2P/Intermediated Payment Systems 282
      E. Sovereign (Central Bank) Cryptocurrencies 282
         1. Benefits, Opportunities, and Risks 285
         2. Benefits and Opportunities 286

3. Challenges   286
IV. Initial Coin Offerings and Tokenization   288
   A. ICO Typology   288
   B. ICOs in Asia   289
   C. Regulation of ICOs in Asia   293
     1. Outright Ban   293
     2. Regulatory Warnings   293
     3. Application of Existing Securities and Investment Product Laws   294
     4. Is DLT the Problem?   294
V. DLT: Risks and Concerns   294
   A. Transparency Risks   294
   B. Cyber Risks   295
   C. Operational Risks   295
   D. Blockchain-Specific Risks   296
VI. Policy Issues and Challenges: Devising Appropriate Regulatory
Responses to DLT   296
   A. International Regulatory Context   296
   B. A Functional Proportional Approach Balancing Risks and
Opportunities   297
   C. Core Strategy and the Role of International Regulatory
Cooperation   298
Appendix: Regulatory Statements in Asia   299

12. Casting Light on Central Bank Digital Currency   307
*Tommaso Mancini-Griffoli, Maria Soledad Martinez Peria,
Itai Agur, Anil Ari, John Kiff, Adina Popescu, and Céline Rochon
with contributions from Fabio Comelli, Federico Grinberg,
Ashraf Khan, and Kristel Poh*
   I. Basics of Central Bank Digital Currency   309
  II. A Conceptual Framework to Compare Different Forms of Money   310
  III. Is There a Role for CBDC? User Perspective   315
  IV. Is There a Role for CBDC? Central Bank Perspective   317
   A. Social Criteria for Money   317
   B. Can CBDC Balance Privacy and Financial Integrity Concerns?   321
   C. Would CBDC Undermine Financial Stability and Banking
Intermediation?   322
     1. Scenario 1: Risk of Disintermediation in Tranquil Times   322
     2. Scenario 2: Run Risk in Times of Systemic Financial Stress   325
   D. Would Monetary Policy Transmission Remain Effective?   326
  V. Central Bank Research and Experiments   327
  VI. Conclusion   331
References   332
Appendix   338

Notes   341
Index   429

Contributors

Itai Agur is an Economist in the Macro-Financial Division in the Research Department of the International Monetary Fund.

Anil Ari is an Economist in the Macro-Financial Division in the Research Department of the International Monetary Fund.

Douglas Arner is the Kerry Holdings Professor in Law and cofounder of the Asian Institute of International Financial Law (AIIFL) at the University of Hong Kong.

Irving Aw is Counsel (Tax Law) in the Legal Department of the International Monetary Fund.

Chris Brummer is a professor at Georgetown University Law Center and the Faculty Director at Georgetown's Institute of International Economic Law.

Ross P. Buckley is the KPMG Kaw—King & Wood Mallesons Chair of Disruptive Innovation, a Scientia Professor, and a member of the Centre for Law, Markets and Regulation at UNSW Sydney.

Nic Carter is a Partner of Castle Island Ventures and the Cofounder and Chairman of Coin Metrics, Inc.

Anton N. Didenko is a Research Fellow and a member of the Centre for Law, Markets and Regulation at UNSW Sydney.

Benjamin Geva is a professor at Osgoode Hall Law School of York University in Toronto, Canada.

Aurelio Gurrea-Martínez is an Assistant Professor of Law at Singapore Management University.

John Kiff is a Senior Financial Sector Expert in the Monetary and Capital Markets Department of the International Monetary Fund.

Trevor I. Kiviat is an associate at Davis Polk & Wardwell LLP, where he advises on the novel strategic, operational, and regulatory issues facing digital currency-based businesses.

Alexander Lipton is the Chief Technical Officer of Silamoney and a Connection Science Fellow at Massachusetts Institute of Technology.

Tommaso Mancini-Griffoli is a Deputy Division Chief in the Monetary and Capital Markets Department of the International Monetary Fund

Alex Marthews is the National Chair of Restore the Fourth—a nonprofit that campaigns against unconstitutional mass government surveillance.

Maria Soledad (Sole) Martinez Peria is Chief of the Macro-Financial Division in the Research Department of the International Monetary Fund.

Jai Massari is a partner in the Financial Institutions Group of Davis Polk & Wardwell, LLP.

Cyn-Young Park is the Director for Regional Cooperation and Integration, Economic Research and Regional Cooperation Department of the Asian Development Bank.

Emilija Pashoska is a research assistant with the ADA Chair in Financial Law (Inclusive Finance) at the Faculty of Law, Economics and Finance of the University of Luxembourg.

Adina Popescu is a Senior Economist in the Strategy, Policy, and Review Department of the International Monetary Fund.

Nydia Remolina León is a research associate at Singapore Management University's Centre for Artificial Intelligence and Data Governance, and a legal advisor for innovation, digital transformation, and policy affairs at Grupo Bancolombia.

Céline Rochon is a Senior Economist in the Strategy, Policy, and Review Department of the International Monetary Fund.

Catherine Tucker is the Sloan Distinguished Professor of Management at MIT and Research Associate at NBER.

Christophe Waerzeggers is Senior Counsel (Tax Law) in the Legal Department of the International Monetary Fund.

Angela Walch is a professor at St. Mary's University School of Law and a Research Fellow at the Centre for Blockchain Technologies at University College London.

Petal Walker is Special Counsel at WilmerHale.

Dirk Zetzsche is a Professor of Law and ADA Chair in Financial Law (Inclusive Finance) at the Faculty of Law, Economics and Finance of the University of Luxembourg, and Director of the Centre for Business and Corporate Law at Heinrich-Heine-University in Düsseldorf.

Bo Zhao is an Economist in the Economic Research and Regional Cooperation Department of the Asian Development Bank.

1

Introduction

Chris Brummer

Rarely a day goes by where the upsides—or downsides—of various cryptoassets are not discussed and debated by financiers, regulators, or technologists in the world's leading newspapers and social media. And the debates can be intense. For some, cryptoassets come close to a technological panacea. Cryptocurrencies such as bitcoin, or smart contracts on the Ethereum platform, promise to swiftly disintermediate traditional finance, and usher in technological revolutions comparable to the rise of the internet. Meanwhile, for others, cryptoassets are at best fraudulent, and at worst sources of financial instability. Internationally renowned economists, such as *l'enfant terrible* of cryptocurrency skepticism, Nouriel Roubini, do not hesitate to describe proponents as "crypto zealots" and "mentally psychotic," and point to the extreme highs—and lows—experienced in cryptoassets markets in 2018 as proof of the flaws underpinning the currency.

Differences in opinion start with the very name of just what to call these new financial products. This book adopts the most neutral appellation—crypto "asset"—though even it inherently raises its own immediate questions. In conversations about any new technology, especially one that can take shape as an investment, utility, or payment instrument, what you call an instrument can necessarily lead to conclusions about whether (and how) one should regulate it. If it's an asset, commentators immediate opine, shouldn't it be taxed like property? Or if you call it a currency (such as "crypto currency" or "virtual currency"), then conceptually, you think about it just as that—and with all the attendant economic, tax, and regulatory consequences for finance ministries and others. And if you call it something else—say a "derivative" to the extent to which any transaction requires time for the delivery of a cryptoasset due to mining or data processing—another regime or framework will come to mind. In all, if you're not careful, the question one poses about cryptoassets quickly becomes the answer, even when you're just grappling with defining what you're trying to study.

What cryptoassets have in common is that they depend primarily on cryptography and "distributed ledger" technologies to memorialize and track transactions. Cryptography refers to algorithmic techniques used to protect information by encrypting it into formats accessible to individuals only if they possess a special key. Distributed ledgers, meanwhile, are databases that store records through a peer-to-peer network of computers that is not confirmed by any one entity, and is managed by multiple participants.

As will be emphasized frequently in this book, cryptoassets are used in many different ways, and are generally catalogued as comprising either a medium of exchange ("digital money" or "cryptocurrency"), devices for accessing an online service ("utility token"), or investments—or all three at once. As a medium of exchange, cryptoassets can take the form of "digital money," and as such may be accepted by persons and market participants in commerce. By contrast, as utilities, cryptoassets are like tokens in a pinball machine in an arcade—you use them to access something you want to use, whether it be an online game or cloud storage facility. Finally, cryptoassets can also constitute investments, and are even used to raise capital. Most notably, cryptoassets can comprise the consideration that developers give to investors in initial coin offerings (ICOs). In these offerings, investors provide developers with government-backed fiat money, or they might deliver to developers other cryptocurrencies that can be traded in for fiat money. In any event, the actual cryptoassets given to investors in return are investments—and expected to appreciate—and might have investment-like features, providing holders with rights to dividends or more.

The operating system driving the way cryptoassets are transferred, and records stored, is a special kind of distributed ledger system called a *blockchain*, which links transactions together as time goes on and more transactions take place. The amount and kind of information that any particular blockchain can store can vary immensely, and range from tracking ownership of referenced assets among pseudonymous participants, as in the Bitcoin blockchain, to the public identification of payers and payees, along with account balances and other transactional details. Certain kinds of blockchains, such as the Ethereum platform, can additionally utilize "smart contracts," or programmable forms of digital money, where payments are made only when certain conditions are satisfied, such as a date passing or a service having been rendered.

Importantly, blockchains do not record individual transactions one at a time. Instead, series of transactions are stored as data in individual blocks. As a result, rules are necessary to show when and under what circumstances a new block can be added to a preexisting one to create a chain of blocks, or blockchain. The rules relied on to dictate how new information is added to these data structures are collectively referred to as a *consensus mechanism*.[1]

Most of the chapters in this book will explore these concepts in greater depth, from different perspectives, but it is useful to note from the outset that "proof of work" is the name given the consensus mechanism used on most blockchains.[2] In a proof-of-work system, members must provide a valid cryptographic hash for a block, or in layman's terms, guess a series of correct cryptographic games by providing the right numeric values for each.[3] The individual (or computer) that correctly identifies the numbers involved in the guessing game is then confirmed by other members of the network and receives cryptocurrency as determined by the blockchain's protocol as a payment, or reward, for "mining" the transaction.[4] Coins that have been credited to the account of the miners can then be sold or transferred via subsequent transactions.

In some blockchains, an alternative "proof of stake" approach is used to validate transactions. In these systems, it is the user's stake, or ownership of a certain number of cryptocurrency units, that empowers and directs the formation of new blocks, distinguishing it from the proof-of-work system, where new blocks are created by performing a certain amount of computational work.[5] Miners for the system, sometimes called "forgers," are expected to put up their "stake" as a kind of operational insurance for other participants; if a forger validates a fraudulent transaction, she loses her holdings, as well as her rights to forge blocks in the future.[6]

Finally, some blockchains are permissionless, while others are permissioned. A permissionless blockchain allows anyone to participate in consensus operations. Such are thus in a sense both open-access and public. Permissioned systems, by contrast, allow only actors blessed by designated authorities to participate in building consensus and validating transactions.

I. Cryptoasset Controversies

Cryptoassets are, if nothing else, controversial. Cryptoasset advocates cite a number of potential benefits associated with cryptoassets that if realized could prove transformative for the payments industry. Blockchains, for example, are often described as immutable—unable to be edited or deleted—thereby allowing in some (though not all) instances greater security than traditional banking systems. Furthermore, because cryptoassets leverage peer-to-peer infrastructures, they enable applications across borders at low costs, and are poised to transform international remittances.

Cryptoassets are also often supported by highly decentralized blockchains and operating processes, enabling open and transparent points of access for stakeholders; all the while, nongovernmental and private cryptoassets operate independently of central banks, and as such are subject, according to proponents, to less political manipulation.

Finally, many proponents contend that cryptoassets have the potential to disintermediate an oligopoly of intermediaries dominating the legacy financial system. Blockchain technology exemplified by Bitcoin provides a novel tool for untrusted parties to come to agreement on a record of transactions, without using a middleman such as a bank.[7] Similarly, smart contracts driven by the

Etherium blockchain could be used such that money—whether it be fiat or a cryptoasset—is only sent from one party to another when certain conditions are satisfied, such as a date passing or a service having been rendered. A host of manual processes can be automated, reducing or eliminating the need for all kinds of intermediaries such as escrow agents and banks, as well as compliance and claims processing.[8]

Yet cryptoassets pose considerable potential risks as well—and have engendered biting criticisms from skeptics. Volatility and market integrity are common concerns: Investments in cryptoassets were valued at $830 billion in early 2018 before collapsing, losing according to some reports over 75% of their market capitalization. Discoveries of fraud jumped as well, as forcing enforcement actions by regulators.

And although markets for cryptoassets are small, especially when compared to the stock and bond markets, the pseudonymity and weak cybersecurity of many blockchains are raising questions about the implications of cryptoassets for financial stability and money laundering.[9] All the while, the increasing institutionalization of cryptoassets—including plans to integrate cryptoasset technologies into capital markets and central banking—are pushing financiers and regulators alike to closely scrutinize cryptoasset applications and underlying value propositions.

As we will see in this book, cryptoassets are not just novel instruments; they also challenge longstanding economic models and regulatory strategies. Traditionally, supervisors tasked with supervising new markets (or under-regulated ones) have identified and catalogued relevant intermediaries, regulated them as gatekeepers, and issued rules relevant to these gatekeepers in order to achieve goals related to efficiency, investor protection, capital formation, and market integrity. In the decentralized ecosystems characterizing many cryptoassets, however, where anyone can play certain key roles impacting the design and operation of a cryptoasset, such models are difficult, and perhaps impossible, to translate into effective regulatory practice resembling anything like earlier iterations.

The puzzle becomes all the more difficult given the virtual nature of these assets, and the fact that they are digital instruments, tradeable and transferable online. Cryptoassets are routinely released and traded throughout the world, and can be accessed in terminals strewn across jurisdictions and to far-flung parts of the world. Different countries may, furthermore, have very different conceptions as to just what a cryptoasset is, and how it should be categorized and regulated. Galvanizing a global, coordinated strategy is difficult, if not impossible, with stakeholders and even countries initiating the regulatory process from very different vantage points.

II. An Overview of This Volume

Against this backdrop of issues, this collection of chapters, written by some of the world's leading experts, attempts to demystify cryptoassets through a series of different investigations, across economics, law, and the social sciences. Given the economic and legal questions raised, a distinctly interdisciplinary approach is deployed, with experts hailing from law firms, technology firms, the academy, and the International Monetary Fund. With its origins tied to Washington's Fintech Week, and the interdisciplinary Crypto Asset seminar cosponsored by the IMF and Georgetown University Law Center, the volume seeks, like the conference, to provide cutting-edge analysis and understanding of cryptoassets—and cryptoasset regulatory policy—for educated generalists.

The book begins with a history of money and payments. in chapter 2, "Cryptocurrencies and the Evolution of Banking, Money and Payments," Benjamin Geva, a professor at Osgoode Hall Law School, discusses cryptocurrencies in the context of a historical perspective on the evolution of money, payment, payment intermediation, and commercial banking. Geva points at the latter as the catalyst for national and global networks for book-based payments. Geva goes on and distinguishes between two types of scriptural money, each being value held on deposit, facilitating both book-based payments and redemption to fiat money/banknotes. The first is held by the public on deposit with commercial banks which is demotivated in and redeemable to fiat money/banknotes. The second is in the form of claims against the central bank being available to commercial banks. The latter may make their own payments with it and both redeem and purchase with it fiat money/banknotes to be sold by them to their customers. He discusses options for making scriptural central bank money directly or indirectly available to the public and distinguishes such options from central bank digital-currency schemes.

A sweeping survey of the evolution of payments systems from antiquity to modern age, is followed in Chapter 2 by an outline of the inauguration of electronic payments and the role of the central bank in issuing fiat money as well as in the architecture of the contemporary payment system. Geva then proceeds to discuss the emergence of digital currencies and explores their impact on money, payments, and the banking industry. He distinguishes between cryptocurrencies and other types of digital currencies, between decentralized and centralized schemes, as well as between digital currencies issued privately and by central banks. He concludes by pointing at the challenge cryptocurrencies present to state-issued currency, and more in general, at both the potential and limits of payment disintermediation by digital means. Geva also points at the unstable value and inefficiency inherent in blockchain technology; he predicts, however, that as technology improves, some confluence of traditional banking and digital services may be possible whereby banks themselves enter into the digital currency space, just as digital currency providers become more active and important services providers for traditional bank customers.

The next chapter, "Deconstructing 'Decentralization': Exploring the Core Claim of Crypto Systems," by Angela Walch, begins a conceptual exploration of the concept of "decentralization." She describes the current use of the word "decentralized" as often used to denote resilient systems that lack power centers, even though the term is in fact, highly contested, ambiguous, and, depending on the circumstances, incorrect. Indeed, as with some other descriptors of blockchain technology, the adjective "decentralized" proves to be an overstatement, Walch argues, and can lead to problematic consequences where authorities rely on an unsubstantiated conclusion that a given blockchain (or blockchains generally) is (are) "decentralized." She thus counsels that courts, regulators, and even potential adopters or users of cryptoassets (whether directly or through other financial products) should use other factors to inform their decisions about a blockchain. Specifically, in examining decentralization, a forensic examination should be undertaken to begin to assess how decision-making authority is exercised within a blockchain system.

Chapter 4, "Cryptoasset Valuation: Theory and Practice," by Nic Carter, provides a much-needed primer on valuation strategies for cryptoassets. Mr. Carter identifies the core features that underpin the value of most cryptoassets as encompassing: (1) the degree of unique access to network services; (2) real asset backing; (3) cash flows from an underlying network, including "proto-equity" linked from business cash flows; (4) consumability; and (5) governance rights.

In the next chapter, "Toward a Stable Tokenized Medium of Exchange," Alexander Lipton argues that existing banking and payment systems are rapidly becoming obsolete and misaligned with the new challenges of the modern economy. While open access internet protocols have unleashed a wave of creativity and growth in numerous fields, banking is not one of them. The reason stems mostly from the fact that internet protocols for money and identity, while needed, are conspicuously absent at present.

In light thereof, Lipton argues that a regulatorily compliant fiat-backed token, which can be viewed as an electronic analogue of cash, can help to fill this gap. According to the author, all decentralized crypto coins are inherently unstable, which makes them less than useful for commercial applications. Indeed, contrary to often-made claims, it is not possible to build a truly decentralized stable token. He thus makes the bold conclusion that any potentially successful stable token has to be at least partially centralized, with varying degrees of decentralization. He then describes four approaches to building stable tokens including fully collateralized custodial tokens, partially collateralized custodial tokens, tokens overcollateralized with cryptos, and dynamically stabilized tokens, and conclude that only fully collateralized tokens can be stable, even under extreme circumstances. The author then introduces narrow banks and describe their important role as anchors of a diverse digital banking ecosystem and potential emitters of central-bank-backed digital cash.

The book then turns to regulatory strategies. Chapter 6, *The Law and Finance of Initial Coin Offerings,* by Aurelio Gurrea-Martínez and Nydia Remolina, covers regulatory strategies currently under development for cryptoasset transactions utilized to raise capital for online projects. These transactions, again called ICOs, entail more than $21 billion raised in 2018. Yet how they should be regulated is raising a myriad number of responses across jurisdictions. Because of their investment-like features, regulators are trying to determine when and under what circumstances the cryptoassets are offered investors in return for their capital constitute securities. Similarly, ICOs—even when they do not involve security-like cryptoassets—are raising novel issues for authorities from an accounting, finance, corporate governance, data protection, anti-money-laundering, and insolvency law perspectives. Along with offering a comparative and interdisciplinary analysis of ICOs, this chapter provides a set of recommendations for approaching ICOs in a way that may promote innovation and firms' access to finance without harming legal certainty, investor protection, market integrity, and the stability of the financial system.

Chris Brummer, Jai Massari, and Trevor Kiviat extend the analysis of ICOs by exploring key questions of transparency in chapter 7, "What Should Be Disclosed in an Initial Coin Offering?." In the chapter, the authors note that disclosures in initial coin offerings (ICOs) have ranged widely from informative to incomplete to fraudulent. This uneven quality has spurred investors, quite understandably, to call for the registration of ICOs in order to facilitate better disclosures.

The authors argue, however, that registration under the 1933 Securities Act is, as currently enacted, a weak mechanism for mandating the disclosures needed for informed investments in ICO tokens. Many ICO issuances offer nontraditional, non-financial rights that require and involve different pricing considerations than traditional common equity and debt, and are embedded in technical systems unanticipated by the New Deal. They thus conclude that ICOs necessitate a reconceptualization of long-standing disclosure obligations and safeguards, as well as a revamped approach toward entities tasked with validating disclosures. To highlight their point, they provide a forensic analysis of key provisions in the Securities Act's Form S-1, crowdfunding's Form C, Form 1-A for Regulation A+, and Rule 144A, highlighting their inadequacy in providing investors with key information relevant to informed investing in cryptoassets.

Petal Walker expands on the question of registration and moves to the institutional backdrop for blockchain technologies in a closely related derivatives sector, in "Blockchains and Risk Management Infrastructure of the Derivatives Industry." To begin chapter 8, Walker examines how (and whether) blockchain technologies would be interoperable enough to function in derivatives markets, and subject to derivatives markets regulations. She then extrapolates ways in which a blockchain-based derivatives market could possibly reduce risk, as well as some of the risk concerns about blockchain raised by market participants, including language gap risks. Finally, she examines how the application of today's risk-based registration regime on tomorrow's market may actually increase risk.

Importantly, Dr. Walker suggests that there may have to be fundamental regulatory changes in order to successfully integrate blockchain technologies into derivatives markets in ways that help achieve both market efficiency and transparency. For instance, she proposes that Congress explore a new registrant category in order to capture contract writers. However, Walker recognizes that there are still significant challenges even here, none perhaps most important than human capital—and an absence of technical expertise at the CFTC (U.S. Commodity Futures Trading Commission), the primary agency tasked with oversight of derivatives markets. Furthermore, blockchains would by their nature introduce unprecedented enforcement challenges. It is, as she notes, highly unlikely that regulators would allow the ultimate owner of a significant segment of market activity to be a computer network in which no individuals can explain errors, answer questions, and ultimately be held accountable. But deciding whom to regulate, especially in a decentralized ecosystem, could prove as difficult as operationalizing enforcement itself.

In chapter 9, "Difficulties in Achieving Neutrality and Other Challenges in Taxing Cryptoassets," Christophe Waerzeggers and Irving Aw seek to provide an overview of the main challenges and key considerations for policymakers designing a tax law framework for cryptoassets. This chapter highlights difficulties tax systems face in achieving neutrality when determining the tax treatment of cryptoassets using existing income tax and VAT principles and concepts. Similar to arguments presented by Brummer et al. and Walker, Waerzeggers and Aw emphasize limitations of existing principles when faced with new technologies and business models.

The chapter begins by explaining the challenges of classification based on the wide variation in the underlying economic functions of tokens. These at times hybrid variations in economic functions have caused many jurisdictions striving toward neutrality to adopt a case-by-case approach toward taxing gains arising from the disposal of cryptoassets. Next, the authors examine key features of securities tokens—cryptoassets that serve as securities. Securities transactions, they observe, are typically exempt from VAT. Among its most interesting insights are the logic of a functional application of VAT principles to cryptoassets, and an which could support an argument for the exemption of a supply of a hybrid token that is both a debt and utility token from VAT, as opposed to the supply of a hybrid token that is an equity and utility token where the administrative difficulties in quantifying the implicit fees in margin-based supplies are not applicable. The chapter then concludes with an examination of the challenges in adopting a realization or disposition basis to the taxation of gains on cryptoassets and in valuing cryptoassets, as well as the challenges of taxing gains derived by miners and validators from ensuring the integrity of the blockchain. Expanding on concepts introduced in Nic Carter's overview of valuation, it considers specific valuation challenges that arise for tax purposes in employment remuneration, hard forks, token airdrops, token pre-financing, and token burning.

In chapter 10, "Blockchain and Identity Persistence," Alex Marthews and Catherine Tucker explore "smart contracts"—programmable forms of digital money, and their implications for privacy. They observe that the unique value proposition of "smart contracts" based on blockchain technology is the creation of a permanent public record of agreed-upon transactions that cannot be changed retroactively. This is, to be sure, attractive in terms of reducing the potential for fraud: persons entering into a smart contract pre-commit both their current self and their future selves, no matter what changes occur to them or to their circumstances. However, Marthews and Tucker argue, even in an age of increasing adoption of distributed ledger technologies, self-reinvention remains important. For individuals, it is important to preserve the ability to assume new identities both formally and informally, and from a surveillance perspective, it is important to prevent governments from reliably associating a particular cryptoasset transaction with a particular person.

Marthews and Tucker instead encourage an expanded and refined understanding of what it means for a blockchain use case to "protect privacy," and in particular, how such use cases can encourage a notion of personal identity that is inflexible and matches poorly with individuals' notions regarding their identities. They review several proposed use cases that present this problem in an especially acute form and highlight good practices to preserve space for self-reinvention.

In chapter 11, the book moves to issues of non-U.S. cryptoasset supervision with "Policy and Regulatory Challenges of Distributed Ledger Technology and Digital Assets in Asia." Authored by Douglas Arner, Ross Buckley, Dirk Zetzsche, Bo Zhao, Anton Didenko, Cyn-Young Park, and Emilija Pashoska, the chapter explores the spectrum of DLT, its major uses (focusing cryptocurrencies and

ICOs), and policy and regulatory responses, particularly in Asia. The authors take the time to demystify key aspects of blockchain systems, while also carefully disentangling concepts that are often (incorrectly) used interchangeably, such as distributed ledgers and blockchains. They also conduct a comprehensive analysis of regulatory statements and disparate policy approaches in Asian countries toward cryptocurrency, blockchain, and ICOs. The chapter provides data on total capital raised through ICOs, in Asia, and analyzes the distribution of ICOs by country and region. The chapter argues that from a policy perspective, the most appropriate regulatory approach to DLT is one based upon function, with different instruments and systems regulated as appropriate given their function, based on a crowdfunding typology around donation, reward / use, currency / payment, and investment. Financial regulation would only focus on those in the latter two categories and leaving the former two to consumer protection, general contract and industry standardization – but noting that these areas need further development in order to support the appropriate development of the market.

In the final chapter, "Casting Light on Central Bank Digital Currency," IMF experts tackle one of the most contested issues in macroeconomics: the desirability of creating central bank digital currencies (CBDCs). CBDCs are effectively a new kind of digital currency, one issued by a central bank and which could be used as legal tender. In the chapter, the authors explain the basic design and functional characteristics of two potential forms of CBDCs: account-based and token-based. They then develop a conceptual framework to differentiate and analyze CBDCs as compared to other forms of money, including commercial bank deposits, "narrow finance" solutions such as pre-funded mobile payments, and cryptocurrencies. This framework is then applied to explore the design considerations critical in the development of an effective CBDC from the perspective of an end user.

After analyzing the utility usefulness of CBDCs from the viewpoint of end users, the authors turn to an assessment of whether CBDCs can advance the public policy goals of the central bank, including the social dimensions of money—improving financial inclusion and efficiency—and considerations for financial integrity, financial stability, and effectiveness of monetary policy transmission. The chapter concludes with an overview of central banks' publicly announced efforts or pilot programs related to CBDCs and the status and common features of these initiatives.

2

Cryptocurrencies and the Evolution of Banking, Money, and Payments

*Benjamin Geva**

I. Introduction

In the modern economy, payments are typically made by means of transfers through bank accounts, and otherwise the delivery of cash in the form of banknotes and coins. As conduits of funds transfers, banks operate as intermediaries between payers and payees. They also distribute to their customers banknotes issued by the central bank. The recent emergence of cryptocurrencies, facilitating payments outside the banking system, as well as in items not created throughout banking operations, has put to test these fundamentals and particularly challenged the architectural premises of the present banking system.

This chapter discusses cryptocurrencies in the context of a historical overview of the evolution of money, banking, and the payment system.[1] Section II addresses money, payment, and payment intermediation. Drawing on my previous work,[2] Section III sets out the evolution of commercial banking to facilitate national and global networks for book-based payments. Section IV takes us to the cyber-age. It addresses both electronic banking as a form of payment intermediation and the availability to the public of central bank balances as a challenge to payment intermediation. Cryptocurrencies, as a type of digital currencies, are discussed in Section V, which goes on to examine the challenge they present to state-issued currency, payment intermediation, and the roles of banks in the payment systems. The Conclusion points at an irony: even as a challenge to banking, cryptocurrencies emerged as an outgrowth of an enhancement to banking. For their parts, centralized digital currencies may be linked to banking and the legacy monetary system. While changes of unknown scope and magnitude may be inevitable, banks, "banking," and payment intermediation are unlikely to disappear, at least in the foreseeable future.

* Professor, Osgoode Hall Law School York University; Counsel, Torys LLP, Toronto, Canada; bgeva@osgoode.yorku.ca. For research assistance in the final preparation of the manuscript I am grateful to Alexander Davis of the 2019 Osgoode graduate class.

II. Money, Payment and Payment Intermediation

Money was defined to consist of anything that widely circulates as a medium of exchange so as to be accepted "in final discharge of debts . . . without reference to the character or credit of the person who offers it and without the intention of the person who receives it to consume it . . . ."[3] Over the centuries, coins and banknotes issued by the authority of the state have become the standard monetary objects in all countries, so as to collectively be called "cash" or "currency."[4]

The earliest coins were struck in Lydia (a city-state in Asia Minor) around 700 B.C.E.[5] During antiquity and the Middle Ages, having evolved from a commodity traded for its use value into currency transferred in payment of debts,[6] the coin became the standard circulating object denoting a prescribed monetary value.[7] It was fundamentally a piece of metal fashioned into a prescribed shape, weight, and degree of fineness, stamped by the issuer under the authority of the sovereign with certain designs, marks, and devices.[8] During the seventeenth century C.E., the banknote appeared as an obligation to pay coins or specie. Originally, the obligor thereon was a goldsmith, the predecessor of the deposit bank in England.[9] Ultimately, in the course of the eighteenth century, following the establishment of the Bank of England in 1694,[10] the promise to pay on banknotes circulating as money became that of the central bank.[11]

At its inception, and in theory[12] until the nineteenth century C.E., the value of a coin, at least in its ideal form, was primarily determined by reference to the weight of the precious metal it contained. At the same time, by definition, inasmuch as they are mere obligations to pay, banknotes are "fiat money," namely, of positive nominal value, notwithstanding the (relatively) worthless intrinsic value of the material of which they are made.[13]

Until the modern era, a monetary unit of account was anchored in the value of a specified weight of a prescribed metal. This gave the monetary unit of account its external value in terms of that metal, and facilitated the establishment of an international system under which the value of each national unit of account could be ascertained by reference to all other national units of account.[14] Furthermore, until the modern era, the issuer's obligation to pay, measured by reference to a unit of account, was to actually pay that amount in specie, at least in coins. In England, this was originally true for banknotes issued by private bankers,[15] and subsequently, to banknotes issued by the Bank of England.[16] For a coin, the issuer's obligation was in the form of a guarantee as to its actual metallic content, or at least the redemption thereof.

To this day, current coins and banknotes are typically issued under state authority; at least for banknotes, the issuer is usually the central bank. However, other than the issue of coins and banknotes under state authority, by modern times, the framework just described above has been eroded. First, in the course of the nineteenth century, the coin reflecting a fraction of the unit of account became a token, that is, a piece of metal of a value lower than which it denotes. The division of the basic unit of account into fixed token denominations at equal abstract subunits[17] is called by economists the "standard formula".[18] Thereunder, the prescribed sum of such token denominations is convertible at a fixed exchange rate to each other denomination and to the basic unit, regardless of their own metallic composition.[19]

Next, in the first half of the twentieth century C.E., convertibility of banknotes ceased to exist; that is, the obligation to pay in specie embodied in a banknote became unenforceable.[20] Thus, at present, banknotes and coins express abstract obligations; they are tokens convertible to other tokens. Finally, during the second half of the twentieth century, even the measurement of the unit of account by reference to a specified quantity of a given precious metal was abolished.[21] The external value of the standard national unit of value is now determined only by reference to the value in which that national unit of value is traded in international financial markets by reference to each other national unit of accounts.

Payment in cash is by physical delivery from one person (payer) to another (payee). This is a face-to-face process that does not requires intermediaries. More specifically, "payment" is "a bilateral act which requires the [payee] to accept the [payer]'s act of tender,"[22] and is completed on the passage of possession in the money[23] when the payee takes delivery, thereby manifesting the acceptance of the tender.[24]

From the beginning, payment in cash had flaws, and under some circumstances was impractical. Particularly, this is due to costs and risks associated with the storage, carriage, and transportation of cash. Other concerns have been scarcity of cash and the inevitable cumbersome process of handling and paying in cash large sums of money. In a nutshell, an effective solution has been in the form of payment made to the payee, under the payer's instructions, by an intermediary who typically owed money to the payer.[25] Such payment would discharge both the payer's debt to the payee and the intermediary's debt to the payer. An optimal such an intermediary was a deposit-taker, that is, banker, being a debtor to all depositors. When payee preferred payment into payee's account with another banker (rather than in cash) the two bankers, that of the payer and that of the payee, settled periodically by paying the balance due for customers' payments going in both directions. Bankers kept funds with each other and ultimately with a central counterparty. Over the centuries, both national and global non-cash payment systems so evolved.

At the heart of such a system stands the commercial bank. The essence of commercial banking has been the taking of deposits (or other repayable funds) from the public and lending.[26] Linked to these functions is the provision of inter-account payment services.[27]

Historically, commercial banking (banking) emerged as a form of financial intermediation between savers (depositors) and borrowers. The banker (or bank)[28] took from the public deposits either in specie or in commodity money; what was deposited was both owed by the banker to the depositors and at least in part available to be lent by the banker to borrowers. Loans were mostly credited into borrowers' deposit accounts with the lending bankers in part to be used by borrowers to make payments. In this environment, payment intermediation in the form of non-cash payment services evolved as an outgrowth of deposit-taking or, more in general, of maintaining deposit accounts for customers, whether the original depositors, or the borrowers who deposited the proceeds of the loan.[29] This business model has been workable as long as not all depositors required payment in specie from the banker at the same time. In normal circumstances, it sufficed for a banker to keep at hand enough specie or cash to satisfy reasonable demand. Monitoring depositors' payment activity in accounts facilitated credit decision-making and led to specialization in advancing information-intensive non-traded loans, which became a principal niche for a profitable commercial banking business as well as effective financial intermediation for the economy as a whole.

Already way back in antiquity[30] the evolution of mechanisms for payments initiated by the issue of payment orders had been part and parcel of the emergence of "banking" as a form of financial intermediation between depositors to, and borrowers from, the depositary.[31] Furthermore, over centuries the architecture of the banking system evolved to satisfy the need to carry out non-cash payment transactions between customers of separate banks by the creation of interbank networks. For its part, lending out of deposits generated a fractional reserve system that necessitated the establishment of liquidity facilities to ensure the smooth flow of payments. Finally, for their part, banknotes, of which at present mainly consist of cash, originated as circulating receipts for deposited funds.

III. Deposit Banking, Payment Services, and Paper Money: Historical Perspective on Payments Intermediation

The modern payment system has been described as consisting of "a complex set of arrangements involving such diverse institutions as currency, the banking system, clearing houses, the central bank, and government deposit insurance."[32] The latter element is helpful but not universally present, and yet all are components of what can broadly be described as a commercial (deposit) banking system.

Notwithstanding the substantial enhancement in complexity and importance of banking in the modern economy, its fundamentals are not at all novel.[33] What follows is an abbreviated account of the evolution of payment intermediation and that of paper money as an outgrowth of deposit banking.

A. Antiquity

Ancient Mesopotamia has been identified as the cradle of banking operations.[34] It earned this title due to the emergence of institutions providing all core banking activities, namely, deposit taking, lending[35] and payment services even prior to the emergence of "monetized" coins. However, this was a secondary activity for such institutions; moreover, credit was made available by depositaries out of their own capital[36] and without dipping into deposits.[37] As well, each customer's deposit may have been physically segregated.[38] Payment and withdrawal orders were inscribed on tablets, and yet could be oral. Each payment order directed the drawee to pay either to a payee known to the drawee or to a payee to be properly identified.[39] Payment was made in specie; there appears to be neither evidence for the execution of non-cash payments from one account to another nor any trace of inter-institutional clearing and settlement.

There is a historical debate on the possible origins of money in the Ancient East, particularly in Mesopotamia; specifically, there is a disagreement on whether distinct items of value were actually used exclusively as means of payments, and thus approximated coins.[40] However, it seems to be universally agreed that nascent "banking operations" in Mesopotamia preceded the emergence of money, in the sense of standardized metallic pieces, in fixed denominations, whose value is certified by the ruler's stamp.[41] Rather, various commodities served as both units of account and means of payment. Based on their comparative or relative value, such commodities served as a basis for a price system, as well as actual means or money of payment. Principal commodities were grain and precious metal, usually barley and silver.[42] Having both (1) actual use value or intrinsic utility, and (2) economic value facilitating their use to provide a standardized means for the measurement of the value of other commodities as well for paying for all such other commodities, such items constituted "primitive money."[43]

The emergence of the bank as a distinct type of institution took place in *Ancient Greece*.[44] More specifically, the process took place in the Mediterranean territory on which Ancient Greek civilization expanded,[45] almost throughout the entire classical period of that civilization.[46]

Thus, in the course of the sixth century B.C.E., shortly after the appearance of coined money as a medium of exchange in commercial transactions,[47] money-changing surfaced as a profession. Shortly thereafter, the money changer came to accept deposits of coined money, mix them,[48] and lend out of them, so as to gradually become a banker. A banker effectively kept a running account for each customer, posting to it each deposit and withdrawal.[49] A withdrawal from a customer's account could be made for the entire or part of a balance due on deposited money, either by the depositor himself, or by a designated payee (or on his behalf) in pursuance of the depositor's instruction.

For each payment to a designated payee, having received the payment order and being in possession of cover, the payer's banker sent a note to the payee. Having made an appropriate entry on his books in the payee's favor, the banker became accountable to the payee, regardless of whether the payee kept an account with that banker. A payee who did not have an account at the payer's bank could demand payment in cash, or where the advice note issued by the banker was made out to the payee "or order," the payee could appoint an agent, usually another banker, to come to the payer's banker and claim on the payee's behalf payment in cash over the counter. Alternatively, the payee's banker may have been prepared to credit the payee's account in advance, on the basis of the advice note issued to the payee by the payer's banker and presented to the payee's banker by the payee, and in anticipation of subsequent payment by the payer's banker. Payment by payer's banker to the payee's banker could be effectuated either in coins, or as part of either bilateral or multilateral setoff. No interbank clearing system, whether bilateral or multilateral, existed in Ancient Greece.[50]

Compared to Ancient Greece, the institutional scene in *Ancient Rome*[51] was more complex;[52] and yet, this complexity did not lead to an overall advancement in banking practices. Nonetheless, in three major respects Roman banking practice went beyond that of the Greek. *First*, the receiver-banker could be treated as the first money transmitter, to whom funds are delivered with the view of making a specific payment. However, money transmission by a receiver-banker may have developed under narrow circumstances, in the context of private auctions,[53] and in any event did not extend to cover payment between geographically distant parties. *Second*, as in Ancient Greece, there was in Ancient Rome neither an intra-city nor intercity multilateral interbank clearing and settlement system.[54] However, nascent interbank correspondent arrangements, under which one bank held funds in an account with the other, developed, particularly in the same city,[55] but also in different cities so as to facilitate payments between geographically distant parties.[56] A non-cash payment could have been carried out between accounts of two depositors, either in the same bank, or in two banks situated in the same small town or within a specific market, whether permanent or periodic.

Third, deposit bankers operated under strict bookkeeping requirements, and were obligated to record their monetary operations in account books called *rationes*. An account book (*ratio* in singular) was also known as a *ratio accepti et expensi* ("an account of deposits and payments") and *ratio implicita proper accepta et data* ("a complex account including both deposits and payments"). A deposit banker was required to make such books available for production in a trial involving a client, even where the deposit banker was not a party to the litigation.[57] For his part, the deposit banker was obligated to maintain books, to account for the various entries, and to state a balance owed between himself and the customer.[58]

Payment services were operated in conjunction with deposit banking in *Greco-Roman Egypt*.[59] Public granaries in Greco-Roman Egypt, connected into a network of grain depositaries, operated a countrywide system of payment in agricultural products, such as oil and wine. Particularly however, they ran grain warehouse banking, facilitating payments out of and into deposits of grain, for both public authorities and individuals.[60] The system maintained grain accounts and recorded transfers. For each yearly harvest of each type of grain the various deposits were physically amalgamated so that credit to an account reflected a claim to a share in the mixture rather than to a physically segregated or separate deposit; it seems though, that no lending was made out of the mixture, so that full reserve was held to back all credits to the deposit accounts.[61]

Book-based transfers could occur between accounts in the same granary, same region, or different regions. For an inter-granary transfer, an adjustment was made not only to transferor's and transferee's accounts, but also over a system of inter-granary accounts.[62] A comprehensive account management system thus existed in each granary, in each region, as well as in Alexandria, from which the entire system was overseen. Effectively, this was the forerunner for a nationwide credit-push giro mechanism,[63] under which payment orders were executed by means of crediting and debiting accounts.[64] The system was however doomed to wither away together with the disappearance of specie and kind as universal mediums of exchange.[65]

So far as the monetary economy of Greco-Roman Egypt[66] was concerned, the banking system formed a network and assumed a key role in carrying out treasury operations for the central government and other public authorities. Each regional royal bank operated in conjunction with a network of village banks, which effectively functioned as branch offices for royal banks or more precisely, as points of collections and disbursements of funds[67] throughout the various districts of the country. However, the Royal Treasury, or the *basilicon*, in Alexandria,[68] did not serve as a central bank;[69] it neither maintained accounts for all deposits throughout the country, nor received surplus balances for such accounts, other than for the king. Nor did the *basilicon* oversee the

operation of the entire network; it did not even maintain accounts for the various royal banks into which adjustments for inter-district transfers could be
made. Rather, each royal bank kept a separate set of records for its own account holders. Effectively, together with its village bank network, a royal bank
operated as a stand-alone independent bank. It follows that there was no infrastructure facilitating a countrywide system for inter-district non-cash payments
from an account in one royal bank to an account in another.

Throughout the Ptolemaic era,[70] both royal and private banks maintained
deposit accounts for individuals.[71] Available documentation supports the existence of funds transfers from one account to another[72] in private banks[73]
as well as for tax payments from accounts maintained in royal banks.[74]
Documentation further supports the existence of bilateral correspondent relations between private banks, namely instances where one bank holds an account with another.[75] At the same time, there is no indication of any multilateral
bank clearing arrangement; and certainly, any claim to the existence in Greco-
Roman Egypt of a "centralized state giro system"[76] is not well founded.

Royal banks in Ptolemaic Egypt pioneered a nascent check system.[77] The
drawer would issue a non-transferable check to the payee and send a "control
note" to the drawee bank, which would match it with the check upon its presentation. Checks were non-transferable. The payee would present the check to the
payer's bank, either in person or through an agent, and be paid usually in cash
Alternatively, payee could have his account credited with the payer's bank. In
the further alternative, where the payer's bank kept an account with the payee's
bank, payee would instruct the payer's banker to draw on the payee's banker
a check payable to the payee. The payee would then present that check to the
payee's bank, which would then debit the account of the payer's bank and credit
that of the payee. Being drawn by one bank on another, the check issued by the
payer's bank was the forerunner of a bank draft or money order.[78] Check use
had been eclipsed in Egypt in the course of the Roman period.[79]

B. Middle Ages

In *West Europe*, during the early centuries of the Middle Ages,[80] the economy
collapsed and trade was reduced to a trickle. The monetary economy survived
only in a rudimentary form[81] and banks disappeared from the West after the
fourth century C.E.[82] Banking services reappeared in Europe in the later part
of the Middle Ages to satisfy the growing demands of trade. "Genoa happens
to preserve the earliest notarial minute books that have survived (from 1154
on) . . . [which] are the first source that contains a fairly large number of
documents showing bankers at work."[83] Deposit banking, in the form of taking

deposits and lending out of them in the depositary's own name, was reborn in Italy and "exported" elsewhere[84] in the course of the twelfth and thirteenth centuries, as part of a commercial revolution that took place as of the eleventh century or so.[85]

As originally in Ancient Greece, it was the money changer who commenced to take deposits, mix them, and lend out of them. By 1350, in becoming bankers,[86] money changers developed a system of local payments by book transfers, with the view of eliminating "[t]he great inconvenience of making all payments in specie, especially the waste of time involved in counting coin."[87] The system that developed was strictly local; no facility for inter-city book transfers is known to have existed throughout the Middle Ages.

Thus, between the late thirteenth and early fourteenth century the money changers of Venice, the *campsores*, became bankers.[88] They accepted deposits, lent out of them, and provided book transfer payment services from and to current accounts kept with them.[89] To eliminate fraud, a book transfer required the attendance of both payer and payee at the bank.[90] Ultimately, in some cases, the payer's attendance could be dispensed with and the payer's banker was prepared to act on the payer's instruction presented by the payee. The Medieval non-transferable check was thus born, as a payment order issued by the payer to the payee instructing the payer's banker to pay to the payee, as well as authorizing the payee to collect from the banker. It was however not widely used.[91]

Bankers held accounts with each other, which possibly allowed for intra-city interbank transfers[92] which may have been settled only on irregular intervals. Each bank kept with it only a fractional reserve, namely, a limited amount of coined money, ready to satisfy an anticipated demand for cash withdrawal; it lent or invested most of the money received on deposit. Availability of payment by book transfers, recognized by early fourteenth century legislation in Venice, allowed banks to reduce cash holdings and increase their investments and credit extensions.

However, throughout the Continent, during the fifteenth century, private deposit banks declined. Repeated bank failures undermined the confidence of merchants and further triggered hostility by public authorities.[93] Together with a chronic shortage of good coins, the increased risk in keeping money with a banker led to a devaluation of "bank money" compared to that of "coined money."[94] Ultimately, in a process that "did not gain momentum until the last quarter of the sixteenth century," public banks gradually replaced private banks in commercial centers.[95] Heralding this development, Venice gave rise to a "distinctive style" of banking, referred to as giro banking, under which the primary purpose of banks was the making of payments on behalf of customers rather than making loans.[96] For its part, the Bank of Amsterdam, "established in 1609 under the guarantee of the city,"[97] was a leader among the post-medieval public banks.[98]

During the late Middle Ages, and to accommodate intercity commerce, exchange banking evolved in Continental Europe side by side with deposit banking.[99] It was practiced by large merchants who lent to exporters located in one market, who in turn sent goods for sale in another market. Repayment was made out of the proceeds of the sale, in the destination market, by the seller's correspondent to the lender's correspondent in that market.[100] This practice gave rise to the bill of payment, being the predecessor of the bill of exchange.[101] For their part, exchange bankers formed an intercity network that gave rise to the emergence of an elaborate multilateral clearing and settlement arrangement, implemented by them periodically in medieval fairs.[102]

C. Post-Medieval Era

Against this background the modern banking system, accommodating the present payment system, was born in post-medieval *England*. Its roots are in the institutional transformation of the goldsmiths' system and the establishment of the Bank of England that followed.[103]

The process involved (1) the transformation of the business of individual goldsmiths into that of deposit bankers who accepted deposits, and lent out of them, including by discounting bills of exchange. As bankers they also facilitated depositors' check payments out of and into the deposits; (2) the existence of a tight network of all such goldsmiths ready to extend credit to each other, so as to allow for reciprocal correspondent banking services. Such services have facilitated interbank debt clearing and settlement, originally on a bilateral and later on a multilateral basis, leading to the establishment of a clearinghouse. This allowed risk reduction, enhanced efficiency, and the generation of common services that brought upon further development;[104] (3) the establishment of the Bank of England, originally as a lender to the government and then, having adopted goldsmiths' practices, gradually evolving in the subsequent two centuries into a modern central bank. As such it maintains settlement accounts for deposit bankers (being the successors of goldsmiths) so as to facilitate interbank final settlement as well as to become a lender of last resort;[105] and (4) the issuance of banknotes, first as circulating obligations of goldsmiths evidencing either deposits or loans, then as paper money issued by the goldsmiths, and ultimately, as paper money, "legal tender," exclusively issued by the Bank of England.[106]

Both correspondent banking and customer payment activity required intensive monitoring by the goldsmith-bankers. In turn, this facilitated credit decision-making and led to specialization in advancing information-intensive non-traded loans. Such lending became a principal niche for a profitable commercial banking business as well as effective financial intermediation for the economy as a whole. In providing such loans, as well as in issuing banknotes and discounting bills of exchange, the goldsmith-bankers came to provide a reliable source of liquidity to the economy.

For its part, in departing from the model of the earlier Continental public bank, the Bank of England complemented private commercial banks without competing with or endeavoring to substitute for them. Rather, being their bank maintaining for them accounts,[107] it became able to furnish them with a source of liquidity so as to be a lender of last resort. As well, it provided them with the efficiency of multilateral settlement in reserve accounts held with it. In both ways, it gradually became as a "central bank" an integral part of the private bank network.[108]

The banknote was issued first by the goldsmith-banker,[109] originally possibly as a "warehouse receipt" for deposited coins, and subsequently against a fractional reserve of coins or metal.[110] The power to issue banknotes was taken over by the Bank of England,[111] with convertibility ultimately ceasing to exist altogether in the course of the twentieth century.[112] Using funds on deposit at the central bank, commercial banks buy banknotes from the central bank and sell them for use to the public, against funds held by their customers on deposit with them. As they are exchanged out of and back into deposits "according to customer payment habits," as a form of cash, banknotes (together with coins), are not the principal form of money, a role now preserved to money deposited in banks[113]

The integration of banks into a banking network, consisting of commercial banks multilaterally clearing in a clearinghouse[114] and settling on the books of the central bank, which is an integral part of this network, has led to a fundamental albeit subtle change in the mode of the creation of money through "banking." Thus, deposits made to commercial banks are typically not anymore in the form of specie or commodity money. Rather, they are primarily created by lending into customers' deposit accounts. For its part, an addition to a bank's liquid assets is typically made not in the form of specie or commodity money, but rather in the form of an increase in the sum credited to that bank's own account; at least for a large bank such increase is in the credit to its account with the central bank.[115] Other than by receiving an interbank payment, liquidity designed to meet deposit obligations is obtained at least by a large commercial bank, in the form of credit posted to its account with the central bank, through borrowing in an interbank market, selling government securities, or as a last resort, borrowing from the central bank.

At the same time, non-cash payment activity continues to be primarily carried out over deposit accounts held in commercial banks. Monitoring depositors' payment activity in accounts continues to facilitate credit decision-making and lead to specialization in advancing information-intensive non-traded loans, so as to continue to be a principal niche for a profitable commercial banking business as well as effective financial intermediation for the economy as a whole.[116] This must be true also in an era where credit information may be available from other sources such as credit bureaus.

The architecture, instruments, and institutions of the English system spread globally. At present, commercial banks take deposits from the public, lend into customers' deposit accounts, and provide payment services in conjunction with deposit accounts. In each country, at least all major commercial banks clear multilaterally and settle over deposit accounts they hold with the central bank.[117] They also maintain correspondent relationships[118] with local small banks as well as with cross-border or overseas large banks, so as to create a global network over which in principle non-cash payments can be made by any account holder to another in any currency. Moreover, as a rule, paper money in the form of banknotes is issued in each country by its central bank.

Banknotes, together with coins for small change, constitute cash (or currency). Payment in cash is typically made face to face, without any intermediation. Non-cash payments, whether face to face or between distant parties, require intermediation. Where payer and payee hold their respective accounts with the same bank a non-cash payment is carried out by that bank debiting the payer's account and crediting that of the payee. Where payer and payee hold their respective accounts at two banks that are correspondents, a non-cash payment involves debiting the payer's account by the payer's bank, crediting the payee's account by the payee's bank, and either debiting the account of the payer's bank by the payee's bank or crediting the account of the payee's bank by the payer's bank. In a domestic payment system, at least all major banks hold their accounts with the central bank so that the interbank component of payment between two such banks is carried out as part of the multilateral interbank settlement on the books of the central bank. Otherwise, a non-cash payment requires a chain of settlements on correspondent accounts, with or without settlement on the books of the central bank, or alternatively, one settlement between correspondent banks followed by another settlement on the books of a central bank. To take a simple example for the latter, the interbank component of a non-cash payment in Australian currency from a customer of Bank A in Canada to a customer of Bank B in Australia, assuming that the two are non-correspondent major banks, is carried out by Bank A using its correspondent, another Australian major bank, which in turn settles with Bank B on the books of the central bank of Australia.

Three principal features characterize payment services facilitated by the modern banking system. *First*, value held on deposit with participating banks, often referred to as "bank money" or more specifically, "commercial-bank money" (or even "ledger money"), is denominated in and is redeemable to fiat money (or banknotes), that is, an official currency or "legal tender." *Second*, such value is in the form of a claim in an account maintained with a bank. Typically, this is an asset account; however, payment may be made by means of a credit card, in which case payment is carried from the payer's credit account rather than asset account having a positive balance in bank money. Also in such a case, payment results in an increase in the sum of bank money available to the payee in the payee's asset account—while the payer becomes obligated to reimburse the payer's bank, typically (if not exclusively) in bank money (originating from the payer's asset account). *Third*, claims against the central bank, often referred to as claims to "central-bank money," are available both to holders of fiat money/banknotes and the banks.[119] The latter multilaterally settle their reciprocal claims on the books of the central bank. Obligations on bank deposits payable on demand are referred to as "scriptural money," being a category covering both commercial and central bank money.[120] In principle, the sum of commercial bank money is a derivative of the sum of central bank money; the former is manipulated by the central bank's power to set interest rates through the sale of government securities to banks and/or lending to banks, primarily with the view of achieving price stability.[121] Gold reserves, which may be assets of a central bank, do not play any explicit role in the creation of the money supply.[122]

The non-cash payment system is then premised on the use of "scriptural money." Its architecture is *centralized*. Thereunder, a bank maintains deposit accounts for customers (who thus keep with it commercial bank money). For its part, a large bank may also maintain deposit accounts (in commercial bank money) for correspondent banks. Finally, the central bank maintains settlement (deposit) accounts at least for large banks (which thus hold with it central bank money).[123] As a whole, the system can be visualized as a pyramid at whose head or apex stands the central bank with which at least large banks hold accounts, and possibly with small banks holding accounts with large banks. Individual and corporate customers are at the bottom or base of the pyramid holding their accounts in banks (whether large or small).[124]

IV. The Coming of the Cyber-Age: Electronic Payments, E-money, and Access to Central Bank Balances

A. The Advent of Electronic Banking and E-money

Historically, payment instructions accessing bank money were either oral or, more typically, in writing. Use of telecommunication, first the telegraph and then the transatlantic cable, goes back to mid-nineteenth century.[125] However, the watershed of electronic banking, where payments are processed as well as transmitted electronically, is a development of the second part of the twentieth century. Once it became possible to transmit instructions electronically, from a computer or computer terminal, the electronic funds transfer was born. Telecommunication in the electronic age was originally on cable or wire;[126] subsequently the wireless option became available,[127] and ultimately, instructions could be transmitted over the internet.[128]

Security in electronic funds transfer has been implemented by the physical protection of network components[129] and more recently by the introduction of tamper-resistant access devices and cryptographic data protection. Broadly speaking, "cryptography" (literally: secret writing) denotes "a method of storing and transmitting data in a particular form so that only those for whom it is intended can read and process it."[130] Strictly speaking, the term points at a specific method to that end, under which "complexity . . . is injected into data so that only those who possess a key . . . can remove the complexity . . . and understand the intended message, while those without the key will not be able to retrieve the hidden message in a timely manner." The "process of applying cryptography to a message so that only its intended readers can understand it" is called "encryption"; the reverse, namely the "process of using a . . . key to recover the intended message from its encrypted form," is called "decryption." Where the sender and receiver of a cryptographic message "share the same key data or mutually deducible key data," encryption is "symmetric." Otherwise, where they do not share the same key data, encryption is said to be "asymmetric." Either way secrecy is achieved by means of the application of mathematical theories. Cryptographic complexity addresses factors relating to the decryption of the message and its result.[131] Security is enhanced by the use of random data[132] to generate keys, since "patterns could be recognized [and] could aid in a brute-force attack."[133] Looking ahead, we note that security will be enhanced by the use of "quantum data," namely, data "marked" by merely being observed so as to alert the ultimate (designated) recipient to the fact that the communication had been intercepted.[134]

Developments exploiting such technological achievements have not been limited to communication. It became also possible to "load" monetary value (that is, value denominated in an official or, in fact, any unit of account) on a tamper-resistant stored-value device such as a card or personal computer. In such a case, the value became known as "*electronic money*" or "*e-money.*" The majority of e-money schemes have involved "balance-based" products. In such products, devices store and manipulate a numeric ledger, with transactions performed as debits or credits to a balance. Accordingly, this type of e-money is a monetary balance or value recorded electronically on and is available from a *stored-value product* (SVP), such as a chips card, or a hard drive in a personal computer, or a server.[135] Such a record, accessible from the device without resort to the bank's computer system, can be viewed as a decentralized bank account.[136] E-money is said to "differ . . . from so-called *access products*, which are products that allow consumers to use electronic means of communication to access otherwise conventional payment services" in and out of bank accounts.[137]

A minority of e-money products may still operate on devices that store electronic "notes" (sometimes called coins or tokens) that are uniquely identified by a serial number and are associated with a fixed, unchangeable denomination. In such a "note-based" model, transactions are performed by transferring notes from one device to another, and the balance of funds stored on a device is thus the sum of the denominations of all notes on the device. However, as in the "balance-based" products, transferability is typically restricted, and consumer cardholders may usually make payments only to merchants who may clear these payments or deposit the accumulated balances exclusively through their acquiring banks.[138] Such a product provides the link between traditional value-transfer systems to innovative circulating digital coins discussed in Section V of this chapter.

Under a variant of a "balance-based" e-money product, monetary value is not loaded on the device; rather, it is available from a master account, belonging to the issuer or someone acting on the issuer's behalf.[139] As in the case of e-money, monetary value is not available from the payer-debtor's own bank account.[140] However, such prepaid value is in a bank account, even if not that of the payer. Its use entails communication to the issuer and requires the cardholder to access a bank account (even if not his or hers). From this perspective, a prepaid product device is more a variant of an access device rather than of an SVP.

According to Crawford, e-money is truly "money" when it may circulate from one person to another, that is, from one SVP to another, without being "cleared" or intermediated by the issuer.[141] This seems to me to be true for both "balance-based" and "note-based" e-money products. However, upon reflection, also e-money, in all its manifestations, is ultimately a variant of "bank money";[142] thus, whether e-money is purchased in cash or by means of a debit to the purchaser's bank account, the issuer has its own bank account credited with the amount sold to the purchaser. Where the e-money is purchased from a bank the account credited is the reserve account of the selling bank. Payment in e-money is forwarded to the payee's bank, which credits the payee's account with the amount of payment and forwards the e-money itself for redemption against the value previously credited to the seller's account. In the final analysis, even where prepaid value or e-money is not issued by a bank, a scheme must facilitate the purchase and redemption through banks.

"Electronic banking" enhanced payment services in several other ways. *First*, it introduced electronic processing also to paper-based instruments such as checks.[143] Second, it facilitated new as well as variations of existing products.[144] Third, new players, such as money transmitters[145] or payment institutions,[146] and e-money institutions[147] entered the scene as end-payment institutions in a payment transaction, facilitating domestic and international payments in small amounts to parties who do not have bank accounts. *Fourth*, the power balance in the partnership between financial institutions and telecommunication carriers has shifted, allowing the latter a greater voice and share in the payment market.[148] *Fifth*, in facilitating instant communication, electronic banking allowed the use of risk reduction methods as well as instant authorization leading to an immediate final credit to the payee's account way ahead of the interbank settlement; such may be the case in domestic large value wholesale payment systems,[149] and retail fast payments networks.[150] This is also the case in a typical credit card payment, even when it is carried internationally.[151]

Electronic banking facilitated branchless banking to the detriment of banks with a large branch network.[152] As well, the possible impact of electronic banking on monetary policy has been fiercely debated.[153] At the same time, none of the various facets of electronic banking has affected the architecture of the payment system even as it expanded its scope and globalized it. No wonder, the law governing wireless instructions is the same as the one governing wire orders.[154] For their part, money transmitters, and payment institutions as well as e-money institutions have been using banks as intermediaries in the transfers in which they participate at either end of the transaction.[155] They thus increased rather than decreased payment intermediation. Furthermore, not treating such institutions as deposit-takers hinges on a "benevolent" strict view of "deposit-taking" so as to exclude the delivery of money for a specific purpose.[156] True, a payment instruction issued from a digital device such as a mobile phone rather than from a computer terminal or computer is often said to result in a mobile payment. When the payment scheme is operated over mobile devices it is even described as involving "mobile money." However, in substance, payment orders initiated from a digital or mobile device is a specie of an electronic funds transfer.[157] For its part "mobile money" is a form of "e-money." It is therefore confusing to treat such developments as reflecting a "digitization of state-issue currenc[y]" even in connection with an online (e-commerce) transaction.[158] Ultimately efficiency is bound either to turn payment institutions into banks or for banks to take over payment institutions, either directly or as subsidiaries, so as to eliminate this unnecessary layer of intermediation. The issue for banks is the adoption of a different level of service rather than the elimination of banks as an essential component in linking between payers and payees.

The broader question however is whether "electronic banking" has not been superseded by "fintech," "snatching" money and payments from the banking system. "Fintech" (stading for 'Financial Technology') refers to the use of technology by IT firms[159] to deliver financial solutions directly to purchasers of financial products such as payment services.[160] Technology designed to deliver financial solutions is however available also to banks whether directly or indirectly by purchase from IT firms. Alternatively, IT firms may become banks and compete with existing banks on equal footing. It is not that "banking" survives while banks die;[161] rather, as an economic model banking has adopted new technologies to be used by old and new types of institutions. Whether and to what extent this remains true in light of subsequent developments is discussed further later on in this chapter.

B. Availability of Central Bank Account Balances and Their Equivalents to the Public

In reviewing the present architecture of the payment system prior to the fintech era Goodfriend opined that "although valuing deposits at par and holding fractional reserves is efficient for individual banks, it had the potential for generating destabilizing systemwide bank runs." In his view this risk is however "remedied efficiently by central bank monetary policy,"[162] as well as by other payment system policies.[163]

Conversely, reviving and building on old ideas,[164] a recent set of proposals will make central bank money deposits available to the public either directly or indirectly Unfortunately it has become common to treat such a proposal as relating to central bank digital currency (CBDC).[165] This is however confusing; contrary to true digital currency schemes, discussed in Section V, such proposals, discussed immediately below, remain premised on both generic value in bank accounts and banks as payment intermediaries.

A typical rationale, for making central bank scriptural money available to the public is premised on new technological developments:

> Central banking evolved at a time when service provision in local branches was integral to providing banking services. In that world it made sense for the central bank to "wholesale" its core exchange settlement and liquidity

support services to banks which would then "retail" them to individuals and businesses via their branches, passbooks and cheque accounts. It was impracticable for central banks' services to be provided to individuals.

At the same time, the rationale goes on, "[m]odern technology enables us to extend some core central banking services to individuals and businesses."[166] As a matter of history, the argument is doubtful, as post-medieval public banks, discussed in Section III(B) of this chapter, "retailed" their services to the public. At the same time, it is true that with the increase in the size and geographical scope of the bank customer base, a centralized system is workable only in an enhanced technology environment. Hence, banking-centralization proposals merit consideration.

One proposal premised on this rationale is the provision of payment services to the public exclusively by a designate government agency that will take deposits from the public but will have restricted investment powers so as to be able to invest only in safe assets such as super-collateralized real estate mortgages. Under that proposal, payment transactions will be carried out over deposit accounts with respect to which the liability of the depositary (the government agency) is effectively secured by investment in high-quality assets. On this basis, such deposits will benefit from unlimited guarantee of the central bank. Under that proposal, commercial banks will be able to lend to customers and sell them investment products but be precluded from providing payment services.[167]

However, one may reasonably suppose that in upsetting the delicate balance between the roles of the public and private sectors in the monetary and payment systems, this proposal will be perceived as going too far (or in fact, nowhere). Certainly, in monopolizing payment services in the hands of a government agency, the proposal will stifle competition and give no incentive to innovate. Furthermore, the proposal is not persuasive in mandating a central bank guarantee on the top of the requirement to invest deposited funds in safe assets. I therefore doubt that in a capitalist economy that proposal will persuade policymakers. At the same time, unclothing it from these objectionable elements, the proposal is reminiscent of an earlier idea, that of "narrow banking"; thereunder payment transactions are carried out over bank deposits of which the proceeds are invested in safe assets.[168] "Narrow banking" does not require the superimposition of a central bank guarantee and in fact does not alter the traditional roles of commercial banks as deposit-takers, providers of payment services, and lenders.

Under another proposal the central bank will open accounts and offer payment services directly to the public. This proposal is however said to impose "a large administrative burden" on the central bank that "could distract it from its other functions in [regulating] and managing monetary policy." It is further acknowledged that under the proposal the central bank, "a state-owned enterprise," would undertake pure market functions, in which it "would have no commercial incentive to innovate [payment] services."[169] To meet these objections, under a variant, it is proposed that public access to scriptural central bank money or its equivalent will be indirect.[170]

There are however two alternative approaches to such a variant. One is premised on "full reserve banking"[171] while the other is of "plain sovereign money."[172] Briefly stated, under the former, the entire quantity of commercial bank money, namely, the total amount of demand deposits with banks, is to be backed by a 100% reserve of central bank money held by commercial banks on deposit with the central bank.[173]

Under the latter, that of "plain sovereign money,"[174] the distinction between the two types of scriptural money is abolished; what exists is only one category of scriptural money: central bank money.[175] It will be available to members of the public in accounts on the books of the central bank; unless operated by the central bank itself, as discussed previously, such accounts will be operated through and managed by commercial banks,[176] possibly in "transaction accounts"[177] that will be distinguished from "investment accounts" of which funds may be invested in designated collections of assets of a broadly similar risk profile. Each investment fund will be a distinct legal and corporate entity. Lending will be carried out of investment funds (possibly as well as from long-term borrowing from the public) and should not create additional money or purchasing power.[178] Investment account holders will bear the risk of nonpayment on the due date, and not being available to them prior to that, sovereign money owed to them will not serve as commercial bank money. Rather, prior to maturity on the investment account, sovereign money deposited in them will be lent by the bank and thus will exclusively be used by borrowers from the bank.[179] Banking will thus fully reclaim its function as an intermediation between savers and borrowers.

Under both approaches commercial banks will cease to create money by lending into customers' deposits. Money creation will be under the exclusive power of the central bank[180] with commercial banks either being limited to issue its "replication" or "shadow" to the public, but not expand its quantity (under the full reserve banking alternative), or being restrained from issuing it at all (under the plain sovereign money alternative).[181] They will however be able to lend and provide payment services.

An analysis of the pros and cons of each alternative, vis-à-vis each other as well as by reference to the current fractional reserve regime, is beyond the scope of this chapter as well as of the competence of this author. At the same time, in relation to the topic at hand, under both alternatives banks will continue to accept deposits, make loans (albeit not out of demand deposits), and provide payment services. For sure, they may face competition from "payment institutions" that do not provide "investment accounts" services as well as lenders providing "investment accounts" but not "payment accounts." However, it is reasonable to expect that such competitors will be regulated, respectively on the payment, and saving and lending sides, so it will be for banks to leverage the combined services they give to their advantage. For example, as now, monitoring the payment activity of a customer will help a bank in making its lending decision regarding that customer. Hence, a reform under any of these lines will not change the role of commercial banks in the payment system.

What may however change is the legal underpinning of the bank's liability for money deposited in the payments or transactions account. At the moment, a bank is liable to a depositor on a simple debt since money deposited belongs to the bank, which can use it as it wishes.[182] Conversely, under a "full reserve banking" scheme, the bank's obligation may be conceptualized by analogy to that of a securities intermediary under Article 8 of the *Uniform Commercial Code* in the United States[183] as well as under the Uniform Securities Transactions Act in Canada.[184] According to this legislation, under the "indirect holding" regime, a securities intermediary is liable to an investor on a "securities entitlement" against which the securities intermediary must maintain a 100% "financial asset."[185] At the same time, under a "plain sovereign money" regime the customers will have an entitlement from their banks under an "irregular deposit," which envisages a claim premised on an unidentified portion of a mixture of fungible assets (e.g., money) to which ownership passed to the depositary from the various depositors.[186]

In the final analysis, technological feasibility does not necessarily lead to economic justification. For example, as pointed out at the beginning of this section, albeit ahead of fintech, Goodfriend was on record highlighting the public's substantial efficiency gains of the fractional reserve at the cost of accepted risks, which are anyway mitigated by monetary policy, central bank lending, and deposit insurance.[187] To say the least, under the present system, banks are able to share with customers $profit realized from lending out of demand deposits; the chance is that, in a regime under which scriptural central bank money is available to the public in any form, payment services will be more costly. Whether and to what extent gains in safety outweigh efficiency losses may be in the eyes of the beholder. This section should be taken as outlining banks' continued role and relative advantage in a central bank scriptural money environment rather than necessarily to unequivocally support of such a regime.

V. Cryptocurrencies: Heralding a New Form of Money and Payment Disintermediation?

Innovations discussed previously were accessing accounts and transacting digitally, expressing value on the screen of a digital device, storing value in an SVP so as to give rise to e-money, and making central bank money or its equivalent available to the public. All have not changed the nature of an interbank transfer as a transfer of scriptural money in the form of a balance of monetary value. Nor have they changed the role of the bank as a payment intermediary.

This does not appear to be the case with the emergence of digital currencies. Very much like an electronic payment instruction, a digital coin consists of encrypted data expressed in strings of bits. However, as "an entity that amounts to a string of bits," a coin's string has a numerical value as well as a unique identity.[188] Like physical coins and banknotes, digital coins are not paid out of bank accounts, so their payment does not appear to require intermediation. And yet exactly as with electronic funds transfers, they are paid over cyberspace.

The ensuing discussion excludes currencies not linked to the real economy[189] and is limited to coins that could be liquefied and redeemed, so as to be available for use in real trading, as well as for purchase of goods and services. Payment by such digital coins has the potential of bypassing both the bank account and the centralized multilateral interbank settlement.

A digital currency may be issued either privately or by a central bank.[190] When it is issued privately it may have its own unit of account.[191] Either way, a scheme in which coins are issued and redeemed under a centralized protocol is said to be centralized.[192] A digital currency that is issued, transferred, and redeemed over a *distributed ledger* is decentralized. Finally, a digital currency transferable over a distributed ledger and yet issued by a centralized operator is hybrid.[193]

The distributed ledger underlying decentralization is an asset database that can be shared across a network of multiple sites, geographies, or institutions.[194] Blockchain is an underlying technology, requiring the internet to support and maintain its peer-to-peer network, that enables digital implementation of a distributed ledger. Being a computerized ledger on a distributed network, it generates a single version of the record on each computer and in essence is:[195]

> a type of a database that takes a number of records and puts them in a block . . . Each block is then "chained" to the next block, using a cryptographic signature. This allows block chains to be used like a ledger, which can be shared and corroborated by anyone with the appropriate permissions.

Accuracy of the ledger is corroborated under a method determined under rules adhered to by participants. Record security and visibility to authorized users is ensured by cryptography.

A "*cryptocurrency*" denotes a digital currency in which encryption techniques are used to regulate the generation of units of currency and verify the execution of payment transactions[196] on a decentralized network. Cryptography is thus used in cryptocurrencies to express and protect the value of the coins (the sequence of the bits), to prevent counterfeiting and fraudulent transactions, as well as to perform the validation and execution of transactions records via a distributed ledger, such as the blockchain. Each block contains a cryptographic hash[197] or algorithm that links it to the previous block along with a timestamp for the transactions from that block. The network allows online payments to be sent directly from one party to another without going through a bank or any other centralized counterparty.[198]

The pioneering digital cash scheme, and the most prominent one so far, is Bitcoin.[199] Being "the first and still the most popular cryptocurrency," it "began life as a techno-anarchist project to create an online version of cash, a way for people to transact without the possibility of interference from malicious governments or banks"[200] It is a virtual,[201] self-anchored[202] cryptocurrency and a peer-to-peer decentralized system.[203] In his seminal paper,[204] its mythological founder Satoshi Nakamoto defined bitcoin as an "electronic coin" consisting of a "chain of digital signatures" transferable from the payer to the payee "by digitally signing a hash of the previous transaction and the public key of the next owner and adding them to the end of the coin." Premised on distributed ledger technology (DLT), Bitcoin was born out of an ambition to create government-independent, censorship-resistant money.

The Bitcoin network consists of independent nodes, each operated by a "miner." Miners then bundle each proposed payment with others and create a new block for the blockchain. The new block is hashed and, together with other data, is rehashed. The data is repeatedly fed through a cryptographic "hash" function. The hash is put into the header of the proposed block and becomes the basis for a mathematical puzzle. The "miners" compete to reach a solution for it, and the first to come up with the right solution, as accepted by the majority of miners who submitted "proof of work."[205] is rewarded with newly "minted" bitcoins. The mathematical puzzle is hard to solve, but once found, it is easy for the network to confirm that the answer is correct. Nodes accept the block, whose header contains the hash of the previous block's header, by adding it to the chain that stretches back to the first Bitcoin block (the genesis block), containing the first transaction in the Bitcoin network. This construction is designed to make the Bitcoin blockchain tamper-proof: if one tries to fake a transaction by changing a block that had already been stored in the blockchain that block's hash would be different and ought to be apparent to all as having been tampered with. The "coin" thus carries with it its entire history so that each payment becomes part of its code.

Payments are made from one Bitcoin *wallet* to another. Each such wallet is a computer file or a software program that has an email address. The wallet stores both the private key (in effect the passcode) and the bitcoin[206] balance controlled by it. What is transferred is "monetary fluid" representing the bitcoin sum accessed from the payer's wallet and originating from *all* Bitcoin "coins" accessed from that wallet.[207] Stated otherwise, a payer is unable to designate and set aside for payment any particular bitcoin. In effect, payment can be made in any sum available from the wallet, and regardless, at the end of the process, new bitcoins become associated with the payee's wallet, while those still associated with the payer's wallet may have changed their value and hence their identity. Transaction output is thus said to differ from transaction input, if only due to the diversified chain of provenance of input (from the payer's wallet). It would have been more accurate to speak of a Bitcoin payment resulting in a "coin" being *transformed* rather than *transferred*, except that each resulting "coin" carries with it identities of its predecessors as well as the impact of its subsequent partial use. Transaction information is stored on the blockchain; strictly speaking, the "coins" themselves are not discrete things and are thus not stored anywhere. As a string of bits they however exist in the wallet so that to access them one needs both the password and control over the physical device or cloud having the wallet. If the device is lost, the use of the bitcoins remains available to the owner only where the wallet has been backed up, and as long as the owner has not been preempted by someone else with access to the passcode, such as anyone who could learn it from information available to one in possession of the device.[208]

It is argued that developers of cryptocurrencies "simply migrated the cryptographic tools used to safeguard communication and applied them to safeguard digital currency".[209] Hence the vulnerability to erosive cryptographic intractability from which Bitcoin suffers, in addition to its vulnerability to potential leadership corruption.[210] Also, its operation, whether in facilitating payments, preventing double spending, or issuing new bitcoins, requires substantial computational energy and is thus said to be wasteful.[211] Bitcoin also suffers from poor scalability, as it can handle at most 7 transactions per second,[212] compared to Visa and Mastercard that clear in a second 2,000 transactions,[213] or even a peak-volume of 10,000 transactions per second.[214]

Certainly, however, Bitcoin is driven not only by technological innovation but also by strong sentiments[215] against currency systems based on bank credit[216] and backed by government.[217] Its promoters cite its non-inflationary basis,[218] partly attributed to the limitation on the number of bitcoins to be generated by its protocol. Indeed, in general, Bitcoin's value is premised on its scarcity;[219] its specific value as a monetary asset, in fact "hard money," is the result of its high ratio of the stock to the flow.[220] At the same time, in the long run, the finite number of bitcoins in existence may prove to adversely affect both prices and liquidity.[221] Furthermore, the current 21 million cap is not engraved in stone and is thus subject to change.[222] Regardless, as a self-anchored digital currency, Bitcoin is a mathematical creature; being unsupported by the economic might of an issuer,[223] its principal weakness lies in the inherent instability of its value.[224] In the absence of any "objective rational[e] for any exchange value" Bitcoin is thus likened to "a game that triggered universal interest . . . [but whose] infirmity is as intrinsic as Monopoly money." Last but not least, a competitor's self-anchored math-based currency may emerge and thereby lower the Bitcoin value. This casts a shadow on the acceptability of Bitcoin as a real substitute to fiat currency.[225]

It has specifically been suggested that to meet its unstable value, Bitcoin should be pegged in one way or another to the value of a specific fiat currency or commodity,[226] albeit this can be done only at a heavy ideological cost to its promoters, who highlight Bitcoin's independence from any outside control on both the quantity and the value.

Other than scalability and an unstable value, the principal hurdle for a universal acceptance of cryptocurrencies in general and Bitcoin in particular as the money of the future is that decentralization and the resulting absence of a trusted central counterparty may be more of a curse than a blessing.[227] In other words, efficiency gains in cutting out intermediaries come at costs that outweigh benefits.[228] According to Saifeadean Ammous, inefficiency is inherent in the blockchain technology in general and Bitcoin in particular:[229]

> Bitcoin has a blockchain not because it allows for faster cheaper transactions, but because it removes the need to trust in third party intermediation: transactions are cleared because nodes compete to verify them, yet no node needs to be trusted. It is unworkable for third party intermediaries to imagine they could improve their performance by employing a technology that sacrifices efficiency and speed precisely to remove third party intermediaries. For any currency controlled by a central party, it will always be more efficient to record transactions centrally. Whether removing third party intermediation is a strong enough advantage to justify the increased inefficiency of distributed ledgers is a question that can only be answered over the coming years in the test of market acceptance of digital currencies. What can be clearly seen is that blockchain payment applications will have to be with the blockchain's own decentralized currency, and not with centrally-controlled currencies.

Elsewhere Ammous explains that it is the high processing power threshold that prevents both hacking and the establishment of a central control. Both achievements secure neutrality and full benefit of decentral structure for Bitcoin, and yet at the cost of a fixed supply of growth that cannot be made to adjust to satisfy a purely market-determined demand and hence results in price instability. At the same time, he observes, attempts in other currencies to bypass the expensive, inefficient and wasteful Proof of Work (PoW), by other settlement mechanisms such as Proof of Stake,[230] consensus, or a trusted notary, compromise the neutrality of the system, enhance the control of the issuer, and/or require a third party verificator, all at the expense of the DLT premises. Hence, he concludes, Bitcoin could be no more than a store of value,[231] while other cryptocurrencies cannot fulfill any monetary feature.[232]

Ammous does not see the deflationary nature of Bitcoin as an impediment to its unit of account function. At the same time, having highlighted Bitcoin's inadequacy to serve as a medium of exchange for everyday transactions, he argues that Bitcoin may be "the best store of value humanity ever invented" so as to be capable of functioning as "a reserve currency" to be held by banks in cold storage.[233] Against the Bitcoin reserve banks will perform payment transactions by debiting payers' accounts and crediting those of payees. With Bitcoin reserve banks will settle. However, other than eliminating the central bank, this model will mimic the role of banks in relation to payments in fiat currencies so that everyday Bitcoin transactions will be carried out "off-chain" in effect through banks or similar deposit-taking institutions.[234]

Drawbacks in the utilization of decentralized digital currency schemes have led the way to the consideration of centralized digital currencies issued by trusted issuers such as either central banks or private issuers. In the ongoing fight against counterfeiters and fraudulent copiers centralized schemes are better positioned to apply superior defense measures in protecting the integrity of the database, as well as enhanced security procedures in both coin and identity verification upon redemption and in trade.[235] This is without mentioning the higher scalability of a centrally issued digital coin scheme.

Centralized digital currency schemes require participation of a central player. They are thus premised on a limited disintermediation—under which money moves between the end parties other than through bank accounts. Here are descriptions of two such technologies:

WingCash is a centralized system, allowing the issuer to determine the reserve requirement, under which a claim-check to fiat currency may be issued.[236] It has a multi-issuer platform using a centralized model, allowing for the ledger to replicate in multiple locations. Each claim-check is in the form of a unique web page with an immutably assigned web address (URL), typically cryptographically signed by the issuer. It is described as a digital bearer instrument with a fixed value that simulates a physical banknote. Each digital bearer instrument has a single "possession" attribute so that only the current holder can reassign "possession" to another entity. The ledger immediately records the update to the "possession" attribute to avoid the double-spending problem. As in the case of physical cash, the change of possession from one holder to another constitutes a payment. Therefore, the ledger keeps a record of the change of "possession" of each bearer instrument. Digital notes may be redeemed to fiat currency in the form of either physical cash or bank money. Among 17 faster payments solutions,[237] WingCash's solution for digital Fednotes[238] came tied in the first place.[239]

The second technology is that of *BitMint* facilitating a centralized scheme for a non-speculative and stable currency, consisting of randomized coins, each expressing a claim-check to a defined quantity of a specific commodity, including a fiat currency.[240] It may also be cascaded so as to be denominated in a unit of account anchored on the value of two or more fiat currencies, commodities, or indices.[241] BitMint money is generated through an economical *quantum mechanical process*,[242] which is energy-efficient and reduces waste. BitMint keeps 100% reserve so that the purchasing commodity or fiat currency is always available for redemption on demand. BitMint is said to be identified as "the only candidate qualifying as a universal digital representation of worldwide currencies."[243]

BitMint currency is protected by quantum physics, not dependent on erosive encryption, and claimed to be indefeasible by cyber threats.[244] It has a Validation Hierarchy under which coins are validated through subordinate nodes and may be tethered[245] so as to be "[m]oney with built-in limitation on its use"[246] such as where a coin is cryptographically linked to the rightful owner.[247] Tethering may also facilitate crypto-fusing contractual terms between payer to payee into the money, so as to disallow any use that is in breach of the contract. BitMint money can be split off or amalgamated at any desired resolution[248] and can be paid continuously on a pay-as-you-go basis, for example, as you pump gas into a car gas tank, rather than separately, for example upon the completion of the service.

In the final analysis a centralized digital currency system is modeled on a "note-based" e-money scheme discussed in Section IV of this chapter, except that due to technological advancements the chance is that it entails higher if not unlimited circulation of coins among a larger if not unlimited number of participants. Facilitating payment from one device to another without communication to a bank may revolutionize both payments and money holding patterns. However, inasmuch as digital coins are to be bought with bank money and ultimately may be redeemed in bank money, a centralized digital currency scheme, while being bound to change means and methods of payment, will arguably not change fundamentals as to the quantity of money and the role of banks in its creation and transmission.[249]

VI. Conclusion

In migrating "cryptographic tools used to safeguard communication and appl[ying] them to safeguard digital currency"[250] cryptocurrency developers effectively engineered payment disintermediation. They did so by means of tools that originally were fashioned to enhance payment intermediation through safeguarding interbank as well as customer-to-bank and bank-to-customer communication. Once issues of volatility, scalability, and deflation are resolved, cryptocurrencies have indeed the potential to generate means of payment "offering much of the anonymity of cash while also allowing transactions at long distances" and yet allowing people to "clear and settle quickly without an intermediary."[251] Ironically then, it is the evolution of a process in banking, enhancing payment intermediation, which could lead to the demise of banks as payment intermediaries. The result will not change even if centralized digital currencies are to supersede cryptocurrencies.

However, in my view, the chance is that the demise of both banks and payment intermediation will not happen or at least not anytime soon. Certainly, we shall see some measure of payment disintermediation in the form of improved cryptocurrencies as well as centralized digital currencies. At the same time, banks have been fighting back to improve their own legacy systems.[252] Thereby they may successfully compete with digital currency payment services providers. For its part, a successful centralized digital currency system is likely to count on commercial banks buying and selling the currencies into and out of accounts maintained with them so as to become a universal "note-based" e-money scheme linked to banks and the legacy monetary system.

Regardless, it is hard to see banks as both depositaries and lenders of money disappearing. Rather, they are likely to get themselves into the digital currency space and provide services as well as be in a position to cover risks that customers would prefer not to incur on their own. Also, there is a good chance that in competing with banks, IT firms that are issuers of digital currencies will become rather than supersede banks. And even if cryptoassets may one day reduce demand for central bank money I doubt that the public will be ready to have control on the quantity of money surrendered to digital currency developers. Whether centralized digital currencies are to be traded with or issued by commercial banks, or whether central banks are to take over from the private sector the issue of digital currencies, whether under a centralized or decentralized scheme, changes to monetary policy will not be substantial even if the use of banks as payment intermediaries will be affected.

Possibly, both practicalities and anti-money-laundering and terrorist financing regulations may limit the size of payments to be made in digital currencies. Furthermore, the chance is that for a large payment, a real-time gross settlement (RTGS) system, with liquidity-saving mechanisms, settled between commercial banks on the books of a trusted central bank, will be preferred by participants over a large peer-to-peer digital cash payment between them. For now, we can only speculate on the scope and magnitude of future developments.[253]

3

Deconstructing "Decentralization"

Exploring the Core Claim of Crypto Systems

*Angela Walch**

Decentralization is what allows Bitcoin to substitute an army of
computers for an army of accountants, investigators, and lawyers.
—Nick Szabo, Twitter.[1]

[B]ased on my understanding of the present state of Ether, the
Ethereum network and its decentralized structure, current offers and
sales of Ether are not securities transactions . . .
—William Hinman, Director, Division of Corporation Finance, SEC,
Remarks at the Yahoo Finance All Markets Summit: Crypto:
Digital Asset Transactions: When Howey Met Gary (Plastic).[2]

I'm a little worried people from government agencies are throwing
around the word "decentralization" like we know what it means and
how to evaluate it.
—Neha Narula, Director, MIT Digital Currency Initiative, Twitter.[3]

So I spent a couple weeks reading everything I could about the term
"decentralization" and have come to a conclusion: we should ditch
the term.
—Tony Sheng, Let's ditch "decentralized," www.tonysheng.com.[4]

* Professor of Law, St. Mary's University School of Law. Research Fellow, Centre for Blockchain
Technologies, University College London. I would like to thank Edmund Schuster, Peter Van
Valkenburgh, Nic Carter, Oliver Beige, Ciaran Murray, Michèle Finck, Michel Rauchs, Gina Pieters,
Stefan Loesch, Frances Coppola, Carla Reyes, Kristin Johnson, Usha Rodrigues, Joan Heminway,
Odysseas Sclavounis, Andrew Glidden, Paolo Saguato, Chris Brummer, Drew Hinkes, Stephen
Palley, Nelson Rosario, Brett Scott, Vlad Zamfir, participants at Fintech Week 2018 at the Institute
for International Economic Law at Georgetown Law School on Nov. 5–8, 2018; participants in the
Cryptoassets and the Law Workshop at the London School of Economics on Sept. 4, 2018; participants
at the 4th Annual Law & Money Conference at Sheffield Law School on Sept. 3, 2018; participants
in the Securities Law section discussion at the Association of American Law Schools 2019 Annual
Meeting on Jan. 5, 2019; students in my Fall 2018 Blockchain Technologies, Cryptocurrencies &
the Law course; and the active crypto Twitterverse for valuable discussions, feedback, and insights.
I thank Rebecca Bredt for excellent research assistance.

Cryptoassets. Chris Brummer.
© Oxford University Press 2019. Published 2019 by Oxford University Press.

On June 14, 2018, William Hinman, Director of the SEC's Division of Corporation Finance, seized the crypto[5] world's attention when he stated that "current offers and sales of Ether are not securities transactions" and linked this conclusion to the "sufficiently decentralized" structure of the Ethereum network.[6]

While one speech of an SEC employee does not binding law make, Hinman's was notable in demonstrating how pervasive the belief that blockchains are "decentralized" has become, and that a blockchain's level of "decentralization" is being used to draw conclusions—and potentially make legal decisions—about these systems.

If this is the case, and "decentralized" is transitioning from a marketing term for cryptoassets to one of legal import, we must be clear about what we mean when we describe blockchain networks or systems as "decentralized."[7] Do we mean they have lots of computer nodes running the software, and that those nodes are distributed across the globe? That the software development process is spread amongst many developers who have similar authority to make changes to the software? That the hashing power of record producers (miners) in the network is not concentrated in a small group?

This chapter does not provide a securities law analysis of Ethereum or any other blockchain system, as it has broader goals. Gaining a deeper understanding of the concept of "decentralization" in blockchain systems is important even if the SEC and the courts decide not to make a blockchain's level of decentralization relevant to a cryptoasset's status as a security.[8] This is because the term "decentralized" is generally being used to describe how power operates in blockchain systems—suggesting that power exercised by people in these systems is diffuse rather than concentrated. This is critically important, as our understanding of how power is exercised within these systems will shape conclusions about how responsibility, accountability, and risk should work for them—that is, pretty much every legal determination we make about them. So, it's simply not good enough to say that a blockchain system is decentralized because, well, blockchains are decentralized, and this is a blockchain. We must decide whether "decentralized" is a meaningful way to evaluate a blockchain system, and if so, we must be precise about what we mean by the term, and which portions of a complex blockchain system we are referring to. The concept of "decentralization" is a foundational, infrastructural one for blockchains—if we gloss over what it means, we risk unintended consequences when these systems do not behave like we expect them to.[9]

In this chapter, I seek to do several things. In Section I, I describe the current use of the term "decentralized" as applied to permissionless blockchains like Bitcoin and Ethereum,[10] and argue that the term has been widely used to suggest that these systems are resilient and that there is a lack of centralized (and therefore accountable) power wielded in these systems. In Section II, I analyze the complex, contested nature of the term, delving into issues such as the different domains where power is exercised in blockchain systems and the fluid nature of power concentration and diffusion in these systems. In Section III, I provide examples of events that reveal sites of concentrated power in permissionless blockchain systems, focusing on the activities of software developers and miners. Finally, in Section IV, I explore the significant implications for law of using a fuzzy term such as "decentralized" to make legal decisions, as misunderstandings about power hidden in the term can lead to flawed decisions across a wide swath of legal fields. I conclude that making decisions based on an unsubstantiated conclusion that a given blockchain (or blockchains generally) is (are) "decentralized" is highly problematic, and that courts, regulators, and even potential adopters or users of cryptoassets (whether directly or through other financial products) should use other factors to inform their decisions about a blockchain. Like many other descriptors of blockchain technology (e.g., immutable, trustless, reflects truth), the adjective "decentralized" as an inevitable characteristic of blockchain technology proves to be an overstatement, and we know that making decisions based on overstatements rather than reality can lead to bad consequences.[11]

I. Mainstream Discourse around "Decentralized" Permissionless Blockchains

Virtually every description of cryptoassets or blockchain technologies includes the adjective "decentralized."[12] Indeed, "decentralization" is viewed as a core feature of blockchain systems, and one of the magic ingredients that is said to enable these systems to generate a record that is very difficult to alter, reliably reflects transactions in the system's native digital token,[13] and does not require trust in a single, central party.

In this Section I, I discuss the mainstream use of the term "decentralized" in blockchain systems, and argue that the term is often used to suggest that blockchain systems are (1) resilient, and (2) free from the exercise of concentrated power. As we will see, this includes Director Hinman's comments about how the decentralization of a blockchain system relates to its token's status as a security.

First, it is important to emphasize how ubiquitous the terms "decentralized" and "decentralization" are in the discourse around blockchain technologies and cryptoassets.[14] The terms are present in academic works of relevant disciplines,[15] in discussions within the crypto space, in conference names galore,[16] and in countless reports by businesses, governments and international organizations. Software applications built on top of the Ethereum blockchain are known as "dapps"—short for "decentralized applications." There are multiple "decentralized exchanges" (known as "DEXs" in the industry) being built, which seek to break up the power that centralized exchanges such as Coinbase and Binance have accrued in the sector.[17] Legislators are using these words in statutory definitions of blockchain technology.[18] In short, the words "decentralized" and "decentralization" are inescapable in discussions about the technology.

Further, in mainstream discourse, it has been rare to see clear explanations of "decentralized" or "decentralization" when they are used. For example, in Arizona's statute that uses the term "decentralized" to define "blockchain technology," there is no definition of "decentralized" to be found.[19] Most mainstream descriptions of blockchain technologies or cryptoassets state simply that blockchains are decentralized. End of story. Decentralized is just something that blockchains are. An inherent characteristic. An essential and identifying feature. As I will discuss in Section II, this reflexive use of "decentralized" contrasts sharply with an active discussion among academics and thought leaders within the crypto space about the problematic nature of the term.

"Decentralized" is used in several senses in mainstream blockchain discourse. First, it is used to describe the network of computers (often referred to as "nodes") that comprise a permissionless blockchain, as these systems operate through peer-to-peer connections between computers, rather than on a central server. A core feature of permissionless blockchains such as Bitcoin or Ethereum is that the record generated by the system is stored on many computers within the network, rather than just on one. The idea is that many of the nodes are independent, so that a failure of one does not mean a failure of many or all. This "decentralized" storage of the record supports claims that the record is highly resilient, as the record is likely to persist so long as at least one of the computers continues to hold it. Of course, many factors could influence the actual resilience of the network, such as the geographical distribution of the nodes (affecting their common vulnerability to weather, natural disasters, and the like) or the common ownership of them (one party may own many and could turn all of its nodes off at once). But, at base, because there is not a central computer maintaining the blockchain record, it is *decentralized* rather than *centralized* (more than one party is involved).

The second way "decentralized" is commonly used is to describe how power or agency works within permissionless blockchain systems.[20] If there is not a single, central party keeping the record, that means that no single party has responsibility for it, and thus no single party is accountable for it. This concept of decentralization, or power diffusion, has more political or ideological undertones to it, and seems tied to the cypher-punk, crypto-anarchist roots of Bitcoin (the first blockchain). In serving as a money outside of state control, Bitcoin was a reaction to the central power of a state, and if those who were part of the system could convince the public (as well as the state) that power was diffuse within the system, then no particular person could be held legally accountable for what happened in connection with the system. In a "decentralized" system like Bitcoin, one could convincingly argue that power was everywhere and nowhere at the same time, that, in Melanie Swan's words, "authority float[s] freely."[21] Those in the permissionless blockchain world talk about seizing power from the state and existing powerful institutions like banks or tech platforms (e.g., Google or Facebook), and building a new "decentralized world," where power has been spread around.[22] Within the crypto space, Bitcoin advocates often criticize other permissionless blockchains as not truly decentralized, pointing to clusters of power or agency within the systems. To be fully decentralized (whatever that means) is viewed as one of the ultimate goals of a permissionless blockchain system, a utopian summit to be scaled.[23]

In picking up the terms from the crypto space, and using them uncritically (or at least with insufficient critical inquiry), the conflations and overstatements embedded in the terms have helped to establish people's beliefs about the characteristics of permissionless blockchain systems. As I argued in an earlier paper, the terminology in the blockchain space is highly problematic and misleading, due to numerous factors.[24] As I will discuss further in Section II, decentralization is inherently both a political concept and a physical description of computer networks. Here, both political (no one has any power, especially not the state) and physical (we have a lot of computers running, so you can't easily knock the entire system out) meanings have melded in mainstream usage of the terms.

Perhaps unsurprisingly, Director Hinman's June 2018 speech reflected these melded meanings of "decentralized," and thus seems representative of the common narrative around decentralization in permissionless blockchains. Here are relevant excerpts from the speech.

> If the network on which the token or coin is to function is sufficiently decentralized—where purchasers would no longer reasonably expect a person or group to carry out essential managerial or entrepreneurial efforts—the assets may not represent an investment contract. . . .
>
> [W]hen the efforts of the third party are no longer a key factor for determining the enterprise's success, material information asymmetries recede. As a network becomes truly decentralized, the ability to identify an issuer or promoter to make the requisite disclosures becomes difficult, and less meaningful. . . .

[W]hen I look at Bitcoin today, I do not see a central third party whose efforts are a key determining factor in the enterprise. The network on which Bitcoin functions is operational and appears to have been decentralized for some time, perhaps from inception. . . .

[B]ased on my understanding of the present state of Ether, the Ethereum network and its decentralized structure, current offers and sales of Ether are not securities transactions. . . .

Over time, there may be other sufficiently decentralized networks and systems where regulating the tokens or coins that function on them as securities may not be required. And of course there will continue to be systems that rely on central actors whose efforts are a key to the success of the enterprise.[25]

In these excerpts, we see an emphasis on (1) networks and (2) difficulty in identifying or "seeing" a central party playing a determining role in the system. In each of these excerpts, "decentralized" is used to describe the *network* of the applicable blockchain (Bitcoin or Ethereum) (e.g., "if the *network* . . . is sufficiently *decentralized*," "as a *network* becomes truly *decentralized*," "[t]he *network* on which Bitcoin functions . . . appears to have been *decentralized* for some time," "based on my understanding of the present state of Ether, the Ethereum *network* and its *decentralized* structure," and "there may be other sufficiently *decentralized networks* and systems"). This phrasing suggests that Hinman is looking at the network of computers that comprise the Ethereum and Bitcoin systems to support his statements that the systems are decentralized—that is, using the physical connotation of "decentralized."

Further, we see in these excerpts statements that it is difficult to find a central party within the systems who is determining what happens in the system (e.g., "[a]s a network becomes truly decentralized, the ability *to identify* an issuer or promoter to make the requisite disclosures becomes difficult . . . ," "when I look at Bitcoin today, I *do not see* a central third party whose efforts are a key determining factor in the enterprise"). The language here is suggestive of vision or sight—Hinman *cannot see* a central third party doing important things in systems such as Bitcoin or present-day Ethereum to ensure the systems' success.

Why is Hinman focusing on the ability to identify a party who could make required disclosures about the token of a blockchain system? Because it is relevant to determining whether an instrument (here, a blockchain token) is a security under the U.S. securities laws.[26] Hinman uses the concept of decentralization to refer to how people exercise power within the Bitcoin and Ethereum systems, consistent with my claim about mainstream usage of the term "decentralized." (Interestingly, he appears to be conflating the physical features of the network (which impact its resilience) with the way power works within the system.) The standard for determining whether a transaction represents an "investment contract" and thereby a security comes from the venerable *SEC v. W.J. Howey Co.,* a 1946 U.S. Supreme Court case about interests in citrus groves.[27] The *Howey* test states that there is an investment contract (and thereby a security) when there is (1) a contract, transaction, or scheme; (2) whereby a person invests money; (3) in a common enterprise; and (4) is led to expect profits solely from the efforts of others.[28] The fourth factor has been expanded over the years to remove the requirement that profits be expected *solely* from the efforts of others. Hinman indicates whose efforts would be relevant in his June 2018 remarks:

> *The important factor in the legal analysis is that there is a person or coordinated group (including "any unincorporated organization" see 5 U.S.C. § 77n(a)(4)) that is working actively to develop or guide the development of the infrastructure of the network.* This person or group could be founders, sponsors, developers or "promoters" in the traditional sense. The presence of promoters in this context is important to distinguish from the circumstance where multiple, independent actors work on the network but no individual actor's or coordinated group of actors' efforts are essential efforts that affect the failure or success of the enterprise.[29]

Hinman also provides a series of questions to guide potential token issuers as to whether their token offering will be considered a securities offering. Several of the questions focus on power exercised by people within the blockchain system, that is, "whether a third party—be it a person, entity or coordinated group of actors—drives the expectation of a return [from the sale of the token]."[30] These questions include:

(1) Is there a person or group that has sponsored or promoted the creation and sale of the digital asset, the efforts of whom play a significant role in the development and maintenance of the asset and its potential increase in value?

(2) Does application of the Securities Act protections make sense? Is there a person or entity others are relying on that plays a key role in the profit-making of the enterprise such that disclosure of their activities and plans would be important to investors? Do informational asymmetries exist between the promoters and potential purchasers/investors in the digital asset?

(3) Do persons or entities other than the promoter exercise governance rights or meaningful influence?[31]

The excerpted portions of Hinman's speech all suggest that the term "decentralized" is being used to describe how power works in a given blockchain system—whether certain actors' actions "are essential efforts that affect the failure or success of the enterprise."[32] Hinman's statement that both the Bitcoin and Ethereum blockchain systems are "sufficiently decentralized" such that their tokens are not securities indicates that, according to his understanding of Bitcoin and Ethereum as of June 14, 2018, neither system contained "a person or coordinated group (including "any unincorporated organization" . . .) that [wa]s working actively to develop or guide the development of the infrastructure of the network."[33] Again, using Hinman's language, he "*do[es] not see* a central third party whose efforts are a key determining factor in the enterprise."[34]

It is unsurprising, therefore, that industry organizations for the crypto and blockchain sector have strongly endorsed Hinman's use of "decentralization" to help to determine whether a blockchain token is a security.[35] The newly formed Blockchain Association, an industry trade organization, has called for "decentralization" to be measured under "The Hinman Token Standard," arguing that the characteristics that both Ethereum and Bitcoin possessed on the day of Hinman's speech (June 14, 2018) should set a ceiling on the requirements for a system to be "sufficiently decentralized" that its token is not a security.[36] The Blockchain Association stated:

> [D]evelopers of open source, public blockchain networks and those in the community that help foster their development should work with counsel to understand that the announced Hinman Token Standard likely *has not set an impossibly or unreasonably high standard for decentralization*. Open-source and cryptocurrency projects often need or choose to have *some* centralized leadership, and at times considerable centralized leadership on their path to decentralization. As demonstrated by both bitcoin and ether, the Hinman guidance has established that having some level of centralized leadership will not condemn a token to being classified as a security on that basis alone.[37]

Tellingly, the Blockchain Association acknowledges the "centralized leadership" present in both Bitcoin and Ethereum, which does support its argument that the SEC has set a low bar to be considered "sufficiently decentralized." I agree with the trade group that the SEC's standard for "sufficiently decentralized" is extremely low,[38] and seek to demonstrate in Sections II and III of this chapter that a deeper analysis of the concept is needed.

* * *

In this Section I, I have painted a picture of the ways "decentralized" is used in common discourse, focusing on the common use of the term within the academic, governmental, and industry domains, and particularly on SEC

Director Hinman's use of the term to support his statement that Bitcoin and Ether are not securities. I argue that the term is used (1) to describe the network features (e.g., number of computers in the network), supporting claims that a blockchain system is resilient; and (2) to describe how power operates in the system, supporting claims that power is diffuse and must therefore be unaccountable. I see both of these common meanings as imprecise, and potentially completely inaccurate (depending on which blockchain system we're talking about), and in Section II, I delve deeper into the meaning of "decentralized" as applied to blockchain systems.

II. The Complex Nature of "Decentralization"

In this section, I analyze the concept of decentralization in permissionless blockchains, in order to demonstrate the complex, contested meaning of the term. It turns out I am far from alone in critiquing the use of "decentralized" to describe blockchain systems. In fact, in the past few years, exploring the concept of "decentralization" has become a trend for thought leaders and academics in the crypto space.[39] Venture capitalists, Ethereum creator Vitalik Buterin, and others have attempted to articulate what "decentralization" means.[40] In this subsection, I provide an overview of these takes, drawing out the important themes. This analysis will buttress my arguments in Section IV about the implications of making legal decisions based on a superficial conclusion that a given permissionless blockchain system is decentralized.

Notable Themes

A. No One Knows What "Decentralization" Means

A pervasive theme of all analyses is that decentralization is often discussed as essential and a feature that differentiates crypto systems from others, yet it is much more complex than commonly realized, and is poorly understood.

Part of the complexity in the concept stems from the complexity of permissionless blockchain systems themselves. Crypto systems are comprised of many different actors, including the developers who write and maintain the software code, the miners (or record producers) who process transactions and add them to the common record, and the nodes, who send transaction to miners and maintain copies of the blockchain record. Many commentators noted that the decentralization level of a crypto system as a whole was dependent upon each subsystem within it being decentralized as well.[41] So, for example, if the software development process is centralized to a small number of developers, the system as a whole could not be considered decentralized, even if mining was widely distributed and there were thousands of nodes spread throughout the globe. Some noted that actors outside the system could also impact the decentralization level of a crypto system. Exchanges were noted as a site of potential centralization, as they have the power to choose whether or not to list a particular token for trading.[42] Holders of tokens were cited by others as potential sites of centralization, as in many crypto systems, ownership is concentrated in a very small number of people (often referred to as "whales"). The number of software implementations of a blockchain system's protocol could also affect centralization, particularly if there is a dominant one.[43] Thus, it is not helpful to describe a blockchain system as decentralized unless one is specific about how he or she is measuring the level of decentralization in each domain of the system.

A number of analyses noted that attempts at quantification of decentralization were more meaningful in certain subsystems than in others. For instance, it is possible to count numbers of computer nodes within a system, and potentially (though not very easily, probably) determine how ownership of the nodes is distributed. Similarly, one could measure percentages of hashing power held by a given miner or mining pool.[44] These domains lend themselves to numeric measurements. Yet, as emphasized by commentators such as Sarah Jamie Lewis, Nic Carter, and Michel Rauchs et al., the governance of the software development process is just as relevant to how decentralized a system is, but is much more difficult to quantify or measure, as it deals with the behavior of individuals and often unwritten norms.[45] Moreover, behind every computer in the network, whether miner or node, there is ultimately a person who controls the computer, whose human unpredictability may bleed into governance of the system in unexpected ways.

B. Satoshi Didn't Invent Decentralization

Although "decentralize all the things" has become something of a rallying cry in the crypto world, commentators noted that the concept of decentralization has a long history, both inside and outside the realm of technology. Finck and Barabas et al. link the current excitement about disrupting large institutions through decentralization to that of the early days of the internet.[46] Carter notes the relevance of political science and sociology literature on decentralized governance, as well as the history of open-source software governance.[47] Atzori's excellent political analysis of blockchain-based decentralized governance explores where it is situated in various strands of political theory.[48]

The political or ideological roots of the concept of decentralization is, unsurprisingly, a common theme. Decentralization is fundamentally about diffusing power by distributing it away from a central point of control—sharing that power among many. The idea of decentralization is, of course, a foundational principle of many of our most basic institutional governance structures, from the federalist system that shares power between the states and federal government in the United States, to the checks and balances inherent in the three branches of the U.S. government, to the principle of subsidiarity in the European Union that pushes power away from the center. Decentralization is often about disruption or revolution—breaking up existing power structures, with hopes of spreading power around. The decentralization mantra around blockchains follows in that vein, including the discussions about "being your own bank" or "owning your digital identity" or creating money not issued by a central bank.

C. Decentralized Does Not Equal Distributed

The terms "distributed" and "decentralized" are often used interchangeably in describing blockchain systems. According to the Cambridge Centre for Alternative Finance's *Distributed Ledger Technology Systems: A Conceptual Framework* (the "CCAF Report"), "decentralized" is used to indicate that the nodes operating in a system are controlled by different parties, rather than by the same entity.[49] The CCAF Report states that "distributed" is used to indicate that "storage or computation . . . is divided into parts and occurs across multiple servers or nodes ("parallelized"), but "may still rely on a central coordinator to act as an authoritative source of records."[50]

D. Decentralization Exists on a Spectrum

The CCAF Report points out that "decentralization" of a distributed ledger technology system (including a permissionless blockchain) "is not a simple binary property," as "the degree of centralization reflects the accumulation of interacting decisions and tradeoffs at various layers. In practice, it is more useful to identify the contributing factors to centralization and decentralization across a spectrum, as pure decentralization is a seldom-achieved ideal at both the hardware and software levels."[51] Indeed, it is helpful to envision a spectrum of centralization, with any change made to a given subsystem (e.g., nodes, developers, miners) moving the system toward greater or lesser centralization, rather than a bright line demarcating centralized versus decentralized.

E. Decentralization Is Dynamic rather than Static

The CCAF Report notes that the "power dynamics" within a blockchain system "can be fluid and evolve over time, which further complicates the task of forming a definitive assessment of the system."[52] Hinman's speech also hints at the dynamic nature of decentralization by stressing that his conclusions about whether Ether is a security are based on its characteristics (i.e., its level of decentralization) as of the date of his speech.

The fluctuating nature of a system's level of decentralization is worth emphasizing, as every passing second could bring massive changes to it. So many factors affect how decentralized a blockchain system is that a change to *any* of those factors can shift the blockchain on the decentralization spectrum. For instance, if a significant miner loses power due to a natural disaster or is shut down by a government, the power dynamics within the mining network will shift. If one of the core developers who has the password to merge changes to a particular blockchain software client loses this privilege because the other core developers no longer trust him, the power dynamics within the software development process will shift. If it becomes prohibitively expensive to run a node, or a rumor circulates that running a node is illegal and many nodes drop out, that will shift the level of decentralization of the system.

The critical takeaway here is that any measurement of decentralization is obsolete immediately after it has been calculated. In a permissionless system, anyone can join, and no one has to stay, so the system's composition is, in theory, always in flux.

F. Decentralization Is Aspirational, Not Actual

Commentators have noted that "decentralization" in blockchain systems is not something that has been achieved yet, but instead is merely a goal of current systems.[53] This emphasizes how immature the development of blockchain technologies is, as well as the limited progress that has been made in building a "decentralized world." Another way of putting it is that at present, decentralization in blockchain systems is "all hat, no cattle."

Some initiatives are open about their current, highly concentrated power structures, noting that they need centralized decision-making and highly coordinated actions to build the system, and *then* expect it to become decentralized.[54] Of course, transforming a centralized institution into a decentralized one will require those who wield power in a centralized organization to give it up, and a widely dispersed, divergent group to pick up pieces of that power—quite a significant ask.

· If decentralization is aspirational for these systems, then they are currently similar to existing institutions with centralized power, but for some reason the builders of these systems claim they are different. Other than having a stated goal of becoming decentralized, there is no more reason to expect them to succeed in becoming decentralized than there is to expect existing institutions (e.g., banks) to transition from centralized to decentralized organizations.

G. Decentralization Can Be Used to Hide Power or Enable Rule-Breaking

Some commentators discussed how decentralization enables groups of people to obscure power and escape consequences for breaking rules.[55] Several discussed BitTorrent, which was able to continue operating despite threats to shut it down, and despite rampant copyright infringement through the use of the protocol.[56] As one former BitTorrent Inc. executive wrote recently, "if you're not Breaking Rules you're Doing it Wrong," in explaining the lessons BitTorrent holds for the crypto world.[57] Morris notes that "Decentralization in the sense it is applied to blockchain technologies . . . means creating an uncensorable system that enables the unfettered breaking of rules."[58]

As is well known, cryptocurrencies were initially associated with the criminal underworld of money laundering and the purchase of illicit goods and services on the Dark Web at sites such as Silk Road. Many still argue that these illegal activities represent the only real use cases for cryptocurrencies in the long term, as any lawful uses do not demand the ability to evade law enforcement, so can use more efficient centralized systems with known and accountable participants.

As I will discuss later on in the chapter, the term "decentralized" is being used to hide actions by participants in the system in a fog of supposedly "freely floating authority," and we must be vigilant not to overlook pockets of authority and power within these systems.

H. Calls to Action

The status quo usage of the terms "decentralized" and "decentralization" is deemed untenable by many commentators, and there are a variety of calls to action in the literature. Some simply call for deeper study of the term,[59] others propose frameworks for better understanding or measuring the decentralization of crypto systems,[60] while one proposes doing away with the terms altogether in discussing crypto systems.[61] The rationale behind these calls to action is that current usage of the term is creating misunderstandings about the capabilities of the technology. Further, it is clearly creating misunderstandings about how power works in these systems, with the potential for error in how law or regulation treats these systems and the people who act within them.

III. Examples of Concentrations of Power in Permissionless Blockchain Systems

Having demonstrated that "decentralization" is a problematic concept when applied to permissionless blockchains, in this Section III, I provide examples of actions within the Bitcoin and Ethereum blockchain systems that undermine claims that either system is particularly decentralized. A similar analysis could be done on every permissionless blockchain that exists (indeed, every single blockchain will be unique in this regard). In essence, I believe that many (including the SEC) are overlooking important sites of concentrated power within the Bitcoin and Ethereum systems (and potentially others), and instead are relying on simplistic views of decentralization to draw conclusions.[62]

These pockets of power include key developers and significant miners within the systems.[63] One could argue that every single line of code actually released to the network is an exercise of power by a particular software developer or small group of developers, as only a small number of developers (known as core developers) within a blockchain system have commit keys that enable them to make changes to the code repository. Every line of code reflects a policy choice about the blockchain system as a whole (e.g., how expensive should it be to participate in the system?) and technical choices about how to best reflect the policy mandate in code. (It is true that developers cannot compel anyone to run the software they release, but it is clear their influence is great.)

Run-of-the-mill software upgrades are not nearly as exciting as crisis software upgrades and clandestine meetings, however. The episodes I discuss later on in this section highlight moments where concentrations of power are vividly clear.[64] In Bitcoin, these moments include emergency rescues of the system by small groups of developers in the fall of 2018 (when a critical software bug was discovered) and in March 2013 (when the blockchain suffered an unintended hard fork). In Ethereum, these moments include the invite-only meetings held by key software developers in the fall of 2018 and the actions key developers took during the July 2016 hard fork in response to the DAO hack.[65] Power concentrations undermining claims of decentralization are also evident in the large portions of hashing power held by mining pools in each network. Finally, a series of 51% attacks on many permissionless blockchains, including the

January 2019 51% attack on Ethereum Classic, demonstrate the power dominant miners wield over these networks. In the following subsections, I discuss
each of these issues in turn.

A. Critical Bug Discovery and Fix in Bitcoin Software in Fall 2018

On September 17, 2018, five developers of Bitcoin software were notified of a
serious bug in several Bitcoin software clients, including Bitcoin Core, Bitcoin
ABC, and Bitcoin Unlimited.[66] The bug could allow a denial of service (DoS)
attack on Bitcoin, which could affect the security of the network. The five
developers quickly shared the information with four other Bitcoin developers,
one of whom realized that the bug actually had two potential implications, the
second even more critical than the DoS vulnerability originally reported.[67] If
exploited, the bug could enable someone to create Bitcoins out of thin air, in
excess of the celebrated cap of 21 million. This "inflation bug" could devastate
the cryptocurrency, undermining the public's faith in its credibility. The incident report from the software developers of Bitcoin Core, published several
days later on September 20, 2018, makes for riveting reading, and includes this
description of what happened after the discovery of the inflation bug (note the
use of the passive voice):

> In order to encourage rapid upgrades, *the decision was made* to immediately
> patch and disclose the less serious Denial of Service vulnerability, concurrently
> with reaching out to miners, businesses, and other affected systems while de-
> laying publication of the full issue to give times for systems to upgrade.[68]

The time log of events makes clear that at the time "the decision was made" to
announce only the less severe bug implication and not the inflation implications,
a maximum of 11 people knew about the inflation bug (it is unclear whether all
the developers mentioned in the incident report knew of the inflation bug, or
whether some were only informed of the DoS aspect of the bug).[69]

To be more explicit: fewer than a dozen people decided on September 17,
2018, to:

- withhold information about the critical implications of a bug from the
  public;
- prepare a patch that would fix both the DoS and inflation vulnerabilities;
- urge miners and nodes within the network to immediately install the
  patch on the basis that it fixed only a DoS bug; and

- disclose the critical inflation bug only after miners and others had upgraded with the ostensibly DoS-bug-only patch.

The developers only disclosed the critical inflation implications of the bug to the public on September 20, 2018—three days later.[70] As a quick reminder of the significance of their actions, on September 17, 2018, a Bitcoin traded for around $6,500 (U.S.), with a market cap of more than $108 billion.[71]

Further demonstrating the power of a select few within the Bitcoin system is the fact that the Bitcoin Core core developers initially contacted the "CEO of slushpool," one of the major Bitcoin mining pools, and within 20 minutes of the communication, the pool had upgraded to the recommended software.[72]

One could write many papers about the implications of this event,[73] but it is relevant to my argument in this chapter because it shows (in Hinman's words) "a . . . coordinated group . . . that is working actively to develop or guide the development of the infrastructure of the network."[74] Indeed, one could easily call the bug-fixing actions of this "coordinated group of [fewer than 12] actors . . . *essential efforts that affect[ed] the failure or success of the [Bitcoin] enterprise.*"[75] If they hadn't fixed the bug immediately, the Bitcoin system faced potentially catastrophic failure. To be clear, I am not criticizing the people involved in the fix for the decisions they made to save the network, but it is evident that their actions are inconsistent with statements that the Bitcoin system is decentralized.

Perhaps one good rule of thumb for policymakers is that if some things have to be kept secret from others, the system is not decentralized. In Hinman's words, secrets held by a small number of developers indicate that "informational asymmetries exist between the promoters [defined broadly by Hinman to include developers] and potential purchasers/investors in the digital asset." Put simply, secrets reveal centralization.

As I have argued previously, moments of crisis uncover where actual power lies in a system.[76] In this case, the resolution of the Bitcoin inflation bug revealed the power concentrated in the hands of a few software developers, strongly undermining any claims that the system is decentralized. While Director Hinman could not have been aware of this particular action by Bitcoin developers when he delivered his June 2018 speech several months before the bug fix, this was not the first time a small group of Bitcoin developers acted to save the system.

B. Bitcoin's March 2013 Hard Fork

A similar rescue by a few Bitcoin developers occurred in March 2013, when Bitcoin experienced an unexpected fork of the network.[77] Nodes in the network were running different versions of software due to uneven upgrading to a new software release, and this caused the network to split in two. Upon discovering the fork, key developers determined which version of the forked ledger should be treated as the "real" Bitcoin and reached out to miners in the network to urge them to support the chosen ledger. To do so, some miners had to adopt the earlier software version, and lost earnings they had made on the rejected ledger. Once enough miners switched over, the network returned to a single ledger.

As with the 2018 inflation bug fix, the few software developers who acted to remedy the 2013 hard fork revealed their power within the Bitcoin system. These developers selected the authoritative ledger, creating winners and losers among the miners, depending on which version of the ledger they had been mining during the fork. Developers were able to communicate with particular miners and persuade them to run a particular version of software. These core developers, again, looked like a "coordinated group of actors . . . (whose) *essential efforts . . . affect[ed] the failure or success of the [Bitcoin] enterprise.*"[78]

C. Secret Meetings of Ethereum Core Developers in Fall 2018

In the fall of 2018, during the DevCon conference in Prague, a group of key Ethereum software developers gathered to discuss potential upgrades to the system. The meeting was invitation-only, and, deviating from common practice for meetings or calls of the core developers, was not live-streamed. When news of the meeting broke to the rest of the Ethereum development community, there were immediate accusations of centralization and power grabs.[79]

In other multibillion dollar enterprises,[80] a strategy meeting of senior decision-makers would raise no eyebrows, but in a nominally decentralized, uncoordinated system that simply maintains open source software, holding analogous meetings is taboo. Amidst the uproar, different positions were aired, with some arguing that invite-only meetings were anathema to the ethos of open-source software development, and others arguing that leading developers needed the privacy to speak freely about possible risks and benefits of changes to the system, without the media immediately reporting and potentially twisting their words.[81] The issue remains unresolved, amidst efforts to better define how governance does and should operate within Ethereum. Notably, at least one Ethereum software developer meeting since the invite-only one was conducted under Chatham House Rules, enabling participants to speak freely without fear of attribution.[82]

Why would these invite-only meetings matter so much, and what do they have to do with the decentralization of the Ethereum system? In a word, everything. Permissionless blockchains like Ethereum run on open-source software and use common practices from grass-roots open-source software development to maintain, fix, and improve the software.[83] The claim made by open-source software developers is that no single person or group of persons are in charge of a given software client, but that changes to the code are made by achieving "rough consensus" about them. With open-source software, if one doesn't like the changes made in one version of the code, one can always copy the code and freely make whatever changes one likes. This process of copying the code and creating a new path for it is known as "forking" the code. In normal open-source software, forking may not have significant effect on others, but in permissionless blockchains, it has critically important effects, as the value of a token is tied to the strength of the network and community that runs its software. As we have learned over the last several years, forks of software in permissionless blockchains (and corresponding forks to networks) create new tokens, which are completely different beasts from the original token.[84] So, the way that software is developed matters hugely in permissionless blockchains, and the process is celebrated as not privileging some developers over others. As I've argued in the past, this is not a fair description of these systems, and disparate power inevitably resides in certain developers within them.[85]

Clearly, the discomfort and uncertainty about the governance process as well as what conversations should be open to the public stem from the importance that Ethereum (and Bitcoin, and really, any tokenized permissionless blockchain) has for those who use its tokens, build smart contracts on it, or otherwise rely on it as infrastructure. Core developers have the weight of the blockchain and its ecosystem on their shoulders, as their recommendations and the code they write can make or break the entire Ethereum system. Ironically, in systems that stemmed from a reaction against the power structures of the state and the financial system, concentrated power structures have re-emerged, forcing those with power to make similar decisions to those in traditional power structures (perhaps Ethereum core developers now have an inkling of why Federal Open Markets Committee Meetings are not held in public, and minutes are only released after a delay).

D. Ethereum's July 2016 Hard Fork

As has now entered crypto lore, the Ethereum blockchain hard forked in the summer of 2016 following the hack of the DAO, an application built atop it.[86] The hacker, exploiting a bug in the DAO's software code, was able to take the equivalent of around $50 million of Ether. The Ethereum developers decided to treat the hack as a theft, crafted a new version of Ethereum software to take the stolen Ether back from the hacker, and sold their solution to the miners and nodes of the Ethereum system. Though an advance poll of Ether holders or miners had sparse participation, the Ethereum developers decided to proceed with the hard fork.[87]

The results were mixed. A significant part of the network upgraded to the revised software and followed the new ledger (keeping the name Ethereum), and a smaller part Ethereum network rejected the upgrade and kept the old ledger (allowing the hacker to keep the stolen tokens) going under the name Ethereum Classic. The Ethereum Classic blockchain, with its token ETC, has since operated as an independent blockchain system.

How did the hard fork reveal concentrated power? The developers made numerous decisions that affected Ether holders and those with applications built on top of Ethereum (including, obviously, the DAO). These included whether to treat the hack as a theft justifying a remedy, how to get the funds back from the hacker, how to code the software to do it, and how to sell the solution to the Ethereum community.[88] Further, some members of the Ethereum community certainly perceived that the core developers had power, alleging that dominant developers had recommended the fork because they had personally lost money in the DAO hack.[89]

E. Hashing Power Concentration and 51% Attacks

The previous examples in this section dealt with concentrated power in small groups of software developers, but record producers (miners) within permissionless networks can also be sites of power. In blockchains such as Bitcoin and Ethereum, there are large mining pools that comprise significant portions of the hashing power of each network. A 2018 paper by Gencer et al. described the centralized nature of the Bitcoin and Ethereum networks, noting that more than 50% of the hashing power of each network was concentrated in just a handful of mining pools.[90] In proof-of-work systems such as Bitcoin and (currently) Ethereum, whoever controls more than 50% of the hashing power of the network effectively controls the validation process, and is able to block transactions from being entered onto the blockchain or even alter old entries on the blockchain (sometimes referred to as a block "reorg").

The power that miners and/or mining pools can wield through control of significant portions of hashing power has been on display over the past year, as a rash of 51% attacks has hit a number of cryptocurrencies (though not, as of this writing, Bitcoin or Ethereum). In January 2019, Ethereum Classic was the most prominent cryptocurrency yet to be hit by such an attack, resulting in a rewriting of its blockchain that enabled the attacker to steal over $1 million.[91] As with the software developers, miners and mining pools who control significant portions of hashing power sound a lot like "a . . . coordinated group . . . whose *essential efforts affect the failure or success of the enterprise*" they participate in.[92]

IV. Using "Decentralized" to Make Legal Decisions about Blockchains

In this section, I examine the implications for law of making decisions about permissionless blockchains based on their level of decentralization. They are significant, so regulators, courts, and lawmakers should tread carefully in using "decentralized" as a legal term. My analysis first draws from the foundations laid in Section II, focusing on the legal implications of (1) the uncertainty of the meaning of the term "decentralized"; (2) the fluid, dynamic nature of the "decentralization" level of a given blockchain; and (3) the aspirational nature of "decentralization" in today's permissionless blockchains. I then consider the implications of using the term "decentralized" to describe how power works in the system, given the many instances of the exercise of centralized power, a few of which are discussed in Section III. I argue that misconceptions about the decentralization of blockchain systems function as a veil over the critical actions of certain parties within the system, effectively shielding them from liability. Further, believing that power is diffuse when it is actually concentrated means that blockchain systems are more vulnerable to change than is commonly believed, which makes the tokens on them malleable rather than fixed. As we will see, this has potentially far-reaching implications.

A. Decentralization's Uncertain Meaning Makes It Ill-Suited for a Legal Standard

As I discussed in Section II, no one is sure what it means for a blockchain system to be decentralized, but they are sure the concept is complex, poorly understood, and difficult to quantify.[93] The system's decentralization is in part a description of its governance and part a description of the numerical, geographical, and ownership distribution of the computers within the network. (With the ownership of nodes relevant, governance seeps back into the node count aspect of decentralization, as well.)

We could certainly come up with complicated formulas to measure the "level of decentralization" of a permissionless blockchain system, as some commentators have suggested.[94] One could propose standards for determining a decentralization level in each of the relevant domains of a blockchain system (e.g., nodes, miners, developers, potentially exchanges), and then an aggregate measure of decentralization for the entire system that incorporates the measurements from all domains. One could propose that a node count over X (perhaps 100? 1,000? 10?) is considered decentralized within the node distribution domain. But, are those nodes controlled by a common party? Are they widely distributed geographically, such that they are less subject to common failure due to a natural disaster or a government action in a particular jurisdiction? For the node number to be meaningful, a lot of information about the nodes must also be collected and analyzed.

Further, how would we quantify the governance of software development? Count the number of developers? Look at how many people have commit access to the software repository? But, how meaningful would such a number be? It could be the case that doing this quantifies and purports to fix the meaning of something that is not measurable or necessarily meaningful.

I fear that making decisions, including legal decisions (as Hinman's speech suggests the SEC is doing), based on a simple assertion that a blockchain is decentralized is falling prey to the observational bias sometimes referred to as the "streetlight effect"—that is, paying attention only to matters that have been illuminated, and not ones remaining in the dark.[95] The name of the effect comes from the parable of the man who looked for his lost glasses only in places illuminated by a streetlight, not because he thought he had lost them there, but because that is where he could see. Here, the fact that the node networks of the Bitcoin and Ethereum systems are extensive and global is relatively well known and nodes are easily countable (in the gleam of the streetlight), while the roles of software developers, miners, and even nodes in governance are complex and poorly understood (in the shadows), so these actors who strongly influence the success or failure of a blockchain system remain unremarked.

Accounting scholars have recently termed this phenomenon "Gresham's Law of Measurement," stating it as: "Easy-to-calculate quantitative metrics tend to crowd out more relevant but difficult-to measure assessments."[96] Ramamoorti et al. note that "succumbing to the Gresham's Law of Measurement means allowing measurability to trump meaningfulness. In other words, easily calculated quantitative metrics may provide the illusion of measurability while in actuality not being meaningful."[97] Here, it is relatively easy to count nodes in a network, but much harder to identify and understand how miners, nodes, and software developers interact in governing a blockchain.[98] As Sarah Jamie Lewis, a privacy advocate and crypto systems expert, has explained, "We need to move beyond naïve conceptions of decentralization (like the % of nodes owned by an entity), and instead, holistically, understand how trust and power are given, distributed and interact . . . Hidden centralization is the curse of protocol design of our age. Many people have become very good at obfuscating and rationalizing away power concentration."[99]

The lesson for the SEC and all others making legal or regulatory decisions about crypto systems is that we should not "regulate by streetlight," but should actively work to discover the facts before making legal or regulatory decisions, even if the facts are hidden and ambiguous.[100] The decentralization of a given blockchain system is such a complex, undefined concept that it is a bad idea to use it to make legal decisions at this point in time. Legal decisions based on the concept will sit on faulty foundations, making them difficult to defend and potentially opening them up to accusations of bias.

B. Decentralization's Dynamic Nature Complicates Its Use as a Legal Standard

The always-changing nature of a blockchain system's level of decentralization also makes it problematic to use "decentralized" as a basis for legal decisions. As I described in Section II, the "decentralization" level of a blockchain system (whatever one determines "decentralized" to mean) is a fluid characteristic.[101] This is because the domains within blockchain systems that are relevant to the concept of decentralization are constantly changing. The number of nodes in a blockchain system fluctuates, as people enter and exit the system at will with their computers (in a "permissionless" system, no permission is needed to participate in or leave the network). The hashing power and its distribution change frequently as miners go on and offline with their hashing power based on whether the price of the cryptocurrency makes it financially attractive to continue to provide transaction processing. The people serving as core developers of crypto systems are also in flux, as people gain or lose the trust of their peer developers or resign due to overwork, low (or no) compensation, or perceived risk of liability. Each of these domains is fluid, and helps to constitute the power distribution of the network. This means that if a system's level of decentralization is used to make legal decisions, each category would arguably need to be measured or evaluated periodically to see if that particular domain remains "decentralized."

Of course, the mere fact that a quantity or characteristic changes over time does not mean that law cannot address it. In a world characterized by constant change, humans have constructed ways for law to address change. For instance, as people age, certain of their legal rights and responsibilities also change. People become able to make binding contracts once they turn 17, for instance (depending on the state), or are able to vote once they turn 18, or are able to qualify for certain retirement benefits once they turn 65. As people's health, employment, income, or marital statuses change, for example, they may qualify for certain government benefits or tax consequences. Certain of these statuses are easily measurable (e.g., there is a magic moment when one turns 18 or becomes married), while others are not (e.g., disability is notoriously hard to measure, and requires input from doctors, the person claiming disability, and others). The question is whether "decentralization" is an easy-to-measure characteristic or a fuzzier, hard-to-measure one. I'd lean toward fuzziness, at least if we incorporate the governance that occurs through the software development process.

If a system's level of decentralization were relevant to a legal status, there would have to be periodic evaluations of the decentralization level of the relevant blockchain system to measure it. This raises questions about what happens if the decentralization level of a system decreases (i.e., the system centralizes) *after* the system has previously been deemed sufficiently decentralized to achieve a particular legal status. Using Hinman's statement that Ether is not a security because Ethereum is "sufficiently decentralized" as just one example of the complications that arise, we wonder, could Ether become a security in the future if it stops being "sufficiently decentralized?" Can something cease to be a security that has already been one?[102] How? What are the rules for trading it? How is secondary market trading of the token managed when the token can fluctuate between security and non-security? And if the measurement and determination of a decentralization level is done periodically to mark the moment when a particular legal status is achieved, then participants in blockchain systems (nodes, miners, developers) may game the standard by taking actions to move along the decentralization spectrum. If the prize is large (as non-security status would be), then anything gameable (including a level of decentralization) will be gamed.

C. If Actual Decentralization Is Now Just a Dream, Wait Till It Comes True

In Section III, I provided examples of events in Bitcoin and Ethereum that belie claims that they are decentralized, while in Section II, I noted the largely aspirational nature of "decentralization" in permissionless blockchains. If this is the case, it is premature to use "decentralization" as a way to make legal decisions. However noble the goals are for a given blockchain system to reach decentralization nirvana, the law must deal with present-day realities rather than hopes or dreams.

D. Decentralization Veils and Malleable Tokens

In this section, I discuss how using the "decentralization" of a blockchain system to make legal and other decisions about its token can result in flawed choices from both a legal and a risk perspective. This is because, when "decentralized" is used in its mainstream sense of inevitably indicating diffused power, it may mischaracterize or overstate how free of concentrated power the system is. Misunderstandings about how power works in the system, masked by simply describing the system as "decentralized," can then infect any decisions based on the decentralization of the blockchain.

Over the course of this chapter, I have sought to convey that despite the common use of "decentralized" to indicate that power is diffuse rather than concentrated in a blockchain system, existing blockchains such as Bitcoin and Ethereum have small coordinated groups who shape how the systems operate. To be explicit, though they are called "decentralized," there are many parts of blockchain systems that are exceedingly centralized. Thus, the meaning commonly conveyed by the word "decentralized" does not match the reality of these systems, with the consequence that misleading, inaccurate information about how power works in a given blockchain system is being conveyed every time someone describes the system as decentralized. This includes regulators, policymakers, and anyone else making decisions about these systems.

In the subsections that follow I argue that misuse of the term "decentralized" can lead to (1) flawed judgments about how accountability or liability of people within a blockchain system should work, effectively providing a liability shield similar to that of limited liability entities; and (2) perceptions that the tokens of a given system are more fixed and less subject to change than they are, potentially impacting any financial product tied to that token as well as other infrastructure built on or related to the blockchain system.

1. Who Needs an Entity When You've Got a Veil of Decentralization?

My argument here is simple: the common meaning of "decentralized" as applied to blockchain systems functions as a veil that *covers over and prevents many from seeing* the actions of key actors within the system. Hence, Hinman's (and others') inability to see the small groups of people who wield concentrated power in operating the blockchain protocol. In essence, if it's decentralized, well, no particular people are doing things of consequence.

Going further, if one believes that no particular people are doing things of consequence, and power is diffuse, then there is effectively no human agency within the system to hold accountable for anything. If you *can't see* people doing things that are "a key determining factor in the enterprise," then how could you hold anyone accountable for illegal actions taken or facilitated by the system, or for failures of the system?[103] There simply are no people to be found to punish or to task with responsibilities, such as, in the context of the securities laws, making disclosures to investors. Law has no reason to reach into such a system, as there is no relevant human behavior to direct. The consequence of casting a veil over the people's actions is that they may not be held accountable for those actions—in effect, that a *Veil of Decentralization* functions as a liability shield akin to the famed corporate veil.[104]

Moreover, being protected by a Veil of Decentralization may even be better than what blockchain participants could get if they actually formed a limited liability entity together. In entities, people making significant decisions that affect others (such as directors, officers, or managers) generally owe fiduciary duties, but, despite my urging, no one has yet decided to treat the core developers or significant miners of blockchain protocols as fiduciaries.[105] What's more, the Veil of Decentralization is helpful to participants in the blockchain because it provides a liability shield without making the blockchain system a legal person that could be sued.[106] With a limited liability entity, the corporation or LLC provides the site of legal personhood, but with a decentralized blockchain system, there is no such site.[107] Thus, if we misapply the term "decentralized," people within "decentralized" blockchain systems get the benefit of limited liability without the cost of certain duties and responsibilities.

Note that I am not arguing that Hinman or other regulators are intentionally creating a variation on the corporate form for decentralized blockchain systems, but that this backdoor entity creation is a byproduct of misunderstandings of how power works in the systems, hidden by the use of the term "decentralized."

Clearly, it is problematic to inadvertently give a group of people acting together what is arguably the core benefit of organizational law[108] without demanding any of the obligations organizational law generally requires in return. As Usha Rodrigues reminds us, "only organizational law can create impermeable barriers to protect the firm's participants from claims outside the firm."[109] Similarly, Dirk A. Zetzsche et al. note,

> First, in general, law covers all relations among people and items owned and controlled by them. There is no carve-out for cooperation in a distributed ledger. Second, no legislature is likely to enact an exception to this catch-all characteristic of law as it would promote irresponsible behavior by those controlling the distributed ledger. No legal system could afford a carve-out for DLT interactions given the loopholes it would create.[110]

Yet, a backdoor "carve-out for cooperation in a distributed ledger" is arguably what blockchain protocol actors receive if they are protected from accountability by the Veil of Decentralization.

This is all occurring as scholars grapple with the appropriate legal treatment for the group of people acting together in a blockchain system.[111] Karen Yeung points out that "[t]he decentralized, distributed nature of public blockchains means that there is no single, centrally controlled and integrated entity which conventional legal systems can readily identify as potential bearers of legal rights and/or duties. This may generate difficulties for conventional law-makers . . ."[112] Yeung explains how a corporate entity gives law an access point to address rights and duties, "[y]et, unlike stakeholders in a corporation, participants in blockchain networks are not recognized by law as bound together in a single, centralized organizational form."[113] Philipp Hacker similarly wrestles with legal accountability within blockchain systems, arguing that permissionless blockchains should adopt a tailored corporate governance framework that specifies the duties of software developers and miners or face legal consequences (in what he terms a "comply or explain" approach).[114]

Solutions to the blockchain entity dilemma have been proposed. Carla Reyes rejects the default partnership as an appropriate legal entity for a blockchain protocol such as Bitcoin or Ethereum because of concerns that holders of the tokens of the blockchain could be treated as partners of the miners, exposing them to unexpected joint and several liabilities.[115] She also worries that the creators of blockchain protocols (i.e., software developers) would similarly be viewed as partners (with accompanying liability), which she believes would stifle innovation.[116] Reyes asserts that the common law business trust would be a better legal form for "certain decentralized or distributed business entities" (which she terms "DBEs"), arguing that the miners act as trustees of the blockchain record through their validation efforts and holders of tokens (such as Ether or Bitcoin) function as beneficiaries.[117] In this way, she envisions the DBE (i.e., the blockchain system) obtaining legal personhood, limited liability, and other benefits equivalent to the corporate form. Another reason Reyes views the business trust as appropriate for blockchain protocols is that some states do not require filings to establish the business trust, which is important because affirmatively availing a "decentralized" blockchain system of state legal structures may be taboo to many participants in the protocol.[118] In this case, the default business trust could come to the rescue of the blockchain participants, unlike the much less protective default partnership.

The State of Vermont has similarly considered the issue and in 2018, enacted legislation that creates a new business entity called the Blockchain-Based Limited Liability Company—the BBLLC.[119] Like the common law business trust Reyes proposes, the BBLLC would provide a blockchain protocol with limited liability. It also would impose concomitant duties on participants in the system.

I do not take a position on which is the best legal form for a permissionless blockchain system, as that is outside the scope of this chapter. What is important to recognize is that policymakers should be doling out entity-type benefits only *after* carefully deliberating and determining an appropriate balance of rights and liabilities. It is critically important to get this designation right, as it will affect the behavior of participants both inside and outside these systems, and may very well determine whether blockchains are a success or a failure. Notably, treating blockchains as de facto limited liability entities for some purposes and not others means that rights and liabilities are not aligned. In all solutions proposed by Reyes, Hacker, and the Vermont BBLLC, there is an effort to balance the benefits of limited liability with certain obligations of those within the system. This will almost certainly not happen if we inadvertently treat the system as providing limited liability due to the Veil of Decentralization.

As we've seen in numerous domains, permissionless blockchains make us rethink our existing structures from the ground up. Here, the core question is how a group of people running a common system should be treated from a legal perspective. Should they all be individually responsible for the actions of the system? Should none of them be individually responsible for the actions of the systems, if there is not a single party with absolute control? The most difficult and interesting question raised by Hinman's suggestion that the decentralization level of a blockchain system should drive legal decisions is how we should treat group activities that do not fit into one of our existing legal categories.

Law generally uses legal fictions such as corporations, limited liability companies, or partnerships to structure how we treat groups of people. This is useful because the legal entities enable the parties operating through them to define precisely their potential liabilities, rights, and responsibilities. We know how to treat the group of people because they have put themselves into a particular box, and we have specified how that box works. Permissionless blockchain systems do not fit obviously into those boxes, or at least the people operating within them have sought to exist outside of them. In deciding which "box" to put these systems in (or whether they need an altogether new box), we must engage intentionally with the question and avoid acting based on misunderstandings. We must peel away the Veil of Decentralization and dig in.

2. If People Wield Unnoticed Power, Tokens
Are Unexpectedly Malleable

The final significant consequence of misusing "decentralized" that I will discuss is the risk it creates due to misunderstandings about how tokens on these blockchain systems behave. Again, my argument here is straightforward. Misunderstandings about how power works in a blockchain system, conveyed through uncritical use of the term "decentralized," can mean the systems (and the tokens on them) may behave differently than we expect them to. If we believe that power is diffuse within the system, then it should be difficult to make changes to the system, and therefore to the token that rides on the system. But, if power is concentrated, then changes to the system are easier to make, and the corresponding tokens may be more fluid than we think.

This is significant, as legal and risk determinations about tokens such as Bitcoin and Ether have generally been based on the view that, while the trading in the token may be subject to manipulation in immature, semi-regulated markets, the tokens themselves have fixed characteristics. For instance, Bitcoin is valued by some because of its famed cap of 21 million tokens, which is treated as a fixed characteristic. The Commodity Futures Trading Commission has deemed Bitcoins to be commodities,[120] implying that the Bitcoin token is a thing with a stable set of characteristics, rather than one whose most basic characteristics could shift based on the whims of a few. This view of tokens as having fixed characteristics undergirds decisions to offer futures contracts based on tokens, and to otherwise integrate tokens such as Bitcoin and Ether into the mainstream financial system, whether as collateral for loans or investments by retail and institutional investors.

Yet, as this chapter has sought to show, power is not necessarily diffuse in a permissionless blockchain just because it is labeled "decentralized." And the consequence of power concentrations may be sudden changes to the system and its tokens. Hacker puts it well:

> [T]he decentralized structure [of a blockchain system] is vulnerable to coalitions of the willing, which combine enough technological prowess, computing power, or force of persuasion to implement their proposals on the development of the blockchain. This leads to erratic, unforeseen and potentially radical changes of the system status as a reaction to external shocks or internal developments.[121]

In his analysis of cryptocurrency systems through the lens of complexity theory, Hacker describes how immature governance within blockchains "leads to an inherent unpredictability of the future development of the protocols when coalitions of major players (core developers, operators of mining pools) can exert disproportionate power to unilaterally push updates they view as personally favorable or generally reasonable."[122] Further, he asserts that "we should expect to see more unpredictable behavior over time; this implies radical uncertainty for cryptocurrencies and token-based ventures built on top of them."[123]

"Radical uncertainty" around systems that serve as infrastructure is a troubling prospect. When blockchain systems such as Bitcoin or Ethereum serve as infrastructure to applications built atop them, and their tokens are integrated into the financial operations of our societies, sudden changes to the infrastructure (tied to the exercise of centralized, unaccountable power) can be destabilizing to everything that rests on the infrastructure.[124] As Vidan and Lehdonvirta note, "one of the key characteristics of infrastructure is its invisibility up to the point of breakdown, when its otherwise taken-for-granted components come under scrutiny. In Bitcoin, these breakdowns reveal centers of power in the ostensibly decentralized machinery of the cryptocurrency."[125]

If the systems and their protocols are highly unpredictable due to unpredictable exercises of centralized power by people within the system, then the characteristics of their tokens are much more fluid than is commonly understood.

A token looks less like a rigid steel box with defined characteristics (analogous to the legal entity structures I discussed earlier), and more like a lump of clay that can be reshaped at any moment. This means that any risk analysis and decision made based on the idea that a token is like a steel box is flawed. If a token is a shapeshifter rather than a "thing" (i.e., it remains constantly subject to alteration by unexpected changes to the underlying protocol), then legal or regulatory judgments that are based on it looking like a steel box (i.e., that it is stable and impervious to human manipulation) are very likely wrong. This misunderstanding could potentially impact the token's status as a commodity, a security, or as money itself. Further, as tokens become integrated into the mainstream financial system through their integration into financial products such as futures or exchange traded funds, or as collateral for loans, or as investments by hedge funds, pension funds, or endowments, the implications become greater.

To be clear, it is the *flawed perception* of the power dynamics of permissionless blockchain systems that is the source of errant risk assessments. If our understandings of the power dynamics within a system were accurate, we would expect fluidity in the characteristics of a token, and therefore factor that fluidity into our risk assessments, our views of the value and potential use cases of the technology, and critically, our legal and regulatory decisions. My argument is that unquestioning use of the term "decentralized" and the romanticization of "decentralization" helps to create, sustain, and spread false beliefs about blockchain power structures. In other words, the Veil of Decentralization strikes again.

V. Closing Reflections

Spurred by Director Hinman's statement that Ether is not a security because Ethereum is "sufficiently decentralized," in this chapter I have argued that the terms "decentralized" and "decentralization" are misleading in suggesting that that permissionless blockchains lack sites of concentrated power and human agency. To the contrary, there have been many actions taken by small, coordinated groups of people that have made pivotal changes to the Bitcoin and Ethereum systems. The bug fixes, secret developer meetings, and mining pool concentration discussed in Section III all reveal sites of concentrated—rather than diffuse—power. Yet in uncritically describing blockchain systems as decentralized, we skip over all of that.

This is no mere pedant's lament. In Section IV, I argued that it is highly problematic to use "decentralized" as a legal standard for a variety of reasons from our poor understanding of the concept, to its inevitably shifting nature. Most critical, however, is the fact that the Veil of Decentralization, as I call it, may lead us to inadvertently provide the benefits of organizational law (limited liability) to a blockchain structure or to make decisions about tokens based on misconceptions of how power operates within a blockchain system. Both of these could potentially cause serious harm, as a lack of accountability without corresponding duties is a recipe for high-risk behavior, and "radical uncertainty" in a token's characteristics could impact every matter tied to that token.

In the end, it is all about obtaining a clear-eyed understanding about how power actually operates within the systems, and making decisions based on that enlightened understanding. As we should know by now, failure to appreciate how power works in a given system can have serious consequences. We are dissatisfied now with how power works on the internet—with the long-unappreciated concentrations of power that have grown up in platforms such as Google and Facebook. This is in large part because we believed that the characteristics of these systems were as they were represented to the public. They were free, about connecting the world, and serving their users. Finding out now that (as long-ignored critics perceived) users of these systems are exploited, manipulated, and surveilled through the platforms is extremely upsetting, and is leading to calls to regulate or break up these platforms. If we had demanded that the data mining and tracking that digital platforms do be openly described and publicly debated, we might have ended up in a different place. (Of course, maybe not, as maybe we as busy humans are too distracted or apathetic to resist the siren song of the free "services" of Facebook or Google.)

We need to be cautious about embracing the new utopianism of "decentralization"—this time through a blockchain world. As others have noted, this feels like a second chance to get the power dynamics of our digital activities *right*. This can only happen, though, through active interrogation of how power operates in *each* blockchain system. We must push back when presented with think pieces and thought leaders that fantasize about the better world we'll have if it is "decentralized." These utopian visions generally gloss over what "decentralization" would really mean in a particular, specific blockchain system, and simply jump to the amazingness of a world based on "decentralization." (So, jumping ahead to the "what if we had it" before figuring out what the "it" is.)

Finally, this chapter does not attempt to define "decentralized" or "decentralization" for blockchain systems. We're just not there yet. It seeks, alternatively, to illuminate how tenuous a grasp we have on the concept, that the reality of existing systems may not match the rhetoric about their decentralization, and the significant consequences of using this concept to make legal and other decisions based on our existing limited understanding. It's possible that I will attempt to define decentralization in permissionless blockchains in future work, but at the moment, I feel too much technology development and research is needed before that would be useful. For now, I'm in full support of Tony Sheng's recommendation that we "ditch [the term] "decentralization.""[126] Maybe, in the end, that would help us lift the veil.

4

Cryptoasset Valuation

Theory and Practice

*Nic Carter**

I. Introduction

The valuation of cryptoassets is a hotly debated topic within both industry and academia.[1] While most conventional models fail to explain why a virtual currency might have any value, absent a central bank or nation-state to backstop it, the last 10 years have provided copious evidence that a non-sovereign currency such as bitcoin can acquire and hold meaningful value. However, the jury is out on whether its value derives from demand for network usage, mere speculation, or even its commodity-like cost of production.

As novel cryptoasset schemes have been dreamed up, a vast array of different models for cryptoassets emerged, further complicating questions of valuation. More extensible platforms such as Ethereum enabled the frictionless creation of scarce tokens underpinned by public-key encryption, settling on global permissionless ledgers and clearinghouses—public blockchains. A vast set of new cryptoassets emerged, including application-specific[2] "utility tokens," wrapped real assets (tokenized gold or dollars), proto-equity linked to cash flows from real businesses, tokens ostensibly representing a virtual commodity such as computation or storage, and even more exotic constructs such as "Distributed Autonomous Organizations."

The core questions the industry and its onlookers are currently grappling with are: Is valuation for a cryptoasset merely *difficult,* or is it outright *impossible*? Should they be disaggregated into different "asset classes," and if so, how should they be split up? Can a virtual, non-sovereign currency achieve a stable valuation without managed exchange rates or a state authority to support it? Can application-specific tokens retain any value whatsoever, even if the applications

* Many thanks to Matt Walsh, Arjun Balaji, and Hasu for their review and feedback.

acquire significant adoption? How important is the usage of these networks in valuation? Can they acquire and retain monetary properties just through the shared beliefs of adherents? And last: Can value accretion be forecasted, or does it simply emerge, and if so, what discount rates are appropriate?

At present, few of those questions have been definitively answered, although the study of cryptoasset valuation has matured significantly in recent years. Bitcoin is now in its tenth year, and offers analysts copious transactional data with which to draw inferences, thanks to its transparent and auditable nature. Multiple billion-dollar raises for novel cryptoassets in 2017 and 2018 catalyzed significant interest around their value drivers, jumpstarting a vibrant debate. And academic perspectives, which tend to lag technological developments, have begun to reckon with cryptoassets and virtual currencies as assets in their own right rather than just as passing manias. While Bitcoin and its peers may yet fail, they have achieved considerable economic significance in the last few years, and as such it is worth unpacking their core value drivers.

This chapter reviews practitioner and academic work on the topic of cryptoasset valuation, introduces a value-driven taxonomy of cryptoassets, and investigates several assets directly to demonstrate how they might be valued.

II. Disaggregating Cryptoassets by Value Drivers

Given that the cryptoasset industry includes tokens that are intended as general-purpose currencies, tokens that represent some wrapped real asset (such as gold or dollars), and tokens that serve as quasi-equity, they must be differentiated for the purposes of valuation. In other words, in providing a theory of valuation, we must ask: Precisely what properties of a cryptoasset endow it with value?

While many cryptoasset taxonomies have been attempted—including, most notably, Burniske and White[3]—complications emerge when cryptoassets satisfy more than one of the features—although this is not unlike equity, which can carry rights to capital return, liquidation preference, and corporate governance. The core features that underpin the value of most cryptoassets are the following:

- Unique access to network services
- Real asset backing
- Cash flows from an underlying network
- Consumability
- Governance rights

A. Unique Access to Network Services

The major value driver for the vast majority of cryptoassets is the guarantee of being able to transact within a given network. Bitcoin, for instance, provides nothing aside from the fact that if you provide a valid private key that accompanies a spendable output, you are entitled to update the ledger (assuming you pay a sufficient fee). Why would anyone go to the effort of using Bitcoin? Because transacting on the network requires no entity's permission. For some individuals—those fleeing capital controls or weak currencies, or those who desire to participate in online gray and black markets—Bitcoin's properties are desirable, as no alternative payment method suffices.

The active network of merchants and individuals that accept bitcoin, alongside the scarcity of the units themselves—and the guarantees that a permissionless peer-to-peer asset provides to transactors—collectively make Bitcoin's ledger entries valuable. In the words of De Filippi and Potts, the primary benefits of cryptoassets "relate to what is no longer required, namely corporate or government permissioning, monitoring and regulation of private finance."[4] It is this stripping of encumbrances where most users see the current value proposition in cryptoassets.

Naturally, variable waves of adoption and fluctuating expectations about the prospects of the cryptocurrency cause significant volatility in exchange rates, but in Bitcoin's case, the asset has maintained a nonzero value for over nine years, indicating that there is demand for the network's services. While academia was slow to apprehend this value proposition, this approach has been formally modeled by Pagnotta and Buraschi,[5] who conclude in their model:

> The bitcoin price (i) increases with the average value of censorship aversion
> θ, (ii) with the average expected size of the future network, and (iii) with the
> current size of the network.

This story is much the same for other cryptoassets; Bitcoin is used here because its value proposition is the best understood of the cohort. For cryptoassets that serve only to give users access to network services, the value drivers are simply:

- The supply of the asset (usually fixed or predictable in issuance); and
- The demand for the asset, which is a function of the size of the asset's economy, and the typical holding preference of a user; and

Given the inelasticity of supply, network-access cryptoassets are thus valued based on expected network usage and expected user behavior. A high transaction throughput is not sufficient to guarantee a sustained high value, however. It is trivial to imagine a cryptoasset that is useful and meaningfully adopted, yet due to the disutility of exposure to a token, individuals only use the length of time for which they wish to transact on the network. For an application-specific token, this could be a matter of seconds—causing the token to have significant turnover, high velocity, and low value. This is the problem of velocity popularized by investor John Pfeffer[6] and others. While some investors distinguish application-specific and general network assets, in this context, they are one and same. Even though cryptoassets such as bitcoin and Ether are widely used, their value still derives from the demand of users to use those distinct networks—Bitcoin and Ethereum, respectively.

In the absence of formalization, many investors have attempted to model the future utility of cryptoasset networks as a valuation exercise. Venture investor Nick Tomaino called generic access tokens "usage tokens," asserting that "the fundamental value of usage tokens is determined by the uniqueness of the resources underlying the digital service and the utility of the decentralized digital service itself."[7] This is true both for Bitcoin—if transacting with the same assurances and network endpoints were possible on another ledger, Bitcoin users might be less willing to store value and transact with it—as well as application-specific tokens. Ark Investments analyst Brett Winton has described the value of utility tokens in much the same way, arguing that "[a] [cryptoasset] network's value is determined by the value of tokens that get held aside in user wallets to facilitate the network's transaction flow."[8]

Most prominently, investor Chris Burniske formalized the concept with a discounted utility model,[9] in which the future utility of a cryptoasset was understood to be the primary value driver. Burniske proposed that cryptoassets launched on an immature network were priced according to the expectation of future utility and pure speculation, and that as the network became more useful and desirable to transact on, a larger share of the cryptoasset's value would derive from utility rather than speculation. As noted by analyst Ashley Lannquist,[10] this model can be critiqued on the basis that it assumes that tokens have moderate (rather than extremely high) velocity.

One question that is commonly posed is why users might want to transact uniquely with one cryptoasset as opposed to another. If there were no network-specific defensibility or moats, why should any single cryptoasset accrue meaningful value? One answer is that transactional assurances vary between networks. In 2018, there have been numerous attacks on smaller cryptoasset networks,[11] made possible through the rental of mining hardware and a low network security expenditure. Transactors on Ethereum Classic, the subject of multiple malicious ledger reversions (nicknamed "51% attacks") have weaker guarantees that their transaction will go through, relative to Bitcoin or Ethereum, for instance.

Another challenge for tokens that derive their value from their monopoly rights over a network (bitcoin, the token, is a monopolist on Bitcoin, the network) is the loss of that status. The chief threat here is economic abstraction: the decoupling of a native token from its network, rendering the token itself spurious for network use. Abstraction threatens the core value proposition of network-specific tokens. If the bitcoin token were no longer required to use Bitcoin (and indeed, it is possible to pay transaction fees in dollars[12]), or Ether were no longer required to pay for network resources on Ethereum, a case could be made for abstraction,[13] and the unique access value proposition might be impaired.

Within the industry, there is rough consensus that the valuation from cryptoassets derives from the demand to use them within their distinct networks; differences of opinion arise over whether sustainable value can accrue to these tokens, in particular relatively frictional ones that only give users access to a single application.[14]

B. Asset-Backed Cryptoassets

This category of refers to cryptoassets that are used as a property registry to track the ownership of some real-world asset held with a custodian or trusted third party. The asset in question could be gold, currency, property, or equity—anything that can be encoded on a blockchain.

The most popular asset-backed tokens at present are dollar-denominated: each token represents a claim on a dollar held in reserve with a custodian. Popular dollar-backed tokens that circulate on public blockchains include Tether, USDC, TrueUsd, Paxos, and the Gemini Dollar. In aggregate these represent—and are backed by—over 2.75 billion dollars at the time of writing. (Dai is more complex and is covered in detail in the Maker case study).

Cryptoassets backed by fiat currencies operate on pegs. That is, the cryptoasset may be pegged at 1:1, equaling a claim on the underlying real-world asset. Or there can be other pegs, depending on the underlying design of the cryptoasset. These assets occasionally break their pegs; in times of excess demand, they may break upward, and when the convertibility is called into question, they can trade at a discount. This happened with the USD-backed coin Tether from October to December 2018,[15] as rumors of the insolvency of their custodian, Noble Bank, spooked traders. Only when Tether obtained a new banking partner and published attestations of their dollars in reserve did the peg return to $1.

Aside from inserting sovereign currency into public blockchains, initiatives are underway to tokenize real estate, equity, and other capital assets. Valuations of these assets are typically tightly coupled to the value of the assets held in reserve, together with assumptions about the convertibility of the tokens and the creditworthiness of the custodial institution.

C. Cash Flows from an Underlying Network

As the cryptoasset industry has matured, assets have emerged that provide token owners rights to cash flows on some underlying network. These rights are rarely codified in traditional formal legal or contractual agreements, as is the case with conventional fixed income of equity securities; instead, they are memorialized in the underlying code of the cryptoasset. Early in the development of the industry, as token offerings became popular, cash flow rights were infrequent, as issuers were sensitive to the prospect of their tokens being considered securities by regulators.[16] While this prospect has not abated, investors have come to value explicit cash flows, and so assets have sprung up to accommodate this.

Importantly, it's worth distinguishing cash flows from the usage of an economic network and yields obtained by diluting other network participants. The latter scenario is commonly referred to as "staking," and involves individuals parking a given cryptoasset for a period of time and being rewarded with new issuance. Individuals that hold the asset and do not stake are diluted at the expense of the stakers.

Although attempts have been made, it is not possible to value a cryptoasset based on yields from some holders diluting others; this seems circular. Imagine 100% of owners in a network engaged in staking: no new value would accrue to the owners of the asset; instead everyone's unit count would increase, but as with a stock split, no new wealth would be created.

Cash flows in a cryptoasset system thus refer to flows relating to genuine economic activity deriving from some underlying network, as is the case with dividend-paying stocks that derive their value from underlying corporate earnings. There are relatively few cases of this mechanic in action. Binance Coin, SiaFund, and MakerDAO are current examples where cash flows are evident and actively employed in valuation models. There is a further distinction between assets with programmatic enforcement of the capital return—as is the case with SiaFund and MakerDAO—and those that rely on the promise of an organization to return capital to tokenholders.

D. Consumability

Another method in which value is putatively returned to tokenholders is through the periodic or programmatic burning of tokens. Done against a backdrop of scarcity, or a commitment not to issue new tokens, the destruction of supply is assumed to be a driver of returns for investors. Unlike commodities, cryptoassets with this feature are not literally consumed in any meaningful sense—no resources are produced as a consequence of the consumption of the tokens—and the consumption is therefore arbitrary. However, burns are introduced to make the asset attractive, and as such must be contemplated as a value driver. It's also worth noting that digital tokens in any public-key system can be destroyed or rendered unspendable—but the cryptoassets listed as having consumable features in our rubric are those where reduction of supply through burning is a core feature of the protocol.

Just as equity buy-backs are considered tantamount to dividends, in that they are an alternative means of returning capital to investors, consuming tokens on the open market is assumed to be value accretive to existing holders. Various means of consuming existing token supply exist: in XRP, each transaction burns a tiny amount of supply; in MakerDAO, the settlement of smart contract operations burns MKR tokens; and in Binance Coin, the administering entity—the cryptocurrency exchange Binance—deliberately burns tokens equivalent to a fraction of its earnings on a quarterly basis. Thus the planned destruction of tokens within a cryptoasset network constitutes a means in which value is returned to tokenholders and as such represents a value driver in some cases.

E. Governance Rights

In addition to the value drivers mentioned previously, some cryptoassets offer investors decision-making control. While popular cryptoassets such as Ethereum, Bitcoin, and Ripple offer investors no such rights, novel schemes encode tokenholder votes, in an attempt to mirror the voting rights that equity holders enjoy. Larger projects that incorporate some notion of programmatic governance rights for tokenholders include Decred, Dash, and Tezos, among others (see Carter[17] for a survey of governance rights assigned to tokenholders; Davidson, Filippi, and Potts,[18] and Paech[19] for discussions of blockchain governance more generally). The core motivation behind tokenholder governance is the creation of mechanisms to efficiently resolve disputes in a manner acknowledged as fair, to coordinate over the allocation of resources, and to establish tokenholders as an interest group with explicit power relative to other stakeholders in the system. For practitioner views on cryptoasset governance, see Zeitz[20] and Ehrsam.[21]

In equities, the value that investors ascribe to voting rights can be apprehended through the premium present in privileged shares when dual classes of shares exist. Voting rights premiums are found in numerous empirical studies: Levy finds evidence in Israeli firms,[22] and Nenova[23] finds meaningful premiums in a diverse set of jurisdictions. Whether through the positive value investors ascribe to decision-making power over the firm, or through the possibility of expropriation as Nenova notes, there is considerable academic support for the notion of governance rights having nonzero economic value within the established equity framework.

What is less understood is whether decision-making power has positive value to investors when those governance rights are poorly codified (as is common with cryptoassets) and far weaker than the full suite of governance rights that stockholders enjoy, for instance. Equally obscure is the question of whether a token that grants owners governance over some underlying protocol can have value qua that decision-making power alone, when the token has no other purpose. This is the case for tokens such as 0x, which is the subject of a case study later in this chapter. And since in practice the rights ascribed to tokenholders are often cosmetic in nature, with real power being vested in the development teams, it remains to be seen whether tokenholders in cryptoassets with formal governance are genuinely independent or merely subservient to the protocol developers.

The institution of programmatic shareholder-style governance for tokenholders is not without its critics: notably, Zamfir,[24] Casey,[25] and Buterin[26] have assailed token-vote schemes by noting the potential for plutocracy, a lack of protection of minority tokenholders, the presence of collective action problems, and the possibility of cartelization.

Even though the economic significance of governance is hotly debated within the cryptoasset industry, and as of yet poorly understood, it is commonly cited as a driver of token utility and value, and as such merits inclusion in the suite of value drivers.

To illustrate the exotic manner in which these value drivers are combined in disparate ways across different cryptoassets, we have assembled a selection of notable cryptoassets and organized them by value drivers in Table 4.1.

| | General purpose money | | | | Wrapped real asset | Network derivative | | | | Application token | |
	Bitcoin	Ethereum	XRP	Decred	Tether	MakerDAO	Siafund	Augur	Binance Coin	0x	BAT
Network/application access rights	X	X	X	X				X	X		X
Asset backing					X						
Cash flows from underlying network						X	X	X	X		
Consumability		X				X			X		
Governance rights				X		X				X	

Key:	
Primary value driver	X
Secondary value driver	X

Table 4.1. Cryptoasset value drivers.

While the vast majority of these cryptoassets are used primarily or second-arily for access to a network, some exist exclusively to grant interested parties governance over an unowned network, such as 0x, which is intended to provide users governance rights over a decentralized protocol for exchanging Ethereum tokens. Others include explicit cash flows or capital return mechanisms from an underlying network—these can be classed as network derivatives, and their value modeled as a function of these cash flows.

Major assets such as Bitcoin and Ethereum are understood as general pur-pose monies; their valuation depends on user demand for access to their re-spective networks. Tether is an example of a "stablecoin"—a token built on top of Bitcoin for which an equivalent number of dollars exist in the bank ac-count of a depository institution. The value of Tethers therefore depends on the dollars held in reserve, as well as the market's belief that the institution in ques-tion will redeem them. We profile valuation approaches for a selection of these assets in the following case studies.

III. Case Studies

To illustrate how these value drivers are interpreted by analysts and investors, several case studies are presented, starting with Bitcoin—the best-understood and most data-rich cryptoasset.

A. Bitcoin and Its Peers

To settle the question of how to value a cryptocurrency, its ontological status must first be apprehended. In a comprehensive study on the topic, Yermack[27] disputes that Bitcoin is a genuine currency, lacking price stability and mean-ingful usage in commercial transactions, as well as exposing users to perma-nent loss, being a bearer instrument. However, it could be argued that Yermack demonstrates that Bitcoin is simply a *poor* currency. The metaphysics of the vir-tual asset remain a lingering source of debate within the finance community.

Equity valuation maven Aswath Damodaran contests this appraisal, maintaining[28] that Bitcoin is neither a capital asset nor a commodity (lacking instrumental usage as a consumable good), and as such must be contemplated as a currency, albeit an immature one. Admitting that currencies have long-term value drivers (there is something, fundamentally, which causes the Swiss franc to hold its value better than the Venezuelan bolivar), Damodaran nev-ertheless disputes that Bitcoin can be meaningfully valued. As the usage of cryptocurrencies has increased, custodial pain points have been alleviated, and merchant adoption has—albeit slowly—trickled upward, there has been a grudging admission that the assets ought to be understood as novel internet-native monies or currencies.

1. Valuation with the Equation of Exchange

The equation of exchange is a tautology that demonstrates a simple relationship between the supply of money and its velocity on the one hand, and the price level and transactions on the other. Its usage has attracted significant controversy, but it is perhaps the most popularly employed framework to value cryptocurrencies, which lack cash flows or any other intrinsic value drivers aside from supply and demand. The equation of exchange is popular since it allows analysts to hold certain variables fixed and explore the effects of sensitivities around other levers (such as aggregate transaction value). The methodology was implicitly used in the very first public attempt to value Bitcoin on the cryptography mailing list two days after Bitcoin was released, by early Bitcoin contributor Hal Finney:[29]

> One immediate problem with any new currency is how to value it. Even ignoring the practical problem that virtually no one will accept it at first, there is still a difficulty in coming up with a reasonable argument in favor of a particular non-zero value for the coins.
>
> As an amusing thought experiment, imagine that Bitcoin is successful and becomes the dominant payment system in use throughout the world. Then the total value of the currency should be equal to the total value of all the wealth in the world. Current estimates of total worldwide household wealth that I have found range from $100 trillion to $300 trillion. With 20 million coins, that gives each coin a value of about $10 million.

Finney here uses an addressable market technique—similar to those employed by early stage venture capital investors—to guess at a unit price, assuming a given market penetration. This line of reasoning was subsequently formalized using the equation of exchange, borrowed from monetary economics:

$$M * V = P * Q$$

Where M is the supply of money, V is its velocity (yearly turnover), P is the average price level, and Q is the quantity of expenditures. The identity is a mathematical way of stating that the aggregate economic expenditure in an economy is equivalent to the value of the output of that economy.

Usefully, M can be easily forecasted (since the supply of bitcoin, and most cryptocurrencies, operates according to a predefined schedule), and historical trends for V can be ascertained from network data. Typically, the equation of exchange is used to hold some variables constant in order to model the effect of the growth of the "Bitcoin economy" on price. For instance, some valuations for Bitcoin estimate an addressable market (say, the 7 trillion USD valuation for gold) and toy with the velocity lever to estimate a future unit price for Bitcoin, while others estimate a target transaction volume and estimate unit price at a range of velocities, understanding that Bitcoin can satisfy arbitrary transaction volumes without a high unit price if its velocity is also high.

These approaches became popular as Bitcoin network usage stabilized and its velocity characteristics became better understood. The key insight behind the equation of exchange approach is that the price of Bitcoin is a joint function of the yearly turnover of Bitcoin units in circulation and the demand for Bitcoin-denominated payments and expenditures. For price to be positive in the long term, users would have to hold Bitcoin for a nonzero amount of time, so velocity had to be capped. Historically, Bitcoin velocity has been relatively rangebound, enabling analysts to make simple extrapolations.

Notable early top-down valuations by investors using this approach were published by Luria and Turner[30] as well as Bogart and Rice.[31] Later, Burniske took up the thread, influentially claiming that "A cryptoasset valuation is largely comprised of solving for M, where M = PQ/V. M is the size of the monetary base necessary to support a crypto-economy of size PQ, at velocity V."[32] It therefore became commonplace to model the economy that a cryptoasset could support as justification for its valuation; for Bitcoin, this has historically consisted

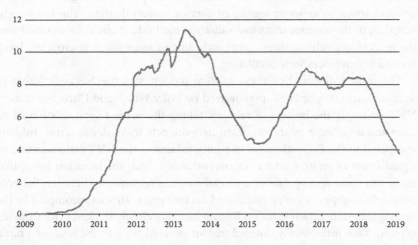

Figure 4.1. Bitcoin velocity, trailing 12 months, adjusted transaction volume.
Source: Coinmetrics.io

of darknet payments, ransomware, remittances, and capital control evasion. Burniske understood all cryptoassets as being the native currency for their local economy, ranging from all-purpose censorship-resistant economies such as that of Bitcoin to smaller application-specific economies such as that of Filecoin.[33]

Importantly, the usage of Bitcoin (and related currencies) as stores of value is consistent with this approach; in that case, velocity is simply presumed to be lower. The forecasting of velocity, initially an afterthought to make the equation balance, came to assume central importance in cryptoasset valuations. In particular, John Pfeffer's analysis[34] zeroes in on velocity as the prime determinant of whether a cryptocurrency would retain long-term value or not. To Pfeffer, transactional currencies or tokens aiming to satisfy some "utility" function within a decentralized network would be afflicted with very high velocities, since users would not want to hold them for any meaningful period of time. Within that view, only assets with low velocities, for which holding preference was paramount, would accrue meaningful value. This became known as the "problem of velocity" for single-purpose assets, echoed by Ethereum-designer Vitalik Buterin.[35]

Valuations with the equation of exchange have been critiqued by monetary economist Warren Weber, who has argued[36] that the model has been frequently misapplied by cryptoasset analysts.

2. Relative Network Usage Models

Rather than forecasting transactional or store-of-value demand, some analysts focused instead on indexing cryptoasset prices to *the relationship of prices with network characteristics*. This approach dispensed with attempts to situate these assets in an external context, and instead treated past as prologue, looking at network usage to generate signals of over-or undervaluation. The key insight was that, in the absence of formal valuation methods, it could be assumed that the market was valuing these assets according to some latent appropriate level, around which prices were oscillating.

The most influential of these relative models was the Network Value to Transactions ratio, or NVT, popularized by Willy Woo[37] and Chris Burniske[38]. NVT is simply the inverse of velocity, taking the market capitalization of an asset and dividing it by the on-chain network activity in dollar terms. Initially compared to the P/E ratio used in equity valuation, the NVT ratio was said to signal times of relative under- or overvaluation, with the intuition being that there was some appropriate or essential baseline relationship between the economic throughput of a cryptoasset and the unit price. This was prompted by the finding that transaction value on Bitcoin had very closely tracked price from inception. Woo influentially claimed that an elevated NVT in the wake of a rapid run-up in price was an indication that Bitcoin was in the midst of a bubble and due to suffer a drawdown.

Other approaches to relative valuation included indexes of price against transaction count and daily active users, proxied by addresses active on the network in a given day. The intuition here was that cryptoassets such as Bitcoin and Ethereum constitute networks and their userbases, imagined as nodes in a network, are the genuine value drivers. This theory was inspired by Robert Metcalfe's principle that the value of a telecommunications network derives from the square of the nodes in the network, which found some empirical support in Zhang et al.[39] Given the availability of user data present in the blockchain itself, this approach became popular among academics and practitioners, and numerous attempts were made to derive an exponent that satisfied the equation comparing active users to market value of cryptoasset networks. Some of the most popular attempts came from Wheatley et al,[40] Clearblocks,[41] and Van Vliet.[42]

The relative value model can be criticized based on its overreliance on historical relationships between network activity and price, its lack of grounding in real-world value drivers, and the relative ease of gaming network metrics. The industry-led attempt to derive entirely novel valuation methodologies based on network usage recalls the excesses of the dot-com era when internet companies came to be valued based on website traffic[43] rather than revenue.

3. Competing Models of Price-Hashrate Dynamics

Considerable debate exists over the role of the cost inputs of mining on the valuation of cryptoassets mined with proof-of-work, so the topic is worth mentioning. In proof-of-work currencies, new coins are periodically issued proportional to miners in the order of most work done. An entity with 30% of the hashrate in a given period should, with some variance, be awarded 30% of the coins. Since these coins have a well-understood market value, mature mining markets tend to equilibrate such that miners will incur costs roughly equal to the value of the block reward. Miner inputs are heterogeneous—some miners have access to discounted energy, cheaper hardware, longer depreciation schedules, cheaper labor, more efficient setups, and so on. So, at any given time, miner margins are dispersed, but the market-wide marginal cost of production is rarely well-below market price—except in periods of rapid price appreciation. Since hashrate is relatively trivial to add to a network, constrained only by hardware scarcity, and there are relatively few barriers to entry in markets for hashrate, significant arbitrage between the market value of new coins minted and the cost of producing them rarely persists for long.

The importance of proof-of-work mining on market price is widely debated; some critics maintain that proof of work is merely a Sybil-resistance[44] mechanism and has little effect on price, while some adherents maintain that the energy inputs to mining through proof of work actually grant cryptocurrencies fundamental or intrinsic value. Broadly, there are three common perspectives that deserve a treatment here:

4. The Cost of Production Is a Determinant in the Value of the Token

The simple version of this model—which is popular with industry practitioners and miners—stipulates that Bitcoin's cost of production is an important driver in price formation. More specifically, it generally relies on the claim that hashrate leads price. The fact that, as mentioned above, cost inputs for miners (electricity, capex, opex) tend to approximate market price, is support for this theory that a genuine "fundamental value" for Bitcoin and other proof-of-work based cryptocurrencies can be apprehended. In this model, the miners themselves are believed to perform important valuation work. This is often set in contrast to high-profile skeptics such as Jamie Dimon[45] and Warren Buffett,[46] as well as Yermack[47] who maintain that there is no fundamental backstop for the price of Bitcoin.

Academic support for the cost-of-production model is found in Hayes,[48] Garcia et al.,[49] and Li and Wang,[50] where the miner-driven input cost is modeled as a lower-bound fundamental value for Bitcoin using econometric methods. While the mining industry is characterized by secrecy, miners themselves often subscribe to the view that the energy irreversibly committed to the Bitcoin minting process through proof of work is not simply a consequence of market price but actually represents the instantiation of that energy into the digital asset. Thus, models of price for assets such as Bitcoin and Ethereum in terms of their electricity inputs are popular: for examples see Barbour[51] and Venturo.[52] Indeed, the first ever exchange rate for Bitcoin, published in October 2009, was derived from the cost to mine a bitcoin by Bitcointalk user NewLibertyStandard—assessed at $0.00076392.[53]

5. Hashrate Follows Price

The cost of production model is not without its critics: put simply, the remarkable correlation between Bitcoin's hashrate and its price is not necessarily evidence that hashrate is causal of price. Indeed, as the economist Paul Sztorc notes, work done to obtain the block reward will always approximate the value of the reward.[54] He suggests that the energy and capex costs incurred to mine Bitcoin are a *consequence* of price, not a cause. The question remains: What is the influence of hashrate—and by extension, the security of the ledger—on market price? Presumably, there is some positive value in maintaining a resistance to arbitrary ledger rewrites (one variant of these is commonly called 51% attacks). To the extent that the difficulty of a conventional attack on a proof-of-work cryptocurrency scales with the security expenditure of mining, and that the market values this property, it can be assumed that expected changes in security (hashrate) would be an important inputs into the valuation of a cryptoasset. This line of reasoning suggests that neither naïve model (price causes hashrate/ hashrate causes price) is appropriate—and that a bicausal model is necessary.

6. Joint Determination

In recent years, more sophisticated analyses of the complex relationship between price and hashrate have emerged. Building on the idea that price and hashrate are bicausal, some academics have begun to construct formal models of Bitcoin and other cryptoassets to reflect just such a relationship. The most influential effort so far is "An Equilibrium Valuation of Bitcoin and Decentralized Network Assets"[55] by Pagnotta and Buraschi. The authors model Bitcoin as an abstract "decentralized network asset" that satisfies user demand for censorship-resistant and trustless exchange, both of which are facilitated by the decentralized nature of the system. Through a theoretical model, Pagnotta and Buraschi attempt to answer the question of how Bitcoin came to be worth anything at all in the first place, finding that a nonzero price equilibrium exists given fast enough adoption of commodity trust provision (through mining).

Importantly, they find that price and hashrate are jointly determined, rather than one being a sole function of the other. By modeling hashrate as the provision of trust for the network, and premising that users value a well-dispersed and non-collusive set of commodity trust producers (miners), the authors determine that the value of the network in the eyes of users varies, ceteris paribus, with the number of miners, not the raw hashrate. In other words, a single dominant miner with overwhelming hashrate—as opposed to a more heterogeneous set of miners with less hashrate—is less-equipped to provide the guarantees of censorship-resistant and trust-minimized transacting that users actually value. It is therefore in the emergent properties of competitive mining that Pagnotta and Buraschi determine value exists, rather than just the accumulation of raw hashes. Accordingly, the authors contest the claim that the cost of mining a unit of Bitcoin constitutes a "price floor" in any sense. Ultimately it is generally acknowledged that a feedback loop between hashrate and price exists, with some diseconomies of scale as hashrate reaches extreme levels—what is the marginal benefit of the seventy-first terahash per second?

Regardless of the precise nature of the causal relationship between market price and hashrate, modeling hashrate on a bottom-up basis is a critical component of the economic analysis of Bitcoin and related cryptocurrencies. One related phenomenon that is worth mentioning is speculative mining; this is the tendency of miners to hoard coins at what they believe are attractive prices, rather than selling them off immediately to pay their electricity costs. Speculative mining—or the tendency of miners to take a directional view on the asset they are producing—is procyclical: during expansionary phases, miners restrict their liquidations of newly mined coins, and during contractions, the dollar value of their takings declines relative to their electricity costs (which are denominated in fiat currencies), so they are forced to sell off a larger fraction of their takings. Miners going out of business may also be committed sellers to settle debts.

Due to the existence of speculative mining, the flow of coins from miners can be understood as a gauge that contracts in a bull market and expands in a bear market. Thus determining key thresholds for producers is part of the economic analysis of Bitcoin production; as with commodities, the relevant thresholds are cash costs and all-in sustaining costs.[56] Miner solvency is also critical to forecasting the health of the network: when a sudden loss of hashrate occurs, as happened October–December 2018, the network performance is impaired as blocks arrive less frequently, with the network as a whole becoming less reliable. Additionally, a sudden reduction in the security expenditure by miners makes attacks on the network cheaper, and potentially opens up a large secondary market of used miner hardware—all of which could degrade the security guarantees of the network. These risks have been noted by Budish[57] and the Bank of International Settlements.[58]

In sum, Bitcoin—and other cryptoassets valued in terms of the strength of their networks and the distinct assurances obtained from transacting on them—are frequently modeled as parallel economies. Important variables commonly employed in valuation include velocity characteristics, expected value stored within the asset, expected economic throughput, and the quality of distinct ledger guarantees that transactors can be expected to enjoy. For proof-of-work coins, miner behavior is paid close attention to; it is contested that the cost of production provides a baseline valuation for the asset directly, but security expenditure is contemplated in many valuation models within the context of the asset's security and user assurances.

B. MakerDAO

Built on Ethereum's ERC20 standard, MakerDAO is the governance token associated with the Dai cryptoasset. The system relies on a dual-token model, with the Dai coin purportedly pegged to the value of the dollar, and the MKR token (which governs the Dai system and derives value from its usage) floating freely. In this context, Dai is the core output of the system—a permissionless, USD-denominated currency that operates on the Ethereum network—with MKR serving to provide crucial administrative inputs, for which MKR owners are rewarded.

Functionally, users that want to engage with the Maker system lock Ether in a contract and are then able to programmatically withdraw dollar-denominated Dai tokens. These are useful for individuals since the contract enables individuals to permissionlessly use interoperable services within the Ethereum network without exposure to the exchange risk of Ether. The downside is that for stability of the Dai token to be maintained, contracts must be overcollateralized (the minimum ratio is 150%), so individuals using the system face liquidation if Ethereum drops significantly against the dollar. Since Dai issued by triggering the contract can be used to buy more Ether on the open market, Maker is popularly used to acquire programmatic leverage on Ether without the use of a counterparty.

The owners of the MKR token are entrusted with the partial stewardship of the network—in particular, the right to set parameters such as stability fees and a ceiling on Dai issuance. In return, MKR tokens are burned when the collateralized debt positions are settled. Against the background of scarcity (only 1 million MKR tokens exist), this burning mechanism is frequently compared to a share buy-back. While the fees paid by users do seem to present revenues, the buy-back analogy is somewhat obscure, as MKR holders cannot be said to own the system or its assets in any meaningful way, as with equity. A model where MKR holders received periodic dividends from the accumulated fees would be more amenable to valuation.

While the system itself is an exotic combination of an automated debt facility and an experiment in internet governance, the value drivers of the MKR token consist of the capital return from MKR buy-backs deriving from the usage of the underlying system and the subjective value of rights over system-wide parameter-setting. As such, funds such as a16z,[59] Placeholder VC,[60] and Vision Hill Advisors[61] have published investment theses for the asset.

MakerDAO (DAO standing for "Decentralized Autonomous Organization") is a useful case study as the token has explicit capital return mechanics that in theory scale with the usage of the underlying network. A formal foundation, based in Zug, Switzerland, develops software for the network, but their business model is more closely linked to the appreciation of the MKR token (which they issued to themselves) rather than the sale of software. The nonprofit, which currently fills an important leadership role, has committed to "gradual decentralization,"[62] aiming for the MKR tokenholders to take a larger role in the governance of the system over the long term. As such, we have a token where holders have at least cursory—and in the future, comprehensive—discretion over the system's parameters, as well as a built-in mechanism for potential capital return.

Maker is noteworthy as it is, today, one of the most popular decentralized applications (dApps) running on Ethereum: 76 million dollars worth of Dai have been issued through the collateralization function to approximately 8,000 distinct active users.[63] The combination of ostensible capital return to holders of the token, the ability to set parameters in a largely autonomous system, and a system providing a desirable service to end users indicates the complexity of token models, while also demonstrating the promise of cryptoasset-native equity-like assets.

C. Binance Coin

Binance Coin (ticker: BNB) is a coin issued by the cryptoasset exchange Binance, currently based in Malta. In July 2017, Binance Coin raised $15 million in an initial coin offering, and the proceeds were used to build the exchange. Binance Coin is worth mentioning here since it conjoins access rights—holders of BNB can trade on the Binance exchange for reduced fees—with implicit cash flows, as earnings from Binance flow to tokenholders through a buy-back program. While there are ancillary uses for BNB,[64] investors who have performed valuations tend to keep their focus on the buy-back mechanism.

BNB is interesting since it represents an informal claim on the earnings from an exchange that is itself loosely regulated, having shuttled around multiple jurisdictions before settling in Malta. Investors in BNB do not enjoy the typical rights of equity holders, and undoubtedly lack liquidation preference or corporate governance rights, but they do have the following promise from Binance: "Every quarter, Binance will use 20% of our profits to buy back BNB and destroy them, until we buy 50% of all the BNB back."[65] True to their word, the exchange has executed buy-backs for six consecutive quarters. These are visible on Ethereum's ledger, which is a source of transparency (although investors nevertheless have to trust that Binance is faithfully reporting their earnings—they do not publish quarterly statements or detailed financial reports).

Investors have not been deterred: the outstanding stock of BNB is worth $1.3 billion at the time of writing and numerous valuations have been published by investors (for examples, see Kang[66] and Neo[67]), with the supposed cash flow dynamic being the focus. While BNB has multiple uses, with Binance heavily evangelizing its usage in fees and in the broader network, investors are most concerned with the buy-backs. Questions abound, however: what will drive value once the buy-back reaches 50% and ceases? How credible are Binance's attestations as to their earnings? How likely is it that Binance continues to buy back the token over the long term, lacking a formal obligation to tokenholders? And last: lacking any liquidation preference or claim to the company's assets, are the buy-backs merely increasing each investor's share of a token that is intrinsically worthless? For the tenth largest cryptoasset to continue to flourish, convincing answers to these questions will need to be found.

D. 0x

0x (sometimes written as ZRX, pronounced "zero x") is the token native to the protocol of the same name. Built on Ethereum, 0x is a protocol that facilitates noncustodial exchange of Ethereum-based tokens by enabling buyers and sellers to communicate on order matching, only broadcasting the final trade to the blockchain.

While 0x was originally intended to be used for fees by relayers[68] (relayers are entities that host orderbooks and present maker trades to the network), fee uptake has been minimal,[69] and many relayers have abstracted away the 0x-denominated fees entirely and do not use 0x for fees.[70] This recalls the notion of economic abstraction discussed earlier—where a token represents a considerable friction in an application context, it is often more convenient to remove it entirely.

Currently, the main use-case for 0x is its governance function, the details of which are still imprecise. Little has been explicitly written on this front, although 0x leadership has proposed the tokens be used in a registry of community-approved relayers, and are pushing for tokenholder votes.[71] Today, 0x tokens represent a claim on future governance rights. Whether that has a nonzero value is obscure, and few frameworks exist to facilitate analysis in that domain. One early attempt was Bonello's[72] proposal to value 0x as the amount a network participant would pay to avert a network fork.

The aggregate value of 0x tokens circulating today exceeds $140 million, so investors either ascribe a positive value to their future governance rights, or they are simply holding the token speculatively.

IV. Conclusion

The ease of creating a token and an upswing of global retail enthusiasm inaugurated a token sale boom in 2017 that eclipsed venture funding for start-ups within the industry. Many of these tokenized projects are nonviable and are in the process of dissolving; a select few will remain after the capital cycle completes. Those with a sustainable value proposition will leave regulators and investors with many questions to answer. Among the most important: Is a token offering a legitimate capital formation mechanism, provided appropriate disclosures are made? What are the appropriate disclosures? Can globalized, permissionless proto-equity (à la BNB) circulating on a blockchain such as Ethereum serve as a replacement for conventional equity financing? And finally, underneath it all, there remains considerable uncertainty over the value proposition and long-term viability of even the best-understood cryptoasset, Bitcoin.

A maturing data environment and the innate transparency of blockchains has led to more sophistication in the analysis of these economic systems; but widely agreed-upon valuation methodologies still do not exist. Perhaps Prof. Damodaran is right and cryptoassets such as bitcoin cannot be valued, only priced. Even so, they might be priced as the local currencies for emerging online economies—and these economies appear to be growing at a rapid clip. After a long period of disbelief, economists have begun to reckon with cryptoassets directly and are probing their value drivers. Practitioners would do well to cross the aisle and work with their academic counterparts on deriving meaningful models for these assets; equally, academia should continue to grant cryptoassets the attention they deserve. After a decade of existence, these quixotic assets are fully entrenched, and clamor for our attention.

5

Toward a Stable Tokenized Medium of Exchange

*Alexander Lipton**

Procedere con estrema cautela nell'accettare brillanti novità tecniche che non siano ancora collaudate da una esperienza pratica sufficientemente lunga . . .

Admiral Domenico Cavagnari[1]

Tres sunt modi, prout michi uidetur, quibus aliquis potest in moneta lucrari, absque hoc quod exponat eam in usu suo naturali: unus per artem campsoriam, custodiam uel mercanciam monetarum, alius est usura, tercius monete mutacio. Primus modus uilis est, secundus malus, et tercius peior.

Nicholas Oresme[2]

I. Introduction

The Global Financial Crisis (GFC) has clearly demonstrated that existing banking and payment systems, while still working, are outdated and are struggling to support the constantly changing requirements of the modern world. It would be an understatement to say that the GFC turned into a wasted opportunity to reorganize the world financial ecosystem. Too-big-to-fail banks dramatically increased (not decreased!) in size, disproportionally amplifying their share of the banking business, while the number of banking institutions significantly

* Chief Technical Officer, Sila Inc and Connection Science Fellow, MIT. Sila is an intuitive, secure, and accessible payment platform for building financial applications. At the heart of Sila is a new regulatory-compliant, fiat-backed tokenized means of exchange—the Sila Token. This token is pegged to the USD via a centralized, 100% reserve held in USD-based instruments, and is guaranteed to be stable and retain its value even in the most extreme volatility environments that afflict financial systems. The Sila token will be used as the base for a fintech API platform that will enable fast, regulatory-compliant payments and other uses of money with minimal reliance on the traditional banking system. Sila's structure and function will resemble that of a narrow bank, while using partnerships with chartered banks to perform day-to-day operations and be regulatory compliant. In the longer run, Sila will apply to get direct access to national payment systems operated by central banks by acquiring the necessary licenses. Further details are given in [49].

Cryptoassets. Chris Brummer.
© Oxford University Press 2019. Published 2019 by Oxford University Press.

decreased. For instance, the size of JPMorgan's balance sheet is presently nearly twice as large as it was at the end of 2006, at the onset of the crisis; similarly, the balance sheets of China's four systemically important banks have more than tripled over the same period. The clearing of many over-the-counter derivatives was mandatorily transferred to a central counterparty (CCP) for clearing; CCPs have become potential points of failure for the system as a whole. This situation is further exacerbated by the high level of interconnectedness of CCPs, due to their having so many general clearing members in common.

While ostensibly better capitalized, banking institutions have increased in complexity to such a degree that their stability and credit worthiness cannot be established with certainty, neither by regulators nor by depositors, investors, and, somewhat surprisingly, by their own management. The balance sheets of Tier 1 banks have become so opaque that their complexity is beyond quantitative analysis. As a result of this complexity, many banks and other financial institutions have become too-big-to-manage. Tier 1 banks have to spend billions of dollars annually (and their smaller competitors hundreds of millions) developing, validating, and maintaining complex models and information technology (IT) systems, which are used to demonstrate to their regulators banks' compliance with capital and liquidity requirements. The Comprehensive Capital Analysis and Review (CCAR) is an annual rite of passage that every systemically important bank has to pass.

The situation is not helped at the macro level by the fact that established macroeconomic tools, such as dynamic stochastic general equilibrium modeling (DSGE), which are routinely used by central banks to model the economy and determine their monetary policies, essentially ignore the banking sector altogether, by viewing it as a mere intermediary for other economic actors.

The frustration of the general public with the status quo is palpable. Manifestations of this frustration can be seen in various aspects of social and economic life and, most directly, in the incredible rise and spectacular fall of cryptocurrencies.

In this chapter we argue that not all is lost. More specifically, we show that, if used deliberately, new technologies, including blockchains and distributed ledgers, can bring much-needed competitive pressures to bear on the incumbents by allowing newly formed fintech companies to enter the market, thus providing considerable benefits to the general public.

In the near future, assuming that newcomers understand banking and its role in society, and with the hope that regulators will finally allow competition between various business banking models, we expect to see hotly contested races between fractional reserve banks and narrow banks (NBs), digital cash and physical cash, fiat currencies and asset-backed cryptocurrencies, and, most important, centralized payment systems and distributed payment systems. The outcome of these races will reshape the entire financial ecosystem going forward. In a few years, it might change beyond recognition.

II. The Banking System

A. Overview

Civilization is not possible without money and banking, and vice versa. For several centuries, banking provided the essential lubrication for the wheels of commerce. However, the very rapid technological developments of the last two decades have made the banking industry in its present form outdated. In addition, taken as a whole, it is no longer sufficiently profitable or attractive to investors [2]. This situation opens a unique opportunity for newcomers, armed with the latest technological tools, to compete with and potentially overtake incumbents, similar to the way Amazon is trouncing retail incumbents.

One of the biggest impediments in the path of unleashing creativity and developing new business models in banking, rather than mending existing legacy businesses, is the absence of successful open access Transition Control Protocols/Internet Protocols (TCP/IP) for money and identity, making money accessible via an application programming interface (API) and transferable like digital packets. While TCP/IP are responsible for the phenomenal proliferation of the internet, which inspired and promoted completely new business models in numerous fields such as commerce, social media, communications etc., banking lags far behind. Moreover, even though the aforementioned technical factor is important, another vital ingredient for developing a new banking infrastructure is missing: many fintech companies, especially in the crypto space, lack a proper understanding of finance in general, and money creation processes in particular. This absence of financial proficiency leads to unfulfilled naïve promises and false jump-starts.

Thankfully, recent technological progress opens an avenue for rectifying this situation. Challengers with a sound command of technology and economics can change the system to the benefit of the general public.

B. Money

Through the ages, money existed in many forms, stretching from the early electrum coins of Phrygia, to the giant stones of Polynesia, the cowry shells of China, the paper money originating with Kublai Khan, the cryptocurrencies of today, and to everything in between. Numerous attempts to understand the true meaning of money and from whence it comes have been undertaken by rulers and their tax collectors, traders, entrepreneurs, laborers, economists, philosophers, stand-up comedians, and ordinary folks.

The Greek philosopher Aristotle articulated legal aspects of money, emphasizing the fact that money is linked to government and government to money, [7]:

But money has been introduced by convention as a kind of substitute for need or demand; and this is why we call it money (νομισμα), because its value is derived, not from nature, but from law (νόμος), and can be altered or abolished at will.

Nicholas Oresme associated money with information and certification rather than law per se, [40]:

When men first began to trade, or to purchase goods with money, the money had no stamp or image, but a quantity of silver or bronze was exchanged for meat and drink and was measured by weight. And since it was tiresome constantly to resort to the scales and difficult to determine the exact equivalent by weighing, and since the seller could not be certain of the metal offered or of its degree of purity, it was wisely ordained by the sages of that time that pieces of money should be made of a given metal and of definite weight and that they should be stamped with a design, known to everybody, to indicate the quality and true weight of the coin, so that suspicion should be averted and the value readily recognized.

Copernicus generally agreed with Oresme and articulated his requirements for sound money as follows, [51]:

1. It must not be changed in value except after ripe deliberation by the government authorities . . . 2. One single place must be chosen for the minting of the money which must be minted in the name of the entire country and not in the name of a single city. . . . 3. When the new currency is issued, the old currency must be de-monetized and withdrawn from circulation. . . . 4. It is essential to have an inviolable and unchangeable rule to mint only 20 marks and no more from a pound of silver, deducting only the quantity of silver necessary to cover the expenses of coinage. . . . 5. Too great a quantity of money must not be issued. . . . 6. All the different kinds of coins should be issued at the same time. . . .

The German sociologist Simmel emphasized that "Money represents pure interaction," the renowned British economist Keynes pointed out that "The importance of money flows from it being a link between the present and the future," while the American economist Kocherlakota argued that "Money is memory"; see [50], [25], [27].

Since late medieval times, money has gradually assumed the form of records in various ledgers. This aspect of money is all-important in the modern world. At present, the vast majority of money in circulation is nothing more than a sequence of transactions, organized in ledgers maintained by various private banks, and by central banks who provide the means (central bank cash) and tools (various money transfer systems) used to reconcile these ledgers.

The role played by money in modern society is multifaceted. However, four main applications are beyond dispute:

- money is a medium of exchange;
- money is a means of payments in general, and taxes in particular;
- money is a store of value;
- money is a unit of account.

In fact, anything taken in lieu of tax eventually becomes money. In view of this fact, in a modern legally compliant economy, money has to be linked to identity one way or the other.

In addition, Graziani, [15], and Keen, [24], argue that in a monetary (as opposite to barter) economy:

- money has to be represented by a token;
- money has to be accepted as a means of final settlement of all transactions, which terminates all credit and debt relationships between the parties;
- money should not grant privileges of seigniorage to any agent making a payment, thus requiring the presence of a bank as a third party to any non-cash transaction.

Okamoto and Ohta, [39], succinctly articulated requirements for electronic money as follows:

- On-line payment—can be securely used online;
- Off-line payment—can be securely used off-line;
- Non-forgeability—cannot be copied and reused;
- Anonymity (or pseudonymity?);
- Transferability—can be transferred to others;
- Divisibility—can be subdivided as needed.

C. Credit Money Creation and Annihilation

The true nature of money creation and annihilation has been a heated topic of debate for a long time. Currently, the so-called modern monetary circuit theory provides the most convincing explanation of the process. The main conclusion of this theory is that money is created by commercial banks when it is lent to their clients, and destroyed by banks when it is repaid, while interest, which, in effect, comes from the next round of borrowing, stays in the system for good, see [4], [30], [35].[3] Unfortunately, understanding money creation and annihilation is far from trivial.[4] Even among prominent economists, confusion reigns supreme. Here is how Paul Krugman approaches the topic, [28]:

> Here's my current thought: in some sense money is a really weird thing, which can look to individuals like a real asset—cold, hard, cash— but is ultimately, as Paul Samuelson put it, a "social contrivance", whose value is more or less conjured out of thin air. Mainstream macroeconomics acknowledges the weirdness—in particular, it makes heavy reliance on the ability of central banks to create more fiat money at will—but otherwise treats money a lot like ordinary goods. But that intellectual strategy doesn't come naturally to many people, so there's always a constituency for monetary cranks.

However, a quick reflection suggests that this intellectual strategy causes some consternation principally because it makes no sense, not least because in the developed capitalist economy money is predominantly (but not exclusively) created by private banks—a fact of life, which mainstream macroeconomics stubbornly ignores. One can only repeat after Hegel, [14]: "*Das Bekannte überhaupt ist darum, weil es bekannt ist, nicht erkannt.*"[5]

D. Bookkeeping and Transactions

In addition to their lending businesses, private banks perform ledger-maintaining and transactional functions for their clients. As part of these efforts, private banks play two very important roles, which central banks are not equipped to perform. They are the system gatekeepers, who provide know-your-customer (KYC) services, and system policemen, who provide anti-money laundering (AML) services. We argue that, in addition to the more obvious areas of application of distributed ledger technology (DLT), such as in digital currencies (DCs) including central bank issued digital currencies (CBDCs), DLT can be used to solve such complex issues as trust and identity, with an emphasis on the KYC and AML aspects. Further, given that all banking activities boil down to maintaining a ledger, judicious applications of DLT can facilitate trading, clearing, and settlement; payments; trade finance; and so on. However, if applied without a clear understanding of the underlying business, DLT can make the situation even less satisfactory than it is at the moment.

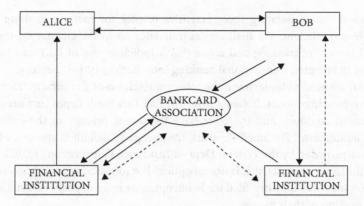

Figure 5.1. A typical credit card transaction between Alice (a buyer) and Bob (the seller). Alice pays Bob by using her credit card. Solid and dashed lines represent the flows of information and funds, respectively. Adapted from [12].

E. Domestic and Foreign Payments

The hallmark of the current financial system is a long chain of middlemen engaged in moving money between a buyer and a seller, not least in the form of correspondent banks. Not surprisingly, middlemen thrive in most situations, especially when foreign exchange transactions are involved. The amount of various fees can easily reach 3% or more, which is a very meaningful amount for most participants.[6] Figure 5.1, adapted from [12], illustrates the payment and information flows for a typical credit card transaction percolating through the clearing and settlement systems. It shows that this system is very inefficient—in order to move money along just three arrows, multiple flows of information are needed. Besides, the actual settlement process takes place using a separate payment network such as Fedwire®.

Obviously, for foreign exchange payments the situation is even more complex and less satisfactory.

F. What Is Wrong with the Current Setup?

The biggest issue afflicting the existing banking system is that it is overly complex because of the commingling of three distinct activities:

- creation and annihilation of credit money through lending;
- record keeping;
- execution of transactions.

It is clear that separating these activities is vital for making banking more nimble and efficient. We shall concentrate later on in the chapter on transactional aspects of banking and argue that a judicious use of DLT can be very helpful in bringing transactional banking into the twenty-first century.

First, we need to understand the inherent riskiness of the current fractional-reserve banking model. It stems from the fact that bank depositors are junior unsecured creditors, and therefore have the lowest priority in the event of a bank liquidation.[7] For small deposits, the danger of default is alleviated by insurance provided by the Federal Deposit Insurance Corporation (FDIC); however, for larger deposits, this is not an option. For instance, when in the summer of 2008 IndyMac Bancorp filed for bankruptcy, its large depositors lost a significant portion of their money.

Though the chance of a major bank collapse is not high, it is non-negligible either. By lending money, banks risk both their own capital and depositors' money. FDIC has deposit insurance funds of only $85 billion, which constitutes a little more than 1% of all existing deposits in the United States.[8] FDIC funds are not sufficient to cover the losses of even one of the largest 23 banks in the United States. In view of this, one has to conclude that depositors implicitly subsidize banks by hundreds of basis points annually by not being paid interest covering their credit risks. During crises, bankers are acutely aware of the riskiness of banks and stop unsecured lending to each other, so that London Interbank Offered Rate (LIBOR) breaks. If banks, who understand the inner workings of their brethren, are reluctant to lend money to each other, why should depositors lend money to them for free?

III. Distributed Ledgers

A. General Considerations

IBM defines a distributed ledger as follows, [22]:

> Blockchain is a shared, distributed ledger that facilitates the process of recording transactions and tracking assets in a business network. An asset can be tangible— a house, a car, cash, land—or intangible like intellectual property, such as patents, copyrights, or branding. Virtually anything of value can be tracked and traded on a blockchain network, reducing risk and cutting costs for all involved.

To appreciate this definition, it is necessary to articulate the differences between centralized and distributed databases. The hallmark of a centralized database is that storage devices are all connected to a common processor, while in a distributed database, they are independent. Write access in a centralized database is tightly controlled; in a distributed database, many actors have writing privileges. As a result, each storage device maintains its own growing list of ordered records, which, if necessary for the sake of efficiency, can be organized in blocks, which explains the name Blockchain (BC). In a traditional centralized ledger, there is a designated gatekeeper, who collects, verifies, and performs the write requests of multiple parties, while in a distributed ledger (DL) these tasks are distributed. It is not always true that making these tasks distributed works best, since centralization has its undeniable benefits.

The utilization of the DL format requires some extra infrastructural provisions. Cryptography has to be used to maintain the integrity of DLs. Only parties possessing private keys can request updates to the relevant parts of the ledger. Miners (also called notaries) have to verify that users' requests are legitimate. After notarizing legitimate updates, miners broadcast these updates to the whole network, thus ensuring that all copies of the distributed database are in synch.

The idea of a BC is old, since BCs naturally occur whenever power, land, or property change hands. The genealogical trees of royal families are the earliest examples of BCs. Modern technology gives the old idea of BC a new lease of life. DLT opens new possibilities for making conventional banking and trading activities less expensive and more efficient by removing unnecessary frictions. Moreover, if built with skill, knowledge, and ambition, it has the potential for restructuring the whole financial system on new principles. We emphasize that achieving this goal requires overcoming not only technical but also epistemological and political obstacles.

In theory, BC-based payment systems can significantly reduce transaction costs to below 1% as they involve significantly fewer middlemen. For instance, Figure 5.2, adapted from [33], illustrates a typical bitcoin transaction and shows that the number of steps needed to execute a transaction is much smaller than in Figure 5.1. However, to do so in practice one needs to overcome several challenges, including regulation, scalability, privacy, and ease of use for all the relevant parties.

Potentially DLT has numerous applications outside of payments. While DCs, including CBDCs, are an obvious venue, other possibilities including exchanges, payments, trade finance, rehypothecation, and syndicated loans, where frictions are particularly high, are attractive candidates as well. However, at present, many applications of DL and related technologies appear to be misguided. In some cases, they are driven by a desire to apply these tools for their own sake, rather than a clear superiority of the result. In other cases, they are driven by a failure to appreciate that some current systems are shaped by business and other considerations much more than by pure technological reasons.

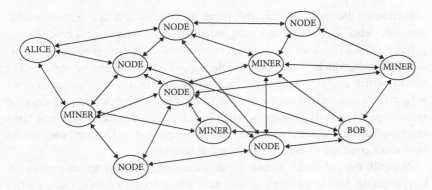

Figure 5.2. A typical Bitcoin transaction, between Alice (a buyer) and Bob (the seller). Alice broadcasts her intention to send some bitcoins to Bob to the entire Bitcoin network. Miners receive her announcement, verify that she has enough funds, and compete with each other to notarize it. The winning miner receives her reward, broadcasts the update to the entire network, and Bob's Bitcoin account is increased, while Alice's decreased.

B. Types of Distributed Ledgers

There are several types of distributed databases or ledgers. We list them in increasing order of complexity:

- traditional centralized ledger;
- permissioned private DL;
- permissioned public DL;
- unpermissioned public DL.

To control the integrity of DL, a variety of mechanisms can be used—proof of work, which can potentially be accelerated by sharding or side chains, proof of stake, quorum verification by third parties, among numerous others, see, [38], [56], [42], [36], [48].

C. Cryptocurrency Creation and Transactions

Cryptocurrencies took the world by storm. Bitcoin (BTC), described in a seminal paper published in 2008 by Satoshi Nakamoto, [38], was the first in a very long line of cryptocurrencies.[9] A major reason for Bitcoin's initial appeal was the fact that its creation was purely algorithmic in nature. In short succession, Ethereum (ETH), a second-generation, secure, decentralized computing system, was introduced by Buterin [10] and Wood [54]. Ripple (XRP), which is not a derivative of Bitcoin and, for a good measure, not a real cryptocurrency, gained considerable popularity as well, see Schwartz et al. [48]. Since then, literally thousands of native cryptocurrencies operating on their own purpose-built ledgers, as well as ERC-20 tokens built on top of existing blockchain platforms, have been launched with varying degrees of success.

D. What Is Wrong with the Current Setup?

Since none of the existing blockchain ecosystems have banks worthy of the name, they have to rely on algorithmic monetary policies for cryptocurrency creation. Regardless of the statements of their creators, in essence, they resurrect, in one way or the other, old ideas of central planning, without fully appreciating the consequences. Moreover, somewhat counterintuitively, newly emerging DLT-based crypto ecosystems suffer from the same drawbacks as the current banking system, because they continue to commingle monetary creation (however primitive and ill-advised) with payments.

Bitcoin, Ethereum, and Ripple have all tried to fill the role of money, but have ended up as a new speculative asset class.[10] In spite of their technical achievements, existing cryptos do not solve the problem for at least four reasons:

- they are not stable enough, even for short transaction times, which prevents their usage for the purposes of conventional commerce;
- they are operationally inconvenient to use for an average economic agent, which is a prerequisite for their wide adoption as money;
- their built-in monetary policies are naïve, simplistic, and inflexible;
- last but not least, they are not truly decentralized, while pretending to be so.

Indeed, the only way for an ordinary person to get a bitcoin is via an exchange, which actually adds rather than removes an extra middleman. Here is what the Goldman Sachs 2018 mid-year economic outlook report, [17], declares:

Our view that cryptocurrencies would not retain value in their current incarnation remains intact and, in fact, has been borne out much sooner than we expected. . . . We expect further declines in the future given our view that these cryptocurrencies do not fulfill any of the three traditional roles of a currency: they are neither a medium of exchange, nor a unit of measurement, nor a store of value.[11]

Not surprisingly, the status quo in the cryptocurrency land is less than satisfactory.

IV. Stablecoins and Their Taxonomy

A. Overview

Recent experience shows that all decentralized crypto coins are inherently unstable and thus unsuitable for commercial applications, see Figure 5.3.

Given this fact, it is not surprising that a lot of attention is being paid to designing stable crypto coins, which can play a role of tokenized cash. Stablecoins come in several flavors. In this section, we give a brief discussion of the most visible types.

It is clear that a properly designed stablecoin can serve as the cornerstone of a fully digital ecosystem, facilitating fast payments on a commercial scale with minimal reliance on the existing banking system, yet doing so in a regulatory compliant fashion. Such a coin addresses the gaping hole in open access TCP/IP [49]. A detailed discussion of technical issues related to TCP/IP and stable cryptocurrencies can be found in [20].

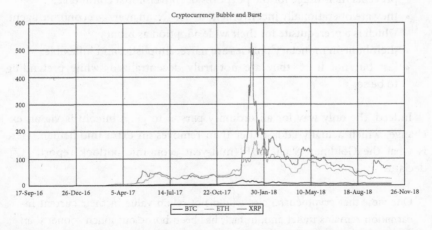

Figure 5.3. The spectacular rise and inevitable fall of BTC, ETH and XRP. All three are normalized to a value of one on January 1st, 2017.

We argue that rather than designing monetary policy on its own, which is a challenging task in practice if not in theory, efficient applications of DLT should initially aim at tokenizing existing stable financial instruments denominated in fiat currencies, such as U.S. dollars. Later on, if these efforts are successful, one should be able to tokenize more diverse asset pools, which can serve as a counterbalance to fiat currencies and be very useful for cross-border transfers.

In our estimation and contrary to numerous claims, it is not currently possible to build a truly decentralized stablecoin. This is partly because the mere determination of the price of a crypto coin in terms of a fiat currency requires an oracle and automatically breaks decentralization. Such oracles are prone to manipulation, and more importantly at odds with the claimed decentralized nature of the coin. Ideally, one should be able to directly observe this price from the blockchain in a distributed fashion. Unfortunately, at present it is not quite possible for both conceptual and technical reasons.[12] Hence, any potentially successful stablecoin has to combine centralized and decentralized features. The degree of centralization versus decentralization can vary, as explained in the next section.

B. Coins Fully Collateralized with Fiat

Custodial coins that are fully collateralized with fiat are relatively centralized as their creation and annihilation is performed by a single party. However, once a coin is created, and before it is destroyed, it can freely move on the corresponding blockchain. Given this semi-centralized design, custodial coins are particularly prone to regulatory influences. In view of this, they must be regulatory compliant in order to be able to survive. Several coins of this nature, including Tether (USDT) and TrueUSD (TUSD), either already exist or are currently being designed; see [47]. We will briefly consider a representative example.

It is easy to see why stablecoins are necessary within the cryptocurrency universe. The vast majority of transactions occur on exchanges that are not fully integrated with the existing banking system.[13] Accordingly, having a stable token in order to get in and out of cryptocurrencies quickly and cheaply is a must. Thus, such tokens have been created in order to provide a link between the crypto universe and existing banking system.

However, all these coins have inherent drawbacks. By construction, they are centralized, so their issuers represent a single point of failure and an irresistible attraction for both regulators and hackers (for different reasons, obviously). Operationally, there is no transparency regarding underlying reserves, which makes it difficult for users to trust these coins. Typically, collateralized coins rely on third parties, most notably banks, to keep the corresponding collateral and execute transactions on their behalf, which makes their actual costs excessive and forces them to impose high transaction fees on users. Ironically, reliance on existing legacy banks brings to the forefront the issue of stability of the banking system itself, which an alternative crypto ecosystem is supposed to rectify in the first place.

Unless very carefully structured, fiat-backed coins suffer from high costs of carry for their collateral, which may require storage, transportation, insurance, etc. Low profitability is a major danger in its own right, which cannot be overestimated. For example, creators of custodial stablecoins that are reliant on bank balance sheets to hold reserves have to pay a high price to effectively rent those balance sheets (and their capital buffers). This fact vastly reduces their cost-effectiveness, and requires a much larger users base to reach profitable scale.

Tether is one of the earliest and best known custodial coins. It is issued on the Bitcoin blockchain through the Omni Layer Protocol [52]. As the name suggests, it is supposed to be linked to the underlying fiat currency, such as USD, by virtue of every tether in circulation being collateralized with a dollar held in a dedicated bank account. While simple in theory, in practice the situation is extremely opaque, mostly because it is not known if the corresponding collateral actually exists, where it is held, or who administers it. Obviously, in view of the above, Tether cannot be viewed as regulatory compliant. Besides, as per Tether's legal disclaimer: "Beginning on January 1, 2018, Tether Tokens will no longer be issued to U.S. Persons." Not surprisingly, all of these issues resulted in USDT recently breaking the peg with the USD.

In spite of its glaring shortcomings, one very impressive feature of Tether emanates from its very nature as an essential instrument for speculators. Namely, USDT has an extremely high velocity. Although its capitalization is about 60 times smaller than Bitcoin, the dollar value of BTC and USDT traded per day is broadly comparable. For instance, on August 8, 2018 BTC capitalization and daily volume were $109 billion and $4.9 billion, respectively, while for USDT, they were $2.4 billion and $3.3 billion. Thus, the velocity of USDT is much higher than the velocity of either BTC or USD. Many observers believe that Tether is actively used to manipulate Bitcoin prices, see, for example, [19], [29].

C. Coins Partially Collateralized with Fiat

Saga is one of a new breed of cryptocurrencies, which are characterized by time-varying degree of collateralization, starting their life as fully collateralized and eventually becoming fully free-floating [45]. In our opinion, such coins cannot be stable in the long run, regardless of the theoretical arguments put forward by their backers. History has been brutal to such schemes—the moment governments start to manipulate the gold content of their coinage, the value of their coins plummets precipitously. The story of the assignats, used as money during the French Revolution, illustrates this point with extreme clarity; see, for example, [16]. In the 1970s inflation was triggered after the United States dropped the gold peg. Paul Volcker eventually brought it under control by using all the tools available to the Fed; see [18]. It is clear that Saga does not have such tools at its disposal and hence is very prone to a death spiral. Saga's approach can be compared to someone building a sturdy table with four legs, and then, when everyone is happy with the table, starting to remove legs one by one, until the table collapses.

D. Coins Overcollateralized with Cryptos

An alternative approach to creating stablecoins is to use unstable native crypto coins, specifically ETH, and smart contracts, which guarantee that stablecoins, representing a sliver of the total, are massively overcollateralized. This collateral cushion is supposed to create a natural floor for the value of the coin. As with many other crypto ideas, this one can be traced back to conventional financial engineering concepts, specifically, trading on the margin and tranching of collateralized debt obligations (CDO). Under normal conditions, the corresponding coins are indeed stable; however, if there is a sudden drop in the value of the underlying asset, the value of the corresponding "derivative" coin will dip below par. Experience suggests that it is not even necessary for the actual breach of the floor to occur—a mere perception of such a possibility is sufficient to make coins value less than par. One does not need to go far in history for a real-life example—the global financial crisis of 2008 was caused to a large degree by the fact that super-senior CDO tranches lost most of their value, even though due to the presence of a massive underlying buffer, they did not suffer any losses,. This illustrates the point that market confidence, which is not explicitly taken into account by theoretical models, does play a crucial role in real life. The CDO tranches eventually functioned as designed, as did LTCM trades, which did not prevent their holders from going bankrupt in the interim.

It should be noted that overcollateralization is the opposite of conventional financial practice, such as trading on margin, which is based on the idea of under-collateralization.[14] It seems that many designers of new crypto coins have totally forgotten why these coins were created in the first place.

In view of the above, crypto-collateralized coins have severe and obvious drawbacks. Since the price evolution of the underlying cryptos, such as ETH, is driven by a jump process, the floor can be breached in the event of a black swan, or more realistically, loss of confidence by the users. Thus, in spite of the fact that coins are overcollateralized, the underlying is so volatile that the peg is not guaranteed. In addition, overcollateralized coins suffer from the negative feedback loop, which arises because forced selling of collateral causes its price to decrease even faster than it would otherwise.

A typical example of stable value coins collateralized by other crypto-currencies is Dai [8], issued by MakerDAO. Dai is supported by a very hefty collateral cushion. In the case when the floor is in danger of being breached, collateral is automatically liquidated by profit-seeking nodes, so that Dai stability is maintained. As was mentioned earlier, see note 15, the amount of collateral needed to keep the scheme going is so large that the underlying economics becomes very challenging.[15]

E. Dynamically Stabilized Coins

While the idea of dynamic stabilization of a coin contradicts common sense and historical experience, it has recently gripped the imagination of the investor community and hence is worth investigating in some detail. There are several obvious issues with algorithmically stabilized coins.

Monetary policies underpinning dynamically stabilized coins are derived from obsolete and outdated economic considerations. Either by necessity or by design these policies are vague and either unproven or actually proven by pre-crypto experiences not to work. At the end of the day, centralized mechanisms, such as a centralized reserve, have to be maintained to ensure price stability anyway.[16] Historically, all the live projects have suffered drops in value, just breaking their stated raison d'etre. In addition, so far no one has been able to design trustless decentralized (price) oracles.

Basis is a representative example of such a coin, see [1]. Stripped of amenities, its algorithm works as follows. If the value of the coin is going up (a relatively easy case), then, not surprisingly, new coins are issued and distributed amongst the holders on a pro-rata basis. If the value of the coin is going down (a more complex case), then bond-like instruments are issued in exchange for coins, which are burned. As a result, the number of coins in circulation goes down and, in theory, their price increases. This is the essence of the concept of seigniorage, as proposed by Robert Sams [46]. When formulated as a cryptocurrency stabilization scheme, this algorithm sounds meaningful. However, if it is rephrased in more familiar terms, for instance, those of a company trying to keep its stock price constant, the algorithm shows its true colors. If the stock price increases, additional stock is issued, thus pushing the stock price down. When the stock price is falling, the company starts to sell bonds, and uses the proceeds to buy its own stock, thus pushing its price up. It is clear that this stabilization scheme represents yet another purely theoretical construction that cannot and does not work in practice, and will collapse when bonds come due—not to mention the fact that selling bonds in the middle of a market panic might be an insurmountable obstacle in the first place.

Algorithms of this type have been known for a long time. For example, Baron Munchausen is famous for using one when pulling himself and his horse out of a mire by his own hair. More recently, similar ideas were entertained by academic economists who proposed a mechanism for fixing the price of gold by a government in terms of its own fiat without keeping any gold in reserve [5]. Obviously, even with all the coercion mechanisms at their disposal, no government was ever able to achieve such a feat. The probability of a crypto algorithm that lacks such mechanisms succeeding is even lower. Without going too far back in history, we note that the current crisis of the Argentinian peso was accelerated by the increase of interest rates to 60%, which, according to the above theory, is supposed to arrest the currency freefall.

As an aside, the Quantity Theory of Money (QTM), which is used as a foundational concept underpinning Basis, has been discredited for decades, and does not pass scientific analysis, not to mention common sense [30]. The only saving grace is that a similar unflattering observation is true for the majority of traditional macroeconomic theories [31]. As was his habit, Keynes put it in characteristically pithy fashion:

> Practical men, who believe themselves to be quite exempt from any intellectual influence, are usually the slaves of some defunct economist. Madmen in authority, who hear voices in the air, are distilling their frenzy from some academic scribbler of a few years back.

F. Coins Collateralized with Assets

While in a stable economic environment it makes sense to collateralize crypto coins with fiat, in some parts of the world it is not a viable option since the local fiat itself is not stable enough. In these instances, coins collateralized with real assets come to the rescue. Recently, several such coins have been proposed by competing start-ups, including Digital Trade Coin (DTC) (of which the present author is a co-inventor), Oilcoin, Sweetcoin, Tiberiuscoin, etc.; see, for example, [34], [35], [53]. These coins have significant utility value for supply-chain financing and in well-defined trading environments, such as oil trading or cross-border financing. In addition, several authors convincingly argue that even in the presence of stable fiat, asset-backed coins have considerable advantages by limiting the freedom of central banks to manipulate their currencies; see, for example, [34].

Fiat currencies, while undeniably useful, are not well suited to the needs of twenty-first century commerce, especially trade and supply chain finance because of high handling and exchange costs. In addition, the USD, being the world reserve currency, causes serious trade imbalances, which can trigger trade wars and exacerbate the international frictions. To alleviate these ills, several financial authorities have suggested that it makes sense to complement fiat currencies with a supranational currency, such as Spanish peso de ocho, or Austrian thalers. This supranatural currency will be insulated from adverse actions by single central banks and other parties. By combining the ideas of narrow banking (for stability), digital currencies (for efficiency and transparency), and use of an asset-backed currency for international trade (to reduce trade distortions and inequality), we see the potential for dramatic improvement in the global financial system. Today, for the first time ever, there is a possibility of designing a digital supranational currency backed by diverse and widely held assets. Such a digital currency could combine the best features of historical currencies, including finality of settlement, partial anonymity, and usability on the web.

Hayek, Keynes, Kaldor, and many other economists advocated reforming the international monetary system by creating an independent international reserve currency, which remains stable in the long run and does not suffer from the inherent deficiencies of credit-based fiat national currencies, [21], [26], [23].

Zhou Xiaochuan, Governor of the People's Bank of China, advocated the need for such a currency as follows, [55]:

I. The outbreak of the crisis and its spillover to the entire world reflect the inherent vulnerabilities and systemic risks in the existing international monetary system. II. The desirable goal of reforming the international monetary system, therefore, is to create an international reserve currency that is disconnected from individual nations and is able to remain stable in the long run, thus removing the inherent deficiencies caused by using credit-based national currencies. III. The reform should be guided by a grand vision and begin with specific deliverables. It should be a gradual process that yields win-win results for all.

Recently, an MIT team (of which the present author is a member) have designed an asset-backed digital currency called DTC that is believed to be well-suited as a medium of trade and exchange for groups of smaller nations or supranational organizations. DTC is largely immune to policies of central banks controlling the worlds' reserve currencies, and consequently has enormous potential to improve the stability and competitiveness of trading and natural-resource producing economies. DTC can serve as a much-needed counterpoint for todays' fiat currencies, and a way forward toward ensuring worldwide financial stability and inclusion; see [34], [35].

G. Narrow Banks as Emitters of Digital Cash

In many countries, including the United States, cash still plays a major role in the economy. Debit cards, which combine digital and physical aspects of cash, are popular as well. The Fed 2015 Diary of Consumer Payment Choice, [13], observed:

> Cash continues to be the most frequently used consumer payment instrument. Cash is widely used in a variety of circumstances. Cash dominates small-value transactions. The average value of cash holdings has grown.

Similarly, Yves Mersch, Member of the Executive Board of the ECB, in a speech given on February 14, 2018, [11], concluded:

> I will conclude by saying that printed euro banknotes will retain their place and their role in society as legal tender for a very long time to come. There is no viable alternative to euro cash. There is good reason to believe that banknotes don't only have to take the form of printed paper, cotton or polymer. However, printed banknotes will remain our core business. And if there is public demand for digital central bank money, this should only be a technical variant of cash.

While cash is facing competition from other payment instruments,[17] results of numerous studies suggest that it remains a resilient form of payment, playing a key and unique role for consumer transactions and other purposes. The amount of currency in circulation, which includes paper currency and coin held both by the public and in the vaults of depository institutions, grows at a healthy pace. While the quantity of currency increases steadily, its velocity currently decreases, meaning that money is being used in a less efficient manner. The velocity of money is the number of times a unit of money is spent to purchase goods and services per unit of time, say quarterly. Increasing velocity of money implies that more transactions are occurring between economic agents, while decreasing velocity indicates the opposite.

The absence of physical cash would alleviate societal ills, such as crime, drug trafficking, and the like, or, at least, make them more difficult to conduct. It would lubricate the wheels of commerce and help the unbanked to become participants in the digital economy through the use of smartphones, benefitting society at large. On the flip side, with cash abolished, interest rates could be set as negative as central bankers liked; rates would be determined only by policymakers.

A properly constructed NB issuing its own digital currency is a much more palatable and practical solution than CBDC by allowing access to full collateral at any time. This suggests that digital currencies, issued by NBs, could become competitive with fiat currencies for everyday use. Such alternative currencies have a long history of usefulness for smoothing bumps in the financial environment, and if backed by a NB could avoid the bankruptcy problems that have traditionally plagued alternative currencies.

NBs keep all depositors' money as liquid cash deposited with a central bank or liquid government bonds, becoming thereby necessary stabilizers and facilitators of the overall global financial system. There is an acute need for such stabilizers after the GFC, which resulted in a massive concentration of assets in a handful of systemically important banks, thus making the overall financial system less robust. In addition to steadying the whole banking sector, NBs naturally perform the role of record keepers in the economy, while refraining from issuing loans. The Great Depression of 1929 made banks' inability to meet their obligations painfully obvious and brought the idea of a NB to the forefront. Although a practical conversion of fractional reserve banks into NBs was rejected in the 1940s under enormous political pressure from fractional reserve banks, the idea has always stayed close to the surface, and gained considerable momentum during and after the S&L crisis in the 1980s and 1990s. Not surprisingly, it gained traction again after the GFC. Further details are given in [3], [33], [41].

Several approaches for designing a NB have been summarized in the literature, see, for example, [41]:

- 100% Reserve Bank (C-PeRB): Assets—central bank reserves and currency. Liabilities—demandable deposits and shareholder equity. Depending on the circumstances, these deposits can either be non-interest-bearing, or interest paying, or interest charging. The latter setup might be necessary if the interest rate paid by the central bank is negative. C-PeRB is financed by a combination of deposits (debt) and shareholders' equity.
- Treasury money market mutual fund (TMMMF): Assets—Treasury bills or repurchase agreements collateralized by Treasury bills.

Liabilities—demandable equity shares having a proportional claim on the assets. TMMMF is financed solely by equity.

- Prime money market mutual fund (PMMMF): Assets—short-term federal agency securities, short-term bank certificates of deposits, bankers' acceptances, highly rated commercial paper, and repurchase agreements backed by low-risk collateral. Liabilities—demandable equity shares having a proportional claim on the assets. As before, PMMMF is financed solely by equity.

A detailed design for a NB, including its international dimensions, is given in the Patent Application [6].

H. Mixing and Tumbling

Early on, it was recognized that Bitcoin does not provide true anonymity of transactions. While at first glance it would seem this is an issue only for those participants engaging in some sort of nefarious activity, a little reflection indicates that honest participants require enhanced anonymity too. For instance, if a merchant payee has a known public address, all its competitors will gain valuable business insight about the payee's financial well-being by monitoring its transactions on a public blockchain. Likewise, a payer with a large amount of stable tokens will automatically attract unwanted attention. Thus, a reasonable level of anonymity is required for perfectly legitimate reasons. While some approaches involve building distributed ledger designed around enhanced anonymity such as Zcash, we find them too radical to use in a regulatory-compliant framework. A suitable mixing service is more appropriate; see, for example, [37].

Given that some centralization is built in to fiat-backed cryptocurrencies from the start, it is natural to benefit from it, and use sponsors as a mixing service. Upon request, they will allow routing of payments via blockchain addresses under their control in a way that will make the original source of funds impossible to deduce for other economic agents. Obviously, legitimate authorities that provide a legally binding demand will be able to trace the flow of funds with the same ease as if mixing was not applied. This approach is designed to solve the anonymity problem for payers. For payees it is solved by using the ring key construct. Recall that by using ring keys one can prove that a transaction was signed within a group of addresses without determining a specific signatory.

I. KYC and AML Considerations

The importance of KYC and AML requirements for regulatory compliance cannot be overestimated. It is necessary to perform KYC/AML procedures when new tokens are issued or existing ones redeemed for fiat. Third-party services can be used for these purposes. In principle, KYC is a relatively inexpensive operation. These procedures can be strengthened further, because the exchange of fiat currencies into stable tokens and vice versa uses existing bank accounts, whose owners have passed the standard KYC procedures performed by their banks.

Given that stable tokens will circulate on the Ethereum blockchain, and subsequently on other blockchains, all of which keep an immutable record of all transactions, AML can be performed indirectly by analyzing the corresponding transaction social graph. In this regard, stable token transactions are more transparent than conventional physical cash transactions, and are on a par with traditional banking transactions.[18]

J. Privacy

There is serious hazard of widely used stable tokens being monitored by a repressive surveillance state. If high volumes of cash transactions are completed on a blockchain, then the government can track a considerable portion of its citizens' payments and exert unprecedented control over their lives. To avoid this situation, small cash-like financial transactions must be anonymous, with exceptions to this anonymity allowed in serious criminal investigations or similar situations. When there is an overriding social imperative to override this anonymity, it could be done by using legal court orders and similar tools. Development of the suitable legal infrastructure is of paramount importance for the successful usage of stable tokens as a medium of exchange.

V. Conclusions

In this chapter, we discussed the current state of the crypto land and argued that stable crypto tokens, which can be viewed as an electronic analogue of cash, can help to augment the existing TCP/IP with a much-needed mechanism in order to bring existing banking and payment systems into the twenty-first century. We described three existing approaches to designing such tokens—fiat collateralization, cryptocurrency collateralization, and dynamic stabilization—and concluded that only regulatorily compliant fiat-backed tokens are viable in the long run. We also discussed asset-backed cryptocurrencies and argued that in some instances they can provide a much-needed counterpoint for today's fiat currencies, and pave a way forward toward ensuring worldwide financial stability and inclusion.

I am deeply grateful to my MIT colleagues Prof. Sandy Pentland and Dr. Thomas Hardjono, to my SilaMoney partners Shamir Karkal, Angela Angelovska-Wilson, and Isaac Hines, to my Numeraire Financial colleagues Dr Marsha Lipton and Stewart Inglis, and to Tim Swanson from Post Oak Labs for extremely useful and insightful discussions of the topics covered in this chapter.

VI. Glossary

Algorithmically stabilized cryptocurrency: A cryptocurrency whose price is pegged to fiat by virtue of an algorithmic monetary policy "emulating" conventional monetary policies of a central bank.

Anti-money laundering (AML): A set of procedures, laws, and regulations designed to stop generating legal income through illegal actions; AML laws have profound implications for financial institutions and intermediaries.

Asset-backed stable cryptocurrency: A cryptocurrency whose price is pegged to a collateral pool in the form of real assets, such as gold, oil, etc.

Continuous audit of reserves: The process conducted by a third party on behalf of the issuer of any collateralized digital token, proving that assets held by the issuer are equal to or greater than their liabilities, which are calculated from the blockchain exposure.

Cryptocurrency: any open source, cryptographically secured, blockchain-based token. See: http://en.wikipedia.org/wiki/Cryptocurrency.

Cryptocurrency platform: A collection of software, hardware, and processes supporting the functioning of a cryptocurrency.

ERC-20 token: Tokens designed and used solely on the Ethereum platform; these tokens are standardized, so that they can be shared, exchanged for other tokens, or transferred from one crypto-wallet to another.

Fiat currency: Currency issue by the central bank of a country or a union of countries.

Fiat-backed stable cryptocurrency: A cryptocurrency whose price is pegged to a collateral in the form of fiat currency.

Know-your-client (KYC): A set of procedures used by banks and other financial intermediaries to avoid being used by criminals for money laundering activities and other illegal activities

Mixer or tumbler: A service used to mix potentially identifiable cryptocurrency transactions with others, in order to obscure the original source of funds; they are used to improve the anonymity of cryptocurrencies, which provide a public ledger of all transactions.

Money market mutual fund (MMMF): An open-ended mutual fund that invests solely in short-term debt securities such as short-dated U.S. Treasury bills and commercial paper; safety profiles of most (but not all) of these funds and bank deposits are comparable.

Narrow bank (NB): A proposed type of bank (also called a safe bank), which holds only central bank cash and liquid and short-dated government bonds; such a bank does not issue any loans (except to the government).

Proof of stake (PoS): An algorithm allowing miners to compete against each other based on the amount of coins they possess, in order to add new blocks to the chain and be rewarded.

Proof of work (PoW): An algorithm requiring miners to compete against each other based on the amount of the computational power they possess, in order to add new blocks to the chain and be rewarded.

Quantity theory of money (QTM): A theory which postulates a direct relationship between the quantity of money in an economy and the level of prices for goods and services.

Seniorage: An algorithm using smart contracts to expand and contract the supply of the price-stable currency, trying to emulate the real-life monetary policies of a central bank.

Treasury money market mutual Fund (TMMMF): a MMMF, which invests solely in U.S. Treasury securities, and seeks to provide current income while preserving shareholders' principal.

Utility-backed cryptocurrency: A cryptocurrency that derives its value partially from its real (or perceived) utility, and partially for speculative reasons.

Velocity of money: The number of times a unit of money is spent to purchase goods and services per unit of time.

VII. References

1. Al-Naji, N., Chen, J., and Diao, L., 2018. Basis: A Price-Stable Cryptocurrency with an Algorithmic Central Bank. White Paper. https://www.basis.io/basis_whitepaper_en.pdf.

2. Begenau, J., and Stafford, E., 2018. Do Banks Have an Edge? SSRN: https://ssrn.com/abstract=3095550.

3. Benes, J., and Kumhof, M., 2012. The Chicago Plan Revisited. Washington, DC: International Monetary Fund.

4. McLeay, M., Radia, A., and Thomas, R., 2014. Money Creation in the Modern Economy. Bank of England Quarterly Bulletin 2014 Q1. SSRN: https://ssrn.com/abstract=2416234

5. Black, F., 1981. A Gold Standard with Double Feedback and Near Zero Reserves. Sloan School, MIT.

6. Burkov, S., Dembo, R., and Lipton, A., 2017 Account Platform for a Distributed Network of Nodes. U.S. Patent Application.

7. Crisp, R. (Ed.), 2014. Aristotle: Nicomachean Ethics. Cambridge University Press.

8. Dai, 2017. The Dai Stablecoin System, December 2017, https://makerdao.com/whitepaper/DaiDec17WP.pdf

9. Danezis, G., and Meiklejohn, S., 2015. Centrally Banked Cryptocurrencies. arXiv preprint arXiv:1505.06895.

10. Ethereum, 2018, A Next-Generation Smart Contract and Decentralized Application Platform. White Paper. https://github.com/ethereum/wiki/wiki/White-Paper.

11. European Central Bank, 2018. The Role of Euro Banknotes as Legal Tender. Speech by Yves Mersch, Member of the Executive Board of the ECB, at the 4th Bargeldsymposium of the Deutsche Bundesbank, Frankfurt am Main, February 14, 2018.

12. Federal Financial Institutions Examination Council, 2016. Retail Payment Systems. IT Examination Handbook.

13. Federal Reserve Bank of San Francisco, 2015. Cash Continues to Play a Key Role in Consumer Spending: Evidence from the Diary of Consumer Payment Choice.

14. Findlay, J. N., and Miller, A.V., 1977. Hegel's Phenomenology of Spirit. Oxford University Press.

15. Graziani, A, 2003. The Monetary Theory of Production. Cambridge University Press.

16. Goetzmann, W. N., 2017. Money Changes Everything: How Finance Made Civilization Possible. Princeton University Press.

17. Goldman-Sachs Investment Strategy Group, 2018. Taking Stock of Our 2018 Outlook: (Un)steady She Goes.

18. Goodfriend, M., and King, R.G., 2005. The Incredible Volcker Disinflation. Journal of Monetary Economics, 52(5), pp.981–1015.

19. Griffin, J. M., and Shams, A., 2018. Is Bitcoin Really Un-tethered? Working Paper.

20. Hardjono, T., Lipton, A. and Pentland, A., 2018. Towards a Design Philosophy for Interoperable Blockchain Systems. arXiv preprint arXiv:1805.05934.

21. Hayek, F. A., 1943. A Commodity Reserve Currency. The Economic Journal, 53(210/211), pp.176–84.

22. Gupta, M., 2018. Blockchain for Dummies. 2nd IBM Limited Edition. John Wiley and Sons.

23. Kaldor N. 2007. Causes of Growth and Stagnation in the World Economy. Cambridge University Press.

24. Keen, S. 2015. What Is Money And How Is It Created? Forbes, https://www.forbes.com/sites/stevekeen/2015/02/28/what-is-money-and-how-is-it-created/#61ab998c7df4.

25. Keynes, J. M., 1936. The General Theory of Employment, Interest, and Money. London: Macmillan.

26. Keynes, J. M., 1943. The Objective of International Price Stability. The Economic Journal, 53(210/211), pp. 185–87.

27. Kocherlakota, N. R., 1998. Money Is Memory. Journal of Economic Theory, 81(2), pp. 232–51.

28. Krugman, P., 2015. There's Something about Money (Implicitly Wonkish), New York Times, Feb. 10, 2015.

29. Leising, M., Rojanasakul, M., Pogkas, D., and Kochkodin, B., 2018. Crypto Coin Tether Defies Logic on Kraken's Market, Raising Red Flags. Bloomberg.

30. Lipton, A., 2016. Modern Monetary Circuit Theory, Stability of Interconnected Banking Network, and Balance Sheet Optimization for Individual Banks. International Journal of Theoretical and Applied Finance, 19(06), p.1650034.

31. Lipton, A., 2016. Macroeconomic Theories: Not Even Wrong. Risk, 30(09), p. 29.

32. Lipton, A., 2018. Blockchains and Distributed Ledgers in Retrospective and Perspective. The Journal of Risk Finance, 19(1), pp. 4–25.

33. Lipton, A., Hardjono, T., and Pentland, S. 2018. Narrow Banks and Fiat-Backed Digital Coins. Capco Journal 47: Digitization, pp. 101–16.

34. Lipton, A., Hardjono, T., and Pentland, A., 2018. Digital Trade Coin: Towards a More Stable Digital Currency. Royal Society Open Science, 5(7), p.180155.

35. Lipton, A., and Pentland, A., 2018. Breaking the Bank. Scientific American, 318(1), pp. 26–31.

36. Mazieres, D., 2015. The Stellar Consensus Protocol: A Federated Model for Internet-Level Consensus. Stellar Development Foundation.

37. Meiklejohn, S., and Mercer, R., 2018. Möbius: Trustless Tumbling for Transaction Privacy. Proceedings on Privacy Enhancing Technologies, 2018(2), pp. 105–21.

38. Nakamoto, S., 2008. Bitcoin: A Peer-to-Peer Electronic Cash System. https://bitcoin.org/bitcoin.pdf.

39. Okamoto, T., and Ohta, K., 1991. Universal Electronic Cash. In: Annual International Cryptology Conference, J. Feigenbaum editor. Springer, Berlin, Heidelberg, pp. 324–37.

40. Oresme, N., 1956. The De Moneta of Nicholas Oresme, and English Mint Documents: Translated from the Latin with Introduction and Notes by C. Johnson. Nelson.

41. Pennacchi, G., 2012. Narrow Banking. Annual Review of Financial Economics, 4(1), pp. 141–59.

42. Raiden, 2018. Raiden Network Documentation. https://raiden-network. readthedocs.io/en/stable/.

43. Rigby, D., 2014. Online Shopping Isn't as Profitable as You Think. Harvard Business Review.

44. Ross, S., 2018, What's Normal for Profit Margin in Retail Sector? Investopedia.

45. Saga, 2018. Saga. White Paper. https://www.saga.org/files/saga-whitepaper.pdf.

46. Sams, R., 2015. A Note on Cryptocurrency Stabilization: Seigniorage Shares. Brave New Coin, pp. 1–8.

47. Schor, L., 2018. Stablecoins Explained. https://medium.com/@argongroup/ stablecoins-explained-206466da5e61.

48. Schwartz, D., Youngs, N., and Britto, A., 2014. The Ripple Protocol Consensus Algorithm. Ripple Labs Inc White Paper.

49. Sila, 2018. Sila: A Stable Fiat-Backed Digital Tokenized Means of Exchange. White Paper.

50. Simmel, G., 2004. The Philosophy of Money. Routledge.

51. Taylor, J., 1955. Copernicus on the Evils of Inflation and the Establishment of a Sound Currency. Journal of the History of Ideas, 16(4), pp. 540–47.

52. Tether, 2016. Tether: Fiat Currencies on the Bitcoin Blockchain. White Paper. https://tether.to/wp-content/uploads/2016/06/TetherWhitePaper.pdf.

53. Tiberiuscoin, 2017. Tiberiuscoin. White Paper. https://www.tiberiuscoin.com/ wp-content/uploads/2018/06/Tiberius-Coin-White-Paper-v3.4.1.pdf.

54. Wood, G., 2015. Ethereum: A Secure Decentralised Generalised Transaction Ledger Homestead Revision. Yellow Paper. http://gavwood.com/paper.pdf.

55. Zhou X., 2009. Reform the International Monetary System. Basel, Switzerland: Bank of International Settlements.

56. Zilliqa, 2018. The Zilliqa Project: A Secure Scalable Blockchain Platform. Position Paper. https://docs.zilliqa.com/positionpaper.pdf.

6

The Law and Finance of Initial Coin Offerings

Aurelio Gurrea-Martínez and Nydia Remolina León*

Initial Coin Offerings (ICOs) are becoming an important source of funding for some capital-hungry firms, especially technology start-ups. In 2018, ICOs raised more than \$21 billion in 2018,[1] surpassing venture capital as a fundraising mechanism.[2] But this development has generated significant skepticism, and according to the Gartner hype cycle of new technologies,[3] one popular metric, blockchain technologies, are, as compared to even other "hot" technologies, *extremely hyped*.[4]

The collapse of the cryptocurrency market in 2018, along with increasingly publicized instances of fraud, have attracted the attention of regulators around the world. Their responses have not, however, been unitary. One reason is that the distinctive features of the blockchain technologies supporting ICO issuances is complex, and relies on novel "decentralized" computer networks that disintermediate or avoid traditional regulated entities such as exchanges and broker dealers. Regulators as such are grappling to first understand the technology supporting ICOs, and then second apply their bespoke legacy regulatory frameworks to it.

In this chapter, we undertake a comprehensive analysis of the legal and financial aspects of ICOs, providing a set of recommendations to enhance the regulatory framework of this new source of finance. The chapter operates thematically, canvassing a wide range of issues, and is organized as follows. In Section I, we examine the concept, features, and structure of an ICO. We note

* For helpful comments and discussions, we would like to thank Chris Brummer, Alfonso Delgado, Scott Hirst, Richard Squire, Felix Steffek, Ricardo Torres, Werner Bijkerk, Jenifer Varzaly, and the participants of various events held at the U.S. Securities and Exchange Commission, Harvard Law School, Cambridge University, ITAM, the Argentinian Securities Commission, the Sao Paulo Stock Exchange (B3), Singapore Management University, the Australian Department of the Treasury, and the International Organization of Securities Commissions (IOSCO), where we had the opportunity to present previous drafts of the paper that became this chapter. This research is supported by the National Research Foundation, Prime Minister's Office, Singapore under its Emerging Area Research Project Funding Initiative.

Aurelio Gurrea-Martínez is Assistant Professor of Law at Singapore Management University. Email: aureliogm@smu.edu.sg.

Nydia Remolina is Research Associate at Singapore Management Uniersity's Centre for Artificial Intelligence and Data Governance . Email: nydiarl@smu.edu.sg.

that because ICOs ultimately run on technology connecting buyers and sellers, or holders of a cryptoasset, they do not feature centralized intermediaries or gatekeepers in their transactions. They thus have no historical precedent and raise challenging questions for authorities tasked with overseeing crypto markets.

In Section II, we analyze different regulatory approaches to deal with ICOs. We argue that none of the existing regulatory models provide an efficient and effective response to the challenges raised by ICOs. For this reason, we will propose a series of reforms to enhance the existing regulatory models. Section III provides an overview of some of the accounting and financial challenges ICOs generate. It will emphasize that the classification of tokens as debt or equity may have several implications from a legal and financial perspective.

In Section VI, we focus on the corporate governance aspects of ICOs. Namely, it will be shown that the purchasers of tokens are highly exposed to the risk of opportunism of the ICO's promoter. As a result, a variety of legal and market devices will be proposed to minimize those agency problems existing between issuers and buyers of tokens. Section V analyzes how ICOs may raise issues related to money laundering, and how regulators and policymakers can deal with these problems.

In Section VI, we provide an overview of the challenges of ICOs from the perspective of privacy law and data protection. Section VII examines how insolvency may affect the issuer and buyer of tokens, and how insolvency jurisdictions should deal with those issues arising in insolvency proceedings involving cryptoassets. Finally, in Section VIII, we discuss the jurisdictional issues arising in ICOs, and why regulators, policymakers, and international organizations such as the International Organization of Securities Commissions (IOSCO) should work together to promote coordination in a variety of issues regarding ICOs. Section IX describes the future of capital markets and corporate governance in a world of tokenized securities. Section X concludes.

I. Concept, Features, and Structure of ICOs

ICOs are a novel method of raising capital where issuers seeking to raise capital do not do so via shares, bonds, or any other traditional financial products. Instead, they issue cryptoassets—digital representations of value utilizing blockchain technologies, where ledgers keep track of ownership using peer-to-peer networks of computers. Usually, ICOs involve the issuance of a particular asset called a "token,"[5] which can entitle the owner to a variety of rights ranging from a financial interest in the company to other non-financial rights, a topic we will return to shortly. But they can also involve the issuance of "currencies" that can be used as means of exchange to purchase goods and services.

In an ICO token issuance, the issuer does not necessarily receive money, as is the case in an issuance of shares or bonds. Instead, it can also receive cryptoassets generally accepted by the public such as Bitcoin or Ether. Moreover, the issuance of tokens is not conducted through the traditional channel in which the regulator and other third parties, such as investment banks, need to intermediate. Instead, it is conducted through a new technology, blockchain, which is the technology used to create cryptoassets such as Bitcoin or Ether.

Finally, unlike what occurs with many other issuances of shares, bonds, or other type of securities, the issuance of tokens does not always require the preparation and registration of a prospectus, unless those tokens are considered securities under a country's securities law. Indeed, in an issuance not involving securities, the issuer will just be required to prepare a simple document, which is not subject to any supervision or imposition of mandatory terms. This document is termed a "white paper." This white paper is the primary disclosure obligation of an ICO provided that the tokens issued by the promoter are not deemed as "securities" under the relevant country's securities law.

This section will provide a common understanding of these and other aspects of an ICO. It also fleshes out in more detail salient differences between ICOs and other traditional fundraises.

A. Tokens

ICOs are also commonly described as "token" sales or "coin" sales.[6] Tokens are basically *digital assets* used in connection with decentralized services, applications, and communities known as token networks. In other words, tokens are digital assets that are recorded on a distributed ledger and can be transferred without an intermediary, and the structuring of the issuance, the pricing of the offer, and the distribution of these instruments do not involve the participation of any regulated entity such as, for example, an investment bank.[7] A common scenario is for tokens to be sold even before the token network is operational. In some of these cases, the tokens will be functional once the platform is developed.

1. The Concept and Features of Tokens

Tokens often differ widely from one another, and different countries adopt different classification schemas to refer to similar tokens. In our opinion, it might be useful to classify tokens by two factors: (1) *functionality* of the token, which focuses on the function and economic substance of the token; and (2) *legal nature* of the token, which is based on the particular features of the token (including its distribution), and the definition of "security" established in a particular jurisdiction.[8] In Section III, we will include a third classification based on the nature of the token from a financial perspective. This latter classification, which categorizes tokens as debt or equity instruments, will be particularly relevant from an accounting and financial perspective, as well as for a variety of legal issues (e.g., covenants, distribution of dividends, or, especially in some civil law countries, directors' duties and liability in situations in which the company's net capital falls below a certain percentage of the legal capital).

i. Functional Classification

Tokens can have a number of different use cases. The Swiss Financial Market Supervisory Authority (FINMA) offers a useful nomenclature for dominant approaches involving the categorization of such use cases. Specifically, FINMA categorizes tokens as (1) payment tokens, (2) utility tokens, and (3) asset tokens.[9] Likewise, they recognize that "hybrid" tokens can also exist.

FINMA defines *payment tokens* as synonymous with cryptocurrencies.[10] Accordingly, these tokens are only used to make payments generally with the issuer—for example, to purchase a future product or service in which the only accepted payment are these "cryptocurrencies" issued by the promoter. The ability of these tokens to serve as a payment method elsewhere will depend on the acceptance of these tokens by third parties.

The concept of *utility tokens* used by FINMA refers to those tokens that are intended to provide digital access to an application or service.[11] Therefore, many companies developing technological products may opt for the issuance of this type of tokens. From a financial and accounting perspective, these tokens seem to reflect the purchase of a future good or service provided by the issuer.

Finally, FINMA defines *asset tokens* as those representing assets enabling token owners' participation in real underlying companies, or earnings streams, or an entitlement to dividends or interest payments.[12] In terms of their economic function, these tokens are analogous to equities, bonds, or derivatives.[13]

ii. Legal Classification

The functional classification is very useful in understanding the features, nature, and economic function of tokens. Likewise, it may provide some guidance about the *tentative* regulations applicable to the tokens. For example, as asset tokens are analogous to debt or equity, these tokens probably fall into the definition of "securities." Nevertheless, this intuitive relationship between the functional classification and the legal classification is just that: intuitive. Indeed, the fact that a token is an "asset token" from a functional perspective does not necessarily mean that, from a legal perspective, the same token is a *security token*—even though it will usually be so.

Perhaps more importantly, the fact that a token is classified as "payment token" or "utility token" from a functional perspective does not mean that these tokens cannot be considered as securities. The classification of a token as a "security token" or a "non-security token," which are legal classifications, will depend on how a particular country defines "securities." [14] In general, this judgment should be made after assessing a variety of factors, including the structure of the token, the functionality of the token, and the way the token was distributed. If, according to a particular legal system, a token is classified as a "security," these tokens will be classified as "security tokens" from a legal perspective, and the issuance of these tokens should comply with existing securities laws. In contrast, if a token does not meet the requirements existing in a particular country to be considered a "security," the token will be classified as a "non-security token" for the purpose of this chapter. Therefore, the issuance will *not* have to comply with existing securities laws.

Sometimes, the features of the token will determine its legal nature. However, as shown by cases such as *Munchee*,[15] the distribution of the token may end up being the defining factor distinguishing a token from a security. Therefore, even though a functional classification of tokens can be useful for several purposes, the legal classification of the token will require a deeper analysis of the token as well as the circumstances surrounding the issuance.

In many situations, issuers will ask third parties (usually lawyers) to provide advice about the nature of the token.[16] In cases in which a formal *legal opinion* is issued, the issuer should enjoy a presumption of *good faith* when analyzing whether it made a mistake in the issuance of tokens—for instance, not complying with securities regulations when it should. However, if it were shown that the third party acted in bad faith or with gross negligence, these "gatekeepers" could be held liable.[17] For this reason, we would recommend that, regardless of the potential use of gatekeepers, regulators should implement a kind of "regulatory sandbox" in which they work with the issuers in order to let them know the nature of their issuance and the applicable law.[18] If issuers follow these steps, good faith derived from their behavior should be an irrebuttable presumption. Moreover, they will receive protection without bearing the costs associated with the issuance of a formal legal opinion.

2. The Presale of Tokens

In some instances, a presale may take place prior to an ICO. A presale or a pre-ICO is a term that refers to the process that takes place before the crowdsale begins. It usually allows the investors to buy tokens before the crowdsale starts. Moreover, this token sale event usually has separate smart contracts from the main crowdsale event.[19]

One purpose of a presale is to provide a discount for prospective purchasers. The buyers that participate in the presale often get cheaper prices per token. As

ICOs impose a minimum and maximum threshold for their token crowdsales, blockchain start-ups often present discounted rates and merits for investors that purchase their crypto tokens at an early stage.[20] Thus, investors in the crowdsale phase of the ICO are required to purchase tokens at a higher rate than early investors. In other words, ICO presales provide benefits for early investors. According to blockchain investment funds and even Ethereum cofounder, Vitalik Buterin, since 2017, the incentivization system for early investors by popular ICOs has led to the network congestion of Ethereum, driving transaction fees above average. When a large number of ICOs are in the works, people will likely buy quantities of Ether so that they can invest in said ICOs—which may drive up the price of the cryptocurrency. During times when Ether's price skyrockets, transaction fees can become more expensive. For instance in March 2017, Ethereum cofounder Vitalik Buterin revealed that an investor in the ICO of BAT spent $2,210 as a transaction fee for one payment to receive the advantages and discounts granted to early investors.[21]

Some companies decide to conduct the presale of tokens only with "accredited" investors, and thus not as public offerings. By some informal accounts, funds from accredited investors make up between 60% and 80% of the total funds raised in a direct token presale.[22] These market players, including accredited investors such as hedge funds, are performing bump-and-dump practices in ICO markets when participating in presales of tokens.[23]

Furthermore, in these token presales, some issuers enter into a Simple Agreement for Future Tokens (SAFT) with these accredited investors. The SAFT is an investment contract whereby investors purchase the right to receive tokens in the subsequent token network launch. In exchange, the company promises to deliver tokens upon the launch of the token network for the investors' promise to pay immediately. Under U.S. law, the SAFT is considered a security.[24]

3. The Crowdsale and Distribution of Tokens to the Public

After the token presale, an issuer can start to develop the project described in its white paper. As of the date of this chapter, no empirical studies have measured the rate of token presales that successfully progress into a real project and what percentage results in an undeveloped idea jeopardizing buyers' interests. Therefore, completion or abandonment rates remain unclear and could be part of a future empirical study regarding ICOs.

Once the project is developed, the company sells part of its tokens in exchange for cryptocurrencies. Generally, such cryptocurrencies would be Bitcoin or Ether. The crowdsale is the core of an ICO. It is the process of raising funds from all type of buyers or investors. Developing a network may sound easy. However, the risk of not developing a project is relatively high—even in the absence of fraud—considering that many of these projects promise to develop some kind of product or service on a blockchain. And the success of these projects could be complex to achieve due to the operational risks and scalability problems of blockchain technology.[25]

For example, the SEC's DAO investigation[26] proved that vulnerabilities in the code can be exploited by hackers to make funds disappear. The DAO, an unincorporated entity, was launched on April 30, 2016, with a 28-day funding window. It proved popular, raising over $100m by May 15th, and by the end of the funding period, the DAO was the largest ICO at the time, having raised over $150 million from more than 11,000 individuals. During the crowdsale, several people expressed concern that the code was vulnerable to attacks.[27] A bug was exploited by a hacker who took more than $3.6 million worth of Ether by mid-June. Additionally, the price of Ether dropped from over $20 to under $13. This situation brought the project to an end.[28] To elaborate, ICOs tend to have a minimum threshold for funding—if this threshold is not met by the end of the funding period, the funds are usually returned to investors automatically in a process called "finalization."[29] In today's ICOs, it is not clear what happens if the project is not developed and what is the enforcement mechanism for holding the developer accountable to the token holders. The degree of accountability also differs if the tokens are security tokens or non-security tokens.

B. Cryptocurrencies as ICO Proceeds

As mentioned earlier, the proceeds from an ICO need not consist of fiat currency. Instead, issuers may receive other cryptocurrencies as consideration or proceeds from a token sale. The cryptocurrencies accepted by issuers in an ICO are normally commonly traded cryptocurrencies such as Bitcoin and Ether. These commonly traded cryptocurrencies may help companies to cash out the proceeds of the ICO. Typically, the issuer specifies in the white paper the type of consideration—whether cash or other cryptocurrencies—to be accepted in exchange for the tokens. For example, if the blockchain network used to develop the issuer's project is Ethereum, the issuer will likely require Ethers.

This represents a potentially enormous difference between ICOs and traditional methods to raise funds. ICOs seeking other cryptoassets as consideration must make an analysis of the assumed price of the cryptocurrency received from token holders. Moreover, the value of the cryptocurrency can vary considerably during the course of the ICO and the development of the project. This feature of ICOs mandates an analysis of the risks and problems companies might face when receiving a volatile asset to fund the development of a project. We will address this issue in Section VII.

C. Blockchain: The Technology behind
Initial Coin Offerings

Historically, data have been stored in centralized databases.[30] A database is a structured collection of data that is stored on a computer, referred to as the server. Centralized databases are maintained by a central administrator and stored in a single server. This administrator is an intermediary that is trusted to maintain the data.[31] In turn, users who want to access the stored data must send a request to the administrator's server. While this centralized databased can reduce costs precisely due to centralization, this same attribute makes it more vulnerable to single point of failure issues[32] and to denial-of-service (DoS) attacks.[33]

In contrast, a distributed database is a collection of multiple databases that are logically interrelated and distributed across a computer network.[34] In these systems, the data can be replicated and stored in separate physical locations to prevent single point of failure issues and DoS attacks. In a distributed peer-to-peer network, the participating computers are commonly referred to as nodes (or peers). Importantly, the tasks are not controlled or coordinated by a central node or an intermediating trusted party. Rather, these tasks are distributed across the nodes that record data into the network. This shared data record is composed of a series of entries that are linked to accounts from users and show every transaction that has been confirmed by the nodes. A protocol provides a set of rules and procedures that nodes must follow to share and verify the data.

Blockchains are a particular kind of distributed database[35] that enables data to be stored and maintained by network users themselves, without having to rely on any "trusted" third parties. In a broad sense, blockchain is as such used to describe the suite of technologies that allow computers in a peer-to-peer network to reach agreement over shared data.[36]

D. The White Paper

ICOs involve the issuance of digital assets, often tokens, which run on a blockchain. To support their issuance, ICO issuers and promoters publish a document, known as a "white paper" that explains how the project is to be funded. A white paper is essentially a business plan. Most ICOs will allow potential investors—along with any interested reader—to download their white paper off their official website. Some websites also serve as databases for the most recent white papers published.[37] White papers are also one of the first elements of a project investors should look at prior to deciding if it is a solid investment or an attractive asset to buy.[38]

The first white paper, and clearly the one that was used as a model for ICOs, is Satoshi Nakamoto's paper on Bitcoin. Since the structure of a white paper has not been regulated, market participants are starting to find a common ground on what should be the content of these documents. According to some empirical studies regarding ICOs and their white papers,[39] there is one consistent characteristic among them: a technical description of the underlying technology for which funding is sought as well as some description of the potential use and benefits of said technology. Basically, it is a general description of the project to be executed and the benefits and disruption that project can bring to the table.

ICO white papers may present certain issues. On the one hand, the paper may provide misleading information. For example, it can state that a token is not a security when it is, or it cannot state the appropriate applicable law.[40] On the other hand, promoters may omit some relevant information: they may disclose only those aspects that can be beneficial to them at the expense of the purchasers of tokens.[41]

These asymmetries of information might be corrected by either setting out which elements should be included as a minimum in the white papers by an overarching body, or letting markets decide the best way to guarantee a certain degree of standardization, for example using analysts or law firms as advisors in structuring ICOs or through peer reviews.[42] Companies might also engage in public discourse, defending the white paper and even advertising an upcoming token sale. As a result of this marketing, advertising, and public discourse, some presales could make many tokens meet the definition of "security" under some countries' securities laws.[43]

When the white paper is first published, usually developers have little more than the description of what they want to achieve after the ICO. However, in some white papers, part of the code is published. Thus, the tokens offered in this stage are not functional for using the platforms. Even though those tokens cannot be utilized, they can still be traded during presales of tokens.

E. Differences between ICOs and Other Methods to Raise Capital

ICOs present some similarities with other financing methods, such as venture capital, angel investment, initial public offerings, and especially crowdfunding. Actually, ICOs are sometimes considered as an application of the crowdfunding mechanism to blockchain-based companies or projects.[44] Since there are no empirical studies determining why companies may prefer ICOs over other fundraising methods, we will try to describe the main differences and similarities between these methods from a functional, finance, and regulatory perspective. Thus, it will be easier to identify those aspects that make an ICO a more or less attractive method to raise capital.

Table 6.1. Differences and similarities between ICOs and other sources of financing

	IPO	Crowdfunding	Venture Capital	ICO
Level of regulatory compliance	IPOs are heavily regulated in all jurisdictions by securities regulations. This process often requires the intervention of an underwriter (one or more investment banks) and law firms.	Crowdfunding is not regulated in most jurisdictions. However, in the United States, UK, and some Continental European countries, it is already regulated. (e.g., U.S. regulations of crowdfunding have been in place since 2012). Some countries in Latin America enacted primary legislation regarding crowdfunding in recent years as well (i.e, Mexico, Argentina Colombia).	Venture capital funds are subject to the same basic regulations as other forms of private securities investments. Additionally, private equity firms often have to register with securities regulators and are subject to some reporting requirements.	ICOs are regulated in some jurisdictions. Only those considered securities are subject to securities regulations.[45] There are almost no barriers to entry for those who wish to conduct an ICO (especially if the token is a non-security token). Some basic coding skills to generate tokens is the only entry barrier.[46]
Limits/caps	No limits.	In almost all jurisdictions, crowdfunding is capped at certain amounts.	No limits in investing but the venture capital funds have a fixed life.	No limits.
"Investors"	Institutional investors and retail investors participate in the distribution of securities through IPOs.	Funds raised from members of the public, many of whom are not professional/institutional investors. However, crowdfunding campaigns generally take place through an intermediating platform that extracts fees from issuers	A venture capitalist is a person who makes venture investments and these venture capitalists are expected to bring managerial and technical expertise as well as capital to their investments. Venture capital funds are typically managed by a venture capital firm, which often employs individuals with technology backgrounds (scientists, researchers), business training, and/or deep industry experience.	None of the regulatory approaches so far have limited ICOs.[47] It follows that current investors would refer to institutional investors and retail investors.

Disclosure requirements	IPOs require the preparation of a prospectus, whose structure and content is highly regulated.	Companies issuing equity (or debt) via crowdfunding platforms are required to disclose essential information to investors	Venture capital funds are accountable to their own investors. This provides an incentive to screen and monitor investments carefully	The content of a white paper is not regulated.
Secondary market of the instruments issued	The securities will have a secondary market, which is determined in the prospectus. The securities, when issued, are registered in a stock exchange.	Securities are privately held and, generally, there is no secondary market to trade them	These funds have a fixed term.	Depending on the structure of the token, some will have a secondary market. This feature could mean in some jurisdictions that the token is a security.
Pricing	IPOs have different mechanisms for pricing: Fixed price, Dutch auction, Bookbuilding (which is the most common method)	The platform is responsible for the valuation and pricing of the projects in almost all jurisdictions. The platform is a supervised entity.	In return for financing one to two years of a company's start-up, venture capitalists expect a 10-times return of capital over five years.[48]	Price comes from issuer and it is subjective. The ICO mechanism allows entrepreneurs to generate buyer competition for the token, which, in turn, reveals consumer value without the entrepreneurs having to know, ex ante, consumer's willingness to pay.

(Continued)

Table 6.1. Continued

	IPO	Crowdfunding	Venture Capital	ICO
What is being sold	Generally shares (equity)	Generally securities that can be classified as equity (equity crowdfunding) or debt (crowdlending).	Generally shares (equity)	Coins or tokens, which can be classified as securities or non-security tokens, and equity or debt, depending on the features of the token.
Accountability	Issuers, law firms and underwriters in an IPO may be liable for misrepresentations or omissions in a prospectus.	The funding portals or platforms are subject to registration and supervision from the securities market authorities.	Venture capital funds are accountable to their own investors. This provides an incentive to screen and monitor investments carefully.	ICOs can be securities offerings and they may need to be registered.

Source: Alfonso Delgado *et al* (2016) and authors' elaboration.

Despite these similarities and substantially different regulatory approaches to ICOs among jurisdictions, which makes the comparison harder, the ICO market was 40% of the size of the IPO market and 30% the size of the venture capital market during the first quarter of 2018.[49] The size of this phenomenon has perked the interest of regulators. The following section analyzes how different jurisdictions and regulators are coping with ICOs and provides a new safe but efficient system to deal with this method to raise funds.

II. Regulatory Approaches to Deal with ICOs

Regulators around the world approach ICOs very differently.[50] For example, some countries, such as China[51] and South Korea,[52] have opted to prohibit ICOs. In other jurisdictions, including the United States,[53] Singapore,[54] and Switzerland,[55] tokens are allowed. However, issuers need to comply with existing securities laws if the token is classified as a "security" under the relevant country's securities law. Finally, in other countries such as Mexico,[56] any issuance of tokens has to be authorized by the regulator. Therefore, regardless whether they are security or non-security tokens, the issuer must attain the approval of the regulator before proceeding with any issuance.

As it will be discussed, all of the existing regulatory approaches present some flaws. For this reason, we will propose a new model to regulate ICOs that, while facilitating the use of ICOs as a source of finance, seeks to (1) enhance the protection of the purchasers of tokens, and (2) create a safe, fair, and efficient regulatory environment.

A. Existing Regulatory Approaches

1. Contractual Approach
One possible approach may consist of excluding tokens from the scope of securities regulation. Under this approach, any issuance of tokens—and the terms provided in the white papers—would be exclusively subject to the law of contracts. In countries with a definition of "securities" based on a closed catalogue of financial products (e.g., shares or bonds), as is the case in Singapore, this approach will be easily achieved. The regulator should not need to enact new legislation. If things remain status quo, all issuances of tokens would be excluded from securities law, unless the token can be classified as a share, bond, or other product included in the definition of security.[57]

By contrast, in countries with a functional concept of securities, as it happens in the United States, where the economic substance prevails over the legal form, an adoption of this model may require action by the regulators. Namely, it may force the regulator to enact legislation prescribing that even if a token meets the requirements to be deemed a security, it will not be subject to securities regulation. This regulatory approach would specifically exclude tokens from securities laws. As a result, ICOs would be exclusively governed by the law of contracts.

This contractual model may reduce regulatory costs associated with an issuance of tokens. Therefore, it can make ICOs a more attractive method to raise capital. However, it would create several problems. First, this approach would not provide a level playing field. By allowing functionally similar products to be subject to different regulatory frameworks, the regulator would unfairly discriminate those products subject to securities laws. Since these latter products would be subject to a higher regulatory burden, the regulatory costs borne by an issuer of tokens would be lower, even when, from a functional perspective, they offer a similar product. Moreover, in countries in which the concept of security is defined from a functional perspective, this approach would also be inconsistent with the definition of security. Therefore, the adoption of this model would also require a modification of the concept of security.

Second, this approach would also be riskier for investors in several ways. On the one hand, since no mandatory disclosure would be required, the issuer would be free to select the amount of information provided to investors and how this information is disclosed. Therefore, the issuer can take advantage of this situation to include obscure terms and omit some relevant information. On the other hand, the lack of mandatory disclosure would also make harder the comparison of ICOs. Therefore, it will be more difficult (or at least costlier) to identify credible, value-creating projects providing a greater level of protection to the purchasers of tokens. Finally, if these products are excluded from the scope of securities regulation, the purchasers of token would not be protected by the securities supervisor. Therefore, unless the power to protect consumers by overseeing the terms of the white papers are transferred to another regulatory agency (for example, a Consumer Protection Bureau), the level of protection to the purchasers of tokens will be significantly reduced. And it will be reduced not only for the higher asymmetries of information potentially created between issuers and token holders, but also for the higher risk of fraud, or at least opportunism, existing in a world in which the issuer knows, from an ex ante perspective, that the issuance and terms associated with the ICO will not be subject to the supervision of any regulatory authority.

2. Bans

Another regulatory approach may consist of banning ICOs. This prohibition may take several forms. First, the regulator may decide to prohibit any type of ICO, as happened in China and South Korea. This prohibition may be due to several factors. For example, the regulator may consider that the risks associated with this new source of finance (especially in terms of fraud, money laundering, and opportunistic behavior over naïve consumers) exceed its benefits. Therefore, it does not make sense to promote this fundraising method, at least while the regulator does not come up with an appropriate regulatory framework to deal with the risks of ICOs. Likewise, the use of ICOs may also have adverse effects for a country's economic and monetary policy. After all, an issuance of tokens not only involves companies raising cryptocurrencies rather than official currencies, but also that purchasers of those tokens have previously acquired cryptocurrencies in order to be allowed to participate in the ICO. Therefore, the amount of official currencies might be significantly reduced, while the investment and consumption in the country may increase or at least remain stable. As a result, the government may lose control over some relevant factors that may affect the economy and monetary policy of the country.

Second, regulators may decide to prohibit ICOs for certain constituencies. For instance, a regulator may decide to prohibit the participation of retail investors due to the higher asymmetries of information that they face, and their vulnerability to potential promoter opportunism. Likewise, a regulator may also ban commercial banks and some institutional investors from purchasing tokens. After all, not only do they manage other people's money, but several reasons mainly associated with systemic risk seem to recommend a more risk-averse investment policy in these entities. And the purchase of tokens is highly risky.

Finally, a regulator may decide to ban the purchase of tokens once certain prudential or other thresholds are met. In other words, it can impose limitations on the amount of tokens potentially acquired by certain purchasers, as seems to be the approach followed in Russia.[58] By implementing this restriction, the regulator would limit the potential losses of token holders involved in a fraudulent or just unsuccessful ICO.

In our view, while the reasons to ban the purchase and issuance of ICOs may seem plausible (especially taking into account that more than 80% of ICOs are scams[59]), this policy followed in China and South Korea may prevent many firms and early-stage ventures from receiving the finances to develop their projects. Moreover, if the primary concerns of the regulator have to do with the risk of fraudulent behavior and the economic and monetary consequences of the risk of ICOs, there are more efficient ways to deal with these issues, as will be discussed in our proposal to create a safe regulatory framework for ICOs.

As for the limitation on the amount of tokens potentially acquired by a single purchaser, we believe that it just solves part of the problem. Namely, it reduces the individual losses potentially borne by a failed (or even fraudulent)

ICO. However, it does not generate any benefit from an aggregate or social-welfare perspective. Issuers can still take advantage of the asymmetries of information faced by consumers, and some fraudulent behavior can be committed. For this reason, we do not find this proposal entirely convincing. In the case of restricting the purchase of tokens to certain actors, for example, the situation might be different. In the context of individuals, we believe that regulators should not ban the purchase of tokens by individuals. Instead, they should invest resources in warning investors, through advertisement and education, about the risks of ICOs. Thus, the regulator would be able to preserve individuals' freedom to purchase tokens while minimizing the risks of being ripped off. For commercial banks and institutional investors, however, we do believe that some bans should be imposed. For this reason, certain limitations for these special market participants will be imposed in our proposal to deal with ICOs, discussed in Part B of Section II, "Toward a Safebut Efficient System of ICO Oversight".

3. Security Token Registration

Many jurisdictions around the world, including the United States, Switzerland, and Singapore, subject the issuance of security tokens to general securities laws. Therefore, if a token is not classified as a security, the issuance of tokens will be exclusively governed by the law of contract. By contrast, if the token is deemed to be a security, the issuance of tokens will be subject to securities law. Therefore, it will be subject to the general rules governing the preparation and registration of prospectus, as well as the supervision of the securities regulator. Likewise, if certain requirements are met, the issuer might enjoy the exemptions generally provided by securities regulators to certain issuances of securities.[60] Therefore, even though it will be subject to the oversight of the securities regulator, it may be waived from the costly procedures generally associated with the preparation and registration of a prospectus.

In our opinion, this model has various advantages. First, it provides a level playing field by not discriminating among functionally similar products. Therefore, regardless of their legal form, products with similar features and functions will be subject to the same rules of the game. Second, by subjecting the issuance of security tokens to securities regulation, the regulator will provide a greater level of protection to the purchasers of security tokens. Finally, the lack of regulation of non-security tokens may reduce the regulatory burden of some tokens that, due to their particular features, might not need the same level of protection existing in security tokens. Therefore, by reducing the regulatory costs associated with the issuance of these tokens, regulators may facilitate fundraising to many ventures that may have trouble getting access to other sources of finance.

Despite the general benefits associated with this regulatory model, we do not find it entirely convincing. On the one hand, it is not clear whether the general framework existing in securities law will be enough to protect security tokenholders. Indeed, even though, from a functional perspective, some tokens can look like securities, the issuance of tokens presents other particular features that cannot be found in other types of securities. First, unlike what happens with shareholders, tokenholders are not protected by corporate law. Second, in the context of ICOs, there is no market for corporate control to discipline managers. That is, the promoter of the ICO cannot be subject to any hostile takeover and ultimately be removed from its position. Therefore, the potential situation of opportunism of issuers vis-à-vis investors will be higher in the context of ICOs, since it is unlikely the promoter will face the risk of being removed for poor governance or performance, as it may happen in equity markets. Third, while equity markets can be relatively efficient, in the sense that they reflect all publicly available information, the same cannot be applied to the market of tokens. In these latter markets, the lack of a deep secondary market (or even the existence of a secondary market) as well the smaller number of analysts and investors will make it very unlikely that the price of a token reflects all publicly available information. As a result, tokenholders will find it more difficult to know the intrinsic value of their assets, and this lack of information may distort their ability to make wise financial decisions. Fourth, tokenholders probably face more asymmetries of information than a regular shareholder in a public company. This is due not only to the complexity of the white project or the project behind the ICO, but more importantly to the inability of the market to project retail investors, as has been mentioned previously. Finally, the cryptocurrency world seems to be involved in a "hype" that may exacerbate the ability of many tokenholders to make thoughtful decisions. Therefore, the risk of making wrong decisions will be higher in the context of ICOs. As a result, perhaps the general rules governing securities law might not be enough to protect investors, and some further steps should be taken by the regulators.

On the other hand, even if it were assumed that the regulatory approach existing in jurisdictions such as the United States, Switzerland, and Singapore provides a reasonable level of protection to security tokenholders, there are still two additional regulatory challenges to be addressed: (1) the protection of non-security tokenholders, and (2) making sure that all security tokens comply with securities laws.

In our opinion, these jurisdictions fail to protect non-security tokens. Indeed, while many steps have been taken to protect security tokenholders, regulators have not seriously thought about the protection of non-security tokenholders. This lack of protection is probably due to the fact that most of the discussion of ICOs has been generated in the capital market space, and the protection of non-security tokens probably exceeds the scope of securities regulators. Therefore, perhaps this discussion should be led by other regulatory authorities. Likewise, we also believe that the regulatory model existing in these countries fail to avoid the problem associated with not subjecting security tokens to securities regulation. On the one hand, the issuer may have perverse incentives to avoid the regulatory burden associated with securities regulation. For this reason, it may classify its tokens as non-security tokens even when they meet all the requirements to be classified as securities. In our opinion, even though this problem will be reduced in countries with an active enforcement department and severe sanctions will be imposed on those issuers failing to comply with securities laws, the deterrence effect created by getting caught and sanctioned might not be enough to prevent misbehavior—especially in a sector where more than 80% of the issuances are scams. Moreover, even if the issuer is caught, it will be difficult to repair the damage to both investors and the market as a whole.

In addition, there will be circumstances in which it is not clear whether a particular token should be classified as a security, as shown in the United States by cases such as *SEC v Howey, Munchee,* or *Reves v Ernst & Young.*[61] Moreover, many issuers acting in good faith might nevertheless fail to comply with existing securities law.

In our opinion, the regulatory model existing in the United States, Switzerland, and Singapore makes it particularly difficult to investigate an ICO if the promoter has not submitted any files or prospectus to the securities regulators. In these situations, the securities regulators will likely hear about the ICO from others, sometimes when something bad has already happened. For this reason, we believe that a system of ex ante control might be needed in these countries. Namely, it will be proposed in Section III that any issuance of tokens, no matter whether they are security tokens or non-security tokens, should be *disclosed* to the security regulators or any other public regulatory agency. Thus, by making it easier to the regulator to facilitate the investigation of all issuance of tokens, issuers will think twice about how to classify their tokens, and, if so, whether they are complying with securities regulation.

4. Comprehensive Token Registration

Other countries, such as Mexico, have opted for imposing a system of full control ex ante over all issuances of tokens.[62] According to this approach, any issuance of tokens should be registered and authorized by the regulator.[63] Then, depending of the type of tokens, existing securities laws may apply or not. Thus while a security token will be subject to the full gamut of disclosure and procedural requirements and obligations existing in securities law, the regulatory burden for an issuance of non-security tokens will be notably reduced.[64]

The Mexican approach solves the problem associated with not having control over the issuance of non-security tokens, or even security tokens not registered before the securities regulator. Therefore, it may fix part of the flaws of the regulatory model existing in the United States, Switzerland, and Singapore. Nevertheless, the solution adopted by Mexico is far from perfect. Among other aspects, it imposes more costs for issuers and regulators. From the perspective of the issuers, the issuance of tokens will probably involve more time and money. From the perspective of the regulator, this model would require more people to be trained and hired to monitor, analyze, classify, and approve the issuance of tokens. Therefore, it will be costlier. And while this investment in hiring and training people to deal with ICOs may be valuable in some cases, there will be many situations in which it is not worth it (e.g., when a token consists of just a redeemable voucher in a company). As a result, even though the Mexican approach solves part of the problems existing in other regulatory models, it creates other costs. For this reason, it does not sound entirely convincing either.

B. Toward a Safe but Efficient System of ICO Oversight

As mentioned previously, all the existing regulatory models intended to grapple with ICOs present significant flaws. For this reason, we propose a new model that, while protecting tokenholders, market integrity, market supervision, and the stability of the financial system, can still facilitate the use of ICOs as an affordable method to raise finance. Our proposal is built on four core pillars.

First, all issuance of tokens, no matter whether they are security or non-security tokens, should be disclosed to the regulator. The way to do so may consist of requiring issuers to submit a simple, harmonized *electronic form* to the securities regulator or any other public authority.[65] This electronic form should contain some basic information about the issuance. This basic information may include the promoter´s location, problem and proposed technology solution, description of the token, blockchain governance, qualifications of the technical team, and risk factors.[66] Likewise, we also believe that the form should include other factors potentially relevant for the purchasers of tokens, including identity of the promoters, legal advisors, accounting and finance aspects of the ICO, and any legal or contractual provisions available to protect tokenholders.

By submitting this electronic form, not only will the regulator be in a better position to monitor any issuance of tokens, but it will also be easier for analysts and investors to compare ICOs since issuers will be required to provide a minimum level of standardized information. Therefore, this comparability could serve as an additional tool to protect tokenholders, while facilitating the analysis of the information provided by the ICO´s promoter by the regulatory authorities . As a result, this higher scrutiny will incentivize promoters to behave in a more honest and diligent manner, since this regulatory model will make it easier for regulators to investigate and, if so, sanction any fraudulent ICOs, as well as those issuances of securities tokens—sometimes publicized as non-security tokens—that fail to comply with securities laws.

Second, as non-security tokenholders are not protected under securities law, we believe that several strategies should be implemented to protect these purchasers. Namely, we argue that regulators should protect non-security tokenholders by implementing some regulatory strategies existing to protect consumers and financial consumers. As it will be discussed in Section V, these strategies will include cooling-off periods, the prohibition of certain terms and products, the imposition of conduct obligations on the issuer, and the use of certain litigation rules to favor the non-security tokenholder in case of a potential lawsuit.

Third, being involved in a presale of tokens is even riskier than participating in other types of ICOs since the tokenholder will be entitled to something that does not exist yet—and based on the number of scams, it seems quite probable that it might not exist ever. Therefore, we believe that *commercial banks* and *pension funds* should not be allowed to purchase these tokens since they invest money from the general public and their potential failure could have severe consequences for the stability of the financial system.[67] Therefore, they should not engage in this type of risky activity.

Fourth, several factors make the purchase of tokens particularly risky, including the high probability of scams, the lack of effective devices to protect tokenholders, the larger asymmetries of information between founders and tokenholders, and the high risk of irrational behavior that might take place in the crypto markets.[68] For this reason, we believe that the regulator should spend more resources and efforts in warning *retail tokenholders* about the risks associated with the purchase of tokens.

III. Accounting and Finance Aspects of ICOs

Another critical aspect raised by the issuance of tokens concerns the accounting and finance aspects of ICOs. In other methods to raise capital, it seems relatively clear, from an accounting and finance perspective, what a company gives to investors, and what the issuer receives in return. For example, in an IPO, a company gives shares (equity) to public investors, and it receives cash in return. In a debenture, a company gives bonds (debt) in exchange for cash. Moreover, in this type of transactions, the way the company's counterparty is classified from an accounting and finance perspective is also relatively clear. In an issuance of shares, the company's counterparties are equity holders. Therefore, they will be part of the company's net assets (or equity) within the balance sheet. In an issuance of bonds, the company's counterparties are debt holders. Hence, they will be part of the company's liabilities. The following Table 6.2 sets forth the registration of a purchase of sale of tokens from an accounting perspective.

Table 6.2. Registration of tokens from an accounting perspective

Issuer's balance-sheet	
Cryptocurrencies (assets)	Tokens (Debt/Equity)
Tokenholder's balance-sheet	
Tokens (assets)	Cryptocurrencies (assets)

The classification of the company's counterparty from an accounting and finance perspective may have different implications. For example, it may affect the company's governance and cost of capital, and more importantly from a legal perspective, the company's financial ratios and covenants.[69] Indeed, since some of the contractual terms potentially agreed between issuers and lenders may specify that the company should maintain certain debt/equity ratios, or even certain levels of current versus non-current liabilities, the classification of an issuance of tokens as debt or equity, or as current liabilities or non-current liabilities, may ultimately affect the company's existing loan agreements. Therefore, it seems particularly relevant to analyze the anatomy of an ICO from an accounting and finance perspective.

As it has been mentioned in previous sections, a promoter issues tokens, and it receives *cryptocurrencies* in return. Therefore, since the cryptocurrencies will represent a right for the company, they will be registered as an *asset* in the company's balance sheet. As a general rule, they will represent a current asset, due to the ability of most cryptocurrencies to be converted into cash in a short period of time.

More problems arise when we analyze the registration of the issuance of tokens. In this case, the *tokens* issued by the company can be classified as equity or debt. In our opinion, this classification will depend on the features of the tokens. When the white paper gives tokenholders economic and political rights similar to those held by shareholders, the tokenholders should be classified, at least from an accounting and finance perspective, as *equity holders*. Therefore, the issuance of tokens will be registered in the company's net assets (equity). By contrast, in those cases in which the features of the token seem to reflect that the tokenholders will be entitled to future services or fixed payments, those tokenholders should be classified as *debt holders*. Therefore, they will be part of the company's liabilities. And depending on the maturity of those rights held by tokenholders, the issuance of tokens will be registered as non-current liabilities (if the maturity is more than a year) or current liabilities (if the maturity is less than or equal to a year).

From the perspective of the tokenholder, the registration of tokens seems a bit clearer. Since tokenholders give cryptocurrencies to the issuer in exchange for acquiring the promoter's tokens, those cryptocurrencies should be registered as a decrease in the tokenholder's assets. Simultaneously, as the tokenholder receives some rights (tokens) in return for the cryptocurrencies, these rights will increase the tokenholder's assets.

Another critical aspect of ICOs from an accounting and finance perspective involves the valuation and, if so, the impairment of value experienced by the cryptocurrencies held in the issuer's balance sheet. This aspect becomes particularly problematic in the context of cryptocurrencies due to their volatility.[70] Moreover, if, as some authors have pointed out,[71] there is a bubble in some cryptocurrencies' markets, and this bubble bursts, the issuer will have to register significant losses in their balance sheet. Therefore, from an accounting perspective, the valuation and impairment of these assets can be particularly relevant not only for the company's financial statements but also for a variety of legal issues. These legal issues may from existing covenants, to distribution of dividends, or—in some jurisdictions—even the duties and liability of directors if the company's net assets fall below a certain amount of the company's legal capital.[72]

Likewise, from the perspective of the *tokenholder*, the fact that many projects fail may force them to register a loss in their assets. Therefore, taking into account that volume and value of ICOs are becoming more and more important, we believe that regulators should pay special attention to the accounting and finance aspects of ICOs. Otherwise, we face the risk of observing something similar to what happened in the 2008 financial crisis: the unexpected registration of losses in many companies' balance sheets may end up harming not only the financial situation of these firms and their investors but also—if the volume of tokens is large enough, and the parties involved are financial institutions—the stability of the financial system.[73]

IV. Corporate Governance Issues

A. The Concept and Nature of Tokenholders

The classification of a tokenholder will mainly depend on the nature, features, and distribution of tokens. From a legal perspective, tokens can be classified as security or non-security tokens. Therefore, the purchasers of security tokens will be classified as "security tokenholders," whereas the holders of non-security tokens will be considered "non-security tokenholders." From an accounting and finance perspective, however, the classification may seem more unclear. On the one hand, non-security tokenholders should generally be classified as debt holders, since they will probably be entitled to future products or services. On the other hand, *security tokenholders* can be classified as either equity holders or debt holders, depending on whether they are entitled to the company's ownership or future returns or just to a fixed return, respectively.

The following Table 6.3 sets forth legal and finance classification of tokenholders

Table 6.3. Legal and finance classification of tokenholders

Legal classification	Finance classification
Security tokenholder	Debt holder/equity holder
Equity-based security token-holders	Equity holders
Debt-based security token-holders	Debt holders
Non-security tokenholder	Debt holder

The fact that a security tokenholder (legal classification) is an equity holder (finance classification) does not mean that these tokenholders should be considered "shareholders," even if they have similar rights. Indeed, in our opinion, unless a particular jurisdiction allows classifying as shares some particular financial products that look like shares but that do not represent a fraction of a company's legal capital, a tokenholder should never be considered a shareholder.[74] We do not believe so for several reasons. First, it is not clear what exactly a shareholder is entitled to. Indeed, while there are some general rights usually held by shareholders (e.g., rights to the company's future returns, rights to the company's residual assets, right to call the shareholders' meeting, right to sue the managers for a breach of fiduciary duties, etc.), the use of preferred shares or dual-class shares structure show that many shareholders can be considered as such without having some rights generally associated with the condition of shareholders (e.g., vote). Therefore, while there are some indicia that may help us identify what a shareholder looks like, it is not always clear.

Second, and perhaps more important, even though financial markets and institutions should be analyzed from a functional approach with particular focus on the economic substance rather than their legal form, this functional analysis does not mean that different legal institutions should be considered similar entities, but instead that they should be subject to similar regulations. For example, in our opinion, even if investment banks and commercial banks were performing similar functions, they should not be considered similar legal entities. Nevertheless, they should be subject to similar regulations. Therefore, a functional approach to financial regulation should not be interpreted as understanding different institutions as equal legal entities but treating functionally equivalent institutions similarly. Therefore, in this context, even though a shareholder should be distinguished from equity tokenholders entitled to similar rights, they both should be subject to a similar treatment. Hence, they both should be part of the company's equity or they both should be subordinated in bankruptcy.

Third, in some countries, existing shareholders have preemption rights with the purpose of avoiding dilution when a company raises capital. Therefore, if a court or regulator interprets ex post that a tokenholder should be considered as a shareholder, existing shareholders can lose a right that, regardless of its desirability, the legislature wants them to have. Therefore, even though the legislature can solve this problem by requiring shareholder vote for any issuance of tokens, this solution might not seem the most desirable one for a fundraising method that was probably, among other aspects, chosen to save transaction costs. Moreover, even in the absence of transaction costs, if old shareholders really want to make tokenholders new shareholders, it may seem more consistent— and more desirable to promote legal certainty for both shareholders and tokenholders—to issue shares rather than tokens.

Finally, the classification of equity tokenholders as shareholders may also make unclear the beneficiaries of managers' fiduciary duties. In other words, it may make even more unclear to whom the managers owe fiduciary duties, and what types of legal rights can be exercised—and by who—in the case of a breach of fiduciary duties. Therefore, this interpretation may not may crease legal uncertainty but it can also reduce the accountability of the board of directors.

For these reasons, we believe that, even when tokenholders have similar rights than those generally held by shareholders, they will just be considered *equity holders* from an accounting and finance perspective, or *security tokenholders* from a legal perspective, but never "shareholders." A different conclusion not only would create legal uncertainty but it would also be inconsistent with the proper application of the functional approach that should prevail in financial regulation. In any case, if, under a particular jurisdiction, financial products similar to shares can be classified as such, and the issuance of shares requires approval via the shareholders' meeting, we would suggest that the issuance of security tokens should be approved at the shareholders' meeting, just in case a court eventually finds that those tokens should be classified as shares, and therefore shareholders' rights can be affected.

B. Protecting Tokenholders from the Promoter's Opportunism

1. Agency Problems in a World of Tokenholders

While the use of ICOs may serve as a new method to allow individuals and firms to raise capital and therefore be able to develop their projects and ideas, the evidence suggests that more than 80% of ICOs are scams.[75] Therefore, the purchase of tokens should be considered a risky activity since the tokenholder is highly exposed to the opportunism of the promoter. In some cases, the promoter might not even pursue the promised projects.[76] In others, the promoters may just waste tokenholders' money when pursuing promoters' own goals. In both cases, there is a type of agency problem, or a higher risk of opportunism, that should be addressed.

This higher risk of opportunism of promoters vis-à-vis tokenholders derives from several factors. First, tokenholders do not usually have the ability to appoint, remove, and remunerate the directors. Therefore, unlike what happens when the suppliers of funds are shareholders entitled to vote, the managers might not have enough incentives to maximize the interests of the tokenholders, since their jobs will not be at risk. Second, white papers may not cover how managers should behave in many cases in which the interests of the tokenholders may be at stake. Moreover, unlike what happens in a typical relationship between directors and shareholders where fiduciary duties may help fill some gaps,[77] promoters do not usually owe fiduciary duties to tokenholders. Therefore, white papers may become more incomplete than a typical corporate contract. Besides, even if they were able to fill these gaps, it is not clear how (if so) the rights potentially provided to the tokenholders in the white paper will be enforced. Third, while managers in listed companies are subject to public scrutiny and a market for corporate control that may encourage them to maximize the value of the firm for the interests of the shareholders,[78] these market forces will unlikely exist in a private company issuing tokens. Fourth, unlike shareholders, tokenholders are not necessarily protected by a country's company laws. In fact, non-security tokenholders do not even get the protection of securities law. Fifth, due to the lower disclosure requirements imposed on promoters and the complexity behind many ICOs, there might be more asymmetries of information between issuers and tokenholders. Sixth, there seems to be a type of market euphoria in the cryptoassets market that may increase the level of irrational decisions made when purchasing tokens.[79] Therefore, all of these factors expose tokenholders to a higher risk of opportunism by promoters.

Several strategies can be implemented to reduce agency problems between promoters and tokenholders. First, managers can be required to buy a certain percentage of tokens. By doing so, they would have more skin in the game, and therefore they would be incentivized to make wiser investment decisions. Otherwise, they might end up losing as much as the tokenholders.

Second, tokenholders may be empowered with some political rights. For instance, they can be allowed to appoint and remove the directors, or even to have a vote on some relevant decisions. Thus, the managers would have more incentives to maximize the interests of the tokenholders. Otherwise, the tokenholders could easily remove the managers.

Third, some market mechanisms can be promoted to protect tokenholders. One of them can be the use of platforms to assess issuers and projects, as well as the use of intermediaries in the token industry. Another market device may consist of the development of secondary markets for tokens. Thus, tokenholders will be protected through the use of an easy exit right—which may lead in return to "price" founders' behavior.

Nevertheless, while these mechanisms may reduce managerial agency problems,[80] they may generate other issues. First, while the fact of requiring insiders to hold a certain percentages of tokens would align the interests of managers and tokenholders, promoters might not have resources to buy enough tokens as to credibly have skin in the game. In fact, that is why they may decide to launch an ICO rather than funding the project by themselves. And even if the promoter were able to keep some tokens for free, this measure would not work either. On the one hand, if the promotor has not paid for those tokens, it would not have enough skin in the game. On the other hand, keeping tokens by founders and/or insiders would generate an opportunity cost, since the more tokens insiders keep, the less cryptocurrencies (and therefore funding) they will be able to raise. Thus, this measure may end up harming the firm's ability to raise funds.

Second, while empowering tokenholders may align the interests of managers and tokenholders, this solution may also generate several problems. On the one hand, this power given to tokenholders may increase "principal costs," that is, the costs associated with letting investors decide.[81] Moreover, these principal costs can be higher in the context of ICOs, since the fact of making business decisions about technical projects may require more expertise than for other businesses. On the other hand, if the white paper confers significant power to the tokenholders, and they have the ability to make some relevant business decisions, tokenholders may face the risk of being considered as de facto directors.[82] And if so, they may end up being liable for some damages. Therefore, tokenholders' rights should be designed in a manner that help reduce managerial opportunism without increasing principal costs or putting tokenholders at risk. Finally, empowering tokenholders will make the managers more accountable to them at the expense of the shareholders. And if so, a type of agency problem among the different suppliers of finance may exist due to their potentially different preferences in terms of risks and returns.[83] For example, while the shareholders, due to their limited liability, variable returns, and diversified portfolios, are usually more inclined to take risks, creditors usually prefer a less risky business strategy. This divergence of interests can be also found between shareholders and tokenholders and even among tokenholders. For instance, if the returns of a group of powerful tokenholders depend exclusively on a single investment project, they may force the managers to invest more time and resources in this project, even if that is not the most desirable strategy for other stakeholders or even the company as a whole. Therefore, a type of "horizontal agency" problem can be created since the managers would be maximizing the interests of a group of investors at the expense of others.[84]

2. Legal Strategies to Protect Tokenholders

One of the primary concerns existing in the ICO markets comes from the lack of effective tools to protect tokenholders. On the one hand, security tokenholders enjoy a type of protection, such as securities law, that might not be enough or even adequate for them due to several reasons, including the lack of an effective market for corporate control to discipline promoters, the higher asymmetries of information probably faced by tokenholders, or the more pronounced irrational behavior that may exist in the crypto market. Moreover, in many circumstances, the purchasers of security tokens might not even enjoy the protection provided by securities laws, since many promoters might not even register their issuance of tokens, alleging that they are issuing non-security tokens. On the other hand, non-security tokenholders are just protected by a private document, such as the white paper, whose ability to be enforced is not even clear. Therefore, it should be a priority for the regulator to implement new legal tools to protect tokenholders.

i. Protecting Security Tokenholders

Security tokenholders are currently protected by two primary mechanisms: (1) the apparatus provided by securities law, which include disclosure obligations, procedural rules, supervision by the securities regulator, and a market of securities lawyers monitoring whether companies are complying with securities laws, so as to otherwise sue them on behalf of investors; and (2) the white paper. Nevertheless, as it has been mentioned, the white paper does not provide an effective tool to protect tokenholders since, due to the absence of mandatory disclosure for white papers, the promotor may just establish and disclose whatever it can be in its interest. Likewise, current securities law might not be enough, or even appropriate, to protect tokenholders. For this reason, we believe that securities regulators should implement a new legal strategy to protect security tokenholders. This strategy, as mentioned in Section II, should consist of requiring promoters to submit an *electronic form* to the security regulator or any other public authority disclosing certain information particularly relevant for the protection of tokenholders. The information provided in this electronic form may include the promoter´s location; problem and proposed technology solution; description of the token; blockchain governance; qualifications of the technical team; risk factors; identity of the promoters, legal advisors, accounting, and finance aspects of the ICO; and legal or contractual provisions available to protect tokenholders (if any). Moreover, the information provided in the electronic form should be based on a system of smart disclosure, in which more attention will be paid to the type of information provided in the form, as well as the way issuers provide this information, rather than the amount of information itself.

ii. *Protecting Non-security Tokenholders*
In addition to the protection provided by the electronic form imposed on any issuance of tokens, we think that other legal devices should be implemented to protect non-security tokenholders. After all, they are not protected by securities laws, as it may happen with security tokenholders. In our opinion, these legal devices to protect tokenholders can be inspired by those generally used to protect *consumers* and more especially *financial consumers*.

First, regulators may impose *cooling-off periods* on any issuance of non-security tokens. Thus, non-security tokenholders will be able to return the token within a given period of time without bearing any cost. This measure not only will protect non-security tokenholders ex post, but it will also encourage many issuers to think twice what they are going to sell.

Second, policymakers may also opt for *regulating products*. Through this mechanism, the regulator may think of prohibiting certain terms particularly obscure or even tokens.

Third, as it has been developed in the context of financial consumers after the failure of some of the previous strategies, regulators may also decide to impose *conduct obligations* on the issuer. Namely, it may require issuers to take into account the interest of tokenholders, avoiding situations in which the issuer seeks to exploit non-security tokenholders' biases and mistakes.

Finally, an additional tool to protect non-security tokenholders may consist of using *litigation rules.* For instance, the legislature may establish that any unclear provision established in the white paper should be interpreted in favor of non-security tokenholders. By doing that, not only will non-security tokenholders enjoy ex post a higher level of protection, but issuers will also have incentives to draft the clauses established in the white paper in a clearer and more protective way to favor the understanding of these clauses by tokenholders.[85]

3. Market Devices to Protect Tokenholders

In addition to the legal and regulatory devices to protect security and non-security tokenholders, we believe that some market mechanisms may also reduce the agency problems existing between issuers and tokenholders. For example, the development of a liquid secondary market for tokens may provide a greater level of protection to tokenholders. Moreover, it would do so in several ways. First, a more liquid market for tokens would make it easier for tokenholders to sell their tokens. Therefore, these "exit rights" could serve as ex post mechanism to protect tokenholders.

Second, the existence of a liquid market may contribute to "price" the behavior of many projects and promoters. Namely, by observing whether tokenholders buy or sell shares, and therefore whether the price of a given token goes up or down, the market can infer the promoters' behavior. Therefore, promoters, or at least those interested in issuing future tokens, will have strong incentives to behave in an efficient and honest manner.

Third, if these markets are developed, there will be more platforms and analysts providing advice and "grading" projects and promoters.[86] Nevertheless, while this market of intermediaries can generate several benefits for tokenholders, regulators should pay close attention to the potential conflicts of interests faced by these actors. Indeed, the lessons learned in the past from auditors,[87] credit rating agencies,[88] and proxy advisors[89] show that these "gatekeepers" can be subject to a variety of conflicts of interests. Therefore, regulators can use some of the regulatory strategies implemented for auditors, credit rating agencies, and proxy advisors to deal with the problems associated with the rise of platforms and analysts in the ICO industry. These strategies may include disclosure obligations (especially when the analyst has been paid by the issuer for any other professional service), and restrictions in the variety of professional services potentially provided by these analysts, as well as liability rules.

V. Anti-money Laundering Implications of ICOs

Tokens created on a blockchain are decentralized and encrypted, sometimes making it harder to track each of the transactions made, and the individuals behind them. Therefore, in theory, anyone with an internet connection and a digital wallet can be part of a token sale event. That can leave room for people to launder money or finance terrorism activities and engage in other fraudulent behaviors. Additionally, taking into account how easy it is to launch a token presale, these mechanisms could be used in countries where illegal activities such as corruption are above average in order to move resources without over-sight. Nonetheless, we could not find available data showing how much money is being laundered through ICOs.

Regulators in the United States and Singapore have been particularly active in highlighting the risks of money laundering and frauds that investors face when buying tokens. Singapore's financial regulatory body and central bank, the Monetary Authority of Singapore (MAS), stated that: "ICOs are vulner-able to money laundering and terrorist financing (ML/TF) risks due to the anonymous nature of the transactions, and the ease with which large sums of monies may be raised in a short period of time."[90] MAS's media release of March 13, 2014, had communicated that while virtual currencies per se were not regulated, intermediaries in virtual currencies would be regulated for ML/TF risks. Specifically, MAS stated that the regulator is "currently assessing how to regulate ML/TF risks associated with activities involving digital tokens that do not function solely as virtual currency."[91]

For MAS, even digital tokens that perform functions that may not be within MAS's regulatory purview for not fitting into the legal category of securities may nonetheless be subject to legislation for combating money laundering and terrorism financing. MAS highlights in particular the following: (1) obligations to report suspicious transactions with the Suspicious Transaction Reporting Office, Commercial Affairs Department of the Singapore Police Force; and (2) prohibitions from dealing with or providing financial services to designated individuals and entities pursuant to the Terrorism (Suppression of Financing) Act and various regulations giving effect to United Nations Security Council Resolutions.

Moreover, issuers of tokens could be subject to licensing requirements under the Securities and Futures Act and the Financial Advisers Act. In addi-tion, platforms facilitating secondary trading of such tokens would also have to be approved or recognized by MAS as an approved exchange or recognized market operator respectively. This regulatory authority also announced the drafting of a new payments services framework that will include rules to ad-dress money laundering and terrorism financing risks relating to the dealing or exchange of cryptocurrencies for fiat or other digital assets such as tokens. Such intermediaries will be required to put in place policies, procedures, and controls to address such risks. These will include requirements to conduct customer due diligence, monitor transactions, perform screening, report suspicious transactions, and keep adequate records.[92]

Along the same lines, United States Authorities delivered similar statements in regard of AML compliance and ICOs. On one hand, the Securities and Exchange Commission (SEC) provided guidelines on its website for investors to consider before participating in token sales. Some of the key points the SEC asks potential buyers to consider are that there are ways to identify fraudulent investment schemes.[93] On the other hand, the Financial Crimes Enforcement Network (FinCEN) published a letter indicating that the U.S. agency will apply its regulations to ICOs. In the letter, FinCEN explained that both developers/issuers/sellers and exchanges involved in the sale of an ICO-derived token would be liable to register as a money transmitter and comply with the relevant statutes around anti-money laundering and know-your-customer rules.[94]

The FinCEN letter recognizes that ICOs vary not only from the functional or legal approach, but also that there are jurisdictional differences depending on the structure of an ICO and its associated token. In sum, as Coincenter has noted, FinCEN asserted that it considers the transmission of newly issued digital tokens derived from ICOs to be subject to the money transmitter rules under the Bank Secrecy Act. This means that developers and exchanges that sell ICO coins or tokens, or exchange them for other virtual currency or something else of value, must register as money services businesses and comply with (1) the Bank Secrecy Act rules regarding Know-Your-Customer obligations, (2) the implementation of an anti-money laundering and combating the financing of terrorism compliance program, and (3) the filing of suspicious activity reports. FinCEN also reminded that U.S. persons must comply with all applicable Office of Foreign Assets Control financial sanctions obligations.

FinCEN reported to the Senate that since 2014 it has examined roughly one-third of the approximately 100 virtual currency businesses that have registered and has initiated several investigations and enforcement actions against firms and individuals. However, it is important to clarify that this letter is not yet a formal FinCEN guidance.

Regarding the European Union, in February 2018, the European Commission launched the European Union Blockchain Observatory and Forum, which highlighted key developments of the blockchain technology, promoted European actors, and reinforced European engagement with multiple stakeholders involved in blockchain activities.[95] Even though tokens and ICOs remain unanalyzed by policymakers and regulators by European central authorities, the Council of the European Union approved the 5th AML

Directive and, among other changes, introduced AML obligations applicable to exchange platforms of virtual currencies.[96] Providers of exchange services between virtual and fiat currencies, and custodian wallet providers, will have to comply with the AML Directive. Despite this, it is doubtful whether these provisions are suitable to put an end to money laundering using virtual currencies, because virtual currencies can still be exchanged between private actors without any monitoring in many jurisdictions. Actually, there is no reference in the Directive to ICOs.[97]

Given the regulatory uncertainty, several crypto exchanges in these jurisdictions where they are clearly subject to AML compliance, and also banks, may refuse to work with ICO projects or ICO founders that do not identify buyers of their tokens. This market behavior will possibly force ICOs to voluntarily comply with the AML regulation, or at least to identify the buyers of the tokens. We do not have available data to confirm this hypothesis though.

This means that regulators still need to work on what the best way is to prevent money laundering when operating on a blockchain where the jurisdictional limits become more confusing or non-existing, and where players operate through online platforms rather than physical markets. Perhaps the understanding of these features will lead to different solutions for preventing money laundering in blockchain-based markets, for example, working with digital identity mechanisms to counter the anonymities of ICOs nowadays.[98]

VI. New Challenges for Privacy Law and Data Protection

The rise of cryptocurrencies, ICOs, and, in general, blockchain use cases, is also generating several issues with regards to privacy law and protection of personal data. The nature of the public blockchain means that every transaction taking place will be published and linked to a published public key that represents a particular user. However, that key is encrypted, and no one would be able to directly identify the users settling transactions on a blockchain.[99] In a blockchain, each block contains a reference to the preceding block by including a cryptographic hash of the data within the preceding block. If the data in a block is altered, the hash of the block changes too, and this falsification of the records can therefore be detected.[100]

However, this operation give rise to some issues regarding personal data, especially in countries that follow the European Union standard of the General Data Protection Regulation Directive (GDPR). Data protection rules do not apply to anonymized data, and some could consider that because of hashing and encryption, blockchain anonymizes data. This could be debated because anonymized qualification of data is very strict, particularly under European rules. Hashing permits records to be linked; thus it will generally be considered a pseudonymization technique, not an anonymization.[101]

Additionally, data stored on a blockchain is tamper-proof, so deleting it later on is not an option. Moreover, transactions on a blockchain are "immutable," which really means that once a blockchain transaction has received a sufficient level of validation, some cryptography ensures that it can never be replaced or reversed.[102] Thus, this data cannot be deleted once it is inserted in blockchain. This feature could also conflict with privacy laws and the Right to be Forgotten or Right to Erasure.[103] This consists in the right to obtain from the controller the erasure of personal data without undue delay. However, it is not clear what *erasure of data* actually means. The GDPR initiative probably did not have in mind a distributed data storage mechanism such as blockchain, but only a centralized or non-distributed data controller. The fact that this unique feature of blockchain technology does not match with privacy rules creates some friction and uncertainty for compliance.

This takes us to the next problem regarding privacy law and blockchain. Who is the data controller on a blockchain? Due to the distributed nature of blockchain, there is not any centralized entity gathering and managing this information. In consequence, more than one party may qualify as controller, which means that several participants of the network could be responsible for compliance with privacy regulations. Governance agreements might be necessary among participants to define the responsibilities as data controllers or data processors.

The applicable jurisdiction can also be a problem for blockchain use cases. Blockchains usually have a cross-border nature, which is an important aspect for privacy laws. In some jurisdictions, privacy law differs from contract law because parties are not allowed to establish the applicable law. The applicable law depends on factors listed in GDPR,[104] for example. As a result, the way blockchain technology operates (based on a system of encryption and hashing) does not seen to be compatible with the traditional system to protect personal data. Therefore, if policymakers want to promote the use of blockchain technologies, as we believe they should, the approach to deal with personal data should be changed. Regarding blockchain use cases in general, there is still a long way for developers and policymakers to go to clarify how blockchain fits into the privacy rules world.

VII. Insolvency

The rise of ICOs may also generate some problems in case of insolvency. Indeed, if the debtor's assets are not sufficient to pay all its debts, the way claims are ranked in the scheme of distribution may become a very sensitive issue.[105] In the world of tokenholders, one may wonder in which position tokenholders should be paid. To answer this question, it seems relevant to distinguish between equity tokenholders and debt tokenholders.

Following the absolute priority rule,[106] it seems clear that debt tokenholders should always be paid ahead of equity tokenholders, since the latter are functionally equivalent to shareholders, and shareholders cannot get paid ahead of the creditors in an event of insolvency. The situation becomes more controversial in the context of debtholders vis-à-vis other creditors, or even between equity holders and shareholders. In these cases, we believe that the solution should depend on whether the white paper mentions something. If the white paper does not specify how debt tokenholders should be paid, they should be paid as general unsecured creditors. Therefore, they will be paid pro rata according to the pari passu principle.[107] Likewise, equity tokenholders would be paid ahead of shareholders, since the latter is the one legally entitled only to the company's residual assets.

However, the white paper may establish the treatment of tokenholders in bankruptcy. In those cases, their treatment will depend on the views taken on insolvency procedures. If a country follows a contractual approach to bankruptcy, these rights should be preserved.[108] Therefore, equity tokenholders may end up getting paid after or along with the shareholders if the white papers says so, and debt tokenholders may be ranked ahead or after general unsecured creditors.

However, it is far from clear that this contractual approach will be applied in practice. Namely, we believe that a subordination clause will probably be applied, since it does not harm other creditors—in fact, it will be for the benefit of the other creditors due to the fact that, following the absolute priority rule, subordinated creditors will only get paid if more senior creditors have been paid in full. More problems may arise, however, if the white paper gives a priority claim to the tokenholders in case of bankruptcy. Under this scenario, unless the insolvency legislation recognizes this priority or "any priority created by contract," this preferential treatment may not be enforceable. Therefore, tokenholders should carefully analyze how they would be paid in bankruptcy, and whether the treatment proposed in bankruptcy would be enforceable under a particular jurisdiction.

In addition to dealing with claims, an insolvency procedure also deals with assets. After all, the assets will determine whether and, if so, how and how much, the creditors are getting paid. In the context of an ICO, the person or entity in charge of managing the insolvency proceeding will face two primary problems: (1) the valuation of these assets associated with the ICO (that is, the cryptocurrencies received in exchange for the tokens), and (2) the ability of those assets to be converted to cash (liquidity). When the cryptocurrencies received by the issuer are generally accepted in the market (e.g., Bitcoin, Ethers, etc.), the liquidity problem is unlikely to exist. Nevertheless, the valuation problem may still be relevant. Indeed, as was mentioned previously, cryptocurrencies are very volatile assets. In other words, their value may rise or drop rapidly. As a result, this volatility may create some problems not only for the trustee or debtor in possession but also for the creditors, whose rights and decisions may be affected by the volatility of these assets. For example, if they know that the cryptocurrencies held by the issuer can be sold to get enough cash to repay their debts, perhaps they may prefer liquidation over reorganization. However, if the liquidation value of the company is not enough to pay even part of their claims (among other reasons, due to the lack of value of the cryptocurrencies), a creditor may have incentives to preserve reorganization over liquidation—especially if the issuer's future cash flows are positive. Therefore, we believe that trustees or debtors in possession should warn creditors about the importance of the volatility of the cryptocurrencies potentially held by the issuer, since it may be a factor potentially relevant for their decisions in bankruptcy.

Additionally, along with the valuation of the cryptocurrencies received by the issuer, another problem potentially existing in the context of ICOs is the valuation of the tokens. While this problem will not be relevant for the insolvency proceeding of the issuer, it will be in the case that the tokenholder becomes insolvent. In these situations, the trustee or debtor in possession will face the challenge of valuing those tokens, which can be particularly difficult in the absence of a secondary market. Therefore, in these circumstances, the trustee or debtor in possession will be required to use some general methods to value assets, including their ability to generate future cash flows. For that purpose, it will be relevant to determine whether the issuer will finally be able to honor the obligations assumed with the tokenholder. If not, the value of the token will be close to zero.

VIII. International Challenges and Cooperation in ICOs

Most securities regulators are issuing some guidance regarding ICOs. In fact, IOSCO has even created a section on its website to include statements issued by many securities regulators around the world with regards to ICOs.[109] This is a desirable initiative to contribute to the understanding and "brainstorming" about how regulators should address ICOs. Namely, by being able to know how other jurisdictions are addressing the same challenge, regulators and policymakers will be able to come up with more ideas to regulate ICOs in a more efficient and effective manner.

However, these initiatives are not enough. On the one hand, it is very costly to analyze each country's regulatory approach to dealing with ICOs. On the other hand, the work developed by international organizations in this space does not analyze the pros and cons of each regulatory solution. For this reason, it would seem desirable if an international organization such as IOSCO issues some guidance on ICOs, as least to establish: (1) the rationale and operation of ICOs, (2) a proposed explanation and classification of tokens, (3) the different regulatory approaches that may be implemented to deal with ICOs; (4) the applicable law that should govern ICOs, (5) the costs and benefits of each regulatory approach, and (6) other issues potentially relevant for securities regulators, such as how to protect tokenholders, or how to deal with other challenges raised by ICOs such as anti-money laundering. Thus, even though each securities regulator will be able to choose one model or another, all of them will have the opportunity to know and assess each model in order to decide which one best fits their financial system, taking into account the priorities of the regulator (e.g., investor protection, innovation, financial stability, prevention of financial crime, etc.), as well as the particular features of the country (e.g., type of investors—institutional or retail—existing in their capital markets, size and expertise of the regulator, etc.). In addition, we also believe that the International Accounting Standards Board (IASB) should also issue an International Financial Reporting Standard (IFRS) to clarity how to register an issuance of tokens.

Finally, we also believe financial cooperation, and the understanding of each country's laws and corresponding regulatory model to deal with ICOs, is relevant as a mechanism to know the scope of each country's jurisdiction. For example, while some countries may apply their laws just to any issuance of tokens taking place in their countries, other jurisdictions may find: (1) their enforcement regimes effective enough to require issuers to comply with their existing securities laws (or at least to submit the proposed form in their countries), (2) they may initiate investigations and enforcement actions because the issuer is registered or incorporated in the country, or (3) the country's laws apply just because some of the tokenholders are from their jurisdiction.

For this reason, and taking into account the different regulatory models existing to deal with ICOs, we think that issuers, regulators, and tokenholders should be aware of the applicable law (and competent regulator) to a given issuance of tokens. Otherwise, the issuance may be subject to legal uncertainty at the expense of not only the issuer but also—and perhaps more important—the tokenholders and the financial authorities in charge of protecting these tokenholders. Therefore, in the absence of a global regulatory framework for ICOs, which seems very unlikely, we propose that an international agreement to deal with some procedural (mainly jurisdictional) aspects of ICOs would be desirable.

IX. Future of Capital Markets, Finance, and Corporate Governance in a World of Tokenized Securities

Tokenization may bring positive paradigm shifts to finance, law, government, and more. It can represent changes in the ways we consume goods or replace traditional investments in capital markets. Perhaps, companies and regulators can learn from ICOs and start thinking about improving markets by using blockchain as a new way for delivering goods and distributing securities.

Due to the absence of financial intermediaries, which means less transactions costs, and the possibility for developers to fund long-term projects where it may take years to capture value,[110] ICOs allow companies to raise an important amount of funds in the early stages of a project. Also, the features of tokens vary, providing founders and investors different types of instruments to offer or buy in these markets. Additionally, since tokens fund networks, the buyers—specially retail buyers—of a token are highly interested in making these networks grow.[111] These characteristics of token sales make us believe that the trend of tokenizing securities or goods is attractive for capital markets.

Essentially, tokenization is a method that converts rights to an asset into a digital token. Blockchain hype made the world interested in exploring ways to successfully tokenize real-world assets. This encompasses usage cases of blockchain that are trying to bring this technology to the traditional registry of shares. For example, in May 2016, the Delaware Blockchain Initiative was launched[112] and is currently in an implementation stage. The Delaware General Corporation Law was amended in order to make it legal for entities incorporated in Delaware to use blockchain technology for record-keeping and administration of stock ledgers.[113] This is impressive since Delaware is regarded as one of the most important states for corporate law in the United States and the world. In 2015, 86% of all IPOs chose to incorporate in Delaware; more than half of all U.S. publicly traded companies and 66% of Fortune 500 companies are incorporated in Delaware as well.[114]

In December 2016, Overstock.com Inc. became the first publicly traded company to issue stock via blockchain thanks to the Delaware Blockchain Initiative.[115] One year later Overstock.com Inc. launched an ICO (only presale) through its subsidiary tZERO to fund the development of an exchange to facilitate the trading of blockchain-based assets, including securities.[116] However, Overstock.com Inc. announced the U.S. Securities and Exchange Commission is investigating the tZERO Coin presale;[117] therefore the project will probably be delayed indefinitely.

Despite the uncertainty that these cases portend for the implementation of blockchain technology for stock ledgers, the advantages of using it should be explored in depth. Initiatives such as Delaware could bring the benefits investors and companies are experiencing with ICOs to a much broader audience and enhance the development of capital markets, finance, and corporate governance. Many years ago, the securities markets went digital, and now there are not many investors holding physical certificates of, for example, shares. However, true benefits of digitization will only reach the securities industry when its layers of settlement processes are finally streamlined, so that securities issuers and investors can again interact directly, which is something that could be achieved by blockchain technology.[118] With blockchain, buyers of shares and corporations are expected to have a clear ownership record, lenders holding security interests in pledged stock are expected to be able to foreclose after a triggering event, and distribution of dividends and payments are expected to be clearer as well.[119] Knowing who owns which shares is a fundamental corporate governance requirement. Blockchain technology should make it easy to know at a specific moment the number of shares that an individual shareholder owns and who exactly are those shareholders. Nowadays corporations—especially publicly traded corporations—rely on intermediaries to know this information (i.e., when using omnibus accounts, central depositories, etc.).

The Dole Food Company, Inc. class action is an example of why accurate stock ownership is not achieved in markets today. In this case, there were more than 36 million shares in the class, but claimants submitted facially valid claims for more than 49 million shares, which is 33% more Dole common stock than those that actually existed. Clearly, no single ledger kept track—in real time—of stock ownership. When an investor buys a share of common stock in a listed corporation, the investor typically does not hold that share directly. Generally, from the corporation's perspective, a company called Cede & Co. (a nominee of the Depositary Trust Company (DTC)[120] is the "record owner" of all the stock, all the time. The investor's broker keeps an entry in its database showing the investor as the stock's beneficial owner, and DTC keeps an entry in its database of the investor broker's ownership.[121]

Dell's 2013 go-private merger highlights another instance where blockchain technology could potentially help prevent proxy voting mistakes derived from direct versus indirect ownership of shares. T. Rowe Price lost standing to seek appraisal even though it had vocally opposed and repeatedly tried to vote against the merger. In order to vote on the Dell buyout, T. Rowe Price had to send its vote through intermediaries. A service provider, which was a third party, later provided an updated record related to the merger. This updated record triggered T. Rowe Price's automated voting system, which was set to vote in favor of any management-recommended merger, as was the Dell merger. Despite T. Rowe Price's intention to oppose the Dell merger, it ultimately voted in favor, losing standing to sue for appraisal. T. Rowe Price ended up paying

$194 million to compensate its clients for actions for loss of appraisal rights derived from this proxy voting mistake.[122]

Using smart contracts opens a world of possibilities for corporations, even for compliance processes and corporate governance matters. For example, a corporation could use blockchain to record directors' votes to ensure they act according to regulation and internal policies. A corporation could also program shares issued in a private placement to be issuable only to the digital wallets of those who qualify as accredited investors. Tokenized shares could also be programmed to facilitate the execution of covenants agreed in financing contracts with creditors. And there are more applications to explore for shares issued in a blockchain as tokens in ICOs.

Some other U.S. states are following Delaware's ideas. Wyoming is one example. The Wyoming Blockchain Coalition is focused on encouraging the adoption of blockchain technology in Wyoming and, so far, has been incredibly successful. In fact Wyoming has approved blockchain-friendly bills defining utility tokens and has also exempted them from the state's money transmission licenses. The coalition has in mind the implementation of a similar initiative to the one passed in Delaware.[123] European markets are being influenced by this initiative. In Germany, for example, models have been developed in which a nominee holds the company's shares as a registered shareholder with tokens. These tokens embed smart contracts that provide for a type of trust agreement between the respective tokenholder and the nominee. The smart contract is supported by traditional legal solutions (written agreements), thus making the tokenholder only an indirect shareholder through the written agreement.[124]

In sum, using blockchain technology in the corporate context could revolutionize corporate record-keeping, governance, finance, and capital markets. The ICOs experience could bring knowledge to the table for regulators and companies to embrace this new technology so as to benefit capital markets development. So far, developers incorporated through a simple Delaware corporation will probably take advantage of the Delaware Blockchain Initiative that would allow the entity to itself incorporate directly on a blockchain.

X. Conclusion

This chapter has sought to provide an understanding of the legal and financial challenges of Initial Coin Offerings. For that purpose, we have started by proposing a concept of tokens based on both their functionality and their legal nature. This chapter argues that the classification of tokens as "utility tokens" or "security tokens" used by many authors and regulators is misleading since it mixes up the functionality of a token and its legal nature. From a legal standpoint,many "utility tokens" can be classified as "security tokens," and a "security token" may functionally be built as an utility, payment, or other type of token Therefore, regulators should abandon the misleading classification of tokens as "utility tokens" and "security tokens". Instead, it would be more convenient to classify tokens according to three different criteria: functionality, legal nature and accounting and financial perspective. From a functional perspective, tokens could be classified as asset tokens, utility tokens, and payment tokens. From a legal perspective, tokens should be classified as security or non-security tokens. Finally, from a financial and accounting perspective, tokens can be classified as equity or debt instruments.

This chapter also canvasses existing regulatory strategies dealing with ICOs, and shows that none are perfect, and that each has its own drawbacks. For this reason, we have proposed a new system to deal with ICOs based on four primary pillars. First, we suggest that any issuance of tokens, regardless of whether they are security or non-security tokens, should be disclosed to the regulator through an electronic form providing a minimum level of information. Second, the purchase of token presales should be prohibited for commercial banks and pension funds. Third, regulators should protect non-security tokens through a variety of tools currently existing to protect consumers. Fourth, regulators should spend more resources in providing information to consumers and investors about the risks associated with ICOs.

After proposing a safe regulatory environment for ICOs, the chapter has also analyzed a variety of their legal and financial aspects, including how to register an issuance of tokens from an accounting perspective, why the classification of tokens as debt or equity can be relevant, how a situation of insolvency may affect the buyers or sellers of tokens, and the particular challenges of ICOs from the perspective of data protection, privacy law, and anti-money laundering. The chapter concludes by analyzing the implications of the tokenization of securities for the future of capital markets. By providing a comprehensive and interdisciplinary analysis of ICOs, this chapter seeks to help regulators and policymakers exercise their regulatory oversight over ICOs in a way that can promote innovation and firms' access to finance without harming key policy objectives such as consumer and investor protection, market integrity, and the stability of the financial system.

7

What Should Be Disclosed in an Initial Coin Offering?

Chris Brummer, Trevor I. Kiviat, and Jai Massari[*]

I. Introduction

Any time spates of fraud and abuse disproportionately involve any particular kind of financial product, advocates for the investing public naturally assume that more regulation is required—especially when it comes to disclosure—in order to restore market integrity. Whether following the stock market crash of 1929 or the 2008 financial crisis, reform-minded critics have, with good reason, demanded in the wake of widespread market shenanigans more abundant, publicly available information to help enable investors to make better-informed capital allocation decisions and reduce their vulnerability to wrongdoers.

Policymakers and regulators have again turned to this solution as they consider Initial Coin Offerings (ICOs or "token sales"). Since their inception in 2013,[1] ICOs have functioned largely as unregulated forms of fundraising that have driven a spectacular spike in funding, with an estimated $5.6 billion (USD) raised worldwide across 435 ICOs in 2017 alone, rivaling traditional venture capital funding.[2] Yet they have also been associated with fraud,[3] failing firms,[4] and alarming lapses in information sharing with investors. These problems are made more complicated by the fact that ICO tokens are associated with a broader class of novel digital assets[5] that operate on "blockchain" infrastructures with varying levels of centralization.[6]

Against this backdrop, the international regulatory community is exploring reforms that involve more explicitly treating ICOs as securities.[7] In the United States in particular, this has meant attempting to bring ICOs within the regulatory perimeter of the Securities Act of 1933 (the "Securities Act") and forcing ICO promoters to undertake the same extensive disclosures that other issuers

* Order is alphabetical. Dr. Brummer is a Professor of Law, Georgetown University Law Center; Mr. Kiviat is an Associate at Davis Polk & Wardwell LLP; Ms. Massari is a Partner in the financial regulatory practice of Davis Polk & Wardwell LLP. We are immensely grateful for our research assistants on the project, Brendan Costello and Amy Larsen.

do when offering securities to the public.[8] Namely, when undertaking a public ICO, an issuer would have to provide key information to prospective purchasers of the tokens as required by SEC regulations, such as the disclosure specified on the SEC's Form S-1, which mandates disclosure required for general public offerings. Or, if a more limited ICO is contemplated, issuers would have to comply with the formalities for crowdfunding or private placement offerings available under SEC regulatory regimes specific to those types of transactions.

For all the value of such discussions, shockingly little study has been devoted to just how well existing disclosure obligations meet the aims of regulators and the needs of ICO token investors (or even ICO sponsors), especially in the United States. Instead, policy conversations largely assume that the robustness of the more developed and proven regulatory scheme provided under U.S. securities laws will translate seamlessly to cryptoassets. Along this line of thought, the expansiveness of the Securities Act—and its explicit application to nontraditional securities, otherwise known as "investment contracts"—should be adequate to tame digital asset markets and in the process bolster informed investor decision-making.

In this chapter, we will unsettle the all-too-common assumption that Securities Act registration and disclosure requirements, as they currently exist, offer adequate remedies for the increasingly obvious shortcomings of ICOs. This chapter instead offers a more tempered conclusion and argues that, as currently constituted, the Securities Act and its accompanying regulations offer, at best, only a partial remedy to the disclosure challenges that ICOs pose. Even if subject to the full panoply of disclosures operative in public offerings, ICO promoters would not necessarily disclose all factors material to evaluating and pricing their tokens. Furthermore, even where disclosures are made, they may not be done in ways that investors can easily understand, and technical disclosures would not be subject to the kind of financial statement audits common in more traditional securities offerings.

To demonstrate, we evaluate the economics of ICOs and argue that many ICO tokens differ from traditional common equity and debt securities in ways that should inform their valuation, especially where they primarily or exclusively afford non-financial or "utility" rights to investors.[9] We show that even assuming total informational efficiency in ICO token markets, the determinants of utility token prices will not be identical to those that inform the prices of traditional securities such as stocks and bonds.[10] Equally important, the New Deal disclosure regime developed over the last 70 years has failed to fully anticipate the technological features that support the growth of ICOs. As a result, disclosures required under U.S. securities laws—from private placements to full-fledged registered offerings—fail to provide investors with the information a typical investor would need to make a reasonably informed investment decision. Instead, they often require information that, though critical for IPOs (Initial Public Offerings), has limited usefulness for ICO token purchasers.

Ultimately, these observations hold important lessons for policymakers. Subsuming ICO fundraises into existing regulatory frameworks may prove helpful as a starting point for proper regulation and market stability, and can provide an important source of discipline for market participants subject to federal antifraud provisions. However, this starting point requires an additional longer-term process of rethinking key applications of both domestic securities concepts and financial economics to the sector. Getting rules right may not require starting from scratch, but it will require more than just extending an existing regulatory regime to a new asset class.

Our chapter proceeds as follows. To set the stage for our analysis, Section II starts with a stylized account of a typical ICO, the type of disclosures commonly provided, and the questions that are often left unanswered. Section III then offers a new theory of ICO pricing, taking account of discrepancies arising where value and profits are no longer tied to claims on an issuer's future profits or revenue. After establishing a theoretical model for pricing, Section IV, the heart of the chapter, reviews existing approaches to disclosure and identifies vulnerabilities and shortcomings in documents relied upon in public and private offerings alike. Section V problematizes "don't mend, just extend" approaches to ICO oversight by highlighting the dearth of key institutional features in virtually all global disclosure regimes, including the absence of standardized auditing mechanisms and procedures for the smart contract code that would be disclosed in public offering documents. In short, we show that even if rules were amended in ways to better reflect the economics of ICO investments, many of the most important but highly technical disclosures would still not necessarily be understood, and securities laws neither require nor provide a framework for auditing them before their release to the public. Finally, Section VI offers policy and legal recommendations for which aspects of the traditional securities disclosure regime are most appropriate in the context of ICO disclosure, as well as how these elements of the regime should be adapted to account for the unique and novel features of the initial coin offering.

II. ICOs: The Shot-in-the-Dark Investment Decision

For context, we begin with a stylized example. Imagine Lambo Laurie, a promising MBA student at Georgetown, receives a call from a friend with an exciting new investment opportunity. "Lambo," her friend declares, "I know you're really into commercial real estate, but I've got an even more exciting investment idea—a blockchain project! You should go online and check it out—there's a guy building a new platform that will disrupt the entire widget industry, and in exchange for some Bitcoin, he'll give you a new digital token that will allow you to use the platform in the future. Even if you don't need it, it's sure to rise in value when the platform revolutionizes the widget market."

Lambo has never invested in ICO tokens, but the mention of a new blockchain project immediately brings to mind the skyrocketing value of cryptocurrencies in 2017.[11] She searches online for more information and navigates to the offering's website. There, a slick landing page highlights several of the token network's features and a large clock displays the time remaining until the ICO goes live. Lambo downloads the only informational document, linked to by a large button labeled "white paper."[12]

The white paper is 30 pages long and the cover page bears the words of the project in small type: "Widget Network." The paper lists a single author, Bo Jackson, whose affiliation is given only as a representative of the Widget Network. A short abstract describes Widget Network as a revolutionary new ecosystem for the community to buy, sell, and exchange digital widgets.

The white paper confidently states that this network will be widely adopted, and implies that such adoption could lead the tokens to appreciate tremendously in value. Lambo is captivated. Early-stage investments in technology that disintermediate the traditional way of doing things seemed like a world open only to elite venture capitalists. It seems like a rare opportunity to get in on the ground floor of something that might end up being the next Uber or Airbnb.

Lambo Laurie reads on and learns that the network is not yet fully developed. In part to finance such development, the Widget Network's promoters plan to raise capital by creating and issuing Widget Network Tokens (WNTs), which they will sell in exchange for Bitcoin and Ether. These tokens will ultimately serve a key economic function on the platform once it is complete. This blockchain will be similar in many respects to that supporting Bitcoin. But, the developers of Widget Network have plans to surpass Bitcoin, which has several perceived shortcomings. For example, some have questioned whether the Bitcoin network can scale effectively.[13] Similarly, Bitcoin has perceived limitations regarding transaction privacy and confidentiality.[14] By contrast, the infrastructure for transferring and using WNT is promised to be faster, more scalable, and more anonymous. And, unlike Bitcoin, WNT is envisioned to be used for more than transacting value—they also allow for "two-way encrypted communication among WNT holders."

Lambo Laurie finds such declarations enticing but the project is still hard for her to conceptualize. The white paper provides a technical description of how the network will function, citing to a website called GitHub, where the developers have made available for inspection all of the Widget Network's code. Lambo navigates to the Widget Network's GitHub page and is somewhat confused by the various files, folders and terms of art (e.g., "commits," "forks," "clones") that it contains. After some digging, Lambo gleans enough to appreciate that this website is where the Widget Network's developers gather to collaborate on the code that underpins the project. Lambo is neither an engineer nor an expert in applied cryptography, so she looks to the narrative to find more clues about how the technology is expected to operate and how exactly the promoters plan to execute their vision.

Reading further into the white paper, Lambo Laurie is left with more questions than answers. Will the token give her any rights or a portion of the project's earnings? The white paper lists the dates of the ICO and the sale price. But it is not clear if there is a cap on fundraising. Will the project raise as much money as people will give to it? How will the money be used? She wonders if her investment will go toward hiring new developers for the project, or if it will be spent on marketing or go directly to the promoters. Even if her capital is used for developing the network, will the promoters be issued tokens that they can then resell for a profit? What about the "advisors" that the white paper touts— will they be compensated, either in tokens or in a more traditional currency?

Further, it is unclear exactly who is running the project. Lambo Laurie is worried about giving her money to a faceless website. She had hoped to be able to put her trust in someone who can make the Widget Network a reality. The person who wrote the white paper does not have a formal title, and the white paper does not otherwise list or provide biographies of the team. She is dubious about the claims the white paper makes about trustless operations. The idea that the Widget Network team is constrained by unchangeable code that all can see sounds good, but is it true?[15]

And the "Widget Network" branding gives one the sense that there is a company involved, but the white paper and website contain no information about how it is organized or managed. Perhaps the white paper authors are partners in a joint venture? Or maybe there is a corporate entity established in the United States or elsewhere to run the project?

Finally, and most importantly, Lambo worries that she might be sending her money into a black hole; she might never realize a return or a functional product from her investment. The white paper asserts with certainty that the project will be a success. But, surely there are ways that the project could go wrong. Lambo has heard about hacks of other ventures in the blockchain space[16] and wonders what the Widget Network is doing to keep its tokens safe. Likewise, she saw a news article recently about an SEC cryptocurrency investigation[17] and actually visited Princeton when Chairman Clayton spoke about ICOs.[18] What is Widget Network doing to make sure it complies with the law? And what if the law changes quickly or unpredictably?

In the end, Lambo Laurie shakes off her doubts and questions about the ICO and decides to take the risk. Crypto-twitter is abuzz about the token offering, and Lambo assumes everyone can't be wrong about such a popular and potentially revolutionary technology. Following the instructions set out on the offering's website, she sends bitcoin from her digital wallet to the receiving address given by the Widget Network's promoters. Lambo Laurie crosses her fingers and hopes for the best. With any luck, she will be transferred a WNT at the end of the sale and the price will appreciate tremendously, or at least she imagines she will be able to sell her WNT to a Widget Network user when it is up and running.

III. Crypto-Economics and Token Pricing

How Lambo Laurie's story ultimately ends is anyone's guess. WNT could appreciate tremendously, replace the U.S. dollar, and allow early investors like Lambo to live their best lives. Or, as in the case of the vast majority of ICOs, the project could fail. Perhaps the technology underpinning the network could prove flawed. Or perhaps the engineers behind the network turn out to not be well trained enough or have adequate technical competency. Or the company could pivot into a completely different direction for which the token is rendered less central, or used for an entirely different and less profitable purpose.

From the standpoint of securities regulation, neither scenario is inherently problematic. Ventures succeed and fail in a capitalist system. And it is not the job of regulators to play favorites, or to ensure that any one investment succeeds. However, what is problematic is the lack of quality information available to Lambo when making her investment decision. Without information, it is difficult, if not impossible, for retail investors like Lambo to hazard an educated guess about both whether to purchase a token and at what price it would be best to do so. Instead of decisions being made based on economic fundamentals, investments in ICOs can be and, according to numerous academic studies, are, in fact, driven by factors such as popularity and social media marketing.[19] This in turn makes the allocation of capital in a society less efficient and raises the specter of investors becoming vulnerable to scams robbing them of as much as their life savings.

But what information would an investor need to know in order to make an informed decision about ICO tokens? Conversations currently imply that it is, at most, the same information as currently demanded by issuers of securities. After all, the energy behind at times heated debates on the status of an ICO token as either a "security" or "commodity" concern whether tokens should be registered and by extension be subject to the same disclosure as stocks and bonds. Under this concept of disclosure, the promoters of WNT would have to share its disclosures with the Securities and Exchange Commission before posting them online, and these disclosures would have to meet the stringent public offering informational requirements of the 1933 Securities Act unless Lambo is deemed to be an accredited investor, in which case less extensive disclosure requirements would be triggered.

Yet notably, the inputs for most ICO token valuations diverge considerably from those informing typical securities. Traditional capital markets require business owners to divest themselves of various rights over their corporation's assets in order to access capital. Issuances of common stock, for example, involve divestitures of ownership. Bond issuances involve interest payments, the creation of credit, and priority rights over assets in the case of default. ICOs, by contrast, routinely offer other kinds of benefits in exchange for capital that allow founders to preserve *both* economic ownership and control. As seen in our example, an ICO typically involves founders offering investors the opportunity to access or acquire assets that in turn operate as access devices to developmental digital infrastructures. Perhaps the token allows access to a distributed cloud storage system, or perhaps it allows consumers to manage their digital identity and monetize their personal data. But again, ownership and control, and even rights over profit streams for debt servicing, need not be sacrificed as a feature of the offering.

Pricing an ICO token offering largely "utility" or "non-financial" rights is consequently an exercise that is fundamentally distinguishable from that undertaken in traditional public securities issuances financings. To be sure, ICO tokens do not escape basic laws of finance. Their price, like that of any financial product (and indeed any object of value) reflects the equilibration of supply and demand. Modeling such equilibria must take into account, however, very different deal dynamics. For equity-based assets such as stocks, prices reflect the discounted value of legal rights to future cash flows. Discounted cash flow (DCF) analysis is not as informative in valuing many ICOs, however, since they do not ordinarily represent rights to future cash flows, and even where they do, future cash flows are not dominant features. Instead, it is the predicted utility value of the token as it is to be used in the future underlying project that drives prices under optimal conditions, together with the features of the ICO token enabling access to that utility value. This future utility value should then be discounted to the present to derive a rational market price at any point, though as in any market, the valuation can fluctuate based on changing prospects of realizing a project and changing circumstances impacting the utility value and future market pricing of that utility.[20]

With these basic points in mind, this section provides an overview of the inputs impacting the token economy. As we will see in subsequent sections, the value of existing disclosure regimes and proposed reforms, should focus on these factors in order to provide a useful basis for investor education and protection.

A. Demand-Side Factors

Market participants may seek to acquire ICO tokens for many purposes: short-term speculation, longer-term investment, or use of the token as part of a network, system, or other technology project that is being developed. Regardless of the purpose of a particular market participant in acquiring the token, the value of any ICO token should—speculative frenzies aside—ultimately reflect the perceived viability and usefulness of the underlying technology solution and the particular rights to access or use that solution represented by the token. Where, for example, a company such as Filecoin offers in its ICO a token promising prospective holders access to a future platform for decentralized data storage, the value of that token should derive its price from the expected utility of such a platform in the sector, the likely number of users of the project's technology, the frequency of that use, and the price one may be able to charge for such a service.

This observation bears some resemblance to pricing dynamics of publicly traded securities. After all, the sale of a company's stock reflects, ultimately, the current and future value of the company, including the demand for its products and utility and value of its services. The more successful and the higher the firm's future revenue, the greater the price of its stock should be. Similarly, the better the fortunes of a company, the less risk of default it will pose, and the price of its outstanding debt should rise to reflect a reduced risk premium.

There are key differences, however, distinguishing ICOs and IPOs (and other public security issuances). First, unlike most issuers that engage in IPOs and other public security issuances after reaching a certain level or stage of development, ICOs routinely involve projects that are themselves not yet operational, and therefore the value of the ICO token will be more speculative. In this respect, ICOs are more similar to early-stage fundraises rather than IPOs or other public securities issuances. The perceived novelty, commercial applicability, and quality of the particular technology solution underlying the token, as well as its technical feasibility, will all be major drivers of success.

Moreover, the product on offer—tokens—may not offer direct profit participation (as traditional equity securities do) or coupon payments and eventual redemption at par value (as traditional debt securities do). Instead, token purchasers receive the means to access a future project once it is completed, more closely anchoring the value of the token in the utility of the project itself. Investment returns for a token will thus rest squarely on the ultimate commercial utility of the technology under development—and the ability of developers to realize optimal results.

For these reasons, the value proposition of a particular ICO token is likely to be more dependent on the ability of a small number of individuals—whether technology developers, managers, or others—to execute the proposed technology solution. Thus, more like a traditional start-up company, the quality of the endeavor's engineers and other technologies may have outsized importance to the venture's success.

The features of a given token, which can vary significantly, will be directly relevant to the market demand for it. How, and under what circumstances, a token provides access to a project's technology solution will shape its utility and, consequently, demand for the token. The logic of tokenization will also be important. The ability to create a token does not mean that a token is necessary in order for a project to be successful; where tokenization facilitates or enhances the value of an underlying project, the market demand for a token (and the project) should rise. Finally, the more rights a token confers to its holder—whether rights to dividends, equity, or governance rights such as the ability to vote on key protocol changes and platform developments—the higher its value should be.

Laws matter, too. As with cross-listings of stock,[21] ICOs subject to a high quality regulatory and property rights environment can enjoy premiums reflecting reduced investor risk. Where, for example, the legal obligations concerning the issuance and transferability of a token are clear, predictable, and trusted, the risk premium attached to buying, using, and trading a token will diminish, which can render it a more attractive investment. Along similar lines, where a founder's intellectual property rights in a project's technology solution are enforceable and protected, the value proposition of the project should increase, and with it the demand for its associated token.

B. Supply-Side Factors

The supply of any token is also important in the operation of a token economy, as well as for the more fundamental issue of token valuation. Supply is driven by a number of important factors, not all of which neatly map onto traditional financing processes. In the case of a stock transaction, a company's board of directors decides to issue new shares, and in the process makes decisions relating to the overall governance and control of the stock.

For tokens, however, supply-side issues are most directly impacted by token founders' initial minting decision, in which a founder determines how many tokens to create, divisibility of the tokens, and whether the founder retains the right to issue more tokens, or conversely, redeem or destroy tokens in the future. This decision may in turn depend on a variety of other considerations, including the expected number of users of the facility or project under development, as well as the amount the founder hopes to raise in the ICO. A large number of users would, all else equal, suggest the minting of large quantities of tokens. So would large fundraising needs, unless the target audience is expected to be able (and willing) to pay large per-token amounts, which presumably would only be possible or desirable if the underlying service is (or is expected to be) expensive enough to warrant it. A large token price would, in short, be expected for accessing expensive or highly valuable technology services.

The retention, or lockups, of tokens by founders will also impact token supply. By agreeing to retain tokens for a specific period, not only can founders signal an aligned interest in maximizing the value and success of the project, but they can also help depress the total number of tokens in circulation, thereby supporting an ICO's price. Similarly, founders can deploy a smart contract that "locks up a portion of minted tokens, taking them out of circulation until some condition is satisfied." Founders could arrange then that once a condition is satisfied, or a benchmark met—potentially enabling or meeting higher buy-side interest—more tokens could be created. Or they could arrange for new systems or applications to be built on top of a platform such that the growing use cases mitigate the increased availability of the cryptocurrency.

Alternatively, founders can introduce caps on future minting, via an ICO token's code, that restrict the total amount of the token that will ever be available. One-time issuances would then be just that, and accordingly purport to remove the possibility of future token creation and inflated supply. However, if decision-making regarding, and access to, the code undergirding the token's economic properties is in the hands of the token's issuers or promoters, any promises regarding current or total circulating supply would not necessarily be written into stone.

Finally, tokens already released can be taken out of circulation, helping to preserve their value much like stock buy-backs undertaken by public companies. The most common method is through "burning" operations where tokens exchanged for services or access to a completed project are not recycled or used by the recipient for future purchases or activities. As such, burning can have a deflationary effect on the price of a token and help sustain its price by ensuring its rarity. It can also, notably, help serve as a buffer against the inflationary impact of future minting.

IV. White Papers as Disclosure Documents

In order for prospective investors to make informed decisions about purchasing tokens, such investors must be apprised of factors that will impact such tokens' supply and demand. To the extent that an investor is not knowledgeable about one or more of these factors, she will be unable to make informed decisions about the wisdom or hazards of participating in a token offering, much less about the price at which participating is advantageous.

As seen in our opening hypothetical, in most instances, ICO disclosures, to the extent they exist at all, are typically communicated through documents generically referred to as "white papers." The term alludes to the first cryptocurrency white paper, written by Satoshi Nakamoto in 2008, which first set forth the core technical features of Bitcoin.[22] Since Nakamoto's publication, it has become routine for details regarding cryptocurrency projects to be communicated through white papers, often not only for explanatory purposes but, particularly in the case of ICO tokens, also for marketing and soliciting interest from potential investors.

A white paper's primary function is to describe the technology problem a particular project is attempting to solve and to articulate a proposed solution along with the features of the accompanying blockchain-backed token used in connection with the solution. Along these lines, technologists and investors active in crypto-fundraises commonly suggest that in their white papers, founders provide an overview of the use applications of the project, the team involved in developing it, and why the project benefits by being placed on a blockchain in the first instance.

However, white papers have been largely and, often incorrectly, understood as unregulated communications that are not subject to any specific rules or governing framework. Consequently, white papers vary enormously, with some white paper disclosures being more extensive than others and with many providing little useful information. At least one academic study has noted that regardless of countless suggestions and developing norms espousing rigorous ICO disclosures, in roughly 32% of token fundraises, it is not possible to identify the issuing entity's or promoter's origin.[23] Our hypothetical with Lambo Laurie was thus already more robust than nearly one-third of the cases. Not only are there few details identifying the individuals behind projects and their contact information, but there may be a complete absence of information pertaining to where the development of a token application is taking place. Complicating things further, only 31% of the ICOs even mention the relevant laws and jurisdictions governing the ICO, leaving potential stakeholders and investors with little indication as to, among other things, where fundraising is occurring or where applications may ultimately be launched and operationalized.[24]

Full disclosure of a project's economic inputs is rare as well. Although white papers typically outline a technology problem and solution, management team and smart-contract vesting features of tokens, along with a timeline for an offering and potential uses of proceeds, this is by no means always the case. Some ICO white papers do not disclose the ownership levels of founders or post-ICO vesting restrictions. Although white papers may boast about the novelty of the technology under employ, they may fail to explain why it is that the application or service under development should be put on a blockchain.

All the while, the information that is made available in white papers is not always accessible to lay readers, making it hard for nonexperts to understand the feasibility and attractiveness of the project. ICO white papers were originally intended to be consumed by other technologically sophisticated software engineers and developers. As such, they showcased highly technical overviews of projects, frequently relying on highly complex statistical models or experimental code to both introduce and explain their projects. According to some commentators, the more obtuse and undecipherable the jargon, the more street cred some projects attracted.[25] This tendency continues to characterize most white papers, even as retail investors have increasingly entered the sector. Not only are challenging concepts explained via complex formulae, but companies also use white papers to establish themselves as experts in a domain, in the hopes that just as they make their pitches for new ICO tokens, competitors may reference their "research."[26]

Finally, there are growing questions as to the utility of the information provided in white papers, even for sophisticated investors. Fraud, falsified identities, and bogus projects are common, as is highlighted by a tide of enforcement cases shaking confidence in the industry.[27] But other less-publicized problems also hamper the utility of information. In a recent study, researchers examined a broad swath of ICO white papers and discovered that where projects made representations about their technology, the source code disclosed was done in the form of byte code.[28] Byte code is, however, notoriously difficult to dissect and involves tracing both the low-level flows of data and arithmetic in order to reconstruct a contract's logic. As such, it requires meticulous attention to each individual machine operation and memory to retain the state of the virtual machine at each step, along with reverse engineering to verify whether the code could actually operationalize features boasted in a white paper. Time-consuming, complicated, and expensive, the disclosures are effectively unauditable.

Collectively, the absence of a robust and credible disclosure regime exacerbates risks already inherent in ICOs. As discussed previously, the vast majority of ICOs are for early stage start-ups, and few have preexisting products. In that sense, ICO investments resemble angel and series A equity investments.[29] In the absence of a comprehensive regulatory framework, white papers fall well short of providing the full array of disclosures most investors would need in order to make sound investment decisions. And once investors have committed their capital, they enjoy few of the protections commonly associated with equity holders such as voting rights, anti-dilution protections, formal auditing mechanisms, and an elected board of directors.

V. ICO Disclosure Models: The Logic, Forms and Limitations

Not surprisingly, given the consistently weak disclosures made by issuers in ICO fundraises, one of today's most popular policy refrains has been to more explicitly situate them within the governing framework for mandatory public offering disclosures. If ICOs are subject to the same rules attached to public offerings of stock and debt, the argument goes, more abundant information will be made available to investors, allowing investors to make more informed investment decisions.

Public offering disclosures are all the more fitting, proponents note, since most ICOs are securities, at least under U.S. law. Though rarely identifiable as common equity, or even bonds, ICO tokens routinely fit the definition of an "investment contract" under the Supreme Court's *Howey* test: they are transactions where an individual "invests his money in a common enterprise and is led to expect profits [primarily] from the efforts of the promoter or a third party."[30] Meeting the definition of investment contracts, ICOs should thus be registered and, by extension, are subject to the mandated securities disclosure regime outlined in the 1933 Securities Act, unless ICOs are privately placed with accredited investors or those capable of "fending for themselves."

This *Howey*-backed argument is also grounded on a subtle, and often overlooked policy rationale touching the very rationale of investor protection. Notably, *Howey*'s criteria are not unitary; that is, it is not any one of its requirements that trigger the activation of U.S. securities laws; it is instead when those factors are combined in any one transaction or deal structure that such a level of investor vulnerability is reached that the protections afforded by U.S. securities laws are needed: where individuals invest their money, they put it at risk and can potentially lose their savings. In addition, *Howey* requires a "common enterprise," which courts have defined as situations in which individuals may be unable, or disincented, from coordinating with one another to access information or bargain collectively with a promoter because their gains may not justify the outlay of individual investigative efforts or taking on the costs of coordinating with large numbers of other investors. The stakes are then only heightened further where investors are additionally dependent on the promoter for their profits. *Howey* stands, at least in part, for the proposition that when such asymmetric information and power imbalances arise, U.S. securities law will step in to fill the void, and allow investors to better price and evaluate investment opportunities.

Against this backdrop, many regulators and practitioners have, of course, long recognized that in many, if not most ICOs, participants invest their money (in the form of Bitcoin, Ether, or fiat currency), and pool their resources in order to fund the development of a project (a common enterprise) from which they expect profits from their tokens, in the form of dividend-like payments or the appreciation of their token for later sale. Investors can thus find themselves in an extremely vulnerable position, especially given the technologically complex nature of many investments. By this logic, the transactions must be registered or privately placed, and appropriate Securities Act disclosures made.

In this section, we complicate the narrative by disentangling the logic of disclosure from how it is operationalized in practice. As we demonstrate, U.S. disclosure requirements do not always map neatly onto token economics and can still fail to meet the disclosure needs of investors of ICO tokens. Thus even where the *Howey* test may be fulfilled, investors may not be protected as courts and policymakers may assume. This is because disclosure forms do not always demand the kinds of information that would optimize the decision-making of ICO token investors. Furthermore, the essentially disclosure-optional regimes associated with private placements rely on assumptions of sophistication and agency that are unlikely to prove as robust for ICO token investors as they might for traditional securities transactions.

A. The "Full" Disclosure Model

The general disclosure document for securities offerings, Form S-1, has its origins in the New Deal. Following the October 1929 stock market crash, and with the U.S. economy still in the midst of the Great Depression, calls for a radical overhaul and implementation of a new regulatory regime had reached a crescendo.[31] Securities transactions in the decades preceding the creation of the federal securities laws were simple, albeit flawed. A company seeking to raise capital would issue and sell securities to the public, often assisted by an investment bank that would help identify an appropriate wholesale and retail market for the securities and potentially underwrite the offering. Brokers would then market shares to the public. And depending on the prestige or notoriety of the company, the firm's shares or bonds would be listed on an exchange or traded over the counter.[32]

This system changed in 1933 with the introduction of the Form A-1. The first general disclosure document, Form A-1,[33] required issuers to provide a narrative description of their business, details of corporate incorporation, management, properties, capital structure, terms of outstanding debt, the purpose of the new issue, and associated expenses.[34] It also demanded disclosure of topics not contained in listing applications, including management's compensation; transactions between the company and its directors, officers, underwriters and promoters; a list of principal shareholders and their holdings; and a description of any contracts not made in the ordinary course of business.[35] The regime's special contribution at the time—and a point of particular emphasis in subsequent agency administration—was the provision and accuracy of a firm's financial statements. In contrast to exchange listing requirements of the time that merely required earnings for the preceding five years, Form A-1 provides a list of more than 40 potentially required line items in the income statement.[36]

Today's disclosure regime has evolved considerably from its New Deal origins. In 1942, a new Form S-1 was introduced as the primary disclosure document for general issuances, and for the following 60 years, it would undergo periodic revision and elaboration in the face of varying scandals and political cycles.[37] The new S-1 also imposes a number of now canonical disclosures, capturing off-balance-sheet arrangements that in the 1990s toppled global companies such as WorldCom, as well as requiring more informational efficiency, business-related disclosures.

For the most part, these disclosures have helped the U.S. regulatory system to earn the reputation of being one of the highest quality in the world.[38] Still, as a product of the New Deal and keyed as responses to specific past crises, the S-1 is built on a number of assumption about securities issuances that are not always applicable to emerging ICO tokens. As discussed in Section III, ICO tokens differ considerably from traditional stock and bonds and the kinds of disclosures that are most relevant when deciding whether or not to purchase these more traditional securities. The S-1, keyed to the kinds of risks and logic of traditional securities offerings, offers some help, but it is not clear in many instances how the expectations should be applied. Below we examine some of the most material elements identified earlier and how the Form S-1 approaches them.

1. Financial Statements

The bedrock of the full disclosure model laid out in Form S-1 is financial disclosure. Modeled to reflect the needs of investors considering investment in industrial firms seeking capital to grow established operations, the form goes to great lengths to require the disclosure of a comprehensive and sometimes overlapping set of S-K items that cover the issuer's financial condition at present, throughout recent history and in the future.

Toward this end, Item 11(a) requires a description of "the registrant's plan of operation for the remainder of the fiscal year," and further descriptions of the cash budget for the next six months.[39] It also requires substantial disclosure about anticipated material acquisitions, research and development (R&D) and financial information about each segment of the business.[40] Item 11(e) requires full financial statements to be prepared that meet the requirements of Reg S-X, with modifications for smaller reporting companies.[41] Items 11(f) and (g) require selected financial data (five years) and supplementary financial information (quarterly for the last two years).[42]

While comprehensive, these financial disclosures may be of limited utility to prospective investors in ICOs. Issuers may not have any historical financial information to share, obviating the very usefulness of a core disclosure requirement relied on by authorities to inform prospective investors. Some of the financial disclosure items are general enough that they might provide some value to ICOs, such as required forward-looking analysis. Item 11(h), for example, requires a discussion of the registrant's financial condition, including "such other information that the registrant believes to be necessary to an understanding of its financial condition."[43] This includes discussion of "material trends" and how they will impact the business.[44] This disclosure item in particular may be important to ICOs since promoters would be required to discuss the health of the company. Still, many ICOs are brand new projects, or projects with very short histories. As a result, there may be no "trends" to identify.

2. Description of Token

Whatever the investment, investors should understand what it is they are purchasing. For investors in ICOs, this means, at a minimum, grasping the rights afforded by a token and comprehending how the token is intended to operate.

Form S-1 aspires to afford an adequate description of rights to investors in securities, but it was not drafted with token investments in mind. There are no explicit references to ICOs in disclosure requirements, and the S-1's general disclosure requirements for traditional securities are an imperfect fit for the most pertinent features of an ICO token.

Arguably the most important disclosure requirement, Item 9, requires a description of the securities to be registered.[45] As a guide, it then lists a series of designated securities, and specifies disclosures concerning issues such as voting rights, dividend rights, and rights concerning liquidation and preemption, among other things.

Still, this disclosure requirement is operationalized to effectuate traditional securities disclosures: critically, the requirements are organized by sections entitled "capital stock," "debt," and "warrants and rights." Meanwhile, for securities not explicitly contemplated, it requires "a brief description (comparable to that required [for capital stock, debt, warrants and rights]) of the rights evidenced thereby."[46] As such, Item 9 suggests a system of disclosure that operates in parallel to the structural features and logic of traditional securities offerings.

Token economics and operations differ from those of capital stock and debt, warrants and rights, however, raising important questions as to whether all salient token characteristics would be required to be disclosed, even in a registered offering. On the one hand, token issuers would certainly have to disclose characteristics that closely resemble those in traditional capital stock or debt. This would presumably include any equity stakes in the project, as well as dividend, fixed income, or other expected payments to token holders. On the other hand, tokens often tout non-financial use rights not present in traditional capital stock or debt. As we mentioned previously, tokens may grant access rights to future services instead of to claims on payments or profits. The extent to which Form S-1 specifies disclosure of the precise functioning of such "utility tokens," even where they are purchased as investments, appears limited.

Disclosure obligations under the Securities Act could also fail to necessitate that issuers provide information to investors about factors impacting the creation and supply of their tokens. One of the most relevant provisions, Item 15, requires disclosure of "all securities of the registrant sold by the registrant within the past three years which were not registered under the Securities Act."[47] As a backward-looking disclosure, this requirement would presumably cover presale offerings and therefore the extant supply of tokens at the time of the ICO. Item 1 requires stating the "amount of securities offered."[48] Thus along with Item 15, Item 1 would require disclosures of an ICO of presale tokens and those introduced by the ICO. Still, Item 1's mandate would only apply to the registered offering and would not address tokens issued in other ways, like those gifted to promoters or minted to fill the issuer's treasury.

Yet perhaps the most challenging disclosure problem concerns future token supply. Information concerning the minting of the tokens, future vesting of tokens, or any caps is particularly relevant to investors in an ICO because each can increase the potential for dilution (or depreciation of value). But no clear obligation requires the disclosure of such information: while Item 6 requires the disclosure of dilution-related costs that may be borne by investors in new issuances, it appears only to apply "when common equity securities are being registered."[49]

Collectively, these omissions indicate that even in a registered offering, key drivers of token supply are, at a minimum, not explicitly required to be disclosed. And in theory, one could infer from the specificity of many disclosure requirements that the absence of a requirement would mean that no disclosures would in fact be necessary for token issuers. This would be, however, as our previous work would suggest, a highly inefficient outcome, and one that would severely undermine the ability of investors to accurately price the tokens.

3. Blockchain Governance

A critical feature of any blockchain project is its system of on-chain governance—that is, how decisions are made concerning a token's blockchain that can alter the rights, structure, or value of the token. For an investor in token securities, this means understanding how decisions are made concerning everything from the modifiability of tokens to the upgrade and integration of blockchain software, and the ability to create new tokens that are incompatible with the issued token's software but share many of its features (e.g., forks).

S-1s do, for their part, require disclosure of an issuer's corporate governance.[50] Item 11 (via Reg S-K item 402) requires the disclosure of directors and key disclosures relating to the compensation of key management officials.[51] Item 11 (via Reg S-K item 407) similarly requires the identification of independent directors, as well as each director who is a member of the compensation, nominating, or audit committee who is not independent under such committee independence standards.[52] Issuers are further required to disclose the total number of meetings of the board of directors (including regularly scheduled and special meetings) that were held during the last full fiscal year.[53]

It is unclear, however, whether the S-1's mandate for corporate governance disclosure would cover governance issues relevant to the governance of a token's blockchain. Changes to a blockchain's protocol are rarely a matter of a simple vote by holders of a virtual currency or a board of directors of a firm. Instead, changes are often the result of the interaction of several actors: the developers of the blockchain's code, miners, and finally, holders of the cryptocurrency. In such circumstances, the blockchain memorializing token transactions has a core software repository that holds the code for the main implementation of its protocol.[54] For code changes to go into effect, the nodes on a blockchain network need to individually update their software to include the updated code.[55] And miners and developers must come to some kind of consensus about the appropriateness of the change.

Because corporate governance focuses on the interaction between management and directors—and more fundamentally, the separation of ownership and control—it is unclear that the interplay of actors in blockchain decision-making must be disclosed in S-1s. Notably, other items may necessitate bits and pieces of relevant on-chain governance disclosure, mitigating some of the gaps arising under Item 1(*l*). Item 9, for example, requires that "if the rights of holders of such stock may be modified otherwise than by a vote of a majority or more of the shares outstanding, voting as a class, so state and explain briefly."[56] This clause could be helpful insofar as it clearly anticipates the disclosure of the modification of holder rights in ways other "than by a vote of a majority or more of the shares outstanding." However, like many other S-1 provisions, these rights and voting disclosures are discussed in terms of capital stock, which likely does not cover tokens issued in an ICO. Whether similar rights would also need to be disclosed for non-equity tokens would instead depend on the interpretation of the catch-all requirement for other security types: "a brief description (comparable to that required [for capital stock].)"[57] Similar limitations arise with Item 11(l), which also requires a description of the process by which security holders can send communications to the board of directors.[58] But for such disclosures to touch on relevant blockchain governance systems for utility tokens, an analogous entity must be found—and core developers and miners would surely not qualify.

4. Management and Technology Team

The human capital involved in any start-up enterprise, and especially an ICO, is often essential. Ideas pitched in white papers (or prospectuses in registered offerings) must ultimately be acted on and realized in order for them to generate value for investors. It is thus critical that investors know who are the individuals connected to the most important aspects of transforming ideas into a real-world, workable technology solution.

The S-1 goes some way to making such disclosures. While on-chain governance may not be covered by Form S-1, governance and management of any existing corporate entity certainly is. As mentioned previously, Item 11(l) requires disclosure of corporate governance.[59] Therefore, this Item would cover governance mechanisms that exist as part of any legally formed entity. This could include the formation of a board of directors, the appointment and removal of officers, or other matters of traditional corporate governance that might be spelled out in a corporate charter or bylaws.[60] Moreover, an S-1 requires that an issuer's management team itself must be carefully detailed. Item 11(k) requires identification of directors and executive officers.[61] It also requires disclosure of the business experience of directors, executive officers, and significant employees.[62] Directors and officers must further disclose involvement in legal proceedings, including criminal proceedings, as do promoters.[63]

In traditional IPOs, such disclosures would invariably cover the most important decision-makers in the firm. However, questions arise as to how sufficient they are for ICOs. In contrast to IPOs, officers and directors might not be the most important, or even the most visible, members of an ICO team. Instead, the technologists who develop a token's nuts and bolts are instrumental to the project. Their names often appear as the author of a project's white paper, or are touted in the offering materials as experienced and esteemed advisors. In the language of *Howey* and its progeny, these non-director, non-officer technologists are often those people from whose efforts investors expect profits.[64] Item 11(k) includes one catch-all that might yet bring in some of these technologists. Even those who do not hold those formal titles are required to be identified if they are significant employees "who make or are expected to make significant contributions to the business of the registrant."[65] Yet even here, the disclosures would presumably relate to their "business experience." The S-1 would not, however, require disclosures of technologists' training in the technological area at issue, or their experience in coding or computer engineering more generally.

5. Secondary Trading

Price appreciation is often facilitated where there is a liquid market for any given financial product. Liquid markets reduce the risk of holding an instrument, and provide investors with the comfort that they will be able to exit their investments quickly. The most liquid markets, at least traditionally, have been exchanges—which gather potential buyers and sellers to enhance the speed and recurrence of capital market transactions. But not all exchanges are the same, and some are subject to very different kinds of rules and oversight by federal authorities.

Because traditional securities, particularly equity securities, are often sold on stock exchanges, disclosure about exchange listing and trading of the security is well contemplated by Form S-1. Item 8, for example, specifically requires issuers to disclose "[i]f the securities are to be offered on an exchange," and if so, to "indicate the exchange."[66]

What this obligation is in practice for an ICO is not entirely clear. In principle, securities are only permitted to be traded on specifically designated "national securities exchanges" that are in turn registered with the Securities and Exchange Commission. However, many ICO tokens trade on digital marketplaces that have not been registered as national securities exchanges, and instead constitute Alternative Trading Systems (ATSs)—broker-dealer driven platforms subject to some, though less intense, regulatory scrutiny and oversight. Yet other marketplaces described as "exchanges" operate under bespoke state licenses, such as New York's bitlicense, that permit limited financial activities beyond the scope of U.S. securities laws.

Along similar lines, the liquidity risks of crypto-infrastructures may escape disclosure obligations under Form S-1. To its credit, Form S-1 correctly recognizes that future developments, both due to and exogenous to an issuer's actions, can have profound effects on secondary market trading. Item 8 requires disclosure of passive market making and stabilization.[67] Item

11(h) requires identification of trends that may affect the liquidity of the registrant and "the course of action that the registrant has taken or proposes to take to remedy."[68] As such, this requirement could be interpreted to mandate disclosures akin to fat tail events in capital markets where demand for an instrument evaporates, leaving investors with no means of exiting their investment. Finally, Item 11(j) requires quantitative and qualitative disclosures about market risk.[69] To the extent exchange rate exposure is included as a market risk, parties must describe "how those exposures are managed . . . a discussion of the objectives, general strategies and instruments, if any, used to manage those exposures."[70]

Still, there are unique risks associated with infrastructure provision in the ICO markets. As described in some detail by the New York Attorney General's office in a recent report on virtual currency exchanges,[71] market-maker duties, pricing, and rebates are often ill-defined, and information regarding exchange policies on these topics is largely not publicly available. Similarly, the ability and efforts of virtual currency exchange to police manipulative trading, including trading that could affect the pricing of exchange-listed assets, vary significantly. In addition, these exchanges—unlike regulated securities exchanges—often do not have publicly available listing standards or other criteria to inform market participants about how and why certain tokens are made available for trading.

The SEC has taken recent action to require the registration of digital marketplaces as ATSs and national securities exchanges. However, even after being registered, many marketplaces will, given the unique features of cryptoassets, likely continue to operate differently from traditional securities exchanges and other securities trading venues. And divergent practices could have material effects on the pricing of ICO tokens listed and traded on these exchanges.

6. Risk Factors

ICOs, which normally involve companies with little or no operating history and a nascent or unproven technological innovation, may present significant risks to investors. A key goal of disclosure should therefore be informing investors about the possible risks they assume when investing in an ICO and the relative likelihood of occurrence of these risks. In this subsection, we address the extent to which the general "risks" disclosure forced by the S-1 addresses key ICO risks. Furthermore, an expansive disclosure in the risk section could remedy some of the holes highlighted in the previous subsections. However, on both counts we find that the S-1 disclosure regime would likely fall short.

Disclosure of risks under the "full disclosure" model is mandated by Item 3 of Form S-1, which requires discussion of "the most significant factors that make the offering speculative or risky," but cautions against "present[ing] risks that could apply to any issuer or any offering."[72] Such risk factors include, but are not limited to: (1) a lack of operating history, (2) a lack of profitable operations in recent periods, (3) the financial position of the issuer, (4) the business or proposed business, or (5) the lack of a market for common equity securities.[73]

The enumerated types of risks seem largely orthogonal to the kinds of risk disclosures relevant for an ICO, with the possible exception of Item 4. Items 1–3 appear somewhat redundant given that they will likely provide the same information as the financial statements required by the S-1: the ICO is likely a new venture with no operating history, past profits, or assets of any kind. Item 5 is inapplicable because tokens issued in an ICO do not typically represent common equity securities.

Still, the general mandate of "significant factors" seems on its face flexible enough to cover many relevant ICO risk disclosures. However, the application of this language may be a bit more limited than it would appear. Although there is "scant caselaw on Item 503," when analyzed, "courts have generally found Item 503 violations to track Rule 10b-5 violations."[74] This implies that "courts typically analyze the sufficiency of Item 503 disclosures with the familiar materiality standard."[75] Therefore, if a risk's omission would not be serious enough to generate a 10(b) claim then it can presumably be excluded from the prospectus. In one particularly on-point case, a court rejected a claim that offering documents were misleading because they "failed to disclose a 'systematic weakness' in the company's proprietary technology."[76] In ruling, the court noted that the offering materials "candidly acknowledge that the proprietary technology could fail if marketplace behavior diverged from prediction," and concluded that "no reasonable investor could disregard these warnings, despite the frequent and laudatory descriptions of the proprietary technology also included in the Offering Documents."[77]

Further, the explicit exclusion of risks that "could apply to any issuer or any offering" could be particularly troubling in the ICO context. There doesn't appear to be any case law that decides whether the "any offering" language should be construed to all types of offerings or more specifically to offerings of similar types of securities. But, if this language was read to prohibit disclosure of risks that could apply "to any ICO," this could remove disclosure of many salient blockchain-specific but common risks. The risk that blockchain technology could fail, or be hacked, are huge and consequential for any token offering. This is a much greater problem than in the context of equity securities, for example, where the risks are generally more tied to the specific business or product being offered.

B. Scaled Disclosure Regimes

Registration under the Securities Act can be burdensome. It usually requires hiring an investment bank to underwrite the securities, as well as lawyers and auditors to help prepare S-K disclosures and financial statements. Such costs not uncommonly can delay a company's access to capital markets, or block any possibility of raising public capital.

For these reasons, efforts have been introduced periodically to reduce the regulatory burden of disclosures for firms. The lynchpin for many of these efforts has been what can be described as a scaled disclosure regime based in part on the economic impact of the issuance—and the exposure of potential investors on an individualized basis. Because of their flexibility, they offer faster, more efficient means for raising capital, though they offer even fewer informational protections to investors.

1. Crowdfunding/Rule 4(a)(6)

The most basic scaled disclosure regime can be found in the SEC's crowdfunding provisions. Memorialized under Title III of the JOBS Act, the provisions exempt crowdfunded securities (e.g., small securities offerings conducted via online platforms) from a range of registration and disclosure requirements that would normally attach wherever stocks and bonds were sold by burgeoning companies online. The rules contain a number of important obligations, including a requirement that all transactions take place online through an SEC-registered intermediary, a limit as to the amount of money permissible to be raised ($1,070,000) in a 12-month period, and limitations on the amount individual investors can invest across all crowdfunding offerings. But for our immediate purposes, what is more relevant are the disclosure requirements, which, against the backdrop of these prudential limitations, are designed to facilitate a lighter-touch disclosure regime.

The key disclosure document for crowdfunding is Form C.[78] In Form C, the instructions outline a range of modified disclosures inspired in part by public offerings, including information about officers, directors, and owners of 20% or more of the issuer; a description of the issuer's business and the use of proceeds from the offering; the price to the public of the securities or the method for determining the price; the target offering amount and the deadline to reach the target offering amount; whether the issuer will accept investments in excess of the target offering amount; certain related-party transactions; and a discussion of the issuer's financial condition.

Under the SEC's crowdfunding provisions, issuers must also disclose a company's financial statements. Just what kind of disclosures depends on the circumstances.

- *Issuers offering $107,000 or less.* Financial statements of the issuer and certain information from the issuer's federal income tax returns, both certified by the principal executive officer. If, however, financial statements of the issuer are available that have either been reviewed or audited by a public accountant that is independent of the issuer, the issuer must provide those financial statements instead and will not need to include the information reported on the federal income tax returns or the certification of the principal executive officer.
- *Issuers offering more than $107,000 but not more than $535,000.* Financial statements reviewed by a public accountant that is independent of the issuer. If, however, financial statements of the issuer are available that have been audited by a public accountant that is independent of the issuer, the issuer must provide those financial statements instead and will not need to include the reviewed financial statements.
- *Issuers offering more than $535,000.* For first-time Regulation Crowdfunding issuers: Financial statements reviewed by a public accountant that is independent of the issuer, unless financial statements of the issuer are available that have been audited by an independent auditor. For issuers that have previously sold securities in reliance on Regulation Crowdfunding: Financial statements audited by a public accountant that is independent of the issuer.

Collectively, the requirements represent a dramatic departure from the kinds of disclosure represented in an S-1. They are much less invasive than those found in the S-1 and enable faster, less legally complex and less costly offerings of securities.

They do, however, present more risks for ICO token investors from an informational standpoint. Financial disclosures are, as previously mentioned, generally less important for start-ups than for established companies doing IPOs, given the former's limited histories. However, whatever financial information is available can be insightful. And while Form C also emphasizes financial disclosure like S-1s, it does so in a way that is substantially less comprehensive. Specifically, Form C requires only abbreviated (and, for smaller offerings, unaudited) financial statements for the two most recently completed periods.[79] Thus in the year prior to an offering, the year most likely in which financial information may be available, a lighter touch to quality control is taken as compared to an S-1.

Form C asks whether the issuer has an operating history[80] and requests a description of the issuer's financial condition.[81] It also demands a general description of the terms of the securities being offered[82] and whether the securities have voting rights.[83] Still, it is unclear whether this would force disclosure beyond the ownership and control rights of traditional securities to the features associated with ICO tokens. As we have described, the rights given to token holders are far different than those given to holders of traditional equity securities.[84] It is unclear whether the simple language commanding an issuer to "describe the terms of the securities being offered" would be enough to force disclosure beyond the simple dividend and voting rights that traditionally answer such questions, to complex and nuanced discussions of token functionality.

Similarly, disclosures about corporate governance, which themselves might not extend to important on-chain governance topics, are even more limited in Form C.[85] The relevant item in Form C asks generally the "risks to purchasers associated with corporate actions," and lists four examples: additional issuances, issuer repurchases, a sale of the issuer or its assets, and transactions with related parties.[86] This disclosure requirement is far more general and less expansive than the equivalent corporate governance section required by Form S-1. The latter, in Item 11(l) noted previously, specifically addresses issues of director independence, board meetings and committees, and shareholder communications,[87] and requires attachment of relevant governance documents such as the certificate of incorporation and bylaws.[88]

Like Form S-1, Form C targets officers and directors in disclosures about a firm's key leadership. The likelihood, however, that technologists would be covered is less than even that in an S-1. An additional demand that disclosures be made for "any persons occupying a similar status or performing a similar function" could arguably pull in technologists.[89] However, while technologists may play high-profile roles in white papers that serve a marketing function, their primary significance is as engineers and coders. Although this will ultimately be a fact-based inquiry, it is difficult to identify their work generically as "performing a similar function" to that of a CEO.

Finally, Form C does not require a discussion of exchange listings. As such, in contrast to the S-1, there is no legal basis for mandating a discussion of a token's ultimate liquidity and the market for the token.

Still, it must be noted that there are several areas where Form C, perhaps due to its more recent creation and the unique features of crowdfunding, arguably provides more suitable ICO disclosures than Form S-1, not less. For example, required disclosure about the terms of the offering is more representative of how an ICO operates. A typical ICO raises an amount of funding that is not perfectly determined ex ante, but rather that falls within certain pre-specified limits. ICOs may cease when the amount raised has hit a set "cap" on fundraising, or shortly thereafter, and the price may vary throughout the offering period. Form C contemplates such flexible offerings, and asks issuers to disclose a range of offering amounts by asking explicitly for both the target and the maximum offering amount, or cap; the "deadline to reach the target offering amount"; and the "method for determining price."[90] By contrast, Form S-1 speaks more narrowly of the "amount of securities offered" and the "offering price."[91] While some allowances are made in the S-1 to disclose offerings on a "minimum/maximum" basis, or a method for determining price (in the event stating a price is impracticable),[92] Form C appears to more explicitly contemplate, and more clearly require disclosure of, the flexible pricing, timeline, and issuance amounts that characterize a typical ICO.

2. Reg A+

Another increasingly important example of scaled disclosure is Regulation A+. A more attractive outlet for offerings as compared to the original Regulation A, Regulation A+, like crowdfunding, was implemented under the JOBS Act to help facilitate capital formation. It offers much more potent tools for fundraises by establishing two tiers of investment: Tier 1, which permits offerings of up to $20 million in a 12-month period; and Tier 2, which permits offerings of up to $50 million in a 12-month period. As in crowdfunded projects, limitations are placed on the amount a non-accredited investor can raise for Tier 2 offerings.

The basic disclosure document for Regulation A+ is Form 1-A, which is intended to be a scaled-down version of an S-1. As such, it includes requirements necessitating a number of disclosures similar to those in public offerings:

- Risk Factors
- Dilution
- Plan of Distribution and Selling Security Holders
- Use of Proceeds
- Description of Business
- MD&A (Mergers, Dispositions & Acquisitions)
- Compensation for Executives
- Security Ownership of Management and Other Security Holders
- Securities Being Offered

The Reg A+ disclosure regime is, as compared to that in crowdfunding, a more fulsome and rigorous application of mandatory disclosure and is routinely categorized as a "mini-IPO." It is, however, less expansive than an S-1. Because Form 1-A is largely a subset of Form S-1, it therefore falls short as an ICO disclosure tool in many of the same ways as Form S-1.

Like Form S-1 and Form C, Form 1-A emphasizes financial disclosures, which, for the reasons articulated previously, may not be particularly relevant in the ICO context. This disclosure, furthermore, is, like the Form C, less comprehensive than Form S-1, requiring only abbreviated and sometimes non-audited financial statements[93] along with a more general discussion of the registrant's financial condition.[94] Likewise, Form 1-A requires a discussion of the rights given by the offered security,[95] but these disclosure items are more tailored to the ownership and control rights of traditional securities than the features associated with ICO tokens. Again, disclosures about corporate governance might not extend to important on-chain governance topics, and Form 1-A's disclosures are even more limited.[96]

Like Form S-1, Form 1-A limits disclosure of relevant team member information primarily to officers and directors. Still, Form 1-A also includes a carveout for "significant employees," who are "expected to make significant contributions to the business," mirroring the language of the S-1.[97] Further, Form 1-A has similar holes in disclosure of secondary market trading that will occur in the ICO tokens. Finally, unlike Form C, Form 1-A does not add to the Form S-1 framework any disclosure items that may be especially relevant to ICOs, such as any targets or caps on the sale.

3. Private Offerings

As the far end of the scaled disclosure regime are private offerings. In contrast to public offerings, where securities are sold to retail investors, private offerings are available only to accredited or sophisticated investors. Typically, private placements are conducted via Regulation D's Rules 504 and 506 and then resold via qualified institutional buyers under Rule 144A.

Private placement issuers have much more flexibility with respect to disclosure than their public offering, Reg A+, and even crowdfunding counterparts. Non-accredited investors must be furnished with a Regulation A circular if the issuer is a nonreporting company; only the balance sheet need be audited. Reporting companies must provide a copy of their annual report, Exchange Act filings, and a brief description of the offering. Meanwhile, there are no disclosure requirements in Rule 504 and 506 offerings made exclusively to accredited investors. Although issuers will often circulate an offering memorandum that tracks disclosures required under the Securities Act, it is industry practice, not SEC regulation, that dictates the memorandum's contents.

With this end run around full disclosure available and increasingly relied upon in ICO token markets, it is worth reflecting on the fact that disclosures in private offerings presume investors are capable of fending for themselves. Either through their income or wealth, or by dint of their access to the same information available in an S-1 and sophistication, participants in private markets are deemed to operate on a level playing field with issuers and, as seen previously, securities laws do not necessitate registration or SEC disclosures. It is, however, not entirely clear that wealth or income, especially at the now modest thresholds at which one qualifies as an accredited investor, are sufficient to ensure either access to relevant information or the ability to bargain for it.[98]

Moreover, even where investors are generally sophisticated about business and financial matters, they may not be technically sophisticated enough to be able to make investment decisions in the novel, computer-driven, and complex context of the ICO.

VI. Beyond Disclosure: "Plain English" Requirements and Third-Party Validators

Our analysis highlights the fact that disclosure, for its own sake, is positive but needs tailoring—as U.S. securities laws have long acknowledged—to the facts and circumstances of a financial product. From this perspective, we see that the mere designation of many ICOs as securities does not immediately place them into a secure and transparent regulatory environment. S-1s, for their part, neglect key aspects of blockchain governance and token burning and would ultimately depend on risk factors or "regulatory risks" to highlight custodial and transfer risks. Even then, these disclosures concerning key parts of the infrastructure might be considered regulatory, and it is unclear to what degree risks relating to both cybersecurity and also operational risks relating to ICO token infrastructures would need to be disclosed.

Of course, disclosure is, in itself, no panacea, even assuming that "full" or "scaled" disclosure regimes are ultimately revised in ways that address their current deficiencies. For disclosures to be meaningful, as well as incorporated into ICO pricing and valuations, two conditions must be met: (1) disclosures must be read and understood by investors, and (2) third-party validators must be available to scrutinize disclosures to ensure their accuracy. The Securities Act does not always provide clear pathways for either, however, when applied to ICOs.

As to the first condition, we saw previously that disclosures made in ICO white papers are often hyperbolic and also highly technical.[99] Developers will, when providing disclosures, routinely delve into highly technical details concerning their projects, for instance citing to code, either directly in the white paper or on the relevant GitHub repository, while offering few clarifying details and statements about such disclosures.[100] Even those with technical backgrounds often struggle to make sense of such disclosures. Accordingly, retail investors with limited sophistication are also left with little actionable information.

Pulling ICOs into the existing securities law perimeter responds in part to the problem. On the one hand, the SEC has advanced "Plain English" disclosure rules designed to reduce the jargon and difficulty often associated with reading registration statements.[101] The most stringent requirements in Rule

421(d) articulate definitive prohibitions against "legal jargon" and "technical terms" in the summary, risk factors, and cover and back pages of a prospectus. Meanwhile, under Rule 421(b), the Commission has outlined a number of norms such as "short sentences whenever possible," "bullet points," and "descriptive headers" while advising that prospectus drafters avoid "legal and highly technical business terms," "legalistic, overly complex presentations," "vague boilerplate," "excerpts from legal documents," and "repetition." As such, the Plain English rules speak to the overly complex business narratives and communications that have traditionally made securities offerings indecipherable for everyday investors.

Whether the rules will make communications more understandable for technological start-ups is questionable, and in some instances they could exacerbate complexity, as opposed to improve clarity. Take, for example, the advisory note that prospectus drafters avoid "relying on glossaries and defined terms." Under normal circumstances, this kind of guidance would help investors avoid the need to sift through disclosures in ways that added to the time and burden of reading disclosures. But for the current state of ICOs, these steps could be extremely useful. Because many ICO terms have multiple or unclear meanings, whether it be "decentralization," "utility," and even "token," defining terms and using the term in the document could prove helpful and perhaps even vital.

At the same time, some of the most rigorous requirements for clarity and simplicity should be extended beyond just the summary and cover and back pages to include parts of the registration statement describing the token itself. Here token's financial and non-financial features, along with minting and burning, should be described in a clear manner, understandable to a lay audience. To supplement these disclosures, the code itself should be archived in a technical format, such as a GitHub repository, for outside scrutiny and evaluation.

This brings us to the second critical problem highlighted previously: the current absence of necessary third-party validators to assist in ensuring the quality of disclosures made by developers in an ICO. Unlike typical securities offerings, where a stable of long-established gatekeepers such as auditors and accountants are available to provide quality control for the most important traditional disclosures, financial statements, the ICO ecosystem enjoys comparatively few gatekeepers to monitor the most important disclosures made in ICO white papers—namely those concerning the underlying technology.[102] In short, there are no systems or entities in place to require the "review of code by experts to determine if the code is secure such as whether there are any existing vulnerabilities, possibilities for future bugs or any errors in coding that could expose users."

This is a problem with real consequences. Recent academic studies have highlighted the fact that retail investors do not read the code presented in white papers or the related GitHub repositories, which given the relative lack of technical sophistication among retail and accredited investors is not altogether surprising.[103] This is not just an academic issue. Source code flaws in certain digital assets or in the smart contracts that support them have been exposed and exploited, and in the process, have either exposed users' personal information, resulted in the theft of users' digital assets or both.[104] Additionally, such flaws in or exploitations of the source code have sometimes, albeit rarely, allowed a malicious actor to take or create money in contravention of known network rules. In other cases, such errors or defects have been publicly found and corrected prior to exploitation.

Accordingly, if smart contracts are used in a token sale, there should be some disclosure around who audited such contracts. Relatedly, ICO promoters should disclose the procedures in place to secure the token sale. For example, such promoters should disclose not only how users obtain tokens, but also what specific security procedures are in place to prevent common attack vectors such as (1) denial-of-service or distributed denial-of-service attacks,[105] (2) social engineering (e.g., phishing, spoofing) attacks,[106] (3) chat channel spamming, (4) fake social media accounts, or (5) man-in-the-middle attacks.[107] Further, ICO promoters, when relevant, should provide detailed disclosures regarding their procedures for securing and storing private keys.

These shortcomings would naturally suggest that bringing ICOs more expressly within the perimeter of U.S. securities laws, where key financial data are reviewed by auditors, could help address what is a considerable market failure. But here too, the mere designation of ICOs as securities would not, in itself, serve as a silver bullet to the absence of auditors for technology- and code-related disclosures. Notably, U.S. securities law anticipates relatively mature industrial companies as issuers and as such requires the involvement of auditors only in the context of the review of a company's financial statements. An ICO issuer's representations relating to the data infrastructure and code driving its technology, something entirely unanticipated as a key disclosure under the New Deal framework of the Securities Act, would not be subject to such a requirement. Thus, even if ICO tokens were designated as securities, the Securities Act would not impose rules requiring the auditing of disclosures relating to the blockchain code referenced in ICOs.

Additionally, even if rules were introduced subjecting code and technological disclosures to an audit by third parties, the firms undertaking validation would not necessarily be subject to any operational, professional, or business conduct standards. Third-party validators are mostly engineering and technology firms, not financial intermediaries. Thus they would only be subject to direct federal regulation if their activities were deemed to constitute investment advising (which would subject them to the 1940 Investment

Advisers Act). Yet even here, regulation as investment advisers would not involve the substantive certification or qualification of auditors. Instead, primary obligations of third-party validators would include disclosing their clients, business practices involving potential conflicts with clients, and "any disciplinary events of the adviser or its employee." Operational guidelines would remain essentially voluntary or left for industry norms to potentially develop.

VII. Conclusion

In this chapter, we have sought to systematically examine the needs of investors in ICOs, and then how extant regulatory disclosure requirements speak to them. In doing so, the chapter carefully problematizes what are all-too-often simple policy prescriptions offered in light of the increasingly high profile and prominent role played by ICO tokens in capital markets and the associated risks posed to investors.

Among this chapter's insights is the observation that merely designating ICO tokens as "securities" will not necessarily improve the disclosures made available to prospective investors such that they will be able to make informed investment decisions. The disclosure regime embodied in the Securities Act is one based on pricing assumptions that, though well-suited to the industrial age, do not map neatly onto the developing field of digital assets. As a result, reliance on Securities Act disclosure forms would prove not only potentially burdensome, but also inadequate for investor protection.

Furthermore, even if Securities Act disclosures were revised to demand more tailored information concerning those features of ICOs most relevant for pricing, macro-level reforms would also be needed to ensure the accessibility of those disclosures to retail investors. Moreover, a system of third-party validation for blockchain code would be needed, along with a supporting regulatory infrastructure for auditors, to ensure the quality of disclosures made in a revamped regulatory ecosystem.

Collectively, these observations suggest that achieving an optimal disclosure regime for ICO tokens necessitates more than one-shot policymaking and rule writing. Designating ICO tokens as "securities" may reflect sound applications of existing policy or Supreme Court case law, but it does not, on its own, constitute the extent of work required to integrate ICO tokens into an operational and efficient regulatory regime. Instead, such decisions comprise, at best, the initiation of a long-term process of regulatory upgrades that will be needed to fine-tune protections for the retail public and preserve the efficiency of capital formation in global financial markets.

Disclosure Item	Form S-1	Form 1-A[108]	Form C[109]
The Offering			
What is it?			
• What exactly are you participating in with this token or coin?	Item 4 [S-K 504] requires stating "the principal purpose for which the net proceeds to the registrant from the securities to be offered are intended to be used," but this might not be sufficient to explain what the purchaser of the token gets in return.	Item 4 asks the issuer to check a box for the type of security offered. This will allow the issuer to affirmatively or negatively state whether the token contains a common equity or debt interest, but beyond that the "other" box only includes a brief line for description. The "use" could be stated there but need not be.	The cover page has a line for "type of security offered," but does not specify the information that must be provided. Presumably, "non-equity token" might be sufficient.
• What right(s) does the token confer?	Item 9 [S-K 202] requires a description of the securities to be registered.	Circular Item 6 requires a statement of "the principal purposes for which the net proceeds to the issuer from the securities to be offered are intended to be used," but this might not be sufficient to explain what the purchaser of the token gets in return.	Q&A 9 asks bluntly "what is the purpose of this offering,"
• A portion of earnings or equity in a project?	For types of securities not explicitly contemplated, it requires "a brief description (comparable to that required [for capital stock, debt, warrants and rights]) of the rights evidenced thereby." This would certainly cover dividend and ownership rights, etc. Still, it is likely not sufficient to cover non-financial (use) rights of tokens.	Circular Item 14 requires an outline of the presence of any of a list of enumerated rights, including dividends, voting, and "any rights of holders that may be modified otherwise than a vote of a majority." Of course, this is likely insufficient to require disclosure of other token-specific rights that do not fall within these traditional financial categories.	Q&A 13 asks for a description of the terms of the securities being offered.
• A current or future utility?			Q&A 14 asks whether the securities have voting rights and Q&A 15 asks about limitations on voting rights.
• A donation to a nonprofit foundation?			
• Potential for dilution	Item 6 [S-K 506] directly addresses dilution, but appears only to apply "when common equity securities are being registered."	Part III Item 17 requires filing as an exhibit "all instruments defining the rights of any holder of the issuer's securities."	
• See below (Insider Dealings)		Circular Item 4 specifically addresses dilution, requiring a comparison of the public contribution and the average cash contribution of officers, directors, promoters, and affiliated persons if there is a material disparity.	

188

Terms and conditions
- What is the fundraising cap?
- What, if any, restrictions are there on the sale?

Item 1 [S-K 501] requires stating the "amount of securities offered," and the "offering price," which together could impute a fundraising cap. Still, this would not be sufficient to explain the functioning of how any coded cap operates.

Item 8 [S-K 508] requires a brief outline of "the plan of distribution of any securities to be registered that are offered otherwise than through the underwriters."

Item 4 requires disclosing the number of securities offered and the price.

Circular Item 19(j) permits the price and maximum number of securities to be listed within ranges.

Circular Item 5 requires a brief outline of "the plan of distribution of any securities being issued . . . otherwise than through underwriters."

Circular Item 5 requires description of any arrangements "for the return of funds to subscribers if all the securities to be offered are not sold," to "limit or restrict the sale of other securities of the same class" or to "stabilize the market."

The cover page requires listing the "target number of securities to be offered," the price "or the method for determining price," the "target offering amount," and whether and how oversubscriptions will be allocate. Notably, it also requests the "maximum offering amount" and the "deadline to reach the target offering amount," which seems better suited for how ICOs actually function than even the S-1 disclosure. Note that there is a bold statement in the form that the offering will be canceled if the target offering amount is not met.

Q&A 12 notes that investors may cancel an investment until 48 hours prior to the deadline identified in the offering materials.

(Continued)

189

Disclosure Item	Form S-1	Form 1-A	Form C
Marketing and Insider Dealing Disclosures			
Promotional activity • Describe the current and future promotional activity including marketing plans for the token sale, token giveaway information, beneficiaries of the giveaways, and more. • Disclosure of celebrity and "influencer" endorsements.	Item 9 [S-K 508] requires identification of "any finder and, if applicable, describe the nature of any material relationship between such finders and the registrant." Item 10 [S-K 509] requires disclosure of the interests of named experts, though this appears to limited to those who "prepared or certified any part [of the registration statement] or a certified a report or valuation for use in connection." Item 11(k) [S-K 401] requires registrants not previously subject to reporting requirements to disclose involvement of promotors in certain legal proceedings (e.g., criminal convictions). Item 11(n) [S-K 404] requires disclosure of "the names of the promoter(s), the nature and amount of anything of value . . . received or to be received . . ." Item 13 [S-K 511] requires a "reasonably itemized statement of all expenses in connection with the issuance," which could perhaps be stretched to cover token giveaways and payments for endorsements and white paper translations, etc. Item 15 [S-K 701] requires disclosure of expenses incurred in connection with the issuance and distribution, including "finders' fees," and indications whether these were to insiders "and their associates" or to those owning ten percent or more.	Item 4 requires disclosure of the fees in connection with the offering, including those by "promotors" and asks the name of the "service provider." Item 6 asks for disclosure of unregistered securities issued in the previous year, which could include giveaways and payments to endorsers.	Q&A 17 asks what other securities of the issuer are outstanding, which could provide insight into token giveaways. Q&A 25 asks about exempt offerings within the last three years, which could provide insight into token giveaways. Q&A 30 asks about convictions of promoters.

Token reserves
- Founder and employee tokens (e.g., reserved for incentive compensation)
- Company and ecosystem (or foundation) tokens (e.g., reserved for working capital and incentivizing new users)
- Advisory tokens (e.g., reserved for advisors)
- Disclosure of advisors

Item 10 [S-K 509] requires disclosure of the interests of named experts, though this appears to limited to those who "prepared or certified any part [of the registration statement] or a certified a report or valuation for use in connection."

Item 11(d) [S-K 201] requires disclosure of "securities authorized for issuance under equity compensation plans," but this appears only to apply "where common equity securities are being offered." Therefore, there may be a hole where token compensation plans need not be disclosed if the tokens are not considered "common equity."

Item 11(l) [S-K 402] requires disclosure of compensation of executive officers and directors. But, in-kind compensation by tokens might be difficult to value presale. Also, many involved (founders, employees, advisors) might not qualify as executive officers to trigger the reporting requirements.

Item 11(m) [S-K 403] requires disclosure of the portion of outstanding shares owned by the directors and executive officers.

Circular Item 6 requires disclosure of whether "the proceeds will be used to compensate or otherwise make payments to officers or directors."

Circular Item 11 requires disclosure of the compensation of each of the three highest-paid persons who were executive officers or directors. Still, it is unclear whether founder and employee tokens would fall within "compensation," as even "other compensation" must be denominated in dollars. A note to Item 11 states that compensation "paid otherwise than in cash . . . state in a note to the table the nature and amount thereof."

Circular Item 12 requires disclosure of any holder who beneficially owns more than 10% of the issuer's voting securities. Note that this might present a problem for tokens with no voting rights.

Circular Item 13 requires disclosure of any experts who prepared or certified the offering statement if they were employed on a contingent basis or have a material interest in the issuer.

Q&A 6 asks for the name of each person who is the beneficial owner of 20 percent or more of the issuer's "outstanding voting equity securities." To the extent the tokens issued are non-equity, this would seemingly exclude disclosure of majority holders of tokens.

(Continued)

Disclosure Item	Form S-1	Form 1-A	Form C
Presale discounts and caps • Disclosure of the exact amounts paid per token by every presale purchaser • Not necessarily entity-level disclosure • Price and quantity disclosure	Item 6 [S-K 506] requires disclosure where "there is substantial disparity between the public offering price and the effective cash cost to officers, directors, and promoters," but appears only to apply "when common equity securities are being registered." Item 15 [S-K 701] requires disclosure for "all securities of the registrant sold by the registrant within the past three years which were not registered under the Securities Act." This would presumably cover presale offerings performed pursuant to a registration exemption.	Item 6 asks for disclosure of unregistered securities issued in the previous year, along with the "aggregate consideration for which the securities were issued." Circular Item 12 requires disclosure of any holder who beneficially owns more than 10% of the issuer's voting securities. Note that this might present a problem for tokens with no voting rights.	Q&A 17 asks what other securities of the issuer are outstanding, which could provide insight into token giveaways. Q&A 25 asks about exempt offerings within the last three years.
Economics and Financial Disclosures			
Supply • Is supply fixed or limited? • Discuss future issuance plans or token burning schemes designed to influence the price of the currency. • Anticipated fully diluted supply curve • How many coins or tokens will be issued and how?	Item 1 [501 S-K] requires stating the "amount of securities offered." Still, this would only apply to the registered offering and would not address tokens issued in other ways. Item 7 [S-K 507] provides that "the amount and (if one percent or more) the percentage of the class to be owned by such security holder after completion of the offering," when securities "are to be offered for the account of security holders." Item 8 [S-K 508] requires disclosure of passive market making and stabilization.	Item 1 requires disclosure of outstanding securities. However, the only boxes provided are for common and preferred equity and debt, so outstanding tokens may not be included. Item 4 asks for a more general number of "securities of that class already outstanding." Item 6 asks for disclosure of unregistered securities issued in the previous year. Circular Item 5 requires a description of any arrangement to stabilize the market.	The cover page requires listing the "target number of securities to be offered," and the "maximum offering amount." Still, this only covers tokens generated in the sale and not supply management thereafter. Q&A 17 asks what other securities of the issuer are outstanding, which could provide insight into token giveaways.

- Who can change this? (see Governance later on in this table)
- Who controls large amounts of coins?

Item 11(m) [S-K 403] requires disclosure of any person "who is known to the registrant to be the beneficial owner of more than five percent of any class of the registrant's voting securities," as well as any arrangements known that could change control in the future. This may not apply to tokens without voting rights. Further, determining unique beneficial owners might be more difficult if they use multiple blockchain wallet addresses.

Q&A 18 and 19 discuss differences between securities, and 20 discusses how the rights of principal shareholders might affect new holders.

Exchange Liquidity

- Which exchanges will list the token after the ICO is complete, and when?

Item 1 [S-K 501] requires disclosing "whether any national securities exchange or the Nasdaq Stock Market" lists the securities offered. It is unclear whether cryptocurrency exchanges would be covered.

Item 8 [S-K 508] states that "if the securities are to be offered on an exchange, indicate the exchange." This is broader than "national securities exchange" in Item 1, but only applies to initial offerings on an exchange and not secondary trading.

Item 9 [S-K 202] notes that "the document should not . . . convey the impression that the registrant may apply successfully for listing of the securities on an exchange . . ."

193

(Continued)

Disclosure Item	Form S-1	Form 1-A	Form C

Token lock-up period and vesting schedules
• Disclose the token lockup period and vesting schedules for any investors, as well as the team and insiders described above.
• Plan for distributing locked-up tokens (e.g., time frames, amounts)
  • Examples: periodic release, one-time release, governed by smart contract, token vesting, milestone based.
• What mechanism assures that proceeds flow according to the distribution budget?
	Item 6 [S-K 506] directly addresses dilution, but appears only to apply "when common equity securities are being registered."
	  Item 4 [S-K 504] requires stating "the principal purpose for which the net proceeds to the registrant from the securities to be offered are intended to be used and the approximate amount intended to be used for each such purpose," but does not necessarily require disclosure of the mechanisms that assure this.
	  Item 15 [S-K 701] requires that after the effective registration date, the issuer will report "the use of proceeds on its first periodic report."
		Circular Item 6 requires a statement of "the principal purposes for which the net proceeds to the issuer from the securities to be offered are intended to be used," but does not necessarily require disclosure of the mechanisms that assure this.
		  Part III Item 17 requires disclosure of "any management contract or any compensatory plan ... deemed material," except those available to employees generally and provides the same method of allocation between management and non-management. This might include plans for deferred compensation and lockup of tokens.	

194

Pre-ICO reporting
- Pro forma financials and projections

Item 11(a) [S-K 101] requires a description of "the registrant's plan of operation for the remainder of the fiscal year," and further descriptions of the cash budget for the next six months. It also requires substantial disclosure about anticipated material acquisitions, R&D, and financial information about each segment.

Item 11(e) requires full financial statements to be prepared that meet the requirements of Reg S-X, with modifications for smaller reporting companies. Items 11(f) and (g) subsequently require selected financial data (five years per S-K 301) and supplementary financial information (quarterly for the last two years per S-K 302).

Item 11(h) [S-K 303] requires a discussion of the registrant's financial condition, including "such other information that the registrant believes to be necessary to an understanding of its financial condition." This includes discussion of "material trends" and how they will impact the business.

Item 1 requires completion of an abbreviated income statement and balance sheet for the most recent fiscal period, and the amount of any outstanding securities.

Circular Item 9 requires a discussion of the registrant's financial condition. This includes discussion of liquidity and capital resources, known trends, and a plan of operation for the 12 months following the offering.

Circular Item F/S requires filing of limited financial statements, which need not be audited in every case.

The cover page requires a barebones listing of several core balance sheet and income statement items for the most recent fiscal year and one prior.

Q&A 27 asks whether the issuer has an operating history.

Q&A 28 asks to describe the financial condition of the issuer.

Q&A 29 asks for additional financial information via financial statements.

(Continued)

Disclosure Item	Form S-1	Form 1-A	Form C
Post-ICO reporting • Will the team file ongoing financial reports and how often? • Will an annual audit be conducted and by whom? • Where will these reports be filed?	Item 11(a) [S-K 101] requires that "if [applicable rules] do not require you to send an annual report to security holders . . . describe briefly the nature and frequency of reports that you will give to security holders and specify whether the reports that you give will contain financial information [that has been audited.]"		Item 2 requires a statement that an issuer must file an annual report, and how it may terminate its reporting obligations in the future. Item 3 specifies the nature of the annual report, including non-audited financial statements certified by the principal executive officer. The back page requires annual reports and provides for termination under certain conditions.

Organization and Operations Disclosures

Disclosure Item	Form S-1	Form 1-A	Form C

Mission, goals, and objectives
• What is the purpose of the sale and how does it fit within the larger mission of the project? What does the team seek to achieve and how?
	Item 4 [S-K 504] requires stating "the principal purpose for which the net proceeds to the registrant from the securities to be offered are intended to be used and the approximate amount intended to be used for each such purpose."
	  Item 11(a) [S-K 101] requires a narrative description of the business, including the "principal products and services rendered," "competitive conditions," etc.
		Item 2 requires the issuer to certify that it is not a development stage company with "no specific business plan or purpose."
		  Circular Item 7 requires a narrative description of the business, including the "principal products and services rendered," and the "status of a product or service if the issuer has made public information about a new product or service that would require the investment of a material amount of assets."
			Q&A 7 asks to "describe in detail the business of the issuer and the anticipated business plan of the issuer."
			  Q&A 9 asks bluntly, "What is the purpose of this offering?"
			  Q&A 10 asks for "a reasonably detailed description" of the intended use of the offering's proceeds.

The team			
The team - Who is working on this project? - Is there a community? - Is it open source? - What is the off-chain governance structure? - Is it centrally controlled? - Description of the founding team - Independent background checks?	Item 11(k) [S-K 401] requires identification of directors and executive officers. Even those who don't hold those formal titles are required to be identified if they are significant employees "who make or are expected to make significant contributions to the business of the registrant." This might sweep in at least some of the team who do not have executive officer titles. Item 11(k) [S-K 401] requires disclosure of the business experience of directors, executive officers, and significant employees. Directors and officers must further disclose involvement in legal proceedings, including criminal proceedings, as do promoters.	Item 3 [Reg A Rule 262] requires certification that no issuer, director, officer, beneficial owner, or promoter is disqualified (e.g., by virtue of criminal conviction). Circular Item 7 requires disclosure of "the total number of persons employed by the issuer, including the number employed full time." Circular Item 10 requires disclosure of the position, age, term of office, and hours per week for each executive officer, directors and significant employees. Significant employees include "persons such as production managers, sales managers, or research scientists . . . who make or are expected to make significant contributions to the business of the issuer." This would likely sweep in much of the technology team. Directors and officers must further provide business experience and criminal convictions.	The cover page requires listing the current number of employees. Q&A 5 asks for the name, title, responsibilities, and business experience for each officer. Notably, it includes "any persons occupying a similar status or performing a similar function," which might sweep in tech advisors who do not hold a traditional officer title. Q&A 30 asks about convictions of directors and officers.
Jurisdiction - Is a legal entity/organization involved? - In what jurisdiction is the legal entity formed? - Is there a principal place of business or geographic area where the organization or its activities are located?	Item 3 [S-K 503] requires disclosure of the mailing address and phone number of "principal executive offices." Item 11(a) [S-K 101] requires description of the business, which includes five years of operating history, the form of the registrant's organization, etc.	Item 1 requires the name of the issuer, the jurisdiction and the address of the principal executive offices. Part III Item 17 requires the charter and bylaws of the issuer to be attached as exhibits.	The cover page requires listing the name of the issuer, its form, jurisdiction, date of organization, and physical address.

(Continued)

197

Disclosure Item	Form S-1	Form 1-A	Form C
Corporate legal structure (off-chain governance) • Who are the primary issuing and supporting organizations for the project? • Where and how are these entities structured? • Organizational documents? • Legal counsel contact info? • Who controls and governs these entities? • Officers and board members? • Audit Committee? • Compensation Committee?	Item 3 [S-K 503] requires disclosure of the mailing address and phone number of "principal executive offices." Item 11(a) [S-K 101] requires description of the business, which includes five years of operating history, the form of the registrant's organization, etc. Item 10 [S-K 509] requires disclosure of the interests of counsel, though this appears to be limited to those who rendered an opinion or certification in connection with the offering. Item 11(k) [S-K 401] requires identification of directors and executive officers. Item 11(l) [S-K 407] provides at-length disclosure about the corporate governance of the registrant. Item 11(l) [S-K 407] requires disclosure of board meetings and "whether or not the registrant has standing audit, nominating and compensation committees." Item 16(a) [S-K 601] requires that articles of incorporation, bylaws, and subsidiaries be appended as exhibits.	Item 1 requires the name of the issuer, the jurisdiction, and the address of the principal executive offices. Part III Item 17 requires the charter and bylaws of the issuer to be attached as exhibits.	The cover page requires listing the name of the issuer, its form, jurisdiction, date of organization, and physical address. Q&A 4 asks for the name and business experience of each director "and any persons occupying a similar status or similar function."

Blockchain governance and amendments (on-chain governance)		
• White paper at token issuance and all historical versions (or links to these)?	Item 11(l) [S-K 407] on Corporate Governance. Corporate governance deals with stocks. Would it be enough to force disclosure about blockchain governance?	Q&A 14 asks whether the securities have voting rights, and Q&A 15 asks about limitations on voting rights.

• What is the on-chain governance structure?
  • Public or private blockchain?
  • What is the consensus mechanism?
  • How are decisions made?
	Item 2 [S-K 502] requires delivery of prospectus by dealers. Would this cover white paper disclosure, especially historical versions?
	
	Item 9 [S-K 202] requires that "if the rights of holders of such stock may be modified otherwise than by a vote of a majority or more of the share outstanding, voting as a class, so state and explain briefly." Note that this references stock, but a later provision requires comparable disclosure for other securities.
		Q&A 16 asks how the terms of the securities being offered may be modified.
		
		Q&A 31 asks for any other material information presented to investors or any information necessary to make the statements not misleading, which could require releasing the white paper.

• What mechanism governs amendments?	Item 11(l) [S-K 407] requires description of the process by which security holders can send communications to the board of directors. To the extent that this allows token holders to communicate with any real-world entity, this may allow for interaction between on-chain and off-chain governance.	

(Continued)

Disclosure Item	Form S-1	Form 1-A	Form C
Custody chain • Who holds the private key(s) to the wallet(s) in which ICO funds will be held? • Who custodies reserve tokens? • Procedures and controls surrounding custody and treasury management.			
Treasury management policy • Plan for managing ETH, BTC, fiat balances raised in the sale? • Hedging instruments for exchange rate risk exposure? • Liquidation plans to cover operating expenses? • Secondary sales rules (e.g., Ripple's periodic liquidation windows)? • Hedging instruments for reserved tokens? • Policies and procedures regarding insider sales and purchases?	Item 11(h) [SK-303] requires identification of trends that may affect the liquidity of the registrant and "the course of action that the registrant has taken or proposes to take to remedy." Item 11(j) [S-K 305] requires quantitative and qualitative disclosures about market risk. To the extent exchange rate exposure is included as a market risk, parties must describe "how those exposures are managed . . . a discussion of the objectives, general strategies, and instruments, if any, used to manage those exposures."		

200

IP/Tech

Web assets (verified)
- E.g., project website, token sale website, GitHub repository

Social media links (to prevent phishing attacks)
- E.g., Twitter, Telegram, Reddit, Slack

Protocol and other IP ownership
- Who owns the copyright and IP for the protocol used by the company?
- Any other IP associated with the token sale?
- Is there an open source reference implementation that describes the licenses (e.g., Creative Commons license) used by the ICO?
- Community information relating to the size of the committer base and the volume of pull requests, along with the total size of the codebase.

Item 11(a) [S-K 101] requires discussion of "the importance to the segment and the duration and effect of all patents, trademarks, licenses, franchises and concessions held." Still, this might not include other IP relevant to a crypto company, and it does not address ownership and use of the IP.

Circular Item 7 requires a discussion of "patents, trademarks, licenses, franchises, concessions or royalty agreements . . ." Still, this might not include other IP relevant to a crypto-company, and it does not address ownership and use of the IP.

Part III Item 17 requires attaching any material contracts as exhibits, which includes "any franchise or license or other agreement to use a patent, formula, trade secret, process or trade name upon which the issuer's business depends to a material extent." This is important because it includes trade secrets, which may well cover much of the IP held by a crypto-company.

The cover page has a place for listing the website of the issuer.

(Continued)

201

Disclosure Item	Form S-1	Form 1-A	Form C
Audits • Independent audits of the smart contracts and security procedures used in the ICO.		Part III Item 17 requires attaching as an exhibit the consent of experts "whose profession vies authority to a statement made by them and who is named in the offering statement as having prepared or certified a report or evaluation whether or not for use in connection with the offering statement." This could conceivably force disclosure of an audit report if such audit is mentioned in the offering statement.	
Risk Factors **Material risks to a purchase of the tokens based on any of the previously mentioned or other factors**	Item 11(j) [S-K 305] requires quantitative and qualitative disclosures about market risk. But, this is only one part of purchaser risk, and the concept of a "market" in the token context may be less well defined. Item 1[S-K 501] requires a cross-reference to the "risk factors section" to be placed on the cover page. Item 3 [S-K 503] requires a discussion "where appropriate" of the most significant factors that make the offering "speculative or risky." This seems flexible enough to cover many crypto-specific risks.	Circular Item 1(h) requires a cross-reference to the risk factors section to be placed on the cover page. Circular Item 3 requires "a carefully organized series of short, concise paragraphs, summarizing the most significant factors that make the offering speculative or substantially risky." Circular Item 14 requires a description of "potential liabilities imposed on securityholders under state statutes or foreign law, for example, to employees of the issuer . . ."	Q&A 8 asks for a discussion of "the material factors that make an investment in the issuer speculative or risky," and instructs to "avoid generalized statements and include only those factors that are unique to the issuer." Q&A 22 asks for the risks relating to minority ownership. Q&A 23 asks for risks associated with corporate actions.

8

Blockchains and Risk Management Infrastructure of the Derivatives Industry

Petal P. Walker

The U.S. derivatives markets serve an important role in the American economy by providing opportunities for hedging and risk management, as well as opportunities for some speculation. Inherent in these diverse markets are various forms of risk. And pursuant to the Commodity Exchange Act (CEA), the U.S. Commodity Futures Trading Commission (CFTC or Commission)—the agency charged with overseeing these markets—has constructed a regulatory infrastructure to address these risks. This infrastructure is multifaceted, involving a web of requirements including, inter alia, mandatory clearing, mandatory trade execution, reporting, and registration. Though end-to-end blockchain-based derivatives markets are not likely in the near future,[1] there is considerable activity suggesting that it will ultimately become a reality. But how adaptive would today's derivatives regulatory infrastructure be to tomorrow's blockchain-based derivatives markets?

This chapter explores vectors necessary for tackling the integration issues posed by blockchain technologies in derivatives markets. To do so, the chapter opens with an overview of a typical derivatives transaction and a discussion of the basic regulatory infrastructure designed to address the risks of the derivatives markets today, including its registration regime. Next the chapter provides an overview as to how blockchain could be applied in the derivatives markets. In a third step, I explore the ways in which a blockchain-based derivatives market could possibly reduce risk, followed by an overview of some of the risk concerns about blockchain raised by market participants and how they may be addressed. The chapter concludes by considering an issue that has escaped considerable attention—how the application of today's risk-based registration regime on tomorrow's blockchain market may actually increase risk.

I. What's a Swap?—A Look at a Basic Transaction

According to the CEA and CFTC regulations, many different kinds of instruments could potentially fall under the CFTC's jurisdiction. This chapter focuses on one kind of instrument that falls under its jurisdiction, a swap. Swaps are generally agreements between two counterparties to exchange cash flows based on the occurrence (or nonoccurrence) of a future event. Examples include interest rate swaps (IRS) where counterparties agree to exchange future interest payments based on a principal amount based, and credit default swaps (CDS) where one party agrees to exchange regular payments in order to pass on its credit risk in case of default. Swaps have traditionally been executed bilaterally, according to very tailored (or "bespoke") terms negotiated by the parties. And today, many swaps are still bespoke and continue to trade bilaterally. However, there are also stops that are fairly standardized, including many IRS, CDS, and foreign exchange (FX) swaps, and energy swaps.

Pursuant to CFTC regulation, virtually all swaps are required to be reported, but several standardized IRS and CDS swaps are also required to be executed on exchange, and cleared. As outlined further later on in the chapter in the description of registration obligations, in order to make these on-exchange trades, end-users typically utilize brokers called introducing brokers (IBs) or futures commission (FCMs) to trade on platforms called Designated Contract Markets (DCMs) or Swap Execution Facilities (SEFs). After the execution of the trade, standardized swaps are then required to be cleared on a derivatives clearing organizations (DCOs). Clearing is when, after the execution of a transaction between two counterparties, a third party (a central counterparty (CCP) that does clearing, of which DCOs are the U.S. registrant) steps in and becomes a buyer to the seller and a seller to the buyer. This process is called novation. After clearing the trade, the DCO then sends the trades to a swap data repository (SDR) for reporting to the market and the Commission.

As also described later in the chapter, swaps that remain off-exchange, or over-the-counter (OTC) trades are often chaperoned by swap dealers (SDs). SDs and the counterparties agree to the terms of initial and variation margin. Initial margin is the amount of collateral that should be paid initially to ensure performance on a contract, and is generally higher than the margin required by DCOs. Variation margin is calculated daily during the life of the contact and is basically the amount necessary to meet the mark-to-market requirements for the contract. OTC swaps may also be sent to clearing, but whether cleared or uncleared, they too must be reported to the SDR.

A. An Overview of Registration Obligations

Many of the intermediaries that participate in the life cycle of swaps, as described earlier in this section, are required to register with the CFTC. While many requirements, such as clearing, trade execution, reporting, antifraud, and anti-manipulation, apply to many swap participants, there are certain participants whose activities in the market are of such significance that they must submit to registration. Registration is central to the CFTC's oversight in that it allows the CFTC to, inter alia:

(1) Identify the key participants in the markets;
(2) Form a regulatory relationship with these key participants;
(3) Require these key participants to meet certain requirements aimed at risk mitigation;
(4) Have ready access to these participants during times of relative peace and crisis; and
(5) Require key participants to self-report significant events.

There are several registration categories required by the CFTC, but the specific ones we will discuss in this chapter are:

(1) *IB*: Subject to certain exceptions, an intermediary who solicits and accepts orders from U.S. customers, but does not hold customer funds, must register as an IB.[2] Relative to other registrants, IBs are not subject to many regulatory requirements—mainly resource requirements and some business conduct standards.[3]

(2) *FCM*: Subject to certain exceptions, an intermediary who solicits and accepts orders from U.S. customers and maintains customer accounts, must register as an FCM.[4] FCMs are subject to several regulatory requirements including financial resource requirements (capital), risk management, supervision, treatment of customer funds, and business conduct.[5]

(3) *SD*: Subject to certain exceptions, an intermediary that basically makes a market in swaps for U.S. customers (over a certain threshold of activity), must register as a SD. SDs are subject to a considerable amount of regulation including capital requirements,[6] margin, risk management, know your customer, portfolio compression, and much more.[7]

(4) *SEF*: Subject to certain exceptions, an entity that provides swaps trading between multiple participants facing multiple participants (as opposed to a single participant facing multiple participants) must register as a SEF. All SEF participants must meet resource requirements (meet the requirements of Eligible Contract Participant). SEFs can only be used to execute swaps. SEFs typically offer electronic trading and voice brokering. SEFs provide for a variety of trading methods, including trading on orderbook and request-for-quote (RFQ) system, which are the only two means through which mandatory swaps must be executed.

SEFs allow limited off-exchange trading. SEFs are self-regulatory organizations (SROs) and subject to numerous regulations including resource requirements, technology requirements, participant access, and more.

(5) *DCM*: Subject to certain exceptions, a trading venue that offers futures and/or swaps to U.S. retail investors must register as a DCM. DCMs allow retail customers to trade futures and swaps that are largely standardized mainly on order book. DCMs allow limited off-exchange trading. As they serve retail investors, DCMs are even more highly regulated than SEFs, and are also SROs.

(6) *DCO*: Subject to certain exceptions, a central counterparty (CCP) that novates swaps for U.S. persons, must register as a DCO. DCOs are highly regulated including resource requirements, access requirements, margin methodology, product and participant requirements, and more. They also serve an important risk management function by determining the initial and daily variation margin for their numerous counterparties.

(7) *SDR*: An entity that reports swaps to the CFTC must register as an SDR.

The registrants described above are integral players in the lifecycle of derivatives contracts. The CEA designates these market participants as registrants because their actions have the potential of impacting enough of the market to justify obligating them to have a direct relationship with the Commission that goes beyond the obligations of the average market participant.

Importantly, throughout the life cycle of a swap contract, there also are entities that play pivotal roles in the derivatives markets that are not required to register with the Commission. These participants include settlement banks, which are regulated by prudential regulators. They also include a wide variety of third-party providers that engage in: pre-trade credit checks for FCMs prior to placing orders on the exchange, compression exercises for the portfolios of market participants, confirmation of the terms of contracts prior to submission to clearing, and much more.

II. How Blockchain Technology Would Transform Derivatives Markets

As has been recounted in earlier chapters, blockchains are databases that link series-level transaction blocks as time goes on and as more transactions take place. They can do so via varying *consensus mechanisms*, where via permissioned or open systems decisions can be made via a community of actors, or nodes, connected to one another through a decentralized, peer-to-peer network.[8] Because of this infrastructure, blockchains present at least the possibility of fully transparent data-management and recording facilities, where all in the system can see transaction data memorialized in an immutable ledger.

Applied to the transaction structure described later on in the chapter, blockchains could transform the delivery of derivatives-related financial services. Surujnath describes it thusly:

> A blockchain-based derivatives contract market would likely involve a system of several interoperable ledgers that use multi-sig smart contracts for effectuating transfers and oracles for asset monitoring and collateral management. Parties to a blockchain derivatives transaction would submit bids and asks as usual. . . . They could upload asks directly to the blockchain and rely on its computing to automatically choose the highest bid. Because of public-key cryptography, the publicly viewable addresses would serve as aliases that conceal identifying information of the counterparties. Once the parties are matched . . . [t]he contracts are then uploaded to the derivatives ledger, which contains the logic and execution algorithms for all the clearing members' agreements. . . . Throughout the lifespan of the agreement, the collateral ledger uses oracles to reference agreed upon external data sources (like Bloomberg) to track price movements in the underlying assets and to automatically adjust positions.[9]

As described a possible end-to-end blockchain-based derivatives market would include a set of interoperable ledgers (or one ledger) that multiple participants can access as nodes on the network. It would have smart contracts that have self-executing properties as well as multi-signature (multi-sig) decision points. Smart contracts are defined as a "series of instructions that execute autonomously based on predetermined inputs."[10] They can be programmed to, inter alia, process customer requests, pull data from oracles, recalculate margin, withdraw and submit value in customer accounts, use oracles to compute exposure, and recalculate variation margin.[11] In a largely automated fashion, these contracts would, inter alia, receive and send messages to counterparties, match trades, assess and reassess collateral, access information from oracles, and reallocate collateral in customer accounts. Additionally, some subset of participants would validate transactions, and all participants, including the CFTC, could see the evolution of the transactions in near real time.

Thus, an end-to-end blockchain would fundamentally change the transaction process in the derivatives markets. Instead of the transaction evolving as it moves from one entity to another in a linear fashion from pre-trade credit check to reporting, the entire life cycle of the contract would take place in one space where all participants can view, and continually validate, the entire history of the contract in near real time. This shift would constitute a fundamental transformation. End-users would no longer have to take a back seat as a range of intermediaries handle the contract from soup to nuts. While free to use intermediaries, all participants, including end users, would have the ability to view the state of the market and the autonomy to transact within it.

III. The Risks and Rewards of Blockchain Technology

As several authors have noted, the risk reduction that would result from a blockchain-based derivatives market are obvious. It would create a "golden record" that all the participants would agree to in real time,[12] thereby avoiding duplication,[13] and reducing, if not eliminating, disputes.[14] It is extremely efficient. Smart contracts would precisely and logically carry out the contract terms without unnecessary interference.[15] And thereby, a blockchain network would provide the opportunity for enhanced collateral management.[16] It would also provide a very direct way for participants to verify transactions; by simply looking at the chain, participants could easily see whether a transaction was illegitimate.[17] Moreover, from a cybersecurity perspective, because all blockchain participants have their own copy of the ledger, it reduces the risk posed by a single point of failure.[18]

A. Newfound Transparency, Supervisory Potential for Regulators

But I would argue that one of the greatest potential risk reduction attributes of a blockchain network is the transformation of the regulator's supervisory potential. The nearly instantaneous reporting that blockchain allows would be a game changer for the CFTC and other regulators. Among other things, blockchains enable a comprehensive record of ownership,[19] and provide enhanced transparency.[20] Blockchains as such could allow regulators to notice irregularities and address wrongdoing.[21] The transparency of blockchains also enhances regulatory oversight and allows for statistical analyses in real time.[22] Blockchains, could thus enable faster reporting capable of retracing transaction histories.[23] Regulators could also able to access that data at any time.[24] Furthermore, blockchains could conceivably enable continuous monitoring, increased efficiency, decreased investigation times, real time insights, and the use of artificial intelligence to better predict systemic risk events.[25]

No longer would the regulator have to wait for market participants to send data at periodic intervals. Rather the regulators could potentially sit on the blockchain itself and see the market as it unfolds in near real time. This would result in changing, among other things, the fundamental dynamics between regulator and market participants by "revolutioniz[ing] financial regulation,"[26] and making it more forward-looking.[27] Therefore, the integration of a blockchain would introduce a whole new level of regulatory oversight. Regulators would be able to not only respond to market conditions but to also work collaboratively with market participants to influence them earlier if they create systemic risk.

B. Common Risk Concerns Raised

Authors have also noted, however, some risks that may be introduced by blockchains. In this subsection I discuss some of those concerns, and comment on the degree to which the current regulatory paradigm may be able to address newly introduced risks.

1. Language Gap Risk

Many authors have cited language issues. The bare truth is that relatively few people in finance, in the market, at the regulator, or in the legal community know how to read code. It looks like gibberish to all but the relatively few people who are versed in the field. This has raised concerns for writers and regulators. *Walch* states it this way:

> [A]s with all software, only a small percentage of the population understands how software works. Software coders have a particular expertise that makes the quality of their code, and even the basic functions it performs, opaque to people who are not experts in the relevant software language. . . . Software coding is truly an area in which knowledge (of code) is power."[28]

Walch goes on to note the risks of centralizing this power in the hands of a few in the context of Bitcoin saying:

> The fact that only a very limited portion of the population truly understands how Bitcoin operates gives rise to systemic operational risks. This is because it requires the population to put extreme amounts of trust in the skill and integrity of the people making decisions about the Bitcoin code and network. . . . We should proceed with caution in building complex, opaque systems that carry out tasks of significant systemic importance.[29]

Authors have specifically identified the gap between coder and non-coder in regard to finance and law.

i. Language Gap between the Coder and the Finance Professional
As one author notes, the typical coder may not be suited to writing financial contracts. Walch notes that "smart contract programming requires an 'economic thinking; perspective that traditional programmers may not have acquired."[30] Walch describes the dilemma, in the context of bitcoin, as an "expertise problem."[31] Authors have also cited the opposite concern: that risk management experts would be unable to understand the code. The European Securities and Markets Authority (ESMA) notes in its 2016 discussion paper that "[u]se of complex encryption techniques . . . could have negative implications from a risk management or oversight perspective . . . the encryption of the information could make it harder to disentangle it and to process it, at least in the short term . . . "[32] Thus, there certainly is a language divide between the coder—the smart contract writer, for instance—and the typical business person. One could see however, how this gap could be addressed by coders and business persons working closely to ensure that they effectively communicate concepts in both directions.

ii. Language Gap between the Coder and the Legal Professional
Many authors have cited the difference between coding language and legal language. For instance, Butler et al. note that "a lawyer can neither understand, nor predict the behavior of, the smart contract code, as there is no intermediate language that bridges the gap."[33] Contracts today are legally complex, [34] and that legal complexity is not going to automatically disappear because they are written in code. Because of its nuance, coders would find it difficult to predict all of the permutations of legal issues that could arise from a contract.[35] And while some aspects of a contract can be reduced to simple "if, then" statements, there are aspects of contract that are inherently nuanced and ambiguous. For instance, Butler et al. note that contracts can be divided into two elements: operational semantics (pertaining to the execution of contract on the platform) and denotational semantics (pertaining to the legal meaning of the contract).[36] And in their 2017 white paper, ISDA/Linklaters similarly makes the distinction between "operational" versus "non-operational" clauses in contracts.[37] They go on to note that the latter, such as dispute resolution and good faith, are not easily expressed in Boolean language.[38] Moreover, it is not beneficial to remove all ambiguity from contracts since some aspects of contract are necessarily contextual and, as the context changes, the parties would benefit from the flexibility that the ambiguity provides.[39]

The gap between compliance counsel and technology providers is not new; there is one now. However, the stakes are far higher in a blockchain network environment because the technology is that much more complicated, interconnected, and partly self-executing, so that it is much more important to get it right. While in an ideal world, single individuals would be fully versed in law and coding, "expecting a lawyer to acquire the type of technological expertise required to code smart contracts is unrealistic"[40] As Butler et al. notes, "trust, by all stakeholders, including regulators, in smart contracts can only stem from the ability of lawyers in financial institutions to understand, express and ultimately validate the denotational semantics of a contract."[41]

In order to have effective compliance, the communication between lawyers and coders needs to be able to flow in both directions. Counsel need to understand what the code means in order to opine on its compatibility with ever-changing laws. And coders need to understand the law enough to integrate it into the code. There are efforts underway to bridge the coder/non-coder divide and create a common language.[42] For instance, ISDA has published its "common domain model," which is "meant to establish some common parameters to allow for interoperability.[43] Efforts such as these are critical for moving the technology forward.

2. Technology Risk

Several authors also raise concerns about risks endemic to virtually all emerging technologies, including blockchain-based technologies. Authors note risks that are inherent to software such as bugs, the need for continual update, and, as noted previously, specialized knowledge.[44] Authors have also noted that private keys could be stolen,[45] and glitches or errors could be catastrophic.[46] Another issue is that since, as noted, an end-to-end system is unlikely in the near future, there will be a transition period in which blockchain structures would have to operate with non-blockchain structures,[47] which could introduce risk.

The most common technology risk cited, however, is cybersecurity. For instance, while acknowledging that blockchains could reduce cybersecurity risk because a copy of the common ledger is held by many entities, not just one,[48] ESMA nonetheless argues that blockchains pose greater cybersecurity issues because, if successful, an attack would increase the likelihood of the contagion since the markets would be so tightly integrated.[49] Importantly, however, blockchain has the benefit of substantial cryptography[50] creating robustness.[51] Moreover, cybersecurity concerns are in every aspect of our lives where technology is involved. While all market participants, blockchain-based or not, should remain vigilant about cybersecurity, it would be an undesirable outcome for these concerns to inhibit the development of efficient systems such as a blockchain-based derivatives market.

3. Permanency Risk

Another risk often cited is the absence of a recourse mechanism.[52] According to this argument, as blockchain data cannot be erased, problems caused by errors or malfeasance cannot be fixed.[53] However, just because a contract cannot be reversed does not mean it cannot be corrected. A court could obligate the losing litigant to enter in an opposite transaction on a blockchain network to address the invalid contract through surrendering keys or the like.[54] A blockchain network does not inhibit correction; it simply keeps a record of all changes to the ledger—including corrections. *Werbach* notes that, in this way, smart contracts clarify that contract law is not about ensuring performance but adjudicating grievances,[55] which can be ably achieved through appropriate programming.

4. Transparency Risk

Several authors, often with the bitcoin model in mind, have raised concerns over transparency risk. They argue that because all the participants can see the movement on a blockchain network, even if they cannot see the name of the participant, they can see major activity and potentially front-run to manipulate the market.[56] However, unlike the bitcoin blockchain, permissioned systems do not have to be fully transparent.[57] The use of pseudonyms, and public addresses (and private keys) allow for anonymity and security.[58] While regulators (and chosen counterparties)[59] may be able to see all the participant information, programming can obfuscate certain information from the rest of the market. Moreover, emerging technologies such as the Lightning Network hold promise for creating private spaces on the broader blockchain where participants can build a transaction and not record it on the ledger until they both agree.[60]

IV. The Risks and Rewards of Registration

As described previously, a major cornerstone of the CFTC's regulatory regime is registration. The CFTC endeavors to require registration of all the significant entities in its market from a risk-creation perspective in order to make sure that they have appropriate risk management practices. But with blockchain, risk shifts. The individuals who were important in the non-blockchain paradigm are not necessarily important within a blockchain paradigm. In a blockchain-based derivatives market, some of the important players are: (1) a blockchain network itself, (2) the smart contract writers, (3) the smart contract itself, (4) oracles, (5) nodes, and (6) validators. And as seen later on in the chapter, the mold of the current registration regime may not fit the future paradigm.

A. The Blockchain Network

The blockchain network itself would clearly be a significant player in these markets. Under the current regulatory regime, a blockchain (or a group of interlocking blockchains) that operates as described previously would, in the first instance, have to register as a SEF or DCM since it is matching customers through a series of smart contracts. The determination of whether it would have to register as either or both would depend on several factors, including: whether its members are all ECPs, whether it trades only swaps, and what methods of execution it employs. But a blockchain network-based derivatives market described above would also have to register as a DCO since it is, inter alia, novating contracts and making margin calls, which are all functions of a DCO. Moreover, since it maintains a regulator node, it is providing reporting data to the regulator and thus would arguably have to register as an SDR as well. In today's derivatives markets, we have examples of financial market infrastructures (FMIs) that share common ownership including DCM/DCO/SDR.[61] But each has separate staff, separate networks, and separate business models. In blockchain-based markets, all of these functions would operate almost simultaneously in the same network, thus creating super-FMIs with transactions moving seamlessly within one network. This raises a number of questions.

Given that the Commission likely would, in this scenario, take the position that the entity could not double count the resources dedicated to one registrant class for another, it would require a considerable amount of capital to support all the multiple functions. And what risk management requirements would the CFTC consider sufficient for an entity of such significance to the marketplace? Would the Commission conclude that the requirements of a DCO would be sufficient for an entity that is a DCM, DCO, and SDR in one?

And what of the concentration charges often leveled at CCPs: If high-volume CCPs today are considered as a concentration of risk then what of a DCM/SEF/DCO/SDR combination? Another solution would be to create another registrant class if Congress determines that the sum is not equal to the collection of its parts—that a DCM/DCO/SDR operating in real time based on blockchain technology creates a unique risk profile with new risks such that it requires a different set of regulatory requirements.

Another important issue for registration is that of personhood. It is highly unlikely that the Commission would be satisfied that the ultimate owner of a significant segment of market activity is a computer network that they can analyze but that cannot be hold accountable. The Commission and other regulators would undoubtedly require access to the individuals who can explain errors,[62] answer questions, and ultimately be held accountable for malfeasance.

So, there would most likely have to be an "owner" of a blockchain network. But who or what would fill that role? Within a permissioned system, blockchains would most likely be sponsored by a consortium of market participants—such as the intermediated CCP. But in the clearinghouse example, the clearinghouse itself is a stand-alone business so the CFTC can require registration of the CCP itself and police its leaders as needed. Thus, the closest parallel would be to form a stand-alone company that constitutes the blockchain network, then people it and resource it in order to meet the requirements of multiple CCP registrations. But with a DCM/DCO/SDR, requiring personhood would encourage centralization, and the concentration concerns that centralization raises.

But what if a blockchain network intends to operate as a classic blockchain— a diffuse network, without a central entity of any kind. Then, the risk formation would be diffuse—the CFTC would not be able to look to one entity to police (and register) regarding activity on a blockchain network, and instead would have to look to the individual nodes. This arrangement would certainly satisfy the concentration concerns, but would the Commission be able to effectively oversee and police the risk of that many players without a central authority?

B. The Smart Contract Writer

As discussed previously, the role of the smart contract writer is incredibly significant. While every contract is forward-looking, it is all the more important to get the smart contract right because many (and, in some cases, all) elements are self-executing.[63] So within the coding, the writer has to insert all current and anticipated risks,[64] including determining which oracles to link to, and determining if and when multi-signatures are required.[65] And importantly, since these contracts would have access to customer accounts, they could affect liquidity.[66] Their importance to risk formation in a block-based derivatives market is undeniable as these smart contracts could affect the entire market as they self-execute over time.[67]

As such, smart contracts shift more of the risk management earlier in the transaction life cycle. In the current market, the DCO calculates risk at the novation of the contract—initial margin, but then the DCO continues to reassess risk over the life of the contract and daily revises that risk and requires variation margin to address it. As circumstances change, the DCO continues to assess and reassess how these circumstances have altered the risk and therefore the risk management necessary.

Another key risk management player in today's market is the FCM. The FCM, as a member of the DCO, continues to engage in a risk management assessment of its customers and requires margin as well. The FCM also vouches for its customers. The DCO and the other clearing members are actually putting their trust in the FCM—its capital holding and its risk management apparatus—when allowing the FCM's customers to trade through the FCM's account.

With a blockchain network, because the contracts are self-executing (or largely self-executing), they are preprogrammed to respond in specified ways to changes in circumstances. Unlike the CCP, which has the benefit of the initial risk assessment and then continual correction, the smart contract writer has to anticipate future risks in a way that the DCO does not since the stakes are much higher. Now there are certainly ways to reassess risk management during the life of the contract for important decisions— for example, smart contracts can require the use of multi-sig to approve meaningful changes to the contract. But the contract writer has to be able to make those choices (e.g., when multi-sig would be necessary) at the initiation of the contract.

The significance of these contracts within the derivatives markets means that the smart contract writers are also extremely significant. The question then becomes: What registrant category, if any, applies to smart contract writers? In truth, there is no current registration requirement for individuals who draft contracts unless they are client-facing. If the contract writer is not engaged in customer-facing activity, then he or she would not have to register in any intermediary category.

But that begs the question: Could the Commission determine that the smart contract writer is engaging in customer-facing activity? When someone codes a contract and puts it on a blockchain network—are they, in essence, soliciting customers? To answer that question, much would likely depend on the coders' mode of compensation. Are they compensated whenever a person chooses to use the contract to transact? Then the Commission may classify them as a swap dealer—someone who is making a market in that commodity. Or the Commission may view them as an introducing broker—by coding the contract, they are soliciting customers to the marketplace—to a blockchain network. And if they are compensated when the customer engages with the exchange, they could be viewed as introducing trades to a registered exchange and therefore acting as an IB.

Another option is for Congress to institute a new registrant category in order to capture contract writers. However, whether the CFTC were to define smart contract writers as captured by a current registration category, or Congress were to create a category for them, it would still pose the same challenge: expertise. In order to regulate someone, you have to understand what that person is doing. When you register someone, you are, in essence, giving that person a seal of approval. So, if the CFTC were to register smart contract writers, the regulator would have to understand enough about the substance of their business—coding—in order to know, inter alia, if they were competent, and if they were violative, as well as what information to ask for, and what to do with the information once received.

Another option is to treat the contract writer as any other technology provider and attempt to hold the customer-facing entity responsible for the risk management of the contract—so that the registrant would police the smart contract.[68] But who would this customer-facing entity be? Arguably, it would most likely be whoever pays the contract writer. So, if a blockchain network, for instance, compensates the contract writer, then the Commission may require a blockchain network owner to ensure that the contract writer is acting in compliance with a blockchain network's regulatory requirements. Or if another intermediary compensates the contract writer then it would have to engage in the policing. Another option is for the CFTC to rely on the registration of another agency that has the expertise to understand the technical activity of smart contract writers and establish appropriate risk management parameters for them.

C. The Contract

In today's derivative markets, it would be laughable to consider registering a contract. But the smart contract is inherently different from today's contract because it not only indicates what must happen, it *acts*. It is self-executing. Once programed, the contract runs itself. It is not like an ISDA agreement where it is only as good as the people who enforce it. In other words, in today's ISDA, if both parties decide to ignore a clause, then the clause has no effect—the contract cannot effectuate itself. But a smart contract is different. What makes it smart is that it can effectuate itself. Even if the participants change their mind about the original program, the contract is preprogrammed to carry out their original wishes. Yet the contract cannot be held accountable for its decisions.

So what registrant categories could a smart contract fall into? That would truly depend on its activity. In truth, if a smart contract is matching customers, or providing a market for all comers, and/or moving monies out of margin accounts, under the current paradigm, it itself could be considered a SEF/DCM, a SD, or a DCO. But subjecting individual contracts to registration under the current paradigm would be burdensome to the technology, and of little use since it cannot be held accountable. A variation on that idea would be to require that a significant contract hold risk-based capital as insurance against its own malfunctioning. A final option would be to hold other registrants—whoever profits from the contract—to policing it.

D. Oracles, Nodes, and Validators

The oracles for the contracts would most likely be established information sources such as Bloomberg or Moody's, which are subject to their own regulatory oversight, and no additional registration would be required. In keeping with the current registration paradigm, nodes and validators could also be subject to registration depending on the interpretation of their actions. Despite the claim that blockchain "eliminates the role of a financial intermediary,"[69] some super-nodes may be considered a kind of intermediary. A super-node that intermediates between other nodes and a blockchain network may be just considered a technology provider or an IB based on the services it provides its node customers. Validators are partly doing the work of exchanges today by validating trades, though arguably their function is also similar to a technology provider, such as those that engage in confirmation, which does not require registration under our current regime.

V. Conclusion

The current regulatory scheme for derivatives markets is calibrated for the risks inherent to today's markets, but it is not fully suited to the risks of tomorrow's blockchain-based derivatives markets. Blockchain technology fundamentally changes the risk profile of the derivatives markets by, inter alia: (1) introducing significant players to the market such as smart contract writers, and the smart contracts themselves, that were not ever anticipated in today's markets; (2) reducing risk through empowering the regulator to engage in more robust engagement with the market; (3) introducing technical languages that require translation; and (4) moving risk management further up the lifespan of the typical contract. By mitigating risk in some areas and introducing different dynamics to the markets, end-to-end blockchain would fundamentally change the way the market does business. And, in order not to inhibit the great promise that blockchain has for market efficiency and transparency, the regulatory infrastructure may have to fundamentally change with it.

9

Difficulties in Achieving Neutrality and Other Challenges in Taxing Cryptoassets

*Christophe Waerzeggers and Irving Aw**

I. Introduction

The recent volatility in cryptoassets prices—booming to almost USD 800 billion in estimated market capitalization early 2018 only to collapse to about a quarter of that value by the time of writing[1]—has generated strong interest from governments and tax administrations in considering the appropriate tax treatment of transactions in, and relevant gains derived by taxpayers from the acquisition and disposal of, cryptoassets. With tech entrepreneurs coming up with evermore innovative ways to harness blockchain technology and established businesses embracing the technology to reinvent how they connect with clients and investors, it becomes imperative that jurisdictions formulate appropriate tax policy responses to the taxation of this emerging industry to ensure consistency in and effectiveness of their tax laws.

Not every jurisdiction has yet proactively addressed the tax treatment of investments in cryptoassets based on the principle of tax neutrality. This is unsurprising at least in part since governments also commonly use taxation as an instrument to discourage behaviors perceived to be harmful or otherwise undesirable. Jurisdictions that are generally supportive of—or at least neutral toward—the crypto industry (for instance, Australia, Singapore, United Kingdom, and Ireland) have typically taken an approach toward the taxation of transactions involving cryptoassets based on first principles in domestic tax legislation to approximate neutrality with comparable "conventional" transactions or activities. However, this approach requires a proper understanding of the facts on a case-by-case basis, including the nature of the cryptoasset in question

* Senior Counsel and Counsel in the Legal Department of the IMF. The views expressed in this chapter are those of the authors and do not necessarily represent the views of the IMF, its Executive Board, or IMF management. The authors are grateful to Mr. Cory Hillier and Ms. Jess Cheng, both Counsels in the Legal Department of the IMF, for their comments on an earlier draft of this chapter.

and the purpose for which the cryptoasset was acquired and disposed. The nature and versatility of cryptoassets as well as the distinctiveness in operations of the crypto industry—driven by the underlying ever-evolving technology—present particular challenges to the application of first principles to transactions involving cryptoassets.

This chapter seeks to provide an overview of the main challenges and key considerations for tax law policymakers wishing to design or benchmark their tax law framework for cryptoassets. It deliberately does not attempt to be exhaustive—in particular because of the evolving nature of the underlying technologies and their applications—but rather seeks to set out a framework of reference based on basic principles of tax law design as these apply to the common forms of activity and transactions in the cryptoasset sphere. The chapter also does not deal in any detail with associated tax administration and other law enforcement challenges such as those related to anti-money laundering and combatting the financing of terrorism. The remainder of this chapter is organized as follows: Section II discusses the classification challenges that tax law policymakers and tax administrations typically face in relation to cryptoassets. Section III proceeds to discuss some of the key tax law considerations when considering basic forms of activities and transactions with respect to cryptoassets. Section IV draws some preliminary conclusions.

II. Challenges in Classification and the Problem of Hybridity

One of the key challenges in achieving neutrality in the tax treatment of cryptoassets derives from the wide variations in their underlying economic functions, which in turn often determine or at least inform their tax law treatment.

A useful starting point in considering the different types of functions that cryptoassets may serve is the Swiss Financial Market Supervisory Authority's (FINMA) classification of tokens for Swiss regulatory purposes.[2] FINMA has identified three main categories under which tokens may fall based on their underlying economic functions, namely: (1) payment tokens, (2) utility tokens, and (3) asset tokens. *Payment tokens* are used as "means of payment for acquiring goods or services or as a means of money or value transfer."[3] *Utility tokens* are meant to provide digital access to applications or services through blockchain technology. *Asset tokens* are digital representations of physical or financial assets. However, such classifications are not mutually exclusive—in many cases, a token is well capable of being classified under more than one of these categories. Such a hybrid token is subject to all the relevant Swiss regulatory requirements for each of the categories under which it may fall.[4]

Unfortunately, adopting such a cumulative approach is not a viable option for tax purposes. While it is often necessary to examine the subjective purpose of a taxpayer against the objective economic substance of a transaction to determine the appropriate tax treatment for that transaction in relation to that taxpayer, this presupposes a proper determination of the nature or substance of that transaction. The wide variations in the underlying economic functions of tokens, exacerbated by the complications caused by hybrid tokens, present particular challenges in determining the objective economic substance of a token transaction. To illustrate the difficulties in classifying a particular token for tax purposes, consider for instance the nature of Ether, which is the native token of the Ethereum platform. As a native token, Ether can be used as "gas"[5] to verify transactions on the Ethereum platform (i.e., as a utility token). Ether could also be staked as an asset by a holder in return for the chance to verify blocks when Ethereum moves to a proof of stake system (i.e., an asset token). In addition, given its acceptance by at least a segment of the public as a means of payment, Ether could be used by holders to pay for goods or services provided by selected merchants and retailers (i.e., a payment token). The tax consequences of a transaction involving Ether therefore vary depending on the underlying economic function played by Ether in that particular transaction.

Given such variations in the underlying economic function performed by a token in any given transaction, it is unsurprising that many jurisdictions that strive toward neutrality have adopted a case-by-case approach toward taxing gains arising from the disposal of cryptoassets.[6] However, the relatively low entry barrier for investments in cryptoassets—and the constant innovation in the applications of distributed ledger technology—means that tax administrations are likely to face significant challenges in assessing cases as crypto transactions become more widespread.[7]

A. Money or Property

The distinction between transactions involving monetary and non-monetary consideration (barter) is important for both value added taxes (VAT)[8] and income/capital gains tax purposes.

In monetary economics, one of the functions of money is to act as a medium of exchange to avoid the problem of double coincidence of wants[9] in bartering. When used as a medium of exchange, the provision of money to obtain goods and services does not amount to a separate taxable transaction for VAT purposes, but instead constitutes payment (or "consideration") for the supply of those goods or services. In other words, money is the measure of consumption expenditure by reference to which the VAT liability in relation to the supply of goods and services is typically determined but is not itself consumed and therefore should not be separately taxed. This is typically achieved by treating the supply of money provided as consideration for a supply as "out-of-scope" or otherwise excluded from the definition of supply.[10] The rationale for such exclusion is also a utilitarian one, as it reduces complexities by preventing VAT from being applied twice to a single transaction.[11] Money exchange transactions, while recognized for VAT purposes,[12] are typically exempt from VAT.[13] This recognizes, on the one hand, that in those circumstances one medium of exchange is simply swapped for another, or that the transaction is pure investment in which case it is also appropriately excluded from the consumption tax base. In addition, exempting the exchange service promotes the unencumbered flow of payments by sidestepping "the difficulties connected with determining the taxable amount and the amount of VAT deductible."[14] However, the treatment is different for money that is numismatic in nature, in which case the supply is typically taxable.[15] This suggests that money is excluded from the scope of VAT only if it is used either as a medium of exchange or as investment, while numismatic money has intrinsic value in and of itself, and should be subject to VAT as a supply of goods.

As an initial point, it is worth clarifying that utility tokens granting participation in a network and whose provisioning serve as proprietary payment mechanism for the delivery of goods or services native to the network do not fall within the category of money since they are akin to prepayments for future goods or services, unless such utility tokens are also used as a medium of exchange in the wider economy.[16] The issuance or supply of utility tokens may thus give rise to VAT liability where there is a sufficiently direct link between the prepayment and specific goods or services.[17]

Currently, bitcoin is arguably the only cryptoasset that can be considered to be widely used as a medium of exchange, given its acceptance by an increasing number of major retailers.[18] It could not however be said to fulfill, at least for now, the other two widely accepted functions of money, namely, store of value and unit of account. We consider these functions to be of little relevance for tax purposes. While the volatility in the price of bitcoin makes it a poor store of value, certain traditional currencies[19] are also subject to the same risks.[20] Most retailers that accept bitcoin as a payment option do not adopt bitcoin as a unit of account and instead choose to price their products or services in traditional currencies. However, it could be counterargued that this is no different from an online retailer that accepts foreign currencies but continues to price its products or services using a local currency. To the extent that tax laws recognize traditional currencies that have poor store of value as unit of account and enable retailers that accept foreign currencies in exchange for goods or services priced in a local currency to treat any gains or losses as foreign exchange gains or losses for income tax purposes—and do not treat the supply of foreign currencies in exchange for goods and services as a separately taxable supply for VAT purposes—bitcoin should be treated in the same manner, if the objective is to achieve neutrality.[21]

For this reason, the Court of Justice of the European Union (CJEU) in the *Hedqvist* case[22] took the view that the exchange of traditional currencies for units of bitcoin and "non-traditional currencies, that is to say, currencies other than those that are legal tender in one or more countries, in so far as those currencies have been accepted by the parties to a transaction as an alternative to legal tender and have no purpose other than to be a means of payment" and vice versa in return for payment of a spread fee is a financial transaction and thus VAT exempt under Article 135(1)(e) of the EU VAT Directive—despite the explicit reference in that provision to "currency, bank notes and coins *used as legal tender*" (emphasis added).[23] It should be noted that the CJEU's decision only concerned exchange transactions between bitcoin and traditional currencies (Swedish kroner, in this case), and that the Court's reasoning can be extended only to cryptoassets that have been subjectively accepted by the parties to a transaction as an alternative to legal tender and objectively have no purpose other than to be a means of payment.[24] The judgement does not provide any further guidance as to which other cryptoassets "have no purpose other than to be a means of payment" and should thus be treated as money for EU VAT purposes.[25] This means that hybrid tokens such as Ether would presumably not fall within the scope of the EU VAT exemption, even as such tokens are increasingly accepted as a means of payment outside their respective platforms.[26] For example, Overstock.com[27] and More Stamps Global[28] now accept all major alt-coins for purchases made on their websites, which includes hybrid tokens such as Ethereum and Qtum.

The payment/barter distinction similarly applies in the context of direct taxation. For income and capital gains tax purposes, the supply of money in exchange for goods or services in a transaction does not constitute a separate transaction giving rise to a separate gain or loss calculation when money is used as a medium of exchange. In contrast, where numismatic money or money that is an investment article is exchanged for other goods or services, it is often treated as a barter transaction such that gains or losses for income or capital gains tax purposes are computed separately in respect of the disposal of the numismatic or investment article money (treated as a property) by a person, as well as that of the goods or services by the counterparty.[29] The income and capital gains tax laws of many jurisdictions also contain special rules relating to the recognition and taxation of gains and losses from currency transactions, which may trigger the recognition of gains and losses for tax purposes in the absence of a disposal event. The classification of cryptoassets as money as opposed to property under domestic income and capital gains tax legislation could therefore also have an impact on when gains or losses in relation to such cryptoassets are taxed.

Most jurisdictions currently treat cryptoassets as property as opposed to money for income and capital gains tax purposes, even when the cryptoasset is used as a means of exchange for goods or services. For example, the United States Internal Revenue Service (IRS) treats all cryptoassets as properties and therefore all transactions involving cryptoassets are treated as barter transactions for federal income tax purposes.[30] Similarly, the Australian Tax Office (ATO) does not consider cryptocurrencies[31] to be foreign currencies for income tax purposes,[32] and treats the use of cryptoassets to obtain goods or services as a capital gains tax event on which capital gains or losses in respect of the cryptoasset are to be recognized (or ordinary income, if the disposal is part of the business carried on by the disposer).[33] On the other hand, the UK's Her Majesty's Revenue & Customs (HMRC) appears to accept that bitcoins and similar cryptocurrencies should be treated as currency for non-individual income tax purposes, and therefore, when accepted by businesses as payment for goods or services, the business should account for profits or losses on exchange movements between its functional currency and the cryptocurrency based on the general rules on foreign exchange.[34]

There is the additional question of whether there is a need to maintain consistency in the classification of cryptoassets as money or property for both income or capital gains tax and VAT purposes. In Australia's case, for instance, certain cryptoassets are treated as currency for VAT purposes as a result of recent legislative changes,[35] but not for income tax purposes. The ATO takes the view that the legislative context and purpose of the rules on foreign exchange gains and losses for income tax purposes require currency to be "monetary unit recognized and adopted by the laws of any other sovereign State as the means for discharging monetary obligations for all transactions and payments in a sovereign State."[36]. This means that, for Australian income tax purposes, a taxpayer that receives a cryptoasset as a medium of exchange for goods or services provided must include the arm's length Australian dollar value of the transaction in calculating assessable income, and must also account for income or capital gains tax on any gain or loss due to fluctuations in the price of the cryptoasset between the time of acquisition and the time of disposal of the cryptoasset.[37]

There is something unsatisfactory about treating a cryptocurrency used in a single transaction differently depending on the tax type involved—if a cryptoasset was in fact used as a medium of exchange, then to treat it otherwise for the purposes of a particular tax type will require a specific policy justification for such deviation. Whatever the reason is for rejecting a cryptoasset as money, be it because it is not issued by a government or not widely accepted enough (whatever that standard entails) as a medium of exchange by the general public, the same reason applies regardless of whether the transaction is being analyzed for income or capital gains tax or for VAT purposes. If a cryptoasset is treated as a property or chattel for income tax purposes because it is not widely accepted enough by the general public as a medium of exchange, then there is no reason it should not be similarly treated as anything other than a barter exchange for VAT purposes.

More important, however, it is the underlying policy consistency—and thus neutrality—that matters. In other words, even if a cryptoasset is treated in the same way—either as money or property—for *both* income tax and VAT purposes, it does not mean that the tax consequences thereof should also be the same. For instance, where a cryptoasset is treated as money for both VAT and income tax, a transaction involving such a cryptoasset should not lead to a separate VAT liability, whereas for income tax purposes parties to the transaction may be required to recognize an exchange gain (or loss) and accordingly be liable to tax on that gain (or receive a deduction for the loss). This is the appropriate outcome, as VAT and income tax have different policy objectives—that is, in the case of VAT, to tax final household consumption (of which there is none simply from exchanging or holding a means of payment) and, in the case of income tax, to tax any net accretion to wealth where a broad definition of income is applied. Conversely, where a cryptoasset is treated as property—and a transaction involving such a cryptoasset is thus treated as barter such as is the case in the United States for instance, the tax consequences are appropriately different for U.S. income tax purposes (gains/loss recognition as discussed previously) and—absent a federal VAT—state sales tax purposes (cryptocurrencies not being separately subject to sales tax as intangible property, which state sales taxes typically do not tax).[38]

B. Securities Tokens

A cryptoasset that is classified as property instead of money could also, depending on the rights embodied therein, serve as securities.[39] To the extent that a jurisdiction aligns its definition of "securities" for both tax and regulatory purposes—whether by statute or through judicial interpretation—the ongoing discussions on whether cryptoassets should be classified as securities for regulatory purposes will also be relevant in determining its domestic tax treatment of cryptoassets. However, given that financial regulations have different objectives—such as investor protection—than tax laws, it would be necessary to separately examine the rationale behind the different tax treatment accorded to securities and how tax laws ought to apply to cryptoassets that have security-like features.

Securities transactions are typically exempt from VAT. Interest payable on a debt comprises compensation for time value of money, a risk premium to cover the risk of loan default, as well as implicit fees representing part of the costs incurred by the lender, such as labor and overheads, in issuing and servicing the loan. While in particular the latter component of interest should arguably be subject to VAT, most VAT systems nonetheless exempt transactions involving debt due to difficulties in quantifying the implicit fees embedded in margin-based supplies.[40] The issuance or supply of equity securities, on the other hand, are typically VAT-exempt transactions on the basis that dividends constitute a return on investment—that is, a mere consequence of ownership as opposed to consideration for a supply—and therefore should not be included in the consumption tax base.

For these reasons, in order for a supply to be exempt from VAT as a security transaction, what is being transferred must necessarily involve a right of ownership over a company or a debt claim against the company.[41] Similarly, the issuance or supply of any cryptoasset should, to the extent that it involves the transfer of a right of ownership over the issuing company or a debt claim against the company, be exempt from VAT. This would obviously preclude utility tokens, which are effectively prepayments for goods or services and confer on their holders neither a right of ownership over, nor a debt claim against, the company.

However, it could be argued that the supply of a hybrid token that is both a debt token and a utility token should nevertheless be exempt from VAT. If the underlying justification for exempting the supply of debt securities is based on the administrative difficulties in quantifying the implicit fees in margin-based supplies, a part of the consideration paid for such a hybrid token will always be attributable to the time value of money, even if part of the consideration serves to prepay goods or services.

On the other hand, there are less compelling reasons for a hybrid token that is both an equity token and a utility token to be exempt from VAT. Such a token could have been acquired for purposes other than investment, that is, as prepayment of goods and services, which should rightly be included in the consumption tax base. The difficulty lies in the fact that a person could well have acquired such a token with an investment purpose. The question then is whether the subjective purpose of the purchaser in such a case should be of relevance in determining if the supply should be exempt from VAT. Taking, for instance, the CJEU's long-standing approach to dealing with complex transactions as a guiding principle, the starting point of the analysis would be to identify, as a matter of fact and having regard to all relevant circumstances of the transaction, the "essential features" of that transaction as viewed from the viewpoint of "a typical customer" investing in or acquiring such assets.[42]

For income tax purposes, passive income derived from securities, such as dividends and interest, are usually taxable in the place where the economic activity giving rise to its payment occurs, as opposed to passive income from non-securities, such as non-immovable property rent and royalty, the taxing right of which generally accrues to the state in which the recipient of the income is resident. These types of incomes are also often subject to different tax rates. The classification of a cryptoasset as a security or non-security, and in the case of a security, as debt or equity, therefore also has important income tax consequences. However, compared to VAT, there are fewer concerns in relation to the income tax treatment of passive income arising from hybrid tokens, since such income arises from the security features of the token, and its nature will not be affected by the fact that the token also serves as a means of payment in its native ecosystem or in the broader economy.[43]

C. Asset-Backed Tokens or Stable Coins

Blockchain technology enhances the divisibility of valuable assets in the real world, such as real estate and precious metals, by allowing investors to acquire a fractional ownership in such assets, thus increasing the liquidity of illiquid assets and lowering entry barriers for potential investors. The ability to invest in particular assets through non-fungible tokens further encourages the tokenization of real world assets.[44]

The holders of a non-fungible token that represents a specific asset are effectively co-owners of the asset, and therefore the tax treatment of any payments arising from ownership of the token should be the same as that of the income arising from the underlying asset. Thus, if the owners of a token representing a specific piece of real estate receive payments that are funded by rental income arising from the real estate, such payments should be taxed as rental income in the hands of the owners and not as distributions of business profit, even if the company operating the blockchain keeps a proportion of the rental income. On the other hand, if the tokens are fungible and represent a fractional ownership of an underlying non-homogenous pool of asset, then any distributions to token owners would be more akin to a distribution of profits by a fund. In such cases, the question arises as to whether such profits should retain their underlying nature or whether they should be seen as a distribution of business income.

The classification of an asset-backed token itself as goods or services could have VAT implications. For one, the place of taxation rules under VAT laws are usually different for goods and services. Goods are usually considered as being supplied where they are physically delivered or made available, whereas the place where services are considered to be supplied is usually determined depending on the type of service or circumstances of the supply, with reference to the place of residence and/or establishment of the supplier, the customer, or where actual delivery takes place, depending on the nature of the service being supplied. If the supply of a token is treated as a supply of services regardless of the nature of the token,[45] and the default place of taxation rule points to the location of the supplier, tokens that represent assets located in Country A supplied by a person with a business of fixed establishment in Country B (and with no relations to Country A whatsoever) will be Country B instead of Country A. Conversely, where the default place of taxation rule is customer location, the challenge will be for the jurisdiction where the customer is located to know that a taxable transaction has occurred, and to be able to collect tax in relation to that transaction. It is noteworthy in this respect that the OECD VAT/GST Guidelines—the only currently existing international standard with respect to the territoriality of VAT systems—do not explicitly consider transactions in cryptoassets.[46]

It is also worth highlighting that tokenization potentially has an impact on stamp duty or similar transfer taxes. Since many jurisdictions impose transfer taxes or stamp duties on securities and other assets, the collection of these taxes and duties could easily be avoided if the transfer of the tokenized forms of securities and assets are not similarly taxable. Neutrality requires the transfer of a tokenized asset or security to be subject to such duty/tax if the transfer of the underlying asset or security represented by the token is taxable.

III. Taxing Increases in Value of Cryptoassets and Other Specific Transactions

A. Disposal Gains

Like the taxation of gains from any other asset, one of the key considerations in the tax treatment of gains from cryptoassets depends on the characterization of those gains as capital or income. Currently, most jurisdictions do not take into consideration how a cryptoasset is classified in determining the appropriate tax treatment, but instead merely look at whether the owner engages in a trade or business, since a token—whether it is a utility token, payment token, or asset token—is capable of being held on capital or revenue account depending on the circumstances. The remainder of this section discusses the common ways in which cryptoassets are acquired.

In terms of timing, taxing gains on cryptoassets on a mark-to-market basis may be attractive to tax administrations during times when the crypto market is doing well, but is tantamount to taxing the paper profits of the taxpayer and would also be problematic for administrative reasons. Apart from the administrative resources required to perform valuation on an annual basis, the tendency for prices of cryptoassets to fluctuate significantly means that tax administrations may well be collecting taxes in one year and refunding it in the next. From a taxpayer's perspective, a liability to pay tax before disposal of the asset can create cash-flow issues and force the holder to dispose of the cryptoasset in order to pay the tax due.

As such, adopting a realization or disposition basis to the taxation of gains on cryptoassets, such that tax liability arises only where the cryptoasset is exchanged for cash or some other goods or services, would be practically more realistic. The difference between a disposition basis and a realization basis is that gains are also taxed when a cryptoasset is exchanged for a like asset in the former case but not in the latter, and thus a realization basis of taxation has additional advantages from an administrative point of view since the cryptoasset acquired has the same tax cost as the cryptoasset disposed. However, there are nonetheless challenges in taxing such exchanges. First, it would be difficult to determine the selling price of each cryptoasset in a token-to-token exchange if it takes place on a peer-to-peer basis or on a direct trading cryptocurrency exchange platform, and no cryptocurrency exchange has exchange rates for both cryptoassets. Second, the cash-flow problem remains for the owners of cryptoassets since they would still be forced to sell the newly exchanged cryptoassets for traditional currencies to discharge their tax liabilities.[47]

It is also worth discussing some of the challenges in valuing cryptoassets. As already mentioned, it is hard to ascribe a value to a cryptoasset that does not have a ready market price. Even if a cryptoasset is accepted on a trading platform or by a broker, crypto exchanges determine exchange rates independently based on the supply and demand needs of their respective users as well as their respective trading volumes, which means exchange rates can vary from exchange to exchange, and therefore tax administrations will need to consider which exchange or exchanges will be relied upon in determining the open market price of a particular cryptoasset. Moreover, unless a cryptoasset is a non-fungible token or NFT, the fungibility of a cryptoasset would require the stipulation of an appropriate method of recovering its cost basis. A taxpayer could avoid the application of the usual accounting methods of last-in-first out (LIFO) or first-in-first-out (FIFO) through the use of multiple wallets for purchasing different lots of the same cryptoasset, and selectively choosing a certain wallet to pay from as a tax mitigating strategy.

B. Mining and Forging

Blockchains currently achieve distributed consensus by one of two main methods: proof-of-work or proof-of-stake.[48]

In a proof-of-work system, miners are rewarded with new coins (known as block rewards), and in some cases fees, for solving complex algorithms as part of the process of verifying the transactions within a block (a process known as hashing). This work is performed by specialized computing equipment powered by electricity. The mining process is reportedly very energy intensive.[49] The likelihood of success in solving the algorithms depends on the miner's "hash rate," which can be increased through the acquisition and use of more and better mining equipment or through participation in "mining pools."[50] Conversely, in a proof-of-stake system, validators "stake" certain numbers of crypto units by holding such units in a special staking wallet—essentially holding such units in escrow—in return for a chance to be selected to validate transactions through the generation of a new block and receive fees (and in some cases, cryptoassets) in return—a process also known as "forging." If a forger validates a transaction that turns out to be fraudulent, its stake will be forfeited. The proof-of-stake system is believed by some to be superior to the proof-of-work system due to, inter alia, its lower adverse environmental impact and its ability to verify blocks of transactions faster, thereby overcoming the scaling difficulties faced by proof-of-work blockchains.

1. Proof-of-Work

One of the key benefits of distributed ledger technology according to blockchain proponents is the elimination of the need for trusted intermediaries and the associated costs for maintaining such trust. This is achieved through the decentralization of functions traditionally performed by such intermediaries. This is particularly evident through the hashing function performed by the miners, which serves to verify transactions, ensures the integrity of the blockchain—collectively substituting for the role performed by traditional intermediaries. However, decentralization could also lead to income tax base erosion, since most jurisdictions impose a requirement that gains be derived in the course of a business or profit-seeking endeavor before they are subject to income tax. Whereas traditional intermediaries such as payment service providers are quite clearly carrying on a business and their profits taxable, the activities of miners in a proof-of-work blockchain ecosystem may or may not amount to the carrying on of a business under the tax rules of different jurisdictions.

To overcome this difficulty, a number of jurisdictions, including the United States,[51] specifically treat tokens derived from mining by any person as income in all circumstances. However, other jurisdictions, such as the UK, Singapore,

South Africa, and Jersey, rely on existing tax law principles and impose income tax on block rewards from mining only if it is carried out in the course of a trade or business. The Netherlands draws a distinction between mining carried out by corporations and that carried out by individuals—block rewards derived in the former case are always treated as income, while those derived in the latter case will only be subject to tax if structurally positive results are achieved from the performance of work that goes beyond mere speculation.

While the issue of whether an activity conducted by a person amounts to a trade or business for income tax purposes is certainly not a new one, the unique nature of crypto mining does create additional complexities. In determining the level of crypto mining activities necessary to amount to the carrying on of a trade or business by a person, as opposed to mere speculation or hobby, it would not be possible to simply rely on an intention to profit, since it would be irrational for one to engage in crypto mining without the hope of making a profit. The Dutch approach of imposing income tax on individual miners only if there are structurally positive results achieved through the performance of work that goes beyond that of a speculative venture does not quite answer the threshold question of *what* constitutes such structurally positive results. Should the combined power of the mining equipment owned and operated by a single taxpayer, plus that of all the mining equipment in a mining pool to which that taxpayer belongs, be used as a bright-line test in determining whether the threshold has been reached?[52] Reliance on a case-by-case factual approach would be equally unsatisfactory. For example, would the purchasing of additional mining equipment by a single miner be sufficient to amount to a trade or business? Does the processing power of the equipment purchased have a bearing on the analysis? Does mere participation in a mining pool evince an intention to engage in a trade or business, and if not, will the size or hashing rate of the mining pool affect the answer? Given these difficulties, there is arguably a case to be made for an irrebuttable presumption treating all miners to be in it for profit and therefore carrying on a business, even if the miner is an individual who had only purchased one mining device that would otherwise be considered insufficient to amount to carrying on of a business.[53] At the very least, this is an area where more detailed taxpayer guidance is needed.

The existence of a business or otherwise also raises interesting international tax considerations as it affects the allocation of taxing rights on block rewards amongst jurisdictions. This is because, where a tax treaty applies, the domestic law of the jurisdiction applying the treaty will generally determine if there is a business,[54] and accordingly, whether there is an enterprise and whether the block reward constitutes business or other profit.[55] Under current international tax conventions, the resident state typically has taxing rights over all profits of its residents that are not covered by a specific provision of the tax treaty. On the other hand, the source of business profit is determined by reference to the location of the assets used and activities undertaken to generate the business profit, that is, the source state has taxing rights over such profit to the extent that it is attributable to a permanent establishment (PE) that the miner has in the source state. Since the assets and activities involved in generating block rewards are the mining equipment, an argument could be made to the effect that the source of such block rewards should rightly be attributed to the location(s) where mining equipment are located. Consideration should then be given to how taxing rights ought to be allocated amongst source states where a miner has equipment in multiple locations and/or is a participant in a mining pool, for example, possibly based on objective criteria such as the aggregate hashing power in each jurisdiction that contributed to the block reward.

This approach toward determining taxing rights could also be criticized in light of the principle of taxation where value is created,[56] in that it may be insufficiently taking into account the value created by those whose cryptoasset transactions form the subject of the verification process resulting in the block reward. While the nexus and allocation rules in the current international tax system have already been identified as inadequate or at least ill-suited in addressing value creation arising from certain digital business models, there is as of yet no international consensus on how such rules should be revised to address the value creation issue more generally, or in relation to taxing block rewards in particular.

The VAT/GST treatment of cryptoassets earned from mining also raises questions, with the approaches of jurisdictions in this regard again varying. UK HMRC consider cryptoassets earned from Bitcoin mining activities to be generally outside the scope of VAT on the basis that there is an "insufficient link between any services provided and any consideration received."[57] Therefore, according to the HMRC, Bitcoin mining activities do not constitute economic activities for UK VAT purposes. The UK tax authorities also consider any service provided by miners in verifying payment transactions through the mining process to be an exempt supply for VAT purposes under Article 135(1)(d) of the EU VAT Directive. The German Federal Ministry of Finance similarly does not consider the supply of services by miners to be taxable supplies, but for a different reason—the absence of an identifiable service recipient indicates that mining services are not provided in the context of an exchange of services for consideration, and that therefore any new bitcoins earned by miners should not be regarded as consideration for services rendered.[58] On the other hand, tax authorities in other jurisdictions such as Ireland and Jersey are more tentative, taking the view that mining services are out of scope of VAT only if they are not carried out in the course or furtherance of business or economic activity.

It seems difficult to argue that in a blockchain that employs a proof-of-work distributed consensus system, mining activities do not amount to economic activities for VAT purposes due to an insufficient link between the services provided and the consideration received. Indeed, but for the block reward, miners would not have engaged in mining activities in the first place. However, for a miner to owe VAT on particular coins earned, a discernable transaction has to be identified. While arguably all coin or token owners rely to some extent on the work of miners to protect the integrity of the blockchain and therefore receive a benefit from the mining activities, the existence of such a benefit might not be enough to amount to a discernable transaction between the miner and one or more identifiable token- or coin holders.[59]

2. Proof-of-Stake

Given that a proof-of-stake system operates quite differently from a proof-of-work system, a separate analysis should apply in determining the tax treatment of any tokens acquired by forgers for verifying transactions. Unlike miners, who engage in a competitive running of hashing algorithms to validate a block of transactions and could be argued to be engaging in a speculative exercise, forgers essentially are given the right to validate transactions through the creation of a new block on the blockchain through ownership in tokens and their willingness to stake such tokens. In this regard, the operations of forgers are arguably analogous to the work performed by a service provider after a successful bidding exercise. The tokens "staked" by a forger are essentially a refundable deposit for the right to participate in a contract. Upon successful selection, the forger performs the service of verifying the transactions. In this regard, the work performed by forgers in a proof-of-stake system is not speculative, and therefore, any tokens received in return for forging a block should be treated as income for services upon which tax should be paid.

It is unclear whether this distinction between mining and forging is sufficient to lead to a different VAT treatment. On the one hand, there is arguably an even stronger link between the verification services performed by forgers and any fees or tokens received in return. On the other hand, it may still be equally difficult to discern one or more identifiable beneficiaries of a forger's activities for those services to amount to taxable services. Finally, as to whether those services—if they were to be found to exist—performed by forgers should be treated as exempt for VAT purposes, this would depend on the existing policy settings of the VAT system in question and the type of cryptoasset involved. Where payment services are broadly exempt—such as under the EU VAT[60]—the services of forgers is likely to receive the same treatment, whereas the outcome is likely to be different under a more limited exemption system for financial services such as under the Australian GST for instance.

C. Token Airdrops

Token airdrops, which can take place before or in conjunction with an initial coin offering (ICO), are increasingly popular amongst token issuers as a marketing tool.[61] In general terms, a token airdrop is a distribution event during which tokens are "airdropped" into existing wallets without any payment in traditional currency or other cryptoassets in return. Pre-ICO token airdrop exercises are designed to generate awareness and excitement about an upcoming ICO, and often require participants to take certain actions in order to qualify for the free tokens, such as watching an advertisement, signing up for the issuer's Telegram or Twitter account, following certain social media accounts, and/or sharing certain posts on social media. Not all pre-ICO token airdrops necessarily require a positive action on the part of the recipient—for example, tokens are sometimes airdropped into active ERC-20 compatible wallets without the need for wallet owners to take further actions, ostensibly as a useful tool to encourage the mass adoption of a token by the public. Token airdrops that are conducted during an ICO serve a similar marketing purpose by providing an additional incentive—a chance to obtain a free token—for potential investors to subscribe to the tokens during the ICO.

One of the salient questions in relation to the tax treatment of token airdrops is whether the tokens received in an airdrop should be treated as income or windfall in the hands of the recipients. The implications of how such tokens are classified are particularly pronounced in jurisdictions where windfall gains are not subject to tax. The difficulty in drawing a bright-line test in this regard is exacerbated by the varying degrees of participation required in each airdrop exercise in order to qualify for free tokens. On the one hand, one could qualify for airdropped tokens merely by holding a number of tokens in an active compatible wallet.[62] On the other hand, and more commonly, a person qualifies for an airdropped token only after taking a certain course of action, the extent of which could range from the passive following of a Twitter or Telegram account or watching an advertisement to positive actions such as actively sharing a post on social media (with a precondition that the user has a minimum number of followers on that social media channel). Neutrality would require a comparison of each such scenario against its conventional equivalent, though as is often the case for crypto transactions, there might not be a ready conventional equivalent. For example, tokens airdropped after watching an advertisement could be considered analogous to gifts received from attending time-share presentations, but the duration and extent of inconvenience of a time-share presentation is considerably more substantial than that of watching an online advertisement.

The sharing of a post on social media could be compared to social media influencers posting a blog or vlog entry in return for free samples and merchandise, although it seems more likely that social media influencers do this as a full-time or at least stand-alone occupation, in contrast to the typical recipient in a token airdrop.

Even if tokens received pursuant to an airdrop are treated as taxable income, there remains the practical issue of valuing these tokens, which typically do not have a readily available open or fair market value. Tokens that are airdropped before an ICO are likely to have no value, since the value of a non-asset-backed token is derived from network effects, with the whole purpose of the token airdrop being to generate such network effect. Therefore, to impose tax on airdropped tokens at the time of receipt is likely to result in effectively no tax collected. This raises then another question: Should a more expansive view of the value created by the recipients of a token airdrop be adopted, so that consideration must be given to more than what was originally done by the recipient, if at all, to qualify for that initial token? If the value of the token is inextricably tied to network effects, the mere fact that an airdrop participant holds and uses that token generates value that results in the appreciation of the token, which raises questions of whether the subsequent gain in value should be treated as income or capital in nature. The answer is probably a mixture of both, but it would be practically difficult to ascertain what proportion of the amount of the gain is attributable to the network effect contributed by the taxpayer, and what is attributable to capital appreciation more generally.

Similar questions arise for VAT purposes, although the issue might often be "solved" through the operation of the VAT registration threshold. To the extent that airdropped tokens are consideration for a supply (for instance, of advertising services) by the recipient of the token, the total value of tokens received by a single recipient—subject, of course, to the same valuation difficulties as highlighted above—might not exceed the VAT registration threshold, in which case the person will not be liable to VAT on the tokens received. A person who is already registered for VAT on the other hand is likely to be liable for VAT on those tokens, unless the activity in relation to which the tokens were received is completely separate and unrelated to the activity for which the person is registered. More generally, airdropped tokens are likely to be viewed as within the scope of VAT where there is some positive action required by the recipient of the token in return for which the token is received; conversely, where the recipient receives the airdropped token merely because that person holds a social media account or relevant crypto wallet, such tokens are less likely to be seen as consideration and therefore not subject to VAT in the hands of the token recipient.

D. Hard Forks

A hard fork involves a change to the software of a cryptoasset that is incompatible with older versions of the software. A lack of consensus in the community on adopting the new protocol following the upgrade results in the creation of a new chain and the retention of the old one, and accordingly, the creation of a new token. Token owners are typically issued an identical number of the new tokens arising from a hard fork. In theory, the value of the original token falls after a hard fork, while the new token acquires a new value. Often, one of the two tokens will eventually fall out of favor, with its value being extinguished, but this is not necessarily the case. The 2017 hard fork in the Bitcoin block chain due to an increase in block size from 1 megabyte to 8 megabytes for scalability reasons is an example where both the original token and the new token Bitcoin Cash (BCH) continue to exist post-event.

The fact that the creation of a new token in a hard fork is not necessarily a zero-sum game means that there may be a net gain or loss to a token holder at the time of the hard fork. The question is whether the receipt of the new tokens should be treated as a taxable event, and if so, how the value of the newly issued tokens ought to be ascertained. In this regard, one might find it intuitive to compare the issuance of new tokens pursuant to a hard fork to a bonus issue in a corporate finance context. Since bonus shares are paid out of cash reserves and the value of the company as well as a stockholder's percentage ownership in the company remain the same even though the total number of shares issued and owned increases after a bonus issue, bonus shares are in fact a notional reward that in itself does not result in net gains to stockholders—although bonus issues could trigger increased market participation that has a short-term positive effect on the market price of the shares. In contrast, the new tokens issued through a hard fork are sui generis and distinct from the original tokens, and therefore it would be practically difficult if not impossible to ascertain the value of the new tokens, and any decrease in the value of the original tokens from any erosion in network effect due to the forking event.

At least one jurisdiction has explicitly considered the issue of how new tokens arising from a hard fork ought to be taxed. The ATO has issued specific guidance on the tax treatment of new tokens received by a taxpayer as a result of a hard fork. Where the original tokens were held as investment, the taxpayer will not be treated as having made a gain at the time of receipt, but will instead be treated as having made a capital gain at the time of disposal. On the other hand, if the original tokens were held in a business carried on by the taxpayer, the new tokens issued will be treated as trading stock and must be brought to account at the end of the income year. In other words, the nature of the new tokens—whether it is income or capital—depends on the purpose for which the original tokens were held by the taxpayer. Those who receive new tokens pursuant to a hard fork in respect of original tokens held on trading account will therefore have a practical problem of valuing the new tokens.

The intervention of a hard fork does not, in and of itself, seem to raise any VAT consequences in the hands of the tokenholders in the absence of a relevant transaction.

E. Employment Remuneration

The general approach of countries with pay-as-you-go (PAYG) or pay-as-you-earn (PAYE) arrangements is that cryptoassets paid by employers to employees as remuneration are subject to withholding at the time of payment. For example, the IRS requires "the fair market value of virtual currency paid as wages [to be] subject to federal income tax withholding."[63] Similarly, the Netherlands requires any cryptoasset paid by an employer to an employee to be converted to euros as at the date that the payment-in-kind is made available to the recipient.[64] The ATO adopts a two-track approach—where there is a valid salary sacrifice arrangement under which an employee agrees to accept cryptoassets as remuneration instead of Australian dollars, the cryptocurrency is taxed to the employer as a fringe benefit, and in the absence of such an arrangement, the employee is taxed and the employer is required to withhold tax on the "Australian dollar value of the cryptocurrency it pays to the employee"[65] under the PAYG system.

The main challenge here is again one of valuation of cryptoassets that do not have a readily available open or fair market value. In such cases, employers would face challenges in determining a proper amount of tax to withhold. This is not an entirely new problem—employers have been known to provide employees with all types of benefits-in-kind that do not necessarily have an available open or fair market value. To alleviate this problem, tax laws often provide for *de minimis* fringe benefits exemptions. In some cases, a different basis could be defined by legislation in substitution of the open or fair market value—for example, a tax on shares in a private company with limited history of transactions could be assessed based on the net book value of the company in the absence of open or fair market value. However, where the value of a cryptoasset is derived principally, if not exclusively, on network effects, there is no inherent underlying value that could act as a satisfactory substitute to its open market price. Where an employer remunerates its employees with payment tokens that it issues, there is the additional question of whether such tokens should be treated as benefit-in-kind or actual payment in a foreign currency.

Another question in relation to the tax treatment of cryptoassets received as employment remuneration is whether cryptoassets issued by crypto companies to their employees be treated in a similar manner as employee stock options and share awards. Employee stock options and share awards are designed to incentivize employees and align their economic interest with those of the firm's. Equity tokens and tokens backed by equities in an employer company given to employees arguably have the same function, but the same argument may not be as readily extendable to other types of tokens issued by the employer.

F. Token Pre-financing

Token pre-financing refers to the raising of funds necessary to create tokens and decentralized infrastructure (including decentralized applications or dApps) during the incubation period of a crypto project.[66] It is essentially a bootstrapping exercise, during which investors contribute traditional currencies or cryptoassets and, in return, acquire the right to subscribe to tokens (at a predetermined discounted price) that will be developed and created with the funds raised. Investors in a token pre-financing exercise are effectively investing in the success of the underlying technology of a company by participating in the risks and rewards of the functional utility or proprietary money supplies that will form the economic activities of the company in the future, as opposed to ownership of the start-up company which is tied to the success of the start-up itself.

From a taxation point of view, there are two sets of concerns. The first involves the appropriate tax treatment of the proceeds from token pre-financing in the hands of the fundraiser. The second relates to the characterization of the cryptoassets as income or capital in nature in the hands of the subscriber.

The economic objective of token pre-financing is analogous to that of reward-based crowdfunding. In determining the proper tax treatment of the proceeds in the hands of the crypto developer raising the funds, it is necessary to consider the specific financing instrument used by, and legal arrangement entered into between, the parties. The Simple Agreement for Future Tokens (SAFT)[67] is one of the instruments used by crypto developers and investors for token pre-financing, under which the crypto developer promises to issue a certain amount of tokens in a future ICO to the investor. Once the predetermined threshold amount has been raised during the pre-financing rounds, there is no recourse for an investor under a SAFT deal if an ICO does not in fact occur. A SAFT arrangement is therefore essentially a prepaid forward contract.[68] In the alternative, an investor could acquire a call option to purchase tokens at a predetermined price upon the occurrence of a future token sale.

Where the future token will be a utility token, the amount invested at the token pre-financing stage should be treated as prepayment of goods or services for tax purposes. However, as with many conventional crowdfunding exercises, the issuer in a token pre-financing exercise is often a start-up and, in many jurisdictions, there is a requirement for a person to be carrying on a business before any income is taxable. In a coin issuance, the issuer often puts forth a white paper that sets out, inter alia, an existing problem that the project seeks to solve, the proposed blockchain product and architecture that will form the solution to this problem, as well as details on the token, such as the number of tokens to be issued, how they will be used, etc. It would probably be possible to ascertain through a perusal of the white paper whether an issuer intends to profit from the exercise and whether there is a business.

If the future token will be a payment token, there is the additional question of whether the transaction is equivalent to the future supply of "money," which should be exempt or excluded for VAT purposes. As discussed earlier, there are good reasons to treat tokens as equivalent to money for VAT purposes if they are subjectively accepted by the parties to a transaction as an alternative to legal tender and objectively have no purpose other than to be a means of payment. However, there is no guarantee, at the pre-financing stage, that a token would be effectively accepted by parties as a medium of exchange or indeed even materialize at all. As such, it would not be appropriate to treat the supply of future payment tokens as money for VAT purposes.

Given that an investment made by an investor in a token pre-financing exercise is similar to any other venture capital investment, except that the investor is participating in the risks and rewards of the technology developed by the start-up company, and not the company itself, the general tax treatment of gains derived by an investor from the disposal of such tokens—whether such gains should be taxed as investment income or capital gains—should follow. Where a jurisdiction provides for preferential tax treatment for venture capital, consideration should be given to the policy question of whether such treatment should be extended to token pre-financing.

G. Token Burning

A number of token issuers[69] have adopted the practice of "token burning" as a means to return value to investors without paying a dividend, usually for regulatory purposes. This involves the issuer company regularly buying tokens back from the market and burning them. In theory, this should result in an increase in value to the remaining tokens due to a diminished supply as well as an increase in ownership percentage with each buyback. There are two sets of gains arising from each round of token burn—a gain realized by the investor in respect of the tokens bought by the company at prevailing market price, as well as an unrealized gain due to an appreciation in the price of the remaining tokens as a result of the deflationary measure.

Although the mechanism of token burning is broadly similar to a share buyback followed by share cancellation, it should be borne in mind that the tokens involved may or may not bear rights similar to those of shares. For example, BNB, the native token of Binance, is essentially a utility token that provides markdowns on and rebates for charges incurred on crypto-to-crypto exchanges on the Binance platform. Of course, where the token involved is a token backed by equities or an equity token, the tax treatment of the realized gains from a round of token burning should be similar to that for share redemptions. Some jurisdictions, such as Canada,[70] deem the gains derived by shareholders from a share redemption as dividends as opposed to capital gains, which are usually taxed more preferentially.

However, where the token involved is not a pure equity token, then the analogy to a share redemption would be less appropriate. Even though token burns are usually contemplated by crypto developers from the very start with an express objective of creating a positive cycle of appreciation through a reduction in the supply of tokens, it does not preclude a person from acquiring the tokens for the functional utility supply that they represent. Using the Binance example, a person could well have purchased a number of BNB for the purpose of using them to pay for crypto-to-crypto exchanges on the platform for lower fees. In any case, the gains derived from any tokens burned in such a case could not be said to have been a tax mitigating or avoidance measure by the issuer to recharacterize a distribution of profits to its investors by adopting the form of a return of capital. The fact that the purchaser knew about one or more scheduled token burns for the tokens purchased does not necessarily turn these tokens into objects of investment.

There appears to be no good reason to tax unrealized gains accruing to tokenholders as a result of an appreciation in value of the remaining tokens due to a token-burning exercise. Even though the number of tokens that can be issued are fixed and hard-coded, which makes the issuance of additional tokens in the future technically impossible (as compared to the share capital of a company that can always be increased with the necessary approval), there are other factors that can affect the price of the remaining tokens between the time of the token burn and the time of eventual disposal by the investor. As such, a deemed realization of the gains in respect of the remaining tokens would be inappropriate.

IV. Conclusion

This chapter attempted to highlight some of the difficulties tax systems face in achieving neutrality when determining the tax treatment of cryptoassets using existing income tax and VAT principles and concepts. In doing so it also highlighted some of the limitations posed by those principles and concepts when faced with new technologies and new business models these have enabled. In this respect, it also illustrated the wider challenges posed to the international tax system by digitalization in the presence of user participation and network effects. As highlighted in the introduction to this chapter, the broader question of whether the tax treatment of transactions involving cryptoassets ought to be guided by the principle of neutrality depends on each jurisdiction's perception of the desirability (or lack thereof) of these assets and the underlying technology, but even where neutrality is considered to be the appropriate approach, it may not be straightforward or even possible to achieve due to limitations posed by existing income tax and VAT principles and concepts or more simply the lack of a "conventional equivalent" for some of these transactions.

Although not the focus of this chapter, the real and serious practical difficulties faced by tax administrations in enforcing tax laws in relation to blockchain transactions should not be forgotten. These difficulties can in and of themselves have a significant impact on tax neutrality, as they may provide strong incentives for taxpayers to adopt distributed ledger technology to carry out transactions or rearrange their business models. One of the main challenges tax administrations face in relation to blockchains is "pseudonymity." Transactions in an open blockchain are transparent but remain anonymous until the address is matched to an identity. This is challenging given the lack of a central register for wallet holders. This problem is exacerbated by the fact that a single user can hold multiple wallets and/or use multiple IP addresses or Tor to anonymize the user's IP address. The emergence of anonymity in open blockchains presents even greater challenges, as the rise of high privacy cryptos, such as Monero, Dash, and Zcash, makes it even more difficult for tax administrations to trace transactions to individuals.[71]

In addition, the traditional response of the international tax system in the face of compliance challenges, which is to rely increasingly on third-party information, may not be as effective in the face of decentralized systems where central authorities and intermediaries play a diminished role in the recording and execution of private transactions. Crypto exchanges, for instance, to which regulators increasingly look to play an enforcement role,[72] will not be able to provide information on peer-to-peer transactions taking place outside of the exchanges, so tax administration will have to rely and invest more in technological tools and solutions to enforce tax laws.[73]

10

Blockchain and Identity Persistence

Alex Marthews[†] and Catherine Tucker[*,‡]

I. Introduction and Definitions

Blockchain technologies are popularly touted as a way to protect individual privacy.[1] Blockchain may indeed help with data security; also, blockchain app developers and theorists, often out of a genuine desire to protect people and their privacy, have devoted considerable efforts to devising ways that the blockchain can be used to verify aspects of a static digital identity. However, these notions of a static, single, and accurate digital identity ignore the reality of how people's identities work, and especially the plural, time-varying, and fictionalizing elements of personal identity. Securing identity from outside discovery and interpretation is important, but privacy covers more territory than securing a static identity.

In this chapter, we chart out ways that people's multiple identities may be affected and undermined by the development of public and unmodifiable ledgers of transactions and contractual undertakings. Following on from this discussion, we apply our clearer model of identity to the blockchain use cases of marriage, money laundering, and criminal justice records, and draw conclusions for regulators, blockchain applications developers, and the general public.

Along the way, we will deal with many new concepts and new technologies, so before we proceed, we offer some definitions and background information about the concepts and technologies we consider.

II. Blockchain

A. What Is Blockchain Technology?

First, we define what it means to say that a mix of "cryptographic proof" and incentives on the blockchain can replace trust and third-party verification.

* *Acknowledgments.* The authors benefited from the comments and assistance of many people while writing this chapter, but especially wish to thank Vipin Bharathan.
† Digital Fourth, Belmont, MA.
‡ MIT Sloan School of Management, MIT, Cambridge, MA.

Cryptoassets. Chris Brummer.

From an economics perspective, blockchain technology implementations tend to have two features in common:

1. A set of shared data: In the case of the well-developed use case of cryptocurrencies, these are digital ledger entries that form an immutable audit trail of all unspent balances and past transactions.
2. An incentive system ("consensus rules") designed to ensure that such shared data can be updated and maintained so as to maintain a record that is consistent between participants in the network.

Think of the shared data as forming a large, "append-only" relational database, where each entry is timestamped and cryptographically linked to all previous entries. Full network participants in a blockchain protocol, sometimes referred to as "nodes," keep a copy of the entire shared data and help broadcast new information to the rest of the network. In systems that rely on "mining" to secure the shared data, a special set of mining nodes also performs wasteful computations—a sunk cost—to make it extremely expensive for an attacker to alter entries in the shared ledger. In a blockchain protocol, the immutability of the records is therefore the result not simply of cryptography, but of the economic incentives targeted at forming and maintaining an honest "consensus" about what the shared data should represent at any moment in time. Participants in a blockchain protocol thus have a strong incentive to collaborate to prevent fraud.

B. What Is the Current State of the Art of Protecting Privacy on Blockchain?

Blockchain technology has often been heralded as a potential means of protecting privacy, because it is a decentralized, trustless system that removes data from the control of a governing authority (Buterin and Weyl, 2018). However, a technology that publishes data for all participants to access in blocks has obvious limitations in how privacy-protective it can be.

Therefore, new technologies have evolved that try to preserve the ability of blockchain to create a trustless consensus by dissociating it from the underlying data it validates. This also has potential efficiency benefits. For example, Zyskind et al. (2015) propose that rather than storing on the blockchain the data itself, organizations can store "pointers to encrypted data." However, "[w]hile this approach is suitable for storage and random queries, it is not very efficient for processing data." They propose methods to "never let a service observe the raw data, but instead, to allow it to run computations directly on the network and obtain the final results." In other words, the individual transactions need not, as they are with an unpruned Bitcoin blockchain, be all visible to all, in order for a consensus ledger to exist; the private cryptocurrency Monero is an instructive example (Khatwani, 2018). "Privacy coins," such as Monero and Dash, focus their efforts on obscuring the connection between a transaction on the blockchain and a particular, static digital identity. Monero does this by explicitly verifying the source of your funds, but including "a handful of decoys" to obscure the funds' origin, a tactic that works much better for isolated transactions than for the kind of repeated patterns of transactions that give rise to a sense of individual identity (Miers, 2019). The most recent solutions, such as Zerocash, do not use decoy transactions, but instead add "new types of transactions that provide a separate privacy-preserving currency, in which transactions reveal neither the payment's origin, destination, or amount."[2]

Other entities, such as the Distributed Identity Foundation, aim to break down the concept of a digital identity into individual "claims" that what they term a "self-sovereign individual" can use in a more layered and controllable way, establishing only the piece of their identity that is most appropriate for the transaction at hand (Braendgaard, 2018). However, the term "self-sovereign individual" obscures significant problems of identity. What is being protected is not "the individual" in itself, but a particular digital identity, which may be attributable to one person or many, may shift over time, and which may contain no accurate information about an individual at all, or at least no information enabling the counterparty to a transaction or a third party to determine that the digital identity in question was legally or morally capable of engaging in the transaction. Even sophisticated identity management schemes on the blockchain can treat these issues as being outside of their scope: for example, (Augot et al., 2017) simply "*assume[s]* [emphasis ours] that [the identity provider] validates a user's real world identity (via a more or less rigorous verification process) and then publishes documents that are correct," and proudly announce as a feature that their system provides "identities that are as indelible as the blockchain itself," rather than confronting the real-world challenges created by indelible, blockchained identities.

Consequently, it is urgent to re-examine the ways in which digital identities, as manifested in the blockchain space, relate to legal and personal, or narrative, identities. We aim to come to a clearer understanding of the risks presented by blockchain technologies as they move beyond cryptocurrencies to a broader set of applications.

III. Digital Identity

We should begin our discussion of identity by noting that "digital identity" is crucial to the operation of blockchain transactions, including both cryptocurrency transactions and smart contracts.

Digital identity comprises a number of different elements:

1. *"registration information"*—copies of a governmental or other officially issued document provided at registration for a service;
2. *"transactional identity"*—the set of facts required to re-authenticate a user before a transaction will be permitted in a particular system at a particular time;
3. *"transaction history"*—the list of transactions in a system over time;
4. *"digital history"*—The combination of transactions conducted in a system and information retained by the system about each user conducting those transactions.

Using these definitions, we may state the following: Though depending on their approach to privacy issues, some cryptoasset exchanges still require no or almost no registration, all define some kind of transactional identity relating to a user, even if not all retain that information. In permissionless public ledger systems, such as Bitcoin, the entire transaction history is public and accessible to any other user (Nakamoto, 2008).

We may conveniently define a person's "digital identity" as the set of digital histories across systems relating to a single legal identity. Especially as instantiated in unmodifiable, public blockchain transaction histories, we argue that digital identities are not simply a documenting or bodying forth of one's nondigital identities, but can, if misused, harm one's sense of narrative identity. Since the work of Bergson before the First World War, philosophers and sociologists have grown used to describing narrative identity as something that can potentially change with every action and interaction (Bergson, 1911), but the conceptualizations of digital identity common in discussions of blockchain technology seem pre-Bergsonian. A digital identity cannot change as if it had never been; it can only be added to. Like a butterfly pinned in a Victorian entomologist's display case, a static and single digital identity is legible, comparable, and useful for automated analysis—but the butterfly is still dead. This kind of digital identity is inimical to notions of the identity in flight, of self-reinvention, or in Christian terms, of being "born again."

The kind of permanent digital identity created in public, unmodifiable blockchain ledgers can be a boon for state control. The more static the representation of identity becomes, the more analyzable it becomes, and therefore the more useful it becomes for the purposes of the state (Scott, 1998). The state needs to document identities for taxation, for law enforcement, and for many other purposes; it needs the ability both to compare identity documents across people at particular points in time, and to compare identity documents for the same person across time. In the "entomologist state," each individual's identity is treated as the reverse of Bergson's: static, unchanging, and controllable. As identity documents have become more digital, they have also become harder to change, either retroactively (Beemyn and Brauer, 2015) or going forward (Donath, 2014); casually conducting financial transactions or traveling under an assumed name used to be unambiguously legal (Sullivan, 2018), but now is less so. Digital identity differs from legal and narrative constructions of identity in another way. Digital identity construction is cheap. Joining a Facebook group has low barriers to entry compared to joining a group in nondigital everyday life, and this difference enables cheaper and much more diverse signaling of affinity with a group. The connection of a greater variety of digital memberships with one legal identity in turn enables the state to develop much more sophisticated profiles, classifying people according to a hundred fields rather than a few. Digital identities allow us "to explore and develop multiple identities rather than to discover a self" (Bauman, 2004); the "opportunities for staging and transforming the self/selves have become nearly limitless" (Abbas and Dervin, 2009); but this exploration comes increasingly at the price of enhancing both state surveillance and the potential for individual citizens to more easily target members of out-groups at scale.

Last, it is routine for elements of your digital identity to be false. It is trivially easy to make false inferences from the avalanche of facts making up the digital identity, so digital identity acts as much as a machine for warping a narrative identity as for keeping it within logical bounds. Your phone may note that it was present at a park at 12:30 p.m. on Saturday, but if your daughter borrowed it to go to the park by herself to watch videos, it has contributed a fact that is not properly connected to you. The search history of your shared home computer may tell you something about the accumulated mishmash of interests in a household. However, it does not enable you to disentangle the threads properly attributed to each individual. This means that aggregated inferential consumer data profiles, such as Acxiom, get even elementary inferences, such as gender, wrong a surprising amount of the time (Neumann et al., 2018).

IV. Legal Identity and Smart Contracts

Your legal identity consists of the official government records about you. These records paint a picture of who you are. The records may in themselves be false in certain ways. There may be unintentional errors. There may be errors that only emerge in retrospect, as in the assignment of a binary gender in a birth certificate to a transperson. There may be records that, while factual, give a false impression of the person they relate to, as with someone falsely convicted of a crime, or truly convicted of a crime such as miscegenation that is now no longer a crime. By omission, your legal record may omit court rulings under seal, such as those involving you as a minor. Under the European Union's new General Data Protection Regulation, or GDPR, the "right to be forgotten" enables individuals to request that information about them in official records, such as bankruptcy proceedings, be eliminated; and if that information is stored in a public blockchain, it may be impossible for that blockchain to comply with GDPR.

Despite all of these limitations to the accuracy of legal identities, the fact that the error rate in your legal identity is lower than for either digital or narrative identities leads society to rely heavily on legal identity and the documents that constitute it.

A careful consideration of "smart contracts" indicates that there are significant clashes between digital identity on the blockchain and legal identity. Smart contracts originated with the intention of being "self-executing"; that is, part of their attraction resided in their ability to function independently of any need for enforcement by external authorities, such as regulatory agency officials, police, or judges; in other words, they are intended to be capable of operating independently of people's legal identities. However, as soon as a cryptoasset transaction or a smart contract has an impact on the real-world income or lives of an individual, it does unavoidably become legally relevant.

We might assume that the digital identity making the transaction, or entering into a contract, is connected to some legal person, whether that be a corporation or an individual, who is further legally entitled to enter into a binding contract. By doing so, even without meaning to, we are making further, broad assumptions about the nature of that legal person—for example, that the legal person is not a child or senile and has not been adjudged to be legally insane. The kinds of registration documents asked for on cryptoasset exchanges would not usually enable exchange administrators to make these kinds of determinations.

Second, even if we assume that the digital identity, as presented, more or less accurately represents the preferences of the underlying legal identity as to what the latter has agreed should happen, there is a further problem. Smart contracts contain within themselves no mechanism whereby their provisions may be updated as the preferences of the contracting parties change. Increasingly, both recommended practice on smart contracts and actual practice have created some processes by which smart contracts can sunset, or where the parties can pre-specify in predefined cases that the contract will become invalid and be replaced by another contract with different terms ((Governatori et al., 2018), highlighting Solidity smart contracts in Ethereum, which have a *selfdestruct* contract operation).

Neither of these tactics, however, resolve the problem at issue, that smart contracts achieve reliability and predictability at the cost of preventing mechanisms within the life of the contract that are intended to situate the contract within broader legal doctrines and social norms, and that are themselves intended to enable a just reappraisal of contractual terms. In the cryptoasset space, it is a matter of deep uncertainty in most countries as to what kinds of transactions are legal. Some countries, such as Bangladesh, Bolivia, China, Colombia, Russia, Taiwan, Thailand, and Vietnam, have outlawed Bitcoin transactions, rendering Bitcoin transactions as part of a smart contract legal at their beginning, pre-ban, and illegal at their end, post-ban. However, there are many more problems than simply the underlying cryptocurrency transaction being made illegal over the course of a contract. As noted in (Mik, 2017), smart contracts assume that "a particular sum has in fact become due." "Tamper-proof enforcement" requires that the initial code be bug-free; but the code may malfunction, leading to incorrect execution of the contract. The smart contract itself may not accurately reflect the parties' agreement or their original intent. Last, and most importantly, a tamper-proof smart contract "requires that all possible events that may occur during its lifetime and affect its operation be anticipated," even where it may become "commercially absurd or illegal." As Governatori et al. (2018) note, smart contracts "mak[e] it difficult to implement legal remedies that reverse the outcome of illegal transactions." They raise the possibility that smart contracts could be written so as to build in "learning mechanisms," but that "this would go beyond the state of the art." Covering all eventualities may require longer smart contracts, introducing a greater probability of error.

Beyond this, the more that smart contract terms are expressed in self-executing and standardized terms, the further their terms diverge from natural language that the humans on either side of the contract might use to understand what they have agreed to. It is currently not possible to translate the natural language of a contract into code via automated systems, and programmers are not trained well enough in law to create templates that will adequately reflect the intent of both parties. Vice versa, lawyers are not typically trained enough in code to produce code that translates legal requirements adequately.

To deal with some of these issues, Marino and Juels (2016) propose standard smart contract code that covers issues such as termination, rescission, and modification of contracts; modification being accomplished, more or less, by agreeing in advance to abandon the original smart contract and migrate to a new iteration of it. But the problem, again, is that it is unlikely that contracting parties will be able to chart out in advance all the circumstances that might lead them to want to abandon the original smart contract. As a last point, perfect enforcement of the law, construed as the obligations undertaken by the two or more digital identities who are party to a smart contract, may not be desirable, and "those deploying automated law-enforcement schemes should be extremely cautious" (Shay et al., 2016). For regular contracts, an aggrieved party in a regular contract sometimes chooses "not to exercise her rights . . . in practice contractual performance is rarely perfect and . . . some breaches are deliberately ignored" (Mik, 2017). Consequently, it seems as if application developers, in-house counsel, and policymakers should be especially cautious about permitting the operation of long-term smart contracts, especially in areas that are least easily susceptible to the rendering of legal obligations as code.

V. Narrative Identity

Separate from, and deeper than, the notions of "digital identity" and "legal identity" is your personal identity, however that may be defined. The advent of blockchain technologies intensifies ways in which digital technologies more broadly affect our notions of identity. It does this in ways that primarily affect the kind of stories we are able to tell ourselves and others about ourselves, and the coherence of our own personal narratives. Building in part on the philosophical work of Ricoeur, psychologists have developed the term "narrative identity" to signify "a person's internalized and evolving life story, integrating the reconstructed past and imagined future to provide life with some degree of unity and purpose" (Mcadams and Mclean, 2013). This kind of self-narration is very different from the strict temporality and unmodifiability of a public register on the blockchain.

The key difference between narrative identity and legal identity is that narrative identity is usually unstable over time. The kind of person you are at 15 and the kind of person you are at 50 are often very different; that process is cumulative, internal, and often not marked in its changes by any external validating authority.

The key difference between narrative identity and digital identity is that your narrative identity may be incompatible with some or all of the digital facts that, in concatenation, form your digital identity. It would be easy to assume that such incompatibilities ought to be resolved in favor of the digital facts, but thanks to the many ways in which digital facts may be inaccurate, this is not necessarily true.

A. Resolving Incompatibilities between Narrative Identity and Blockchain Records

In Ridley Scott's dystopian 1982 movie *Blade Runner*, the android Rachael's identity depends in part on implanted memories transferred from her creator's niece, which seem to her to be real. "She" believes them to be so; but to make her belief that her identity is real the measure of whether it is, begs the question that it seeks to answer—How can an unreal identity be the agent that renders an unreal memory real, and thereby create a real identity out of an artificial one? The director urges us to consider the fact that the memory appears to her to be real as evidence that she is a "real person"; the same, consistent narrative point is made in Mary Shelley's *Frankenstein* and in *Pinocchio*.

As humans, we tell each other, on average, something like two hundred lies a day (Jellison, 1977). We do this, in part, in the service of telling ourselves coherent stories about ourselves; preferably ones where (1) the world makes sense, (2) what we do in the world makes sense, and (3) we are at least reasonably moral actors within that world. Popular culture supports the generation and moral validity of such narratives, even if they rest in part on beliefs that contradict material facts.

It appears, therefore, that there is some informal but broad cultural consensus that your identity is as real or as coherent as you narrate it to be, and that there is something commonly held to be wrong or unfair about treating an identity as invalid merely because it rests in part on false beliefs.

Reijers and Coeckelbergh (2018) partially endorse this perspective, by identifying ways that "delegat[ing] transactions to blockchain technologies" may transform our "social relations" into something "rigid, irreversible and non-negotiable, [. . .] reduc[ing] the freedom and the responsibility of humans interacting with the blockchain." They offer the example that reducing human relations to code could lead a health insurance company to "block coverage according to automatically detected violations of the ;smart contract', disregarding the personal contexts affected by the technology's configurations." The process of reducing narrated experience to a strict order of contractual events leads to a replacement of people by "quasi-entities," and of coherent, if not always factual, narratives by mere catalogs. These "quasi-entities," in our taxonomy, could be described as a reification of the narrative identity that, stripped of context, is forced into compatibility with the digital identity.

Going one step further, the philosopher Deleuze argues that the narrative identity has its own validity even if the imagination is "bent on the absurd, the fantastical and the evil" (Sheerin, 2009). Narrative identity involves a necessary blending of history and fiction in order to constitute a coherent self. This self is fragile, especially in the face of inconsistencies between itself and the digital identity; nonetheless, Deleuze held this fragile narrative self to be primary over the external dictates of society even with respect to the fictions it tells about itself. More moderately, Kearney (1998) asserts that "[t]he transcendental ego only secures its sense of oneness insofar as the imagination first proposes a horizon of identity and permanence." For the purposes of this discussion, it is enough to observe that the narrative self is vital to a sense of personal identity, that it is constituted by a formulation and continual reconstruction of memory, and that people are likely to bend, reorder and reinterpret facts in order to "retcon"[3] a self that is morally tolerable and coherent to themselves.

Even if the law is unlikely to look positively on efforts to sustain absurd, fantastical, or evil narrative identities, it is still surprisingly routine for the law to accommodate to people having more than one narrative identity, or more than one "face" that they present to the world, even if Facebook, for example, disfavors such practices. It is common in the United States for a married woman to use her birth surname in professional contexts and her married surname in personal contexts. It is also common for Chinese people and the Chinese diaspora to use a "Chinese" name in personal contexts and a "European" name in professional contexts. These kinds of variety in usage point to an idea that when we speak of privacy, we may mean in part "face-keeping" (Lahlou, 2008): The ability to keep narrative identities separate, and to present different "faces" in different social contexts. If blockchain implementations shift to an environment where there is "one person, one ID," the variety and play of different narrative identities is artificially suppressed.

A particularly acute expression of this incompatibility problem relates to trans rights. The transperson's gender identity rests on a narrative where their physical body does not match, and never matched, who they are inside; and that their legal identity should be formally changed, along with their bodies or not the body, to match their narrative identity. However, if a statement of their prior legal gender is placed on the blockchain by any party, that statement cannot then be altered after the transperson's decision to transition. The need to retroactively render past digital or legal records compatible with a present-day narrative identity is one that cannot be addressed through the blockchain.

VI. Use-Cases

As blockchain technology spreads, start-ups are devising new use cases for blockchain. We shall consider three of these: marriage, money laundering, and criminal records. Each of these poses unique issues for the maintenance of a narrative identity in the context of blockchain technology that may give pause to efforts to spread blockchain technology to new areas.

A. Marriage on the Blockchain

The start-up Bitnation, billing itself as the "world's first decentralized border-less voluntary nation," conducted its first marriage under its "SmartLove" application in 2016. It permits participants to choose witnesses and arbitrators for eventual disputes, establishes a multi-signature escrow to hold mutual assets such as money, tokenized land titles, and car assets, and sets up a "Pseudo-Anonymous Reputation System as [an] incentive for contract compliance." Bitnation's founder, Susanne Templehof, suggests that a blockchain-based marriage offers two advantages over a government-issued marriage license. First, it fulfills a need "in the LGBT, inter-faith and polyamorous communities around the world" (D'Anconia, 2016), and second, it can be done quickly, in "ten minutes between writing the contract and timestamping it." Templehof warns, however, that "the intrinsic immutability of blockchain systems means it could be very hard to get a divorce, suggesting short term marriage contracts of four or five years at a time." (Allison, 2011). This nicely illustrates some broader issues that emerge as conflicts arise between smart contracts and narrative identity.

In most Western nations, if you get married, perhaps under duress, and then immediately regret it—a change in the "narrative identity" of who you feel yourself to be inside—there are long-standing mechanisms in place that permit the adjustment of your legal identity through the legal system. A smart contract-enforced marriage, by contrast, becomes void only at a pre-specified time, meaning that, for example, an abusive party knows that their abusive treatment of their spouse cannot result in divorce, and consequent removal of access to the spouse's assets, before a date certain. This presents significant safety risks that people entering into a smart contract-enforced marriage may not be well placed to quantify in advance. Further, unlike with a legal marriage, a digital record of a marriage placed on a public blockchain register can never be deleted, altered, or obscured, other than by the obliteration of the entire register.

Second, the blockchain may not care whether you are LGBT, but it also will not care whether you are both in your right mind, or are brother and sister, or are an adult and a child. Politically negotiated and legally mediated restrictions on who may marry, matter in ways that should give us pause when considering the spread of marriage contracts on the blockchain.

Third, as outlined in (Sullivan and Burger, 2017) a marriage recorded on Bitnation could be undertaken for the purpose of digitally registering a name change; that name change could then be used to register a new digital identity under a national identity registration scheme such as India's Aadhaar, and that new digital identity could give rise to a new legal identity that could then be used for criminal (or non-criminal) purposes.

Fourth, it is conceptually questionable whether something that consists only of a contract between any number of people involving the financial disposition of assets is recognizably a "marriage." What makes a contract a *marriage* contract may in fact be the legal and communal and, for the subset of religious marriages, religious validation of a previously existing relationship. In that sense, the term "marriage" as Bitnation uses it may, for marketing purposes, confuse the concept of a marriage with the concept of a prenuptial agreement.

This example tells us that smart contracts are unlikely to be appropriate for use in matters as sensitive as family relations. They may operate better as contracts between people at arm's length who are not personally acquainted, and who have a low prior level of trust in each other and in intermediary institutions who might otherwise enforce a legal contract.

B. Money Laundering on the Blockchain

The preceding example naturally gives rise to the question: How arm's length is too arm's length? More precisely, how anonymous and delinked from an individual legal identity can a digital identity on the blockchain become, before its arm's length nature becomes its chief merit, and it begins to be used primarily for money laundering or other illegal activities?

Exchange operators rightly point out that it is not necessary for each human to operate one and only one user account on a cryptoasset exchange; nor is it necessary, as regulators in South Korea and elsewhere have done, to link registration on an exchange to an extensive set of government identity documents coupled with biometric indicators of identity. Allowing users to maintain multiple user accounts actively assists in the preservation of their narrative identit(ies). We can see from examples of people using cryptocurrency to preserve their assets in the Venezuelan hyperinflationary environment, that cryptoassets may serve as an important safety valve against government abuses and confiscations (Bambrough, 2018), and that governmental perceptions of what constitutes criminal financial activity can often merit pushback. However, regulators of cryptoasset exchanges are also right be concerned about the relationship of the digital identities of exchange users to the legal identities of those users.

Money-laundering regulations make it extremely difficult to use permissionless systems in banking environments (Azouvi et al., 2017). Most countries have "Know Your Customer" regulations that require connection of the digital to the legal identity via registration documents, normally issued by governments. There are several projects underway to build a reliable, decentralized Know Your Customer platform oriented toward cryptocurrencies, such as SelfKey and Civic, based around the concept of a "self-sovereign identity"; but none of these projects have yet launched fully, and it is as yet unclear how they will be able to partner with banks to find new customers under current law.

The Estonian E-Residency program, launched in 2014, has received more scholarly attention than any other attempt to digitize national identity. It allows individuals with no prior connection to Estonia to become "e-residents," and to gain access to Estonian government services for company formation, banking, payment processing, and taxation. It also gives the e-resident a smart card which they can use to sign documents. Applicants fill out an online form and include a copy of their passport; before approval, they must present themselves to an Estonian embassy for an interview. The services offered allow, for example, a non-EU entrepreneur to process payments as from within the EU. The economic effects over its four years of operation have been positive for Estonia—government estimates suggest a tenfold return to GDP from the cost of the program—but there have been recent reports of significant flows of laundered money, involving sales of Russian stocks and bonds through nonresidents' bank accounts (Mardiste and Jensen, 2018).[4]

As of December 2017, the e-Residency program launched detailed planning efforts for using cryptoassets to bolster Estonia as a destination for quality initial coin offerings (ICOs). These plans included a proposal for an "identity estcoin" (Korjus, 2017), conceiving of one of its main benefits as allowing e-Residency to operate with "remote verification," so that applicants would no longer have to attend the embassy in person. This is the furthest, to our knowledge, that any country has gone in advancing blockchain technology as a substitute for Know Your Customer bank identification requirements.

These new proposals would decouple Estonian e-Residency from most of the elements of a legal identity, while still maintaining a link to the legitimizing presence of the Estonian state. It offers individuals a way to advance and maintain plural residencies, rather than a single digital identity, and therefore bolsters concepts of narrative identity. However, serious concerns still remain. Multiple identities established via a blockchain, such as by using a faked passport to become an e-resident, could, through mutual recognition of another EU government, "contaminate" non-blockchain identity systems that are premised on the assumption of a single and consistent digital identity. Such risks could lead in the future to bigger money-laundering problems for Estonia, as it proceeds down the path toward becoming a "digital nation."

C. Criminal Justice Records on the Blockchain

In a sense, enforcement of laws is an intervention by the state, nominally on behalf of the people or of the common good, to disrupt and rework the narrative identity of the individual in a way that ensures that they accepts responsibility for things that they have done. The accused may have excused, justified, elided, forgotten, or unconsciously suppressed their culpability as part of their own narrative identities. "Rehabilitation" may then be deemed to have occurred when the lawbreaker has integrated into their narrative identity the fact that they broke the law, feels remorse for it, and has made amends for it to others or to the state.

Asserting the primacy of the digital over the narrative identity subjects all individuals to a law-enforcement-like process whereby the elements of their identity that are discordant with respect to the digital facts assigned to them are forcibly suppressed.

The notion of adding criminal justice records to an unmodifiable blockchain ledger is one that is at an earlier stage than either legal residency or marriage. We are not aware of any start-ups focusing on this process, but there has been significant recent discussion of the possibility. Graski and Embley (2018) argue for a ledger that would be updated by, among others, "prosecutors, courts and criminal-history repositories," and that would "tie charges to ultimate dispositions," reducing the effort needed to maintain accurate and up-to-date criminal histories in multiple areas of the criminal justice system. With similar enthusiasm, (Miller, 2018) advocates for a semiprivate ledger, offering that "[c]riminal charges could be shared and tracked in a ledger that law enforcement, prosecution, courts, probation, defense attorneys, and corrections organizations could access. When charges are added or dropped by law enforcement, prosecution, or courts, that information would be posted to the ledger as well, with the expected result being faster, more efficient administration of justice."

These suggestions exhibit a considerable faith in the procedures of (at least) the U.S. criminal justice system. We can well understand the use of private blockchain ledgers for improving the tracking of, say, where prisoners are in the prison system, or the logistical demands of tracking police equipment purchases. However, such a scheme reaches what feels to us to be a natural limit when it forms a longitudinal and unmodifiable record of a person's life.

The problems inherent in smart contracts recur here. A criminal charge may be brought that, it emerges later, ought not to have been brought. Someone may be convicted of a crime, and actually be guilty of it under the law, but the law may change such that their conduct is no longer a crime. If enough breakers of a law, such as draft-dodgers or undocumented immigrants, take political action that results in both a law's repeal and a change in society's judgment as to whether the law was ever fair, they may sometimes succeed in shifting their criminal justice records to match their narrative identities, in a way that is not possible if their records were on the blockchain. Sometimes, the process also works in reverse, where a criminal expresses remorse to a parole board, and the fact that their narrative identity appears to have shifted to match the external judgement of their legal identity, operates to allow their release. A criminal justice record may show that a person pled guilty to a crime before trial— most cases in the United States end that way—but that individual may have had plenty of reasons to plead guilty without being guilty in fact. The person committing a crime may be a minor, and ideas over who is and is not a minor also shift (generally upward) over time. The court records in our current system may be properly under seal. There are many situations, easily envisioned, that would wreak havoc in people's lives if transferred to an unmodifiable ledger.

VII. Decentralized Identifiers and Verified Claims

One suggestion for how to limit the potential of blockchain applications to damage people's narrative identities by acting as an unchangeable identity register has been the idea of "decentralized identifiers," or "DIDs." These are facts about ourselves whose creation, management, distribution, and reuse is wholly under our control, unlike, say, our phone numbers or email addresses. Addressing the issue of presenting multiple "faces," each entity may have as many DIDs as they wish. There is now a standardized protocol for how DIDs are registered, resolved, updated, or revoked (Reed et al., 2018). A DID is like a URL, but without any centralized registry or certificate-issuing authorities. Unlike a URL, however, it "contains cryptographic information that enables au-thentication of an entity associated with the DID," such as public keys corre-sponding to private keys controlled by the entity. Any changes to the DID are timestamped. The ledger thereby created is immutable, but procedures for rev-ocation must be included. If the private key is compromised or lost, you cannot regain control of a DID. For organizations or people not equipped to deal with securing cryptographic keys, there are "web of trust" protocols that allow key recovery from several or a quorum of trusted parties (Garcia, 2018).

Dunphy and Petitcolas, 2018 review existing DID-based apps that seek to manage identity on the blockchain in a more privacy-protective manner. One challenge that they note is that users may "pu[t] representations of per-sonally identifiable information on a [distributed ledger] designed to priori-tize immutability and transparency of data." Indeed, after the immense effort invested in the pre-blockchain biometric identity system of Aadhaar in India (Solomon, 2018), there are now systems being developed to serve low-income people in the developing world, that systematically encourage the connection of biometric identifiers to the blockchain ((Hajialikhani and Jahanara, 2018), discussing "UniqueID"). This objection to DID systems applies with more force to Ethereum and Bitcoin's blockchains than to more modern public distributed ledgers designed with identity issues in mind, such as Sovrin. Sovrin's co-founder and CEO Tim Ruff, quoted in Macknight (2018), describes the Sovrin system as follows:

> The problem lies in defining identity, which means so many different things in different contexts. Sovrin is actually a "claims exchange" system, where a claim is a piece of information that makes an attestation about some fact, and stretches beyond simple identity. [. . .] No longer do I have an identity that I carry with me, but I have dozens, hundreds, or even thousands of claims in a digital wallet that I can use in different contexts, depending on where I need to establish trust [. . . Then all that is] needed is a standardised way to digitally sign these claims and verify the signatures.

Solutions such as Sovrin and Selfkey are an attempt to solve the issues described in Section I, where the digital identity is assumed to be a true representation of the self, that needs then to be verified externally in a trustless way. They do this by atomizing the claims made about the identity into individual, reusable pieces of information ("verifiable claims"), each attesting to a fact without containing that fact within itself. Macknight notes that "verifying the party with whom data is shared, remains a challenge, which is partly addressed through the web-of-trust, the governance of the Sovrin Foundation and the reputation of the stewards." To this extent, then, existing identity solutions have not yet resolved the original hopes of blockchain enthusiasts that it might be possible to devise blockchain-based identity verification systems that are truly trustless and that reliably protect registration information from being compromised.

VIII. Conclusions

This discussion has been intended to grapple with some of the issues attendant on converting pre-blockchain digital and legal records to the blockchain. What has emerged over the course of the discussion is that though blockchain offers great promise, a host of problems arise when one tries to use blockchain to develop and interpret a consistent narrative about individuals.

We used the concept of "narrative identity" to locate more precisely the nature of the privacy violation involved. We asserted that blockchain app developers may understandably have been more focused on the technical problems of identity verification in a trustless environment than on whether blockchain applications might pin human identity down unnecessarily. We advocated against systems that collapse narrative identity into the digital identity, a single narrative that best fits a set of externally imposed, digitally timestamped facts that itself is subject to significant possibilities of inaccuracy and corruption. We used examples of marriage, money laundering, and criminal justice records to discuss some of the negative consequences of blockchain going beyond dealing with movements of assets and physical goods to maintaining an authoritative, longitudinal record of people.

An important caveat to place here is that, even though blockchain registers are designed to be unmodifiable, and to be distributed across thousands or millions of devices, their permanence is not thereby assured. Digital devices rapidly become outdated and are replaced; the continued accessibility of a particular blockchain register depends in part on the continued existence of a community or a company responsible for that accessibility. Many forms of digital storage from 30 or 40 years ago are now prohibitively complicated to access. The rate of technological progress may therefore serve as its own limiting factor for the problems outlined in this chapter, but over a timescale that is generally unhelpful for those confronted with these problems in the near future.

Blockchain continues to be an exciting and rapidly developing space. The concept of decoupling individuals from required membership in a physical national community is a liberating one, and cryptoassets are already providing an important safety valve against oppressive regimes. We explore new ideas, such as decentralized identifiers and verified claims, that are helping to accommodate the need to preserve a narrative identity to the blockchain age; and we draw on insights from psychology, philosophy, computer science, law, and transgender studies to understand the importance of preserving space in our social and technological systems for people to reinvent themselves.

References

Abbas, Y. and F. Dervin (2009). *Digital technologies of the Self.* Cambridge Scholars.

Allison, I. (2011, September 29). Decentralised Government Project Bitnation Offers Refugees Blockchain IDs and Bitcoin Debit Cards. *International Business Times.*

Augot, D., H. Chabanne, T. Chenevier, W. George, L. Lambert, G. Navarro-Arribas, H. Hartenstein, and J. Herrera-Joancomart'i (2017). A User-Centric System for Verified Identities on the Bitcoin Blockchain. In *Data Privacy Management,*

Cryptocurrencies and Blockchain Technology, Cham, pp. 390–407. Springer International.

Bambrough, B. (2018, Aug. 20). Bitcoin Believers Speak Out in Venezuela as Maduro Makes Historical Devaluation. *Forbes.*

Bauman, Z. (2004). *Identity: Conversations with Benedetto Vecchi.* Cambridge: Polity Press.

Beemyn, G. and D. Brauer (2015). Trans-Inclusive College Records: Meeting the Needs of an Increasingly Diverse US Student Population. *Transgender Studies Quarterly 2*(3), 478–87.

Bergson, H. (1911). *Creative Evolution.* London: Macmillan.

Braendgaard, P. (2018, January 24). Different approaches to Ethereum Identity Standards. *Medium.*

Buterin, V. and G. Weyl (2018, May 21). Liberation through Radical Decentralization. *Medium.*

D'Anconia, F. (2016, Nov. 24). Bitnation Releases Marriage App, Smartlove, on Ethereum Blockchain. *Cointelegraph.*

Donath, J. (2014, Apr. 25). We Need Online Alter Egos Now More than Ever. *Wired Magazine.*

Dunphy, P. and F. Petitcolas (2018, January 10). A First Look at Identity Management Schemes on the Blockchain. In *Security & Privacy*, Volume 16, pp. 20–29. IEEE.

Garcia, P. (2018). Biometrics on the Blockchain. *Biometric Technology Today*, 5–7.

Governatori, G., F. Idelberger, Z. Milosevic, R. Riveret, G. Sartor, and X. Xu (2018). On Legal Contracts, Imperative and Declarative Smart Contracts, And Blockchain Systems. *Artificial Intelligence and Law Online*, 1–33.

Graski, D. and P. Embley (2018, October 15). When Might Blockchain Appear in Your Court? National Center for State Courts: Court Technology Bulletin (blog post).

Hajialikhani, M. and M. Jahanara (2018, June). UniqueID: Decentralized Proof-of-UniqueHuman. *ArXiv e-prints.*

Jellison, G. (1977). *I'm Sorry, I Didn't Mean to, and Other Lies We Love to Tell.* New York: Chatham Square Press.

Kearney, R. (1998). *The Wake of Imagination: Toward a Postmodern Culture.* New York: Fordham University Press.

Khatwani, S. (2018, May 10). 9 Anonymous Cryptocurrencies You Should Know About. *Coin-sutra.*

Korjus, K. (2017, December 19). We're Planning to Launch Estcoin—and That's only the Start. *Medium.*

Lahlou, S. (2008). Identity, Social Status, Privacy and Face-Keeping In Digital Society. *Social Science Information 47*(3), 299–330.

Macknight, J. (2018). Will Technology Solve the Identity Crisis? *The Banker: Cybersecurity*, 98.

Mardiste, D. and T. Jensen (2018, May 25). Police Says $13 Billion Laundered through Estonia. *Reuters*.

Mcadams, D. and K. Mclean (2013, June). Narrative Identity. *Current Directions in Psychological Science 22*(3), 233–38.

Miers, I. (2019). Blockchain Privacy: Equal Parts Theory and Theater. *Tokendaily*.

Mik, E. (2017). Smart Contracts: Terminology, Technical Limitations and Real World Complexity. Available at SSRN: https://ssrn.com/abstract=3038406 or http://dx.doi.org/10.2139/ssrn.3038406. Unpublished.

Nakamoto, S. (2008). Bitcoin: A Peer-to-Peer Electronic Cash System. Available at https://bitcoin.org/bitcoin.pdf.

Neumann, N., C. Tucker, and T. Whitfield (2018). How Effective Is Black-Box Digital Consumer Profiling and Audience Delivery?: Evidence from Field Studies. *Mimeo, MIT*.

Reed, D., M. Sporny, D. Longley, C. Allen, R. Grant, and M. Sabadello (2018). Draft Community Group Report – Decentralized IDentifiers (DIDs) v0.11: Data Model and Syntaxes for Decentralized IDentifiers (DIDs). Technical report, W3C.

Reijers, W. and M. Coeckelbergh (2018). The Blockchain as a Narrative Technology: Investigating the Social Ontology and Normative Configurations of Crypto-currencies. *Philosophy & Technology 31*(1), 103–30.

Scott, J. C. (1998). *Seeing Like a State: How Certain Schemes to Improve the Human Condition Have Failed*. New Haven, Conn.: Yale University Press.

Shay, L. A., W. Hartzog, J. Nelson, D. Larkin, and G. Conti (2016). *Confronting Automated Law Enforcement*. Cheltenham: Edward Elgar.

Sheerin, D. (2009). *Deleuze and Ricoeur: Disavowed Affinities and the Narrative Self*. London: Continuum Press.

Solomon, B. (2018, Sept. 28). Op-ed: Digital IDs Are More Dangerous Than You Think. *Wired Magazine*.

Sullivan, C. (2018). Digital Identity—From Emergent Legal Concept to New Reality. *Computer Law & Security Review 34*(4), 723–31.

Sullivan, C. and E. Burger (2017). E-residency and Blockchain. *Computer Law & Security Review: The International Journal of Technology Law and Practice 33*(4), 470–81.

Zyskind, G., O. Nathan, et al. (2015). Decentralizing Privacy: Using Blockchain to Protect Personal Data. In *Security and Privacy Workshops (SPW), 2015 IEEE*, pp. 180–84. IEEE.

11

Policy and Regulatory Challenges of Distributed Ledger Technology and Digital Assets in Asia

Douglas Arner,* Ross P. Buckley,** Dirk Zetzsche,*** Bo Zhao,**** Anton N. Didenko,† Cyn-Young Park,♦ and Emilija Pashoska

1. Introduction

Since the launch of Bitcoin in 2009,[1] cryptocurrencies and their underlying blockchain technology have risen to global attention. It is now clear Bitcoin and a number of other cryptocurrencies were the focus of one of the largest speculative bubbles in history: during 2017, the price of Bitcoin and other cryptocurrencies increased dramatically before falling steeply in 2018.

Since 2017, there has also been an explosion in tokenization of assets by ICOs (Initial Coin Offerings). ICOs can be seen as a conjunction of crowdfunding and blockchain. They typically use blockchain to offer and manage tokens that confer various rights.

The hallmarks of a speculative bubble were certainly present with ICOs in 2017 and 2018, but this does not mean they are without substance: at the height of the dot.com bubble, few expected Amazon and Google to become as significant as they are today. As is often the case in hype cycles, while the initial excitement is overdone, frequently the long-term impact is underestimated.

* Kerry Holdings Professor in Law, University of Hong Kong.

** KPMG Law—King & Wood Mallesons Chair of Disruptive Innovation, Scientia Professor, and member, Centre for Law, Markets and Regulation, UNSW Sydney.

*** Professor of Law, ADA Chair in Financial Law (Inclusive Finance), Faculty of Law, Economics and Finance, University of Luxembourg, and Director, Centre for Business and Corporate Law, Heinrich-Heine-University, Düsseldorf, Germany.

**** Economist, Economic Research and Regional Cooperation Department, Asian Development Bank

† Research Fellow and Member, Centre for Law, Markets and Regulation, UNSW Sydney.

♦ Director for Regional Cooperation and Integration, Economic Research and Regional Cooperation Department, Asian Development Bank.

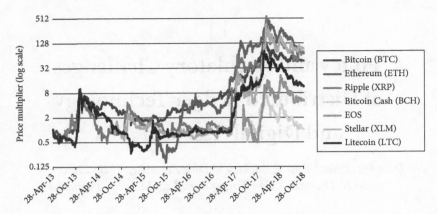

Figure 11.1. Major cryptocurrency price over time. Price Multiplier (price on a certain day/price on the day of inception).

Note: the price multiplier shows the price change of each cryptocurrency since inception. A value above 1 (below 1) indicates the price has increased (decreased) by the factor.

Data source: Coinmarketcap.

Period: 28th April 2013–31st October 2018.

In Asia, interest in digital assets and related technologies has been very high. Asia has become a leading player in many aspects, from cryptocurrency investment to launching and participating in ICOs. A range of countries have made development of blockchain and distributed ledger technology (DLT) a national priority. Many financial institutions are investing heavily in proof-of-concept demonstrations and the rollout of pilot applications of DLT. At the same time, many jurisdictions in Asia as well as around the world have become concerned about risks, particularly concerning cryptocurrencies and ICOs.

Part of the attraction of DLT lies in transcending regulation, and perhaps even providing an alternative trust solution to those traditionally provided by sovereign states. DLT is frequently portrayed as offering unbreakable security, immutability, and unparalleled transparency. Proponents argue this provides a framework of trust based upon technology rather than human-based arrangements (e.g., states), so regulation is seen as unnecessary.[2] Yet, while the law may be dull and the technology exciting, the impact of sovereigns and their institutions cannot be simply wished away. Risk will remain, from both the legal and technological standpoint.[3]

A. DLT, Blockchain, and Cryptocurrencies in Asia

Interest in DLT has exploded with technology companies, scholars, industry practitioners, and policymakers, promoting DLT as a transformative

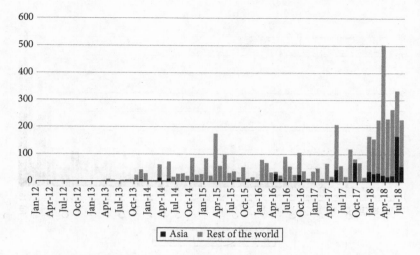

Figure 11.2. Monthly VC investment (US$M) by DLT Company Location.

Data source: Coindesk 2018; calculated by the authors. June 2018 saw a significant spike in venture capital investment in Asia, correlating with a significant investment in Alibaba's Ant Financial in China.

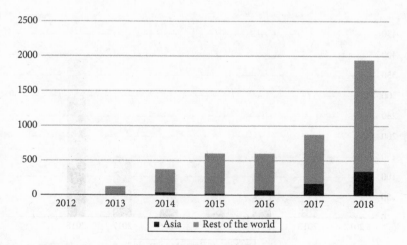

Figure 11.3. Yearly VC investment (US$M) by DLT Company Location.

Data source: Coindesk 2018; calculated by the authors. Yearly venture capital investment continues to increase, with Asia closely following this trend.

technology.[4] Figures 11.2 to 11.6 highlight venture capital investment in DLT since 2013, by amount raised and location of the fundraising firm. These charts highlight increasing global volumes (in orange) and substantial investment both from Asia and in firms in Asia (in blue).

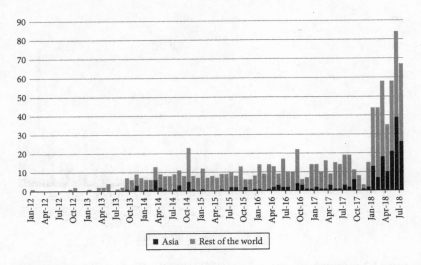

Figure 11.4. Monthly Number of VC investment rounds by DLT Company Location.
Data source: Coindesk 2018; calculated by the authors.

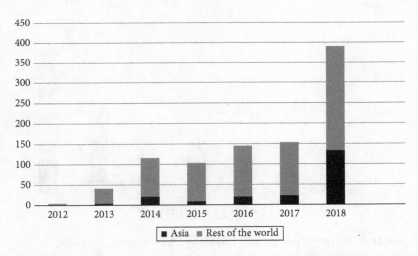

Figure 11.5. Yearly Number of VC investment rounds by DLT Company Location.
Data source: Coindesk 2018; calculated by the authors. 2018 saw a significant spike in total venture capital investment rounds for DLT, with Asia now constituting close to one third of global rounds. Each set of figures above clearly indicates significant, fast-paced growth in investment in DLT across Asia. However, the amount of venture capital investment varies significantly by jurisdiction. In this regard, the key players over the past several years have proven to be China, South Korea, Japan and Singapore. Figure 4 below highlights the breakdown of venture capital investment by jurisdiction in Asia.

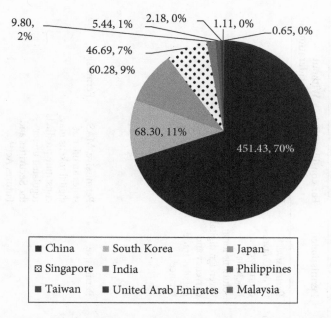

9.80, 2% 5.44, 1% 2.18, 0% 1.11, 0% 0.65, 0%
46.69, 7%
60.28, 9%
68.30, 11%
451.43, 70%

■ China   ■ South Korea   ■ Japan
⊠ Singapore   ■ India   ■ Philippines
■ Taiwan   ■ United Arab Emirates   ■ Malaysia

Figure 11.6. VC Investment in DLT in Asia (US$M) Jan. 2012–July. 2018. *Data source*: Coindesk 2018; calculated by the authors.

B. Recent Developments and Policy Responses

The hype cycle has resulted in various policy and regulatory responses across the region. (See Appendix for a summary of the major statements in Asia regarding cryptocurrencies and ICOs.) While there are common features in the regulatory responses (such as issuance of cautions in most jurisdictions in relation to the investment risks associated with ICOs and a slow shift toward regulation of these applications), policy approaches are diverse across jurisdictions.

For example, in 2013, both China and South Korea announced cryptocurrencies would be treated as "virtual commodities" and not currencies. This restrictive approach has continued to date with their banning of ICOs. By way of contrast, Japan and Singapore have taken permissive approaches, with early steps toward regulating these technologies. In 2014, Japan began developing cryptocurrency regulations, and in 2016 recognized virtual currency as a legal means of payment subject to AML and KYC requirements. In Singapore, cryptocurrencies have been regulated since 2014.

Other jurisdictions have taken less active approaches and have instead only issued cautions about associated risks, such as Macao SAR and Malaysia.

Table 11.1 summarizes the policy approaches taken by jurisdictions in Asia toward cryptocurrencies, blockchain, and ICOs.

Table 11.1. Policy approaches in China, Singapore, South Korea, Japan, Hong Kong, and Indonesia (October 31, 2018)

	Cryptocurrency		Blockchain		Initial Coin Offerings	
	Sovereign	Non-Sovereign	Public	Permissioned	For consideration	Without consideration
China	Permissive. People's Bank of China (PBOC) is developing its own digital currency[5]	Permissive for Chinese investors only. Investors are free to hold cryptocurrencies including Bitcoin. China has prohibited the use of cryptocurrency exchanges and financial institutions from providing cryptocurrency services[6]	Permissive. In 2017 more than half blockchain-related patent applications were from China; 12 out of 26 listed banks have adopted blockchain applications[7]	Permissive. PBOC favors centralized blockchain solutions for a sovereign digital currency and possibly trade finance[8]	Banned. Domestic ICOs are banned and rules block online trading in offshore ICOs[9]	Banned.
Singapore	Permissive. Monetary Authority of Singapore (MAS) is hesitant to issue a digital currency but open[10]	Permissive. The current scale of trading does not pose risks[11]	Permissive. Public and private. For example, Project Ubin has tested DLT for clearing and settlement of payments and securities[12]	Permissive.	Permissive. MAS states an offer of digital tokens may constitute products regulated under the Securities and Futures Act[13]	Permissive.

South Korea	Permissive. The Bank of Korea has a taskforce investigating issuing a central bank digital currency (May 2018)[14]	Permissive. The use of anonymous bank accounts for virtual coin trading was banned from January 30, 2018 to stop cryptocurrencies being used in money laundering and other crimes[15]	Permissive. The Ministry of Economy and Finance has allocated 1.6 trillion won toward "Growth through Innovation" investment plan focusing on big data, AI, and blockchain (August 2018)[12]	Permissive.	ICOs banned from September 29, 2017. The government is considering ending the ban and issuing guidelines[13]	Currently banned.
Japan	Permissive. Bank of Japan Deputy Governor states there are no plans to issue a cryptocurrency as at October 20, 2018[16]	Permissive. From April 2017 the Payment Services Act defines cryptocurrencies as property values stored electronically and are not currency. Crypto exchanges must be registered[17]	Permissive. Blockchain widely used beyond financial services. The government supports the use of DLT in its Future Strategy 2017[18]	Permissive.	Permissive. Regulations are currently being developed. Selling tokens requires a license[19]	Permissive.

(Continued)

Table 11.1. Continued

	Cryptocurrency		Blockchain		Initial Coin Offerings	
	Sovereign	Non-Sovereign	Public	Permissioned	For consideration	Without consideration
Hong Kong	Permissive. Hong Kong Monetary Authority (HKMA) has no plan to issue a central bank digital currency as of May 30, 2018[20]	Permissive. Cryptocurrencies are considered virtual commodities[21]	Permissive. Public and private sector. A DLT or blockchain-based cross-border trade and trade finance platform is being developed by the HKMA and MAS[22]	Permissive.	Permissive. SFC regulates ICOs involving "securities" and wrote to seven exchanges. Most confirmed compliance with the SFC regulatory regime and others ceased offering tokens to Hong Kong investors (February 2018)[23]	Permissive.
Indonesia	Permissive. Bank of Indonesia is considering issuing a cryptocurrency or digital rupiah. Study to be completed by 2020[24]	Banned for payments only and not legal currency. Financial institutions banned from trading. Otherwise permitted and may be considered a commodity[26]	Permissive. Five banks are considering implementing blockchain. An Indonesian Blockchain Association and Hub have been established[28]	Permissive. The Bank of Indonesia is considering using a centralized system for the digital rupiah[30]	Permissive. Regulations being considered for crypto exchanges[31]	Permissive.

| India | Permissive. Reserve Bank of India (RBI) investigating launching a digital currency (August 2018)[25] | Currently permissive but regulations are being devised to ban private cryptocurrencies. Crypto exchanges are legal but because banks are prohibited from dealing with crypto exchanges the business model is becoming increasingly unviable[27] | Permissive. The government has stated it will use blockchain proactively for ushering in digital economy (February 1, 2018)[29] | Permissive. | Permissive. ICOs are not regulated but the ban on banks engaging in cryptocurrency activities limits the market. One of the largest exchanges closed in September 2018[32] | Permissive. |

Generally speaking, these jurisdictions remain supportive of DLT, but some are conservative toward its two highest profile applications: cryptocurrencies and ICOs. This divergence reflects rational policy choices but also highlights the confusing nature of much of the terminology and a general lack of understanding of some of these new technologies.

For instance, Singapore, in particular, has been welcoming of ICOs and cryptocurrencies, as it seeks to establish itself as the preeminent FinTech hub in the region. Other jurisdictions such as China have been strictly opposed to cryptocurrencies and ICOs, partly due to the perceived importance of protecting sovereign control over the domestic currency and the financial system, while welcoming DLT technology more generally. Approaches in other regional countries have tended to fall within these two poles.

II. DLT and its Applications: Evolution and Typology

The differences in regulatory approaches taken to date toward DLT reflect some confusion as to the meaning of DLT itself and the distinctions between its applications. Regulators seeking to address the concerns arising from these technologies must of course first have a clear understanding of what they are and the purposes for which they may be applied. The best way to understand this field is to begin with the relevant underlying technology, before considering its applications.

A. Centralized and Distributed Ledgers

Distributed ledgers are best understood in contrast to their counterpart, the centralized ledger, as demonstrated in Figure 11.7.

A centralized ledger stores data and is maintained by a trusted administrator, recording transfers of assets upon receipt of verified notifications. Financial sector examples include most securities clearing and settlement systems as well as large value payment systems including RTGS (real time gross settlement) systems. Centralized structures are typically characterized by security (because they are controlled by a single entity that can focus on this aspect) and speed of execution.

However, risks exist in centralized structures. A ledger stored on a network server can be destroyed, or more likely, hacked, so the original data are held for ransom or manipulated and replaced by inaccurate data. Mathematical approaches can be used to determine how much effort is necessary to manipulate any given server. Every server *can* be manipulated with sufficient computing power.

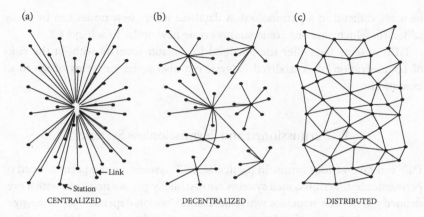

(a)   (b)   (c)

←—Link

←—Station

CENTRALIZED   DECENTRALIZED   DISTRIBUTED

Figure 11.7. Distributed Communication Networks: Definition of Redundancy Level.
Source: Mougayar 2015 referring to Baran 1962, p. 4.

Centralized structures thus concentrate risk but use that concentration to focus security and management. Central counterparties (CCPs) are an example, providing a trusted central party for transactions, reducing counterparty risk and interconnections with potential systemic implications. However, CCPs also concentrate risk and thus arguably create a new forms of finanical sector risk, including systemic risk as highlighted in the development of various international regulatory approaches by the Financial Stability Board and others.

Distributed ledgers[33] address these problems by raising the barriers for manipulation of stored data. In distributed ledgers many data storage points (nodes) are connected with each other and store all data simultaneously, together constituting the common ledger. DLT requires consensus of those nodes. The technical details of how to achieve consensus vary from proof of work[34] and proof of stake to proof of authority.

To illustrate, assume there are N nodes and E describes the effort necessary to break into any single server. Provided all other conditions (e.g., security of each server) are equal, the efforts necessary to manipulate all servers would be N x E rather than 1 x E. The number of servers that will need to be manipulated depends on the number of servers necessary for consensus (C). If C>1 the distributed ledger is more secure than the centralized one. This assumes equal security of each server. However, in practice, security of the central node on a centralized ledger is likely to be far superior to each distributed node. This also assumes manipulation of existing nodes is necessary for consensus, whereas consensus can be steered by other factors (e.g., control of the majority of processing power in a proof-of-work system). Furthermore, the calculation will be more difficult in a permissionless database where new nodes can be easily added (in which case one could simply create new nodes to achieve C).

DLT systems thus offer the potential for greater security without the risks of concentration of centralized ledgers, but also suffer in terms of speed of execution.

B. Permissioned and Permissionless Systems

DLT can take various forms. In particular, DLT systems can be permissioned or permissionless. Permissioned systems are essentially private networks with a predefined governance structure where data authorization depends upon the agreement of multiple predefined servers. Hyperledger Fabric is probably the leading example, with R3's Corda being the leading example in the financial sector.

In contrast, permissionless DLT systems such as Bitcoin operate on public domain software and allow anyone who runs the software to participate. In some cases even the code is further developed in the public domain. The participants may not know who else is running a node at any given time, creating additional security: if the number of overall nodes is known, a cyberattack may be planned with greater certainty. The other leading example of a permissionless system is other Ethereum..

Permissionless systems arguably present the greatest opportunity to create alternative trust solutions, as they are open to all and often designed to be self-perpetuating. However, they raise risks concerning administration and control of data, and permissioned systems are far more common, particularly in the financial context.

C. Blockchain

"Blockchain" refers to how data are stored on the ledger. Rather than being stored individually, a single block contains multiple data points and all blocks are stored in a specific order (the "chain"). Each block includes a timestamp and a link to the previous block. Rather than manipulating one data point alone, a cyberattack must manipulate the whole block of data as well as—due to the timestamp and link—all linked blocks. The level of resilience provided by this linkage varies depending on the blockchain's design. In the Bitcoin blockchain, the link is generated by hashing[35] the data in the preceding block, which means the attacker must manipulate not only the desired block, but also every block after it—while outpacing the network of Bitcoin miners (due to the proof-of-work consensus algorithm).

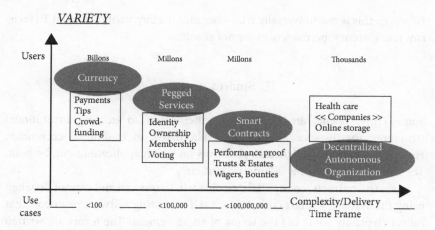

Figure 11.8. Blockchain applications: End-user view.[36]

Blockchain's key benefit is tamper-evidence: in a hash-based blockchain any modification of data will generate a different hash and any change will become evident. As a result, blockchain may be particularly useful in services that benefit from robust record-keeping, such as smart contracts. Figure 11.8 illustrates the sorts of uses the technology can facilitate.

Blockchain can underpin smart contracts or be used to generate, store, and distribute a cryptocurrency, ICO or other digital asset. For instance, Bitcoin is a blockchain-based cryptocurrency. Ethereum is a blockchain-based system that includes a cryptocurrency but also an open platform that can be used to design applications. In this chapter, we treat DLT as covering the full range of applications of blockchain operating on distributed ledgers.

D. Technology-Based Trust Solutions

The basic argument in favor of DLT is that it provides trust solutions involving enhanced security, transparency, and permanence. Suitable applications may include asset finance, back-office clearing and settlement, trade processing and settlement, insurance claims tracking, and smart contracts. Among the best-known applications are cryptocurrencies and ICOs.

At the heart of many arguments in favor of DLT is that it can provide an alternative platform for many core functions in modern economies, from money (e.g., cryptocurrencies) to identity (e.g., permanent public storage system independent of state control). DLT certainly has long-term potential to redesign many systems and offer an alternative platform for institutional frameworks.

However, this is not universally true—because the key attributes of DLT (security, transparency, permanence) are not absolute.

E. Smart Contracts

Some DLT systems are designed as alternatives to existing institutional structures, for instance Bitcoin as an alternative to traditional currencies. However, others are designed as platforms on which applications can be built. The key to such platforms is "smart contracts."

In smart contracts, code will determine what users can and cannot do when using the system.[37] Smart contracts are self-executing software protocols that reflect (typically some of) the terms of an agreement. The terms are written in code and operate on DLT. This permits transactions to be carried out without an external enforcement mechanism. As long as the code does not provide for a reversing procedure, transactions are traceable, transparent, and irreversible.

The key impact of smart contracts is to disintermediate. Human intervention can delay administrative processes if they exclusively depend on "if–then" binary conditions. In contrast, a computer that detects when an "if–then" condition is met can automatically execute the protocol. For instance, if settlement depends on payment, a computer can check quickly and accurately whether the condition has been met. This could have multiple uses in collective investment schemes and networked market structures such as syndicated loans and securities settlement.

F. DLT Use Cases and Investment Trends

DLT use cases have moved beyond cryptocurrencies, and their application is now being explored across the financial system, from capital raising to insurance claims processing and digital identity authentication.

Figure 11.9 shows the areas where DLT was believed to have the greatest potential impact in 2016. Seventy-seven percent of respondents believed DLT would have the greatest impact in finance.

The key benefit of DLT lies in its ability to address the storage trust issue. DLT ensures the validity of data sets by spreading data over many nodes, which have to agree to confirm data as correct. DLT (in particular blockchain) can ensure better than other technologies that data are not manipulated and that the party making a transfer has title to the asset being transferred. This is leading

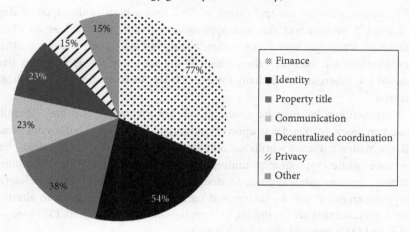

Leading sectors expected to be impacted by blockchain
technology globally (2016 Survey)

Figure 11.9. Leading sectors expected to be impacted by blockchain technology globally (2016 Survey).

Data source: Statista.

to a range of innovative applications, including Everledger for the diamond market.

Everledger was launched in Australia in 2016 to connect suppliers and retailers of diamonds using a blockchain-based framework. The application aims to track gemstones throughout the supply chain from the source, providing digital provenance tracking and certification.

In the developing country context, Papua New Guinea (PNG) has been piloting a blockchain-based device to facilitate digital identification to underpin delivery of services and payments. The IDbox, as it is called, may prove to be a cost-efficient device allowing people in developing countries to create a unique digital identity based on a wallet that allows users to store ETH—the cryptocurrency that operates on the Ethereum blockchain. It is targeted for use in developing countries with low internet access, limited electricity, and limited smart phone penetration. Funds are sent and traced using blockchain to make sure they reach the intended beneficiaries and are spent on nominated services. The pilot was supported by the Central Bank of Papua New Guinea, the Australian government, and some PNG banks. However, the device does place heavy reliance on only one fingerprint, so there must be concerns about both its robustness and resilience.

III. Cryptocurrencies

Cryptocurrencies are an application of DLT and a high profile type of digital asset.[38] Bitcoin was the first application of DLT, designed as an alternative to sovereign-issued currencies.[39] This led to an explosion of other cryptocurrencies, such as Ether, which is the currency for applications that run on the Ethereum blockchain. Over 2,000 cryptocurrencies have now been created.

Cryptocurrencies may be sovereign or non-sovereign and are generally based on blockchain and rely upon cryptography. However, this does not mean all alternative currencies utilizing cryptography will be cryptocurrencies. For instance, while cryptography underpins the "gold" used in many computer games, these are generally not treated as cryptocurrencies.[40] In this chapter "cryptocurrencies" will be interpreted narrowly, and used to refer to alternative currencies that are (1) digital, (2) cryptographically protected, (3) based on DLT, and (4) convertible into fiat currency.

A. Non-Sovereign: Alternative Currencies and Payment Systems

Cryptocurrencies can also be used as alternative currencies to sovereign-issued currencies. Alternative currencies create "alternative payment systems" that may coexist with legally recognized payment systems. They can enjoy varying levels of convertibility into fiat currency and can be either centralized (i.e., with a single center of issuance) or decentralized (i.e., without such a center).[41]

Table 11.2 highlights the top cryptocurrencies by founder location. Six of these are based in Asia, predominantly China.

Table 11.2. Top 20 cryptocurrencies by founder company location

No.	Name	Location	Asia	Market Cap
1	Bitcoin	N/A		$113,923,794,526
2	Ethereum	Switzerland		$23,043,040,037
3	Ripple	U.S.		$21,507,352,542
4	Bitcoin Cash			$9,139,198,331
5	EOS	Cayman Islands		$5,148,876,432
6	Stellar	United States		$4,632,485,681
7	Litecoin	N/A		$3,452,238,359

Table 11.2. Continued

No.	Name	Location	Asia	Market Cap
8	Tether	Hong Kong	Yes	$2,798,061,303
9	Cardano	Switzerland		$2,135,494,787
10	Monero	N/A		$1,891,106,160
11	IOTA	Germany		$1,555,435,741
12	Dash	Canada		$1,513,558,032
13	TRON	China	Yes	$1,443,110,342
14	Binance Coin	China	Yes	$1,214,870,601
15	NEO	China	Yes	$1,184,528,771
16	Ethereum Classic	Switzerland		$1,173,913,323
17	NEM	Singapore	Yes	$959,534,752
18	Tezos	United States		$805,787,507
19	VeChain	Singapore	Yes	$715,268,205
20	Dogecoin	United States		$667,038,134

Source: Coinmarketcap.

Cryptocurrencies are often presented as decentralized alternatives to existing sovereign-issued currencies. Bitcoin's launch followed the 2008 global financial crisis, during a period that was characterized by FinTech—"financial technology"—seeking to develop better alternatives to traditional financial institutions and approaches. However, governments and central banks have often reacted negatively, particularly around concerns about consumer and investor protection, both in terms of a perceived lack of transparency and uncertainty around the value of such currencies. Thus jurisdictions in Asia and elsewhere have developed various regulatory approaches, ranging from facilitative frameworks (e.g., Japan) to outright bans (e.g., China).

Much discussion centers around whether cryptocurrencies are in fact money or currency. From a functional standpoint, money plays three major roles: unit of account, store of value, and means of exchange. Cryptocurrencies do in some cases fulfill these functions but their volatility in value has so far largely limited their utility regarding all three aspects and particularly the first two, meaning cryptocurrencies have functioned more like speculative commodities than currency.

From a legal standpoint, whether something is money or currency is determined by law, with many jurisdictions providing a monopoly for the national currency (e.g., China). In such jurisdictions, absent a change in law, cryptocurrencies will not be legal forms of money. Other jurisdictions have been more facilitative (e.g., Japan, Singapore, and Hong Kong SAR) in allowing alternatives to the domestic currency, including cryptocurrencies (e.g., Japan, Singapore).

Overall, whether or not to allow the use of cryptocurrencies for payment and settlement is largely a domestic policy question. To date, Bitcoin has been most popular in economies with very volatile currencies.

In jurisdictions that have determined not to regulate cryptocurrencies as money, other potential approaches apply, beyond prohibition or bespoke regulation. The central issue is whether cryptocurrencies can be recognized as a part of the formal payment system, which in most jurisdictions draws regulatory scrutiny. As a term, "payment system" is broader than currency. Cryptocurrencies do form payment systems—but "alternative" payment systems. Whether a cryptocurrency is part of the formal payment system will depend on how it is meant to be used: Bitcoin often falls outside, while Ripple often falls within the system. This is because formal payment systems are generally closed-loop systems. If some cryptocurrencies can be integrated into the formal payment system, then they can be used as a settlement vehicle.

Other jurisdictions may classify cryptocurrencies as commodities (e.g., the United States) or simply apply consumer protection laws. Overall, the key for any jurisdiction is to consider the potential risks and develop a proportional approach to the risks that arise.

B. Alternative Currencies: Legal Status and Regulatory Implications

Only certain types of alternative currencies have triggered a regulatory response. Unlike their freely convertible counterparts, alternative currencies operating within closed virtual systems and semi-convertible alternative currencies (popular in computer games) remain unregulated.[42]

Regulatory treatment of freely convertible alternative currencies (including many cryptocurrencies) is more complicated. Clear links to the real economy and entry points to the formal payment system are causes for concern. The most popular reaction has been in the form of warnings and prohibitions on their use in the formal payment system. Some jurisdictions have gone further, attempting to subject cryptocurrencies to comprehensive domestic regulation.[43] The effectiveness of these measures hinges on clear definitions being used—yet most regulators reuse the existing terminology and therefore fail to achieve the required clarity.

Cryptocurrencies issued by central banks might further complicate the existing taxonomy.

Alternative currencies present challenges for monetary policy and financial regulation. Particular attention is paid to the areas of monetary stability, consumer protection, and taxation. From the standpoint of monetary policy, the main question is whether alternative currencies pose risks to the central banks' or monetary authorities' ability to manage the economy and maintain the integrity of the national monetary system. Appropriate macroeconomic policy (together with stable inflation and a prudent fiscal position) should reinforce trust in the domestic currency, removing the need for non-sovereign alternatives. Although the volatility of cryptocurrencies has been very high, so far there appears to be little linkage to the traditional financial system, thus minimizing potential sources of systemic risk. The Financial Stability Board has concluded there is as yet no "material risk to global financial stability."[44] However, monitoring of cryptocurrency markets is certainly valuable. Second, alternative currencies may not be adequately captured by existing regulatory instruments in the area of financial fraud and crime. Financial authorities should issue regulatory guidance based on thorough investigation of the associated benefits and risks of alternative currencies. It is still unclear which, if any, alternative currencies should be regulated and, if so, how.

Finally, alternative currencies raise tax issues and challenges. In 2014, the U.S. Internal Revenue Service announced its intention to treat convertible virtual currency—such as Bitcoin—as property for tax purposes. If Bitcoin is treated as property, the use of Bitcoin will be subject to capital gains tax. For example, a taxpayer who pays for something with Bitcoin needs to treat it as disposing of a property, meaning that she will have to realize income if the value of Bitcoin has appreciated. This may further discourage the use of Bitcoin as a payment method due to unfavorable tax consequences. As such, potential tax consequences and pitfalls of treating any type of alternative currency as property rather than currency need to be carefully reviewed against the benefits of their potential use.

C. Sovereign Digital Currencies and Cryptocurrencies

It would be naïve to expect governments and regulators to idly sit back and observe cryptocurrencies, which have the potential to challenge fiat currency. Since direct regulation of cryptocurrencies built on a permissionless blockchain can be impractical, if not impossible (especially in the absence of a coordinated *international* response), a number of countries are rethinking their approach to cryptocurrencies. Instead of attempting to regulate elusive cryptocurrencies with no issuer or center of operation, a paradigm shift is beginning toward considering offering end users government-issued or government-backed digital currencies. These could be more resilient and useful than unregulated cryptocurrencies and may even come with benefits for regulators (such as automated taxation).

We envisage three alternative approaches: (1) central bank accounts with general access, (2) central bank accounts with intermediated access, and (3) new digital forms of fiat currency.[45]

D. Central Bank P2P/Intermediated Payment Systems

Alternative options for storing value in the form of official currency were previously not technologically feasible. However, now, there are increasingly proposals to allow broader access to central bank accounts for the public and non-financial institutions. Such access can be provided to end users *directly* or *via intermediaries* (e.g., private operators guaranteed by central banks).[46]

Such discussions raise a major policy question: If the technology is now available to replace interbank large value payment systems, should we? The major central banks that have faced this question so far (e.g., Bank of England and Bank of Canada) have chosen not to take this leap. From a policy standpoint, the arguments in terms of efficiency and macroeconomic and macroprudential monitoring capability for the central bank are compelling, as is the possibility of removing the traditional public good of providing payments from the banking system. However, the existing system is familiar and arguably robust. Payment systems in major markets functioned without issue throughout the 2008 crisis. Further, there is real concern about the impact on the banking system—and the important roles it plays in financial intermediation and savings.

E. Sovereign (Central Bank) Cryptocurrencies

The prospect of an "official" cryptocurrency has begun to attract attention, with Venezuela being the first country to officially create one.[47] A summary of countries taking steps in this direction is highlighted in Table 11.3.

Table 11.3. Summary table of central bank cryptocurrencies: Existing and announced projects

Country	Currency/Project	Description	Source
Brazil		Researching digital fiat currencies and related architecture	Central Bank of Brazil July 2018[48]
Canada		Central bank studying key design questions relating to a central bank digital currency (CBDC)	Bank of Canada Oct. 1, 2018[49]
China		Central bank (PBOC) developing a digital currency	Library of Congress[50]
East Caribbean	Digital East Caribbean dollar	Considering issuing a digital currency by the East Caribbean Central Bank; cooperation of eight national central banks	Forbes May 2018[51]
Ecuador	Dinero electronico (decommissioned)	Legislation passed in September 2014 with Dinero becoming spendable in February 2015. Decommissioned in Dec 2017	Cato Institute[52]
Estonia		Central bank decided against issuing a digital currency (Estcoin)	Bloomberg June 2018[53]
Hong Kong		Central bank (HKMA) has no plan to issue a digital currency	The Government of Hong Kong
India		Central bank (RBI) investigating issuing a digital currency	Reserve Bank of India
Indonesia	Digital Rupiah	Central bank (BoI) considering issuing a digital rupiah.	The Jakarta Post
Israel		Central bank does not recommend issuing a digital currency (E-Shekel)	Bank of Israel November 2018[54]
Japan		No plan to issue a digital currency	Reuters quoting Bank of Japan— October 2018[55]

(Continued)

Table 11.3. Continued

Country	Currency/Project	Description	Source
Kazakhstan	CryptoTenge	Creating sovereign cryptocurrency tied to fiat	Cointelegraph— May 2018[56]
Kyrgyzstan		Creating gold-backed digital currency	Forbes
Marshall Islands	SOV	Sovereign digital currency based on blockchain and issued by the Minister of Finance given legislative backing on February 26, 2018	Nitijela— Parliament of the Republic of the Marshall Islands[57]
Netherlands		Central bank (DNB) critical of CBDCs	DNB Annual Report 2017[58]
Papua New Guinea		Blockchain is supported. Central bank states blockchain could lead to CBDC issuance	BankPNG 2016 and 2017[59]
Russia	Cryptoruble	Government considering issuing a CryptoRuble	New York Times 2018[60]
Senegal	eCFA	Supported by Senegalese Central Bank and issued by regional bank, Banque Regionale De Marches, eCFA is a West African Economic and Monetary Union (cross-border) digital currency based on the franc	BRM November 2016[61]
Singapore		Central bank (MAS) hesitant to issue a digital currency, but leaves the issue open for further consideration	Straits Times[62]
South Africa		Central bank states it is too risky to issue a CBDC	South African Reserve Bank August 2017
South Korea		Central bank (BoK) investigating the possibility of a digital currency	The Korea Times[63]
Sweden	E-krona	Central bank seriously considering issuing a digital currency	Riksbank October 2018[64]

Table 11.3. Continued

Country	Currency/Project	Description	Source
Thailand	Project Inthanon	Central bank (BoT), with a number of banks, developing a wholesale CBDC to facilitate interbank settlements by Q1 2019	Bank of Thailand August 21, 2018[65]
Tunisia	e-Dinar	Government-sponsored and implemented by La Poste Tunisienne (Tunisian Post Office), Monetas (Swiss Tech firm) and DigitUs (Tunisian startup).	Carnegie Middle East Centre; e-dinar.poste.tn 2017[66]
United Kingdom		Not considering issuing a digital currency	Bank of England[67]
Uruguay		Central bank (CBoU) conducted a pilot of a digital Uruguayan peso	Central Bank of Uruguay November 2017[68]
United States		U.S. Fed states there is no compelling reason for a Fed-issued digital currency	Federal Reserve May 2018
Venezuela	Petro	Government launched a sovereign digital currency supported by a basket of commodities in February 2018	Government of Venezuela February 2018[69]

A central-bank-issued cryptocurrency is an attempt to marry the benefits of certain alternative currencies and central bank money. DLT (especially in the form of blockchain) offers various advantages for digital central bank money, such as its tamper-evident record of each transaction and elimination of intermediaries and corresponding risks. Universal acceptance within the formal payment system is ensured while middlemen are eliminated. The key disadvantage of existing forms of digital central bank money is removed as it becomes directly accessible for the majority of end users, not simply the commercial banks.[70]

1. Benefits, Opportunities, and Risks

A number of governments have begun preparations for launching sovereign digital currencies. The very small number of countries working in this space suggests governments are either (1) concerned cryptocurrencies may upset the duality of central bank and commercial bank money in existing payment systems and wish to create better alternatives, or (2) see sufficient benefits from new sovereign digital currencies (or both). Sovereign digital currencies can also be used for raising money by the state—a feature of Venezuela's Petro.[71] Petro was launched by the government of Venezuela in 2018. It is an asset-backed cryptocurrency, backed by raw materials such as oil and gold. The Petro was designed to supplement Venezuela's ailing economy and raise capital and attract investment by circumventing U.S. sanctions.

2. Benefits and Opportunities

First, sovereign digital currencies may reduce the risks associated with the circulation of fiat money in digital form, which today is routinely through commercial bank accounts. Direct access to central bank money generally remains a privilege for a limited number of entities, but sovereign digital currencies may offer much broader access. Central banks could act as the ultimate trusted intermediary that is immune to insolvency, replacing commercial banks. A truly disintermediated sovereign digital currency is conceivable in theory, but seems unlikely in practice, since regulators would have to relinquish control over transaction confirmation and record-keeping.

Second, integration of blockchain into the sovereign digital currency offers enhanced record-keeping. Tracing functionality would enhance the quality of data on the national economy compiled by central banks. Ironically, this enticing benefit for regulators may be seen as unnecessarily intrusive by end users and could promote the use of "real" cash instead.

Third, sovereign digital currencies could be used as a vehicle for critical national expenditure (public procurement, government subsidies) to bypass commercial banks completely. This could substantially reduce systemic risks associated with commercial banks, lower the impact of collapse of any given financial institution, and, consequently, diminish incentives to bail out failed banks.

Fourth, central banks and governments could modernize their aging wholesale payment systems with advanced functionality such as supporting smart contracts.[72]

Fifth, sovereign digital currencies have the potential to dramatically alter the financial inclusion landscape, provided the necessary infrastructure is in place, including providing enhanced control for regulators over benefits distribution.

3. Challenges

Regulatory challenges relating to sovereign digital currencies can be grouped into three categories.

The first covers technical issues involved in setting up a sovereign digital currency, particularly in the absence of accepted international standards on DLT and blockchain. Regulators are faced with a multitude of possible design choices, yet may have inadequate resources or only limited access to the required expertise. There are many technical questions regulators must answer. Should the system utilize DLT and, if so, using what consensus algorithm? Will the database be a blockchain and, if so, how will the blocks be linked together? What cybersecurity protections should be put in place? Can each unit of sovereign digital currency be traced back to its source, and, if so, how would such system scale over time? How can mistakes/erroneous payments be rectified? Which algorithm or regulator/authority/group of entities will control issuance? What information about users and their transactions will be public, and what only available to the regulator? How do end users access their balances: via biometric/multifactor identification or otherwise?

The second concerns the impact of a sovereign digital currency on the payment system, financial market, and economy as a whole. Regulators should perform a comprehensive ex ante analysis of the system, identifying entities that may end up in direct competition with the state once it implements an "official" cryptocurrency (e.g., commercial banks, electronic money issuers). Excessive competition from the state may require some to rethink their business model, relocate, or cease operations altogether. Uncontrolled implementation of sovereign digital currencies may lead to commercial bank runs and upset the duality of central bank and commercial bank money, which forms the basis of most payment systems. Regulators might consider collaboration, such as by utilizing existing infrastructure of commercial banks by agreement. On the other hand, regulators may implement measures to create a level playing field—or even artificially make sovereign digital currencies less attractive by establishing upper limits or otherwise (at least initially). While partnership with private entities reduces the time to implement new currency systems, the impact of involving private entities must be carefully considered if they will acquire proprietary information. Regulators must also consider any implications for money supply and whether the new currency will be issued via an ICO or in exchange for other forms of sovereign money (e.g., cash) or commercial bank money (or both) and design corresponding conversion mechanisms.

Third are legal challenges concerning the need to introduce the concept of sovereign digital currency into the national regulatory system. These may, in turn, alter the existing approach to regulation of non-sovereign cryptocurrencies.

A trusted central bank cryptocurrency would likely be attractive in a range of other DLT applications. In particular, there are significant discussions regarding "stable coins"—cryptocurrencies backed by fiat currencies. Rather than issuing a sovereign cryptocurrency, a central bank might allow the creation of a stable coin, backed by deposits of fiat currency with the central bank, which could effectively serve as sovereign currency in specific systems, for instance applications developed on Corda.FaceBook's proposed cryptocurrency likewise appears to fall into this categaory.

IV.   Initial Coin Offerings and Tokenization

ICOs are one application of DLT and typically represent a combination of distributed ledgers and crowdfunding. A digital token evidences (or at least purports to evidence)[73] some right or interest. ICOs—like crowdfunding—take a number of forms, depending on what sort of token or digital asset is being offered.

A.   ICO Typology

Donation ICOs are tokens offered in exchange for donations in support of something, mirroring donation-based crowdfunding, for instance on GoFundMe.com.

Rewards ICOs tokenize some sort of advance purchase or entitlement to the outcomes of a project, mirroring reward-based crowdfunding, for instance on KickStarter.com. These are frequently labeled as "usage" or "utility" tokens but this label is frequently applied in too expansive a manner to try to avoid characterization as a financial product. The key to a rewards ICO is that it entitles the tokenholder to use something in the future, such as paying in advance for a software license.

Investment ICOs involve issuance of tokens for investment opportunities generating financial return, typically involving income or potential profits through the appreciation of the value of the token. Investment ICOs raise the same issues and risks as any other form of financial product, albeit with the addition of issues raised by the application of DLT. Investment ICOs in the United States, and increasingly in other jurisdictions, are being characterized as securities, and subject to the full rigor of securities laws.[74]

Cryptocurrency ICOs raise funds to develop or distribute new cryptocurrencies. These are often combined with some aspect of blockchain, tokenization, and/or smart contracts. As such, they are often, in reality, investment ICOs, with pure cryptocurrency ICOs being uncommon. For pure cryptocurrency ICOs, the typical regulatory treatment is under currency, payment, or commodity rules, resulting in a lower regulatory burden than investment ICOs. Cryptocurrency ICOs that confer upon the tokenholder the right to an amount of cryptocurrency could also be classified as derivatives, as the value of the ICO derives from the value of the underlying cryptocurrency.

ICOs can also be asset-backed. In a rewards structure, the token might take the form of a digital coupon that could be presented for an underlying asset (e.g., pizza). In an investment structure, the token could represent an investment asset (e.g., a security). In a cryptocurrency ICO, the token could represent another cryptocurrency. Such tokens highlight an important element of the broader potential of blockchain: the use of digital tokens to provide liquidity, transparency, and permanence for real assets that were previously largely illiquid or where ownership and/or providence concerns are high. Asset-backed tokens and security tokens ("STOs") form a rapidly growing percentage of investment ICOs.

From this typology, an ICO can be seen as an application of blockchain or DLT, in the context of fundraising. ICOs may or may not involve cryptocurrency but will typically involve the conferral of rights that are issued and managed on a blockchain.

B. ICOs in Asia

Asia has been a substantial source of both investment in and offerings of ICOs, as highlighted in Figures 11.10 to 11.14.

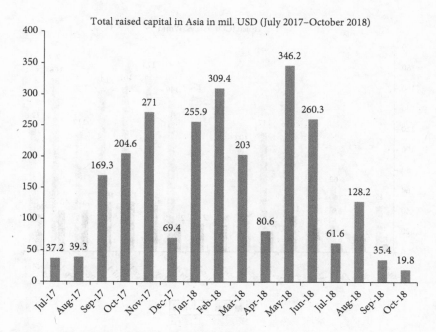

Figure 11.10. Total raised USD in Asia in mil USD.
Source: TrackICO (web-scraped); 422/188 observations.[75]

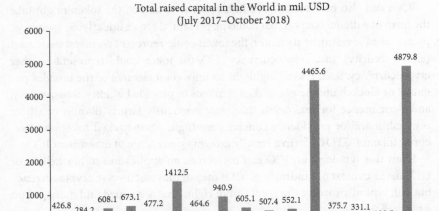

Figure 11.11. Total raised USD worldwide in Mil USD.

Source: TrackICO (web-scraped); 704 full observations.

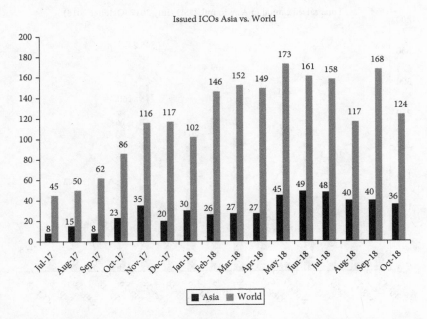

Figure 11.12. Issued ICOs—Asia vs. World (period: 01.07.2017–31.10.2018).

Source: TrackICO (web-scraped); Asian sample includes 477 ICOs, world sample includes 1,926 ICOs.

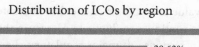

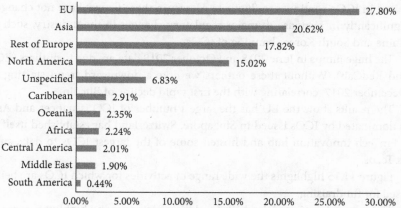

Figure 11.13. Distribution of ICOs by region: World and Asia (period: July 2017–October 2018).

Source: TrackICO (web-scraped); sample of 892 ICOs.

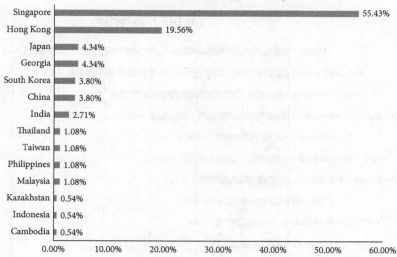

Figure 11.14. Distribution of ICOs by country (Asia).

Source: TrackICO (web-scraped); sample of 184 ICOs.

Just as the value of cryptocurrencies has fluctuated over time, the total capital raised in ICOs continues to fluctuate. However, these figures have not changed significantly in response to major regulatory changes in the industry, such as China and South Korea's banning of ICOs.

The huge jumps in June 2018 and October 2018 data are due to outliers (EOS and RedCab). Without these outliers we note a downward trend starting in December 2017, correlating with the first rapid decline of Bitcoin.

The results show the EU has the largest number of ICO issuances and Asia is dominated by ICOs issued in Singapore. Switzerland has established itself as a FinTech innovation hub and hosted some of the largest ICOs to date, such as Tezos.

Figure 11.15 highlights the wide range of activities for which ICOs are being used for fundraising.

The range of projects for which fundraising is occurring highlights some of the greatest potential benefits of the combination of blockchain and crowd-funding, as highlighted in Figure 11.16.

ICOs thus are a form of raising finance built around the "tokenization" of assets. Distributed ledgers store and allocate tokens among ICO participants. The technology offers transparency of entitlements offered and shared across

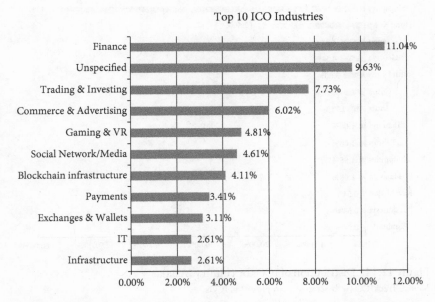

Figure 11.15. Distribution of ICOs by industry: Asia (July 2017–October 2018).
Source: dataset hand-compiled based on ICO whitepapers by the authors; sample size 996 ICOs.

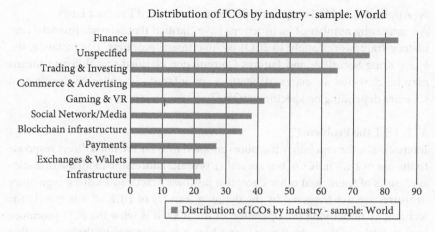

Figure 11.16. Distribution of ICOs by industry: World.
Source: dataset hand-compiled based on ICO whitepapers by the authors; sample size 996 ICOs.

the entire ledger. Coupled with blockchain, it also allows better tracking of such entitlements, since each transfer will be recorded in order.[76] DLT-based cryptocurrencies are often used as consideration in exchange for ICO tokens, but consideration can generally take the form of any valuable asset.[77]

C. Regulation of ICOs in Asia

Regulators in Asia have adopted a range of responses to ICOs.

1. Outright Ban

In light of the SEC's investigations into "pump and dump" ICO schemes in the United States,[78] China and South Korea issued outright bans on ICOs in September 2017, although South Korea's position has since softened to some extent.

2. Regulatory Warnings

Other regulators in Asia have adopted a more cautious approach, issuing warnings stressing the risks of investment in ICOs. The Monetary Authority of Singapore for instance proposed the "ask–check–confirm" approach: (1) ask questions to understand the investment opportunity, (2) check whether the information provided is true, and (3) confirm the seller's credentials (Monetary Authority of Singapore 2017b).

3. Application of Existing Securities and Investment Product Laws

An increasing number of jurisdictions have clarified that relevant financial regulatory frameworks apply to ICOs as investment products. For instance, the Hong Kong Securities and Futures Commission clarified that different tokens may be classified as shares, debentures, or interests in collective investment schemes depending on specific criteria.[79]

4. Is DLT the Problem?

Interestingly, the regulatory measures adopted thus far are not a direct response to the use of DLT in ICOs, but are rather prosaic: addressing inadequate disclosure, risks of fraud, and other deceptive business practices. Existing regulatory measures are not triggered by the defining features of DLT, as it is merely the technology underlying the operation of the ICO. It is what the ICO promises, how it discloses the risks it poses, and how it is promoted to the market, that will determine how it falls for regulation.

V. DLT: Risks and Concerns

Despite the prospective benefits offered by DLT, implementation of this technology has been fraught with difficulties that highlight its potential weaknesses. The starting point is that "risk does not vanish if financial services are provided via distributed ledgers."[80] Three major types of risk are most relevant for DLT: ledger transparency risks, cyber risks, and operational risks.

A. Transparency Risks

The key concept underlying DLT—that the same data are distributed among all data nodes—promotes transparency as well as security. The data that end up being distributed across the entire ledger can be repackaged or encrypted, but remain accessible by every node operator. This makes DLT systems potentially ideal for dealing with issues concerning money laundering.

At the same time, this creates obvious complications whenever shared data must remain confidential. Even where data do not reveal a person's identity (e.g., a Bitcoin wallet owner) because a private key is required, there is a risk the information from the user's profile can be used to reconstitute such identity. Repersonalization of pseudonymous data on distributed ledgers has already become a rapidly growing area of business.[81]

Increased transparency puts a higher emphasis not only on the protection of data but also on its structure and content. Distribution of personal data is restricted under data protection laws in some countries, and penalties for violations may be severe. This also raises problems in the cross-border context, as data protection legislation varies from jurisdiction to jurisdiction. This raises the potential need for regional cooperation in addressing data issues—and also for technological solutions, including through DLT.

B. Cyber Risks

DLT does not result in an immediate reduction of cyber risks, and in some cases even enhances them.

First, inaccurate data distributed across a distributed network will remain inaccurate, and its visibility within the entire network may increase the likelihood of others acting upon such data. The use of DLT does not rectify inaccurate data.

Second, DLT offers increased safety of data compared to a centralized ledger only when the cybersecurity of the central node is lower than the resilience of the number of nodes sufficient to establish consensus. This assumption is often inaccurate—for instance, not all nodes of a distributed ledger are equally secure. Ledgers that require a majority of nodes to vote for a consensus may be more easily manipulated if attacks are targeting nodes with the weakest level of cybersecurity.[82]

While the use of DLT is proliferating in Asia, there are to date no applicable systems of certification. While DLT is attractive, the reality is that different applications of the same technology are not created equal.

C. Operational Risks

Operational risks are another area where DLT's strengths may turn into weaknesses. Any errors in the ledger's code are replicated across the entire network. Outdated or otherwise insecure code can be abused by attackers in widescale attacks.[83] At the same time, the consensus mechanism used to reconcile data across nodes may itself be inadequately coded and, consequently, exploited.

The distributed nature of a ledger does not reduce the end users' reliance on experts who understand how the system operates. When mistakes happen or expectations associated with DLT are not met, questions as to who is responsible will arise.

It is important to note that simply because Bitcoin has proven famously robust, not all applications of DLT will be. There is a need for a certification system to differentiate the quality of DLT-based systems, for instance through the International Standards Organization's (ISO) certification processes.

D. Blockchain-Specific Risks

Blockchain's key distinguishing feature is the sequential order of data that is split into portions ("blocks"). This structure allows information to be added, but not removed. Changes to a single block in the chain require alteration of the whole sequence of later blocks. Depending on the consensus algorithm implemented on a distributed ledger, this feature may make reversal of records extremely difficult, creating a semblance of immutability.

The append-only nature of blockchain is at odds with the "right to be forgotten" granted in some jurisdictions.[84] It may also preclude effective implementation of certain remedies, in cases where records need to be reversed. For example, if a fraudulent transfer of title occurs, the title could be subsequently transferred back to the rightful owner, but the block recording the fraudster's transaction would remain on the chain. At the same time, consensus algorithms could be adjusted to provide for transaction reversal where necessary.

VI. Policy Issues and Challenges: Devising Appropriate Regulatory Responses to DLT

Regulatory measures addressing technological innovation take time to develop, and governments often silently observe trends and assess risks underlying new technologies. While regulators are waiting, businesses develop new business models and products implementing the new technologies. If successful, this implementation may delay or eliminate the need for new regulation. However, if new—especially systemic—risks emerge, a regulatory response may be needed swiftly. Urgent measures generally target specific business models or products, rather than technologies, such as regulatory responses that currently target ICOs, rather than DLT.

A. International Regulatory Context

The main regulatory challenge for DLT applications lies in its multifaceted nature. Some legislatures are attempting to provide a firm legal basis for distributed ledgers by implementing definitions in statutes.[85] Others focus specifically on blockchain.[86] The majority, however, are silent on both concepts.

This does not mean, however, that DLT systems operate in a legal vacuum. Both regulators and lawyers apply already existing legal principles, including but not limited to company, contract, tort, and property law. It is likely jurisdictions will approach the matter differently in the absence of international rules.[87]

Early attempts to regulate DLT have been fraught with problems of terminology. "Blockchain" has proven difficult to define, culminating in rules that are overly simplistic or even misleading. For example, Arizona's new blockchain law claims data stored on a blockchain are *"immutable,"* creating a qualitative test that is extremely difficult for any DLT application to fulfill, since absolute immutability remains unrealistic in practice. One of the latest attempts to fix the terminology barrier is the creation of a dedicated ISO Committee focusing on the development of a range of international standards.[88]

We recommend regulators first prioritize regulating the principal applications of DLT, focusing on digital assets such as cryptocurrencies, and ICOs, and do not devote substantial resources to regulating the technology itself. The regulation of technology is arduous (given its rapid development) and rarely necessary.

B. A Functional Proportional Approach Balancing Risks and Opportunities

The potential of DLT in any particular context varies with the needs and requirements of the individual use-case, and whether the core attributes of DLT (security, transparency, permanence) are beneficial. DLT is not the solution to all problems but may in some contexts constitute an appropriate—or even transformative—platform technology.

Use-cases that benefit from security, transparency, and permanence include registration or ownership of property and property rights as well as the execution of standard transactions (e.g., clearing and settlement systems). Use-cases where a chain of custody are significant include trade in goods, artworks, jewelry, and diamonds. For areas where speed, anonymity, and fungibility are central (such as securities trading), DLT solutions are far less likely to be suitable.

Over time, perhaps the greatest impact of DLT may be that it encourages a wide range of people to reconsider the design of underlying systems and infrastructure and how new technologies, whether DLT-based or not, might allow the redesign of these systems. Many companies have outdated software systems and DLT is providing an impetus for their replacement to be considered.

Nonetheless, even if DLT is suitable, there are wide variations in design and governance.

Whether individual jurisdictions will need specific legislation to support DLT depends on: (1) the features of that legal system and its policy choices, (2) the robustness of consumer protection legislation and enforcement arrangements, and (3) data protection rules (given data are stored by multiple nodes simultaneously).

Where legislation could provide additional certainty is in the field of conflicts of law where multiple nodes from multiple jurisdictions interact. National legislation could clarify which law applies to DLT solutions that involve multiparty contracts and partnerships, and more precisely what type of connecting factor determines the applicable law.

There will also be a need to consider how specific applications fall into functional categories that draw additional regulatory attention, such as payment, credit provision, and insurance. In each case, DLT should be treated according to the applicable general principles (e.g., financial stability, financial integrity, and competition considerations).

Finally, exchanges and similar arrangements should be subject to specific attention, with differential treatment depending on the type of digital asset involved (in particular, digital financial products).

C. Core Strategy and the Role of International Regulatory Cooperation

In summary, we recommend the following approach:

1. Policymakers and regulators should treat DLT as a platform technology that can be used across a variety of functional areas.

2. There should be a system of categorization and certification (e.g., through the ISO) combined with the general legal system, and in particular consumer protection, data protection, choice of law, and competition frameworks.

3. Regulatory treatment should vary depending on the context, but for now, the priority should be regulating applications of DLT, focusing on digital assets and markets, including cryptocurrencies, cryptocurrency exchanges, and ICOs.

4. There must be a focus on public interactions with DLT and the role of intermediaries, as this is where the greatest risks have arisen and are likely to arise in the future (with digital asset exchanges the most urgent focus so as to address the largest range of market integrity, consumer protection, and financial stability risks).

5. Policymakers and regulators should strive to better understand individual use-cases and systems, balancing the innovative opportunities presented with a prudent perspective on risk. This will require substantial investment in tech expertise.

Appendix:
Regulatory Statements in Asia

Table 11.4. Major policy and regulatory events concerning cryptocurrencies and ICOs in China, Singapore, South Korea, Japan, Hong Kong, Macau, Malaysia, Thailand, and Indonesia (end of October 2018)

	Date	Event
China	12/5/2013	People's Bank of China (PBOC) announces a ban on financial institutions transacting in Bitcoin from April 2014 Bitcoin is defined as a virtual commodity that is not a currency. Banks are requested to extend their money-laundering supervision to institutions providing cryptocurrency services. Citizens can trade in Bitcoin online but are warned of the risks
	5/7/2014	PBOC warns banks to tighten monitoring of virtual currency trades, notably Bitcoin
	1/20/2016	PBOC plans to issue a sovereign digital currency following studies beginning in 2014
	1/11/2017	PBOC announces Bitcoin exchanges will be inspected for regulatory compliance breaches
	9/4/2017	China bans all domestic ICOs following a PBOC report that states 90% are fraudulent. ICO rules prohibit financial institutions and nonbank payment institutions from directly or indirectly providing cryptocurrency services
	9/15/2017	China officially bans all domestic virtual currency exchanges. PBOC issues a joint statement that cryptocurrencies do not have the legal status of money
	11/20/2017	China says people are free to participate in the Bitcoin market
	1/17/2018	PBOC orders financial institutions to shut down payment services that trade virtual currencies
	2/5/2018	PBOC states regulations will be tightened to ban domestic investors transacting in overseas ICOs and virtual currencies. Measures strengthened to block online platforms (domestic and offshore) engaged in virtual currency trading and ICOs
Singapore	1/8/2014	Singapore states Bitcoin is not a currency for taxation purposes
	3/13/2014	Monetary Authority of Singapore (MAS) states virtual currency intermediaries will be regulated to address potential money laundering and terrorist financing risks
	8/25/2016	MAS proposes a new regulatory framework for digital payments to capture virtual currency intermediaries

(Continued)

Table 11.4. Continued

	Date	Event
	11/16/2016	Singapore announces development of a blockchain proof-of-concept pilot project ("Ubin") for inter-bank payments
	8/1/2017	MAS announces plans to regulate ICOs that are deemed "securities" under the Securities and Futures Act
	8/10/2017	Singapore issues consumer advice on investment schemes involving digital tokens including virtual currencies
	11/14/2017	MAS issues Guide to Digital Token Offerings
	11/21/2017	Singapore releases a proposed Payment Services Bill and consultation paper to regulate payment activities including virtual currency services
	12/19/2017	MAS cautions against investments in cryptocurrencies
	5/24/2018	MAS warns ICO issuers trading in digital tokens that are deemed securities that they need MAS authorization
	8/24/2018	MAS and SGX partner with Anquan, Deloitte, and Nasdaq to harness blockchain for settlement of tokenized assets
South Korea	12/10/2013	Bank of Korea, Financial Supervisory Service, Ministry of Strategy and Finance, and Financial Services Commission (FSC) state Bitcoin and other virtual currencies are not legal currency
	12/12/2013	President of the Bank of Korea recommends Bitcoin should be regulated
	11/18/2016	FSC launches task force and convenes a meeting of supervisors to discuss the regulation of digital currencies and crypto exchange licensing rules
	7/3/2017	Bill introduced to amend the Electronic Financial Transactions Act that requires traders, brokers, or other businesses involved in cryptocurrency transactions to obtain regulatory approval from the FSC
	9/29/2017	FSC bans all forms of cryptocurrency-based money raising activities (including ICOs) over concerns of fraud and speculation
	12/6/2017	FSC issues a directive banning securities firms from intermediating in Bitcoin futures transactions
	12/19/2017	FSC warns public about risks of investing in virtual currencies
	1/11/2018	Justice Minister states regulators are preparing legislation to halt cryptocurrency trading—this never eventuates
	1/18/2018	FSC states the government is considering a ban on all virtual currency exchanges—never eventuates Bank of Korea reiterates cryptocurrencies are not legal currency
	1/30/2018	Korea Financial Intelligence Unit (KFIU) issues Virtual Currency Anti-Money Laundering Guidelines

Table 11.4. Continued

	Date	Event
		Cryptocurrency trading must occur through real-name bank accounts linked to crypto exchanges
	1/31/2018	Finance Minister states government's immediate task is to regulate exchanges
	2/20/2018	Financial Supervisory Service states the government supports "normal" cryptocurrency trading and encourages financial institutions to facilitate transactions with cryptocurrency exchanges
	5/28/2018	Government plans to allow ICOs by suggesting a legislative and policy proposal with consumer protections
	6/8/2018	Korean Policy Advisory Council meets to develop a regulatory framework for cryptocurrency exchanges
	6/27/2018	FSC announces a revision to Virtual Currency Anti-money Laundering Guidelines, effective from July 10, 2018
	7/17/2018	FSC announces creation of the Financial Innovation Bureau (temporary body with a two-year life span) tasked with policy initiatives and responding to new developments with cryptocurrencies
	8/20/2018	Government considers ending the ICO ban and creating an ICO guideline
	10/11/2018	Government states it is likely to announce its position on ICOs in November 2018
Japan	6/19/2014	Financial Services Agency (FSA) starts to develop cryptocurrency regulations following the failure of Mt. Gox—a Bitcoin exchange
	3/4/2016	Virtual currencies recognized as a legal means of payment (not a currency) from April 1 2016
		Bitcoin exchanges will be legally subject to anti-money laundering/know-your-customer rules
		Banks prohibited from dealing in Bitcoins or acquiring a virtual exchange. Banks not prohibited from investments in financial products that incorporate Bitcoin
	5/25/2016	Japan amends the Payment Services Act to define cryptocurrencies and require virtual exchange operators to be subject to financial conditions, such as separating customer assets and undergoing external auditing
	4/1/2017	Amendments to the Payment Services Act take effect Cryptocurrencies are defined as property stored electronically that excludes currency and currency-denominated assets
		Virtual currency (or cryptocurrency) exchange service providers are permitted subject to licensing requirements
	9/30/2017	FSA grants first cryptocurrency exchange licenses
	10/27/2017	FSA issues user and business operator warnings about risks of ICOs

(*Continued*)

Table 11.4. Continued

	Date	Event
	1/30/2018	FSA requests all cryptocurrency exchanges review system-risk management plans and report results
	3/8/2018	FSA creates research group to investigate virtual currency exchanges
	4/5/2018	Government proposes guidelines for ICOs to facilitate stronger consumer protections More stringent registered exchange operator standards proposed pursuant to the Financial Instruments and Exchange Act to oblige separation of customer funds and introduce insider trading rules
	8/6/2018	Virtual Currency Exchange Association, a self-regulatory body, which represents all 16 approved crypto exchanges, successfully applies for FSA certification
Hong Kong	11/16/2013	Hong Kong Monetary Authority (HKMA) states Bitcoin is a virtual commodity, not a currency
	1/8/2014	Government states Bitcoin and other virtual currencies are virtual commodities
	1/9/2014	HKMA issues circular on virtual commodity risks
	1/16/2014	Securities and Futures Commission (SFC) issues circular on the money laundering and terrorist financing risks associated with virtual commodities
	1/29/2014	Insurance Authority issues a letter to authorized insurers on the money laundering and terrorist financing risks associated with virtual commodities
	3/14/2014	Government warns public of the risks associated with virtual commodities
	3/21/2014	SFC issues another circular on the money laundering and terrorist financing risks associated with virtual commodities
	3/21/2014	Insurance Authority issues another letter on virtual commodity money laundering and terrorist financing risks
	4/30/2014	HKMA issues letter to all authorized institutions warning of virtual commodity risks
	2/11/2015	HKMA warns of risks associated with Bitcoin
	3/25/2016	Government indicates no need to regulate or ban trading in Bitcoin or other virtual commodities
	9/5/2017	SFC states digital tokens offered in an ICO may be "securities" and therefore subject to the Securities and Futures Ordinance
	11/8/2017	Government says digital tokens should be considered virtual commodities rather than currencies
	12/11/2017	SFC issues reminder on cryptocurrency-related products and derivatives
	2/9/2018	SFC warns of cryptocurrency exchange and ICO risks

Table 11.4. Continued

	Date	Event
	6/1/2018	SFC issues circular to cryptocurrency intermediaries on compliance with notice requirements
Macau	9/27/2017	Macau issues alert on risks of virtual commodities and tokens
Malaysia	9/7/2017	Malaysia issues caution to investors on the risks of ICOs
	1/19/2018	Malaysia issues caution that ICO issuers may be subject to securities and banking laws
Thailand	10/27/2017	Thailand issues regulatory approach to ICOs
Indonesia	02/06/2014	Bank of Indonesia (BOI) states Bitcoin and other virtual currencies are not currencies or legal payment instruments
	11/09/2016	BOI prohibits payment system operators from processing virtual currencies for payment system activities
	12/19/2017	BOI prohibits financial technology operators from processing payments using virtual currencies
	01/13/2018	BOI warns the public concerning risks of virtual currencies and reiterates virtual currencies including Bitcoin not allowed to be used for payments
	01/23/2018	Minister of Finance warns virtual currencies are high-risk and speculative investments that cannot be legally used for transactions
	06/04/2018	Commodity Futures Trading Supervisory Agency states cryptocurrencies will be treated as futures or commodities and that regulations are being developed to govern the operation of crypto exchanges. Financial Services Authority states the financial industry is barred from trading cryptocurrencies and Bitcoin
India	12/24/2013	Reserve Bank of India (RBI) cautions users, holders, and traders of virtual currencies including Bitcoins about financial, operational, legal, customer protection, and security-related risks
	2/01/2017	RBI states that it has not issued any licenses or authorized any entity to operate schemes or deal in Bitcoin or virtual currencies. (However, it is not illegal to do so)
	4/12/2017	Ministry of Finance constitutes an Inter-Disciplinary Committee to examine the virtual currency regulatory and legal framework and suggest measures for dealing with virtual currencies including consumer protection and money-laundering issues
	12/29/2017	Ministry of Finance cautions the public against the risks of investing in virtual currencies
	2/1/2018	Minister of Finance states the government does not consider cryptocurrencies as legal tender and will take all measures to eliminate their use in financing illegitimate activities or as part of the payment system

(Continued)

Table 11.4. Continued

Date	Event
4/5/2018	RBI states its Inter-Disciplinary Committee will study and provide guidance on the feasibility and desirability of issuing a central bank digital currency RBI states regulated entities shall not deal in virtual currencies from July 6, 2018
4/6/2018	RBI again cautions against virtual currency risks RBI again states regulated entities shall not deal in virtual currencies
10/30/2018	Financial Stability and Development Council briefed to devise an appropriate legal framework to ban the use of private cryptocurrencies while encouraging the use of DLT

Sources:

1. 'Regulators' Statements on Initial Coin Offerings' (*IOSCO*) <www.iosco.org/publications/?subsection=ico-statements> accessed 27 November 2018
2. 'Regulation of Cryptocurrency Around the World' (Library of Congress, China, Korea, and Japan) <www.loc.gov/law/help/cryptocurrency/> accessed 27 November 2018
3. Daniel Holman and Barbara Stettner, 'Anti-Money Laundering Regulation of Cryptocurrency: U.S. and Global Approaches' (ICGL TO: Anti-Money Laundering, Allen & Overy, 2018) 30-31 <www.allenovery.com/publications/en-gb/Documents/AML18_AllenOvery.pdf> accessed 29 November 2018
4. Shen Wenhao and Michael Kim, 'Cryptocurrency laws and regulations in Asia' (*Asia Business Law Journal*, 16 July 2018) <www.vantageasia.com/cryptocurrency-law-asia/> accessed 29 November 2018
5. 'Digital Currencies: International Actions and Regulations' (Perkins Coie LLP, June 2018) <www.perkinscoie.com/en/news-insights/digital-currencies-international-actions-and-regulations.html> accessed 27 November 2018
6. 'China Central Bank Warns Banks on Bitcoin' *Wall Street Journal* (Beijing, 7 May 2014) <www.wsj.com/articles/china-central-bank-warns-banks-on-bitcoin-1399454876> accessed 18 June 2019
7. Xie Yu , 'China orders banks to stop financing cryptocurrencies as noose tightens around disrupter' *South China Morning Post* (Hong Kong and Shanghai, 6 February 2018) <www.scmp.com/business/banking-finance/article/2129645/pboc-orders-banks-halt-banking-services-cryptocurrency> accessed 18 June 2019
8. Monetary Authority of Singapore, *MAS clarifies regulatory position on the offer of digital tokens in Singapore* (1 August 2017) <www.mas.gov.sg/News-and-Publications/Media-Releases/2017/MAS-clarifies-regulatory-position-on-the-offer-of-digital-tokens-in-Singapore>; *Consumer Advisory on Investment Schemes Involving Digital Tokens (Including Virtual Currencies)* (10 August 2017) <www.mas.gov.sg/News-and-Publications/Media-Releases/2017/Consumer-Advisory-on-Investment-Schemes-Involving-Digital-Tokens.aspx>; and *Reply to Parliamentary Question on banning the trading of bitcoin currency or cryptocurrency* (5 February 2018) <www.mas.gov.sg/News-and-Publications/Parliamentary-Replies/2018/Reply-to-Parliamentary-Question-on-banning-the-trading-of-bitcoin-currency-or-cryptocurrency.aspx> accessed 29 November 2018
9. Financial Services Commission (Korea), *Revision to Virtual Currency Anti-Money Laundering Guidelines* (27 June 2018) <www.fsc.go.kr/eng/new_press/releases.jsp?menu=01&bbsid=BBS0048> accessed 18 June 2018
10. Dahee Kim and Cynthia Kim, 'South Korea considers shutting down domestic cryptocurrency exchanges' *Reuters* (Seoul, 18 January 2018) <www.reuters.com/article/us-southkorea-bitcoin/south-korea-considers-shutting-down-domestic-cryptocurrency-exchanges-idUSKBN1F706T>; 'South Korea says no plans to ban cryptocurrency exchanges, uncovers

$600 million illegal trades' *Reuters* (Seoul, 31 January 2018) <www.reuters.com/article/us-southkorea-bitcoin/south-korea-says-no-plans-to-ban-cryptocurrency-exchanges-uncovers-600-million-illegal-trades-idUSKBN1FK09J>; and Cynthia Kim and Heekyong Yang, 'Uproar over crackdown on cryptocurrencies divides South Korea' *Reuters* (Seoul, 12 January 2018) <www.reuters.com/article/us-southkorea-bitcoin/uproar-over-crackdown-on-cryptocurrencies-divides-south-korea-idUSKBN1F10YG> accessed 18 June 2019

11. Yoon Yung-sil , 'S. Korean Financial Authorities Ban Bitcoin Futures Trading' *BusinessKorea* (7 December 2017) <www.businesskorea.co.kr/news/articleView.html?idxno=20022>; 'National Assembly Calls for Measures to Allow ICOs' *BusinessKorea* (29 May 2018); <www.businesskorea.co.kr/news/articleView.html?idxno=22613>; and 'ICOs, Blockchain High on Agenda of Korea's National Assembly Extraordinary Session' *BusinessKorea* (20 August 2018) <www.businesskorea.co.kr/news/articleView.html?idxno=24403> (accessed 18 June 2019)

12. Eun-Jee Park , 'Government to introduce regulations for Bitcoin' *Korea Joongang Daily* (18 November 2016) <http://koreajoongangdaily.joins.com/news/article/Article.aspx?aid=3026364> accessed 18 June 2019

13. Yoo-chul Kim, 'Korea to allow ICOs with new regulations' *The Korea Times* (8 March 2018) <www.koreatimes.co.kr/www/biz/2018/03/367_245242.html> accessed 18 June 2019

14. Hyung-ki Park, 'Korea decides not to recognise Bitcoin as real currency' *Korea Herald* (10 December 2013) <www.koreaherald.com/view.php?ud=20131210000673> accessed 18 June 2019

15. Sung-mi Ahn, 'Gov't likely to announce ICO stance in Nov' *The Investor* (11 October 2018) <www.theinvestor.co.kr/view.php?ud=20181011000606> accessed 18 June 2019

16. Financial Services Agency (Japan) *Establishment of "Study Group on virtual currency exchange industry ect"* (8 March 2018) <www.fsa.go.jp/news/30/singi/20180308.html> accessed 29 November 2018

17. Stacey Steele and Tetsuro Morishita, 'Lessons from Mt Gox: Practical considerations for a virtual currency insolvency' in Douglas W. Arner, Wai Yee Wan, Andrew Godwin, Wei Shen, and Evan Gibson (eds), *Research Handbook on Asian Financial Law* (forthcoming, Edward Elgar 2019)

18. Masakazu "Masa" Masujima, 'Japan's Virtual Currency Regulation and its Recent Developments' p. 21. (Mori Hamada & Matsumoto, April 2018) 21 <https://events.eventact.com/ki2/crypto/Masakazu%20Masujima%20(Mori%20Hamada%20&%20Matsumoto)-Japans%20Virtual%20Currency%20Regulation%20and%20its%20Recent%20Developments.pdf> accessed 18 June 2019

19. 'Regulation of Cryptocurrencies and Initial Coin Offers (ICOs) in Japan' (*Charltons Quantum*, August 2018) <https://charltonsquantum.com/regulation-cyrptocurrency-initial-coin-offerings-ico-japan/> accessed 18 June 2019

20. Yuki Hagiwara and Yuji Nakamura, 'Japan Unveils Guidelines For Allowing Initial Coin Offerings' *Bloomberg* (5 April 2018) <www.bloomberg.com/news/articles/2018-04-05/japan-plans-first-step-toward-legalizing-initial-coin-offerings> accessed 18 June 2019

21. The Government of Hong Kong, *LCQ 1: Monitoring the use of bitcoins* (8 January 2014) <www.info.gov.hk/gia/general/201401/08/P201401080357.htm>; *Hong Kong Government warns public of the risks associated with virtual commodities* (14 March 2014) <www.info.gov.hk/gia/general/201403/14/P201403140751.htm>; LCQ4: Regulation of trading activities of bitcoin (25 March 2015) <www.info.gov.hk/gia/general/201503/25/P201503250463.htm>; *LCQ15: Regulation of offering and trading of digital tokens* (8 November 2017) <www.info.gov.hk/gia/general/201711/08/P2017110800405.htm>; and *LCQ5: Issuance of cryptocurrency* (30 May 2018) <www.info.gov.hk/gia/general/201805/30/P2018053000387.htm> accessed 29 November 2018

22. Securities and Futures Commission (Hong Kong), *Circular to Licensed Corporations and Associated Entities—Anti-Money Laundering / Counter-Terrorist Financing Money Laundering and Terrorist Financing Risks Associated with Virtual Currencies* (16 January 2014) <www.sfc.hk/edistributionWeb/gateway/EN/circular/anti-money-laundering/doc?refNo=14EC2>; *Circular to Licensed Corporations and Associated Entities—Anti-Money Laundering / Counter-Terrorist Financing Money Laundering and Terrorist Financing Risks Associated with Virtual Currencies* (21 March 2014) <www.sfc.hk/edistributionWeb/gateway/EN/circular/anti-money-laundering/doc?refNo=14EC14>; *Statement on initial coin offerings* (5 September 2017) <www.sfc.hk/web/EN/news-and-announcements/policy-statements-and-announcements/statement-on-initial-coin-offerings.html>; and *SFC warns of cryptocurrency*

risks (9 February 2018) <www.hk/distributionWeb/gateway/EN/news-and-announcements/news/doc?refNo=18PR13> accessed 29 November 2018

23. Hong Kong Monetary Authority, *Risks associated with virtual commodities* (9 Janaury 2014) <www.hkma.gov.hk/media/eng/doc/key-information/guidelines-and-circular/2014/20140109e1.pdf>; *Risks associated with virtual commodities* (30 April 2014) <www.hkma.gov.hk/media/eng/doc/key-information/guidelines-and-circular/2014/20140430e1.pdf>; *The HKMA reminds the public to be aware of the risks associated with Bitcoin* (11 February 2015) <www.hkma.gov.hk/eng/key-information/press-releases/2015/20150211-3.shtml>; and The Government of Hong Kong, *Hong Kong and Singapore launch a joint project on cross-border trade and trade finance platform* (15 November 2017) <www.info.gov.hk/gia/general/201711/15/P2017111500600.htm> accessed 18 June 2019

24. Office of the Commissioner of Insurance (Hong Kong), *Money Laundering and Terrorist Financing Risks Associated with Virtual Currencies* (29 January 2014) <www.ia.org.hk/en/legislative_framework/circulars/antimoney_laundering/files/cir_aml_20140129.pdf>; and *Money Laundering and Terrorist Financing Risks Associated with Virtual Currencies* (21 March 2014) <www.ia.org.hk/en/legislative_framework/circulars/antimoney_laundering/files/cir_aml_20140321b.pdf> accessed 29 November 2018

25. , 'Legality by Country (Asia) - Indonesia' *Coinnewsasia* <www.coinnewsasia.com/legality-by-country-asia/> accessed 29 November 2018

26. Bank of Indonesia, *Statement of the Bank of Indonesia Related to Bitcoin and Virtual Currency Offers* (6 February 2014) <www.bi.go.id/id/ruang-media/siaran-pers/Pages/sp_160614.aspx>; and *The Bank of Indonesia Warns not to Sell, Buy or Trade Virtual Currencies* (18 January 2018) <www.bi.go.id/id/ruang-media/siaran-pers/Pages/sp_200418.aspx> accessed 29 November 2018

27. Ministry of Finance (Indonesia), *Minister of Finance: Bitcoin is Not in Line with Law* (25 January 2018) <www.kemenkeu.go.id/en/publications/news/minister-of-finance-bitcoin-is-not-in-line-with-law/> accessed 29 November 2018

28. 'Cryptocurrencies decided as future trading commodity' *The Jakarta Post* (Jakarta, 4 June 2018) <www.thejakartapost.com/news/2018/06/04/cryptocurrencies-decided-as-future-trading-commodity.html> accessed 18 June 2019

29. Andita Rahma, 'OJK: Indonesia Bans Bitcoin, Other Virtual Currencies' *Tempo.co* (Jakarta, 25 January 2018) <http:/en.tempo.co/read/news/2018/01/25/056915174/OJK-Indoensia-Bans-Bitcoin-Other-Virtual-Currencies> accessed 18 June 2019

30. Beo Da Costa and Tabita Diela, 'Indonesia central bank warns over cryptocurrencies' *Reuters* (13 January 2018) <www.reuters.com/article/us-markets-bitcoin-indonesia/indonesia-central-bank-warns-over-cryptocurrencies-idUSKBN1F20A7> accessed 18 June 2019; Reserve Bank of India, *RBI cautions users of Virtual Currencies against Risks* (24 December 2013) <https://rbi.org.in/Scripts/BS_PressReleaseDisplay.aspx?prid=30247>; *RBI cautions users of Virtual Currencies* (1 February 2017) <https://rbi.org.in/Scripts/BS_PressReleaseDisplay.aspx?prid=39435>; *Statement on Development of Regulatory Policies* (5 April 2018) <https://rbi.org.in/Scripts/BS_PressReleaseDisplay.aspx?prid=43574>; and *Prohibition on dealing in Virtual Currencies (VCs)* (6 April 2018) <https://rbi.org.in/Scripts/NotificationUser.aspx?Id=11243> accessed 29 November 2018

32. Government of India, Ministry of Finance, *Government constitutes an Inter- Disciplinary Committee chaired by Special Secretary (Economic Affairs) to examine the existing framework with regard to Virtual Currencies* (12 April 2017) <www.pib.nic.in/newsite/PrintRelease.aspx?relid=160923>; and *19th Meeting of the Financial Stability and Development Council (FSDC) held under the Chairmanship of the Union Finance Minister, Shri Arun Jaitley reviewed the current global and domestic economic situation and financial sector performance; The Council decided that the Regulators and the Government would keep a close watch on the developing situation and take all necessary measures* (30 October 2018) <www.pib.nic.in/newsite/PrintRelease.aspx?relid=184478> accessed 18 June 2019

33. Arun Jaitley (Minister of Finance, India), 'Budget 2018-2019, Speech of Arun Jaitley' (1 February 2018) <www.indiabudget.gov.in/ub2018-19/bs/bs.pdf> accessed 18 June 2019

34. 'Government Cautions People Against Risks in Investing in Virtual 'Currencies'; Says VCs are like Ponzi Schemes' *Press Information Bureau (Government of India)* (Delhi, 29 December 2017) <www.pib.nic.in/PressReleseDetail.aspx?PRID=1514568> accessed 29 November 2018

12

Casting Light on Central Bank Digital Currency

Tommaso Mancini-Griffoli, Maria Soledad Martinez Peria, Itai Agur,
Anil Ari, John Kiff, Adina Popescu, and Céline Rochon*

The impact of digitalization is widespread and profound. It is changing the nature of jobs, education, commerce, innovation, and product life cycles. Demographics are accelerating these developments. Millennials now outnumber baby boomers (Tilford 2018) and are steering the economy toward their world—one in which digital platforms are central, and nearly second nature.

Payments, and more fundamentally money, are also undergoing tremendous change.[1] Technology, new employment arrangements, and the growing decentralized service economy, as well as evolving social attitudes, are driving efforts to build new and more decentralized forms of money. These offer peer-to-peer transactions, micropayments, and easy-to-use interfaces integrated with social networks. Payments are increasingly being diverted toward privately run solutions. Even cryptoassets such as Bitcoin—still early in their development cycle—offer competing forms of money.

Deep and pressing questions consequently arise. Is there a role for cash, or a cash-like form of money, in the digital world? Should central banks offer new forms of money? If so, what are the implications for monetary policy and financial intermediation, stability, and integrity?

* With contributions from Fabio Comelli, Federico Grinberg, Ashraf Khan, and Kristel Poh. An earlier version of this chapter was originally published as IMF Staff Discussion Note 18/08. The views expressed in this chapter are those of the author(s) and do not necessarily represent the views of the IMF, its Executive Board, or IMF management. Reprinted with permission. Gratefully acknowledged is the guidance of Dong He, Giovanni Dell'Ariccia, and Vikram Haksar, and comments by seminar participants at the IMF and Inter-American Development Bank, as well as by IMF reviewing divisions, and also by Tobias Adrian, Jihad Alwazir, Tamim Bayoumi, Pelin Berkmen, Luis Brandao Marques, Jess Cheng, Chris Colford, Ulric Eriksson von Allmen, Gaston Gelos, Masaru Itatani, Nigel Jenkinson, Tanai Khiaonarong, Darryl King, Amina Lahreche, Ross Leckow, Rodolfo Maino, Fabiana Melo, Aditya Narain, Maurice Obstfeld, Luca Ricci, James Roaf, Herve Tourpe, Romain Veyrune, and Froukelien Wendt. Karen Lee provided excellent research assistance. We are indebted to Joe Procopio for copyediting the document.

Central banks are taking these questions seriously. Several are actively investigating the possibility of issuing a central bank digital currency (CBDC). This new central bank liability would be a widely accessible digital form of fiat money, intended as legal tender. One day, it could fully replace physical cash. CBDC seems to be a natural next step in the evolution of official coinage (from metal-based money, to metal-backed banknotes, to physical fiat money).

Against this backdrop, this chapter aims to answer a simple question: Does CBDC offer benefits? On the demand side, would it satisfy end user needs better than other forms of money? And on the supply side, would issuing CBDC allow central banks to more effectively satisfy public policy goals, including financial inclusion, operational efficiency, financial stability, monetary policy effectiveness, and financial integrity? In short, is CBDC a desirable form of money given existing and rapidly evolving alternatives? Although its adoption appears more promising in some circumstances than in others, a final decision requires careful evaluation of country-specific circumstances, including a review of technological feasibility and costs, factors that are beyond the scope of this chapter.

This chapter includes a summary of pilot projects and studies from central banks exploring the possibility of issuing CBDC. The analysis is based on publicly issued materials and discussions with staff members at central banks and technology providers around the world.

Our analysis contributes to a growing body of literature on CBDC. Others have already explored this topic, including international organizations such as the Bank for International Settlements[2] and several central banks (Bank of Canada, People's Bank of China, Bank of England, Bank of Finland, Norges Bank, Danmarks Nationalbank, Sveriges Riksbank),[3] as well as academics and policymakers (Raskin and Yermack 2016; Rogoff 2016; Bordo and Levin 2018; He 2018; He and Khan 2018; Kahn, Rivadeneyra, and Wong 2018). Those analyses discuss the pros and cons of CBDC adoption and, in some cases, make policy recommendations. Our study departs from these earlier analyses in three ways. First, it emphasizes the perspective of users—and their preferences for different features of money—in addition to the goals of central banks. Second, it considers policy responses to CBDC adoption to mitigate ensuing risks. Finally, it offers a one-stop reference on views and ongoing and future plans of some central banks from around the world regarding CBDC.

The chapter is organized in five sections. Section I covers the basics of CDBC. Section II lays out a conceptual framework to compare different forms of money from the standpoint of end users and the central bank. Section III puts the approach to use, evaluating whether there might be a role for CBDC from the perspective of users. Section IV considers that question from the viewpoint of central banks, and in so doing explores different options for designing CBDC. Part of this section is devoted to gauging the impact of CBDC on financial integrity, financial stability, and monetary policy transmission. Section V offers an overview of central bank investigations, and the last section concludes and raises questions for future research on how CBDC might affect cross-border payments.

I. Basics of Central Bank Digital Currency

CBDC would be a new form of money, issued digitally by the central bank and intended to serve as legal tender;[4] however, it would differ markedly from other forms of money typically issued by central banks: cash and reserve balances. CBDC designed for retail payments would be widely available while, in contrast, reserves are available only to selected institutions, mostly banks with accounts at the central bank.[5] Clearly, CBDC is not intended to have a physical form as does cash. But as with cash, it would be widely accessible to a country's residents—and potentially to individuals and organizations abroad.[6] CBDC could be used as easily for person-to-person, person-to-business, and business-to-business transactions of any amount, a notable improvement over cash.[7] Reserves, by contrast, settle wholesale interbank payments only.

CBDC could take account- or token-based forms, the former involving the transfer of a claim on an account and the latter of a token between wallets.[8] A transaction in account-based CBDC would resemble today's transactions between commercial bank depositors, except that accounts would be held with the central bank. A payer would log in to an account at the central bank—for example, through a web page or an app on a mobile device—and request a transfer of funds to a recipient's account, also at the central bank (Figure 12.1).

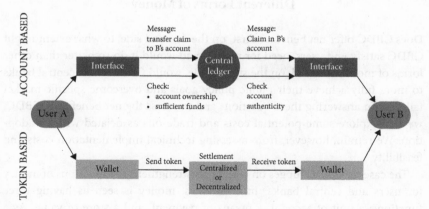

Figure 12.1. Account- and Token-Based CBDC, Basic Mechanics.
Source: IMF staff

The central bank would ensure settlement by updating a master ledger, but only after verification of the payer's authority to use the account, availability of sufficient funds, and authenticity of the payee's account. The exchange of information would therefore be substantial.

Although transactions using token-based CBDC would involve more steps than exchanging cash, they would offer the convenience of not having to meet in person. Unlike cash—the prime example of a traditional token-based form of money—CBDC tokens would be too complex to be distinguished from counterfeits by parties to the transaction. Settling a transaction using token-based CBDC would require external verification of the tokens. As a result, transactions might not be entirely anonymous, as is cash. The extent of anonymity would depend on whether wallets are registered and transaction information is recorded.

Verification of the tokens and settlement could be centralized or decentralized, depending on the technology used. Decentralized settlement is possible via the use of distributed ledger technology (DLT); however, although the technology is evolving, it currently falls short in scalability, energy efficiency, and payment finality (He and others 2017). One potential option for DLT is the use of a closed ("permissioned") network managed by the central bank. But there are other types of centralized settlement technology that may prove more efficient. These approaches would check the validity of the tokens' serial numbers, then reassign numbers once tokens change wallets to avoid the risk of double spending.

II. A Conceptual Framework to Compare Different Forms of Money

Does CBDC offer net benefits? First, on the demand side, to what extent might CBDC satisfy end users' need for money, and would it do so better than other forms of money? Second, on the supply side, would CBDC allow central banks to more fully achieve their public policy goals and overcome specific market failures? In answering these questions and to assess the net benefits of CBDC, we also explore some potential costs and trade-offs associated with its adoption. We refrain, however, from assessing technical implementation costs and feasibility.

The case for CBDC hinges on whether it strengthens the functions of money for users and central banks. In economics, money is seen as having three functions: a unit of account, a means of payment, and a store of value. As a unit of account, money serves as a measuring stick ideally linked to the same basket of goods over time. As a means of payment, it facilitates transactions. As a secure store of value, it provides refuge from various sources of risk, defined later in this chapter.[9]

Users will seek a form of money that maximizes private benefits and minimizes associated costs and risks,[10] and they will use a variety of criteria to evaluate these different forms of money. Figure 12.2 lists these criteria, placing emphasis on the means of payment and store of value functions of money, for which criteria are more diverse. The relative weight of each criterion will vary by country and user.

Of these, one important criterion stands out: the ability to make anonymous transactions. In the context of money, anonymity covers the extent to which identity and transactions are, or can be, disclosed to transaction parties, third parties, and the government. There are legitimate reasons why people may prefer at least some degree of anonymity—potentially when it comes to everyone except the government, and regarding the government unless a court order unlocks encrypted transaction information. It is a way to avoid customer profiling—commercial use of personal information, for example, to charge higher mortgage rates to people who purchase alcohol. Another advantage of anonymity is that it potentially limits exposure to hacking. Moreover, anonymity is often associated with privacy—widely recognized as a human right (as stated in the Universal Declaration of Human Rights [Article 12] and elsewhere).

On the supply side, central banks play a pivotal role and ensure that money delivers on its three functions. For central banks, this role means two things: First, because they are accountable to the public, central banks must design the money they issue—and regulate private forms of money—in a way that satisfies the user needs stated earlier. Second, because they are public policy

	Means of payment	Store of value
Maximize benefits	• *Liquidity:* Payment on demand • *Scalability:* Payment of any size (no limits) • *Acceptance :* Person to person, person to business, business to business to and from any device; no network limitation • *Extra services:* Preferential access to other financial services (loans, advice, etc.)	• *Returns:* Nominal interest payments[11]
Minimize costs	• *Transaction:* Ease of use; fees • *Disclosure:* Degree of anonymity	
Minimize risks	• *Settlement:* Lag between agreeing to a transaction and actual receipt of funds	• *Theft:* Ability to reverse fraudulent transactions, exposure to fraud/cyber risk • *Loss:* Ability to claim ownership or recover access if lost • *Default:* of the money issuer

Figure 12.2. User Criteria to Judge Different Forms of Money.

institutions, they must ensure that money also meets important social criteria (illustrated in Figure 12.3 and discussed in Box 12.1):

- As a *unit of account,* money is an important public good that requires price stability in all economic circumstances. The design of money can favor, or interfere with, this goal. For instance, because cash pays no interest, central banks find it difficult to offer deeply negative interest rates following sharp recessions (discussed more fully in Section IV of this chapter).
- As a *means of payment,* money must be universally available and verifiable as well as efficient, while ensuring appropriate consumer protection and minimal cost to taxpayers.
- As a *store of value,* money must be as secure as possible, but it must also allow for efficient allocation of resources.

In addition to these criteria, central banks will prefer forms of money that support, or at least do not undermine, three other public policy goals: financial integrity, financial stability, and monetary policy effectiveness.[11] In turn, each of these further supports the three functions of money. Financial integrity covers, among other things, anti-money laundering and combating the financing of terrorism (AML/CFT) rules, including customer due diligence measures and additional measures aimed at fighting corruption and fostering good governance.

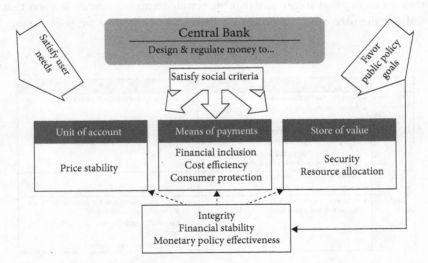

Figure 12.3. The Central Bank's Criteria to Evaluate Different Forms of Money.

Box 12.1. The Birth of Central Banking—a Quest for Efficient, Low-Cost, and Safe Money

There is a fascinating historical account of the birth of central banking in Europe in Kahn, Quinn, and Roberds (2014). Coins were the predominant form of money in medieval times and during the early Renaissance. Although they were a relatively efficient means of payment and allowed immediate settlement, transportation costs grew substantially as commerce spread geographically. Bills of exchange were introduced to decrease these costs; merchants could purchase bills drawn on the foreign banks where they intended to do business. However, bills carried substantial counterparty risk, as debtor banks often did not pay. The Bank of Amsterdam was established in 1609 to reduce the risks inherent in bills of exchange, following earlier (though smaller-scale and private) models, such as the Taula de Canvi in Barcelona (1401), Banco di San Giorgio in Genoa (1408), and Banco di Rialto in Venice (1587). The Bank of Amsterdam stood ready to pay high-quality Dutch guilders against the receipt of bills. In 1683, it offered account balances to settle bills of exchange on its books, and soon thereafter suspended the right of coin withdrawals entirely, thereby shifting the unit of account from commodity money to its liabilities, as in a system with metal-backed banknotes. At its peak in the mid-1700s, yearly turnover through the accounts at the Bank of Amsterdam was more than 2.5 times Dutch GDP.

This evolution highlights ongoing efforts to establish increasingly efficient, secure, and lower-cost forms of money. The Bank of Amsterdam first reduced the risks and costs of payments by offering immediate and final settlement. Then it did more by offering liquidity backstops to merchant banks that were funded with bills of exchange. Without this backstop, merchant banks would have faced a trade-off. They either had to offer a secure store of value by storing the cash received for their bills of exchange or efficiently allocate funds by lending the cash. This would expose them and their creditors to the liquidity risk associated with maturity mismatches. The Bank of Amsterdam's innovation underscores the role of the state in enhancing the safety of private payment systems without contravening their efficiency. Bank supervision, lender of last resort functions, and deposit insurance do much the same today.

Finally, we turn to competitors to CBDC. These fall into four categories, but will vary by country: cash, commercial bank deposits, narrow finance, and cryptoassets. All except cash are evolving and rapidly gaining market share.

Commercial bank deposits are going through notable improvements. Traditionally, payments have been facilitated by debit card networks. Today, two continuing transformations are notable, especially in advanced economies. The first stems from "wrapper" technology—such as Venmo in the United States—which allows transactions to take place between mobile devices (bypassing expensive point-of-sale terminals) and adds a layer of security.[12] The other is central-bank-provided fast-payment solutions ("fast payments").[13] These allow payments of any size and type (person-to-person, person-to-business, business-to-business) to be settled instantaneously by the central bank in reserve money through a dedicated platform running continuously at negligible cost.[14]

We introduce the term "narrow finance solutions" to capture the various new forms of private money backed one for one by central bank liabilities, either cash or reserves. These forms offer stable nominal value, security, liquidity, and potentially close to a risk-free rate of return. The parallel here is with currency boards (such as in Hong Kong SAR) or metal-backed banknote systems (such as the gold standard). Two versions of narrow finance solutions are relevant. The first is *stored value facilities*[15] such as AliPay and WePay in China, PayTM in India, M-Pesa in Kenya, and Bitt.com in the Caribbean. These provide *private e-money* to users against funds received and placed in custodian accounts. Transactions occur between electronic wallets installed on mobile devices, can be of any size (although they are usually not large), and are centrally cleared, but are restricted to participants in the same network. However, holding these forms of money entails some risk.[16] Nonetheless, this segment is gaining widespread and very rapid acceptance. The second version of narrow finance solutions—*narrow banks*—is only beginning to materialize. This form covers institutions that invest client funds only in highly liquid and safe government assets—such as excess reserves at the central bank—and do not lend. However, they allow payments in their liabilities through debit cards or privately issued digital money.[17]

Cryptoassets—for example, Bitcoin, Ether, and Ripple—differ along many dimensions and struggle to fully satisfy the functions of money, in part because of erratic valuations. These currencies are not the liability of any institution and are not backed by assets. Their value is usually volatile because most have rigid issuance rules. Some new cryptoassets attempt to stabilize their value by controlling issuance according to a function of price deviations from a fiat currency or commodity (as in an exchange rate peg), including examples such as Basecoin and Stablecoin.[18] In all cases, cryptoassets transactions are settled in a decentralized fashion using distributed ledger technology.

III. Is There a Role for CBDC? User Perspective

Competing forms of money can be ranked according to the criteria described earlier. The evaluation is presented visually in Figure A1.1 of Appendix I, in the form of "spider charts," and explanations are provided in the subsequent Table 12.A1.1. Higher scores are captured by points farther from the center. The more attractive the form of money, the larger the surface covered by the spider chart. All monies were deemed liquid, so that criterion was left aside. Some conclusions regarding the forms of money are as follows:

- *Cash* is not an especially attractive means of payment given its high transaction costs (the need to meet in person and withdraw cash, which may be difficult in remote locations), vulnerability to theft, and lack of returns in the form of interest. However, cash offers immediate settlement, no default or cyber risk, and—importantly—full anonymity, a potentially attractive feature to users.
- Cryptoassets are the least attractive option, receiving a low score in settlement speed because of current technological limitations (which may eventually be overcome). Their main advantage is anonymity.
- *Private e-money* provided by *stored value facilities* scores high on several fronts. It offers widespread acceptance, low transaction costs via user-friendly interfaces designed by customer-centric firms, and full-service bundling with other financial as well as social services. *Narrow banks* could further reduce default risk—and possibly enhance scalability by offering larger-value payments, although potentially lower ease of use, depending on design.
- *Commercial bank deposits*, as they were traditionally structured, offered average value. On the positive side, they provided security from theft and loss, and integration with additional services, while on the negative side there was only limited acceptance (cumbersome peer-to-peer payments requiring checks or wire transfers) and scalability (floors on debit card payments). However, recent reforms and innovations, including *fast payments,* have improved the attractiveness of commercial bank deposits considerably. Deposits with fast payment are completely scalable and are widely accepted, without network limits; have no settlement risk; and offer limited default risk where deposit insurance is available.[19] Transaction costs (fees and ease of use) are minimal.

It is apparent that CBDC would not strictly dominate any of these alternative forms of money. As evident in Figure 12.A1.1, CBDC would closely compete with evolving commercial bank deposits and e-money. CBDC stands out only when it comes to anonymity and default risk. There are two sets of features to be discussed when assessing the design of CBDC: fixed features, for which the central bank does not have discretion, and flexible features.

- *Fixed design features:* CBDC would be on par with fast-payment solutions regarding acceptance (person-to-person, person-to-business, business-to-business without network restrictions), settlement risk, and transaction cost (to the extent that mobile interfaces are well designed). CBDC would probably be superior regarding default risk, although in many jurisdictions only marginally. Instead, CBDC would score poorly in terms of offering additional services (although banks could provide the front-end applications to manage CBDC and could cross-sell services).
- *Flexible design features:* CBDC could offer competitive interest returns, protection from theft and loss, scalability, and anonymity, though not all at once as these features depend on one another. As discussed earlier, anonymity could be provided to different degrees: relative to transaction parties, third parties, and/or the government. But the greater the anonymity, the harder it is to reverse fraudulent transactions (risk of theft) and claim ownership (risk of loss). And central banks may be prepared to offer full anonymity only with strict and low limits on CBDC holdings, thus undermining scalability. Finally, CBDC could offer interest. If it paid the policy rate, it would be as attractive as narrow finance solutions, although commercial banks could still offer higher rates on deposits (and recoup profits by charging higher lending rates).

In summary, demand for CBDC will depend on its design. Demand may not be high in more advanced economies, except as a cash replacement, but could be very attractive elsewhere. Commercial bank deposits with fast payments, and to some extent narrow banking solutions, will rival CBDC and could be superior in some areas. CBDC could excel only regarding anonymity, although at some cost to scalability and security. As such, it would compete mostly with cash, by allowing small-value transactions with at least some degree of anonymity. Someday CBDC may, indeed, be introduced as a replacement for paper bills, which will become increasingly anachronistic as economic activity grows ever more digital. However, in jurisdictions with limited banking penetration and unreliable settlement platforms, CBDC may be more attractive to users, especially in the absence of stored value facilities.

IV. Is There a Role for CBDC? Central Bank Perspective

This section gauges whether central banks could benefit from CBDC to more fully achieve public policy goals. These goals include satisfying the social dimensions of money's three functions, as well as improving financial integrity, financial stability, and monetary policy effectiveness.

A. Social Criteria for Money

CBDC is unlikely to offer near-term assurance of price stability in all economic circumstances—as needed to bolster the *unit of account* function of money. The global financial crisis starkly illustrated that interest rate policy can be constrained by the presence of cash. Policy rates cannot be brought significantly below zero without risking a massive shift into cash, which ensures zero returns (see Dell'Ariccia and others (2017) for a full discussion, and Habermeier and others (2013) for an overview of unconventional monetary policy). However, cash is unlikely to go away anytime soon, for political reasons. Only over the longer term, if CBDC is adopted widely, would cash be eliminated, much as happened with metal coinage. In that scenario, policy rates could go deep into negative territory. But this would happen only to the extent that CBDC also charged negative rates and did not replace cash as a means to circumvent policy. In the interim, other measures have been proposed to allow for deeply negative policy rates, but with questionable feasibility and without necessarily requiring CBDC.[20]

CBDC could help ensure equal access to a *means of payment* for all citizens, thereby favoring financial inclusion; however other solutions also exist and may be more efficient. Much of the utility of CBDC in this regard depends on the barriers to financial inclusion. For one, cash may be difficult to obtain and use in underpopulated and rural areas. As a majority of the population shifts to digital forms of money, the infrastructure for cash (such as distribution networks, counting machines, and armored services) may deteriorate, and businesses may resist dealing with it. As in other cases of negative externalities, government intervention may be warranted. One approach may involve subsidizing the provision of cash in underserved areas. CBDC may not be a viable solution if access to technology is limited. If the problem is instead the supply of bank accounts—which banks deem unprofitable or require unaffordable or nonexistent technology—the question is whether the private sector can offer alternative solutions. M-Pesa in Kenya and PayTM in India are examples of successful initiatives, although with some state support in the case of M-Pesa (from the UK Department for International Development). Alternatively, the government could subsidize the deployment of bank branches. Or—short of direct intervention—it could facilitate the development of online banking and communication infrastructure in rural areas and reduce the cost of bank-intermediated small-value transactions by deploying fast payments. Where these solutions are not feasible, CBDC could provide an alternative. However, if barriers to financial inclusion stem from an aversion to formalization, neither CBDC nor other initiatives would prove satisfactory.

Instead, CBDC may help reduce costs associated with the provision of cash, thereby ensuring an *efficient means of payment* from a public policy perspective. Issuing and managing cash are expensive. Hasan, De Renzis, Schmiedel (2013) estimate the cost to be 0.5% of GDP for the euro area, similar to the cost in Canada (Kosse and others 2017) and Uruguay (Alvez, Lluberas, and Ponce 2018). These costs fall mostly on banks, firms, and households. Although introducing and maintaining CBDC would probably entail substantial fixed costs, marginal operational costs would likely be low, despite the need for customer service. On this basis alone, the business case to adopt CBDC would probably be better for larger jurisdictions able to absorb the fixed costs.

CBDC would not help resolve the tension central banks face between offering a *secure store of value* and promoting financial intermediation. Narrow finance solutions offer a liquid and secure store of value at the cost of financial intermediation. This is because payments must be entirely prefunded, as explained earlier. Fractional reserve banks, however, pool the liquidity buffers households and firms maintain to respond to payment shocks. And because not all shocks materialize at once (at least not most of the time), they can lend a portion of the funds, keeping only a fraction in highly liquid and safe assets. Even though central banks should be concerned if narrow banking solutions grow substantially, CBDC would not help reverse the trend. CBDC is also, after all, a form of money that requires full pre-funding. Instead, fast payments would help fractional reserve banks offer money that competes with that offered by stored value facilities and other narrow finance solutions.

Other potential benefits of CBDC must be seen against the backdrop of a reduction in the use of cash. The trend is already evident in some countries and is expected to become more widespread—Sweden is probably the most striking example.[21] In other countries, cash in circulation as a share of GDP has actually increased in the past decade, as documented in Bech and others (2018). However, a second look reveals that such movements are largely cyclical and can be partly explained by low interest rates. As shown in Box 12.2, the preference for cash has mostly been decreasing or has remained unchanged except in reserve currency countries (Switzerland and the United States). In addition, the demand for cash is likely to diminish as older generations give way to more technology-adept generations. Merchants and banks in both advanced and developing economies are also trying to discourage cash transactions, given the related costs.

Box 12.2. A Closer Look at the Demand for Cash

In many countries, currency in circulation has increased significantly in the past decade (Figure 12.4a).[22] However, much of that increase seems cyclical, because it can be explained in good part by lower interest rates, higher uncertainty, and economic recoveries.[23] Figure 12.4b shows that in selected countries the unexplained (residual) component of cash in circulation—loosely associated with preferences—has often decreased or remained stable. Only in Switzerland and the United States has this component increased markedly over the past decade, in part thanks to those countries' reserve currency status.

However, cash still accounts for a large share of transaction volumes, though not of value, even in advanced economies. The use of cash is subject to habit, increases with age, and decreases with education and income. It is generally lowest in countries with the most developed payment systems.[24]

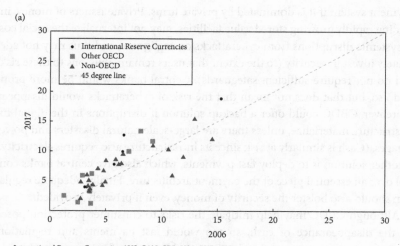

(a)

International Reserve Currencies: AUS, CAN, GBR, USA, EUR, JPN
Other OECD: CZE, DNK, HUN, ISL, ISR, KOR, NOR, POL, SWE
Non-OECD: BRA, BUL, CHL, CHN, COL, HRV, IDN, IND, KWT, MLS, MEX, NGA, PHL, ROM, RUS, SRB, SGP, ZAF, THA, TUR, UKR, ARE, URY

Figure 12.4a. Cash in Circulation (as percent of GDP).
Source: IFS, Haver

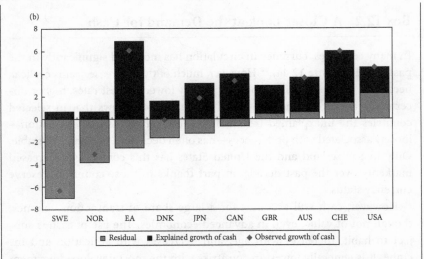

Figure 12.4b. Growth of Real Cash Balances (in percent, annualized growth rates).
Sources: Staff calculations

As the use of cash wanes, there is greater concern about the security of the payment system if it is dominated by private firms. Private issuers of money, including rapidly growing stored value facilities, may not internalize the social cost of systemic disruptions from cyberattacks or negligence, and thus may not adequately invest in security (to the extent that users remain oblivious to these risks and do not require sufficient safeguards). Central banks would be more prone to do so, but that does not mean that the risk of cyberattacks would disappear. Moreover, CBDC could offer a backup solution if disruptions in the digital infrastructure materialize, unless there are large-scale natural disasters and power outages. (Cash is similarly at risk since its infrastructure also requires electricity.) Another solution is to deploy fast payments, which also give central banks control over an essential piece of the payment architecture. Finally, adequate regulation should also bolster the security of money, even if privately provided.

Although CBDC may help mitigate the risks to consumer protection posed by the disappearance of cash, so too would fast payments and regulation. Modern payment systems are often operated by only a few commercial banks and by even fewer clearinghouses and messaging services. Payment systems tend to become natural monopolies, reflecting strong network externalities (the value of using a given payment network is greater the larger the user community), decreasing average costs (savings from netting transactions over a large user base), high fixed development and maintenance costs, and significant gains from aggregating data, which—to an individual—is worth little. However, private monopolistic providers will tend to offer inadequate and expensive services and could take unfair advantage of data. The prevalence of cash as an attractive and low-cost competitor may have limited the monopoly power of private monies. In the future, if antitrust regulation and data protection prove insufficient, CBDC could serve that same purpose; however, so too could the deployment of low-cost fast payments.

In summary, while central banks could benefit from CBDC to more fully satisfy some of the social criteria of money, in many countries there are also other solutions. CBDC may be a way to reduce the cost to society associated with the use of cash. Financial inclusion may also benefit if private sector solutions and policy efforts do not bear fruit; however, CBDC will not support efficient allocation of resources. It could, under some circumstances, help central banks bolster the security of payment systems and consumer protection. But, where possible, fast-payment platforms could offer compelling alternatives to satisfy these goals.

B. Can CBDC Balance Privacy and Financial Integrity Concerns?

In designing money, national authorities face a trade-off between satisfying legitimate user preferences for privacy and mitigating risks to financial integrity. Cash protects privacy because it is anonymous: No account is necessary, and there is no record of transactions. However, it also facilitates criminal financial transactions such as money laundering, financing of terrorism, corruption, and tax evasion. Most of the cash in circulation is in the top two largest denominations, often associated with illicit payments or store of value.[25]

Recent discussions on the trade-off between financial integrity and privacy for cash could prove useful for CBDC design. Eliminating cash would undermine privacy; moreover, it is unlikely to improve financial integrity since illicit transactions would presumably migrate to another form of money (McAndrews 2017). Ironically, those seeking anonymity for legitimate purposes might even adopt the parallel money, contributing to its liquidity and attractiveness for criminal use—a pattern that may be visible in the adoption of cryptoassets. Proposals to do away with high-denomination bills seem more appealing (Rogoff 2016 and references therein). Remaining small-denomination bills could in part satisfy legitimate preferences for privacy but would pose risks for illicit transactions.

Depending on its design, CBDC can strengthen or undermine financial integrity. For example, financial integrity could be strengthened if authorities impose strict limits on the size of transactions. Alternatively, CBDC can be designed to facilitate effective identity authentication and tracking of payments and transfers. Identities would be authenticated through customer due diligence procedures, and transactions recorded. But unless required by law, users' information could be protected from disclosure to third parties and governments, while criminals could be deterred by the risk of investigation and prosecution. Although promising on paper, these solutions would have to be further evaluated, and questions answered. For instance, would users trust the safeguards established to protect their privacy? Would central banks be held responsible for compliance failures, even if customer due diligence procedures were outsourced? And to what extent could authorities benefit from the ability to scrutinize transaction information for illicit activity in real time? On the other hand, CBDC offering full anonymity and large-value transactions would undermine financial integrity relative to cash and current non-cash fund transfer systems. Whatever design is chosen, it should accommodate the implementation of effective AML/CFT measures.

C. Would CBDC Undermine Financial Stability and Banking Intermediation?

CBDC could affect financial stability and banking intermediation if it competes with bank deposits. Hence, in what follows we assume CBDC will possess characteristics similar to those of bank deposits, namely traceability and protection from loss or theft. In a world of diverse consumers, it is reasonable to assume that some will prefer and adopt CBDC. Two hypothetical scenarios are considered. The first is a tranquil period following the introduction of CBDC. In this scenario, questions arise such as how banks will respond, what will happen to bank intermediation and funding, and how central banks might react. The second scenario assumes a period of systemic financial stress in a world with CBDC. The key question in this case is what happens to run risk—the potential for a significant shift of deposits from banks to CBDC.

1. Scenario 1: Risk of Disintermediation in Tranquil Times
Banks will likely react to the introduction of CBDC, but their ability to defend their business model depends on market power. As some depositors leave banks in favor of CBDC, banks could increase deposit interest rates to make them more attractive.[26] But the higher deposit rates would reduce banks' interest margins. As a result, banks would attempt to increase lending rates, though at the cost of loan demand.[27] The greater banks' market power, the less

credit demand would contract, and the more effectively banks could respond to CBDC by preserving profits (see Box 12.3).

Alternatively, banks could try to replace the deposits that shift to CBDC with other forms of funding. Potential alternatives are commercial paper, bonds, and equity. All are market (wholesale) types of funding. There are three likely

---

Box 12.3. Banks' Response to CBDC—Higher Rates on Deposits and Lending[28]

The introduction of CBDC draws deposits away from banks, leading to an upward shift in the deposit supply curve (Figure 12.5a). Banks counteract some of the impact on their deposit bases by raising deposit interest rates (Figure 12.5b). Moreover, banks pass part of this deposit rate hike on to their loan interest rates. When banks have more market power in lending (also reflected in thee steepness of the demand curve for deposits), they can better insulate their profits by passing the deposit rate hike on to loan rates. Banks with little market power adjust more aggressively in quantity, exhibiting a larger contraction in deposit and loan volume.

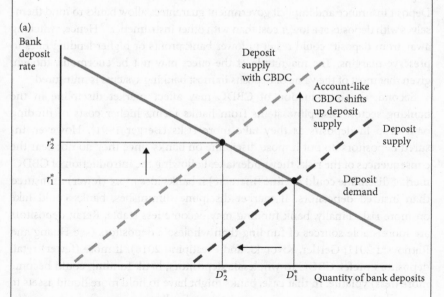

Figure 12.5a. Introduction of CBDC.
Source: IMF staff

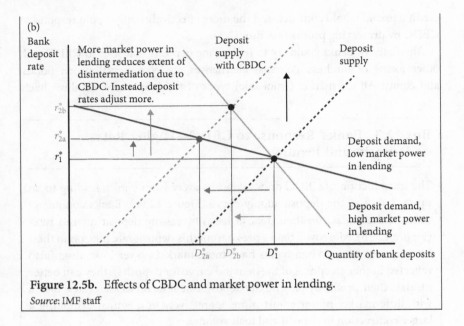

Figure 12.5b. Effects of CBDC and market power in lending.
Source: IMF staff

implications to such a shift: First, bank funding would become more expensive. Deposit insurance and implicit government guarantees allow banks to fund themselves with deposits at a lower cost than with other instruments.[29] Hence, switching away from deposits could result in lower bank profits or higher lending rates to preserve margins. The magnitude of the effect may not be enormous, though, given that most of the value of deposits in most banking systems is uninsured.

Second, the introduction of CBDC may affect market discipline in the banking sector. Discipline stems from banks facing higher costs of funding or a drop in deposits as they take more risks (Berger 1991). However, insured depositors do not impose discipline on banks since they do not bear the consequences of the risks they undertake. Following the introduction of CBDC, market discipline could decline (increase) if banks lose more (fewer) uninsured than insured depositors. If market discipline diminishes, banks could take on more risk. Finally, bank funding may become less stable. Retail depositors are more stable sources of funding than wholesale depositors (see Huang and Ratnovski 2011; Gertler, Kiyotaki, and Prestipino 2016). If more (fewer) retail depositors prefer CBDC to wholesale depositors, bank funding could become more (less) volatile. In that case, banks might have to hold more liquid assets to meet regulatory requirements or cut back on lending.

The extent of disintermediation will be greater among banks in more direct competition with CBDC. For example, CBDC would likely be in greater competition with retail than with wholesale deposits, which require larger-value payments. Thus, banks with a larger share of retail deposits will face tougher competition following the introduction of CBDC and may not be able to raise lending rates to preserve profits. Greater presence of nonbank loan providers would add to competitive pressure on banks.

In the event of disintermediation, central banks can respond in several ways, although some are not especially palatable over the medium term and would imply a dramatic step away from central banks' typical mandates. One option is that the central bank could limit the decline in bank deposits and lending by setting limits on individual CBDC holdings or discouraging (such as through fees) convertibility from bank deposits to CBDC. In addition, the central bank could lend the funds diverted from deposits back to banks. This would allow banks to keep lending, although the central bank could require more capital or collateral, with possible implications for the cost and volume of lending. Moreover, the central bank's balance sheet would grow, it would systematically take on credit risk, and it would have to decide how to allocate funds across banks.[30]

At the margin, central banks could help maintain the ties between customers and banks by allowing banks to manage CBDC. As discussed earlier, banks could offer wallets to hold and make transactions in CBDC and could offer customer support.

2. Scenario 2: Run Risk in Times of Systemic Financial Stress

CBDC may facilitate a generalized run on banks by offering a readily available, safe, and liquid alternative to deposits,[31] but in many cases, this effect will be muted. First, the introduction of CBDC would not facilitate idiosyncratic runs from one bank to another. Such movement can already take place electronically at the click of a button. Second, if a banking crisis coincides with a more general economic (currency or sovereign) crisis, funds will be withdrawn from all local assets, including CBDC.[32] Third, even short of a general crisis, CBDC is unlikely to matter much if very safe and liquid alternatives already exist. These include reserves-only narrow banks or Treasury-only mutual funds[33] or, in some cases, state banks with healthy balance sheets or explicit and credible state guarantees.[34]

In some cases, CBDC could even help the central bank ease liquidity pressures and thus contain bank runs.[35] The provision of extensive liquidity support is pervasive during banking crises. For example, central banks provided liquidity assistance to banks in almost 96% of the 151 crisis episodes studied by Laeven and Valencia (2018). Liquidity can be provided by increasing reserves (to replace funding) and cash (to allow banks to meet deposit withdrawals). Having CBDC will not affect the central bank's ability to increase reserves since this can already take place electronically. In geographically vast countries where transporting cash to bank branches and ATMs might be a costly and time-consuming endeavor, CBDC could facilitate the process of providing liquidity to banks and resolve runs faster.[36]

Even if the introduction of CBDC increased the risk of systemic bank runs, deposit insurance could alleviate the effects. Liquidity provision needs are smaller in countries with deposit insurance before a banking crisis.[37] Countries adopting CBDC should, therefore, have a deposit insurance scheme to lower the probability of runs.[38] The effectiveness of such schemes in mitigating runs, however, will depend on the credibility of the fiscal backstop and the extent of coverage.

D. Would Monetary Policy Transmission Remain Effective?

The introduction of CBDC is unlikely to significantly affect the main channels of monetary policy transmission under plausible CBDC designs.[39] The effects on these four channels are as follows:

- The basic *interest rate channel* may be the most affected and could strengthen. Changes in policy interest rates induce households and firms to rebalance investment and consumption between the future and the present, especially if these are exposed to interest-sensitive borrowing and saving instruments. To the extent that CBDC increases financial inclusion—thus access precisely to such instruments—monetary policy transmission could strengthen (Mehrotra and Nadhanael 2016). Gains would be most evident if CBDC were interest bearing.
- The *bank lending channel* could also strengthen. Through this channel, policy interest rates and their expectation affect bank balance sheets and profits—ultimately their creditworthiness and thus their non-deposit funding cost and lending rates.[40] This channel would strengthen if CBDC increased the share of banks' wholesale funding, as argued earlier.
- The *credit channel* is unlikely to be affected much. This channel is related to the one just described; policy rates affect asset prices and collateral values of borrowers, thus their creditworthiness and costs of borrowing.[41] However, CBDC should not markedly impinge on these effects.
- Likewise, the *exchange rate channel*—through which changes in policy rates bring about rebalancing between foreign and domestic assets, and a commensurate variation in the exchange rate affecting exports and imports—is unlikely to be affected.

This relatively benign view depends on the expectation that central banks would remain in a position to affect market interest rates relevant to the channels previously described. First, central banks should be able to affect term spreads through communication as before, such as by releasing and discussing their interest rate projections. Second, central banks should be able to retain control of interest rates on reserves. As long as banks demand reserve balances to pay each other—ultimately, as long as banks intermediate payments—the central bank should be able to set their marginal price.[42] This is key, since the price of reserves determines the opportunity cost for banks to lend funds to each other, and by extension the rates set in the much larger money markets. In turn, these affect rates on riskless, and ultimately risky, assets. Clearly, the presence of banks across these markets, as well as arbitrage and lack of market segmentation, is key to transmission. CBDC, however, is not expected to markedly affect any of these conditions under most design scenarios.

One scenario, however, would significantly test the standard transmission channels, but could be resolved with a change in operating framework. If banks were no longer involved in intermediating payments, having lost the business to CBDC (or stored value facilities, depending on how these are regulated), demand for reserves would disappear. This scenario resembles the "cashless world" considered by Woodford (2000). In this world, though, monetary policy has the means to remain effective. Woodford argues that "perfect control over overnight rates would still be possible, through adjustments of the rate paid on central bank balances." In the digital world, the insight translates into paying interest on CBDC. Doing so would put a floor on interest rates if CBDC is provided without limit. Indeed, no one with access to CBDC would lend at a rate below that offered by CBDC, which would remain the safest and most liquid asset available. This is akin to controlling monetary policy by paying interest on reserves when these are in excess of what is demanded by the banking sector for precautionary purposes (referred to as a "floor system").

V. Central Bank Research and Experiments

Many central banks, in both advanced and emerging market and developing economies, are considering the pros and cons of issuing CBDC. Table 12.1 summarizes the jurisdictions in which central banks are (or have been) actively exploring CBDC for retail use based on publicly available information.

Some sovereigns have issued, or may issue, retail digital currencies, though these are not CBDC because they are not issued by central banks as their liability. For example, the Marshall Islands has discussed launching the SOV, a cryptoasset that will become legal tender along with the U.S. dollar, with the

Table 12.1. Jurisdictions where retail CBDCs are being actively explored[43,44]

Australia (on hold)	Bahamas
Brazil	Canada
China (and here)	Curaçao and Sint Maarten
Eastern Caribbean	Ecuador (pilot complete)
Denmark (rejected)	Israel
Norway (ongoing)	Philippines
Sweden	United Kingdom (on hold)
Uruguay	

Sources: Central banks or various news sources (Information has not been verified through official channels.)

apparent intention to raise funds for the government. Likewise, Venezuela is planning to issue the petro, a commodity-backed cryptoasset.

Central banks are considering CBDC for two main reasons: declining use of cash in advanced economies and financial inclusion in emerging market and developing economies. These and other objectives mentioned by central banks are summarized in Table 12.2. None of the central banks surveyed cite seigniorage preservation or monetary policy effectiveness at the zero lower bound as rationales for CBDC adoption, with papers by the Bank of Canada emphatically denying the latter.[45] The main rationale for advanced economies seems to be countering the growth of private forms of money (operational risk and monopoly distortions) and reducing costs associated with managing cash (cost efficiency). For example, Sweden points to increasing payment system single-point-of-failure risk associated with diminishing cash usage. In emerging market economies, the main interest in CBDC seems to be fostering financial inclusion by reaching out to the unbanked segments of the population. Only China cites monopoly distortions as a justification. Cost efficiency is also behind China's investigations, Ecuador's CBDC issuance (launched in early 2015 though shut down in early 2018), and Uruguay's six-month trial.[46] Some developing economy central banks have also mentioned reducing the costs and risks associated with the distribution of physical cash.

Some central banks are reportedly no longer pursuing CBDC, citing factors such as small benefits for central banks and potential disintermediation and bank run risks (Australia, Denmark, European Central Bank, New Zealand, Switzerland).

In terms of design, most central banks seem to be contemplating forms of account-based CBDC, with various levels of anonymity; although some token-based solutions also exist. The Eastern Caribbean Central Bank and the People's

Table 12.2. Rationales for Exploring CBDCs via Publicly Available Information

	Diminishing Cash Usage				
	Monopoly Distortions	Operational Risks	Cost Efficiency	Financial Inclusion	Other
Bahamas				X	Countering derisking
Canada	X				
China	X	X	X	X	
CBCS			X	X	
ECCB		X	X	X	
Ecuador				X	
Norway	X				
Senegal				X	
Sweden	X	X			
Tunisia				X	
Uruguay			X	X	

Monetary policy was not cited as a rationale by any of the central banks surveyed. It was not possible to ascertain the rationales, based on publicly available information, for Australia, Bahrain, Denmark, the European Union, Hong Kong SAR, India, Indonesia, Jamaica, South Korea, and Switzerland.

Sources: Central banks or various news sources. Information has not been verified through official channels.

Note: CBCS = Central Bank of Curaçao and Sint Maarten; ECCB = Eastern Caribbean Central Bank.

Bank of China could offer both account- and token-based CBDC, with accounts managed by commercial banks and/or other licensed financial institutions. The People's Bank of China is also considering fully anonymous token-based wallets, albeit with low payment limits. However, other central banks seem to be shying away from such solutions because they would not meet Financial Action Task Force requirements.[47] Most central banks are considering anonymous CBDC when it comes to transacting parties and third parties but not in the case of the government. This is the situation of the People's Bank of China. (Wallets with greater anonymity, however, would have lower payment limits.) Protecting users against risks of theft and loss was considered important to many of the central banks mentioned.

A number of central banks surveyed indicated that CBDC should be available 24 hours a day, seven days a week, to mimic the accessibility of cash. In this regard, Canada, China, and Sweden are looking into CBDC with offline capability. This would be offered by preloading tokens onto a wallet while online, then validating transactions via encrypted messaging to point-of-sale terminals, similarly to cash cards. In all cases, central banks are considering limits to such transactions. Functionality could be temporarily available during electricity or infrastructure breakdowns but still be susceptible to catastrophic events.[48] Even cash is not particularly resilient in such circumstances, as its distribution and use require electricity (to operate automated teller machines, vending machines, and other cash dispensers), and cash can be destroyed easily in a catastrophe.

None of the central banks surveyed are seriously considering interest-bearing CBDC. Central banks appear to be concerned with financial intermediation, lending contraction, and heightened bank balance sheet volatility. Some, such as the Reserve Bank of New Zealand and Uruguay simply assert on principle that CBDC should be fungible. Central banks contemplating token-based CBDC suggest that paying interest would present a technical challenge, though not an insurmountable one. Others raise the hurdle of tracking interest payments for tax purposes. However, Sweden's proposed CBDC, the e-krona, will have the built-in ability to pay interest if the central bank decides to do so.

The central banks surveyed are studying ways of managing and funding CBDC infrastructure. Although marginal costs of managing physical cash are likely higher than those of CBDC, the high upfront fixed costs may favor CBDC adoption in larger economies. Some central banks are exploring the option of building and maintaining CBDC in-house, but most are planning to outsource these onerous tasks, despite the risks involved. Some central banks are contemplating cost-sharing mechanisms. For example, China may make third-party wallet providers bear part of the development costs in return for keeping a cut of any fees charged and benefiting from cross-selling opportunities. The Uruguay pilot appears similar. China is also thinking about charging fees on large transactions, just as for large cash withdrawals.

Similarly, various central banks surveyed plan to outsource CBDC development while maintaining close supervision. For example, the Uruguay CBDC pilot turned to the Roberto Giori Company to develop digital notes, IN Switch Solutions for wallets, and Redpagos for "storefront" operations (cashing e-pesos in and out). Tunisia used Monetas for digital notes and DigitUS for wallets, but developed the user interface itself (according to The Tunisian Post). Senegal used eCurrency Mint for the notes, while the Banque Régionale de Marchés provided the wallets and user interface.[49]

For the most part, central banks are focused on CBDC applications for the domestic economy, rather than on cross-border issues. Only Canada and China mentioned cross-border issues, but more as complications than opportunities. Canada seemed focused on accessibility by tourists. China cited cross-border capital management. Other projects focus more on intermediating wholesale payments across borders, such as a joint project among the Bank of Canada, the Monetary Authority of Singapore, and the Bank of England.

VI. Conclusion

CBDC is a digital form of existing fiat money, issued by the central bank and intended as legal tender. It would potentially be available for all types of payments and could be implemented with a variety of technologies. As such, CBDC could be the next milestone in the evolution of money. The history of money suggests that, while the basic functions of money might not change, the form does evolve in response to user needs. Digitalization of many aspects of economic activity is prompting central banks to seriously consider the introduction of CBDC.

This chapter has introduced a three-step conceptual framework to assess CBDC's potential to create value both for end users and for central banks. The first step is to identify the criteria with which users evaluate different forms of money. The second step involves establishing the public policy goals of central banks with respect to money. The third step lays out the competitive landscape, comprising existing and evolving forms of money.

Applying this framework, we find no universal case for CBDC adoption as of yet. From the perspective of end user needs, we find that demand for CBDC will depend on the attractiveness of alternative forms of money. In advanced economies, there may be scope for the adoption of CBDC as a potential replacement for cash for small-value, pseudo-anonymous transactions. But in countries with limited banking sector penetration and inefficient settlement technology, demand for CBDC may well be greater. From a central bank perspective, the case for CBDC is likely to differ from country to country. CBDC may reduce the costs to society that are associated with the use of cash. Moreover, CBDC may improve financial inclusion in cases of unsuccessful private sector solutions and policy efforts. It could also help central banks bolster the security of, and trust in, the payment system and protect consumers where regulation does not adequately contain private monopolies. But regulation and, where possible, novel payment solutions could offer compelling alternatives to satisfy these goals.

For countries that decide to introduce CBDC, appropriate design and policies should help mitigate the ensuing risks. Monetary policy transmission is unlikely to be significantly affected and may even benefit from greater financial inclusion. Moreover, though it will not eliminate illicit activity, CBDC may in some situations enhance financial integrity. Conversely, CBDC entails risks for financial integrity if badly designed. In addition, although CBDC could increase the cost of funding for deposit-taking institutions and intensify run risk in some jurisdictions, design choices and policies can help ease such concerns. Nevertheless, operational and reputational risks arising from malfunctions of the digital infrastructure or cyberattacks are likely to remain as challenges.

Looking ahead, the cross-border implications of CBDC raise a multitude of new questions that merit investigation. For instance, from a practical standpoint, how would tourists be able to make payments in a foreign country that has adopted CBDC? Should foreigners have access to CBDC? To what extent would this complicate know-your-customer and AML/CFT compliance, and could standardized information be requested across countries? Would access to CBDC in a reserve currency (such as e-dollars) facilitate currency substitution in countries that have weak institutions? And to what extent might safe-haven flows be encouraged, potentially draining resources from countries that face banking, sovereign, or currency crises? Finally, if CBDC were used for cross-border transactions, how might central banks be required to cooperate? Would they absorb some of the functions of correspondent banks and thus take on additional liquidity, credit, and foreign exchange rate risk—or might tokens be created for cross-border payments among particular central banks, commercial banks, or firms? These deep and difficult questions have far-reaching implications and provide ample opportunities for further exploration.

References

Acharya, V., D. Anginer, and A. Warburton. 2016. "The End of Market Discipline? Investor Expectations of Implicit Government Guarantees." https://ssrn.com/abstract=1961656 or http://dx.doi.org/10.2139/ssrn.1961656.

Adler, G., and E. Cerutti. 2015 "Are Foreign Banks a Safe Haven? Evidence from Past Banking Crises." IMF Working Paper 15/43, International Monetary Fund, Washington, DC.

Agarwal, R., and M. Kimball. 2015. "Breaking through the Zero Lower Bound." IMF Working Paper 15/224, International Monetary Fund, Washington, DC.

Agur, I., A. Ari, and G. Dell'Ariccia. Forthcoming. "Central Bank Digital Currencies: Design Tradeoffs and Implications." IMF Working Paper, International Monetary Fund, Washington, DC.

Ali, R. 2018 "Cellular Structure for a Digital Fiat Currency." MIT Digital Currency Initiative. https://dci.mit.edu/digital-fiat-currency.

Alvez, M., R. Lluberas, and J. Ponce. 2018. "The Cost of Using Cash and Checks in Uruguay." Unpublished.

Arango-Arango, C., Y. Bouhdaoui, D. Bounie, M. Eschelbach, and L. Hernandez. 2018. "Cash Remains Top-of-Wallet! International Evidence from Payment Diaries." *Economic Modelling* 69 (January): 38–48.

Bennett, B., S. Schuh, and S. Schwartz. 2014. "The 2012 Diary of Consumer Payment Choice." Federal Reserve Bank of Boston Research Data Report.

Bagnall, J., D. Bounie, and K. Huynh. 2016. "Consumer Cash Usage and Management: A Cross-Country Comparison with Diary Survey Data." *International Journal of Central Banking* 12 (4): 1–61.

Barajas, A., and R. Steiner. 2000. "Depositor Behavior and Market Discipline in Colombia." IMF Working Paper 00/214, International Monetary Fund, Washington, DC.

Barrdear, J. and M. Kumhof. 2016. "The Macroeconomics of Central Bank Issued Digital Currencies." Bank of England Working Paper 605, Bank of England, London.

Bech, M. L., U. Faruqui, F. Ougaard, and C. Picillo. 2018. "Payments Are A-Changin' but Cash Still Rules." BIS *Quarterly Review* (March):67–80.

Bech, M. L., and R. Garratt. 2017. "Central Bank Cryptocurrencies." BIS *Quarterly Review*. September.

Berger, A. 1991. "Market Discipline in Banking." In *Proceedings of a Conference on Bank Structure and Competition*. Federal Reserve Bank of Chicago.

Bernanke, B. 2007. "Inflation Expectations and Inflation Forecasting." Speech delivered at the Monetary Economics Workshop of the National Bureau of Economic Research Summer Institute, Cambridge, MA.

Bordo, M., and A. Levin. 2018. "Central Bank Digital Currency and the Future of Monetary Policy." *Monetary Policy and Payments* 3:143–78.

Brown, M., I. Evangelou, and H. Stix. 2017. "Banking Crises-Bail-ins and Money Holdings." Central Bank of Cyprus Working Paper 2017-2.

Calomiris, C. 2008. "Testimony Before the Committee on Oversight and Government Reform." U.S. House of Representatives, December 9.

Calomiris, C., and G. Gorton. 1991. "The Origins of Banking Panics: Models, Facts, and Bank Regulation." *Financial Markets and Financial Crises*. University of Chicago Press.

Caprio, G. Jr., and D. Klingebiel. 1996. "Bank Insolvencies: Cross-Country Experience." World Bank Policy Research Working Paper Series 1620, World Bank, Washington, DC.

Carney, Mark. 2018. "The Future of Money." Speech at the inaugural Scottish Economics Conference, Edinburgh University, March 2.

Committee on Payments and Market Infrastructures (CPMI). 2016. "Fast Payments—Enhancing the Speed and Availability of Retail Payments." CPMI Report 154, Basel.

Committee on Payments and Market Infrastructures (CPMI). 2018. "Central Bank Digital Currencies." CPMI Report 174, Basel.

Covitz, D., N. Liang, and G. Suarez. 2013. "The Evolution of a Financial Crisis: Collapse of the Asset-Backed Commercial Paper Market." *Journal of Finance* 68 (3): 815–48.

Das, A., and S. Ghosh. 2004. "Market Discipline in the Indian Banking Sector: An Empirical Exploration." https://econwpa.ub.uni-muenchen.de/econ-wp/fin/papers/0410/0410020.pdf.

Dell'Ariccia, G., V. Haksar, T. Mancini-Griffoli, K. Eckhold, S. Gray, F. Han, G. H. Hong, E. Lundback, H. Oura, H. Poirson, P. Rabanal, and D. Sandri. 2017. "Negative Interest Rate Policies—Initial Experiences and Assessments." IMF Policy Paper, International Monetary Fund, Washington, DC.

Diamond, D., and P. Dybvig. 1983. "Bank Runs, Deposit Insurance, and Liquidity." *Journal of Political Economy* 91 (3): 401–19.

Eichengreen, B. 2018. "Why 'Stable Coins' Are No Answer to Bitcoin's Instability." Project Syndicate, September 11. https://www.project-syndicate.org/commentary/stable-coins-unviable-cryptocurrencies-by-barry-eichengreen-2018-09.

Engert, W., and B. Fung. 2017. "Central Bank Digital Currency: Motivations and Implications." Bank of Canada Staff Discussion Paper 2017-16, Ottawa.

Esselink, H., and L. Hernández. 2017. "The Use of Cash by Households in the Euro Area." Occasional Paper Series 201, European Central Bank, Frankfurt.

Europol. 2015. "Why Cash Is King? A Strategic Report on the Use of Cash by Criminal Groups as a Facilitator for Money Laundering." https://www.europol.europa.eu/publications-documents/why-cash-still-king-strategic-report-use-of-cash-criminal-groups-facilitator-for-money-laundering.

Financial Action Task Force (FATF). 2015. "Money Laundering through the Physical Transportation of Cash." Paris.

Flannigan, G., and S. Parsons. 2018. "High-Denomination Banknotes in Circulation: A Cross-Country Analysis." Reserve Bank of Australia *Bulletin*, March.

Fung, B., and H. Halaburda. 2016. "Central Bank Digital Currencies: A Framework for Assessing Why and How." Bank of Canada Staff Discussion Paper 2016–22, Ottawa.

Gertler, M., N. Kiyotaki, and A. Prestipino. 2017. "A Macroeconomic Model with Financial Panics." International Finance Discussion Paper 1219, Federal Reserve Board, Washington, DC.

Goldstein, I., and A. Pauzner. 2005. "Demand–Deposit Contracts and the Probability of Bank Runs." *Journal of Finance* 60 (3): 1293–327.

Goodhart, C. 2011. "The Macro-Prudential Authority: Powers, Scope and Accountability." *Market Trends* 2011-2, Organisation for Economic Co-operation and Development, Paris.

Gorton, G., and E. Tallman. 2016. "How Did Pre-Fed Banking Panics End?" NBER Working Paper 22036, National Bureau of Economic Research, Cambridge, MA.

Grym, A., P. Heikkinen, K. Kauko, and K. Takala. 2017. "Central Bank Digital Currency." Bank of Finland *Economics Review* 5.

Gürtler, K., S. Nielsen, K. Rasmussen, and M. Spange. 2017. "Central Bank Digital Currency in Denmark," Analysis 28, Danmarks National Bank.

Habermeier, K., L. Jacome, T. Mancini-Griffoli, C. Baba, T. Bayoumi, J. Chen, G. Dell'Ariccia, S. Gray, M. Ismael, T. Mondino, A. Pescatori, T. S. Sedik, S. Sgherri, H. Tanimoto, K. Ueda, N. Valckx, and F. Valencia. 2013. "Unconventional Monetary Policies—Recent Experiences and Prospects." IMF Policy Paper, International Monetary Fund, Washington, DC.

Hasan, I., T. De Renzis, and H. Schmiedel. 2013. "Retail Payments and the Real Economy." European Central Bank Working Paper 1572, Frankfurt.

Hasan, I., K. Jackowicz, O. Kowalewski, and L. Kozlowski. 2013. "Market Disciplines during Crisis: Evidence from Bank Depositors in Transition Countries." *Journal of Banking and Finance* 37 (12): 5436–51.

He, D. 2018. "Monetary Policy in the Digital Age." *Finance and Development* 55 (2).

He, D., K. Habermeier, R. Leckow, V. Haksar, Y. Almeida, M. Kashima, N. Kyriakos-Saad, H. Oura, T. Saadi Sedik, N. Stetsenko, and C. Verdugo-Yepes. 2016. "Virtual Currencies and Beyond: Initial Considerations." IMF Staff Discussion Note 16/03, International Monetary Fund, Washington, DC.

He D., and A. Khan. 2018. "Central Bank Digital Currencies." In *Global Financial Stability Report*, Chapter 1, International Monetary Fund, Washington, DC, April.

He, D., R. Leckow, V. Haksar, T. Mancini-Griffoli, N. Jenkinson, M. Kashima, T. Khiaonarong, C. Rochon, and H. Tourpe. 2017. "Fintech and Financial Services: Initial Considerations." IMF Staff Discussion Note 17/05, International Monetary Fund, Washington, DC.

Hori, M., Y. Ito, and K. Murata. 2009. "Do Depositors Respond Rationally to Bank Risks? Evidence from Japanese Banks during Crises." *Pacific Economic Review* 14 (5): 581–92.

Huang, R., and L. Ratnovski. 2011. "The Dark Side of Bank Wholesale Funding." *Journal of Financial Intermediation* 20 (2): 248–63.

International Monetary Fund (IMF). 2011. "Euro Area Policies: 2011 Article IV Consultation—Staff Report; Public Information Notice on the Executive Board Discussion; and Statement by the Executive Director for Member Countries." IMF Country Report 11/184, International Monetary Fund, Washington, DC.

Jobst, C., and H. Stix. 2017. "Doomed to Disappear: The Surprising Return of Cash across Time and across Countries." CEPR Discussion Paper 12327, Centre for Economic Policy Research, London.

Judson, R. 2017. "The Death of Cash? Not So Fast: Demand for U.S. Currency at Home and Abroad, 1990–2016." Paper presented at the 3rd International Cash Conference, Deutsche Bundesbank, April.

Kahn, C., S. Quinn, and W. Roberds. 2014. "Central Banks and Payment Systems: The Evolving Trade-off between Cost and Risk." Paper presented at the Norges Bank Conference on the Uses of Central Banks: Lessons from History, June 5–6.

Kahn, C. M., F. Rivadeneyra, and T.-N. Wong. 2018. "Should the Central Bank Issue e-Money?" Unpublished.

Kahn, C., and W. Roberds. 2009. "Why Pay? An Introduction to Payments Economics." *Journal of Financial Intermediation* 18 (1): 1–23.

Kelly, B., H. Lustig, and S. van Nieuwerburgh. 2016. "Too-Systemic-to-Fail: What Option Markets Imply about Sector-Wide Government Guarantees." *American Economic Review* 106 (6): 1278–319.

Kosse, A., H. Chen, M.-H. Felt, V. D. Jiongo, K. Nield, and A. Welte. 2017. "The Costs of Point-of-Sale Payments in Canada." Bank of Canada Staff Discussion Paper 2017-4, Ottawa.

Kroszner, R. 2016. "A Review of Bank Funding Cost Differentials." *Journal of Financial Services Research* 49 (2): 151–74.

Krüger, M. 2016. "Pros and Cons of Cash: The State of the Debate." In *2016, Cash on Trial*, edited by C. Beer, E. Gnan, and U. Birchler. SUERF Conference Proceedings 2016/1, SUERF—The European Money and Finance Forum, Vienna, 45–67.

Kumhof, M., and C. Noone. 2018. "Central Bank Digital Currencies—Design Principles and Balance Sheet Implications." Bank of England Staff Working Paper 725, London.

Laeven, L., and F. Valencia. 2018. "Systemic Banking Crises Revisited." IMF Working Paper 18/206, International Monetary Fund, Washington, DC.

Lovett, R.A. 2011. "What If the Biggest Solar Storm on Record Happened Today?" National Geographic News, March 4 https://news.nationalgeographic.com/news/2011/03/110302-solar-flares-sun-storms-earth-danger-carrington-event-science/.

McAndrews, J. 2017. "The Case for Cash." ADBI Working Paper 679, Asian Development Bank Institute, Manila.

Meaning, J., B. Dyson, J. Barker, and E. Clayton. 2018. "Broadening Narrow Money: Monetary Policy with a Central Bank Digital Currency." Bank of England Staff Working Paper 724, London.

Mehrotra, A., and G. Nadhanael. 2016. "Financial Inclusion and Monetary Policy in Emerging Asia." In *Financial Inclusion in Asia*, edited by S. Gopalan and T. Kikuchi. London: Palgrave Macmillan, 93–127.

Davoodalhosseini, S. 2018. "Central Bank Digital Currency and Monetary Policy." Bank of Canada Staff Working Paper 2018-36, Ottawa.

Mondschean, T., and T. Opiela. 1999. "Bank Time Deposit Rates and Market Discipline in Poland: The Impact of State Ownership and Deposit Insurance Reform." *Journal of Financial Services Research* 15 (3): 179–96.

Monetary Authority of Singapore. 2017. "Consultation Paper on Proposed Payment Services Bill." http://www.mas.gov.sg/News-and-Publications/Consultation-Paper/2017/Consultation-Paper-on-Proposed-Payment-Services-Bill.aspx.

Norges Bank. 2018. "Central Bank Digital Currencies." Norges Bank Paper 1, Oslo.

Raskin, M., and D. Yermack. 2016. "Digital Currencies, Decentralized Ledgers, and the Future of Central Banking." NBER Working Paper 22238, National Bureau of Economic Research, Cambridge, MA.

Rogoff, K. 2014. "Costs and Benefits to Phasing Out Paper Currency." NBER Working Paper 20126, National Bureau of Economic Research, Cambridge, MA.

Rogoff, K. 2016. *The Curse of Cash*. Princeton, NJ: Princeton University Press.

Schmidt, L., A. Timmermann, and R. Wermers. 2016. "Runs on Money Market Mutual Funds." *American Economic Review* 106 (9): 2625–57.

Semenova, M. 2007. "How Depositors Discipline Banks: The Case of Russia." Economics Education and Research Consortium Working Paper Series 07-02e, Kiev.

Sibert, A. 2013. "Deposit Insurance after Iceland and Cyprus." VoxEU.org, April 2. https://voxeu.org/article/deposit-insurance-after-iceland-and-cyprus.

Sisak, B. 2011. "What Drives Cash Demand? Transactional and Residual Cash Demand in Selected Countries." Magyar Nemzeti Bank Working Paper 10, Budapest.

Sveriges Riksbank. 2017. "The Riksbank's E-krona Project Report 1." September. https://www.riksbank.se/globalassets/media/rapporter/e-krona/2017/rapport_ekrona_uppdaterad_170920_eng.pdf.

Tilford, C. 2018. "The Millennial Moment." In Charts, *Financial Times*, June 6. https://www.ft.com/content/f81ac17a-68ae-11e8-b6eb-4acfcfb08c11.

Tsesmelidakis, Z., and R. Merton. 2013. "The Value of Implicit Guarantees." https://ssrn.com/abstract=2231317 or http://dx.doi.org/10.2139/ssrn.2231317.

Ueda, K., and W. di Mauro. 2013. "Quantifying Structural Subsidy Values for Systemically Important Financial Institutions." *Journal of Banking and Finance* 37 (10): 3830–42.

Ungan, A., and S. Caner. 2004. "Depositor Behaviour and Market Discipline in Turkey." https://ssrn.com/abstract=495122.

Wakamori, N., and A. Welte. 2017. "Why Do Shoppers Use Cash? Evidence from Shopping Diary Data." *Journal of Money, Credit and Banking* 49 (1): 115–69.

White. 2018. "The World's First Central Bank Electronic Money Has Come—And Gone: Ecuador, 2014–2018." Cato Institute, Washington, DC.

Woodford, M. 2000. "Monetary Policy in a World without Money." NBER Working Paper 7853, National Bureau of Economic Research, Cambridge, MA.

Yifei, F. 2018. "Some Considerations about Central Bank Digital Currency." YICAI News Service, January 25. https://www.yicai.com/news/5395409.html.

Appendix

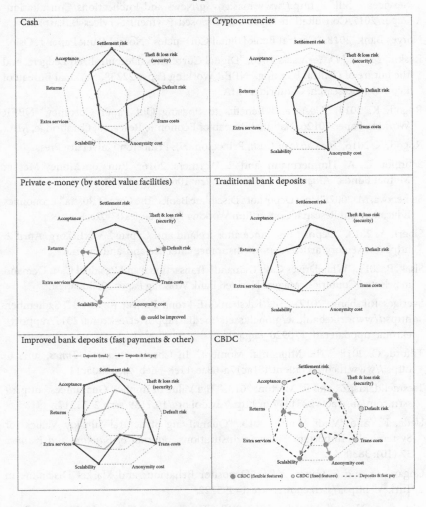

Figure 12.A1.1. Attractiveness to Users of Different Forms of Money.

Table 12.A1.1. Scores by Criteria

	Cash	Traditional bank deposits	Cryptoassets*	Private e-money (by stored value facilities)	Bank deposits with fast payment
Scalability	M: not for large-value transactions	M: not for small- or micro-value transactions	L: not for large payments	M: could be expanded to large-value transactions	H: all transactions possible
Extra services	L: none	H: access to all bank services	L: limited services through exchanges	H: integration with social and financial services	H: like bank deposits
Interest returns	L: zero yielding	M: interest, though below policy rate	L: none	L: usually none, though could be offered	M: interest
Acceptance	M: limits to change; some merchants reject	L: only person to business and business to business, point-of-sale terminals needed	L: only few retailers accept	M: person-to-business, business-to-business, person-to-person, but only within network	H: like stored value facilities but no network limit
Settlement risk	H: none; immediate settlement	M: some delay	M: lags; struggle to establish finality for some	M: like bank deposits	H: instantaneous in central bank money (reserves)
Theft & loss risk	M: hard to recover/ claim; no cyber risk	M: can reverse transaction & claim ownership	L: hard to recover/ claim due to anonymity	M: like bank deposits	M: like bank deposits
Default risk	H: none, a central bank liability	M: deposit insurance	H: to the extent code is solid, not a liability	M: no deposit insurance, though some safeguards	M: like bank deposits
Transaction costs	L: need to physically meet	M: service fees	L: high energy requirements	H: very easy to use, cheap	H: very easy to use, cheap
Anonymity costs	H: full anonymity	L: not anonymous	H: full anonymity	L: not anonymous	L: not anonymous

Note: Scores are H (high), M (medium), and L (low) to the extent the corresponding criteria are desirable for the end user. For instance, a high mark for transaction costs means that costs are low and thus attractive to users. *Rapidly evolving technological advances could improve scores.

Notes

Chapter 1

1. Jonathan Rohr & Aaron ⌐Wright, *Blockchain-Based Token Sales, Initial Coin Offerings, and the Democratization of Public Capital Markets* 8 (Cardozo Legal Stud. Research Paper No. 527, 2017), https://papers.ssrn.com/sol3/papers.cfm?abstract_id=3048104.
2. For many blockchains, "a valid hash for a block must have a predefined number of leading zeroes, which can only be generated through a computationally difficult, brute force guessing game—often referred to as proof of work. The proof of work guessing game requires that a computer repeatedly execute a hashing algorithm until the algorithm outputs a valid hash with a sufficient number of leading zeros. Members of a blockchain-based network (known as miners) play this proof of work guessing game and expend computational resources to generate a valid hash." *Id.* at 9.
3. Shaan Ray, *What Is Proof of Stake?*, HackerNoon (Oct. 7, 2017), https://hackernoon.com/what-is-proof-of-stake-8e0433018256.
4. *Id.*
5. *Id.*
6. *Id.*
7. *How Blockchain Could Disrupt Banking*, CBInsights (Dec. 12, 2018), https://www.cbinsights.com/research/blockchain-disrupting-banking/.
8. *Id.*
9. *Crypto-asset Markets: Potential Channels for Future Financial Stability Implications*, Fin. Stability Bd. (Oct. 10, 2018), http://www.fsb.org/wp-content/uploads/P101018.pdf.

Chapter 2

1. It has its genesis in "Banking in the Digital Age—Who is Afraid of Payment Disintermediation?" presented in Frankfurt, Germany, on February 23 and 24, 2018 at the EBI Global Annual Conference on Banking Regulation), European Banking Institute Working Paper Series 2018—no. 23, 59 Pages Posted: 2 Apr 2018; can be downloaded from http://ssrn.com/abstract=3153760.
2. Particularly chapters 2, 3, 8, and 10 of Benjamin Geva, *The Payment Order of Antiquity and the Middle Ages: A Legal History* (Oxford and Portland, OR: Hart, 2011
3. *Moss* v. *Hancock* [1899] 2QB 111, 116. To the same effect see also: *Reference Re Alberta Statutes* [1938] S CR 100, 116, as well as Johnson v. State, 52 So. 652 (Ala. 1910) and State v. Finnegean, 103 N.W. 155 (Iowa, 1905).

4. Both are not terms of art, so to speak. See, e.g., in B.A. Garner, ed. in chief, *Black's Law Dictionary*, 9th ed. (St. Paul, MN: West, 2009) at 245, 440.

5. This is the conclusion, confirming the conventional wisdom on the matter, of the thorough study by D. Kagan, "The Dates of the Earliest Coins" (1982) 86:3 Journal of Archeology 343.

6. For a comprehensive account, see, e.g., P. Gardner, *A History of Ancient Coinage* 700–300 BC (Chicago: Ares, 1974, being unchanged reprint of the Edition: Oxford, 1918).

7. Roughly speaking, antiquity comes to an end with the beginning of the Middle Ages, usually marked by the fall of Rome in 476 C.E. The Middle Ages are commonly dated from the fifh century fall of the Western Roman Empire until the fall of the Eastern Roman Empire in the fifteenth century.

8. See in general definitions of "coin" in J. Burke, *Jowitt's Dictionary of English Law*, 2nd ed. (London: Sweet & Maxwell, 1977) vol. 1 at 368. "Coin in French, signifieth a corner, and from thence hath its name . . . " See M. Hale (d. 1676), *The History of the Pleas of the Crown*, 1st American ed. by W.A. Stokes & I. Ingresoll (Philadelphia: RH Small, 1847) vol. 1 at 187, n.2.

9. J.M. Holden, *The History of Negotiable Instruments in English Law* (London: Athlone Press, 1955; rep. Holmes Beach, FL: Gaunt, 1993) at 70–73 and A. Feavearyear, *The Pound Sterling—A History of English Money*, 2nd ed. by EV Morgan (Oxford: Clarendon Press, 1963) at 107–08.

10. 5 & 6 Will & Mar. c. 20 s. XIX.

11. An act of 1708, 7 Ann. c. 30 s. 66 forfeited the private note-issuing power of banking firms. Subsequently, under *Country Bankers Act, 1826* (U.K.), 7 Geo. IV, c. 46, the note-issue power was restored to a non-London bank. Ultimately, this power was severely curtailed and subsequently disappeared following the passage of the *Bank Charter Act*, 7 & 8 Vict., c. 32 in 1844. See Holden, *supra* note 9, at 87–94, 195–96.

12. For an unequivocal legitimization of the king's power to control the metallic content of a coin irrespective of its denomination see *Le Case de Mixt Moneys* (1605), Davis 18, 80 E.R. 507.

13. See Glossary in T.J. Sargent & F. Velde, *The Big Problem of Small Change* (Princeton, NJ, and Oxford: Princeton University Press, 2002) at 375. The term is not conceptually different from "token money" referring to a coin not having the intrinsic value for which it is current. Ibid. at 376.

14. For the history of the international monetary system, see, e.g., R. Lastra, *Legal Foundations of International Monetary Stability* (Oxford: Oxford University Press, 2006) at 345–70.

15. Such notes "accounted among merchants as ready cash." See *Tassell and Lee v. Lewis* (1696), 1 Ld. Raym. 743 at 744, 91 E.R. 1397 at 1398. However, "the acceptance [by a creditor] of . . . [such a] note is not actual payment." Rather, "when such a note is given in payment, it is always intended to be taken under this condition, to be [absolute] payment [only] if the money be paid [in coin] thereon . . . " The condition was dispensed with upon the creditor's failure to demand payment in coin from the issuer "in convenient time." *Ward v. Evans* (1702), 2 Ld. Raym. 928 at 930, 92 E.R. 120 at 121.

16. Payment in Bank of England notes was held to be as good as "payment . . . in gold" so as to amount to absolute discharge. See *Currie v. Misa* (1875), LR 10 Ex 153 at 164. See also *The Guardians of the Poor of the Lichtfield Union v. Greene* (1857), 26 LJ Ex. 140 at 142. At the same time, while being legal tender under s. 6 of the *Bank of England Act 1833* (U.K.), 3 & 4 Will. 4, c. 98, actual convertibility to specie "had been an essential feature of the Bank of England Act 1833." Charles Proctor, *Mann on the Legal Aspect of Money*, 6th ed. (Oxford: Oxford University Press, 2005) at 65.

17. E.g., one dollar for 100 pennies (each of one cent), 20 nickels (each of five cents), 10 dimes (each of 10 cents), or four quarters (each of 25 cents).

18. See Sargent & Velde, *supra* note 13, at 5 (as well as Preface at XVII), specifically drawing on C.M. Cipolla, *Money, Prices, and Civilization in the Mediterranean World, Fifth to Seventh Century* (New York: Gordian Press, 1956) at 27. The triumph of the standard formula in the course of the nineteenth century is set out by Sargent & Velde, *supra*, at 306–19.

19. That is, 100 pennies, 20 nickels, 10 dimes, or four quarters are convertible to one dollar. Two nickels are converted to a dime, etc. Each such conversion is irrespective of the metallic content of the subunit denominations (that is, the penny, nickel, dime, or quarter). The "standard formula" preceded the cessation of convertibility (discussed in the immediately following paragraph); yet, as it is understood today, the "standard formula" does not rule out (nor does it require) that the basic unit, for example, the dollar, be convertible or at least anchored to the value of a specified quantity of a given precious metal.

20. In England, abolition of convertibility goes back to the *Gold Standard Act, 1925* (U.K.), 15 & 16 Geo. 5, c. 29. Abolition was strengthened in *Gold Standard (Amendment) Act, 1931* (U.K.), 21 & 22 Geo. 5, c. 46. See Holden, *supra* note 9, at 279.

21. The "cutoff" date is August 15, 1971. On that day the United States ceased to maintain the purchasing power of the U.S. dollar in terms of a specified amount of gold. Thereby it effectively abolished the gold (or any other commodity) standard as the yardstick for the international monetary system. Until then, all currencies had been measured by reference to the U.S. dollar, which is turn, had been assessed in gold. See Lastra, above note 14, at 362–63.

22. David Fox, *Property Rights in Money* (Oxford: Oxford University Press, 2008) at 28.

23. Hence, contract alone cannot transfer the legal title to money. Ibid. at 87.

24. Ibid. at 79–86, and further, at 87–95.

25. Alternatively, having paid the payee, an intermediary who did not owe money to the payer, became owed by the payer.

26. See, e.g., definition of "credit institution" in Article 4(1)(1) of Regulation (EU) No 575/2013 of the European Parliament and of the Council of 26 June 2013 on prudential requirements for credit institutions and investment firms and amending Regulation (EU) No 648/2012, http://eur-lex.europa.eu/legal-content/EN/TXT/?uri=celex:32013R0575, accessed Dec. 22, 2017.

27. http://eur-lex.europa.eu/legal-content/EN/TXT/?uri=celex:32013R0575, accessed December 22, 2017.

Edwin Green, *Banking: An Illustrated History* (New York: Rizoli, 1989) at 11. For a similar judicial discussion on the characteristics of banking see Lord Denning MR judgment in *United Dominion Trust v. Kirkwood* [1966] 2 QB 31 (CA) at 445-447.

28. Grammatically, "banker" is the professional individual, while "bank" is the institution. Until incorporation, there was no real difference, and this chapter will use the two terms interchangeably. Note also that "commercial banking," "banking," and "deposit banking" are, generally speaking, synonyms, and unless indicated otherwise are used in this chapter interchangeably.

29. See, e.g., Meir Kohn, "Early Deposit Banking" (February 1999) Department of Economics Darmouth College, Working Paper 99-03, http://sites.dartmouth.edu/mkohn/files/2017/03/99-03.pdf, accessed Jan. 9, 2018; and James McAndrews & William Roberds, "Payment Intermediation and the Origins of Banking" (Aug. 1999) Federal Reserve Bank of Atlanta, Working Paper 99-11, https://www.frbatlanta.org/research/publications/wp/1999/11.aspx, accessed Jan. 9, 2018. Both studies cover the Middle Ages and overlook antiquity.

30. As stated in n. 7, *supra*, roughly speaking, antiquity comes to an end with the beginning of the Middle Ages, usually marked by the fall of Rome in 476 C.E.

31. For an insight into the process, though well into the later Medieval period, see, e.g., Abbot Payson Usher, *The Early History of Deposit Banking in Mediterranean Europe* vol. 1 (Cambridge, MA: Harvard University Press, 1943) particularly at 3–25.

32. M.S/Goodfriend, "Money, Credit, Banking, and Payment System Policy", in David B. Humphrey, *The US Payment System: Efficiency, Risk and the Role of the Federal Reserve* (Boston: Kluwer Academic, 1990) at 247.

33. But cf. William Linn Westermann, "Warehousing and Trapezite Banking in Antiquity" (1951) 3 Journal of Economic and Business History 30 at 31 who highlights "a sound contrast between the relatively simple services rendered by the bank and the banker in antiquity . . . and the commanding position and complex character of banking as a function of credit in the economic system of today." No doubt, such a contrast really exists, and yet it is not on point in tracing the roots of the modern bank to its predecessor in Ancient Greece.

34. Raymond Bogaert, *Les Origines antiques de la banque de dépôt* (Leyde: A. W. Sijthoff, 1966) at 129 [Bogaert, *Les Origines*]. Roughly speaking, at 41–129, Bogaert surveys a period extending over 1,500 years commencing at the end of the twenty-first century B.C.E. and covering the Ur III Empire (2112–2004 B.C.E.), the Old Babylonian Period (2000–1600 B.C.E.), which included the reign of Hammurabi (1792–1750 B.C.E.), the Middle Assyrian and Middle Babylonian Periods (1200–750 B.C.E.), and the Neo-Assyrian and Neo-Babylonian Kingdoms (745–539 B.C.E.). Elsewhere in the book, at 43, Bogaert specifically discounts the existence of any comparable role to Pharaonic Egypt, the other Ancient Near Eastern civilization.

35. A complex system of lending is traced back in Mesopotamia to the first half of the 2nd millennium B.C.E. See in general, Katrien De Graefe, "Giving a Loan Is Like Making Love . . . " in Koenraad Verboven, Katelijn Vandorpe & Véronique Chankowski, eds, *Pistoi Dia Tèn Technèn-Bankers, Loans and Archives in the Ancient World: Studies in*

Honour of Raymond Bogaert (Leuven: Peeters, 2008) at 3 [Verboven et al., *Ancient World*].

36. Bogaert, *Les Origines, supra* note 34, at 174.

37. The gradual erosion during the first millennium B.C.E., culminating approximately at the first part of its second half, is noted by Francis Joannès, "Les activités bancaires en Babylonie" in Verboven et al., *Ancient World, supra* note 35, at 17, 19. The claim is set out in Alexander Lipton & Alex "Sandy" Pentland, "Breaking the Banks: New Financial Networks Could Stop the Concentration of Wealth and Increase Participation in the Economy—But only if Handled with Care" (January 2018) 318:1 Scientific American 26 who identify the origins of fractional lending out of deposits "more than 5,000 years ago in the Mesopotamian city of Ur" is supported by neither Joannès, *supra*, nor Bogaert, *Les Origines, supra* note 34, to whose expertise I prefer to defer.

38. Bogaert, *Les Origines, supra* note 34, at 59, 84 n.236, 99 and nn. 311–313 & text, *supra*.

39. Ibid. at 99. For written orders issued by a lender temple directed to a warehouse or granary at the locality of the payee-borrower see ibid. at 54. An order to a non-depositary obligor could be either written or oral. Ibid. at 100.

40. Proponents include M. Balmuth, "The Monetary Forerunners of Coinage in Phoenicia and Palestine" in A. Kindler, ed., *The Patterns of Monetary Development in Phoenicia and Palestine in Antiquity* (Tel Aviv: Schocken, 1967) (Proceedings of the International Numismatic Commission, The Israeli Numismatic Society, International Numismatic Convention, Jerusalem 1963) at 25; M. Balmuth, "The Critical Moment: The Transition from Currency to Coinage in the Eastern Mediterranean" (1975), 6 World Archeology 293; and J. Dayton, "Money in the Near East Before Coinage" (1974), 23 Berytus Archaeological Studies 41. For a critique see M.A. Powell, "A Contribution to the History of Money in Mesopotamia prior to the Invention of Coinage" in B. Hruška & G. Komoróczy, eds., Festschrift Lubor Matouš, Volume 2 (Budapest: Eötvös Loránd Tudományegyetem, Ókori Történeti Tanszek 1978) at 211. Another skeptic is P. Grierson, *The Origins of Money* (London: The Athlone Press, 1977, being the Creighton Lecture in History, 1970) at 8 & n.7.

41. The earliest coins were struck in Lydia (a city-state in Asia Minor) around 700 B.C.E. See Section II of this chapter.

42. See in general R.F.G. Sweet, *On Prices, Money and Money Uses in the Old Babylonian Period* (Unpublished Ph.D dissertation submitted to the Department of Oriental Languages and Civilizations of the University of Chicago, IL, 1958, available through UMI Dissertation Services, Ann Arbor, MI); and M.A. Powell, "Identification and Interpretation of Long Term Price Fluctuations in Babylonia: More on the History of Money in Mesopotamia" (1990), 17 Altorientalische Forschungen 76. See also J.N. Postgate, *supra* note 10, who in discussing (at 202–05) currency, observed (at 204) that "In the early second millennium, silver was the preferred currency of the merchant classes and perhaps of the administration, but even in the Old Babylonian times . . . the administration and the private sector regularly used [also] barley to fulfil much the same function, and other commodities are also attested."

43. According to P. Einzig, *Primitive Money*, 2nd ed. (Oxford: Pergamon Press, 1966) at 317, primitive money was "a unit or an object conforming to a reasonable degree to some standard of uniformity, which is employed for reckoning or for making a large proportion of the payments customary in the community concerned, and which is accepted in payment largely with the intention of employing it for making payments." For primitive money see also A.J. Toynbee, *A Study of History*, Abridgement of Volumes VII–X by D.C. Somervell (London: Oxford University Press, 1957) at 60 and in this chapter, Section I, particularly Section I.B.

44. The ensuing discussion draws on Raymond Bogaert, *Banques et banquiers dans les cités grecques* (Leyde: A.W. Sijthoff, 1968) at 50–60 and 331–45 [Bogaert, *Banques et banquiers*]; Bogaert, *Les Origines, supra* note 34, at 130–58; Edward E. Cohen, *Athenian Economy and Society: A Banking Perspective* (Princeton, NJ: Princeton University Press, 1992) at 8–11, 14–18, 62–66, and 111–21.

45. Roughly speaking this territory covers Mainland Greece, Greek Islands (together roughly coinciding with the area of modern-day Greece), and the western coast of Asia Minor or Anatolia (the latter of which is part of modern-day Turkey).

46. The Classical Period is said to have lasted between 500 and 336 B.C.E. It was preceded by the Archaic Period (stretching from 750 to 500 B.C.E.) and followed by the Hellenistic Period (taking place between 336 and 146 B.C.E.). The latter commences with Alexander the Great (336 to 323 B.C.E.) under whose reign Greek civilization extended eastward where it met and mingled with Eastern civilization. For time periods in the history of Ancient Greece you may visit http://en.wikipedia.org/wiki/Timeline_of_ancient_Greece, accessed December 27, 2017.

47. Both the production and use of coined money were expanded toward the end of the sixth and beginning of the fifth century B.C.E. See in general, Arthur R. Burns, *Money and Monetary Policy in Early Times* (New York: A.M. Kelley, 1965, reprint of 1927) at 43–45.

48. On the theory that the depositary thus became indebted for the amount of the deposit rather than to return it in specie, Bogaert, *Banques et banquiers, supra* note 44, at 333 treats such a deposit as "irregular" in the sense subsequently given to it by the Romans. In the view of Cohen, *supra* note 44, at 112–13 this is however an anachronism.

49. On the evolution of accounting in Greece, see, e.g., Léopold Migeotte, "La compatabilité publique dans les cités Grecques: l'exemple de Délos" in Verboven et al., *Ancient World, supra* note 35, at 59, and Véronique Chankowski, "Banquiers, caissiers, comptables. À propos des méthodes financières dans les comptes de Délos" in Verboven et al., *supra*, at 77.

50. Bogaert, *Banques et banquiers supra* note 44, at 344–45 and 413.

51. Between around 500 b.c.e. and 30 c.e. the Roman Republic grew from a city-state to dominate first Italy, then the Western Mediterranean and, finally, the entire Mediterranean basin. In the process, Rome had undergone a fundamental change in its system of government and came to be the Roman Empire. The City of Rome ultimately fell at 476 c.e., an event that marks the end of the Roman period in the West. An outline of Roman history can be found, for example, at http://

www.forumromanum.org/history/, accessed December 28, 2017. In 320 C.E. Emperor Constantine chose Byzantium (present-day Istanbul) as the new capital of the Empire and renamed it Constantinopolis. He officially divided the Empire into an Eastern and Western Empires in 395 C.E. The Eastern Empire survived for close to 1,000 years after the fall of Rome, until Constantinopolis fell to the hands of the Ottoman Turks in 1453 C.E., except that particularly as of the rise of Islam at the seventh century C.E. it had been considerably weakened long before its ultimate fall.

52. For this institutional framework, see, e.g., Jean Andreau, *Banking and Business in the Roman World* (Cambridge: Cambridge University Press, 1999) at 30–49 [translated by Janet Lloyd] [Andreau, *Banking*] at 30–49; as well as Koenraad Verboven, "Faeneratores, Negotiatores, and Financial Intermediation in the Roman World (Late Republic and Early Empire)" in Verboven et al., *Ancient World, supra* note 35, at 211; and Koenraad Verboven, "The Sulpicii from Puteoli, *argentarii* or *faeneratores?*" in Pol Defosse, ed., *Hommages à Carl Deroux; III—Histoire et épigraphie, Droit* (Bruxelles: Éditions Latomus, 2003) at 429. See also Peter Temin, "Financial Intermediation in the Early Roman Empire" (2004) 64.3 Journal of Economic History 705.

53. See in general, Hubert Cancik & Helmuth Schneider, eds, *Brill's New Pauly Encyclopedia of the Ancient World: Antiquity*, vol. 2 (Leiden-Boston: Brill, 2003) at 331 (v. "Auctiones"). See also G. Humbert, "Auctio," in Charles Victor Daremberg and Edmond Saglio, eds, *Dictionnaire Des Antiquités Greques et Romaines* vol. 1, Part 1 (Graz: Akademische Durck- u. Verlagsanstalt, 1969) at 543. For the controversy as to the role the banker played in a public auction, see, e.g., Fritz Sturm, "Stipulation argentaria" in Felix Bernard Joseph Wubbe & Johan Albert Ankum, *Mélanges Felix Wubbe: offerts par ses collègues et ses amis à l'ocassion de son soixante-dixiéme anniversaire* (Fribourg: Éditions universitaire, 1993) at 453, 460–63; Hans Ankum, "Quelques problèmes concernant les ventes aux enchères en droit romain classique," *Studi in onore di Gaetano Scherillo*, vol. 1, 377 (Milan: Cisalpino-La goliardica, 1972); and J.A.C. Thomas, "The Auction in Roman Law" (1957) Juridical Review 42.

54. Notwithstanding Sam Maxwell, *De la délégation en droit romain* (Bordeaux: Imprimerie Vᵉ Cadoret, 1895) at 111.

55. See Andreau, *Banking, supra* note 52, at 43, who specifically claims that in the Roman world "[t]here was no system of institutionalized compensation between banks of the same city."

56. See Jean G. Platon, *Les Banquiers dans la législation de Justinien* (Premiére partie) (Paris: Librairie Recuil Sirey, 1912) at 108–09.

57. See Adolf Berger, *Encyclopedic Dictionary of Roman Law* (Philadelphia: American Philosophical Society, 1953) at 366–67 (v. "Argentarii").

58. Edmond Guillard, *Les Banquiers Athéniens et Romains suivis du Pacte de Constitut en Droit Romain* (Paris, Lyon: Guillaumin, H. Georg, 1875) at 52 sets out these obligations and discusses them at length in 52–79.

59. Following the death of Alexander the Great in 323 B.C.E., and after the ensuing partition of his empire, Egypt fell into Ptolemy's hands. His successors, the Ptolemies, ruled Egypt until 30 B.C.E. when the country was conquered by the Romans.

With the partition of the Roman Empire in the course of the fourth century C.E., the Byzantines succeeded the Romans; they stayed in power until 642 C.E., when the Arabs took over and the Islamic epoch commenced. For Egypt, the entire era of close to a millennium, between Alexander the Great and the introduction of Islam, is loosely referred to as Greco-Roman. This historical sketch draws on http://www.sis.gov.eg/section/0/701?lang=en-us, accessed December 27, 2017, and http://en.wikipedia.org/wiki/Alexander_the_Great, accessed December 27, 2017. See also http://en.wikipedia.org/wiki/Roman_Empire, accessed December 27, 2017, and http://en.wikipedia.org/wiki/Muslim_conquests, accessed December 27, 2017.

60. The system is concisely described by Claire Préaux, *L'Économie royale des Lagides* (Bruxelles: Édition de la Fondation Égyptogique, 1939) at 142, as well as by Michael Rostovtzeff, *The Social and Economic History of the Hellenistic World*, vol. 2 (Oxford: Clarendon Press, 1941) at 1287. See also Gyles Davies, *A History of Money: from Ancient Times to Present Day*, 3rd ed. (Cardiff: University of Wales Press, 2002) at 52–55 and Westermann, *supra* note 33, at 32–33. The authoritative text relied by all is in German: Friedrich Preisigke, *Girowesen im griechischen Ägypten* (Strassburg: Verlad von Schlesier & Schweikhardt, 1910) [Reprinted: Hildesheim, New York: Georg Olms Verlag, 1971], discussing the grain giro system at 62–184, particularly at 89–92, 101–02, and 128–30 (see also relevant translated documents reproduced at 147–173), in connection with which I had the benefit of a partial unofficial translation.

61. For this understanding of the system (on the basis of Westermann's article, *supra* note 33) see Jeffery Williams, "Fractional Reserve Banking in Grain" (1984) 16 Journal of Money, Credit and Banking 488 at 488 n.1.

62. For example, a transfer from a Depositor A in Granary A to a depositor B in Granary B resulted not only in an adjustment of Depositors' accounts, but also in an adjustment that reflected the claim of Granary B on Granary A where the grain in the amount of the transfer remained kept.

63. "Giro" (coming from Greek "*gigros*," and meaning ring, circular, or cyclical) usually narrowly denotes a "credit-push" mechanism for a non-cash payment between two accounts (as in http://en.wikipedia.org/wiki/Giro, accessed December 27, 2017). Alternatively, it may more broadly denote any bookkeeping transfer (as in Westermann, *supra* note 33, at 49) or transfer operations (as in Rostovtzeff, *supra* note 60, at 1279). In this latter (broad) sense it is any non-cash payment between two bank accounts, regardless of whether it is a "credit-push" or "debit-pull" mechanism.

64. Possibly also, circulating credit notes attesting to credit posted to a grain account are said to have been used as payment devices. See, e.g., Roger S. Bagnall and Raymond Bogaert, "Orders for Payment from a Banker's Archive: Papyri in the Collection of Florida State University" (1975), in Raymond Bogaert, *Trapezitica Aegyptiaca: Recueil de recherches sur la banque en Égypte Gréco-Romaine* (Firenze: Edizioni Gonelli, 1994) at 240 [*Trapezitica*]. No mention of such credit notes appears in Preisigke, *supra* note 60.

65. And yet, a temporary revival of grain banking, consisting also of lending out of amalgamated deposits, occurred in Chicago in the course of the nineteenth century. See Williams, *supra* note 61.

66. Bogaert researched and wrote extensively on the subject. His work, consisting of 20 articles, mostly in French, to 1994 (originally published elsewhere) is collated in *Trapezitica, supra* note 64. Six subsequent articles (which are thus not part of the collection) are Raymond Bogaert, "Liste géographic des banques et des banquiers de l'Égypte romaine, 30A-284" (1995) 109 Zeitschrift-für Papyrologie und Epigraphik 133; Raymond Bogaert, "La Banque en Égypte Byzantine" (1997) 116 Zeitschrift-fur Papyrologie und Epigraphik 85; Raymond Bogaert, "Les opérations des banques de l'Égypte Ptolémaïque" (1998) 29 Ancient Society 49; Raymond Bogaert, "Liste géographique des banques et des banquiers de l'Égypte Ptolémaïque" (1998) 120 Zeitschrift-für Papyrologie und Epigraphik 165; Raymond Bogaert, "Les opérations des banques de l'Égypte romaine" (2000) 30 Ancient Society 135; and Raymond Bogaert, "Les documents bancaires de l'Égypte Gréco-Romaine et Byzantine" (2001) 31 Ancient Society 173. Bogaert commenced the first of these last six articles ("Liste geographic" (1995), *supra* at 133 text at n.1) by conceding that for health reasons he had abandoned his plan to synthesize his extensive research on banks in Greco-Roman Egypt into a monograph. Since then, he unfortunately passed away (in October 2009). A recent work covering the first part of the period is Sitta von Reden, *Money in Ptolemaic Egypt: From the Macedonain Conquest to the End of the Third Century BC* (Cambridge: Cambridge University Press, 2007) at 257–96.

67. From a modern perspective, they were not "bank branches" as, per explanation that immediately follows, they did not maintain on their books the principal accounts of their customers.

68. Bogaert's tentative statement to that effect in Bogaert, "Le statut des banques en Égypte Ptolémaïque" (1981), *Trapezitica, supra* note 64, at 56 as well as in Bogaert, "Recherches sur la banque en Égypte Gréco-Romaine" (1987), *Trapezitica, supra* note 64, at 6 is expressed more confidently in Bogaert, "Les opérations des banques de l' Égypte Ptolémaïque" *supra* note 66, at 117.

69. Among others, this has been a contested point. The present analysis follows Bogaert, who on this issue determined against the existence of a central bank in Alexandria. For his view on the point, in conjunction with a survey of the debate, see, e.g., Bogaert, "Le statut des banques en Égypte Ptolémaïque" ibid. at 47.

70. The Ptolemies ruled Egypt following the death of Alexander the Great in 323 B.C.E. until 30 B.C.E. when the country was conquered by the Romans. See note 59 *supra*.

71. Bogaert, "Les opérations des banques de l'Égypte Ptolémaïque", *supra* note 66 respectively at 113–16, 124–28, 135–42.

72. Bogaert, *supra* note 66.

73. *Ibid.* at 136–37.

74. *Ibid.* at 115.

75. *Ibid.* at 135.

76. Davies, *supra* note 60 at 92.

77. Bogaert, *Banques et banquiers, supra* note 44 at 340–41, particularly at text at n.206; Bagnall & Bogaert, *supra* note 64, at 219.

78. For legal aspects of these instruments under modern law see, e.g., Benjamin Geva, "Irrevocability of Bank Drafts, Certified Cheques and Money Orders" (1987), 65 Can. Bar Rev. 107.

79. For a check from Roman Egypt from 125 c.e., giving rise to a dispute involving the unavailability of funds to cover payment, see R. Bogaert, "Recherches sur la banque en Égypte Gréco-Romaine" (1987), *Trapezitica, supra* note 64, at 6, 23.

80. The fall of Rome in 476 c.e. marks the end of antiquity and the beginning of the Middle Ages. For Western Europe, the end of the Middle Ages is marked by the discovery of the New World in 1492, or perhaps slightly later, in the early sixteenth century, by the division of Western Christianity in the Reformation, the rise of humanism in the Italian Renaissance, and the beginnings of European overseas expansion. These propositions are common knowledge. See in general e.g. http:// simple.wikipedia.org/wiki/Middle_Ages, accessed December 27, 2017.

81. Robert S. Lopez, "The Dawn of Medieval Banking," in Center for Medieval and Renaissance Studies, University of California, Los Angeles, ed., *The Dawn of Modern Banking* (New Haven, Conn. and London: Yale University Press, 1979) at 1, 3–5. For payments in kind assessed in monetary value and on occasion supplemented with low-value coins that took place in the Carolingian Empire (eighth century c.e.), see, e.g., Alexander Murray, *Reason and Society in the Middle Ages* (Oxford: Clarendon Press, 1978, rep. 2002) at 31–35.

82. Bogaert, *Les Origines, supra* note 34, at 163–65.

83. Lopez, *supra* note 81, at 10.

84. See, e.g., André-E Sayous, "Les opérations des banquiers Italiens en Italie et aux Foires de Champagne pendant le XIIIe siècle" (1932) 170 Revue Historique 1 [Sayous, "banquiers Italiens"]; and M. Prestwich, "Italian Merchants in Late Thirteenth and Early Fourteenth Century England" in Centre for Medieval and Renaissance Studies, University of California, Los Angeles, ed., *The Dawn of Modern Banking* (New Haven, Conn. and London: Yale University Press, 1979) at 77.

85. The revolution occurred in the aftermath of the feudal anarchy of the manorial economy of the Dark Ages. For a detailed discussion on this general context, see Raymond de Roover, "Chapter II: The Organization of Trade", in M. M. Postan, E. E. Rich & E. Miller, eds., *The Cambridge Economic History of Europe Volume 3: Economic Organization and Policies in the Middle Ages* (London: Cambridge University Press, 1963, rep. 1979) at 42 [de Roover, "The Organization of Trade"].

86. Raymond de Roover, "New Interpretations of the History of Banking", in Julius Kirshner, ed., *Business, Banking, and Economic Thought in Late Medieval and Early Modern Europe: Selected Studies of Raymond de Roover* (Chicago and London: University of Chicago Press, 1974, Phoenix Edition 1976) at 213 [de Roover, "New Interpretations"].

87. See Raymond De Roover, "What Is Dry Exchange?" in Julius Kirshner, ed., *Business, Banking, and Economic Thought in Late Medieval and Early Modern Europe: Selected Studies of Raymond de Roover* (Chicago and London: University of Chicago Press, 1974, Phoenix Edition 1976) 183 at 184 [de Roover, "Dry Exchange"].

88. Sir William S. Holdsworth, *A History of English Law*, vol. 8 (London: Methuen & Co., Sweet and Maxwell, 2nd ed.: 1937, rep. 1966) at 178.

89. See in detail: Reinhold Mueller, "The Role of Bank Money in Venice, 1300–1500", in Fondazione Giorgio Cini et al., eds., *Studi veneziani* (NS) vol. 3 (Pisa: Giardini, 1979) at 47.

90. De Roover, "New Interpretations", *supra* note 86, at 215, 216; R. De Roover, *L'Evolution de la Lettre de Change* XIVᵉ–XVIIIᵉ siècles (Paris: Librairie Armand Colin, 1953) [hereafter: De Roover, *lettre de change*] at 208. See also at 212–13. In these three pages he summarizes the views of Bartolo Da Sassofferato (1314–1357); Baldo Degli Ubaldi (1327–1400); and Giasone Del Maino (1435–1519). De Roover acknowledges (*supra* at 208) Bartolo's text to be "obscure" but claims to follow its usual interpretation including by the two other jurists. *Supra* at 85–87. See also Usher, *Deposit Banking*, *supra* note 31, at 90, speaking of "the custom of transacting all important business in person if possible" as facilitated by "[t]he compactness of medieval and early modern towns and the concentration of the commercial community . . . "

91. See in general, De Roover, "New Interpretations," *supra* note 90, at 216–17 as well as Usher, *Deposit Banking*, *supra* note 31, at 90–94. For an extensive discussion, see M. Spallanzani, "A Note on Florentine Banking in the Renaissance: Orders of Payment and Cheques" (1978), 7:1 Journal of European Economic History 145. The author points out (e.g., at 146) the difficulty in identifying with certainty those payment orders that are checks. Furthermore, his definition of "cheque" (at 148), as "an order of payment issued on a bank . . . by someone who has funds available" is too broad and in effect does not distinguish between cheques and other payment orders. At the same time, my overall impression from the article is that he speaks of a "cheque" in the correct sense.

92. But contrary to Mueller, *supra* n. 89 . at 74–76, Mark Manning, Eriend Nier & Jochen Schanz, eds., *The Economics of Large-value Payments and Settlement: Theory and Policy Issues for Central Banks* (Oxford: Oxford University Press, 2009) at 24 find "no conclusive evidence" for interbank transfers in medieval Venice.

93. De Roover, "New Interpretations," *supra* note 57, at 219.

94. Frederic C. Lane, *Venice, A Maritime Republic* (Baltimore: John Hopkins University Press, 1973) at 328–29 [Lane, *Venice*]; for the same phenomenon in Venice at a later period see *supra* at 402. See also Frederic C. Lane, "Venetian Bankers, 1496–1533: A Study in the Early Stages of Deposit Banking" (1937) 45 Journal of Political Economy 187 at 200–01 [Lane, "Venetian"].

95. de Roover, "New Interpretations," *supra* note 57, at 223. For a discussion of the public bank in Venice as a successor of the private bank system that failed primarily due to excessive lending by means of simple book entries, see Charles F. Dunbar, "The Bank of Venice" (1892) 6 Quarterly Journal of Economics 308; and Gino Luzzatto, "Les banques publiques de Venise (Siècles XVI–XVIII)" in Johannes Gerard van Dillen, ed., *History of the Principal Public Banks* (London: Frank Cass, 1964, being 2nd impression of the 1934 1st edition, The Hague: Martinus Nijhoff, 1934) at 39.

96. Lane, *Venice, supra* note 94, at 147. See also Lane, "Venetian" *supra* note 94, at 187 specifically rejecting earlier such institutions and stating that "*Giro* banks did not come into existence until the late sixteenth century, at Venice in 1584 . . . "

97. Adam Smith, *The Wealth of Nations* (Chicago: University of Chicago Press, 1976; being the 1776 original text, edited by E. Cannan and prefaced by G. J. Stigler, "Two Volumes in One") vol. 1 at 504.

98. See, e.g., Johannes Gerard van Dillen, "The Bank of Amsterdam", in van Dillen, ed., *supra* note 95, at 79; Smith, *supra* note 97, at 503–13; Pit Dehing & Marjolein C. 't Hart, "Linking the Fortunes: Currency and Banking, 1550-1800" in Marjolein 't Hart, Joost Jonker & Jan Luiten van Zanden, eds., *A Financial History of the Netherlands* (Cambridge: Cambridge University Press, 1997) at 45–51; and Stephen Quinn & William Roberds, "The Big Problem of Large Bills: The Bank of Amsterdam and the Origins of Central Banking" (2007) [For a former version, see Federal Reserve Bank of Atlanta, Working Papers Series, Working Paper 2005-16, August 2005 (albeit the latter contains lots of econometrics that are inaccessible to a nonspecialist such as myself)]. For money and banking in Amsterdam see also Jan De Vries & An van der Woulde, *The First Modern Economy: Success, Failure, and Perseverance of the Dutch Economy, 1500–1815* (Cambridge: Cambridge University Press, 1997) at 81–91 and 129–34.

99. Raymond de Roover, "Banking and Credit in the Formation of Capitalism," Fifth International Conference of Economic History Leningrad 1970 (Paris, 1979) at 9. See in detail, Raymond de Roover, *Money, Banking and Credit in Mediaeval Bruges: Italian Merchant Bankers, Lombards and Money Changers: A Study in the Origins of Banking* (Cambridge, Mass: The Medieval Academy of America, 1948; republished, London: Routledge/Thoemmes Pres, 1999 as vol. II of The Emergence of International Business, 1200–800).

100. For a detailed analysis in a broad context, see de Roover, "The Organization of Trade," *supra* note 85, at 42.

101. De Roover identifies three stages in the history of the bill of exchange from its inception to the end of the eighteenth century: De Roover, *lettre de change, supra* note 90, at 18–19. He enumerates two subsequent periods, one of expansion, in the nineteenth century during which the bill of exchange became discountable, followed by a subsequent contraction in terms of actual use. For the early bill of payment as a notarial instrument, see, e.g., André-E Sayous, "L'origine de la lettre de change" (1933) 12 (Ser. 4) Revue historique de droit français et étranger 66; André-E Sayous, "Note sur l'origine de la lettre de change et les débuts de son emploi á Barcelone (XIVᵉ siècle)" (1934) 13 (Ser. 4) Revue historique de droit français et étranger 315; and André-E Sayous, "Les méthodes commerciales de Barcelone au XVᵉ siècle, d'après des documents inédits de ses archives" (1936) 15 (Ser. 4) Revue historique de droit français et étranger 255 at 274–86 [Sayous, "méthodes commerciales XV"] at 274–86. With the disappearance of the notarial requirement, the instrument nevertheless retained some formal language: Marie-Thérèse Boyer-Xambeu, Ghislain Deleplace & Lucien Gillard, *Private Money & Public Currencies: The 16th Century Challenge*, translated by Azizeh Azodi (New York and London: M. E. Sharpe, 1994) at 30.

102. See Boyer-Xambeu et al., *supra* note 101, at 91–94 as well as at 70–91. See also de Roover, *lettre de change, supra* note 90, at 74–82; Usher, *supra* note 31, at

110–33; and Paul-Louis Huvelin, *Essai historique sur le droit des Marchés & des Foires* (Paris: Arthur Rousseau, 1897) at 534–93.

103. See, e.g., Richard D. Richards, *The Early History of Banking in England* (New York: A. M. Kelley, 1965, reprint of 1929 edition). For a succinct summary, see Holdsworth, *supra* note 88, at 185–92.

104. See in detail, Stephen Quinn, "Balances and Goldsmith-Bankers: The Co-ordination and Control of Inter-banker Debt Clearing in Seventeenth-Century London," in David Mitchell, ed., *Goldsmiths, Silversmiths and Bankers: Innovation and the Transfer of Skill, 1550 to 1750* (London: Alan Sutton Publishing and Centre for Metropolitan History, 1995) at 53.

105. See H. V. Bowen, "The Bank of England during the Long Eighteenth Century, 1694–1820" in Richard Roberts & David Kynaston, eds., *The Bank of England: Money, Power, and Influence 1694–1994* (Oxford: Clarendon Press, 1995). See also Richard D. Richards, "The First Fifty Years of the Bank of England (1694–1744)", in van Dillen, ed., *supra* note 95, at 201; Richard Roberts, "The Bank of England and the City" in Richard Roberts & David Kynaston, eds., *The Bank of England: Money, Power, and Influence 1694–1994* (Oxford: Clarendon Press, 1995) at 152, 153. For its origins see also James E. Thorold Rogers, *The First Nine Years of the Bank of England* (Oxford: Clarendon Press, 1887).

106. Notes of the Bank of England were made legal tender in England and Wales for all payments (except for by the Bank itself) over five pounds by s. 6 of the *Bank of England Act, 1833*, (U.K.), 3 & 4 Will. IV, c. 98.

107. While certainly there was rivalry the fact is that "many goldsmiths opened accounts with the Bank within a few months of its creation"; Holden, *supra* note 9, at 93.

108. See, e.g., Ben Norman, Rachel Shaw & George Speight, "The History of Interbank Settlement Arrangements: Exploring Central Banks' Role in the Payment System" (2011) Bank of England, Working Paper No 412, https://www.ecb.europa.eu/home/pdf/research/Working_Paper_412.pdf, accessed Dec. 27, 2017.

109. See, e.g., Richard D. Richards, *The Early History of Banking in England* (New York: A. M. Kelley, 1965, reprint of 1929 edition) at 40–43 [Richards, *Early History*]; Holden, *supra* note 9; Albert Feavearyear, *The Pound Sterling: A History of English Money*, 2nd ed. by E. V. Morgan (Oxford: Clarendon Press, 1963) at 107–08; JK Horsefield, "The 'Stop of the Exchequer' Re-visited" (1982), 35 Economic History Review 511 at 523 [Horsefield, "Exchequer"]; *Tassell and Lee v. Lewis* (1695), 1 Ld. Raym. 743 at 744, 91 E.R. 1397 at 1398 (K.B.).

110. Notes were issued by banks either against deposit of specie, that is, precious metal or coins, or against the negotiation, and hence in discount, of bills of exchange, as well as of promissory notes; Smith, *supra* note 66; George Tucker, *The Theory of Money & Banks Investigated* (New York: A. M. Kelly, 1964, reprint of 1839 original) at 161, 164.

111. See, e.g., Holden, *supra* note 9, at 92.

112. Convertibility was abolished for good in the UK under the *Gold Standard (Amendment) Act*, 1931, 21 & 22 Geo. V, c. 46.

113. Joseph Huber, "The Chicago Plan (100% Reserve) and Plain Sovereign Money" (Jan. 2015), http://www.academia.edu/31071041/The_Chicago_Plan_100_Reserve_and_Plain_Sovereign_Money, accessed Dec. 28, 2017.

114. For the origins and early history of the London Clearing House, see, e.g., William Howarth, *Our Clearing System and Clearing Houses* (London: Effingham Wilson, 1884); and Phillip W Matthews, *The Bankers' Clearing House: What It Is and What It Does* (London: Pitman & Sons, 1921). For a modern perspective on the scope of operation of a clearing house, see, e.g., Herbert L. Baer, Virginia G. France & James T. Moser, "What Does a Clearinghouse Do?" (Spring 1995) 1 Derivatives Quarterly 39. See also: James T. Moser, "What Is Multilateral Clearing and Who Cares?" Chicago Fed Letter, Nov. 1994 (No. 87, Federal Reserve Bank of Chicago).

115. See Michael McLeay, Amar Radia & Ryland Thomas, "Quarterly Bulletin 2014 Q1: Money Creation in the Modern Economy" (2014) Bank of England, https://www.monetary.org/wp-content/uploads/2016/03/money-creation-in-the-modern-economy.pdf, accessed Dec. 27, 2017.

116. Goodfriend, *supra* note 32, at 252–57.

117. CPSS, *Core Principles for Systemically Important Payment Systems* (Basel: BIS, Jan. 2001) at 34–36, https://www.bis.org/cpmi/publ/d43.pdf, accessed Dec. 27, 2017.

118. See in general, CPMI, *Correspondent Banking* (Basel: BIS July 2016) https://www.bis.org/cpmi/publ/d147.pdf, accessed Dec. 27, 2017.

119. For the distinction between "commercial-bank money" and "central-bank money" see, e.g., Manning, Nier & Schanz, *supra* note 92, at 4.

120. For this term see: Antonio Sáinz de Vicuña, "An Institutional Theory of Money", in Mario Giovanoli & Diego Devos, eds., *International Monetary and Financial Law: The Global Crisis* (Oxford: Oxford University Press, 2010) at 517 and 527.

121. See, e.g.: Michael McLeay, Amar Radia & Ryland Thomas, "Money in the Modern Economy: An Introduction" BOE Quarterly Bulletin 2014 Q1 at 4; Michael McLeay, Amar Radia & Ryland Thomas, "Money in the Modern Economy" BOE Quarterly Bulletin 2014 Q1 at 14; and B. Friedman, "The Future of Monetary Policy: The Central Bank as an Army with Only a Signal Corps?" 2:3 International Finance 261, (1999).

122. For their function, see, e.g., Ronan Manly, *Why the World's Central Banks Hold Gold—In their Own Words*, posted on March 20, 2018, https://www.bullionstar.com/blogs/ronan-manly/worlds-central-banks-hold-gold-words/, accessed October 5, 2018.

123. On moving away from this tiering structure, see, e.g., Evangelos Benos, Gerardo Ferrara & Pedro Gurrola-Perez, "The Impact of De-tiering in the United Kingdom's Large-Value Payment System" (2017) Bank of England, Working Paper No 676.

124. See, e.g., E Gerald Corrigan, "Luncheon Address: Perspectives on Payment System Risk Reduction", in David B. Humphrey, ed., *The U.S. Payment System: Efficiency, Risk and the Role of the Federal Reserve* (Boston: Kluwer Academic Publishers, 1990) at 129–30. See also Hans J. Blommestein & Bruce J. Summers, "Banking and the Payment System", in Bruce J. Summers, ed., *The Payment System: Design, Management and Supervision* (Washington, D.C.: International Monetary Fund,

1994) at 15 and 27; and Bruce J. Summers, "The Payment System in a Market Economy", in Summers, *supra*, at 1–5.

125. See Douglas W. Arner, Janos N. Barberis & Ross B. Buckley, "The Evolution of Fintech: A New Post-Crisis Paradigm?" at 4, https://papers.ssrn.com/sol3/papers.cfm?abstract_id=2676553, accessed Dec. 28, 2017.

126. For an early discussion on the subject see Israel Sendrovic, "Technology and the Payment System," in Summers, ed., *supra* note 124, at 178.

127. See Gianni Bonaiuti, "Economic Issues on M-Payments and Bitcoin" in Gabriella Gimigliano, ed., *Bitcoin and Mobile Payments Constructing a European Union Framework* (London: Palgrave, 2016) at 27.

128. See CPSS, *Innovations in Retail Payments* (Basel: NIS, May 2012), https://www.bis.org/cpmi/publ/d102.pdf, accessed Dec. 27, 2017. See also: CPSS, *Survey of Developments in Electronic Money and Internet and Mobile Payments* (Basel: BIS, Mar. 2004), https://www.bis.org/cpmi/publ/d62.pdf, accessed Dec. 27, 2017.

129. Gideon Samid, *Tethered Money: Managing Digital Currency Transactions* (London: Academic Press, 2015) at 80–81.

130. See definition of "cryptography": http://searchsoftwarequality.techtarget.com/definition/cryptography, accessed December 28, 2017.

131. For definition of "cryptographic complexity" (as well as "cryptographic equivocation"), see Samid, *supra* note 129, at 139–40 (Glossary).

132. For the superior protection of randomness premised on "a cipher which use[s] no mathematical complexity but instead call[s] for large amounts of randomness" see, e.g., Carsten Stöcker & Gideon Samid, "Randomness: The Fix for Today's Broken Security," https://medium.com/@cstoecker/randomness-the-fix-for-todays-broken-security-39ea7dc3a89b, accessed Jan. 9, 2018.

133. CPSS and the Group of Computer Experts of the Central Banks of the Group of Ten Countries, *Security of Electronic Money* (Basel: BIS, 1996) at 16, https://www.bis.org/cpmi/publ/d18.pdf, accessed Dec. 2017. A brute-force attack occurs when "An outsider could try to discover the plaintext by testing all possible decryption keys." Ibid. at 58.

134. Samid *supra* note 129, at 106.

135. CPSS, *Security, supra* note 133, particularly at 5. See also information on "electronic money" at https://en.wikipedia.org/wiki/Electronic_money, accessed Dec. 27, 2017.

136. Alan L. Tyree, "The Legal Nature of Electronic Money" (1999) 10 Journal of Banking and Finance Law and Practice 273 at 276 .

137. CPSS, *Implications for Central Banks of the Development of Electronic Money* (Basel, Oct. 1996) at 1 (emphasis in the original); https://www.bis.org/publ/bisp01.pdf, accessed Oct. 07, 2018.

138. CPSS, *Security, supra* note 133, particularly at 5.

139. For the view that this is in fact e-money in the true sense, see: Nadia F. Piffaretti, *A Theoretical Approach to Electronic Money* (Feb. 1998). FSES-302. Available at SSRN: https://ssrn.com/abstract=70793 or http://dx.doi.org/10.2139/ssrn.70793.

140. Unfortunately, the confusion between these two types of payment products is rampant. For a definition of "e-money" that does not include the prepaid

product, see Ben Fung, Miguel Molico & Gerald Stuber, "Electronic Money and Payments: Recent Developments and Issues" (2014) Bank of Canada Discussion Paper 2014-2, http://www.bankofcanada.ca/wp-content/uploads/2014/04/dp2014-2.pdf, accessed Dec. 27, 2017.

141. Bradley Crawford, "Is Electronic Money Really Money?" (1997), 12 Banking and Finance Law Review 399.

142. I am thus not persuaded by the classification of CPMI, *Digital Currencies* (Basel: BIS, Nov. 2015) at 6, https://www.bis.org/cpmi/publ/d137.pdf, accessed Mar. 11, 2018, under which e-money is lumped with digital currencies as "E-money (broad sense)" so as to be contrasted with commercial bank money.

143. See in general e.g., Benjamin Geva, "Is Death of the Paper Cheque upon Us? The Electronic Presentment and Deposit of Cheques in Canada" (2014) 30 BFLR 113; and Benjamin Geva, "From Paper to Electronic Order: The Digitalization of the Check in the USA" (2015) 4 Penn State Journal of Law and International Affairs 96.

144. Such as preauthorized debits (PADs) replacing the delivery of a series of postdated checks; the debit card complementing the credit card and to a large extent substituting for both cash and checks; preauthorized credits (PAPs) substituting for paychecks.

145. See, e.g., Section 102 (14) of the Uniform Money Services Act (UMSA), http://www.uniformlaws.org/shared/docs/money%20services/umsa_final04.pdf, accessed Dec. 28, 2017, under which "Money transmission" is defined to mean "selling or issuing payment instruments, stored value, or receiving money or monetary value for transmission . . . "

146. Defined in Article 4 (4) of the Directive (EU) 2015/2366 of the European Parliament and of the Council of 25 November 2015 on payment services in the internal market, amending Directives 2002/65/EC, 2009/110/EC and 2013/36/EU and Regulation (EU) No 1093/2010, and repealing Directive 2007/64/EC, Official Journal of the European Union 23.12. 2015, L 337/35, http://eur-lex.europa.eu/legal-content/EN/TXT/?uri=celex:32015L2366, accessed Dec. 28, 2017 to mean: "a legal person that has been granted authorisation in accordance with Article 11 to provide and execute payment services throughout the [European] Union." The term does not include credit institution (bank), electronic money institution, or post office giro institutions. See Article 1(1).

147. Defined under Article 2(1) of the DIRECTIVE 2009/110/EC of the European Parliament and of the Council of 16 September 2009 on the taking up, pursuit, and prudential supervision of the business of electronic money institutions amending Directives 2005/60/EC and 2006/48/EC repealing Directive 2000/46/EC, Official Journal of the European Union, 10.10. 2009. L 267/7, http://eurlex.europa.eu/legal-content/EN/TXT/?uri=CELEX%3A32009L0110, accessed Dec. 27, 2017, to mean: "a person that has been granted authorisation under Title II to issue electronic money."

148. See, e.g., document issued by the Canadian Bankers Association (CBA), Canadian NFC Mobile Payments Reference Model, Version 1.03, May 14, 2012, https://

www.cba.ca/Assets/CBA/Files/Article%20Category/PDF/msc_20120514_mobile_en.pdf, accessed Dec. 28, 2017.

149. See, e.g., the large value wholesale payment system in Canada where finality of payment is guaranteed by the central bank prior to the completion of settlement. CPSS, *Core Principles, supra* note 117, at 30, https://www.bis.org/cpmi/publ/d43.pdf, accessed Dec. 28, 2017.

150. See, e.g., CPMI, *Fast Payments—Enhancing the Speed and Availability of Retail Payments* (Basel: BIS, Nov. 2016), https://www.bis.org/cpmi/publ/d154.pdf, accessed Dec. 28, 2017.

151. For the legal nature of the credit card payment see in general: Benjamin Geva, "The Processor and the Contractual Matrix in a Card Scheme: How Privity Fell and Resurrected in *Aldo v. Moneris*" (Oct. 2013) 32:5 Nat'l Banking L Rev 73.

152. Hanno Beck, "Banking Is Essential, Banks Are Not. The Future of Financial Intermediation in the Age of the Internet" (2001) 3:7-22 Economic Research and Electronic Networking, https://link.springer.com/content/pdf/10.1023%2FA%3A1009927623530.pdf, accessed Jan. 9, 2018.

153. See, e.g., Benjamin J. Cohen, "Electronic Money: New Day or False Dawn?" (2001) 8:2 Review of International Political Economy 197, https://www.researchgate.net/publication/233010154_Electronic_money_New_day_or_false_dawn, accessed Jan. 9, 2018.

154. See, e.g., Benjamin Geva, "The Wireless Wire: Do M-Payments and *UNCITRAL* Model Law on International Credit Transfers Match?" (2011) 27:2 BFLR 249.

155. See, e.g., CPSS and the World Bank, *General Principles for International Remittance Services* (Basel: BIS and the World Bank, Jan. 2007), https://www.bis.org/cpmi/publ/d76.pdf, accessed Dec. 28, 2017.

156. For a critical analysis, see, e.g., Benjamin Geva & Muharem Kianief, "Reimagining E-Money: Its Conceptual Unity with Other Retail Payment Systems" (2005) 3 Current Developments in Monetary and Financial Law 669 and 677–79.

157. Whether from (or into) an asset account, credit line, or stored-value—as the case may be.

158. Notwithstanding Joshua S. Gans & Hanna Halaburda, "Some Economics of Private Digital Currency" (2013) Bank of Canada, Working Paper 2013-38, http://www.bankofcanada.ca/wp-content/uploads/2013/11/wp2013-38.pdf, accessed Dec. 28, 2017.

159. Generally speaking, IT (standing for Information Techonology) "deals with the technology part of any information system, and as such deals with hardware, servers, operating systems and software etc." See, e.g., http://www.differencebetween.com/difference-between-information-systems-and-vs-information-technology/, accessed Dec. 28, 2017.

160. A broader definition under which Fintech "refers to the use of technology to deliver financial solutions," as in Douglas W. Arner, Jànos Barberis, and Ross P. Buckley, *Fintech and Regtech in a Nutshell, and the Future in a Sandbox,* (CFA Research Foundation Briefs, 2017), at 2, https://www.cfainstitute.org/-/media/documents/

article/rf-brief/rfbr-v3-n4-1.ashx , will encompass the use of technology by banks such as in electronic banking, and hence is unhelpful for the purposes of this chapter.

161. As claimed by "clever consultants" according to "Unresolved," The Economist (Sept. 8, 2018) 20 at 21.

162. Goodfriend, *supra* note 32, at 248.

163. Ibid. at 261.

164. For detailed discussions see references in sources cited in notes 126 and 127 *supra*.

165. See, e.g., see Michael D. Bordo & Andrew T. Levin, "Central Bank Digital Currency and the Future of Monetary Policy" (2017) NBER, Working Paper 23711, http://www.nber.org/papers/w23711, accessed Dec. 28, 2017 See also: Norges Bank, *Norges Bank Papers: Central bank digital currencies* (18 May 2018) https://static.norges-bank.no/contentassets/166efadb3d73419c8c50f9471be26402/nbpapers-1-2018-centralbankdigitalcurrencies.pdf?v=05/18/2018121950&ft=.pdf, accessed May 24, 2019; Sveriges Riksbank , *The Riksbank's e-krona project* Report 2, (October 2018)   https://www.riksbank.se/globalassets/media/rapporter/e-krona/2018/the-riksbanks-e-krona-project-report-2.pdf , accessed May 24, 2019; Bank of Israel: *Report of the team to examine the issue of Central Bank Digital Currencies* (November 2018) https://www.boi.org.il/en/NewsAndPublications/PressReleases/Documents/Digital%20currency.pdf , accessed May 24, 2019; and John D Murray, *Central Banks and the Future of Money* (CD Howe Institute Commentary No. 540, April 2019) https://www.cdhowe.org/sites/default/files/attachments/research_papers/mixed/Final%20Commentary_540.pdf , accessed May 24, 2019.

166. Nick Gruen, *Central Banking for All: A Modest Proposal for Radical Change* (London: Nesta, Mar. 2014) at 7, https://www.nesta.org.uk/sites/default/files/central_banking_for_all.pdf,accessed Dec. 28, 2017.

167. Ibid, *passim*. In the UK, he designates the National Savings and Investments (NS&I) as the appropriate governmental agency. At the moment the NS&I accepts deposits from the public (up to prescribed ceilings) and places them in savings accounts from which payment services cannot be provided. In Gruen's words, "what is being proposed is to allow super-collateralised loans to be treated as part of the monetary system rather than the financial system." Ibid. at 9.

168. The term is said to be coined by Robert Litan, *What Should Banks Do?* (Washington, DC: Brookings Institution, 2005). See Patrizio Lainà, "Proposals for Full-Reserve Banking: A Historical Survey from David Ricardo to Martin Wolf," Economic Thought 4:2 (2015) at 12, http://et.worldeconomicsassociation.org/files/WEA-ET-4-2-Laina.pdf, accessed Dec. 28, 2017. Litan discusses "narrow banking" *supra* at 6, 169–78 and 186–87.

169. Ben Dyson & Graham Hodgson, *Digital Cash: Why Central Banks Should Start Issuing Electronic Money* (London: Positive Money, 2016) at 15, http://positivemoney.org/wp-content/uploads/2016/01/Digital_Cash_WebPrintReady_20160113.pdf, accessed Dec. 28, 2017.

170. Ibid. at 16.

171. See, e.g., Jaromir Benes & Michael Kumhof, "The Chicago Plan Revisited" (2012) International Monetary Fund, Working Paper WP/12/202, https://www.imf.org/external/pubs/ft/wp/2012/wp12202.pdf, accessed Dec. 28, ; William R. Allen, "Irving Fisher and the 100 Percent Reserve Proposal" (1993) 36:2 Journal of Law and Economics 703, http://www.journals.uchicago.edu/doi/pdfplus/10.1086/467295, accessed Dec. 28, and Lainà, *supra* note 123.

172. See, e.g.: Huber, *supra* note 82; Phillipe Bacchetta, *The Sovereign Money Initiative in Switzerland: An Economic Assessment* (Sept. 26, 2017) https://people.unil.ch/philippebacchetta/files/2017/06/Vollgeld_5.pdf, accessed Dec. 28, 2017. For a blueprint see Ben Dyson, Graham Hodgson & Frank van Lerven, *Sovereign Money—An Introduction* (London: Positive Money, 2016), http://positivemoney.org/wp-content/uploads/2016/12/SovereignMoney-AnIntroduction-20161214.pdf, accessed Dec. 28, 2017.

173. There are at least two variants as to the rules that will govern the conduct of monetary policy under such a regime, particularly as to the role of discretion by the central bank. For a summary see Huber, *supra* note 82, at 3.

174. Beware of inconsistent use of terminology. Andrew Jackson, *Sovereign Money—Paving the Way for a Sustainable Recovery* (London: Positive Money, Nov. 2013), https://positivemoney.org/wp-content/uploads/2013/11/Sovereign-Money-Final-Web.pdf, accessed Dec. 28, 2017, uses the term to denote central bank money distributed directly to a business to fund infrastructure projects.

175. However, it does not make sense to me to have a hybrid system under which *scriptural* money is available to the public in both commercial and central bank money, as I read Dyson & Hodgson, *supra* note 124, at 28–30, to suggest.

176. For a precedent from Sri Lanka, albeit for investors' securities accounts operated by intermediaries on the books of the central bank, see *Payment & Settlement Systems Act*, No. 28 of 2005, Chapter II Securities Accounts (Secs 6-10), http://www.cbsl.gov.lk/pics_n_docs/09_lr/_docs/acts/Paymt_&_setmt_sys_act.pdf, accessed Dec. 28, 2017.

177. For these two options see Bordo & Andrew Levin, *supra* note 165.

178. Where required to meet demand further, lending may be done by the creation of new money by the central bank to be lent to banks and other lending institutions for the purposes of relending it to borrowers in the real economy. See Dyson, Hodgson & van Lerven, *supra* note 172, at 36.

179. Legally of course on maturity of the investment account the bank will be liable to depositors and investors regardless of possible default by borrowers, in which case it will be up to the bank to find sovereign money from other sources to fund its liability to depositors and investors.

180. In connection with sovereign money see, e.g., Dyson, Hodgson & van Lerven, *supra* note 172, at 28–37. One proposal for full reserve banking is for the central bank to act as a "currency board" in issuing new money only against a basket of available assets (of which gold is only one); see Warren Coats, "My Political Platform for the Nation—2017" (Dec. 31, 2016), *Warren's Space* (blog), https://wcoats.wordpress.com/2016/12/31/my-political-platform-for-the-nation-2017/,

accessed Dec. 28, 2017 (see section on Monetary and Financial Policies); Warren Coats, "Real SDR Currency Board" (2011) 22:2 Central Banking Journal, https://works.bepress.com/warren_coats/25/, accessed Dec. 28, 2017.

181. For the view that "both logically and according to the International Accounting Standards, sovereign money cannot be considered to be a debt of the state. Instead, sovereign money conforms to the classification of equity," see Ben Dyson & Graham Hodgson, *Accounting for Sovereign Money: Why State-Issued Money Is Not "Debt"* (London: Positive Money, 2016) at 9, http://positivemoney.org/wp-content/uploads/2016/03/AccountingForSovereignMoney_20160309.pdf, accessed Dec. 28, 2017.

182. The locus classicus for this proposition is *Foley v. Hill* (1848), 2 HLC 28, 9 ER 1002.

183. See Uniform Commercial Code (UCC) Article 8 (1994) Sections 8-501 to 8-511, in conjunction with definitions in Section 8-102, https://www.law.cornell.edu/ucc/8, accessed Dec. 28, 2017.

184. See Uniform Securities Transfer Act (USTA) (2004), Sections 106–116 in conjunction with definitions in Section 1, https://www.ulcc.ca/en/uniform-acts-new-order/current-uniform-acts/761-securities-transfer/2049-secbities-transfer-act, accessed Dec. 28, 2017.

185. See in general, e.g. Benjamin Geva, "Securities Transfers in the Indirect Holding System—Law Reform in Canada in the Footsteps of UCC Article 8" (2007) 18 Journal of Banking and Financial Law and Practice (Australia) 72–77.

186. In general, for the irregular deposit, see Robert W. Lee, *The Elements of Roman Law with a Translation of the Institutes of Justinian*, 4th ed. (London: Sweet & Maxwell, 1956) at 295 and R. Zimmermann, *The Law of Obligations: Roman Foundations of the Civilian Tradition* (Cape Town: Juta, 1990) at 215–19.

187. Goodfriend, *supra* note 32, at 261. Bank regulation could be added to the listed items.

188. Samid, *supra* note 129, at 105–06.

189. Such are:

> (i) closed/"in-game only" schemes, in which a link to the real economy or fiat currency hardly exists; (ii) schemes with unidirectional flow, under which the currency may originally be purchased with a fiat currency but may not be converted back to it, such as Facebook Credits, and even; (iii) schemes with a bidirectional flow, envisaging conversion in both directions, albeit usually not used in entirely open loops throughout the entire economy, such as air miles in Frequent Flyer Programs.

> See European Central Bank/Eurosystem, *Virtual Currency Schemes* (October 2012) at 12–15, https://www.ecb.europa.eu/pub/pdf/other/virtualcurrencyschemes 201210en.pdf, accessed Mar. 12, 2018. For an explanation as to why such a currency will not "migrate" to the real economy, see, e.g., Gans & Halaburda, *supra* note 158.

190. For the latter, see, e.g., CPMI, *Central Bank Digital Currencies* (Basel: BIS, Mar. 2018), https://www.bis.org/cpmi/publ/d174.pdf, accessed Oct. 7, 2018). See also Norges Bank Papers NO 1. 2018: Central Bank Digital Currency, https://static.norges-bank.no/contentassets/166efadb3d73419c8c50f9471be26402/

nbpapers-1-2018-centralbankdigitalcurrencies.pdf?v=05/18/2018121950&ft=.pdf, accessed Oct. 7, 2018.

191. Denomination in its own unit of account appears to be an element in the definition of "virtual currency" (that is, privately issued digital currency) in IMF Staff Discussion, *Virtual Currencies and Beyond: Initial Considerations* (Jan. 2016), at 7, https://www.imf.org/external/pubs/ft/sdn/2016/sdn1603.pdf accessed Sept. 21, 2016].

192. I am using this term here in a different sense than Liam Pak Nian & David Lee Kuo Chuen in David Lee Kuo Chuen, ed., *Handbook of Digital Currency: Bitcoin, Innovation, Financial Instruments and Big Data*, (Amsterdam etc.: Elsvier, 2015), at 7, who uses it to denote "closed system[s} with transactions within specific entities" in such items as loyalty points or air miles.

193. For this tripartite classification, see IMF Staff Discussion, *Virtual Currencies, supra* note 191 (where a third criterion is added viz., "mechanisms to implement and enforce internal rules on the use and circulation of the currency").

194. UK Government Office for Science, "Distributed Ledger Technology: Beyond Block Chain" (2016) at 17–18, https://www.gov.uk/government/uploads/system/uploads/attachment_data/file/492972/gs-16-1-distributed-ledger-technology.pdf, accessed Dec. 28, 2017.

195. Ibid. at 17. See also, e.g., CPMI, *Distributed Ledger Technology in Payment, Clearing and Settlement System—An Analytical Framework* (Basel: BIS, Feb. 2017), http://www.bis.org/cpmi/publ/d157.pdf, accessed Dec. 28, 2017; and David Mills et al., "Distributed Ledger Technology in Payments, Clearing and Settlement" (2016) Federal Reserve Board Division of Research & Statistics and Monetary Affairs Finance and Economics Discussion Series 2016-095, https://www.federalreserve.gov/econresdata/feds/2016/files/2016095pap.pdf, accessed Dec. 28, 2017.

196. This definition slightly modifies the one from https://medium.com/@Wolfofcrypto/basic-cryptocurrency-starter-guide-8f2071ea85de; particularly, I replace "transfer of funds" by the "execution of payment transactions" to point at payment by the transmission of "coins" rather than "generic value" in the forms of funds.

197. "Hashing" was defined to be "a cryptographic technique to generate a unique code to represent [a] document which keeps the contents of that document confidential [so as] to verify that [it] exists and has not been tampered with." See: "Discussion Paper on Distributed Ledger Technology" Financial Conduct Authority Discussion Paper DP 17/3 at 18, https://www.fca.org.uk/publication/discussion/dp17-03.pdf, accessed Dec. 28, 2017.

198. See, e.g., Nian & Chuen, supra note 192, at 5 and 8.

199. In the broader context of subsequent "plenty of alternatives," see, e.g., Andreas Hanl, "Some Insights into the Development of Cryptocurrencies" (2018) MAGKS Joint Discussion Paper Series in Economics No 04-2018, https://www.uni-marburg.de/fb02/makro/forschung/magkspapers/paper_2018/04-2018_hanl.pdf, accessed Mar. 12, 2018.

200. "Bitcoin and other cryptocurrencies are useless," The Economist (Aug. 30, 2018) at 14.

201. See, e.g., definition in s.102(23) of the *Uniform Regulation of Virtual Currency Businesses Act*, http://www.uniformlaws.org/Act.aspx?title=Regulation%20of%20 Virtual-Currency%20Businesses%20Act, accessed Dec. 28, 2017, under which "[v]irtual currency" is "a digital representation of value that is used as a medium of exchange, a unit of account, or a store of value; and is not legal tender . . . " "Legal tender" is defined in s.102(8) as "the medium of exchange or unit of value, including the coin or paper money of the United States, issued by the United States or by another government."

202. Namely, its value is not pegged to that of a financial asset or commodity.

203. See, e.g., Stuart Hoegner, "What Is Bitcoin?" in Stuart Hoegner, ed., *The Law of Bitcoin* (Bloomington IN: iUniverse, 2015) at 1; Neil Guthrie, "The End of Cash? Bitcoin, the Regulators and the Courts" (2014) 29 BFLR 355. For its mechanics, see Jonathan Levin, "Bitcoin: New Plumbing for Financial Services," *coindesk* (Nov. 29, 2014), http://www.coindesk.com/bitcoin-new-plumbing-financial-services/, accessed Dec. 28, 2017. See also Nicholas Wenker, "Online Currencies, Real-World Chaos: The Struggle to Regulate the Rise of Bitcoin" (2015) 19 Texas Review of Law & Politics 145; and Jacob Hamburger, "Bitcoins vs. State Money Transmission Laws: Protecting Consumers or Hindering Innovation?" (2015) 11 Journal of Law Econ & Policy 229. *See also*: https://en.wikipedia.org/wiki/Bitcoin, accessed Dec. 28, 2017; http://www.coindesk.com/information/what-is-bitcoin/, accessed Dec. 28, 2017; http://www.wired.com/2011/11/mf_bitcoin/, accessed Dec. 28, 2017; and "The Great Chain of Being Sure About Things" (Oct. 31, 2015) The Economist. See also European Central Bank/Eurosystem, *supra* note 189, at 21–24 and https:// en.bitcoin.it/wiki/How_bitcoin_works, accessed Dec. 28, 2017.

204. Satoshi Nakamoto, "Bitcoin: A Peer-to-Peer Electronic Cash System" (2008) at 2, https://bitcoin.org/bitcoin.pdf, accessed Dec. 28, 2017.

205. "Proof of Work" is defined to require "that the decentralized participants that validate blocks show that they have invested significant computing power in doing so." See Fintechblue, "What Is Proof of Work?" *fintechblue*, http://www.fintechblue.com/ 2016/06/what-is-proof-of-work/, bDec. 28, 2017. According to Satoshi Nakamoto, ibid., "[p]roof-of-work is essentially one-CPU-one-vote," rather than "one-IP address-one-vote."

206. Conventionally, "Bitcoin" (capitalized) refers to the technology and network whereas "bitcoins" (lowercase) refers to the currency, units, and "coins."

207. A participant may have more than one wallet. In any event, note that what is described in the text is the direct holding of bitcoins. Alternatively, in an indirect holding system, a participant keeps bitcoins with an intermediary. See Ryan J. Straus & Matthew J, Cleary, "The United States" in Hoegner, ed., *supra* note 203.

208. For Bitcoin mechanics, see Levin, *supra* note 164. For more technical information see, e.g., https://bitcoin.stackexchange.com/questions/39101/what-happens-to-bitcoin-wallet-bitcoins-if-pc-is-stolen; https://bitcoin.stackexchange.com/questions/1600/

where-are-the-users-bitcoins-actually-stored; and https://bitcoin.stackexchange.com/questions/1600/where-are-the-users-bitcoins-actually-stored, all accessed Jan. 9, 2018.

209. Samid, *supra* note 129, at 26. See also ibid. at 101 for an argument against extrapolating cryptotools for transient communication to shielding digital currency.

210. For details on the main bitcoin principles, see ibid. at 108–116.

211. See details at e.g. Christopher Malmo, "Bitcoin Is Unsustainable" (June 29, 2015) *Vice: Motherboard*, http://motherboard.vice.com/read/bitcoin-is-unsustainable, accessed Dec. 28, 2017; See also, e.g., John Quiggin, "Bitcoins Are a Waste of Energy—Literally" (Oct. 5, 2015), *ABC News*, http://www.abc.net.au/news/2015-10-06/quiggin-bitcoins-are-a-waste-of-energy/6827940, accessed Dec. 28, 2017.

212. See, e.g., https://en.bitcoin.it/wiki/Scalability_FAQ#What_is_this_Transactions_Per_Second_.28TPS.29_limit.3F, accessed Dec. 28, 2017.

213. Saifedean Ammous, "Blockchain Technology: What Is It Good For?" (Aug. 8, 2016) at 2, https://poseidon01.ssrn.com/delivery.php?ID=69700112712607411512711140771 23080074103024036044086003100075101125124080023124089029110032053022 10904900312000806809609807011511608309402208612006810312212502511309 80050650670200931231181110290040710920170230921210000250640041121230 79076114065120009100&EXT=pdf, accessed Dec. 28, 2017.

214. Timothy B. Lee, "Bitcoin Needs to Scale by a Factor of 1000 to Compete with Visa. Here's How to Do It" (Nov. 17, 2005), *The Washington Post*, https://www.washingtonpost.com/news/the-switch/wp/2013/11/12/bitcoin-needs-to-scale-by-a-factor-of-1000-to-compete-with-visa-heres-how-to-do-it/?utm_term=.f6e09d78860d, accessed Dec. 28, 2017.

215. For an overview, citing the sources as immediately below, see European Central Bank/Eurosystem, *supra* note 189, at 22–23.

216. Murray N. Rothbard, *Economic Depressions: Their Cause and Cure* (Auburn, AL: Ludwig von Mises Institute, 2009).

217. Friedrich A Hayek, *Denationalisation of Money*, 3rd ed. (London: The Institute for Economic Affairs, 1976).

218. European Central Bank/Eurosystem, *supra* note 189.

219. As pointed out by Saifedean Ammous, *The Bitcoin Standard: The Decentralized Alternative to Central Banking* (Hoboken, NJ: Wiley, 2018) at 177, speaking of Bitcoin designer Nakamoto as the inventor of "digital scarcity." For scarcity as the source for the value of a monetary asset see Karl Polyani, "The Semantic of Money Use" in G/Dalton (ed.), *Primitive, Archaic and Modern Economies: Essays of Karl Polyani*, (Darden City, NY: Doubleday, 1968) at 175, 197.S.

220. Ammous, *supra* note 219, at 56, 23, 155, and 199–200.

221. Samid, *supra* note 129, at 113.

222. Hoegner, ed., *supra* note 203, at 1, 9 n.57.

223. Samid, *supra* note 129, at 14-16.

224. For a discussion on the nature of Bitcoin value, see, e.g., William J. Luther, "Is Bitcoin Intrinsically Worthless?" (July 2017), https://papers.ssrn.com/sol3/papers.cfm?abstract_id=3000068, accessed Dec. 28, 2017.

225. Samid, *supra* note 129, at 14–15 (for an illustration of instability), and 109–10 (for connection between self-anchoring and instability). The quotation is from p. 15.

226. Ibid. at 114–21. Cf. e.g., NationCoin, being a proposed Regulated and Sovereign Backed Cryptocurrency (RSBC). Its scheme envisages crypto-coins, which as in Bitcoin, will be created by and transacted over a blockchain. However, upon their creation, crypto-coins will be stored, and released to the public by a Digital Asset Reserve, as RSBC, at the fixed value of the national unit of account. Transactions are to be verified by "miners" who will be paid freshly minted crypto-coins. See Kartik Hegadekatti & Yatish S. G., "Generation, Security and Distribution of MationCoins by a Sovereign Authority" (Jan. 7, 2017), https://papers.ssrn.com/sol3/papers.cfm?abstract_id=2888347, accessed Dec. 28, 2017.

227. For an interesting historical study on the lessons from the misfortune of such absence see, e.g., Isabel Schnabel & Hyun Song Shin, Money and Trust: Lessons from the 1620s for Money in the Digital Age (Basel: BIS, Feb. 2018), https://www.bis.org/publ/work698.pdf, accessed Mar. 12, 2018.

228. A point highlighted by in Mark Carney, *Speech: The Future of Money* (Bank of England, Mar. 2, 2018) at 6–9, https://www.bankofengland.co.uk/-/media/boe/files/speech/2018/the-future-of-money-speech-by-mark-carney.pdf?la=en&hash=A51E1C8E90BDD3D071A8D6B4F8C1566E7AC91418.

229. Ammous, *supra* note 213, at 2.

230. For the difference between proof of work and proof of stake, see, e.g.: https://www.google.ca/search?rls=com.microsoft:en-CA:IEAddress&dcr=0&q=what+is+the+difference+between+proof+of+work+and+proof+of+stake?&spell=1&sa=X&ved=0ahUKEwj38Knl1azYAhUm94MKHekWAF8QvwUIJigA&biw=1094&bih=625, accessed Dec. 28, 2017., accessed Dec. 28, 2017.

231. Not everybody is in agreement. For considering Bitcoin to be an "imperfect store of value" due to its volatility see Aaron Kumar & Christie Smith, "Crypto-currencies—An Introduction to Not-so-Funny Moneys" (Nov. 2017) Reserve Bank of New Zealand Analytical Note Series, AN2017/07 at 2, https://www.rbnz.govt.nz/-/media/ReserveBank/Files/Publications/Analytical%20notes/2017/an2017-07.pdf, accessed Jan. 9, 2018.

232. Saifedean Ammous, "Can Cryptocurrencies Fulfill the Functions of Money?" (Aug. 2016), https://poseidon01.ssrn.com/delivery.php?ID=8980310680690200130841000940011151130240080490680, accessed Oct. 5, 2018. But see Saifedean Ammous, "Can Bitcoin's Volatility Be Tamed?" The Journal of Structured Finance, Spring 2018 at 53 who argues that volatility is a market description reflecting limited use and not of an inherent feature contradicting it being hard.

233. Ammous, *The Bitcoin Standard, supra* note 219, at 198 and 207, respectively. For predicting that upon achieving gold parity Bitcoin will continue to gain value thereby percipitating a decline in gold value see, e.g., Katrik Hegadekatti, "Blockchain Technology—An Instrument of Economic Evolution?" (2017) MPRA Paper No 82852, https://mpra.ub.uni-muenchen.de/82852/1/MPRA_paper_82852.pdf, accessed Mar. 12, 2018. Not everybody is in agreement: Tony Klein, Pham Thu Hien & Thomas Walther, "Bitcoin Is Not the New Gold: A Comparison of Volatility, Correlation, and Portfolio Performance"

(2018), 59 International Review of Financial Analysis, https://poseidon01.ssrn.com/delivery.php?ID=9220050651100020730180717070125012100030050050078068020092085104072067006101008083103029001033127027001029092103085029064020094016039074000002097115015012065025020107058092077002030098027120091103021017102001100070113069122066113117069065099031115022117&EXT=pdf, accessed Oct. 7, 2018.

234. For a more moderate hypothetical variation, under which currency issued under the Bitcoin standard will consist of Bitcoin, as well as fiduciary currencies issued by central banks and commercial bank money, both backed by Bitcoin, and in which central banks will continue to be lenders of last resort, see Warren E. Weber, "A Bitcoin Standard: Lessons from the Gold Standard" (2016) Bank of Canada, Staff Working Paper 2016-14, https://www.bankofcanada.ca/wp-content/uploads/2016/03/swp2016-14.pdf, accessed Jan. 9, 2018.

235. See, e.g., Samid, *supra* note 129, at 92–94 and cf. ibid. at 125–27 as well as at 25, 98–100, albeit focusing on the advantage of paying with digital coins over that of paying in scriptural money, which may expose account data to hackers.

236. For some information visit www.wingcash.com, accessed Dec. 28, 2017 as well as www.wingcash.org, accessed Dec. 28, 2017.

237. "Strategies for Improving U.S. Payment System" (Jan. 26, 2015) Federal Reserve System, https://fedpaymentsimprovement.org/wp-content/uploads/strategies-improving-us-payment-system.pdf, accessed Dec. 28, 2017.

238. WingCash (Proposer), "Faster Payments QIAT" (Feb. 21, 2017) at 11 and 14https://drive.google.com/file/d/0B_CNPQWTRQwuZWhqbDUzNVJsNGc/view, accessed Dec. 28, 2017. For extensive information, see documents ibid. at 13: http://fasterpaymentsnetwork.com/, accessed Dec. 28, 2017; https://drive.google.com/file/d/0B_CNPQWTRQwuc1hhWlAzOEljNGs/view, accessed Dec. 28, 2017; and https://drive.google.com/file/d/0B_CNPQWTRQwuZWhqbDUzNVJsNGc/view, accessed Dec. 28, 2017.

239. See "The U.S. Path to Faster Payments FINAL REPORT PART TWO: A CALL FOR ACTION" (July 2017) Faster Payments Task Force at 13, https://fasterpaymentstaskforce.org/wp-content/uploads/faster-payments-task-force-final-report-part-two.pdf, accessed Dec. 28, 2017.

240. For detailed information on BitMint (not to be confused with BitMinter), see, e.g.: http://www.bitmint.com/, accessed Mar. 12, 2017; http://finder.startupnationcentral.org/company_page/bitmint/, accessed Mar. 12, 2017, and sites and videos accessible through it; and https://medium.com/@bitmintnews, accessed Mar. 12, 2017, and associated articles.

241. Samid, *supra* note 129, at 22.

242. On this process, see, e.g., https://en.wikipedia.org/wiki/Introduction_to_quantum_mechanics, accessed Dec. 28, 2017.

243. Helmut Scherzer, "Chapter 36: On the Quest to the Ultimate Digital Money" (Springer © 2018) in Linnhoff-Popien, Claudia, Ralf Schneider, and Michael Zaddach. *Digital Marketplaces Unleashed.* Springer. © 2018.Skillsoft. <http://ezproxy.library.yorku.ca/sso/skillport?context=138044> (Accessed May 23, 2019) at 36.6. For how BitMint works see ibid. at 36.5.

244. For details, see Gideon Samid, "Bitcoin.BitMint: Reconciling Bitcoin with Central Banks," BitMint, LLC, https://eprint.iacr.org/2014/244.pdf, accessed Dec. 28, 2017. See also e.g., http://www.bitmint.com/bitcoin.htm, accessed Dec. 28, 2017.

245. Samid, *supra* note 129, at 108.

246. Ibid. at 140 (Glossary).

247. Ibid. at 50 and 100.

248. For details on randomized or entropic coins, see ibid. at 106–08.

249. For a similar conclusion regarding (broadly and loosely defined) central bank digital currency, see Jack Meaning, Ben Dyson, James, Barker & Emily Claydon, *Broadening Narrow Money: Monetary Policy with a Central Bank Digital Currency*, Staff Working Paper no. 724, Bank of England, May 2018, https://www.bankofengland.co.uk/-/media/boe/files/working-paper/2018/broadening-narrow-money-monetary-policy-with-a-central-bank-digital-currency.pdf?la=en&hash=26851CF9F5C49C9CDBA95561581EF8B4A8AFFA52accessed May 21, 2019.

250. Samid, *supra* note 129, at 26. See text at *supra* note 209.

251. Donge He, "Monetary Policy in the Digital Age," IMF Finance & Development 13 (June 2018).

252. See e.g. : Bank of Canada, Bank of England, and Monetary Authority of Singapore, *Cross -Border Interbank Payments and Settlements: Emerging opportunities for digital transformation* (November 2018) particularly at 28-31 (Models 1 and 2). *http://www.mas.gov.sg/~/media/ProjectUbin/Cross%20Border%20Interbank%20Payments%20and%20Settlements.pdf* (accessed May 24, 2019).

253. See, e.g., Walter Engert & Ben S. C. Fung, "Central Bank Digital Currency: Motivations and Implications," Bank of Canada, Staff Discussion Paper 2017-16 at 16–17, https://www.bankofcanada.ca/wp-content/uploads/2017/11/sdp2017-16.pdf, accessed Jan. 9, 2018.

Chapter 3

1. Nick Szabo (@nickszabo4), TWITTER (Sept. 3, 2015, 11:57 PM), https://twitter.com/NickSzabo4/status/639663431918850048. Nick Szabo is considered the inventor of "smart contracts."

2. William Hinman, Dir., Div. of Corp. Fin., SEC, Remarks at the Yahoo Finance All Markets Summit: Crypto: Digital Asset Transactions: When Howey Met Gary (Plastic) (June 14, 2018) [hereinafter Hinman Speech].

3. Neha Narula (@neha), TWITTER (June 15, 2018, 6:03AM), https://twitter.com/neha/status/1007579383417188353. Ms. Narula is Director of the MIT Digital Currency Initiative.

4. Tony Sheng, *Let's ditch "decentralized,"* TONY SHENG (Sept. 3, 2018) https://www.tonysheng.com/decentralized-definition.

5. With apologies to those for whom "crypto" is short for "cryptography," I am using the term here to refer to cryptocurrencies and related distributed ledger technologies.

6. Hinman Speech, *supra* note 2.

7. This chapter focuses on permissionless blockchains such as Bitcoin and Ethereum. A separate analysis of "decentralization" would be necessary for permissioned blockchains, which share few characteristics with permissionless blockchains.

8. For the sake of clarity, I use the terms "decentralized" and "decentralization" somewhat interchangeably, where appropriate. For example, in order to avoid having to say that use of the terms "decentralized" and "decentralization" is problematic, I would say that use of the term "decentralized" is problematic, intending to pull in both terms. In a chapter on confusion in terminology, I recognize the irony of this endnote.

9. This chapter focuses on the concept of decentralization in permissionless blockchain systems such as Bitcoin or Ethereum. It does not examine decentralization with respect to applications built atop these core protocols, such as DAOs or other smart contracts.

10. This chapter does not focus on private or permissioned blockchain systems, as the exercise of power within these systems differs from that in permissionless blockchains, and the consortium agreements underpinning the operation of permissioned blockchains purport to manage the exercise of power by participants in these systems. Note that in prior works I have referred to systems like Bitcoin and Ethereum as "public blockchains." However, the terminology appears to be evolving as some permissioned networks are private (do not reveal the record to everyone) and some are public (reveal the record to everyone). Because of this evolving distinction, I believe it is clearer to refer to systems such as Bitcoin and Ethereum as permissionless rather than public.

11. This chapter builds on previous work I have done on blockchain terminology, where I have focused on the misleading nature of terms such as "immutable" and "trustless." *See* Angela Walch, *The Path of the Blockchain Lexicon (and the Law)*, 36 REV. BANKING & FIN. L. 713 (2017) [hereinafter *The Path of the Blockchain Lexicon*] (analyzing "immutable); Angela Walch, *In Code(rs) We Trust: Software Developers as Fiduciaries in Public Blockchains, in* REGULATING BLOCKCHAIN: TECHNO-SOCIAL AND LEGAL CHALLENGES (Philipp Hacker et al. eds., forthcoming 2019) [hereinafter *In Code(rs) We Trust*] (analyzing "trustless").

12. *See, e.g.,* Vitalik Buterin, *The Meaning of Decentralization*, MEDIUM (Feb. 6, 2017), https://medium.com/@VitalikButerin/the-meaning-of-decentralization-a0c92b76a274 ("'Decentralization' is one of the words that is used in the crypto-economics space the most frequently, and is often even viewed as a blockchain's entire raison d'être . . . "); Balaji S. Srinivasan & Leland Lee, *Quantifying Decentralization*, EARN.COM (July 27, 2017), https://news.earn.com/quantifying-decentralization-e39db233c28e ("The primary advantage of Bitcoin and Ethereum over their legacy alternatives is widely understood to be *decentralization*.") (emphasis added).

13. As the topic of this chapter makes clear, the terminology of the crypto world is problematic and in flux. In the chapter, I use the terms "token" or "coin" or "cryptoasset" interchangeably to represent the made-up unit tracked on permissionless blockchain systems. Ether and bitcoin are examples of these tokens.

14. Here, I use the term "blockchain technologies" to pick up all related technologies that go by names such as distributed ledger technologies, shared ledger technologies,

cryptocurrencies, crypto-systems, etc. I and others have previously discussed the amorphous nature of the term "blockchain" and other terms in the space. *See generally The Path of the Blockchain Lexicon, supra* note 11; Angela Walch, *Blockchain's Treacherous Vocabulary: One More Challenge for Regulators*, 21(2) J. INTERNET L. 1 (2017); Adrienne Jeffries, *"Blockchain" Is Meaningless*, THE VERGE (Mar. 7, 2018), https://www.theverge.com/2018/3/7/17091766/blockchain-bitcoin-ethereum-cryptocurrency-meaning; Nic Carter, *Blockchain Is a Semantic Wasteland*, MEDIUM (Oct. 5, 2018), https://medium.com/s/story/blockchain-is-a-semantic-wasteland-9450b6e5012.

15. *See, e.g.*, Benito Arruñada & Luis Garicano, *Blockchain: The Birth of Decentralized Governance* (Pompeu Fabra Univ., Econ. & Bus. Working Paper Series, Paper 1608, 2018), https://ssrn.com/abstract=3160070 (business and economics perspective); Andrea Gaggioli, *Blockchain Technology: Living in a Decentralized Everything*, 21 CYBERPSYCHOLOGY, BEHAVIOR, & SOCIAL NETWORKING 65 (2018) (psychology perspective); Marcella Atzori, Blockchain Technology and Decentralized Governance: Is the State Still Necessary? (Dec. 1, 2015) (unpublished manuscript), https://ssrn.com/abstract=2709713 (political science perspective).

16. *See, e.g.*, d10e, http://d10e.biz/ (last visited June 7, 2019) (describing itself as "the leading conference on decentralization"); Decentralized, https://www.decentralized.com/ (last visited June 7, 2019) ("120+ international speakers analyzed the steps towards a "Decentralized Future" at Europe's Premier Blockchain Conference"); dappcon, https://www.dappcon.io/ (last visited June 7, 2019) ("DappCon is a nonprofit global developer conference focusing on decentralized applications, tooling, and foundational infrastructure on Ethereum.").

17. *See* Will Warren, *What Is a Decentralized Exchange?*, COIN CENTER (Oct. 10, 2018), https://coincenter.org/entry/what-is-a-decentralized-exchange; Scott Winges, *Decentralized Exchanges 101: All You Need to Know*, COINMARKETCAP (Sept. 6, 2018), https://blog.coinmarketcap.com/2018/09/06/decentralized-exchanges-101-all-you-need-to-know/.

18. *See, e.g.*, Act of Sept. 21, 2006, ch. 26, ARIZ. REV. STAT. ANN. § 44-7003 (2006) (amended by 2017 Ariz. Sess. Laws 2417), https://legiscan.com/AZ/text/HB2417/id/1528949 (defining blockchain technology as "distributed ledger technology that uses a distributed, *decentralized*, shared and replicated ledger, which may be public or private, permissioned or permissionless, or driven by tokenized crypto economics or tokenless.") (emphasis added). The statute does not define "decentralized." Arizona's definition has served as a model for blockchain legislation in other U.S. states.

19. *Id.*

20. *See* Adem Efe Gencer et al., *Decentralization in Bitcoin and Ethereum Networks*, ARXIV 1 (Mar. 29, 2018), https://arxiv.org/pdf/1801.03998.pdf ("Decentralization is a property regarding the fragmentation of control over the protocol.")

21. Atzori, *supra* note 15, at 11 (citing Melanie Swan as "We are not used to governance being a personal responsibility and a peer-to-peer system as opposed to something externally imposed by a distant centralized institution . . . Authority floating freely has already happened in other industries such as information . . . ").

22. *See, e.g.,* Chris Dixon, *Why Decentralization Matters,* MEDIUM (Feb. 18, 2018), https://medium.com/s/story/why-decentralization-matters-5e3f79f7638e (arguing that the decentralization inherent in crypto platforms will enable the building of Web 3.0, breaking up the power held by big tech platforms such as Google, Amazon, and Facebook); Jimmy Song, *Why Bitcoin Is Different,* MEDIUM (Apr. 2, 2018), https://medium.com/@jimmysong/why-bitcoin-is-different-e17b813fd947 (arguing that Bitcoin's decentralization is a distinguishing feature from other coins and strengthens its status as money).

23. *See* Atzori, *supra* note 15, at 7 (describing arguments of blockchain proponents as "[d]ecentralization aims to reduce or prevent such concentration of power and it is a fundamental condition for citizens to achieve political efficacy, equality, transparency, and freedom.").

24. The multidisciplinary nature of blockchain technology leads to cross-discipline communication problems, as each discipline brings its own jargon and knowledge frameworks. Further, the rapid changes in the technology, along with the discarding and adoption of terminology for marketing purposes, have been factors in shaping the lexicon. *See The Path of the Blockchain Lexicon, supra* note 11, at 723–28.

25. Hinman Speech, *supra* note 2.

26. As stated in the introduction, this chapter is not focused on providing a securities law analysis of tokens, but on exploring the meaning of "decentralization" in blockchain systems and potential legal implications. For securities law analyses related to crypto and tokens, see, for example, Jonathan Rohr & Aaron Wright, *Blockchain-Based Token Sales, Initial Coin Offerings, and the Democratization of Public Capital Markets,* (Cardozo Legal Studies Research Paper, Paper 527, 2018), https://ssrn.com/abstract=3048104; SEC Release No. 81207, Report of Investigation Pursuant to Section 21(a) of the Securities Exchange Act of 1934: The DAO (July 25, 2017), https://www.sec.gov/litigation/investreport/34-81207.pdf.

27. SEC v. W.J. Howey Co., 328 U.S. 293 (1946).

28. *Id.* at 298–99.

29. Hinman Speech, *supra* note 2, n.3 (emphasis added).

30. Hinman Speech, *supra* note 2.

31. *Id.*

32. Hinman Speech, *supra* note 2, n.3.

33. *Id.*

34. Hinman Speech, *supra* note 2 (emphasis added).

35. *See, e.g.,* David Benger, *A Top SEC Official Said That Ether Is Not a Security,* COIN CENTER (June 14, 2018), https://coincenter.org/link/a-top-sec-official-said-that-ether-is-not-a-security (calling Hinman's speech "pro-innovation" and stating that "Director Hinman's analysis was based on an appreciation for the nuances of how decentralized technology really works"). Coin Center is "the leading non-profit research and advocacy center focused on the public policy issues facing cryptocurrency and decentralized computing technologies like Bitcoin and Ethereum." *About Us,* COIN CENTER, https://coincenter.org/about (last visited Jan. 30, 2019).

36. Blockchain Association, *Understanding the SEC's Guidance on Digital Tokens: The Hinman Token Standard*, MEDIUM (Jan. 10, 2019), https://medium.com/@BlockchainAssoc/understanding-the-secs-guidance-on-digital-tokens-the-hinman-token-standard-dd51c6105e2a.

37. *Id.*

38. See Section III of this chapter for examples of concentrations of power in Bitcoin and Ethereum that suggest they are quite centralized.

39. And I don't want to be left out.

40. For recent academic work on decentralization that relates to blockchain systems, see Carmela Troncoso et al., *Systematizing Decentralization and Privacy: Lessons from 15 Years of Research and Deployments*, 2017 PROCEEDINGS ON PRIVACY ENHANCING TECHNOLOGIES 404 (2017); CHELSEA BARABAS ET AL., DEFENDING INTERNET FREEDOM THROUGH DECENTRALIZATION: BACK TO THE FUTURE?, The Ctr. for Civic Media & The Digital Currency Initiative, MIT Media Lab (2017); Florian Glaser, *Pervasive Decentralisation of Digital Infrastructures: A Framework for Blockchain Enabled System and Use Case Analysis*, 2017 PROCEEDINGS OF THE 50TH HAWAII INT'L CONFERENCE ON SYS. SCI. 1543 (2017); Nic Carter, A Cross-Sectional Overview of Cryptoasset Governance and Implications for Investors (2017) (unpublished MSc dissertation, University of Edinburgh Business School) (https://coinmetrics.io/papers/dissertation.pdf); MICHEL RAUCHS ET AL., DISTRIBUTED LEDGER TECHNOLOGY SYSTEMS: A CONCEPTUAL FRAMEWORK, Cambridge Centre for Alternative Finance (Aug. 2018); Sunoo Park, *Decentralize All the Things?*, MEDIUM (Aug. 20, 2017), https://medium.com/mit-media-lab-digital-currency-initiative/decentralize-all-the-things-84702944f3fe; For industry work on decentralization in blockchain systems, see Srinivasan & Lee, *supra* note 12; Meltem Demirors, *Decentralization Is a Myth*, TWITTER (Aug. 19, 2018, 9:46am), https://twitter.com/Melt_Dem/status/1031190564639830016 (9-part tweetstorm); Sarah Jamie Lewis, *Tweetstorm on Decentralization*, TWITTER (Aug. 13, 2018, 10:43pm), https://twitter.com/SarahJamieLewis/status/1029212002953060352 (17-part tweetstorm) [hereinafter *Lewis Tweetstorm*]; Sarah Jamie Lewis, *On Emergent Centralization*, FIELD NOTES (July 14, 2018), https://fieldnotes.resistant.tech/defensive-decentralization/; Spencer Bogart, *The Long Game in Crypto: Why Decentralization Matters*, MEDIUM (Apr. 25, 2018), https://medium.com/@Bitcom21/the-long-game-in-crypto-why-decentralization-matters-fd681ff5ed0; Matt Corallo, *Why Bitcoin's Decentralization Matters*, BLUEMATT'S BLOG (Jan. 14, 2016), https://bluematt.bitcoin.ninja/2016/01/14/decentralization/; Buterin, *supra* note 12; Sheng, *supra* note 4; Simon Morris, *If You're Not Breaking Rules You're Doing It Wrong—Bittorrent Lessons for Crypto (2 of 4)*, MEDIUM (Dec. 28, 2018), https://medium.com/@simonhmorris/if-youre-not-breaking-rules-you-re-doing-it-wrong-bittorrent-lessons-for-crypto-2-of-4-72c68227fe69; John Backus, *Resistant Protocols: How Decentralization Evolves*, MEDIUM (July 25, 2018), https://medium.com/@jbackus/resistant-protocols-how-decentralization-evolves-2f9538832ada, Peter Van Valkenburgh, *What Could "Decentralization" Mean in the Context of the Law?*, COIN CENTER (June 15, 2018), https://coincenter.org/entry/what-could-decentralization-mean-in-the-context-of-the-law.

41. *See, e.g.*, Srinivasan & Lee, *supra* note 12; RAUCHS ET AL., *supra* note 40; Glaser, *supra* note 40; *Lewis Tweetstorm, supra* note 40.

42. *See, e.g.*, Srinivasan & Lee, *supra* note 12;

43. *See, e.g., id.*

44. *See, e.g.*, Gencer et al., *supra* note 20 (citing percentages of hashing power held by miners in Bitcoin and Ethereum over a defined period of time and concluding "both platforms rely heavily on very few distinct mining entities to maintain the blockchain").

45. *See, e.g., Lewis Tweetstorm, supra* note 40; Carter, *supra* note 40; RAUCHS ET AL., *supra* note 40.

46. MICHÈLE FINCK, BLOCKCHAIN REGULATION & GOVERNANCE IN EUROPE 36 (2018); BARABAS ET AL., *supra* note 40.

47. Carter, *supra* note 40. *See also* Angela Walch, *Open-Source Operational Risk: Should Public Blockchains Serve as Financial Market Infrastructures?, in* 2 HANDBOOK OF BLOCKCHAIN, DIGITAL FINANCE & INCLUSION, (David LEE Kuo Chuen & Robert Deng eds., 2017) (discussing the role common open source software governance practices play in public blockchain governance).

48. Atzori, *supra* note 15.

49. RAUCHS ET AL., *supra* note 40, at 45. *See also* Troncoso et al., *supra* note 40, at 308–09 (distinguishing between distributed and decentralized).

50. *Id.*

51. *Id.* at 44.

52. *Id.* at 45.

53. Nick Grossman of venture capital firm Union Square Ventures discussed the dilemma of building a decentralized system, with the inevitable need to begin centralized and hope that decentralization later emerges, giving examples of Blockstack and FileCoin. *See* Patrick Stanley, *Nick Grossman on Tensions Inherent to Building on Blockchains*, BLOCKSTACK (Jan. 23, 2019), https://blog.blockstack.org/nick-grossman-on-tensions-inherent-to-building-on-blockchains/ (transcribing talk by Nick Grossman at Blockstack conference).

54. *Id.*

55. *See Lewis Tweetstorm, supra* note 40 ("Hidden centralization is the curse of protocol design of our age. Many people have become very good at obfuscating and rationalizing away power concentration."); Troncoso et al., *supra* note 40, at 307 ("To some extent decentralization was originally a response to the threat of censorship."). *Cf.* FINCK, *supra* note 46, at 41 (discussing the use of software code to escape compliance with legal rules).

56. Barabas et al., *supra* note 40; Carter, *supra* note 40.

57. Morris, *supra* note 40.

58. *Id.*

59. *See, e.g., Lewis Tweetstorm, supra* note 40.

60. *See, e.g.*, Srinivasan & Lee, *supra* note 12; Buterin, *supra* note 12; Carter, *supra* note 40.

61. Sheng, *supra* note 4.

62. *See also* FINCK, *supra* note 36, at 183 ("It is conventionally assumed that blockchains are decentralized both at software and hardware level"); Atzori, *supra* note 15, at 31 ("the idea of a blockchain-based authority "floating freely" . . . turns out to be deceptive, since authority is in fact proven to morph into more subtle or hidden centralized forms."); Philipp Hacker, *Corporate Governance for Complex Cryptocurrencies? A Framework for Stability and Decision Making in Blockchain-Based Organizations*, *in* REGULATING BLOCKCHAIN: TECHNO-SOCIAL AND LEGAL CHALLENGES (Philipp Hacker et al., eds., forthcoming 2019) at 16 ("[public blockchain governance] allows for the coordinated actions of a few major stakeholders or developers to take control of the rules for constructing the blockchain"); Gili Vidan & Vili Lehdonvirta, *Mine the Gap: Bitcoin and the Maintenance of Trustlessness*, 21 NEW MEDIA & SOC'Y 42, 42 (2019) ("In contrast to the discourse [around Bitcoin], we find that power is concentrated to critical sites and individuals who sometimes manage the system through ad-hoc negotiations, and who users must therefore implicitly trust.").

63. Software developers and miners/validators are not the only potential sites of centralized power relevant to permissionless blockchains. As noted earlier in Section II of this chapter, other sites of centralization could include parties acting outside the systems, such as exchanges or other infrastructure providers. However, in this chapter, I focus on actors *within* permissionless blockchain systems.

64. The examples of power concentrations I discuss in Section III in no way represent an exhaustive list of signs of centralization in Bitcoin or Ethereum, but merely a few compelling examples.

65. The actions Ethereum core developers took in January 2019 in coordinating and rapidly calling off the Constantinople software upgrade to the network provide another example of centralized power, but publication deadlines prevent full discussion in this chapter. *See* Nikhilesh De & Christine Kim, *Ethereum Clients Release New Software in Wake of Hard Fork Delay*, COINDESK (Jan. 15, 2019), https://www.coindesk.com/ethereum-new-software-hard-fork-delay-constantinople.

66. *CVE-2018-17144 Full Disclosure*, BITCOINCORE (Sept. 20, 2018), https://bitcoincore.org/en/2018/09/20/notice/ (providing a description of the bug disclosure and resolution process). For news coverage of the event, see Jordan Pearson, *A Major Bug in Bitcoin Software Could Have Crashed the Currency*, MOTHERBOARD (Sept. 19, 2018), https://motherboard.vice.com/en_us/article/qvakp3/a-major-bug-in-bitcoin-software-could-have-crashed-the-currency (reporting on the potential effects of the bug as originally publicly disclosed by Bitcoin developers, prior to their disclosure on September 20, 2018 that it was actually also an inflation bug); Alyssa Hertig, *The Latest Bitcoin Bug Was So Bad, Developers Kept Its Full Details a Secret*, COINDESK (Sept. 21, 2018), https://www.coindesk.com/the-latest-bitcoin-bug-was-so-bad-developers-kept-its-full-details-a-secret; Aaron van Wirdum, *The Good, the Bad and the Ugly Details of One of Bitcoin's Nastiest Bugs Yet*, BITCOIN MAG. (Sept. 21, 2018), https://bitcoinmagazine.com/articles/good-bad-and-ugly-details-one-bitcoins-nastiest-bugs-yet/.

67. *CVE-2018-17144 Full Disclosure*, *supra* note 66. Note that I am assuming this description to be true, but I have no way of knowing if it is.

68. *Id.* (emphasis added).

69. *Id.*

70. *Id.*

71. COINMARKETCAP, historical data for Sept. 17, 2018, https://coinmarketcap.com/currencies/bitcoin/historical-data/?start=20180115&end=20190115 (last visited Jan. 15, 2019).

72. *CVE-2018-17144 Full Disclosure, supra* note 66.

73. As one example, this bug-fixing incident supports my argument that core developers of public blockchain systems function as fiduciaries of those who rely on these systems. *See In Code(rs) We Trust, supra* note 11.

74. Hinman Speech, *supra* note 2, n.3.

75. *Id.*

76. *See In Code(rs) We Trust, supra* note 11, at 6–7.

77. For discussions of the actions by Bitcoin developers and miners related to the March 2013 hard fork, see *In Code(rs) We Trust, supra* note 11, at 7; Angela Walch, *The Bitcoin Blockchain as Financial Market Infrastructure: A Consideration of Operational Risk*, 18 N.Y.U. J. LEGIS. & PUB. POL'Y 837, 866, 873 (2015); Walch, *supra* note 47, at 260–61; Hacker, *supra* note 62, at 12.

78. Hinman Speech, *supra* note 2, n.3 (emphasis added).

79. *See* Rachel Rose O'Leary, *Ethereum Developers Are Quietly Planning an Accelerated Tech Roadmap*, COINDESK (Nov. 23, 2018), https://www.coindesk.com/ethereum-developers-are-quietly-planning-an-accelerated-tech-roadmap; Adriana Hamacher, *The Whistle-Blowing Wizard*, DECRYPT (Dec. 7, 2018), https://decryptmedia.com/2018/12/07/greg-colvin-ethereum-developer-interview/; *Ethereum [ETH]—Tensions Rise as Ethereum Devs Try to Streamline Coordination*, CRYPTO ECONOMY (Nov. 25, 2018), https://www.crypto-economy.net/en/ethereum-eth-tensions-rise-as-ethereum-devs-try-to-streamline-coordination/

80. In October and November 2018, ETH's market cap fluctuated between $11 and $20 billion. COINMARKETCAP, historical data for October–November, 2018, https://coinmarketcap.com/currencies/ethereum/historical-data/?start=20181015&end=20190115 (last visited Jan. 15, 2019).

81. Lane Rettig, *How Open Is Too Open?*, MEDIUM (Dec. 30, 2018), https://medium.com/@lrettig/how-open-is-too-open-bfc412cf0d24; Dani Putney, *An Exercise in Ethereum Governance; Transparency, Chatham House Rule, And Ethereum 1.x*, ETHNEWS (Nov. 30, 2018), https://www.ethnews.com/an-exercise-in-ethereum-governance-transparency-chatham-house-rule-and-ethereum-1x.

82. *Eth 1.x Proposal Sync 1 Notes*, GITHUB (Nov. 30, 2018), https://github.com/ethereum/pm/blob/master/All%20Core%20Devs%20Meetings/Eth1x%20Sync%201.md (providing a summary of the Nov. 30, 2018 meeting of the core developers of Ethereum held under Chatham House Rules).

83. *See* Walch, *supra* note 47, at 251–67 (describing grass-roots open source software and the ways its governance practices create operational risks for public blockchains).

84. For example, the Ethereum Classic token (ETC) trades at a different valuation to Ether (ETH), and has a different group of miners and software developers. The situation is the same for forks of Bitcoin (BTC), including Bitcoin Cash (BCH), Bitcoin SV, and others.

85. *See* Angela Walch, *Call Blockchain Developers What They Are: Fiduciaries*, AMER. BANKER (Aug. 9, 2016), https://www.americanbanker.com/opinion/call-blockchain-developers-what-they-are-fiduciaries [hereinafter *Call Devs Fiduciaries*]; *In Code(rs) We Trust, supra* note 11.

86. Joon Ian Wong & Ian Kar, *Everything You Need to Know About the Ethereum "Hard Fork,"* QUARTZ (July 18, 2016), https://qz.com/730004/everything-you-need-to-know-about-the-ethereum-hard-fork/.

87. Vitalik Buterin, *Notes on Blockchain Governance*, VITALIK BUTERIN'S WEBSITE (Dec. 17, 2017), https://vitalik.ca/general/2017/12/17/voting.html.

88. A counterargument to my claim that Ethereum developers and miners exercised power is that parties who did not wish to proceed were able to continue with the Ethereum Classic blockchain. However, Ethereum Classic had much less mining power devoted to it so was more vulnerable to attack, as well as having to assemble a new team of software developers to keep it going.

89. *See* Ray Jones, REDDIT (June 29, 2016), https://www.reddit.com/r/ethereum/comments/4qiqq8/ethereum_protocol_developer_holds_114877_worth_of/d4th8ce/ ("The simplest solution would be for all people in positions of influence who are in favor of a hard fork to openly declare their DAO token holdings"); Aakil Fernandes, REDDIT (June 29, 2016), https://www.reddit.com/r/ethereum/comments/4qiqq8/ethereum_protocol_developer_holds_114877_worth_of/d4tm9o5/ ("We should care when people have conflicts of interest. That applies to lawyers, judges, bankers, politicians and yes it applies to developers. Humans are humans."); Justin Camarena, TWITTER (June 17, 2016), https://twitter.com/juscamarena/status/744008754459475968 ("I'd agree with a rollback for protocol level hacks . . But this isn't that at all. Core devs own DAO").

90. *See* Gencer et al., *supra* note 20. *See also* Lin William Cong et al., Decentralized Mining in Centralized Pools (Apr. 10, 2018) (unpublished manuscript) (*available at* https://www.gsb.stanford.edu/sites/gsb/files/fin_11_19_cong.pdf, Nov. 2018 draft).

91. *See* Russell Brandom, *Why the Ethereum Classic Hack Is a Bad Omen for the Blockchain*, THE VERGE (Jan. 9, 2019), https://www.theverge.com/2019/1/9/18174407/ethereum-classic-hack-51-percent-attack-double-spend-crypto.

92. Hinman Speech, *supra* note 2, n.3.

93. *See supra* Section II.A.

94. *See* Srinivasan & Lee, *supra* note 12.

95. *See* David H. Freedman, *Why Scientific Studies Are So Often Wrong: The Streetlight Effect*, DISCOVER (Dec. 10, 2010), http://discovermagazine.com/2010/jul-aug/29-why-scientific-studies-often-wrong-streetlight-effect.

96. Sridhard Ramamoorti et al., *The Gresham's Law of Measurement and Audit Quality Indicators: Implications for Policy Making and Standard Setting*, 29 RESEARCH IN ACCOUNTING REG. 79, (2017).

97. *Id.*

98. For a useful description of the complexities of blockchain protocol governance, see FINCK, *supra* note 46, at 182–209.

99. *Lewis Tweetstorm, supra* note 40. *See also* Troncoso et al., *supra* note 40, at 322 ("[T]here are no coherent quantitative metrics to characterize decentralization.").

100. *Cf. The Path of the Blockchain Lexicon, supra* note 11 (discussing how regulators must learn the facts about a new technology before regulating and the difficulties blockchain's misleading vocabulary raises in learning the facts).

101. *See supra* Section II.E.

102. *See* Robert Rosenblum et al., *Why the SEC Thinks Most Tokens Are Securities and When the SEC Thinks a Token Might Stop Being a Security*, WILSON SONSINI GOODRICH & ROSATI PRACTITIONER INSIGHT (Aug. 1, 2018), https://www.wsgr.com/WSGR/Display.aspx?SectionName=publications/PDFSearch/Practitioner-Insight-tokens.htm (discussing the shift from a security to a non-security and back again). Hinman also suggested in his "When Howey Met Gary Plastics" speech that an instrument's status as a security is flexible, just like the *Howey* test. *See* Hinman Speech, *supra* note 2.

103. *See* Vidan & Lehdonvirta, *supra* note 62, at 55 ("[I]n the blockchain mode of trustlessness, decentralization through a collapse of users and their [computers] further removes human agency from the visible operations of the system. There is no banker, bureaucrat, or even software developer at which the finger could easily be pointed.").

104. *See* Thomas K. Cheng, *Form and Substance of the Doctrine of Piercing the Corporate Veil*, 80 MISS. L.J. 497 (2010) (providing an overview of the doctrine of corporate veil piercing). One could argue that FinCEN's treatment of miners, software developers, and users of blockchain tokens represents another example of the Veil of Decentralization protecting actors within a blockchain. *Cf.* Rebecca Bredt, Heigh-Ho, Heigh-Ho, Money Transmitters, or No? Why Bitcoin Miners Should Be Considered Money Transmitters Under the Bank Secrecy Act, (Dec. 10, 2018) (unpublished manuscript) (on file with author) (arguing that Bitcoin miners should be treated as money transmitters due to the transaction fees they receive for validation efforts).

105. *See Call Devs Fiduciaries, supra* note 85; *In Code(rs) We Trust, supra* note 11. *But see* Rodrigo Seira, *Blockchain Protocol Developers Are Not Fiduciaries: An Analysis of the Cryptoeconomics of Open Source Networks and the Role of Protocol Developers in Public Blockchain Network Governance*, GOOD AUDIENCE (Nov. 26, 2018), https://blog.goodaudience.com/blockchain-protocol-developers-are-not-fiduciaries-49bf436a20ca (arguing that blockchain protocol developers should not be treated as fiduciaries); Carla Reyes, (Un)Corporate Crypto-Goverance, Fordham L. Rev. (forthcoming 2019); Raina Haque et al., Blockchain Development & Fiduciary Duty, Stanford J. of Blockchain L. & Pol'y (forthcoiming 2019).

106. Of course, the lack of legal personhood to represent a blockchain protocol system as a whole means that a blockchain can't sue or enter into contracts as a legal person either.

107. Potentially the foundations that fund software development in some public blockchains (such as Ethereum's Ethereum Foundation) could serve as a site of legal accountability.

108. Usha R. Rodrigues, *Law and the Blockchain*, 104 IOWA L. REV. 679, 692 (2019) ("Traditionally, the corporation's chief virtue was seen to lie in the unique protection against liability that it provides for shareholders.").

109. *Id.* at 688 (citing Henry Hansmann & Renier Kraakman, *The Essential Role of Organizational Law*, 110 YALE L.J. 387 (2000)).

110. Dirk A. Zetzsche et al., *The Distributed Liability of Distributed Ledgers: Legal Risks of Blockchain*, 2018 U. ILL. L. REV. 1361 (2018). In the reference, "DLT" is short for "distributed ledger technology," of which blockchain technology is one type.

111. *Cf.* Andrew Verstein, *Enterprise Without Entities*, 116 MICH. L. REV. 247 (2017) (exploring how reciprocal insurance exchanges operate without the use of legal entities, obtaining similar benefits through the use of contracts and insurance law).

112. Karen Yeung, *Regulation by Blockchain: The Emerging Battle for Supremacy Between the Code of Law and Code as Law*, MODERN L. REV (forthcoming 2019), at 7, *available at* https://ssrn.com/abstract=3206546.

113. *Id.* at 8.

114. Hacker, *supra* note 62.

115. Carla L. Reyes, *If Rockefeller Were a Coder*, 87 GEO. WASH. L. REV. [ ] at 23–24 (forthcoming 2019), *available at* https://ssrn.com/abstract=3082915.

116. *Id.* at 24–25.

117. *Id.* It is unclear where the software developers who create and maintain the protocol fit into the business trust conception, though presumably they would be considered trustees of the blockchain along with the miners.

118. *Id.*

119. *See* VT. STAT. ANN. tit. 11, § 4172 (2018).

120. *See In re Coinflip, Inc.*, CFTC No. 15-29 (Sept. 17, 2015) (finding that Bitcoin was a commodity).

121. Hacker, *supra* note 62, at 16.

122. *Id.*

123. *Id* at 17.

124. *See* Walch, *supra* note 47, at 259–66 (discussing the role changes in software pose to blockchain systems and systems built atop them).

125. Vidan & Lehdonvirta, *supra* note 62, at 47 (citing Susan Leigh Star, *The Ethnography of Infrastructure*, 43 AM. BEHAVIORAL SCIENTIST 377 (1999)).

126. Sheng, *supra* note 4.
Bank Digital Currency: Motivations and Implications," Bank of Canada, Staff Discussion Paper 2017-16 at 16–17, https://www.bankofcanada.ca/wp-content/uploads/2017/11/sdp2017-16.pdf, accessed Jan. 9, 2018.

Chapter 4

1. "Cryptoassets," "tokens," and "cryptocurrencies" are used interchangeably in this chapter.

2. This term refers to tokens that are used to unlock a specific decentralized application—think of a car wash token or an API key.

3. See generally Chris Burniske & Adam White, *Bitcoin: Ringing the Bell for a New Asset Class*, ARK INVEST & COINBASE (2017), https://research.ark-invest.com/hubfs/1_Download_Files_ARK-Invest/White_Papers/Bitcoin-Ringing-The-Bell-For-A-New-Asset-Class.pdf.

4. Sinclair Davidson, Primavera De Filippi & Jason Potts, 14 *Blockchains and the Economic Institutions of Capitalism*, J. INST. ECON. 1, 11 (2018).

5. Emiliano Pagnotta & Andrea Buraschi, An Equilibrium Valuation of Bitcoin and Decentralized Network Assets 16 (Mar. 21, 2018) (unpublished manuscript) (on file with Imperial College London).

6. John Pfeffer, An (Institutional) Investor's Take on Cryptoassets (Dec. 24, 2017) (unpublished manuscript) (on file with author), https://s3.eu-west-2.amazonaws.com/john-pfeffer/An+Investor%27s+Take+on+Cryptoassets+v6.pdf.

7. Nick Tomaino, *On Token Value*, THE CONTROL (Aug. 6, 2017), https://thecontrol.co/on-token-value-e61b10b6175e.

8. Brett Winton, *How to Value a Crypto-Asset—A Model*, MEDIUM (Sept. 15, 2017), https://medium.com/@wintonARK/how-to-value-a-crypto-asset-a-model-e0548e9b6e4e.

9. Chris Burniske, *Cryptoasset Valuations*, MEDIUM (Sept. 24, 2017), https://medium.com/@cburniske/cryptoasset-valuations-ac83479ffca7.

10. Ashley Lannquist, *Today's Crypto Asset Valuation Frameworks*, BLOCKCHAIN AT BERKELEY (Mar. 6, 2018), https://blockchainatberkeley.blog/todays-crypto-asset-valuation-frameworks-573a38eda27e.

11. Alyssa Hertig, *Blockchain's Once-Feared 51% Attack Is Now Becoming Regular*, COINDESK (June 9, 2018, 10:30 AM), https://www.coindesk.com/blockchains-feared-51-attack-now-becoming-regular.

12. BITCOIN WIKI, TRANSACTION ACCELERATOR, https://en.bitcoin.it/wiki/Transaction_accelerator (last modified Aug. 26, 2018, 12:12 PM)

13. https://docs.ethhub.io/questions-about-ethereum/is-ether-needed-for-transaction-fees/. (last visited Feb. 5, 2019).

14. It is often suggested that application-specific tokens simply rely on a more popular network such as Ethereum or Bitcoin for value transfer, rather than introducing an additional token that users must acquire to use the network.

15. Andrea Tan, Nejamin Robertson & Matthew Leising, *Why Crypto Traders Are So Worried About Tether*, BLOOMBERG (Oct 14, 2018, 4:40 AM), https://www.bloomberg.com/news/articles/2018-10-14/why-crypto-traders-are-so-worried-about-tether-quicktake-q-a.

16. Nic Carter, A Cross-Sectional Overview of Cryptoasset Governance and Implications for Investors 44 (2017) (unpublished dissertation, University of Edinburgh Business School) (on file with author), https://coinmetrics.io/papers/dissertation.pdf.

17. *Id.* at 45-52.
18. See generally Davidson, de Fillipi & Potts, *supra* note 4.
19. Philipp Paech, *The Governance of Blockchain Financial Networks*, MODERN L. REV. (2017)
20. See Peter Zeitz, *Blockchain Governance*, 0x BLOG (Sept. 27, 2018), https://blog.0xproject.com/blockchain-governance-7ff89e6ec383.
21. Fred Ehrsam, *Blockchain Governance: Programming Our Future* MEDIUM (Nov. 27, 2017), https://medium.com/@FEhrsam/blockchain-governance-programming-our-future-c3bfe30f2d74.
22. *See generally* Haim Levy, *Economic Evaluation of Voting Power of Common Stock*, 38 J. FIN. 79 (1983).
23. *See generally* Tatiana Nenova, *The Value of Corporate Votes and Control Benefits: A Cross-Country Analysis*, 68 J. FIN. ECON. 325 (2003).
24. Vlad Zamfir, *Against On-Chain Governance, Refuting (and Rebuking) Fred Ehrsam's Governance Blog*, MEDIUM (Dec. 1, 2017), https://medium.com/@Vlad_Zamfir/against-on-chain-governance-a4ceacd040ca.
25. *See* Michael J. Casey, *It's Too Soon for On-Chain Governance*, COINDESK (July 2, 2018 12:00 PM), https://www.coindesk.com/soon-chain-governance.
26. *See* Vitalik Buterin, *Notes on Blockchain Governance*, VITALIK BUTERIN'S WEBSITE (Dec. 17 2017), https://vitalik.ca/general/2017/12/17/voting.html.
27. *See generally* David Yermack, *Is Bitcoin a Real Currency* (Nat'l Bureau of Econ., Working Paper No. 19747, 2013), https://www.nber.org/papers/w19747.pdf.
28. Aswath Damodaran, *The Bitcoin Boom: Asset, Currency, Commodity or Collectible?*, MUSING ON MARKETS (Oct. 24, 2017, 4:26 PM), http://aswathdamodaran.blogspot.com/2017/10/the-bitcoin-boom-asset-currency.html.
29. Hal Finney, *Re: Bitcoin v0.1 Released*, MAIL-ARCHIVE (Jan. 11, 2009), https://www.mail-archive.com/cryptography@metzdowd.com/msg10152.html.
30. *See generally* GIL LURIA & AARON TURNER, BITCOIN INVESTMENT TRUST (GBTC) (July 9, 2015), https://www.scribd.com/doc/271095696/GBTC-Initiation-2015-07-09.
31. *See generally* SPENCER BOGART & KERRY RICE, THE BLOCKCHAIN REPORT: WELCOME TO THE INTERNET OF VALUE (2015), https://www.weusecoins.com/assets/pdf/library/The%20Blockchain%20Report%20-%20Needham%20(Huge%20report).pdf.
32. Chris Burniske, *Cryptoasset Valuations*, MEDIUM (Sept. 24, 2017), https://medium.com/@cburniske/cryptoasset-valuations-ac83479ffca7.
33. Filecoin is the cryptoasset designed to facilitate transaction on the forthcoming Filecoin network, an incentivized file storage and transfer network
34. *See generally* Pfeffer, *supra* note 6.
35. *See* Buterin, *supra* note 26.
36. Warren Weber, *The Quantity Theory of Money for Tokens*, COINFUND (Feb. 26.2018), https://blog.coinfund.io/the-quantity-theory-of-money-for-tokens-dbfbc5472423.

37. Willy Woo, *Introducing NVT Ratio (Bitcoin's PE Ratio), Use It to Detect Bubbles*, WOOBULL (Oct. 5, 2017), https://woobull.com/introducing-nvt-ratio-bitcoins-pe-ratio-use-it-to-detect-bubbles/.

38. Laura Shin, *Bubble? So What? Token Summit Marks Cryptocurrency's Revitalization*, FORBES (May 26, 2017 2:52 PM), https://www.forbes.com/sites/laurashin/2017/05/26/bubble-so-what-token-summit-marks-cryptocurrencys-revitalization/#1cbb19fd17b5.

39. *See generally* Xing-Zhou Zhang, *Tencent and Facebook Data Validate Metcalfe's Law*, 30 J. COMP. SCI & TECH. 246 (2015), https://link.springer.com/article/10.1007/s11390-015-1518-1.

40. *See generally* Spencer Wheatley, Didier Sornette, Tobias Huber, Max Reppen, & Robert N. Gantner, *Are Bitcoin Bubbles Predictable?* Combining a Generalized Metcalfe's Law and the LPPLS Model *1* (Swiss Fin. Inst. Working Paper No.18-22, 2018), https://arxiv.org/abs/1803.05663.

41. ClearBlocks, *Valuing Bitcoin and Ethereum with Metcalfe's Law*, MEDIUM (Feb. 13, 2018), https://medium.com/@clearblocks/valuing-bitcoin-and-ethereum-with-metcalfes-law-aaa743f469f6.

42. *See generally* Ben Van Viet, *An Alternative Model of Metcalfe's Law for Valuing Bitcoin*, ECON. LETTERS (2018), https://www.sciencedirect.com/science/article/pii/S0165176518300557.

43. Erick Schonfeld, *How Much Are Your Eyeballs Worth? Placing a Value on a Website's Customers May Be the Best Way to Judge a Net Stock. It's Not Perfect, but on the Net, What Is?*, FORTUNE MAG. (Feb.21, 2000), http://archive.fortune.com/magazines/fortune/fortune_archive/2000/02/21/273860/index.htm.

44. Sybils are participants on a network that can costlessly interfere with it; Proof of Work adds Sybil-resistance to cryptocurrencies because it makes ledger entries costly (and hence expensive to game)

45. Hugh Son, Hannah Levitt & Brian Louis, *Jamie Dimon Slams Bitcoin as a "Fraud,"* BLOOMBERG (Sept. 12, 2017, 6:59 PM), https://www.bloomberg.com/news/articles/2017-09-12/jpmorgan-s-ceo-says-he-d-fire-traders-who-bet-on-fraud-bitcoin.

46. Tae Kim, *Warren Buffett Says Bitcoin Is "Probably Rat Poison Squared,"* CNBC (May 5, 2018, 2:55 PM), https://www.cnbc.com/2018/05/05/warren-buffett-says-bitcoin-is-probably-rat-poison-squared.html.

47. *See* generally Yermack, *supra* note 27.

48. *See generally* Adam Hayes, *Bitcoin Price and Its Marginal Cost of Production: Support for a Fundamental Value*, 26 APPLIED ECON. LETTERS (2019).

49. *See generally* David Garcia, Claudio J. Tessone, Pavlin Mavrodiev & Nicolas Perony, *The Digital Traces of Bubbles: Feedback Cycles Between Socio-Economic Signals in the Bitcoin Economy*, J. ROYAL SOC'Y INTERFACE (2014), https://royalsocietypublishing.org/doi/full/10.1098/rsif.2014.0623.

50. *See generally* Lin William Cong, Ye Li & Neng Wang, *Tokenomics: Dynamic Adoption and Valuation* (Columbia Business School, Working Paper No. 18-46, 2018).

51. Steve Barbour (@SGBarbour), TWITTER (Jan. 7, 2019, 10:55 AM), https://twitter.com/SGBarbour/status/1082350109340270592.

52. Brian Venturo, *ETH Issuance—Part 2—Deflation*, MEDIUM (Aug. 27, 2018), https://medium.com/@brianventuro/eth-issuance-part-2-deflation-13775c651a42.

53. http://newlibertystandard.wikifoundry.com/page/2009+Exchange+Rate & https://truthmegasite.com/new-liberty-standard-publishes-first-exchange-rate-on-bitcoin-of-1309-03-btc-to-one-u-s-dollar-0-0008btc/ (last visited Feb. 5, 2019).

54. Paul Sztorc, *Nothing Is Cheaper than Proof of Work*, TRUTHCOIN (Feb. 28, 2019), http://www.truthcoin.info/blog/pow-cheapest.

55. Emiliano Pagnotta & Andrea Buraschi , *An Equilibrium Valuation of Bitcoin and Decentralized Network Assets*, unpublished, available at SSRN (https://papers.ssrn.com/sol3/papers.cfm?abstract_id=3142022) (2018).

56. *Provable Solvency Report #58*, COINFLOOR (Jan. 28, 2019), https://blog.coinfloor.co.uk/post/182376261211/provable-solvency-report-58-january-2019.

57. *See generally* Eric Budish, *The Economic Limits of Bitcoin and the Blockchain* (NAT'L BUREAU OF ECON., Working Paper No. 24717, 2018), https://faculty.chicagobooth.edu/eric.budish/research/Economic-Limits-Bitcoin-Blockchain.pdf.

58. *See generally Raphael Auer, Beyond the Doomsday Economics of "Proof-Of-Work" in Cryptocurrencies* (Bank of Int'l Settlements, Working Paper No. 765, 2019), https://www.bis.org/publ/work765.pdf.

59. Jesse Walden & Katie Haun, *Maker*, A16ZCRYPTO (Sept. 24, 2016), https://a16zcrypto.com/2018/09/maker/.

60. Chris Burniske & Joel Monegro, *Maker Investment Thesis*, PLACEHOLDER (Jan. 23, 2019), https://www.placeholder.vc/blog/2019/1/23/maker-investment-thesis.

61. Vision Hill Advisors, *A MakerDAO Case Study*, MEDIUM (Feb 5, 2019), https://medium.com/@visionhill_/a-makerdao-case-study-47a31d858be5.

62. MakerDAO, *Foundation Proposal v2*, MEDIUM (Aug. 20,2018), https://medium.com/makerdao/foundation-proposal-v2-f10d8ee5fe8c.

63. MakerDAO, *Dai in Numbers*, MEDIUM (Feb. 7, 2019), https://medium.com/makerdao/dai-in-numbers-2710d8a5633a.

64. Binance, *What Is BNB?*, https://www.binance.com/en/blog/292158287506071552/6th+Binance+Coin+Burn (last visited Feb. 19, 2019).

65. *Id.*

66. Andrew Kang, *An In-Depth Valuation & Analysis of Binance Coin (BNB)—Fairly Valued and a Potential Store of Value?*, MEDIUM (Aug. 5, 2018), https://medium.com/@Rewkang/an-in-depth-valuation-analysis-of-binance-coin-bnb-fairly-valued-and-a-potential-store-of-61e828b93f53.

67. Leonard Neo, *Token Analysis (BNB)—Binance Growth and Adoption Indicates an Intrinsic Valuation of $22.80*, MEDIUM (Sept. 11, 2018), https://medium.com/astronaut-capital/token-analysis-bnb-binance-growth-and-adoption-indicates-an-intrinsic-valuation-of-22-80-95163008eca0.

68. Will Warren & Amir Bandeali, *0x 0x: An Open Protocol for Decentralized Exchange on the Ethereum Blockchain*, 0XPROJECT.COM (2017), https://0x.org/pdfs/0x_white_paper.pdf.

69. Jason Choi (@mrjasonchoi), TWITTER (Jan. 3, 2019 5:21 PM) https://twitter.com/mrjasonchoi/status/1080997511530070016.

70. *Are 0x Relayers Using ZRX? Yes and No*, THE BLOCK (2018) https://www.theblockcrypto.com/tiny/are-0x-relayers-using-zrx-yes-and-no/.

71. Will Warren, *Governance in 0x Protocol*, MEDIUM (Mar. 27, 2018), https://blog.0xproject.com/governance-in-0x-protocol-86779ae5809e.

72. Phil J. Bonello, *A Framework for Valuing Governance Tokens: 0x*, HACKER NOON (Apr. 19, 2018), https://hackernoon.com/a-framework-for-valuing-governance-tokens-0x-49d2cf2ef5bc.

Chapter 5

1. "Proceed with extreme caution in accepting brilliant technical innovations that are not yet tested by a sufficiently long practical experience . . . " Admiral Domenico Cavagnari (1876–1966).

2. "It seems to me that there are three ways in which profit may be made from money, without laying it out for its natural purpose; one is the art of the moneychanger, banking or exchange, another is usury, a third alteration of the coinage. The first way is contemptible, the second bad and the third worse." Nicholas Oresme (1320–1382).

3. In the case when a borrower defaults, money is not destroyed as expected but remains in the system forever, which is tantamount to forgery.

4. An astute (if somewhat tangential) observation by Lord Palmerston (1784–1865) springs to mind: "The Schleswig-Holstein question is so complicated, only three men in Europe have ever understood it. One was Prince Albert, who is dead. The second was a German professor who became mad. I am the third and I have forgotten all about it."

5. "Quite generally, the familiar, just because it is familiar, is not cognitively understood."

6. For example, web-only retailers often see net margins from as low as 0.5% to 3.5%, see, e.g., [43], [44].

7. Devaynes v Noble (1816) 35 ER 781.

8. See https://www.fdic.gov/bank/analytical/qbp/2017mar/qbpdep.html#1.

9. "Was this the face that launched a thousand ships/And burnt the topless towers of Ilium?" Christopher Marlowe, Doctor Faustus, Act V, Scene I.

10. "We wanted the best, but it turned out as always." Viktor Chernomyrdin (1938–2010).

11. Ironically, this view did not preclude Goldman from joining a number of other traditional financial players who have set up their own crypto trading desks.

12. Attempts to estimate the consensus price via the so-called Schelling point scheme are impractical at best, since there are no mechanisms to align this price with its external value.

13. This is partly by necessity, and partly by design.

14. Thus, to get $1 worth of a stable coin, a user needs to have $2 or even $3 worth of ETH. This situation should be compared with the conventional margin trading, where a user can have an exposure of $10 worth of equities by posting $1 collateral (say).

15. Dai is not unique in this regard. A typical smart contract requires so much collateral, that its underlying economic rationale is difficult to fathom.

16. See, e.g., Preston Byrne's blog: https://prestonbyrne.com/2017/10/13/basecoin-bitshares-2-electric-boogaloo/.

17. At the same time, cash is facing competition from other payment instruments. For instance, between 2012 and 2015, the percentage of consumer transactions made with cash decreased by eight percentage points, from 40 to 32%. This can be explained by increasing consumer comfort with payment cards and the growth of online commerce.

18. It is worth noting that when Bitcoin and Ethereum had just been introduced, criminal elements were extremely excited about illicit usage of cryptocurrencies. However, with time, they realized that the immutable record of transactions has opened new avenues for law enforcement agencies to monitor and prosecute their activities. Hence, at present, they are tending back to cash transactions.

Chapter 6

1. *See Cryptocurrency ICO Stats 2018*, COINSCHEDULE, https://www.coinschedule.com/stats.html?year=2018 (last visited Feb. 5, 2019); *see also Initial Coin Offerings Have Become Big Business*, ECONOMIST (Sept. 1, 2018), https://www.economist.com/technology-quarterly/2018/09/01/initial-coin-offerings-have-become-big-business; *Blockchain Start-Up Raises More than $4bn*, FIN. TIMES (June 2, 2018), https://www.ft.com/content/69abdb66-666c-11e8-b6eb-4acfcfb08c11 (pointing out that *block.one*, a Cayman Islands-based company, raised more than 4 billion through a single ICO).

2. Betsy Verecky, *Is a Cryptocurrency a Security? Depends*, MIT SLOAN SCH. OF MGMT. (May 4, 2018), http://mitsloan.mit.edu/newsroom/articles/is-a-cryptocurrency-a-security-depends.

3. The hype cycle is a branded graphical presentation developed and used by the American research, advisory, and information technology firm Gartner to represent the maturity, adoption, and social application of specific technologies. The hype cycle provides a graphical and conceptual presentation of the maturity of emerging technologies through five phases.

4. *See Mike Walker, Hype Cycle for Emerging Technologies, 2018*, GARTNER (Aug. 6, 2018), https://www.gartner.com/doc/3885468/hype-cycle-emerging-technologies-

5. Cryptoassets, tokens, or digital assets are usually used as synonyms. For example, the Mexican Fintech law refers to these instruments as "virtual assets." In Singapore, the regulator uses the term "digital token." In Switzerland and the United States, the securities regulator uses the expression "tokens." In the United Kingdom, the regulator uses "crypto-assets," which are then classified in different types of "tokens."

6. Media Release, Int'l Org. of Sec. Comm'ns, IOSCO Board Communication on Concerns Related to Initial Coin Offerings (Jan. 18, 2018), https://www.iosco.org/news/pdf/IOSCONEWS485.pdf.

7. Alfonso Delgado et al., *Towards a Sustainable ICO Process: Community Guidelines on Regulation and Best Practices*, EXTROPY.IO (2016), http://extropy.io/publications/bluepaperioc.pdf.

8. Some authors and jurisdictions distinguish between "security tokens" and "utility tokens." *See, e.g., Guidance on Cryptoassets* (U.K. Fin. Conduct Auth., Consultation Paper No. CP19/3), https://www.fca.org.uk/publication/consultation/cp19-03.pdf; *see also* Sabrina T. Howell, Marina Niessner & David Yermack, *Initial Coin Offerings: Financing Growth with Cryptocurrency Token Sales* (Euro. Corp. Governance Inst. Finance Working Paper No. 564/2018), https://ecgi.global/sites/default/files/working_papers/documents/finalhowellniessneryermack.pdf.   In our opinion, this classification adopted by many authors and countries confuses the function of the token with its legal nature. Therefore, it should be abandoned. Otherwise, it can be misleading, since "utility tokens" from a functional perspective can actually be considered "security tokens" from a legal perspective and vice versa.

9. *See* Press Release, FINMA, FINMA Publishes ICO Guidelines (Feb. 16, 2018), https://www.finma.ch/en/news/2018/02/20180216-mm-ico-wegleitung.

10. *Id.*

11. *Id.*

12. *Id.*

13. *See id.*

14. For example, in the United States, securities are defined according to the "Howey test," which basically requires the existence of four elements: (1) an investment of money, (2) the expectation of profits from that investment, (3) the existence of a common enterprise, and (4) the generation of profits derived from the efforts of a promoter or third party. For a detailed analysis of the "Howey Test," and more generally the concept of security in the United States, see JOHN COFFEE, JR. & HILLARY A. SALE, SECURITIES REGULATION: CASES AND MATERIALS, 246–327 (12th ed. 2012). This definition of security follows a functional approach, and it is focused on the economic substance of the investment rather than its legal form. In countries in which the concept of security is defined following this functional approach, it will be easier that an investment is considered a "security." However, this is not always the case. In some countries, the concept of security is established in a more formalistic way. Namely, the legislature may establish the type of financial instruments that can be considered a security (e.g., shares, bonds, etc.), as it happens in Singapore. As a result, any financial instrument that is not specially mentioned in legislation would be excluded from the scope of securities regulation. Finally, other countries may follow an intermediate approach: to facilitate the identification of a security, they may establish a list of financial instruments that are always deemed a "security," but they also allow other financial instruments that may meet certain requirements to be considered "securities." This latter approach is followed, for example, in Spain. See Spanish Securities Market Act art. II (2015). The approach followed by a legal system to define "security" will have great implications in the context of ICOs. For instance, while countries with a flexible concept of securities, as it happens in the United States, will make it easier to include a token within the scope of securities regulation, those countries defining securities by reference to a given list of financial instruments will unlikely allow a token to be classified as a security unless the legislation is amended to especially include tokens (or a particular type of tokens)

as securities. For a useful analysis of a variety of tokens to see whether they meet the requirements to be considered "securities" under Singapore law, see *A Guide to Digital Token Offerings*, MONETARY AUTH. OF SING. 10–19 (Nov. 14, 2017), http://www.mas.gov.sg/News-and-Publications/Monographs-and-Information-Papers/2017/Guidance-on-Digital-Token-Offerings.aspx.

15. Munchee was a California-based company that was seeking $15 million in capital to improve an existing iPhone app focused on restaurant meal reviews. It sought to create an "ecosystem" in which Munchee and other companies would buy and sell goods and services using the tokens. The company communicated through its website, a white paper, and other means how the proceeds were used to create the ecosystem, including payments in tokens to users for writing food reviews and selling both advertising to restaurants and "in-app" purchases to app users in exchange for tokens. According to the white paper, during the offering, the company and other promoters emphasized that investors could expect that efforts by the company and others would lead to an increase in the value of the tokens. Based on this statement made by the company, the SEC decided to open an investigation for violation of federal securities regulation. Munchee consented to the SEC's cease-and-desist order without admitting or denying the findings. *See* Press Release, Sec. & Exch. Comm'n, Company Halts ICO After SEC Raises Registration Concerns (Dec. 11, 2017), https://www.sec.gov/news/press-release/2017-227.

16. These "third parties" are often called "gatekeepers." In general, a gatekeeper can be defined as a professional who is positioned so as to able to prevent wrongdoing by withholding necessary cooperation or consent. *See* Reinier H. Kraakman, *Gatekeepers: The Anatomy of a Third-Party Enforcement Strategy*, 1 J.L. ECON. & ORG. 53 (1986). For an analysis of the concept of "gatekeepers" and how lawyers, auditors, securities analysts, credit rating agencies, and investment bankers can serve as such players, see JOHN COFFEE, JR., GATEKEEPERS: THE PROFESSIONS AND CORPORATE GOVERNANCE (2006).

17. Liability for legal opinions is a controversial issue. In general, it will depend on the jurisdiction and the role played by legal opinions in that particular jurisdiction. In the United States, for example, see Joseph L. Johnson, *Liability of Attorneys for Legal Opinions Under the Federal Securities Laws*, 27 B.C.L. REV. 325 (1986).

18. This approach seems to have been followed by the Spanish Securities Market Authority (CNMV) in the ICO launched by Home Meal. *See La CNMV, dispuesta a colaborar con Home Meal, dueña de Nostrum, para lanzar su ICO en España*, EUROPAPRESS (Feb. 28, 2018, 4:42 PM), http://www.europapress.es/economia/finanzas-00340/noticia-cnmv-dispuesta-colaborar-home-meal-duena-nostrum-lanzar-ico-espana-20180228164239.html.

19. *See How Is the Presale Different from the Crowdsale?*, HACKERNOON (Feb. 27, 2018), https://hackernoon.com/how-is-the-presale-different-from-the-crowdsale-f369f484794d.

20. These discount rates can go up to 30%. For example, in the ICO of the messaging application Kik, the pre-ICO sale allowed Blockchain Capital, Pantera Capital and Polychain Capital to purchase kin tokens at a 30% discounted rate. *See* Jon Russell,

Chat App Kik to Raise $125M Through an ICO in September, TECHCRUNCH (Aug. 29, 2017), https://techcrunch.com/2017/08/29/kik-ico-september-125-million/; u/ripcurldog, *ICO's MUST Stop Institutional Investors from Pre-sale ICO Discounts!!!!*, REDDIT (Oct. 3, 2017, 5:03 PM), https://www.reddit.com/r/KinFoundation/comments/743eim/icos_must_stop_institutional_investors_from/.

21. *See* Joseph Young, *Hedge Funds Investing Early in ICOs Is Abusive: Cryptocurrency Investor*, CCN (Sept. 10, 2017), https://www.ccn.com/hedge-funds-investing-early-in-icos-is-abusive-cryptocurrency-investor/.

22. *See* Juan Batiz-Benet, Jesse Clayburgh & Marco Santori, *The SAFT Project: Toward a Compliant Token Sale Framework*, PROTOCOL LABS & COOLEY LLP, at 4 (2017), https://saftproject.com/static/SAFT-Project-White paper.pdf.

23. Young, *supra* note 21.

24. This has been used only in presales of non-security tokens. Batiz-Benet et al, *supra* 22.

25. *See Blockchain Risk Management—Risk Functions Need to Play an Active Role in Shaping Blockchain Strategy*, DELOITTE (2017), https://www2.deloitte.com/content/dam/Deloitte/us/Documents/financial-services/us-fsi-blockchain-risk-management.pdf.

26. A DAO is a Decentralized Autonomous Organization. Its goal is to codify the rules and decision-making apparatus of an organization, eliminating the need for documents and people in governing, creating a structure with decentralized control. "The DAO" is the name of a particular DAO, conceived of and programmed by the team behind German start-up Slock.it—a company building "smart locks" that let people share their things (cars, boats, apartments) in a decentralized version of Airbnb.

27. *See* David Siegel, *Understanding the DAO Attack*, COINDESK (June 25, 2016, 4:00 PM), https://www.coindesk.com/understanding-dao-hack-journalists/.

28. Delgado, *supra* note 7, at 26.

29. *Id.* at 9.

30. Sebastian Meunier, *Blockchain Technology—A Very Special Kind of Distributed Database*, MEDIUM (Dec. 29, 2016), https://medium.com/@sbmeunier/blockchain-technology-a-very-special-kind-of-distributed-database-e63d00781118.

31. *See* Alfonso Delgado & Nydia Remolina, *Foundations of Blockchain Technology*, IIDF Working Paper Series (2019).

32. A single point of failure (SPOF) is a part of a system that, if it fails, will stop the entire system from working. SPOFs are undesirable in any system with a goal of high availability or reliability, be it a business practice, software application, or other industrial system. *See* KEVIN DOOLEY, DESIGNING LARGE SCALE LANs: HELP FOR NETWORK DESIGNERS 31 (2009).

33. Where an external attacker temporarily prevents legitimate users from accessing the database by flooding the network with superfluous requests. *See* Delgado & Remolina, *supra* note 31.

34. In distributed systems, not all storage devices are attached to a common processor.

35. In 2008 Satoshi Nakamoto, a pseudonym used by the inventor(s) of blockchain, published the Bitcoin paper and the source code on the internet. In January 2009, New Liberty Standard opened the first Bitcoin trading platform. The initial exchange rate was 1,309.03 Bitcoin for one U.S. dollar; in February 2010, the first payment in Bitcoin was processed at a price of 10,000 (more than $140 million at today's exchange rate). The first large companies to accept Bitcoin were WordPress, Overstock. com, Zynga, and TigerDirect. *See* Satoshi Nakamoto, *Bitcoin: A Peer to Peer Electronic Cash System* (Nov. 2008), https://bitcoin.org/bitcoin.pdf.

36. *See* Peter Van Valkenburgh, *What Is "Blockchain" Anyway?*, COINCENTER (Apr. 25, 2017), https://coincenter.org/entry/what-is-blockchain-anyway; See Delgado & Remolina, *supra* note 31.

37. *E.g.*, WHITEPAPER DATABASE: CRYPTOCURRENCY ICO WHITEPAPERS, http:// whitepaperdatabase.com/ (last visited Feb. 7, 2019).

38. As we will see in the following sections, not all tokens are investments. For example, some of them only grant access to a platform or a discount. These tokens should not be considered necessarily as an investment contract.

39. Dirk A. Zetzsche, Ross P. Buckley, Douglas W. Arner & Linus Fôhr, *The ICO Gold Rush: It's a Scam, It's a Bubble, It's a Super Challenge for Regulators* (Euro. Banking Inst. Working Paper Series No. 18/2018), https://papers.ssrn.com/sol3/ papers.cfm?abstract_id=3072298.

40. Only 31% of the ICOs in a sample of 450 ICOs mention the law applicable to the ICO. In 37.7% of the cases the white paper excluded investors from certain countries from participation. In 86.5% of the cases there is no information at all as to the regulatory status of the ICO. This also included cavalier disregard of the need to inform a participant as to where precisely their funds are going. *See* Zetzsche, *infra* note 40.

41. The risks of selective disclosure and the benefits associated with harmonization and comparability may justify mandatory disclosure in capital markets. For a discussion on this issue, see JOHN ARMOUR ET AL., PRINCIPLES OF FINANCIAL REGULATION 164–67 (2016); Luca Enriques & Sergio Gilotta, *Disclosure and Financial Market Regulation*, *in* THE OXFORD HANDBOOK ON FINANCIAL REGULATION 511–25 (Eilis Ferran, Niamh Moloney & Jennifer Payne eds., 2015); Merrit Fox, *Retaining Mandatory Securities Disclosure: Why Issuer Choice Is Not Investor Empowerment*, 85 VA. L. REV. 1335 (1999); Zohar Goshen & Gideon Parchomovsky, *The Essential Role of Securities Regulation*, 55 DUKE L.J. 711 (2006). Pointing out the benefits of standardization in some particular rules (e.g., accounting), see JOHN ARMOUR ET AL., THE ANATOMY OF CORPORATE LAW: A COMPARATIVE AND FUNCTIONAL APPROACH 19 (2017). Likewise, using Akerlof's seminal work about asymmetries of information, it can be argued that the lack of enough information about all issuers may lead to an adverse selection problem: investors will not be able to distinguish "good" and "bad" issuers. Therefore, they might be reluctant to provide finance, or they will do so at a higher cost for everyone, considering that, in the absence of mandatory (and standardized) disclosure, many "bad issuers" may decide to provide just "selective disclosure" of what it can be only in their interest. *See generally* George A. Akerlof, *The Market for "Lemons": Quality Uncertainty and the Market Mechanism*, 84 Q.J. OF

ECON. 488 (1970). In the context of ICOs, Professor Chris Brummer has advocated for standardizing disclosure in white papers. *See* David Hollerith, *Congressional Hearings: We Must Distinguish Digital Commodities from ICOs*, BITCOIN MAG. (Mar. 14, 2018, 9:36 PM), https://bitcoinmagazine.com/articles/congressional-hearings-we-must-distinguish-digital-commodities-icos/.

42. Some advisors and law firms are specialized now in review ICO papers, and some of them are "certified" by a peer review.

43. The SAFT transaction might rely on Rule 506(c) of the Securities Act (United States federal securities regulation), which allows for general solicitation of investors, but requires that the offering must be limited, in the end, only to verified accredited investors.

44. Delgado, *supra* note 7.

45. We will describe the different regulatory approaches in Section II.

46. The Ethereum's introductory tutorial teaches this basic coding skills. *See* Delgado, *supra* note 7.

47. This statement excludes jurisdictions that have prohibited ICOs, such as China.

48. Bob Zider, *How Venture Capital Works*, HARV. BUS. REV. (Nov. 1998), https://hbr.org/1998/11/how-venture-capital-works.

49. Caitlin Long, *6 Facts Institutional Investors Should Know About Crypto* (Apr. 24, 2018), https://caitlin-long.com/2018/04/24/6-facts-institutional-investors-should-know-about-crypto/.

50. *See* Regulators' Statements on Initial Coin Offerings, INT'L ORG. SEC. COMM'NS, https://www.iosco.org/publications/?subsection=ico-statements (last accessed Feb. 8, 2019) (listing statements of many securities regulators regarding ICOs).

51. The details of this prohibition can be found in several sources. *See, e.g.,* Gabriel Wildau, *China Central Bank Declares Initial Coin Offerings Illegal*, FIN. TIMES (Sept. 4, 2017), https://www.ft.com/content/3fa8f60a-9156-11e7-a9e6-11d2f0ebb7f0.

52. *See* Cynthia Kim, *South Korea Bans Raising Money Through Initial Coin Offerings*, REUTERS (Sept. 28, 2017), https://www.reuters.com/article/us-southkorea-bitcoin/south-korea-bans-raising-money-through-initial-coin-offerings-idUSKCN1C408N (analyzing the recent ban by South Korea).

53. *Initial Coin Offerings (ICOs)*, SEC. & EXCH. COMM'N, https://www.sec.gov/ICO (last visited Feb. 8, 2019).

54. *A Guide to Digital Token Offerings*, MONETARY AUTH. OF SING. (Nov. 14, 2017), http://www.mas.gov.sg/News-and-Publications/Monographs-and-Information-Papers/2017/Guidance-on-Digital-Token-Offerings.aspx.

55. FINMA, *supra* note 9.

56. See Mexico Fintech Law (In Spanish: Ley para regular las Instituciones de Tecnología Financiera). *Available at*: http://www.senado.gob.mx/sgsp/gaceta/63/3/2017-10-12-1/assets/documentos/Iniciativa_Ejecitvo_Federal.pdf.

57. While this is very unlikely in most jurisdictions, where shares or bonds are defined in a more formal way rather than on a functional basis, this scenario can be possible under Singapore law. *See* MONETARY AUTH. OF SING., *supra* note 53, at 3. (allowing tokens to be considered "shares" when it confers or represents ownership interest in a

corporation). Therefore, if a token confers or represents ownership interest in a corporation, it can be considered a "share." And if so, it will be a security.

58. *See* Allen Scott, *Russia Unveils ICO Regulations, Underpinned by the Ruble*, BITCOINIST (Apr. 2, 2018, 5:00 AM), http://bitcoinist.com/russia-unveils-ico-regulations-ruble/.

59. *See* Ana Alexandre, *New Study Says 80 Percent of ICOs Conducted in 2017 Were Scams*, COINTELEGRAPH (July 13, 2018), https://cointelegraph.com/news/new-study-says-80-percent-of-icos-conducted-in-2017-were-scams.

60. *See generally* JOHN ARMOUR ET AL., PRINCIPLES OF FINANCIAL REGULATION 167–73 (2016). For a U.S. perspective, see COFFEE & SALE, *supra* note 14, at 328–407. In the European Union, see Regulation (EU) 2017/1129 of the European Parliament and of the Council of 14 June 2017 on the prospectus to be published when securities are offered to the public or admitted to trading on a regulated market, and repealing Directive 2003/71/EC with EEA relevance, 2017 O.J. (L 168) 12. This regulation repealed the Directive 2003/71/EC, which governed the offer of securities in the European Union since 2005. In Singapore, an offer may be exempt from the Prospectus Requirements where, amongst others, the offer is a small offer of securities of an entity, or units in a CIS, that does not exceed S$5 million (or its equivalent in a foreign currency) within any 12-month period, subject to certain conditions; the offer is a private placement offer made to no more than 50 persons within any 12-month period, subject to certain conditions; the offer is made to institutional investors only; or the offer is made to accredited investors, subject to certain conditions. *See* MONETARY AUTH. OF SING., *supra* note 54, at 5–6. Similar requirements apply in other jurisdictions.

61. These cases were decided in the United States. For the concept of "security" in the United States, see JOHN COFFEE, JR. & HILLARY A. SALE, SECURITIES REGULATION: CASES AND MATERIALS, 246–327 (12th ed. 2012); HAL S. SCOTT & ANNA GERLPERN, INTERNATIONAL FINANCE: TRANSACTIONS, POLICY AND REGULATION (21st ed. 2016). For a comparison between the United States and Europe, see Philipp Hacker & Chris Thomale, *Crypto-Securities Regulation: ICOs, Token Sales and Cryptocurrencies Under EU Financial Law*, EURO. CO. & FIN. L. REV. (forthcoming) (manuscript at 17–36), https://papers.ssrn.com/sol3/papers.cfm?abstract_id=3075820##. For the concept of security in Singapore, for example, see HANS TJIO, WAN WAI YEE, & YEE KNOW HON, PRINCIPLES AND PRACTICE OF SECURITIES REGULATIONS IN SINGAPORE (3d ed. 2017). For an analysis of the concept of securities in the United Kingdom, Australia, South Africa, and India, see Frederick H. C. Mazando, *The Taxonomy of Global Securities: Is the U. S. Definition of a Security Too Broad?*, 33 Nw. J. INT'L L. & BUS. 121, 148–76 (2012).

62. However, Mexico's Fintech law only mentions "digital assets." It does not refer to ICOs or tokens. Nonetheless, "digital assets" is broad enough to consider tokens and ICOs subject to Mexican Fintech law according to our interpretation.

63. Interestingly, in Mexico, the issuance of tokens does not have to be authorized by the securities regulator but by the central bank.

64. It is not clear how the Mexican approach will operate in practice. While this chapter was being written, Mexico had just enacted a Fintech Law saying that any issuance of "cryptocurrencies" will be subject to the authorization of the regulator.

65. Moreover, companies required to prepare and submit financial statements should be required to mention in the notes any issuance of tokens.

66. This basic information has been suggested for white papers. *See* Chris Brummer, *What Should Be in an ICO White Paper? Expert Take*, CoinTelegraph (Mar. 14, 2018), https://cointelegraph.com/news/what-should-be-in-an-ico-white-paper-expert-take. For a deeper analysis, see Chris Brummer, Trevor Kiviat & Jai R. Massari, *What Should Be Disclosed in an Initial Coin Offering?* (2018), https://papers.ssrn.com/sol3/papers.cfm?abstract_id=3293311.

67. Due to the size and the particular features of these institutions, their failure may generate various negative externalities, including lack of confidence, contagion, connectedness, and more generally systemic risk. For an analysis of these concepts, see Hal Scott, Connectedness and Contagion: Protecting the Financial System from Panics (2016); Steven L. Schwarcz, *Systemic Risk*, 97 Geo. L.J. 193 (2008); Viral Acharya, *A Theory of Systemic Risk and Design of Prudential Bank Regulation*, 6 J. Fin. Stability 224 (2009). For an analysis of the importance of pension funds and other institutional investors in capital markets, see Ronald J. Gilson & Jeffrey N. Gordon, *The Agency Costs of Agency Capitalism: Activist Investors and the Revaluation of Governance Rights*, 863 Colum. L. Rev. 928 (2013).

68. *See* Delgado, *supra* note 8, at 26–28.

69. For a pioneer study about the impact of the capital structure on the value of the firm, see Franco Modigliani & Merton Miller, *The Cost of Capital, Corporation Finance and the Theory of Investment*, 48 Amer. Econ. Rev. 261 (1958). These authors establish that the value of the firm was independent of the capital structure. However, they make this assertion in a world without asymmetries of information, transaction costs, taxes, and costs of bankruptcy. Once these variables are included in the model, the use of debt seems to generate more benefits for firms. *See* Michael C. Jensen, *Agency Cost of Free Cash Flow, Corporate Finance, and Takeovers*, 76 Amer. Econ. Rev. 323 (1986); Richard Brealey, Steward Myers & Franklin Allen, Principles of Corporate Finance 460–62 (10th ed. 2011); Aurelio Gurrea-Martínez, *The Impact of the Tax Benefits of Debt in the Capital Structure of Firms and the Stability of the Financial Systems*, Oxford Bus. L. Blog (Mar. 30, 2017), https://www.law.ox.ac.uk/business-law-blog/blog/2017/03/impact-tax-benefits-debt-capital-structure-firms-and-stability. For a general analysis of the capital structure of firms from a legal and finance perspective, see Eilis Ferran & Look Chan Ho, Principles of Corporate Finance Law (2d ed. 2014).

70. The best example can be found in the bitcoin. For the evolution of its price, see Bitcoin Volatility Index, https://bitvol.info/ (last visited Feb. 9, 2019).

71. These authors include Professor Robert Shiller. John Detrixhe, *Robert Shiller Wrote the Book on Bubbles. He Says "The Best Example Right Now Is Bitcoin,"* Quartz (Sept. 5, 2017), https://qz.com/1067557/robert-shiller-wrote-the-book-on-bubbles-he-says-the-best-example-right-now-is-bitcoin/.

72. *See* Luca Enriques & Jonathan Macey, *Creditors Versos Capital Formation: The Case Against the European Legal Capital Rules*, 86 CORNELL L. REV. 1165 (2001); Aurelio Gurrea-Martínez, *The Impact of the Tax Benefits of Debt in the Capital Structure of Firms and the Stability of the Financial Systems*, OXFORD BUS. L. BLOG (Mar. 30, 2017), https://www.law.ox.ac.uk/business-law-blog/blog/2017/03/impact-tax-benefits-debt-capital-structure-firms-and-stability.

73. This situation would create a problem of correlation and connectedness. For an analysis of these concepts, see HAL SCOTT, CONNECTEDNESS AND CONTAGION: PROTECTING THE FINANCIAL SYSTEM FROM PANICS (2016).

74. Our opinion seems to differ here from the Monetary Authority of Singapore. *See* MONETARY AUTH. OF SING., *supra* note 54, at 3 (allowing tokens to be considered "shares" when a token confers or represents ownership interest in a corporation, represents liability of the tokenholder in the corporation, and represents mutual covenants with other tokenholders in the corporation inter se). However, in Singapore, the law seems to distinguish between "stocks" and "shares"—this latter concept seems to be broader. See section 2(1) of the SFA, read with section 4(1) of the Companies Act (Cap. 50), expressing that "share" means "a share in the share capital of a corporation and includes stock except where a distinction between stocks and share is expressed or implied." *See also* Ricardo Torres, *Problemática jurídica de las ICOs: Un análisis desde el Derecho de sociedades*, BLOG DEL INSTITUTO IBEROAMERICANO DE DERECHO Y FINANZAS (Mar. 20, 2018), http://derechoyfinanzas.org/blog/problematica-juridica-de-las-icos-un-analisis-desde-el-derecho-de-sociedades/.

75. Some authors even speak about "Initial Coin Scams." *See* Nouriel Roubini, *Initial Coin Scams*, PROJECT SYNDICATE (May 10, 2018), https://www.project-syndicate.org/commentary/ico-cryptocurrency-scams-by-nouriel-roubini-2018-05.

76. Corporate governance is, after all, about promises between managers and investors. *See* JONATHAN MACEY, CORPORATE GOVERNANCE: PROMISES KEPT, PROMISES BROKEN (2008).

77. A corporate contract is, by definition, an incomplete contract. The parties cannot agree ex ante on any single contingencies. For these reasons, fiduciary duties and other general provisions may help fill some of the gaps existing in corporate contracts. For an analysis of the literature about incomplete contracts in the context of the firm and a firm's capital structures, see OLIVER HART, FIRMS, CONTRACTS, AND FINANCIAL STRUCTURE (1995); Oliver Hart & John Moore, *Property Rights and the Nature of the Firm*, 98 J. OF POL. ECON. 1119 (1990); Oliver Hart & John Moore, *Foundations of Incomplete Contracts*, 66 REV. OF ECON. STUD. 115 (1999); Philippe Aghion & Patrick Bolton, *An Incomplete Contracts Approach to Financial Contracting* 59 REV. OF ECON. STUD. 473 (1992).

78. *See* Henry G. Manne, *Mergers and the Market for Corporate Control*, 73 J. POL. ECON. 110 (1965); Frank H. Easterbook & Daniel R. Fischel, *The Proper Role of the Target's Management in Responding to a Tender Offer*, 94 HARV. L. REV. 1161 (1981).

79. Delgado, *supra* note 7, at 26–28.

80. Michael C. Jensen & William H. Meckling, *Theory of the Firm: Managerial Behavior, Agency Costs and Ownership Structure*, 3 J. FIN. ECON. 305 (1976).

81. For a novel explanation of principal costs, and how corporate governance should reduce both agency costs and principal costs, see Zohar Goshen & Richard Squire, *Principal Costs: A New Theory for Corporate Law and Governance*, 117 COLUM. L. REV. 767 (2017). For an article providing various arguments to empower the board, see Stephen M. Bainbridge, *Director Primacy: The Means and Ends of Corporate Governance*, 97 Nw. U. L. REV. 547, 573 (2003). *See also* Martin Lipton, *Takeover Bids in the Target's Boardroom*, 35 BUS. LAW. 101 (1979); Martijn Cremers & Simone M. Sepe, *The Shareholder Value of Empowered Boards*, 68 STAN. L. REV. 67 (2016). For an article in favor of empowering investors, however, see Lucian A. Bebchuk, *The Case for Increasing Shareholder Power*, 118 HARV. L. REV. 833 (2005); Aurelio Gurrea Martínez, *New Agency Problems: New Legal Rules? Rethinking Takeover Regulation in the US and Europe* (Ibero-American Institute for Law and Finance, Working Paper Series No. 3/2016), https://papers.ssrn.com/sol3/papers.cfm?abstract_id=2766208.

82. For an analysis of this concept, see ROY GOODE, PRINCIPLES OF CORPORATE INSOLVENCY LAW 641–47 (4th ed. 2011).

83. For an analysis of these conflicts among shareholders, see John Armour, Henry Hansmann & Reinier Kraakman, *Agency Problems and Legal Strategies*, in JOHN ARMOUR ET AL., THE ANATOMY OF CORPORATE LAW: A COMPARATIVE AND FUNCTIONAL APPROACH 29–30 (2017); Mark J. Roe, *The Institutions of Corporate Governance*, in HANDBOOK OF NEW INSTITUTIONAL ECONOMICS (Claude Ménard & Mary M. Shirley eds., 2005).

84. For the concept of "horizontal agency problems" in corporate governance, see Roe, *supra* note 83, at 371–77.

85. For a general view about the challenges faced by consumer when they make decisions and how regulators can improve consumer protection, see OREN BAR-GILL, SEDUCTION BY CONTRACT: LAW, ECONOMICS, AND PSYCHOLOGY IN CONSUMER MARKETS (2012); and OMRI BAN SHAGAR & CARL E. SCHNEIDER, MORE THAN YOU WANTED TO KNOW: THE FAILURE OF MANDATED DISCLOSURE (2014). Focusing on financial consumers, and different regulatory approaches to protect financial consumers, see ARMOUR, *supra* note 41, at 205–23, 255–71.

86. Some of these platforms already exist, as it can be the case of websites such as "icoratings.com," "icoalert.com," and "icomonitor.io." *See* Delgado, *supra* note 8, at 27.

87. Arieh Goldman & Benzion Barlev, *The Auditor-Firm Conflict of Interests: Its Implications for Independence*, 49 ACCT. REV. 707 (1974); Matthew J. Barrett, *Enron and Andersen—What Went Wrong and Why Similar Audit Failures Could Happen Again*, in ENRON: CORPORATE FIASCOS AND THEIR IMPLICATIONS 155–68 (Nancy B. Rapoport & Bala G. Dharan eds., 2004); Walter Doralt et al., *Auditor Independence at the Crossroads—Regulation and Incentives*, 13 EURO. BUS. ORG. L. REV. 89 (2012).

88. Frank Partnoy, *How and Why Credit Rating Agencies Are Not Like Other Gatekeepers, Financial Gatekeepers: Can They Protect Investors?* (San Diego Legal Studies Paper No. 07-46) (2006); Carol Ann Frost, *Credit Rating Agencies in Capital Markets: A*

Review of Research Evidence on Selected Criticisms of the Agencies, 22 J. ACCT., AUDITING & FIN. 1 (2007).

89. The conflicts of interest of proxy advisors have not been that evident. They were identified more recently. *See* Guy Rolnik, *The Powerful Private Regulator and the Effects of Conflicts of Interest*, PROMARKET (May 3, 2017), https:// promarket.org/powerful-private-regulator-effects-conflicts-interest/; Tao Li, *Outsourcing Corporate Governance: Conflicts of Interest Within the Proxy Advisory Industry*, MGMT. SCI. (2018); *Discussion Paper—An Overview of the Proxy Advisory Industry: Considerations on Possible Policy Options* (Euro. Sec. & Mkt. Auth. Discussion Paper No. 2012/212) (2012), https://www.esma.europa.eu/sites/default/ files/library/2015/11/2012-212.pdf.

90. Press Release, Monetary Auth. of Sing., MAS Clarifies Regulatory Position on the Offer on Digital Tokens in Singapore (Aug. 1, 2017), http://www.mas.gov.sg/News-and-Publications/Media-Releases/2017/MAS-clarifies-regulatory-position-on-the-offer-of-digital-tokens-in-Singapore.aspx.

91. *Id.*

92. MONETARY AUTH. OF SING., *supra* note 54.

93. The SEC even launched a fake ICO in May 2018, pre-selling a coin called Howey Coin, to show how easy it is to scam investors. *See* Sally French, *The SEC Created a Fake ICO Website to Show Just How Easy It Is to Scam Investors* (May 16, 2018), https://www.marketwatch.com/story/the-sec-created-a-mock-ico-website-to-show-just-how-easy-it-is-for-investors-to-get-fleeced-2018-05-16; HOWEYCOIN, https://www.howeycoins.com/index.html (last visited Feb. 9, 2019).

94. *See* Letter from Fin. Crimes Enforcement Network to U.S. Senate Comm. on Fin (Feb. 13, 2018), https://coincenter.org/files/2018-03/fincen-ico-letter-march-2018-coin-center.pdf.

95. *See* Press Release, Euro. Comm'n, European Commission Launches the EU Blockchain Observatory and Forum (Feb. 1, 2018), http://europa.eu/rapid/press-release_IP-18-521_en.pdf.

96. Neither tokens nor ICOs.

97. It seems that the definition of exchanges does not encompass ICO companies as they do not—generally, but with some exceptions—enable their users to change their tokens into fiat money. It also seems that they do not fall within the definition of wallet providers as the funds, which they receive within the ICO, belong to the company, not to the tokenholders. Developers do not hold their users' private keys for the users' wallets, but only hold private keys for their own wallets.

   However, most developers exchange the raised cryptocurrencies to fiat and deposit them at a bank account for their operational needs. Therefore some could argue that they facilitate an exchange from cryptocurrencies to money. *See* Nejc Novak, *EU Introduces Anti-money Laundering Regulation*, MEDIUM (Jan. 2, 2018), https:// medium.com/@nejcnovaklaw/eu-introduces-crypto-anti-money-laundering-regulation-d6ab0ddedd3.

98. *See Digital Identity: On the Threshold of a Digital Identity Revolution*, WORLD ECON. FORUM (Jan. 2018), http://www3.weforum.org/docs/White_Paper_Digital_

Identity_Threshold_Digital_Identity_Revolution_report_2018.pdf; *see also* Bernard Lunn, *Digital Identity Is the Key to the Blockchain Economy*, DAILY FINTECH (Mar. 24, 2018), https://dailyfintech.com/2018/03/24/digital-identity-is-the-key-to-the-blockchain-economy/; Ana I. Segovia Domingo & Álvaro Martín Enríquez, *Digital Identity: The Current State of Affairs* (BBVA Res. Working Paper No 18/01), https://www.bbvaresearch.com/wp-content/uploads/2018/02/Digital-Identity_the-current-state-of-affairs.pdf.

99. *See* Leah Brown, *How Blockchain Encryption Works: It's All About Math*, TECHREPUBLIC (Nov. 20, 2017), https://www.techrepublic.com/article/how-blockchain-encryption-works-its-all-about-math/.

100. *See What Is Hashing? Under the Hood of Blockchain*, BLOCKGEEKS, https://blockgeeks.com/guides/what-is-hashing/ (last accessed Feb. 9, 2019).

101. *A Guide to Blockchain and Data Protection*, HOGAN LOVELLS (Sept. 2017), https://www.hlengage.com/_uploads/downloads/5425GuidetoblockchainV9FORWEB.pdf.

102. *See* Gideon Greenspan, *The Blockchain Immutability Myth*, COINDESK (May 9, 2017), https://www.coindesk.com/blockchain-immutability-myth/.

103. *See* Council Regulation 2016/679 of the European Parliament and of the Council on the Protection of Natural Persons with Regard to the Processing of Personal Data and on the Free Advancement of Such Data, and Repealing Directive 95/46/EC, art. 17, 2016 O.J. (L 119) 1.

104. *See id.* at art. 3.

105. This work uses the terms "bankruptcy procedures" and "insolvency proceeding" as synonyms.

106. According to this principle existing in most insolvency jurisdictions, junior creditors cannot get paid until senior creditors have been paid in full, and shareholders cannot get any value out of the firm until the company's creditors have been paid in full. For a deeper analysis of this principle, see DOUGLAS G. BAIRD, ELEMENTS OF BANKRUPTCY 71–77 (5th ed. 2010).

107. For an analysis of this principle, see ROY GOODE, PRINCIPLES OF CORPORATE INSOLVENCY LAW 235–40 (4th ed. 2011).

108. However, this is not the general rule. Most insolvency jurisdictions provide a mandatory state-provided set of bankruptcy rules. So far, the contractual approach has been proposed just in the literature. *See* Robert Rasmussen, *Debtor's Choice: A Menu Approach to Corporate Bankruptcy*, 71 TEX. L. REV. 51 (1992); Alan Schwartz, *A Contract Theory Approach to Business Bankruptcy*, 107 YALE L.J. 1807 (1998).

109. *See* IOSCO, *supra* note 10.

110. Since ICOs mostly fund blockchain-based projects. Some of these ideas promise to be disruptive in many markets or industries as use cases of this new technology. Because of this, the implementation of the use cases could take some time to be accepted as a mainstream in many industries. *See also* Delgado, *supra* note 8.

111. This statement is probably not applicable to qualified investors, particularly those funds that are known for participating in presales of tokens and then dumping their investments only to make profits.

112. In May, 2016 Jack Markell—governor of the State of Delaware—announced an initiative by the State of Delaware to embrace the emerging blockchain and smart contract technology industry, which can help the public and enterprises lower their transactional costs, speed up and automate manual processes, and reduce fraud. This announcement took place in the Consensus 2016 conference, which is currently one of the most important international conferences on blockchain. *See* CoinDesk, *Introducing the Delaware Blockchain Initiative*, YouTube (Sept. 30, 2016), https://www.youtube.com/watch?v=-mgxEhIvSTY. Analyzing the features and challenges of this initiative, see Nydia Remolina, *La incorporación de blockchain en el Derecho de sociedades de Delaware*, Blog del Instituto Iberoamericano de Derecho y Finanzas (Aug. 28, 2017), http://www.derechoyfinanzas.org/la-incorporacion-de-blockchain-en-el-derecho-de-sociedades-de-delaware/.

113. *See* Michael Greene, *Delaware Eyeing Blockchain to Improve Corporate Processes*, Bloomberg L. (Apr. 5, 2017), https://www.bna.com/delaware-eyeing-blockchain-n57982086257/.

114. *See* 2015 Annual Report, Del. Div. of Corp., https://corp.delaware.gov/Corporations_2015%20Annual%20Report.pdf.

115. *See* Michael Del Castillo, *Overstock Could Rise $30 Million with Blockchain Stock Offering*, Coindesk (Nov. 21, 2016, 2:05 PM), https://www.coindesk.com/overstock-raise-30-million-blockchain-stock-offering/.

116. *See* Bradly Dale, *The Next Step in Overstock's Master Blockchain Plan Is Underway*, Coindesk (Dec. 19, 2017, 9:00 AM), https://www.coindesk.com/tzeros-ico-one-part-overstocks-master-blockchain-plan/.

117. Overstock.com Inc. (2018). Form 8-K 2018.

118. For a detailed explanation of the Delaware Blockchain Initiative, see Andrea Tinianow & Caitlin Long. *Delaware Blockchain Initiative: Transforming the Foundational Infrastructure of Corporate Finance*, Harv. L. Sch. F. Corp. Governance & Fin. Reg. Blog (Mar. 16, 2017), https://corpgov.law.harvard.edu/2017/03/16/delaware-blockchain-initiative-transforming-the-foundational-infrastructure-of-corporate-finance/; *see also* Nydia Remolina, *La incorporación de Blockchain en el Derecho de Sociedades de Delaware.* Blog del Instituto Iberoamericano de Derecho y Finanzas (2018), http://derechoyfinanzas.org/blog/la-incorporacion-del-blockchain-en-el-derecho-de-sociedades-de-delaware/.

119. Wonnie Song, *Bullish on Blockchain: Examining Delaware's Approach to Distributed Ledger Technology in Corporate Governance Law and Beyond.* Harv. Bus. L. Rev. (Jan. 3, 2018), http://www.hblr.org/2018/01/bullish-on-blockchain-examining-delawares-approach-to-distributed-ledger-technology-in-corporate-governance-law-and-beyond/.

120. Cede and Company, also known as "Cede and Co." or "Cede & Co.," is a specialist U.S. financial institution that processes transfers of stock certificates on behalf of the Depository Trust Company, the central securities depository used by the United States National Market System, which includes the New York Stock Exchange, Nasdaq, and other exchanges together with associated clearinghouses. Cede & Co. owns substantially all of the publicly issued stock in the United States. Thus, investors

do not themselves hold direct property rights in stock, but rather have contractual rights that are part of a chain of contractual rights involving Cede. *See Company Overview of Cede & Company*, BLOOMBERG, https://www.bloomberg.com/research/stocks/private/snapshot.asp?privcapId=22429124 (last visited Feb. 9, 2019).

121. *See* Matt Levine, *Dole Food Had Too Many Shares; It's Enough to Make You Wish for a Blockchain*. BLOOMBERG (Feb. 17, 2017), https://www.bloomberg.com/view/articles/2017-02-17/dole-food-had-too-many-shares; *see also* Joshua Ashley Klayman et al., *Why the Delaware Blockchain Initiative Matters to All Dealmakers*, FORBES (Sept. 20, 2017), https://www.forbes.com/sites/groupthink/2017/09/20/why-the-delaware-blockchain-initiative-matters-to-all-dealmakers/#2ee375f27550; *In re* Dole Food Co. Inc., No. CV 8703-VCL, 2017 WL 624843 (Del. Ch. Feb. 15, 2017).

122. *In re* Appraisal of Dell Inc., 143 A.3d 20 (Del. Ch. 2016).

123. *See* WYOMING BLOCKCHAIN COALITION, http://wyomingblockchain.io/ (last accessed Feb. 8, 2019).

124. *See* André Eggert & Yamila Eraso, *Delaware Blockchain Initiative: Revitalizing European Companies' Funding Efforts*, HARV. L. SCH. F. CORP. GOVERNANCE & FIN. REG. (Sept. 21, 2017), https://corpgov.law.harvard.edu/2017/09/21/delaware-blockchain-initiative-revitalizing-european-companies-funding-efforts/.

Chapter 7

1. Although many cite the Ethereum presale in 2014 as the first ICO, this title likely goes to Mastercoin, which was introduced in 2013 by developer J.R. Willet in a white paper he called *The Second Bitcoin White Paper*. In this document, Willet suggested using Bitcoin's blockchain as a base protocol layer, on top of which new protocols with new rules would be constructed. In other words, Mastercoin would serve as an interim layer between the Bitcoin blockchain and new decentralized applications. Mastercoin introduced one of the key characteristics of an ICO token vis-a-vis the broader universe of digital assets: the "premine." A premine means that a number of coins are set aside for the founders to hold or sell, either for compensation or to fund ongoing operating expenses. Mastercoin also laid the foundation for some important economic arguments raised in favor of ICOs: (1) that building and testing one's own blockchain is less efficient than creating a new application with its own protocol rules on top of an existing blockchain, and (2) that new protocol layers on top of a main blockchain, such as the Bitcoin blockchain, will increase the underlying asset's (e.g., Bitcoin's) value since this activity expands the underlying asset's utilization.

2. COINGECKO, QUARTERLY CRYPTOCURRENCY REPORT: Q1 2018, at 15, https://assets.coingecko.com/reports/Q1-2018-Cryptocurrency-Report-by-CoinGecko-large.pdf.

3. *E.g.*, John Biggs, *Exit Scammers Run Off with $660 Million in ICO Earnings*, TECHCRUNCH (Apr. 13, 2018), https://techcrunch.com/2018/04/13/exit-scammers-run-off-with-660-million-in-ico-earnings.

4. *E.g.*, David Z. Morris, *Nearly Half of 2017's Cryptocurrency "ICO" Projects Have Already Died*, FORTUNE (Feb. 25, 2018), http://fortune.com/2018/02/25/

cryptocurrency-ico-collapse; *see also, e.g.,* DEAD COINS, https://deadcoins.com (last visited May 23, 2019).

5. Some digital assets, such as Bitcoin or Litecoin, are widely regarded as decentralized stores of value or mediums of exchange due to certain common economic features that support these functions; these are sometimes referred to as "pure cryptocurrencies." Other digital assets, such as Monero or Zcash, are a subset of pure cryptocurrencies that also possess certain features designed to enhance transaction privacy and confidentiality ("privacy-focused coins"). Beyond pure cryptocurrencies and privacy-focused coins, there exists a broad array of general purpose digital assets ("platform coins"), such as Ethereum, NEO, and Ravencoin, which are designed to facilitate various peer-to-peer activity, from decentralized software applications to "smart" contracts to digital collectibles, such as CryptoKitties. Platform coins also enable the creation of new digital assets called "tokens," which are typically developed for a specific purpose or application—for example, (1) "utility tokens," which generally have some software-based functionality beyond mere use as a medium of exchange or stored value and are situated within a broader platform or service; and (2) "security tokens," which are designed to represent more traditional interests such as equity, debt, and real estate with the added benefit of certain features of the digital asset markets, such as 24/7 operations, fractional ownership, and rapid settlement.

6. For a detailed discussion of decentralization, *see* Vitalik Buterin, *The Meaning of Decentralization,* MEDIUM (Feb. 6, 2017), https://medium.com/@VitalikButerin/the-meaning-of-decentralization-a0c92b76a274.

7. Wulf Kaal, *Initial Coin Offerings: The Top 25 Jurisdictions and Their Comparative Regulatory Responses* STAN. J. BLOCKCHAIN L. & POL'Y (2018), https://stanford-jblp.pubpub.org/pub/ico-comparative-reg.

8. *See, e.g., In re* Munchee Inc., No. 3-18304 (SEC Dec. 11, 2017) (order instituting cease-and-desist proceedings pursuant to Section 8A of the Securities Act of 1933), https://www.sec.gov/litigation/admin/2017/33-10445.pdf.

9. This chapter focuses primarily on the enigmatic class of ICO tokens often referred to as "utility tokens." It is not intended to be applicable to (1) cryptocurrencies that are not distributed through an offer and sale as ICO tokens, (2) crytocurrencies that are complete and useful as currency immediately upon network launch with fully completed system architectures, or (3) security tokens, which due to their characteristics fall squarely within the existing disclosure regime. However, we suspect that in some limited cases, useful lessons may be gleaned, and we invite further review.

10. Again, we exclude vanilla security tokens (e.g., those with dividends, offering equity, etc.) from our pricing analysis since by definition their pricing determinants would overlap strongly with traditional securities. However, even here, many of our disclosure observations would still be applicable given the technological features of tokenization.

11. *See, e.g.,* SAIFEDEAN AMMOUS, THE BITCOIN STANDARD: THE DECENTRALIZED ALTERNATIVE TO CENTRAL BANKING (2018) (describing the rise of Bitcoin, including its historical context and the economic properties that have facilitated its growth).

12. The following project is fictional, but it is based largely on our review of the white papers of recent ICOs. The sample we reviewed included the top 10 ICO raises through June 1, 2018, excluding duplicates and ICOs with no publicly available white paper, from *ICO/Token Sales*, SMITH + CROWN, https://www.smithandcrown.com/sale. GitHub, *EOS.IO Technical White Paper v2*, (2016), https://github.com/EOSIO/Documentation/blob/master/TechnicalWhitePaper.md. (the EOS white paper; $895 million raised); Protocol Labs, *Filecoin: A Decentralized Storage Network*, (2017), https://filecoin.io/filecoin.pdf.; L.M. GOODMAN, TEZOS—A SELF-AMENDING CRYPTO-LEDGER WHITE PAPER (Sept. 2, 2014), https://tezos.com/static/papers/white_paper.pdf (the Tezos white paper; $234 million raised); SIRIN LABS, FINNEY SECURE OPEN SOURCE CONSUMER ELECTRONICS FOR THE BLOCKCHAIN ERA, https://sirinlabs.com/media/SIRINLABS_-_White_Paper.pdf (last visited May 23, 2019) (the Sirin Labs white paper; $158 million raised); EYAL HERTZOG ET AL., BANCOR PROTOCOL: CONTINUOUS LIQUIDITY AND ASYNCHRONOUS PRICE DISCOVERY FOR TOKENS THROUGH THEIR SMART CONTRACTS; AKA "SMART TOKENS" (May 30, 2017), https://www.bancor.network/static/bancor_protocol_whitepaper_en.pdf (the Bancor white paper; $148 million raised); GAVIN WOOD, POLKADOT: VISION FOR A HETEROGENEOUS MULTI-CHAIN FRAMEWORK DRAFT 1, https://icobazaar.com/storage/campaigns/42/whitepaper.pdf (Last visited May 23, 2019) (the PolkaDot white paper; $144 million raised); NADER AL-NAJI ET AL., BASIS: A PRICE-STABLE CRYPTOCURRENCY WITH AN ALGORITHMIC CENTRAL BANK (June 4, 2018), https://basis.io/basis_whitepaper_en.pdf (the Basis white paper; $125 million raised); PUMAPAY: A FULLPAYMENT PROTOCOL WHITE PAPER—DRAFT V1.9 (2018), https://pumapay.io/docs/pumapay_whitepaper.pdf (the PumaPay white paper; $117 million raised); Quoine Pte. Ltd., LIQUID BY QUOINE: PROVIDING LIQUIDITY TO THE NON-LIQUID CRYPTO ECONOMY (Oct. 30, 2017), https://s3-ap-southeast-1.amazonaws.com/liquid-site/quoine-liquid_v1.9.pdf (the QASH white paper; $108 million raised); THE STATUS NETWORK: A STRATEGY TOWARDS MASS ADOPTION OF ETHEREUM (June 15, 2017), https://status.im/whitepaper.pdf (the Status white paper; $101 million raised).

13. Simon Barber et al., *Bitter to Better—How to Make Bitcoin a Better Currency*, LECTURE NOTES IN COMPUTER SCIENCE 399 (2012). *But see* JOSEPH POON & THADDEUS DRYJA, THE BITCOIN LIGHTNING NETWORK: SCALABLE OFF-CHAIN INSTANT PAYMENTS (Jan. 14, 2016) (proposing the Lightning Network to improve Bitcoin scalability), https://lightning.network/lightning-network-paper.pdf; Sandra Upson, *The Lightning Network Could Make Bitcoin Faster—and Cheaper*, WIRED (Jan. 19, 2018) (explaining the possible improvements from the Bitcoin Lighting Network), https://www.wired.com/story/the-lightning-network-could-make-bitcoin-faster-and-cheaper.

14. *See* ANDREW POELSTRA ET AL., CONFIDENTIAL ASSETS (noting that "even small amounts of personally identifiable information may completely break [Bitcoin] users' privacy"), https://blockstream.com/bitcoin17-final41.pdf (last visited May 23, 2019), *see also* Barber et al., *supra* note 13 (discussing both perceived anonymity and security limitations of Bitcoin).

15. In fact, promises made in a white paper are often not implemented in the code in a way that is binding. One study of 50 top-grossing ICOs found that many issuers did not actually manifest their promises in code. More troublingly, "a significant fraction of issuers retained centralized control through previously undisclosed code permitting modifications of the entities' governing structures." Shaanan Cohney et al., *Coin-Operated Capitalism* (Working Paper July 17, 2017), https://papers.ssrn.com/sol3/papers.cfm?abstract_id=3215345.

16. *E.g.*, Jen Wieczner, *Hackers Just Stole $7 Million in a Brazen Ethereum Cryptocurrency Heist*, FORTUNE (July 18, 2017), http://fortune.com/2017/07/18/ethereum-coindash-ico-hack/.

17. *E.g.*, Nathaniel Popper, *Subpoenas Signal S.E.C. Crackdown on Initial Coin Offerings*, N.Y. TIMES (Feb. 28, 2018), https://www.nytimes.com/2018/02/28/technology/initial-coin-offerings-sec.html.

18. *SEC Chairman on Cryptocurrencies and Initial Coin Offerings*, PRINCETON UNIVERSITY (May 31, 2018), https://jrc.princeton.edu/news/sec-chairman-cryptocurrencies-and-initial-coin-offerings.

19. *E.g.*, Mercer Bullard, *The Law and Economics of Crowdfunding: An Empirical Analysis*, Draft on File with Authors (finding that in a set of crowdfunding filers, 90 percent of the variance in the amount raised was explained by social media engagement); Camila Russo & Olga Kharif, *The Hottest ICOs Are the Ones That Have Done the Least Amount of Work*, BLOOMBERG (Dec. 11, 2017), https://www.bloomberg.com/news/articles/2017-12-12/want-to-issue-a-red-hot-ico-rule-no-1-is-do-very-little-work.

20. *See, e.g.*, Chris Burniske, *Cryptoasset Valuations,* MEDIUM (Sept. 24, 2017), https://medium.com/@cburniske/cryptoasset-valuations-ac83479ffca7.

21. *See* John Coffee, *Racing Towards the Top?: The Impact of Cross-Listings and Stock Market Competition on International Corporate Governance* (Columbia University Center for Law and Economic Studies Working Paper # 205, May 2002).

22. SATOSHI NAKAMOTO, BITCOIN: A PEER-TO-PEER ELECTRONIC CASH SYSTEM (2009), https://nakamotoinstitute.org/static/docs/bitcoin.pdf.

23. Dirk Zetzsche et al., *The ICO Gold Rush, It's a Scam, It's a Bubble, It's a Super Challenge for Regulators* (Working Paper, Nov. 16, 2017), 12.

24. *Id.*

25. Melissa Dylan, *5 Mistakes You're Making in Your Token White Paper*, MEDIUM (Jan. 6, 2018), https://medium.com/new-alchemy/5-mistakes-youre-making-in-your-ico-white-paper-8d7fba3fc83f

26. Bennett Garner, *How to Read a Cryptocurrency White Paper*, COINCENTRAL (Mar. 10, 2018) https://coincentral.com/cryptocurrency-white-paper/

27. For a list of SEC cyber enforcement actions involving digital assets, see *Cyber Enforcement Actions,* SEC, at https://www.sec.gov/spotlight/cybersecurity-enforcement-actions (Last visited May 23, 2019).

28. Cohney et al., *supra* note 15, at 43–44

29. Thomas Bourveau et al., *Initial Coin Offerings: Early Evidence on the Role of Disclosure in the Unregulated Crypto Market* (Working Paper, June 9, 2018), at 14, https://papers.ssrn.com/sol3/papers.cfm?abstract id=3193392.

30. *See* SEC v. W.J. Howey Co., 328 U.S. 293 (1946).

31. Franklin Roosevelt himself promised in his presidential nomination acceptance speech to "let[] in []the light of day on issues of securities, foreign and domestic, which are offered." JOEL SELIGMAN, THE TRANSFORMATION OF WALL STREET: A HISTORY OF THE SECURITIES AND EXCHANGE COMMISSION AND MODERN CORPORATE FINANCE (3d ed. 2003).

32. *See* Donald C. Langevoort & Robert B. Thompson, *"Publicness" in Contemporary Securities Regulation After the JOBS Act,* 101 GEO. L.J. 337, 353 (2012) (noting that listing on certain exchanges was "a means of signaling quality to potential traders").

33. *See* Release 33-5 (1933).

34. Paul G. Mahoney & Jianping Mei, *Mandatory Versus Contractual Disclosure in Securities Markets: Evidence from the 1930s* (Working Paper, Feb. 23, 2006), https://papers.ssrn.com/sol3/papers.cfm?abstract_id=883706.

35. *Id.*

36. *Id.*

37. Release 33-2887 (1942).

38. *See generally,* Coffee, *supra* note 21.

39. Form S-1, at Item 11(a) (pointing to Reg S-K § 229.101).

40. *Id.*

41. *Id.* at Item 11(e).

42. *Id.* at Item 11(f) (pointing to Reg S-K § 229.301); *id.* at Item 11(g) (pointing to Reg S-K § 229.301).

43. *Id.* at Item 11(h) (pointing to Reg S-K § 229.303).

44. *Id.*

45. *Id.* at Item 9 (pointing to Reg S-K § 229.202).

46. Reg S-K § 229.202.

47. Form S-1 at Item 15 (pointing to Reg S-K § 229.701).

48. *Id.* at Item 1 (pointing to Reg S-K § 229.501).

49. *Id.* at Item 6 (pointing to Reg S-K § 229.506).

50. *Id.* at Item 11(*l*) (pointing to Reg S-K §229.402 and §229.407).

51. *Id.*

52. *Id.*

53. *Id.*

54. Nate Maddrey, *The Three Branches of Blockchain Governance,* MEDIUM (Aug. 23, 2018). https://medium.com/digitalassetresearch/the-three-branches-of-blockchain-governance-75a29bf98880.

55. *Id.*

56. Form S-1 at Item 9 (Pointing to Reg S-K § 229.202).

57. *See* text accompanying *supra* note 46.

58. Form S-1 at Item 11(*l*) (pointing to Reg S-K § 229.407).

59. *Id.*

60. *Id.* at Item 16(a) (pointing to Reg S-K § 229.601) (requiring that articles of incorporation and bylaws be appended as exhibits).

61. *Id.* at Item 11(k) (pointing to Reg S-K § 229.401).

62. *Id.*

63. *Id.*

64. *See generally* Howey, *supra* note 30.

65. Form S-1 at Item 11(k) (pointing to Reg S-K § 229.401).

66. *Id.* at Item 8 (pointing to Reg S-K § 229.508 (Item 508)).

67. *Id.*

68. *Id.* at Item 11(h) (pointing to Reg S-K § 229.303).

69. *Id.* at Item 11(j) (pointing to Reg S-K § 229.305).

70. *Id.*

71. OFFICE OF THE NEW YORK STATE ATTORNEY GENERAL, VIRTUAL MARKETS INTEGRITY INITIATIVE REPORT (Sept. 18, 2018), https://ag.ny.gov/sites/default/files/vmii report.pdf.

72. Form S-1 at Item 3 (pointing to Reg S-K § 229.503(c)).

73. *Id.*

74. City of Roseville, 814 F. Supp. 2d 395 (S.D.N.Y. 2011), 426.

75. *Id.*

76. Seow Lin v. Interactive Brokers Group, Inc., 574 F. Supp. 2d 408, 418 (S.D.N.Y. 2008).

77. *Id.* at 420.

78. SEC, *Form C Under the Securities Act of 1933*, https://www.sec.gov/files/formc.pdf (Last visited May 23, 2019).

79. Form C at 14 (Q&A 29).

80. *Id.* at 13 (Q&A 27).

81. *Id.* (Q&A 28).

82. *Id.* at 10 (Q&A 13).

83. *Id.* (Q&A 14); *id.* (Q&A 15).

84. *See* Section III.A, *supra.*

85. *Compare id.* at 12 (Q&A 23) (asking how corporate actions might present risks to security purchasers) *with* Form S-1 at Item 11(*l*) (pointing to Reg S-K § 229.407; requiring extensive disclosure of corporate governance).

86. Form C at 12 (Q&A 23).

87. *See* text and source accompanying *supra* notes 50–58.

88. *See* text accompanying *supra* note 60.

89. Form C at 6 (Q&A 5).

90. *Id.* at 1.

91. Form S-1 at Item 1 (pointing to Reg S-K §229.501).

92. *Id.*

93. Form 1-A at Item 1; *id.* at Circular Item 9.

94. *Id.* at Circular Item 9.
95. *Id.* at Item 4; *id.* at Circular Item 14; *id.* at Circular Item 17.
96. *Compare id.* at Part III Item 17 (requiring charter and bylaws to be attached as exhibits) *with* Form S-1 at Item 11(*l*) (pointing to Reg S-K § 229.407 requiring extensive disclosure of corporate governance beyond provision of governing documents).
97. Form 1-A at Circular Item 10. *See also* text accompanying *supra* note 65. By contrast, note that this mirrored language is not present in Form C, which instead has a carveout for persons "occupying a similar status or performing a similar function." *See supra* note 89.
98. Notably, the threshold for qualifying as an accredited investor has not tracked inflation. When the SEC adopted Regulation D in 1982, accredited investors were defined as individuals with a net worth in excess of $1 million or annual income above $200,000, which climbs to $300,000 for couples. This number has not moved—and if adjusted for inflation would be well over $2 million in today's dollars.
99. *See* Section II, *supra* and the latter part of Section VI, *infra.*
100. *Id.*
101. SEC, A PLAIN ENGLISH HANDBOOK: HOW TO CREATE CLEAR SEC DISCLOSURE DOCUMENTS (Aug. 1998), https://www.sec.gov/pdf/handbook.pdf.
102. For an overview of auditors and the New Deal framers of the Securities Acts, see JEREMEY WIESEN, THE SECURITIES ACT AND INDEPENDENT AUDITORS: WHAT DID CONGRESS INTEND? (1978), http://3197d6d14b5f19f2f440-5e13d29c4c016cf96cbbfd197c579b45.r81.cf1.rackcdn.com/collection/papers/1970/1978_0301_WiesenIntend.pdf.
103. Cohney et al., *supra* note 15.
104. *See, e.g.,* IVICA NIKOLIĆ ET AL., FINDING THE GREEDY, PRODIGAL, AND SUICIDAL CONTRACTS AT SCALE (2018), https://arxiv.org/abs/1802.06038.
105. A denial-of-service attack, or DoS attack, is a cyberattack whereby the attacker attempts to cause a machine or network resource to be rendered unavailable to its intended users. The attacker does this by disrupting, either temporarily or indefinitely, the services of a host connected to the internet. Such attacks are typically accomplished by flooding the targeted machine or network resource with superfluous requests in order to overload systems, thereby preventing some or all legitimate requests from being fulfilled. A distributed denial-of-service attack, or DDoS attack, is largely the same except that the incoming traffic directed at the target originates from many different sources, effectively making it impossible to stop the attack by simply blocking a single source. Such attacks commonly target unsuspecting ICO promoters, primarily as a smokescreen for more dangerous security breaches. For example, a DoS attacker may also attempt to access the control panel of the website through an attack on the site administrator in order to change the wallet address associated with the token sale to one controlled by the attacker. Or, a DoS attacker may combine this with a social engineering attack in order to direct ICO purchasers to a fake website for the token sale controlled by the attacker.
106. Social engineering attacks refer generally to any type of psychological manipulation that causes the target to perform certain actions or divulge confidential

information to the benefit of the attacker. One such type of attack is a phishing attack, in which the attacker fraudulently attempts to obtain sensitive information (e.g., login credentials, private keys) from the target. Phishing may be carried out through email spoofing or through instant messaging (e.g., using a mobile chat application or social media platform). In February 2018, it was reported that the ICO for Bee Token was the target of a phishing attack, whereby the attackers acquired an email address list of investors who had indicated interest in the token sale, and sent fraudulent emails to such investors using email addresses with the domain "@ thebeetoken.com" with instructions to send Ether to wallet addresses controlled by the attackers, rather than the ICO promoters. The attackers made off with roughly $1 million in Ether in just over 25 hours.

107. A man-in-the-middle attack is one where the attacker fraudulently alters the communication between two parties who believe they are communicating directly with each other. For example, an attacker might alter data on a trusted website by accessing an unsecured, or poorly secured, WiFi router (e.g., a public WiFi hotspot) in order to serve targets a fraudulent website designed to mimic an ICO website.

108. Note that Form 1-A provides alternative formats for Part II of its disclosure requirements. The Form 1-A column in this table focuses on the disclosure required under the most straightforward option: following the requirements in Part II (the offering circular) of Form 1-A itself. Alternatively, issuers could instead follow Part I of the Form S-1 (the requirements of which are included in this sheet) or Part I of Form S-11.

109. Form C notes that issuers must include "information required by Rule 201 of Regulation Crowdfunding (§ 227.201)." The only mandatory parts of Form C are a cover page and three items, but the form provides an optional "Question and Answer Format" for an issuer to provide the remaining required disclosure. This chart relies on the Q&A section to map out the required disclosure, and references each Q&A item accordingly.

Chapter 8

1. *See* ESMA. ISDA reply to ESMA's discussion paper on the distributed ledger technology applied to securities markets, at 10. Retrieved from https://www.esma.europa.eu/press-news/consultations/consultation-distributed-ledger-technology-applied-securities-markets (June 2, 2016).

2. 7 U.S. Code § 1a(31) (1992).

3. See NFA. "Introducing brokers," *available at* https://www.nfa.futures.org/members/ib/index.html (last visited February 14, 2019).

4. 7 U.S. Code § 1a(28) (1992).

5. 7 U.S. Code § 1a(49) (1992).

6. Capital rules are not yet finalized for U.S. swap dealers, though proposed.

7. 17 C.F.R 23 (2013).

8. Jonathan Rohr & Aaron Wright, "Blockchain-Based Token Sales, Initial Coin Offerings, and the Democratization of Public Capital Markets" Hastings Law Journal, Vol. 70: 463, pg. 8.

9. Surujnath, R. (2017). "Off the Chain: A Guide to Blockchain Derivatives Markets and the Implications on Systemic Risk." *Fordham Journal of Corporate and Financial Law*, 22(257), 9.

10. Ryan, R. & Donohue, M. (2017–2018). "Securities on Blockchain." *Business Lawyer*, 73, 141.

11. *See* O'Brien, Matt. "Blockchain Technology Will Profoundly Change the Derivatives Industry.", *available at* https://bitcoinmagazine.com/articles/blockchain-technology-will-profoundly-change-the-derivatives-industry-1464368431/ (last visited February 14, 2019).

12. "The Future of Derivatives Processing and Market Infrastructure," at 22–23. *White Paper*. ISDA, Sept. 2016, https://www.isda.org/a/UEKDE/infrastructure-white-paper.pdf.

13. Mainelli, M. & Milne, A. "The Impact and Potential of Blockchain on the Securities Transaction Lifecycle," at 17. *Working Paper No. 2015-007*. Swift Institute, May 9, 2016.

14. *See* ESMA. ISDA Reply to ESMA's Discussion Paper on the Distributed Ledger Technology Applied to Securities Markets.", p. 9.

15. Metjahic, L. (2018). "Deconstructing the DAO: The Need for Legal Recognition and the Application of Securities Laws to Decentralized Organizations." *Cardozo Law Review*, 39(1533), 192.

16. *See* ESMA. "ISDA Reply to ESMA's Discussion Paper on the Distributed Ledger Technology Applied to Securities Markets." at 9. Retrieved from https://www.esma.europa.eu/press-news/consultations/consultation-distributed-ledger-technology-applied-securities-markets (last visited February 14, 2019).

17. Svikhart, R. (2017). "Blockchain's Big Hurdle." *Stanford Law Review Online*, 70(100), 134 (n.12).

18. *See* ESMA. (June 2, 2016). "Discussion Paper: The Distributed Ledger Technology Applied to Securities Markets.", at 17. Retrieved from https://www.esma.europa.eu/press-news/consultations/consultation-distributed-ledger-technology-applied-securities-markets (last visited February 14, 2019).

19. *See* ESMA. "ISDA Reply to ESMA's Discussion Paper on the Distributed Ledger Technology Applied to Securities Markets.", at 8. Retrieved from https://www.esma.europa.eu/press-news/consultations/consultation-distributed-ledger-technology-applied-securities-markets (last visited February 14, 2019).

20. *See* ESMA. "ISDA Reply to ESMA's Discussion Paper on the Distributed Ledger Technology Applied to Securities Markets," at 8. Retrieved from https://www.esma.europa.eu/press-news/consultations/consultation-distributed-ledger-technology-applied-securities-markets.

21. Batog, C. (2015). "Blockchain: A Proposal to Reform High Frequency Trading Regulation." *Cardozo Arts & Entertainment Law Journal*, 33, 166.

22. Batog, C. (2015). "Blockchain: A Proposal to Reform High Frequency Trading Regulation." *Cardozo Arts & Entertainment Law Journal*, 33, 165.

23. *See* ESMA. (June 2, 2016). "Discussion Paper: The Distributed Ledger Technology Applied to Securities Markets," at 11. Retrieved from https://www.esma.europa.eu/press-news/consultations/consultation-distributed-ledger-technology-applied-securities-markets.

24. *See* ESMA. "ISDA Reply to ESMA's Discussion Paper on the Distributed Ledger Technology Applied to Securities Markets," at 8. Retrieved from https://www.esma.europa.eu/press-news/consultations/consultation-distributed-ledger-technology-applied-securities-markets.

25. Arner, D. W., Barberis, J., & Buckley, R. P. (2017). "Fintech, Regtech, and the Reconceptualization of Financial Regulation." *Northwestern Journal of International Law and Business*, 37, 341.

26. Arner, D. W., Barberis, J., & Buckley, R. P. (2017). "Fintech, Regtech, and the Reconceptualization of Financial Regulation." *Northwestern Journal of International Law and Business*, 37, 350.

27. Arner, D. W., Barberis, J., & Buckley, R. P. (2017). "Fintech, Regtech, and the Reconceptualization of Financial Regulation." *Northwestern Journal of International Law and Business*, 37, 355.

28. Walch, A. (2015). "The Bitcoin Blockchain as a Financial Market Infrastructure: A Consideration of Operational Risk." *NYU Journal of Legislation and Public Policy*, 18(837), 281.

29. Walch, A. (2015). "The Bitcoin Blockchain as a Financial Market Infrastructure: A Consideration of Operational Risk." *NYU Journal of Legislation and Public Policy*, 18(837), 282.

30. Butler, T., Al Khalil, F., Ceci, M. & O'Brien, L. (2017). "Smart Contracts and Distributed Ledger Technologies in Financial Services: Keeping Lawyers in the Loop." *Banking & Financial Services Report*, 36(9), 407

31. Walch, A. (2015). "The Bitcoin Blockchain as a Financial Market Infrastructure: A Consideration of Operational Risk." *NYU Journal of Legislation and Public Policy*, 18(837), 285–86.

32. *See* ESMA. (June 2, 2016). "Discussion Paper: The Distributed Ledger Technology Applied to Securities Markets," at 19. Retrieved from https://www.esma.europa.eu/press-news/consultations/consultation-distributed-ledger-technology-applied-securities-markets.

33. Butler, T., Al Khalil, F., Ceci, M., & O'Brien, L. (2017). "Smart Contracts and Distributed Ledger Technologies in Financial Services: Keeping Lawyers in the Loop. *Banking & Financial Services Report*, 36(9), 409.

34. "Smart Contracts and Distributed Ledger—A Legal Perspective," at p. 12. *White Paper*. ISDA, Aug. 2017, https://www.isda.org/a/6EKDE/smart-contracts-and-distributed-ledger-a-legal-perspective.pdf.

35. "Smart Contracts and Distributed Ledger—A Legal Perspective," at p. 12. *White Paper*. ISDA, Aug. 2017, https://www.isda.org/a/6EKDE/smart-contracts-and-distributed-ledger-a-legal-perspective.pdf.

36. Butler, T., Al Khalil, F., Ceci, M., & O'Brien, L. (2017). "Smart Contracts and Distributed Ledger Technologies in Financial Services: Keeping Lawyers in the Loop." *Banking & Financial Services Report*, 36(9), 409

37. "Smart Contracts and Distributed Ledger—A Legal Perspective," at p. 11. *White Paper*. ISDA, Aug. 2017, https://www.isda.org/a/6EKDE/smart-contracts-and-distributed-ledger-a-legal-perspective.pdf.

38. "Smart Contracts and Distributed Ledger—A Legal Perspective," at p. 11. *White Paper*. ISDA, Aug. 2017, https://www.isda.org/a/6EKDE/smart-contracts-and-distributed-ledger-a-legal-perspective.pdf.

39. "Smart Contracts and Distributed Ledger—A Legal Perspective," at p. 13. *White Paper*. ISDA, Aug. 2017, https://www.isda.org/a/6EKDE/smart-contracts-and-distributed-ledger-a-legal-perspective.pdf.

40. Butler, T., Al Khalil, F., Ceci, M., & O'Brien, L. (2017). "Smart Contracts and Distributed Ledger Technologies in Financial Services: Keeping Lawyers in the Loop." *Banking & Financial Services Report*, 36(9), 411.

41. Butler, T., Al Khalil, F., Ceci, M., & O'Brien, L. (2017). "Smart Contracts and Distributed Ledger Technologies in Financial Services: Keeping Lawyers in the Loop." *Banking & Financial Services Report*, 36(9), 409.

42. Butler, T., Al Khalil, F., Ceci, M., & O'Brien, L. (2017). "Smart Contracts and Distributed Ledger Technologies in Financial Services: Keeping Lawyers in the Loop." *Banking & Financial Services Report*, 36(9), 409–10.

43. "ISDA Common Domain Model Version 1.0 Design Definition Document," October 2017, *available at* https://www.isda.org/a/gVKDE/CDM-FINAL.pdf.

44. Walch, A. (2015). "The Bitcoin Blockchain as a Financial Market Infrastructure: A Consideration of Operational Risk." *NYU Journal of Legislation and Public Policy*, 18(837), 277–78.

45. *See* ESMA. (June 2, 2016). "Discussion Paper: The Distributed Ledger Technology Applied to Securities Markets," at 17. Retrieved from https://www.esma.europa.eu/press-news/consultations/consultation-distributed-ledger-technology-applied-securities-markets.

46. *See* ESMA. (June 2, 2016). "Discussion Paper: The Distributed Ledger Technology Applied to Securities Markets," at 18. Retrieved from https://www.esma.europa.eu/press-news/consultations/consultation-distributed-ledger-technology-applied-securities-markets.

47. Mainelli, M. & Milne, A. "The Impact and Potential of Blockchain on the Securities Transaction Lifecycle, at 20. *Working Paper No. 2015-007*. Swift Institute, May 9, 2016.

48. *See* ESMA. (June 2, 2016). "Discussion Paper: The Distributed Ledger Technology Applied to Securities Markets," at 17. Retrieved from https://www.esma.europa.eu/press-news/consultations/consultation-distributed-ledger-technology-applied-securities-markets.

49. *See* ESMA. (June 2, 2016). "Discussion Paper: The Distributed Ledger Technology Applied to Securities Markets," at 17. Retrieved from https://

www.esma.europa.eu/press-news/consultations/consultation-distributed-ledger-technology-applied-securities-markets.

50. Werbach, K. & Cornell, N. (2017). "Contracts Ex Machina." *Duke Law Journal*, 67(313), 227.

51. Mainelli, M. & Milne, A. "The Impact and Potential of Blockchain on the Securities Transaction Lifecycle, at 18. *Working Paper No. 2015-007.* Swift Institute, May 9, 2016.

52. *See* ESMA. (June 2, 2016). "Discussion Paper: The Distributed Ledger Technology Applied to Securities Markets," at 15. Retrieved from https:// www.esma.europa.eu/press-news/consultations/consultation-distributed-ledger-technology-applied-securities-markets.

53. *See* ESMA. "ISDA Reply to ESMA's Discussion Paper on the Distributed Ledger Technology Applied to Securities Markets," at 12. Retrieved from https:// www.esma.europa.eu/press-news/consultations/consultation-distributed-ledger-technology-applied-securities-markets.

54. Werbach, K. & Cornell, N. (2017). "Contracts Ex Machina." *Duke Law Journal*, 67(313), 244.

55. Werbach, K. & Cornell, N. (2017). "Contracts Ex Machina." *Duke Law Journal*, 67(313), 224.

56. *See* ESMA. (June 2, 2016). "Discussion Paper: The Distributed Ledger Technology Applied to Securities Markets," at 18. Retrieved from https:// www.esma.europa.eu/press-news/consultations/consultation-distributed-ledger-technology-applied-securities-markets.

57. Ross, E. S. (2017). "Nobody Puts Blockchain in a Corner: The Disruptive Role of Blockchain Technology in the Financial Services Industry and Current Regulatory Issues." *Catholic University Journal of Law & Technology*, 25, 104.

58. Batog, C. (2015). "Blockchain: A Proposal to Reform High Frequency Trading Regulation." *Cardozo Arts & Entertainment Law Journal*, 33, 165.

59. Ryan, R. & Donohue, M. (2017-8). "Securities on Blockchain." *Business Lawyer*, 73, 144.

60. *See* https://lightning.network/. There are a host of other risks raised by authors not discussed here:

   (1) Enforceability: There is also the risk that blockchain contracts will not be enforceable in a cross-border context. Blockchains are easily international so in the occurrence of a conflict, different jurisdictions and therefore different laws may apply. *See* ESMA. (June 2, 2016). "Discussion Paper: The Distributed Ledger Technology Applied to Securities Markets," at 16. Retrieved from https://www.esma.europa.eu/press-news/consultations/consultation-distributed-ledger-technology-applied-securities-markets. Despite claims that the smart contracts are a law onto themselves, or as one author noted, "it is the code that is law," "borderless enforceability" is not practical. *See* Ross, E. S. (2017). "Nobody Puts Blockchain in a Corner: The Disruptive Role of Blockchain Technology in the Financial Services

Industry and Current Regulatory Issues." *Catholic University Journal of Law & Technology*, 25, 103.

(2) Block trading limitation: While that technology is not fully developed now, promising technology that could potentially allow separate lines of communication between consenting parties to transact until they both agree to post to blockchain. *See* https://lightning.network/.

(3) Netting limitation: ISDA has opined on potential solutions. *See* ESMA. "ISDA Reply to ESMA's Discussion Paper on the Distributed Ledger Technology Applied to Securities Markets," at 12. Retrieved from https://www.esma.europa.eu/press-news/consultations/consultation-distributed-ledger-technology-applied-securities-markets. ("[F]unctionally embedded into the blockchain—are able to transpose the gross level information in to a net movement . . . daily 'lock down' process that nets all cash flows to be exchange on a given value date to be locked and then it becomes a case of merely funding your accounts . . . ").

(4) Margin finance limitation: But smart contracts could potentially be coded to record a transaction at one point, but not retrieve the funds until a later date.

(5) Short-selling limitation: ISDA has proposed a potential solution to make lendable securities available. *See* ESMA. "ISDA Reply to ESMA's Discussion Paper on the Distributed Ledger Technology Applied to Securities Markets," at 13. Retrieved from https://www.esma.europa.eu/press-news/consultations/consultation-distributed-ledger-technology-applied-securities-markets.

61. Three SDRs and are also both DCMs and DCOs.

62. *See* ESMA. (June 2, 2016). "Discussion Paper: The Distributed Ledger Technology Applied to Securities Markets," at 16. Retrieved from https://www.esma.europa.eu/press-news/consultations/consultation-distributed-ledger-technology-applied-securities-markets.

63. Werbach, K. & Cornell, N. (2017). "Contracts Ex Machina." *Duke Law Journal*, 67(313), 243.

64. Werbach, K. & Cornell, N. (2017). "Contracts Ex Machina." *Duke Law Journal*, 67(313), 240.

65. Werbach, K. & Cornell, N. (2017). "Contracts ex machina." *Duke Law Journal*, 67(313), 243.

66. Mainelli, M. & Milne, A. "The Impact and Potential of Blockchain on the Securities Transaction Lifecycle," at 31. *Working Paper No. 2015-007*. Swift Institute, May 9, 2016.

67. Some recommend starting with "dumb short contracts" instead of "smart long contracts" in order to minimize risk. *See* Mainelli, M. & Milne, A. "The Impact and Potential of Blockchain on the Securities Transaction Lifecycle," at 30. *Working Paper No. 2015-007*. Swift Institute, May 9, 2016.

68. *See* CFTC. (September 2018). "Technology Based Innovations for Regulatory Compliance ("Regtech") in the Securities Industry, A Report from FINRA," at 7-8.

69. Ross, E.S. (2017). Nobody Puts Blockchain in a Corner: The Disruptive Role of Blockchain Technology in the Financial Services Industry and Current Regulatory Issues. *Catholic University Journal of Law & Technology*, 25, 103.

Chapter 9

1. CoinMarketCap, *Top 100 Cryptocurrencies by Market Capitalization*, https://coinmarketcap.com/ (accessed November 8, 2018).
2. Swiss Financial Market Supervisory Authority, *Guidelines for Enquiries Regarding the Regulatory Framework for Initial Coin Offerings (ICOs)* (February 16, 2018), https://www.finma.ch/en/~/media/finma/dokumente/dokumentencenter/myfinma/1bewilligung/fintech/wegleitung-ico.pdf (accessed November 8, 2018).
3. *Id.* at 3.
4. *Id.* at 3.
5. "Gas" is the unit of measurement used in the Ethereum ecosystem to measure the computational effort required to execute certain operations.
6. For example, the Irish Tax and Customs consider that "the treatment of income received from/charges made in connection with activities involving cryptocurrencies will depend on the activities and the parties involved" and that "[e]ach case must be considered on the basis of its own individual facts and circumstances." Irish Tax and Customs, Tax and Duty Manual, Part 02-01-03, *Taxation of Cryptocurrency Transactions*, 2, https://www.revenue.ie/en/tax-professionals/tdm/income-tax-capital-gains-tax-corporation-tax/part-02/02-01-03.pdf (accessed November 8, 2018). Similarly, the UK HM Revenue & Customs (HMRC) have taken the view that "[w]hether any profit or gain is chargeable or any loss is allowable will be looked at on a case-by-case basis taking into account the specific facts." HMRC, *Policy Paper, Revenue and Customs Brief 9 (2014): Bitcoin and Other Cryptocurrencies (March 3, 2014)*, https://www.gov.uk/government/publications/revenue-and-customs-brief-9-2014-bitcoin-and-other-cryptocurrencies/revenue-and-customs-brief-9-2014-bitcoin-and-other-cryptocurrencies (accessed November 8, 2018) ("2014 Paper"). This approach was again followed by the HMRC in a more recent policy paper on taxation of cryptoassets for individuals: "As with any activity, the question whether cryptoasset activities amount to trading depends on a number of factors and the individual circumstances. Whether an individual is engaged in a financial trade through the activity of buying and selling cryptoassets will ultimately be a question of fact." HMRC, *Policy Paper, Cryptoassets for Individuals (December 19, 2018)*, https://www.gov.uk/government/publications/tax-on-cryptoassets/cryptoassets-for-individuals (accessed December 19, 2018) ("2018 Paper").
7. While tax administrations—and law enforcement agencies more generally—face real practical challenges in dealing with cryptoassets transactions primarily because of the "pseudonymity" and anonymity enabled by the underlying technology, those challenges and their emerging responses are largely unaddressed in this chapter, which focuses on substantive tax issues.

8. The term "VAT" or "value added tax" is used here in a generic way to encompass all broad-based non-cascading multistage consumption taxes.

9. This refers to the need for both parties to a barter transaction to agree to sell and buy each other's commodity or services.

10. For instance, money is not a supply for Australian goods and services tax (GST) purposes. A New Tax System (Goods and Services Tax) Act 1999 ("Australian GST Act"), §9-10(4). Similarly, "money" is excluded from the definition of "goods" for Singapore GST purposes. Goods and Services Tax Act (Cap. 117A, 2005 Rev Ed) ("Singapore GST Act"), §2(1).

11. See, e.g., Explanatory Memorandum, A New Tax System (Goods and Services Tax) Bill 1999, para 3.7: "Money that is provided as consideration (payment) for a supply is not in itself a supply—§9-10(2). Otherwise money supplied as payment for a supply could be a taxable supply in itself."

12. For instance, the "non-supply" treatment under Australian law at *supra* note 11 does not apply where "money is provided as consideration for a supply that is a supply of money." Australian GST Act, §9-10(4). Apart from its almost circular drafting, this legal approach to recognizing exchange transactions for VAT purposes is rather unusual, in that the relevant transaction or supply that is usually recognized is not the supply of money for money, but the service of exchanging one currency for another, with the consideration being the commission or "spread."

13. In Australia, currency exchange transactions are treated as "input taxed" (i.e., exempt) financial supplies. A New Tax System (Goods and Services Tax) Regulations 1999, subregulation 40-5.09(3). Similarly, transactions "concerning currency, bank notes and coins used as legal tender" are exempt from VAT in the European Union (EU). Council Directive 2006/112/EC of 28 November 2006 ("EU VAT Directive"), Article 135(1)(e).

14. See the judgment of the Court of Justice of the European Union (CJEU) in *Skatterverket v. David Hedqvist* Case C-264/14 ("*Hedqvist*") at para. 36. See also the Opinion of the Advocate General in the *Hedqvist* case at paras. 38 and 39, where she noted that "the objective of the exemption for transactions concerning means of payment is to not impede the convertibility of pure means of payment by levying VAT," and that "in the interest of the smooth flow of payments, the conversion of currencies is as unencumbered as possible".

15. See, e.g., the definition of "money" in §2 of the Singapore GST Act and §195-1 of the Australian GST Act. Similarly, the EU VAT Directive excludes collectors' items such as coins of numismatic interest from the scope of the exemption for currency transactions. EU VAT Directive, Article 135(1)(e). This distinction between money as a medium of exchange and as a *rem* is also recognized in other areas of law. For example, in the UK case of *Moss v Hancock* (not a tax case), a gold five-pound piece that has legal tender status was considered to have been sold to a dealer in old and curious things as a subject of sale, and did not pass in currency. [1899] 2 QB 111 at 116–17.

16. This distinction between widely used cryptoassets and those that are used only on their native platforms has been acknowledged for regulatory purposes in some jurisdictions. See, e.g., Singapore's proposed Payment Services Bill that distinguishes

between widely used virtual currencies and limited purpose virtual currencies. A cryptoasset that satisfies the general definition of "virtual currency" as a medium of exchange accepted by the public or a section of the public, as payment for goods or services or the discharge of a debt, may nevertheless be described as a "limited purpose virtual currency" if it is or is intended to be, *inter alia*, "used only for payment of or part payment of, or exchange for, goods or services, or both, provided by the issuer of the digital representation of value, or provided by such merchants as may be specified by the issuer." Payment Services Bill, Second Schedule, Part II, http://www.mas.gov.sg/~/media/resource/publications/consult_papers/2017/Annex%20B%20to%20Consultation%20on%20Proposed%20Payment%20Services%20Bill%20MAS%20P0212017.pdf (accessed November 8, 2018).

17. Alternatively, utility tokens could be viewed as vouchers, the issuance or subsequent supply of which may trigger a VAT liability where the VAT treatment of the goods or services for which the voucher is redeemable is sufficiently known in advance, for instance, in the EU. Council Directive (EU) 2016/1065 of 27 June 2016 amending Directive 2006/112/EC as regards the treatment of vouchers.

18. Examples include Microsoft, Expedia, Newegg, Dish Network, OKCupid, and eGifter. However, some commentators have taken the view that bitcoins are not used as a medium of exchange but rather a speculative store of value. See e.g. Rosa Maria Lastra and Jason Grant Allen, Policy Department for Economic, Scientific and Quality of Life Policies *Virtual Currencies in the Eurosystem: Challenges Ahead*, Monetary Dialogue July 2018, p. 21, http://www.europarl.europa.eu/committees/en/econ/monetary-dialogue.html (accessed November 8, 2018).

19. In this chapter, we use the term 'traditional currency' to refer to official currencies (i.e. currencies issued by central banks or other official or officially sanctioned issuers) and deposits in the books of commercial banks (which are contractual claims on official currency).

20. As noted by the Advocate General in her Opinion to the European Court of Justice in the *Hedqvist* case, the "legal tender is also subject to [the risks of lack of stable value and vulnerability to fraud of bitcoins] to the same extent." *Supra* note 14.

21. Australia, which has amended its GST legislation to treat digital currencies like money for GST purposes, is an example of a growing trend toward recognizing certain types of cryptoassets as a medium of exchange for tax purposes; We stress that this paper does not advocate that as regards governmental policy toward the use of currencies, tax neutrality is an absolute objective. There may be non-tax policy reasons why countries may wish to tax cryptocurrency transactions less (or more) preferentially. However, where tax neutrality is pursued, the conclusion above stands.

22. *Supra* note 14.

23. *Supra* note 14. The Court was able to apply a purposive approach to interpreting this provision because of discrepancies between different language versions—not every language version of Article 135(1)(e) requires each currency (in whatever form) concerned by the transactions to have legal tender status. Given that imposing VAT on exchange transactions involving "non-traditional currencies" such as bitcoin would create the same difficulties with respect to determining the taxable amount and the

amount of VAT deductible, the Court concluded that not extending the exemption to "currencies (that) have been accepted by the parties to a transaction as an alternative to legal tender and have no purpose other than to be a means of payment" would deprive Article 135(1)(e) of part of its effect. *Hedqvist*, 48–53.

24. This would probably include all altcoins that forked from the original Bitcoin blockchain, such as Bitcoin Gold.

25. Hence, the HMRC has taken the position that no VAT is due on the value of bitcoin or "similar cryptocurrencies" when exchanged for fiat currencies. 2014 Paper, *supra* note 6.

26. Alternatively, where a cryptoasset is not sufficiently akin to a means of payment to be treated like money for VAT purposes, it could be argued that it should then be viewed as a pure investment asset like gold, which, on that basis, should be excluded from the base of the tax. While it is true that most VATs will not tax—either by way of exemption or zero-rating—the supply of certain investment grade precious metals (for instance, in the EU, investment gold of at least 99.5% purity), it seems difficult to argue for most if not all cryptoassets that their functionality—including the way in which they are created and traded—is so akin to pure gold, for instance, that they should be awarded the same VAT treatment. At the very least, such treatment could only be achieved under any of the VAT systems that we are familiar with subject to a prior law change.

27. See *Overstock.com Now Accepts All Major Alt-Coins Including Bitcoin Cash through Integration with Shape Shift (August 08, 2017)*, http://investors.overstock.com/mobile.view?c=131091&v=203&d=1&id=2292540 (accessed November 8, 2018).

28. See https://www.morestamps.global/ (accessed November 8, 2018).

29. Where the disposal and acquisition of a cryptoasset is treated as a barter transaction, it is necessary to have a specific rule to recognize any taxable amounts in the tax cost of the cryptoasset acquired so as to address the problem of double taxation on its subsequent disposal.

30. See IRS, Notice 2014-21, https://www.irs.gov/pub/irs-drop/n-14-21.pdf (accessed November 8, 2018).

31. Cryptocurrencies are a subset of virtual currencies. Virtual currencies are 'digital representations of value, issued by private developers and denominated in their own unit of account' which 'can be obtained, stored, accessed, and transacted electronically, and can be used for a variety of purposes, as long as the transacting parties agree to use them'. Cryptocurrencies are decentralized virtual currencies using techniques from cryptography for their operations. See Dong He, Karl Habermeier, Ross Leckow, Vikram Kyriakos-Saad, Hiroko Oura, Tahsin Saadi Sedik, Natalia Stetsenko, Concepcion Verdugo-Yepes, Virtual Currencies and Beyond: Initial Considerations, IMF Staff Discussion Note SDN/16/03, Jan. 2016, https://www.imf.org/external/pubs/ft/sdn/2016/sdn1603.pdf (accessed November 8, 2018).

32. See ATO, Tax Determination TD 2014/25, *Income Tax: Is Bitcoin a "Foreign Currency" for the Purposes of Division 775 of the Income Tax Assessment Act 1997*, http://law.ato.gov.au/atolaw/DownloadNoticePDF.htm?DocId=TXD%2FTD201425%2FNAT%2FATO%2F00001&filename=pdf/pbr/td2014-025.pdf&PiT=99991231235958 (accessed November 8, 2018).

33. See ATO Tax Determination TD 2014/26, *Income Tax: Is Bitcoin a "CGT Asset" for the Purposes of Subsection 108-5(1) of the Income Tax Assessment Act 1997?*, http://law.ato.gov.au/atolaw/DownloadNoticePDF.htm?DocId=TXD%2FTD201426%2FNAT%2FATO%2F00001&filename=pdf/pbr/td2014-026.pdf&PiT=99991231235958 (accessed November 8, 2018).

34. See 2014 Paper, *supra* note 6. The HMRC has clarified in the 2018 Paper that cryptoassets are not considered currency or money for individual income tax purposes, but it is unclear if the same position will be adopted for businesses. 2018 Paper, *supra* note 6.

35. This is the case for those cryptoassets that meet the newly introduced definition of "digital currency," that is, essentially any digital unit of value that has all of the following characteristics: (1) fully interchangeable with another unit of the same digital currency for the purpose of its use as payment, (2) can be provided as payment for any type of purchases, (3) generally available to the public free of any substantial restrictions, (4) not denominated in a country's currency, (5) the value is not derived from or dependent on anything else, and (6) does not give an entitlement or privileges to receive something else; Australian GST Act, §195-1, as amended in 2017. The definition was framed deliberately broadly and focuses on functionality as currency rather than technology, requiring in particular that "the value of a digital currency must derive from the market's assessment of the value of the currency for the purposes of exchange, despite it having no intrinsic value". Explanatory Memorandum, Treasury Laws Amendment (2017 Measures No. 6) Bill 2017, para. 1.21.

36. *Supra* note 32 at para. 33.

37. *Supra* note 32 at paras. 35 and 36.

38. Of course, taxable property and services sold for cryptoassets should be subject to sales tax; see, e.g., New York State Department of Finance and Taxation, *Tax Department Policy on Transactions Using Convertible Virtual Currencies*, Technical Memorandum TSB-M-14(5)C, (7)I, (17)S, https://www.tax.ny.gov/pdf/memos/multitax/m14_5c_7i_17s.pdf (accessed November 8, 2018).

39. This should be distinguished from a token whose value is backed by a security, which is essentially a "secondary."

40. See, e.g., the EU cases of *Velvet & Steel Immobilien und Handels GmbH v Finanzamt Hamburg-Eimsbüttel* Case C-455/05 at para. 24 and *Skandinaviska Enskilda Banken AB Momsgrupp v Skatteverket* Case C-540/09 at para. 21.

41. Thus, in *Granton Advertising BV v Inspecteur van de Belastingdienst Haaglanden/kantoor Den Haag* Case C-461/12, the CJEU held that cards that entitled their holders to a certain number of goods and services on preferential terms from retailers and businesses (commonly referred to as "vouchers") do not constitute "securities" for the purpose of the EU VAT exemption.

42. See, by analogy, the analysis of the CJEU in *Card Protection Plan Ltd vCommissioners of Customs and Excise* Case C-349/96 in relation to complex transactions involving several elements—in that case, both exempt insurance services and other taxable card holder services.

43. Of course, to the extent that both traditional debt and equity features are embedded in a cryptoasset, the usual debt/equity hybrid mismatch concerns remain.

44. For example, ATLANT tokens (ATL) allow investors to buy unique, property-specific tokens that represent partial ownership of a particular real estate asset, and investors are paid a portion of their rental income from those properties.

45. For example, Singapore currently treats the supply of "virtual currencies" as provision of services. See Inland Revenue Authority of Singapore, Sale of Virtual Currency, https://www.iras.gov.sg/IRASHome/GST/GST-registered-businesses/Specific-business-sectors/e-Commerce/#title5 (accessed November 8, 2018).

46. OECD (2017), *International VAT/GST Guidelines*, OECD Publishing, Paris, https://doi.org/10.1787/9789264271401-en (accessed November 8, 2018).

47. Unless, of course, tax authorities were to accept tax payment in cryptoassets—something that has reportedly been under consideration in several U.S. states; see, e.g., Bitcoin Center New York City, Cryptocurrency & Law: A Comprehensive Overview of 50 States' Guidance and Regulations on Blockchain and Digital Currency (March 6, 2018), https://bitcoincenternyc.com/bitcoin-news/bitcoin-blockchain-cryptocurrency-laws-50-states/ (accessed November 8, 2018).

48. It is understood that other methods of achieving distributed consensus are also currently being researched and developed.

49. It has been estimated that the Bitcoin network currently consumes at least 2.55 gigawatts of electricity, and the consumption could reach 7.67 gigawatts in the future. See Alex de Vries, *Commentary: Bitcoin's Growing Energy Problem*, Joule, Volume 2, Issue 5 (May 16, 2018) at pp. 801–05, https://www.cell.com/action/showPdf?pii=S2542-4351%2818%2930177-6 (accessed November 8, 2018). In addition, mining equipment, which has a relatively short useful life, generates electronic waste.

50. Mining pools consist of miners that pool their resources together for the purposes of increasing their collective computational power in mining a cryptoasset (and accordingly, the likelihood of finding a block) and splitting the block reward based on the amount of work contributed by each miner.

51. See Internal Revenue Service, *Notice 2014-21*, 4, https://www.irs.gov/pub/irs-drop/n-14-21.pdf (accessed November 8, 2018).

52. Such an approach faces an additional difficulty—that the network hashrate is not constant but fluctuates constantly.

53. Consideration should also be given to the treatment of losses that may arise due to market fluctuations in the price of the cryptoasset, resulting in the costs of carrying out mining operations exceeding the value of the block reward.

54. See OECD (2017), Model Tax Convention on Income and on Capital: Condensed Version 2017, OECD Publishing, Paris, https://doi.org/10.1787/mtc_cond-2017-en ("OECD Model Convention"), 97.

55. Block rewards received by miners are unlikely to qualify as royalty, since the legal arrangement is not one where the community rewards the miners for using their equipment, but one where the community incentivizes the miners to achieve a certain outcome, so Article 12 of United Nations Model Double Taxation Convention

between Developed and Developing Countries (which, unlike the OECD Model Convention, still includes payments for use of equipment) does not apply.

56. See OECD (2018), *Tax Challenges Arising from Digitalization—Interim Report 2018: Inclusive Framework on BEPS*, OECD/G20 Base Erosion and Profit Shifting Project, OECD Publishing, Paris, http://dx.doi.org/10.1787/9789264293083-en (accessed November 8, 2018).

57. 2014 Paper, *supra* note 6.

58. See Bundesministerium der Finanzen, *Umsatzsteuerliche Behandlung von Bitcoin und anderen sog. virtuellen Währungen; EuGH-Urteil vom 22. Oktober 2015, C-264/14, Hedqvist,* https://www.bundesfinanzministerium.de/Content/DE/Downloads/BMF_Schreiben/Steuerarten/Umsatzsteuer/Umsatzsteuer-Anwendungserlass/2018-02-27-umsatzsteuerliche-behandlung-von-bitcoin-und-anderen-sog-virtuellen-waehrungen.pdf;jsessionid=4A4C61D8AEBF97211362455DDD2BF211?__blob=publicationFile&v=1 (accessed November 8, 2018).

59. An analogy could be drawn here with the situation of a farmer who, in return for compensation, agreed to discontinue milk production under an EU agricultural policy scheme; the CJEU ruled that the farmer did not make a taxable supply of services—that is, the service of agreeing not to do something—and so did not owe VAT on the compensation received. In making the payment to the farmer the Court found that the EU did not acquire a particular service for its own use, but instead "acted in the common interest of promoting the proper functioning of the Community milk market" in thus for the Community as a whole; see *Jürgen Mohr v Finanzamt Bad Segeberg* Case C-215/94, para. 21.

60. For a transaction to be covered by the payment exemption under Article 135(1)(d) of the VAT Directive, the services provided must, viewed broadly, form a distinct whole and effectively fulfill the specific essential functions of the process of transfer of funds itself, i.e. the service must not merely be an input to the exempt payment service, but must be the exempt service itself. This would involve, *inter alia*, the assumption of 'liability as regards the achievement of the changes in the legal and financial situation that are characteristic of the existence of an exempted transaction of transfer or payment' by the provider of the service. See *Bookit Ltd v Commissioners for Her Majesty's Revenue and Customs* Case C-607/14 and *National Exhibition Centre Ltd v Commissioners for Her Majesty's Revenue and Customs* Case C-130/15. In a proof-of-stake system, the forger validates the transactions that form the next block in the blockchain, which is essential for the accuracy of the transactions and for the avoidance of the problem of double-spending. Until the block is added by the forger, the transaction is not validated, and payment is not effected. As such, the services of the forger arguably constitute the actual payment and are likely to be exempt.

61. There is a separate issue of whether such marketing expenses should be deductible against the taxable income of the issuer, and how to quantify the amount deductible, but this will not be discussed in this chapter.

62. This also raises a problem of involuntariness—should a person who receives a token in the course of an airdrop exercise be taxed on such gain even though that

person has done nothing to obtain that token and does not subjectively want to receive that token? This same problem also applies to crypto transactions more generally, since the owner of a digital wallet cannot reject a payment made by another person to the public address or key of that digital wallet. In jurisdictions where a gift tax is levied on the giver instead of the recipient, an argument could be made that the incidence of tax should fall on the issuer or payer of the token, rather than the recipient.

63. *Supra* note 51.

64. See Letter from the State Secretary for Finance to the permanent commission of Finance dated May 28, 2018.

65. See ATO, *Cryptocurrency Used in Business* (last modified: June 29, 2018), https://www.ato.gov.au/General/Gen/Tax-treatment-of-crypto-currencies-in-Australia---specifically-bitcoin/?page=3#Cryptocurrency_used_in_business (accessed November 8, 2018).

66. ICOs can be a form of token pre-financing but can also be an offering of tokens that have already been created. It usually refers to issuance of tokens by businesses with no or little track record. The term "reverse ICO" refers to the raising of funds through the issuance of tokens as opposed to shares by existing real-world businesses. The focus of the discussion here is on token pre-financing only.

67. See template SAFT for token presale, https://saftproject.com/static/Form-of-SAFT-for-token-pre-sale.docx (accessed November 8, 2018).

68. A SAFT is not a debt as it lacks a maturity date and interest rate, and there is no recourse for the investor if the network launch does not take place.

69. Notable examples include Binance and Iconomi. In the case of Binance, the company has committed to buying back tokens with profits until 50% of the tokens have been repurchased and burned.

70. See § 84(3) of Canada's Income Tax Act, which deems a shareholder to have received a dividend in the event of a share redemption to the extent that the redemption price of the share exceeds its paid-up capital.

71. Although at least one expert is of the view that cryptography might be cracked in the future, and as long as the records are preserved, transactions can be traced. See http://www.businessinsider.com/cambridge-academic-cryptocurrency-users-anonymity-will-not-last-2018-1?r=UK&IR=T. (accessed November 8, 2018).

72. See, e.g., in relation to AML/CFT regulations: Financial Action Task Force (FATF), Statement on Regulation Virtual Assets, Paris, France (October 19, 2018), http://www.fatf-gafi.org/publications/fatfrecommendations/documents/regulation-virtual-assets.html (accessed November 8, 2018).

73. There are studies that show that third-party web trackers and cookies may overcome blockchain privacy. See, e.g., Steven Goldfelder, Harry Kalodner, Dillon Reisman, and Arvind Narayanan, *When the Cookie Meets the Blockchain: Privacy Risks of Web Payments via Cryptocurrencies*, https://arxiv.org/pdf/1708.04748.pdf (accessed November 8, 2018).

Chapter 10

1. For example, Forbes magazine recently argued that "Blockchain technology's disruptive force innovates the way our data are stored, allowing users to fully control personal details they would like to share in public. Leveraging the potential of blockchain technology and decentralization may well be the key to protecting our privacy." July 31, 2018, https://www.forbes.com/sites/shermanlee/2018/07/31/privacy-revolution-how-blockchain-is-reshaping-our-economy/#45929f701086 (accessed July 7, 2019).

2. http://zerocash-project.org/how_zerocash_works, accessed March 1, 2019.

3. "Retconning," or the imposition of "retroactive continuity," is a term from the world of comic books, where long-running characters" origin stories are shifted so as to enable new, internally consistent interpretations of that character.

4. It is unclear whether the reference to "non-residents" in that article applies specifically to e-residents.

Chapter 11

1. This chapter draws on a larger report from the same authors for the Asian Development Bank: *Distributed Ledger Technology and Digital Assets: Policy and Regulatory Challenges in Asia* (Asian Deveopment Bank, June 2019). It does not represent the views of the Asian Development Bank https://papers.ssrn.com/sol3/papers.cfm?abstract_id=3414408 (last visited July 10, 2019). The Asian Development Bank is the sole owner of the copyright in ADB Contribution developed or contributed for this Work, and has granted permission to the Publisher to use said ADB-copyrighted Contribution for this Work (, and to make the Contribution available under an open access license.) The views expressed in this publication are those of the authors and do not necessarily reflect the views and policies of the Asian Development Bank (ADB) or its Board of Governors or the governments they represent. ADB does not guarantee the accuracy of the data included in this publication and accepts no responsibility for any consequence of their use. By making any designation of or reference to a particular territory or geographic area, or by using the term "country" in this document, ADB does not intend to make any judgements as to the legal or other status of any territory or area.

2. For discussion of this viewpoint, see Dirk Zetzsche, Ross Buckley, and Douglas Arner, "The Distributed Liability of Distributed Ledgers: Legal Risks and Blockchain, 2018 Illinois Law Review, p. 1361.

3. Ibid., p. 1407.

4. Focusing on legal and governance issues only: Trautman, L. J. 2016, "Is Disruptive Blockchain Technology the Future of Financial Services?," *The Consumer Finance Law Quarterly Report*, vol. 69, pp. 232–42; Reyes, C. 2016, "Moving Beyond Bitcoin to an Endogenous Theory of Decentralized Ledger Technology Regulation: An Initial Proposal," *Villanova Law Review*, vol. 61, no.1; Wessel, R, O'Brolcháin, F., and Haynes, P. 2016, "Governance in Blockchain Technologies & Social Contract Theories," *Ledger*, vol.1, pp. 134–51; Kiviat, T. I. 2016, "Beyond Bitcoin: Issues in Regulation Blockchain Transactions," *Duke Law Journal*, vol. 65, pp. 569–608; Cohen, R. L., and Tyler, D. C. 2016,

"Blockchain's Three Capital Markets Innovations Explained," *International Financial Law Review*, http://www.iflr.com/Article/3563116/Blockchains-three-capital-markets-innovations-explained.html.; International Organization of Securities Commissions (2017), *Research Report on Financial Technologies (Fintech)*. Available at: https://www.iosco.org/library/pubdocs/pdf/IOSCOPD554.pdf; European Securities and Markets Authority (2015), *Report—The Distributed Ledger Technology Applied to Securities Markets*. Available at: https://www.esma.europa.eu/system/files_force/library/dlt_report_-_esma50-1121423017-285.pdf; Medcraft, G, Australian Securities and Investments Commission (2015), *Op-ed: Blockchain* [Press release]. Available at: http://asic.gov.au/about-asic/media-centre/asic-responds/op-ed-blockchain/. It has been estimated that "distributed ledger technology could reduce banks' infrastructure costs attributable to cross-border payments, securities trading and regulatory compliance by between $15–20 billion per annum by 2022": see Santander InnoVentures, Oliver Wyman and Anthemis Group 2015, The Fintech 2.0 Paper: Rebooting Financial Services, http://santanderinnoventures.com/fintech2/; World Economic Forum (with Deloitte) (2016), *The Future of Financial Infrastructure—An Ambitious Look at How Blockchain Can Reshape Financial Services.*, Available at: www3.weforum.org/docs/WEF_The_future_of_financial_infrastructure.pdf. *See also* IBM (2017), *IBM Blockchain*. Available at: https://www.ibm.com/blockchain/ (last visited July 10, 2017); DuPont, Q., & Maurer, B. 2015, "Ledgers and Law in the Blockchain," *King's Review*, http://kingsreview.co.uk/articles/ledgers-and-law-in-the-blockchain/>; Micheler, E., & von der Heyde, L. 2016, "Holding, Clearing and Settling Securities through Blockchain/Distributed Ledger Technology: Creating an Efficient System by Empowering Investors," *Journal of International Banking & Financial Law*, vol. 31, no. 11; Paech, P. 2016, "Securities, Intermediation and the Blockchain: An Inevitable Choice between Liquidity and Legal Certainty?," *Uniform Law Review*, vol. 21, no. 4.

5. Wenhao, S, and Kim, M. (2018) *Cryptocurrency Laws and Regulations in Asia*. Available at: https://www.vantageasia.com/cryptocurrency-law-asia/; Library of Congress, *Regulation of Cryptocurrency: China*. Available at: https://www.loc.gov/law/help/cryptocurrency/china.php.

6. Wenhao & Kim, ibid.

7. James, A. 2018, "China Leads World In Blockchain Patent Applications." Bitcoinist. Available at: http://bitcoinist.com/china-leads-world-in-blockchain-patent-applications/>; Zhao, W. 2018, "12 Chinese Banks Say They Deployed Blockchain in 2017," *Coindesk*. Available at: https://www.coindesk.com/12-chinese-banks-adopted-blockchain-apps-in-2017-filings-show/.

8. Wenhao, S. and Kim, M. 2018, *Cryptocurrency Laws and Regulations in Asia*. Available at: https://www.vantageasia.com/cryptocurrency-law-asia/; "People's Bank of China to Build Blockchain and Crypto Research Centre to Test Digital Currencies," *Cyrptoslate* 2018. Available at: https://cryptoslate.com/peoples-bank-of-china-to-build-blockchain-and-crypto-research-center-to-test-digital-currencies/; Zhao, W. 2018, "PBoC-Backed Blockchain Trade Finance Platform Enters Test Phase," Coindesk. Available at: https://www.coindesk.com/pboc-backed-blockchain-trade-finance-platform-enters-test-phase/.

9. Library of Congress, *Regulation of Cryptocurrency: China*. Available at: https://www.loc.gov/law/help/cryptocurrency/china.php; Wenhao, S. and Kim, M. 2018,

Cryptocurrency Laws and Regulations in Asia. Available at: https://www.vantageasia.com/cryptocurrency-law-asia/.

10. Lee, J. (2018), "Singapore Wary of Issuing Digital Currencies to Public: MAS Chief Ravi Menon," The Straits Times, January 15. Available at: https://www.straitstimes.com/business/companies-markets/singapore-wary-of-issuing-digital-currencies-to-public-mas-chief.

11. Monetary Authority of Singapore. 2018, Reply to Parliamentary Question on Banning the Trading of Bitcoin. http://www.mas.gov.sg/News-and-Publications/Parliamentary-Replies/2018/Reply-to-Parliamnetary-Question-on-banning-the-trading-0f-bitcoin-currency-orcryptocurrency.aspx.

12. Ibid.

13. Monetary Authority of Singapore. 2017. *MAS Clarifies Regulatory Position on the Offer of Digital Tokens in Singapore,* [Press release]. August 1. Available at: http://www.mas.gov.sg/News-and-Publications/Media-Releases/2017/MAS-clarifies-regulatory-position-on-the-offer-of-digital-tokens-in-Singapore.

14. Yoo-Chul, K. 2018, *BOK Eyeing Digital Currencies,* The Korea Times, http://www.koreatimes.co.kr/www/news/biz/2018/05/602_248317.html.

15. Financial Services Commission. 2018. [Press release]. Available at: https://www.fsc.go.kr/eng/new_press/releases.jsp?menu=01&bbsid=BBS0048.

16. Keihara, L. 2018, "BOJ Deputy Governor Doubts Digital Currency Will Enhance Monetary Policy', Reuters, October 20. Available at: https://www.reuters.com/article/us-japan-economy-boj-cryptocurrency/boj-deputy-governor-doubts-digital-currency-will-enhance-monetary-policy-idUSKCN1MU07X?il=0.

17. Library of Congress, *Regulation of Cryptocurrency: Japan,* https://www.loc.gov/law/help/cryptocurrency/japan.php (last visited June 18, 2019).

18. Government of Japan, https://www.japan.go.jp/abenomics/innovation/index.html. (last visited June 18, 2019).

19. Masujima, M. 2017. *Japan's Virtual Currency Regulations and Its Recent Developments.* Mori, Hamada, and Matsumototo,. Available at: https://events.eventact.com/ki2/crypto/Masakazu%20Masujima%20(Mori%20Hamada%20&%20Matsumoto)-Japans%20Virtual%20Currency%20Regulation%20and%20its%20Recent%20Developments.pdf.

20. Norman T.L. Chan, "Crypto-assets and Money", Keynote Speech at Treasury Markets Summit 2018, Sep. 21, 2018, available at: https://www.hkma.gov.hk/eng/key-information/speech-speakers/ntlchan/20180921-1.shtml (last visited July 10, 2019).

21. The Government of Hong Kong (2014) *LCQ1: Monitoring the Use of Bitcoins* [Press release], January 8. Available at: https://www.info.gov.hk/gia/general/201401/08/P201401080357.htm.

22. Hong Kong Monetary Authority (2017), *Hong Kong and Singapore Launch a Joint Project on Cross-Border Trade and Trade Finance Platform* [Press release], November 15. Available at: https://www.hkma.gov.hk/eng/key-information/press-releases/2017/20171115-6.shtml.

23. Securities and Futures Commission (2018), *SFC Reprimands and Fines Huatai Financial Holdings (Hong Kong) Limited $800,000 over Naked Short Selling* [Press release], September 17. Available at: https://www.sfc.hk/edistributionWeb/gateway/EN/news-and-announcements/news/doc?refNo=18PR106.

24. Gorbiano, M. I. 2018, "Digital Rupiah Study to Be Completed in 2020: BI," The Jakarta Post, February1. Available at: http://www.thejakartapost.com/news/2018/02/01/digital-rupiah-study-to-be-completed-in-2020-bi.html; (2018), "Bank Indonesia Studies Use of Blockchain," Fintech News, May 17. Available at: https://www.fintechnews.org/bank-indonesia-studies-use-blockchain/.

25. Reserve Bank of India (2018), *Annual Report*. Available at: https://rbi.org.in/scripts/AnnualReportPublications.aspx?Id=1229.

26. Ministry of Finance: Republic of Indonesia (2018), *Bitcoin Is Not in Line with Law*" [Press release], January 1. Available at: https://www.kemenkeu.go.id/en/publications/news/minister-of-finance-bitcoin-is-not-in-line-with-law/; "Cryptocurrencies Decided as Future Trading Commodity." *The Jakarta Post,* June 4, 2018. Available at: http://www.thejakartapost.com/news/2018/06/04/cryptocurrencies-decided-as-future-trading-commodity.html.

27. Reserve Bank of India (2018), *Prohibition on Dealing in Virtual Currencies (VCs),* Available at: https://rbi.org.in/Scripts/NotificationUser.aspx?Id=11243.

28. Okoritas Jasa Keuangan (2017), *OJK Issues Regulation on IT-Based Lending Services,* [Press release], January 10. Available at: https://www.ojk.go.id/en/berita-dan-kegiatan/siaran-pers/Pages/Press-Release-OJK-Issues-Regulation-on-It-Based-Lending-Services.aspx; Ariffin, E. (2018), *Indonesia Embraces Blockchain,* The Asean Post, August 23. Available at: https://theaseanpost.com/article/indonesia-embraces-blockchain; "How Is Indonesia Implementing Blockchain Technology?," Fintech News Singapore April 10, 2018. Available at: http://www.fintechnews.sg/18744/indonesia/blockchain-use-case-indonesia/.

29. Jaitley, A. (2018), Minister of Finance, Budget 2018, Speech of Minister of Finance, Parliament of India. Available at: https://www.indiabudget.gov.in/ub2018-19/bs/bs.pdf.

30. Ibid.

31. "Cryptocurrencies Decided as Future Trading Commodity," The Jakarta Post, June 4, 2018. Available at: http://www.thejakartapost.com/news/2018/06/04/cryptocurrencies-decided-as-future-trading-commodity.html.

32. Reserve Bank of India (2018), *Prohibition on Dealing in Virtual Currencies (VCs)*, [Press release], April 6. Available at: https://rbi.org.in/Scripts/NotificationUser.aspx?Id=11243; Ghoshal, D. 2018, "One of India's Biggest Cryptocurrency Exchanges Is Shutting Down," Quartz India, September 28. Available at: https://qz.com/india/1405918/zebpay-a-major-indian-bitcoin-exchange-is-closing/

33. Zetzsche, D., Buckley, R., and Arner, D. W. 2018., "The Distributed Liability of Distributed Ledgers: Legal Risks of Blockchain," University of Illinois Law Review, vol.4, pp. 1361–406.

34. In a proof-of-work system, multiple servers ("nodes") all try to solve one (generally complex and resource-intensive) mathematical problem. The first node to solve the problem is compensated for the "work" it has performed, while all others use the solution provided by the first node to verify that the problem has been correctly solved; thereby the solution to the mathematical problem assumes the function of a unique, one-time-use code.

35. Hashing is a form of cryptography that converts data into a unique string of text.

36. Mougayar, W. 2015, *Understanding the Blockchain, O'REILLY*. Available at: https://www.oreilly.com/ideas/understanding-the-blockchain.

37. *See* Szabo, N. 1997, *The Idea of Smart Contracts*. Available at: http://www. fon.hum.uva.nl/rob/courses/InformationInSpeech/CDROM/Literature/ LOTwinterschool2006/szabo.best.vwh.net/idea.html; Szabo, N. 2002, *A Formal Language for Analyzing Contracts*. Available at: http://www.fon.hum.uva.nl/rob/Courses/ InformationInSpeech/CDROM/Literature/LOTwinterschool2006/szabo.best.vwh.net/ contractlanguage.html>; Casey, A. J., and Niblett, A. 2017, *Self-Driving Contracts*. Available at: https://ssrn.com/abstract=2927459, pp. 26–32; Fairfield, J. A. T. 2014, "Smart Contracts, Bitcoin Bots and Consumer Protection," *Washington & Lee Law Review Online*, vol. 71, no 2. pp. 36–41; Kõlvart, M., Poola, M„ and Rull, A, 2016, "Smart Contracts" in Kerikmäe, T., and Rull, A. (eds.) (2016), *The Future of Law and eTechnologies*. Springer pp. 133–49; Koulu, R. 2016, "Blockchains and Online Dispute Resolution: Smart Contracts as an Alternative to Enforcement," *SCRIPTed*, vol. 13, no. 1; Levy, K. E.C. 2017, "Book-Smart, Not Street-Smart: Blockchain-Based Smart Contracts and the Social Workings of Law," *Engaging Science, Technology, and Society*, vol. 3, no. 1 Lim, C., Saw, T.J., and Sergeant, C. 2016, *Smart Contracts: Bridging the Gap Between Expectation and Reality*, Oxford Legal Stud. Res. Paper, July 11, 2016. Available at: https://www.law.ox.ac.uk/business-law-blog/blog/2016/07/smart-contracts-bridging-gap-between-expectation-and-reality; Werbach, K, and Cornell, N. 2017, "Contracts Ex Machina," *Duke Law Journal*, vol. 67, no. 313. Available at: https://ssrn.com/abstract=2936294>; Wright, A. and De Filippi, P. 2015. *Decentralized Blockchain Technology and the Rise of Lex Cryptographia*. Available at: https://papers.ssrn.com/sol3/papers.cfm?abstract_id=2580664, pp. 10–12.

38. See Didenko, A., and Buckley, R. P. 2018, "The Evolution of Currency: Cash to Cryptos to Sovereign Digital Currencies," *Fordham International Law Journal*, vol. 42. Available at: https://ssrn.com/abstract=3256066.

39. https://coinmarketcap.com/.

40. Ibid. at 40–41.

41. Ibid. at 36–39.

42. Didenko and Buckley, pp. 41–42.

43. Ibid. p. 42.

44. Financial Stability Board (2018), *Crypto-Asset Markets: Potential Channels for Future Financial Stability Implications*, Available at: https://www.fsb.org/2018/10/crypto-asset-markets-potential-channels-for-future-financial-stability-implications/ (last visited July 10, 2019). A cryptoasset is defined as "a type of private asset that depends primarily on cryptography and distributed ledger or similar technology as part of their perceived or inherent value" p. 1.

45. For a more detailed discussion of available approaches see Didenko and Buckley, R. P., pp. 49–50.

46. Didenko and Buckley, pp. 47–49.

47. Wandhöfer, R. 2017, *The Future of Digital Retail Payments in Europe: A Role for Central Bank Issued Crypto Cash?* Available at: http://www.ecb.europa.eu/pub/conferences/ shared/pdf/20171130_ECB_BdI_conference/payments_conference_2017_ academic_paper_wandhoefer.pdf>; Bech, M., and Garratt, R. 2017. *"Central Bank Cryptocurrencies,"* BIS Quarterly Review. Available at: https://www.bis.org/publ/ qtrpdf/r_qt1709f.htm>; Barrdear, J., and Kumhof, M., 2016, *The Macroeconomics of Central Bank Issued Digital Currencies*, Bank of England Staff Working Paper

No 605. Available at: https://www.bankofengland.co.uk/-/media/boe/files/working-paper/2016/the-macroeconomics-of-central-bank-issued-digital-currencies.pdf?la=en&hash=341B602838707E5D6FC26884588C912A721B1DC1; Koning, J. P. 2016, *Fedcoin: A Central Bank-Issued Cryptocurrency.* Available at: https://www.r3.com/wp-content/uploads/2017/06/fedcoin_central-bank_R3.pdf; Engert, W. and Fung, B. 2017, *Central Bank Digital Currency: Motivations and Implications,* Bank of Canada Staff Discussion Paper 2017-16. Available at: https://www.bankofcanada.ca/wp-content/uploads/2017/11/sdp2017-16.pdf   ; Danezis, G., and Meiklejohn, S. 2016, *Centrally Banked Cryptocurrencies.* Available at: https://eprint.iacr.org/2015/502.pdf.; Didenko and Buckley, pp. 49–50.

48. Burgos, A., and Batavia, B. 2018, *Currency in the Digital Era,* Central Bank of Brazil, Working Paper. Available at: https://www.bcb.gov.br/htms/public/inovtec/Currency-in-the-Digital-Era.pdf.

49. Lane, T. 2018, *Decrypting "Crypto,"* Bank of Canada. Available at: https://www.bankofcanada.ca/2018/10/decrypting-crypto/.

50. Library of Congress, *Regulation of Cryptocurrency: China,* Available at: https://www.loc.gov/law/help/cryptocurrency/china.php.

51. Kori, H.2018), "Cryptocurrencies Filling The Caribbean Banking Void," *Forbes,* May 2018. Available at: https://www.forbes.com/sites/korihale/2018/05/29/cryptocurrencies-filling-the-caribbean-banking-void/#521dda9f5efa.

52. White, L. (2018), *The World's First Central Bank Electronic Money Has Come—And Gone: Ecuador, 2014–2018,* Cato Institute. Available at: https://www.cato.org/blog/worlds-first-central-bank-electronic-money-has-come-gone-ecuador-2014-2018.

53. Ummelas, O. (2018), "Estonia Scales Down Plan to Create National Cryptocurrency," *Bloomberg,* June 1. Available at: https://www.bloomberg.com/news/articles/2018-06-01/estonia-curbs-cryptocurreny-plan-that-drew-rebuke-from-draghi.

54. Bank of Israel (2018), *The Bank of Israel Published a Summary of the Work of the Team to Examine Central Digital Bank Currency,* [Press release], November 6. Available at: https://www.boi.org.il/en/NewsAndPublications/PressRelease/Pages/6-11-18.aspx.

55. Kihara, L. (2018), "BOJ Deputy Governor Doubts Digital Currency Will Enhance Monetary Policy," *Reuters,* October 20. Available at: https://www.reuters.com/article/us-japan-economy-boj-cryptocurrency/boj-deputy-governor-doubts-digital-currency-will-enhance-monetary-policy-idUSKCN1MU07X.

56. Preiss, R. M. (2018), "National Government Digital Currencies versus Globally Distributed Cryptocurrencies: In Depth," Cointelegraph, May 21. Available at: https://cointelegraph.com/news/national-government-digital-currencies-versus-globally-distributed-cryptocurrencies-in-depth.

57. Republic of the Marshall Islands Parliament, "Declaration and Issuance of the Sovereign Currency Act 2018." Available at: https://rmiparliament.org/cms/images/LEGISLATION/PRINCIPAL/2018/2018-0053/DeclarationandIssuanceoftheSovereignCurrencyAct2018_1.pdf

58. De Nederlandsche Bank (2017), *2017 Annual Report,* pg. 82. Available at: https://www.dnb.nl/en/binaries/DNB%202017%20Annual%20Report_tcm47-374121.pdf.

59. Bank of Papua New Guinea (2017), *Speech by Governor Loi M. Bakani, CMG at the Blockchain Seminar at PNG Institute of Banking & Business Management (IBBM)*

Auditorium. Available at: https://www.bankpng.gov.pg/announcement/governor-loi-m-bakani-cmg-speech-at-blockchain-seminar-at-png-institute-of-banking-business-management/.

60. Popper, N. (2018), "Russia and Venezuela's Plan to Sidestep Sanctions: Virtual Currencies," *The New York Times*, January 3. Available at: https://www.nytimes.com/2018/01/03/technology/russia-venezuela-virtual-currencies.html.

61. Banque Régionale de Marchés (BRM) (2016), [Press release]. Available at: https://www.ecurrency.net/static/news/201611/press_release-BRM-translated.pdf

62. Lee, J. (2018), "Singapore Wary of Issuing Digital Currencies to Public: MAS Chief Ravi Menon," *The Straits Times*, January 15. Available at: https://www.straitstimes.com/business/companies-markets/singapore-wary-of-issuing-digital-currencies-to-public-mas-chief.

63. Yoo-Chul, K. (2018), "BOK Eyeing Digital Currencies," *The Korea Times*, December 12. Available at: https://libguides.ioe.ac.uk/harvard/newspaperonline.

64. Sveriges Riksbank (2018), *The Riksbank's E-krona Project.* Available at: https://www.riksbank.se/globalassets/media/rapporter/e-krona/2018/the-riksbanks-e-krona-project-report-2.pdf.

65. Bank of Thailand (2018), *Announcement of Project Inthanon Collaborative Partnership* [Press release], August 21. Available at: https://www.bot.or.th/Thai/PressandSpeeches/Press/News2561/n5461e.pdf.

66. Yerkes, S. and Polcari, J. (2017), *An Unexplored Opportunity, Carnegie MEC.* Available at: https://carnegie-mec.org/diwan/75071; La Poste Tunisienne, "Dinar Electronique." Available at: http://e-dinar.poste.tn.

67. Bank of England, *Digital Currencies.* Available at: https://www.bankofengland.co.uk/research/digital-currencies (last visited June 18, 2019).

68. Banco Central Del Uruguay (2018), *Lanzamiento de prueba piloto del billete digital del BCU.* Available at: https://www.bcu.gub.uy/Comunicaciones/Conferencias/20171103_BCU_Billete_Digital.pdf.

69. *Petro: Towards the Economic Digital Revolution,* (2018, Gobierno Bolivariano de Venezuela (Government of Venezuela) White Paper https://www.petro.gob.ve/whitepaper_eng.html .

70. Hampl 2017, p. 2.

71. Government of Venezuela Petro White Paper 2018, p. 14.

72. Bech, M., and Garratt, R. (2017), *Central Bank Cryptocurrencies*, IS Quarterly Review. Available at: https://www.bis.org/publ/qtrpdf/r_qt1709f.htm>, pp. 66–67.

73. The enforceability of tokens is ultimately a matter of law.

74. For a list of regulators that have issued statements on ICOs, see *Regulator's Statement on Initial Coin Offerings,* IOSCO (International Organization of Securities Commissions). Available at: https://www.iosco.org/publications/?subsection=ico-statements.

75. Data is based on disclosures taken from TrackICO; ICOs where raised capital was not disclosed were excluded from the sample.

76. Dirk Zetzsche, Ross Buckley, Douglas Arner and Linus Fohr, 2019. Harvard International Law Journal, vol. 63, no. 2, pp. 18–19.

77. Ibid., p. 10.
78. Roberts, J. J. (2017), "SEC Warns Scammers Are Using ICOs to Pump and Dump," *Fortune*, August 29. Available at: http://fortune.com/2017/08/29/sec-blockchain-ico-scam/.
79. Securities and Futures Commission 2017; Davis Polk 2018.
80. Zetzsche et al. 2018, p. 1369.
81. See, e.g., *Elliptic Offers Bitcoin Forensic Services That Draw on "Extensive Number of Both Public and Privately Accessible Sources of Information in Order to Identify Real-World Identities on the Bitcoin [sic] Blockchain"* , Elliptic. Available at: https://www.elliptic.co/what-we-do?hsCtaTracking=66b61351-d3ad-4fc5-9518-a31527e547d1%7Cce44b826-4995-4d71-a9e5-0f9901e96d62 (last visited June 18, 2019).
82. Zetzsche et al. 2018, p. 1378.
83. Ibid. p. 1377.
84. See also Zetzsche, Buckley and Arner 2018, p. 1376.
85. See *Russian Federal Draft Law "On Digital Financial Assets"* §§ 419059-72018 (2018), defining a "distributed ledger of digital transactions."
86. See Arizona, House Bill 2417, An Act Amending Section 44-7003, Arizona Revised Statutes; Amending Title 44, Chapter 26, Arizona Revised Statutes, By Adding Article 5; Relating To Electronic Transactions § 2 AZ HB2417 (2017).
87. Didenko, A, and Buckley, R. P. (2018). Available at: https://ssrn.com/abstract=3256066.
88. See International Organization for Standardization 2016, *Blockchain and Distributed Ledger Technologies*, ISO/TC 307b. Available at: https://www.iso.org/committee/6266604.html.

Chapter 12

1. See He and others (2017) for a discussion of the impact of financial technology on financial services.
2. See the report produced by the Bank for International Settlements Committee on Payments and Market Infrastructures (CPMI 2018).
3. Fung and Halaburda (2016); Bech and Garratt (2017); Engert and Fung (2017); Davoodalhosseini (2018); Yifei (2018); Carney (2018); Kumhof and Noone (2018); Grym and others (2017); Norges Bank (2018); Gürtler and others (2017); and Sveriges Riksbank (2017).
4. Change in legislation may be needed for CBDC to be legal tender. The definition of legal tender—usually applied to banknotes and coins issued by central banks—varies slightly across jurisdictions. For instance, a creditor is not obligated to accept payment in legal tender in all jurisdictions. See He and others (2016) for details.
5. Reserves can be interpreted as a wholesale form of CBDC used exclusively for interbank payments.
6. The cross-border implications of CBDC are not considered here, but some important questions are put forth in the concluding section for future work.

7. Person-to-person transactions are deliberately defined as person to person and not peer to peer. The first suggests that payments can be made seamlessly between individuals, such as when splitting a dinner bill. The second, however, is often used to denote payments in cryptoassets for which transaction parties, or "peers," are also involved in settlement.

8. The distinction between accounts (intangible property) and tokens (tangible property) is emphasized in Kahn and Roberds (2009). See also Kahn, Rivadeneyra, and Wong (2018) for a discussion of different forms of token-based CBDC.

9. These three properties are not entirely independent. If money is not a store of value, it will certainly not offer a satisfactory means of payment and will consequently not be a satisfactory unit of account. Money offers substantial efficiency gains by helping coordinate the specification of financial contracts. See He and others (2016) for a discussion of money versus "currency," a term used for money issued by governments as legal tender.

10. Kahn, Rivadeneyra, and Wong (2018) adopt a similar approach—"convenience, costs, and safety"—in their phrasing.

11. Other goals of central banks regarding CBDC include measures to stem the loss of seigniorage from the growth of new forms of private money. CBDC would in fact preserve seigniorage and possibly increase it if the central bank's balance sheet grew, depending on whether CBDC earned interest. However, because seigniorage is small in many countries, we do not entertain this line of argument further.

12. Touchless technology also facilitates debit card transactions. There is wrapper technology, such as PayPal, for credit card transactions as well, but credit-based transactions lie outside the scope of this note.

13. The largest-scale project is the European Central Bank's Target Instant Payment Settlement service, introduced in November 2018. There are already other similar initiatives, such as Hong Kong SAR's Faster Payments introduced in August 2018, Sweden's Swish, Denmark's Straksclearing, and Australia's New Payments Platform. Other so-called fast or instant payment solutions are also being rolled out exclusively by commercial banks (see CPMI 2016).

14. Fast payments can be thought of as a form of CBDC offered through a public-private partnership, because they allow people to settle in central bank reserves at will, at any time, through banks (resembling the proposal in Bordo and Levin 2018). The central bank, then, offers the means of payment function of money and banks the store of value function. Together, they offer money's three functions. From a technological standpoint, fast payments would however differ, even if account-based. Fast-payment engines are optimized for interoperability with real-time gross settlement systems (in which banks keep liquidity and borrow funds to settle intraday payments) and, by extension, with private banks. This integration would not be necessary for account-based CBDC.

15. The terms "stored value facilities" and "e-money" are taken from the Monetary Authority of Singapore (2017); e-money is defined as "electronically stored monetary value in a payment account that can be used to purchase goods or services, or to transfer funds to another individual."

16. These depend on whether the stored value facility has access to the funds in the custodian account, whether it can invest them in illiquid assets, and the degree to which e-money issuance can exceed reserves. Both of these examples invite the question of why users would choose to exchange or forgo a safe and liquid asset such as cash or a government bond for another provided by a private intermediary. The answer lies in the ease with which users can initiate payments on private platforms, and potentially access other services. Note that new players—such as large tech firms, including Amazon, Apple, Google, and Facebook—may well enter this space. They could offer e-money to purchase their goods at a discount, in exchange for valuable information.

17. See Ali (2018) for instance for a solution based on privately issued digital money. Note that firms in the narrow finance category do not create money, unlike fractional reserve banks. In a world of CBDC alone, only the central bank could create money. Today most money creation is "outsourced" to commercial banks, which create deposits when they extend credit. The process of money creation nonetheless responds to interest rates set by central banks.

18. See, however, Eichengreen (2018) for doubts about the ability to maintain a peg, short of full backing by fiat currency as in the narrow finance example (referred to as a currency board).

19. Insurance limits nonetheless should ensure that funds earmarked for payments—not all those held as savings—are protected. Households—large firms to a lesser degree—have the option of splitting deposits across accounts.

20. Cash could be prohibited altogether as argued in Rogoff (2014), made costly to hold as suggested in Bordo and Levin (2018), or made to depreciate against CBDC, which would become the sole legal tender, as in Agarwal and Kimball (2015). Note that if CBDC were not interest bearing, the effective lower bound could bind at even higher rates of interest, as CBDC could be stored more cheaply than cash. CBDC has also been touted as a means to implement aggressive monetary stimulus known as a "helicopter drop" by crediting CBDC accounts or wallets holding CBDC tokens. However, doing so would not necessarily reach all citizens. Moreover, the issue of legitimacy remains: How does the central bank decide how much to transfer to each household given the notable and very explicit redistributional consequences? Finally, helicopter drops would continue to be viewed as a form of monetary financing, thus undermining central bank independence.

21. Cash in circulation as a share of GDP is currently half its value 10 years ago, representing merely 6% of central bank liabilities and 2% of the money supply.

22. See also Bech and others (2018) and Jobst and Stix (2017).

23. The baseline is a regression of the log of real cash in circulation on deposit rates and the log of real GDP. Results are robust to inclusion of the log of stock prices (to capture wealth effects), different measures of uncertainty (Chicago Board Options Exchange Volatility Index and uncertainty indices), and country-by-country and panel estimates.

24. For related analysis, see Flannigan and Parsons (2018); Arango-Arango and others (2018); Esselink and Hernández (2017); Wakamori and Welte (2017); Bagnall, Bounie, and Huynh (2016); Krüger (2016); Bennet, Schuh, and Schwartz (2014); and

Sisak (2011). For example, the cash share of payments is 82% by volume in Austria (63% by value), but 46% in the United States (23% by value).

25. Judson (2017); sample includes Australia, Brazil, Canada, the euro area, Hong Kong SAR, India, Japan, Mexico, Singapore, South Arabia, South Korea, Sweden, Switzerland, Turkey, Russia, the United Kingdom, and the United States. See also Europol (2015).

26. Banks could also respond by providing more and better complementary financial services.

27. In addition, central banks could lower policy rates to counter the tighter financial conditions stemming from banks' higher lending rates, so that the banks' response to CBDC would be less contractionary for the economy. Moreover, the net impact of CBDC adoption on interest rates will depend on how the central banks introduce the CBDC, where an injection of CBDC via the sale of government bonds could, under specific circumstances, lead to lower rates (Barrdear and Kumhof 2016).

28. This discussion of the reaction of banks to CBDC adoption is based on a model by Agur and others (forthcoming) assuming an oligopolistic market structure in lending markets.

29. Ueda and di Mauro (2013) estimate that government guarantees have reduced bank funding costs between 60 and 80 basis points in recent decades. Other studies quantify the impact of government guarantees on bank funding costs by analyzing funding cost differentials for banks deemed too big to fail (Tsesmelidakis and Merton 2013; Acharya, Anginer, and Warburton 2016; Kelly, Lustig, and van Nieuwerburgh 2016; Kroszner 2016).

30. A situation in which the central bank does not recycle deposits back to banks, but instead takes on the direct role of maturity transformation and intermediation, would mean an even larger departure from the central bank mandate and could give rise to a sovereign–central bank nexus, if the monetary authority is pressured to lend to the government.

31. Bank run models, such as Diamond and Dybvig (1983) and Goldstein and Pauzner (2005) and references therein, emphasize information asymmetries regarding liquidity mismatches on banks' balance sheets, and liquidity needs of depositors, as the driving forces behind runs. Depositors may also run because of concerns about solvency rather than illiquidity (Calomiris and Gorton 1991).

32. In more general economic crises, depositors may also fear losses in real terms because of high inflation and currency depreciation and may thus attempt to hold foreign assets, leading to capital outflows. In fact, almost 30% of banking crises coincide with currency and/or sovereign crises (Laeven and Valencia 2018). Emerging market and developing economies are more susceptible to these twin or triple crises (Caprio and Klingebiel 1996; Laeven and Valencia 2018). Advanced economies are not immune to these episodes as is evident in the recent European sovereign debt crisis (IMF 2011; Brown, Evangelou, and Stix 2017; Sibert 2013).

33. Schmidt, Timmermann, and Wermers (2016) document runs from money market mutual funds following the collapse of Lehman Brothers in 2008, showing that while most prime money market mutual funds experienced outflows, those invested

in Treasury bills observed strong inflows "as investors sought the liquidity of the U.S. government market as part of a flight-to-safety."

34. Barajas and Steiner (2000), focusing on depositor behavior in Colombia, and Mondschean and Opiela (1999), considering Poland, find that state banks are perceived as safer and have an advantage in attracting deposits relative to private banks. However, a large number of studies, focusing on a diverse set of countries, do not offer corroborating evidence (Adler and Cerutti 2015; Hasan, Jackowicz, Kowalewski, and Kozlowski 2013; Semenova 2007; Das and Ghosh 2004; Ungan and Caner 2004; Hori, Ito, and Murata 2009).

35. The absence of a lender of last resort has been associated with U.S. banking panics in the pre–Federal Reserve era (Calomiris 2008; Gorton and Tallman 2016).

36. For similar reasons, central banks should not impose aggregate limits on CBDC in circulation. These could induce price distortions as a result of scarcity premiums. These limits could also accelerate runs as there is an attempt to purchase CBDC before others do and the aggregate limit is reached. Note also that the trigger for a run could become more unpredictable; when the run is to CBDC rather than to cash it will be harder for depositors to observe the signal of others' liquidity needs or information about the bank as there will be no lining up outside branches.

37. In the Laeven and Valencia (2018) sample of crises, the median peak liquidity provision was 15.3% in countries with deposit insurance; it was 22.4% of deposits for countries without it. In addition, there is evidence that uninsured wholesale depositors are more predisposed to runs (Covitz, Liang, and Suarez 2013).

38. In fact, some runs, such as the case of the run on Northern Rock in the United Kingdom in 2007, have been associated with gaps in deposit insurance coverage for small depositors (Goodhart 2011).

39. Similar conclusions are suggested in Meaning and others (2018) and in CPMI (2018). Another unexplored, though interesting, channel is the potential for CBDC to facilitate the resetting of prices and thus weaken transmission. A more remote option requiring attention is for CBDC to allow for interest rates to differ across individuals or regions.

40. See Bernanke (2007) and references therein for a full description of the bank lending channel. Older versions of this channel, originating in a period with higher reserve requirements and credit market segmentation, suggested that a higher supply of reserves increased deposits—loanable funds—and hence bank lending.

41. It could weaken if fintech innovations, beyond just CBDC, reduce information asymmetries inherent in the markups charged to borrowers.

42. Some adjustments may nevertheless be necessary to central banks' operating frameworks. CBDC is likely to displace cash, but could also partially drain reserves from commercial banks if customers withdraw deposits to hold CBDC. To the extent that banks need the reserves for precautionary purposes, central banks would still be able to replenish these by engaging in liquidity-injecting open market operations. Ultimately, demand for precautionary reserves might actually decrease, because CBDC could attenuate the variance of payment shocks (unlike cash, CBDC does not require lumpy withdrawals from costly visits to ATMs) or increase their

predictability. But even if the shape and position of the demand curve for reserves change, central banks should be able to adapt their supply of reserves to stabilize interest rates. In the interim, movements between deposits and CBDC could be volatile and require more frequent liquidity-injecting open market operations—perhaps on a fixed-rate full allotment basis—to stabilize interest rates. A floor system could also be considered to stabilize interest rates, since the demand for liquidity does not need to be accurately forecast.

43. "Active" means central banks that have convened projects to seriously explore CBDC or that have undertaken pilots. Some central banks have publicly indicated that they are investigating CBDC but have provided little to no detail. These include central banks in Bahrain, Barbados, Egypt, the Euro Area (and rejected), Hong Kong SAR, India, Indonesia, Israel, Jamaica, Korea (and rejected), Lebanon, New Zealand (on hold), Russia, and Switzerland.

44. There is doubt about Senegal's and Tunisia's CBDC, which appear to be fiat-collateralized cryptoassets. In the case of Senegal's e-CFA e-currency, the only connection to the central bank seems to be that the e-currency complies with the e-money regulations of the Banque Centrale des Etats de l'Afrique de l'Ouest. In Tunisia, the post office has been operating an e-dinar digital money wallet since 2000, and in 2016 it partnered with Monetas and DigitUs to offer a crypto-powered payment app, but there has been no central bank involvement.

45. Engert and Fung (2017) conclude that "reducing the effective lower bound does not provide a compelling motivation to issue CBDC."

46. Ecuador's main rationale was to avoid the costs of managing physical dollars in its fully dollarized economy. However, user acceptance was very low, seemingly because of lack of trust in the central bank (White 2018).

47. The Financial Action Task Force is an independent intergovernmental body that develops and promotes policies to protect the global financial system against money laundering, terrorism financing, and the financing of proliferation of weapons of mass destruction. It has set out recommendations for customer due diligence (for instance, identity verification) implementation, record-keeping, and suspicious transaction reporting requirements for financial institutions and designated nonfinancial businesses and professions.

48. A recurrence of the 1859 Carrington Event could knock out communications and power for up to a year and render digital money useless (Lovett 2011).

49. The International Telecommunications Union is working on standardized terms and conditions for the design of digital fiat currencies, including currencies issued by central banks and managed by private entities.

Index

For the benefit of digital users, indexed terms that span two pages (e.g., 52–53) may, on occasion, appear on only one of those pages.

Page numbers followed by *b, f* and *t* refer to boxes, figures, and tables, respectively.

Aadhaar, 257–58
access products, 24–25
Acxiom, 247
algorithms, 104–5
AliPay, 314
Alternative Trading Systems (ATSs), 176
Amazon, 91, 263
AML requirements. *See* anti-money laundering requirements
Ammous, S., 34–35
anonymization, 148–49
anonymous transactions, 311
anti-money laundering (AML) requirements, 94, 110, 312
append-only data, 244
Aristotle, 92
Arizona, 297
Ark Investments, 72
Asia, digital assets in. *See* digital assets in Asia
asset-backed cryptocurrencies, 90
asset-backed tokens, taxation of, 227–28
asset tokens, 220
ATM, 325–26
ATO. *See* Australian Tax Office
ATSs. *See* Alternative Trading Systems
auditors, 145
Augot, D., 245
Australia, 219–20, 224, 233, 277, 328
Australian Tax Office (ATO), 224, 236–37
automated law enforcement, 249–50

baby boomers, 307
Banco di Rialto, 313*b*
Banco di San Giorgio, 313*b*
Bangladesh, 249
Bank for International Settlements, 308
banking system, 91–96
    and bookkeeping/transactions, 94
    and credit money creation/
        annihilation, 93–94

domestic vs. foreign payments in, 95
    and history of money, 91–93
    problems with current, 95–96
bank lending channel, 326
banknotes, 21
Bank of Amsterdam, 19–20, 313*b*
Bank of Canada, 282, 308, 328, 330–31
Bank of England, 12, 20–21, 282, 308, 330–31
Bank of Finland, 308
banks and banking
    in Ancient Greece, 15–16
    in Ancient Mesopotamia, 15
    in Ancient Rome, 16–17
    deposit, 18–19
    and financial system, role in, 13–14
    fractional reserve, 90
    giro, 19–20
    in Greco-Roman Egypt, 17–18
    as intermediary, 29
    narrow, 28, 90, 314
    and payment systems, features of, 23
    in Ptolemaic Egypt, 18
    response of, to central bank digital
        currencies, 323*b*
    too-big-to-manage, 90
    in Venice, 19
Banque Régionale de Marchés, 330
Barabas, C., 48
barter transactions, 223–24
Basecoin, 314–15
basilicon, 17–18
BCH. *See* Bitcoin Cash
Bech, M., 318
Bergson, H., 246
bespoke terms (swaps), 203–4
bills of exchange, 313*b*
Binance, 41–42, 75, 86–87, 240
Bitcoin, 3–4, 32, 52, 170, 307, 314–15
    and capital gains tax, 281
    crypto-anarchist roots of, 42–43

Cryptoassets. Chris Brummer.
© Oxford University Press 2019. Published 2019 by Oxford University Press.

Bitcoin (*Cont.*)
  equilibrium valuation of, 83
  fall 2018 bug fix, 53–54
  governance rights of, 75–77
  hard fork (2013), 54–55
  hard fork (2017), 236
  mining, 32
  Nakamoto's white paper on, 167
  network usage models in, 80–81
  payments in, 32–33
  sale of tokens for, 122–23
  software upgrades to, 52–53
  and taxation, 222–23
  and transaction privacy, 160
  transactions via, 98*f*
  valuation of, 33, 71, 77–84
  wallet, 32–33
Bitcoin Cash (BCH), 236
BitMint, 36
Bitnation, 253–54
Bitt.com, 314
BitTorrent, 51
black swans, 104
Blade Runner (film), 251
blockchain, 2, 96–97
  in Bitcoin, 274
  consensus mechanisms, 206–7
  and criminal justice, 256–57
  and data blocks, 274
  and decentralization, 40, 42
  defined, 2, 243–44
  and derivatives markets, 212–14
  and distributed ledger technologies, 274–75,
    296
  end-to-end, 207–8
  and Ethereum platform, 275
  and initial coin offerings, 124, 153–54,
    174–75
  and language gap risk, 209–11
  origins of, 97
  as paradigm, 212
  and permanency risk, 211–12
  permissioned vs. permissionless, 274
  proof-of-work in, 230
  protocols as fiduciaries, 63
  radical uncertainty in, 66
  risks and concerns in, 209–12
  and tamper-proofing, 32
  and tamper proofing, 275
  and technology risk, 211
  and transparency risk, 212
  See also derivatives markets; identity
    persistence with blockchain

Blockchain Association, 46
Blockchain-Based Limited Liability Company,
    64–65
Bloomberg, 217
BNB. *See* Binance
Bolivia, 249
bonds, 136–37
Bonello, P. J., 87
Boolean operators, 210
bootstrapping, 238
Brazil, 283*t*
BTC. *See* Bitcoin
Buraschi, A., 71, 83
Burniske, C., 70
Burniske, Chris, 72, 79–80
business-to-business transactions, 309
business-to-person transactions, 309
Buterin, V., 47, 76, 98–99, 121–22

Cambridge Centre for Alternative Finance, 49
campsores, 19
Canada, 240, 283*t*, 318, 329–31
capital gains tax, 281
capitalism, 162
Caribbean, 283*t*, 314
cartelization, 76
Carter, Nic, 48
Casey. M. J., 76
cash
  central bank digital currencies and demand
    for, 319*b*
  elimination of, 321
  as form of payment, 315
cash flows, and valuation of cryptoassets, 74
Cavagnari, Domenico, 89
CBDCs. *See* central bank digital currencies
CCAR. *See* Comprehensive Capital Analysis
    and Review
CCPs. *See* central counterparties
CDOs. *See* collateralized debt obligations
CDS. *See* credit default swaps
CEA. *See* Commodity Exchange Act
central bank digital currencies (CBDCs), 94,
    307–32
  account- and token-based, 309*f*
  and banking disintermediation, 322–26
  banks' response to, 323*b*
  and comparison of different forms of
    money, 310–15
  and demand for cash, 319*b*
  and equal access, 317–18
  and financial stability, 322–26
  fixed vs. flexible design features of, 316

fundamentals of, 309–10
and monetary policy transmission, 326–27
and origins of central banking, 313b
potential role for, 315–16
and privacy vs. financial integrity, 321–22
purpose of, 309
and research/experiments by central banks,
327–31, 328t, 329t
and social criteria for money, 317　–21
Central Bank of Papua New Guinea, 277
central banks (central banking), 21
and administrative burden, 28–29
history of, 22–23
and monetary stability, 311–12
origins of, 313b
central counterparties (CCPs), 89–90, 206,
213–14, 273
centralized settlement technology, 310
CFTC. See Commodity Futures Trading
Commission
chat channel spamming, 186
Chatham House Rules, 55
checks, in Ptolemaic Egypt, 18
China, 272
AliPay in, 314
banning of Bitcoin in, 249
banning of ICOs in, 292
and CBDC adoption, 328, 329–31
central bank cryptocurrency in, 283t
cryptocurrencies treated as virtual
commodities in, 267
first use of money in, 91
and Global Financial Crisis, 89–90
initial coin offerings in, 129, 130–31
opposition to cryptocurrencies in, 279–80
policy approaches in, 268t
regulatory statements, 299t
CJEU. See Court of Justice of the
European Union
closed networks, 310
Coeckelbergh, M., 251
coinage, 313b
Coinbase, 41–42
collateralization of tokens
with assets, 105–7
with cryptocurrency, 103–4
by fiat, 101–3
collateralized debt obligations (CDOs), 103
Colombia, 249
commercial bank deposits, 314, 315
commercial banks and banking, 13–14, 23, 136,
287. See also banking system
Commodity Exchange Act (CEA), 203, 206

Commodity Futures Trading Commission
(CFTC), 65–66, 203, 204–6, 207, 208, 212,
213–14, 215–16
Comprehensive Capital Analysis and Review
(CCAR), 90
conduct obligations (initial coin offerings),
144–45
consensus mechanism, 2
consensus rules, 244
contracts
investment, 169
smart, 248–49, 276
cooling-off periods, 144
Corda, 274, 287–88
Council of the European Union, 147–48
Court of Justice of the European Union (CJEU),
223
Crawford, B., 25–26
credit card transactions, 95f
credit channel, 326
credit checks, pre-trade, 206
credit default swaps (CDS), 203–4
credit rating agencies, 145
criminal justice records, 256–57
crowdfunding
and initial coin offerings, 179–82
SEC regulation of, 179–80
crowdsales, of tokens, 122–23
crypto-anarchism, 42–43
cryptoassets
benefits and risks of, 3–4
and commodities, 75
defined, 2
risks of, 3–4
taxation standards in, 228–29
valuation with asset-backed, 73–74
and value-added tax (VAT), 232
crypto-collateralized coins, 103–4
cryptocurrencies
and algorithms, 104–5
as alternative currency, 278–80, 278t
Asian interest in, 264
and banking system, 101–2
central bank, 282–88, 283t
and central bank P2P/intermediated
payment systems, 282
defined, 31–32
and distributed ledger technology, 278–88
fiat backed, 287–88
legal status and regulatory implications of,
280–81
as non-sovereign payment
alternatives, 278–80

cryptocurrencies (*Cont.*)
    origins of, 31–32
    pros and cons of, 315
    regulation of, by nation, 268*t*
    regulatory implications of, 280–81
    sovereign digital, 281–82, 283*t*
    and sovereign digital currencies, 281–88
    top 20, 278*t*, 283*t*
cryptocurrency market collapse (2018), 117
crypto-economy, 79–80
cryptographic proof, 243–44
cryptography, 1–2, 24, 211
crypto-to-crypto exchanges, 240
crypto tokens. *See* tokens
crypto wallets. *See* wallet(s)
crypto zealots, 1
currency(-ies)
    decentralized, 35
    non-sovereign, 69
    state-issued, 11
custody, 297
customer due diligence, 312
customer profiling, 311
cypher-punks, 42–43

Dai tokens, 84–85
Damodaran, A., 77–78
Danmarks Nationalbank, 308
DAO hacks, 52–53
DAOs. *See* decentralized autonomous
    organizations
dapps. *See* decentralized applications
Dark Web, 51
Dash, 75, 241, 244–45
data validity, distributed ledger technologies
    and, 276–77
Davidson, S., 75
DBEs. *See* distributed business entities
DCF. *See* discounted cash flow
DCMs, 206, 212–13
DCM trade platforms, 216
DCOs. *See* derivatives clearing organizations
DCs. *See* digital currencies
debit card networks, 314
debt/equity ratios, 137
debt holders, 137–38
decentralization, 39–68
    as aspirational goal, 50–51
    complexity of, 47–52
    and concentrations of power in
        permissionless blockchain systems, 52–58
    and cryptocurrency network structure, 44
    defined, 41–42
    dynamic nature of, 50

legal complexities of, 60–61
    and legal decision making, 58–67
    and malleable tokens, 65–67
    spectrum of, 49
    terminology related to, 41–47
    veil of, 61–65
decentralized applications (dapps), 41–42, 238
decentralized autonomous organizations
    (DAOs), 56–57, 85
decentralized currency, drawbacks of, 35
decentralized exchanges (DEXs), 41–42
decentralized identifiers (DIDs), 257
decentralized network assets, 83
Decred, 75
decryption, 24
De Filippi, P., 71, 75
Delaware Blockchain Initiative, 153, 155
Delaware General Corporation Law, 153
Deleuze, Gilles, 251–52
Dell, 154–55
demand, and initial coin offerings, 164–65
de minimis fringe benefits tax exemptions, 237
denial-of-service (DoS) attacks, 53, 124, 186
Denmark, 328
Department for International Development
    (UK), 317–18
Depositary Trust Company (DTC), 154
deposit banking, 18–19
deposits
    central bank digital currencies and, 323*b*
    commercial bank, 314, 315
De Renzis, T., 318
derivatives clearing organizations (DCOs), 204,
    206, 212–15, 216
derivatives markets, 203–17
    and blockchain network, 212–14
    potential transformation of, by blockchain
        technology, 206–8
    registration in, 212–17
    and risks/rewards of blockchain
        technology, 208–12
    transactions in, 203–7
DEXs. *See* decentralized exchanges
Diary of Consumer Payment Choice, 107
DIDs. *See* decentralized identifiers
digital assets in Asia
    initial coin offerings, 289–93
    policy approaches, 268*t*
    recent developments and policy
        responses, 267–72
    and regulation of ICOs, 293–94
    regulatory statements, 299*t*
digital currencies (DCs), 94
digital history, 246

digital identity
  and criminal justice, 256–57
  and marriage, 254
  permanent, 246–47
  static, 243
digital identity, blockchain and, 246–47
Digital Trade Coin (DTC), 105–6
DigitUS, 330
disclosure
  full disclosure model, 170–78
  models of, for initial coin offerings, 169–84
  scaled, 179–84
  and white papers, 167–69
discounted cash flow (DCF), 163
disintermediation, 322–26
  and smart contracts, 276
  in times of systemic financial stress, 325–26
  in tranquil times, 321–25
disposal gains, taxation of, 228–29
distributed autonomous organizations (DAOs),
    69, 123
distributed business entities (DBEs), 64
distributed databases, 124
distributed denial-of-service attacks, 186
Distributed Identity Foundation, 245
distributed ledgers, 96–100
  and cryptocurrency creation/
    transactions, 98–99
  and problems with current blockchain
    ecosystems, 99–100
  types of, 98
distributed ledger technologies (DLTs), 1, 31,
    94, 263–98, 310
  in Asia, 264–65
  balancing risk and opportunity, 297–98
  and blockchain, 274–75
  blockchain specific risks in, 296
  centralized ledgers vs., 272–74
  and centralized ledgers vs., 272–74
  conferral rights in, 289
  and cryptocurrencies, 278–88
  cyber risks in, 295
  and data manipulation, 273
  and data validity, 276–77
  and decentralization, 31
  evolution and typology of, 272–77
  and initial coin offerings, 288–94
  international regulation of, 296–97
  and investment, 276–77
  operational risks in, 295
  in permissioned vs. permissionless systems,
    274
  policy issues related to, 296–98
  risks and concerns with, 294–96

and smart contracts, 276
and sovereign digital currencies, 285–86
and tokenization, 292–93
transparency risks in, 294–95
and trust solutions, 275–76
types of, 98
use cases and investment trends, 276–77
distributed ledger technology (DLT), 32
DLTs. See distributed ledger technologies
Dole Food Company, 154
DoS attacks. See distributed denial-of-service
    attacks
dot.com bubble, 263
DSGE. See dynamic stochastic general
    equilibrium modeling
DTC. See Depository Trust Company; Digital
    Trade Coin
due diligence, customer, 312
Dunphy, P., 257–58
dynamic stochastic general equilibrium
    modeling (DSGE), 90

Eastern Caribbean Central Bank, 328–29
Ecuador, 283t, 328
eCurrency Mint, 330
Egypt
  Greco-Roman, 17–18
  Ptolemaic, 18
electronic banking
  origins of, 26–27
  and technology, 27
electronic forms, 135–36, 143–44
electronic money (e-money)
  advent of, 24–26
  balance based, 25
  history of, 24–25
Eligible Contract participants, 205–6
Embley, P., 256
e-money. See electronic money
employee stock options, 238
employment remuneration, taxation of, 237–38
encryption, 24
end-to-end blockchain, 207–8
equal access, central bank digital currencies
    and, 317–18
equity holders, 137–38, 140–41
ERC-20 standard, 84, 234
ERC-20 tokens, 98–99
E-residency program (Estonia), 255
ESMA. See European Securities and Markets
    Authority
Estonia, 255, 283t
ETH. See Ethereum
Ether, 123, 170, 221, 314–15

Ethereum (ETH)
   and anti-money laundering, 110
   and blockchain technology, 3–4, 123,
      275, 278
   and decentralization, 46
   as form of money, 307
   governance rights of, 75–77
   hard fork (2016), 56–57
   and initial coin offerings, 121–22
   introduction of, 98–99
   as permissionless system, 274
   price evolution of, 104
   secret developer meetings for, 55–56
   selfdestruct contract option with, 248–49
   and smart contracts, 2
   software upgrades to, 52–53
   transactors on, 72–73
Ethereum Classic, 52–53, 57–58
European Central Bank, 328
European Securities and Markets Authority
      (ESMA), 210, 211
European Union, 148–49, 223, 247–48, 255, 292
European Union Blockchain Observatory and
      Forum, 147–48
European Union VAT Directive, 232
Everledger, 277
exchange rate channel, 326

Facebook, 42–43, 246–47, 252
face-keeping, 252
face-to-face transactions, 13
fast payments, 314, 315
FCMs. See futures commissions
Federal Deposit Insurance Corporation
      (FDIC), 96
Federal Ministry of Finance (Germany), 232
Federal Open Markets Committee, 56
Fedwire, 95
fiat, collateralization of tokens by, 101–3
fiat currency, 12, 102, 170
FIFO. See first-in-first-out
51% attacks, 52–53, 57–58
Filecoin, 164
Financial Action Task Force, 328–29
Financial Advisers Act, 146–47
financial consumers, 144
Financial Crimes Enforcement Network
      (FinCEN), 147
financial crisis (2008), 282
financial integrity, central banks and, 312
financial market infrastructures (FMIs), 212–13
Financial Market Supervisory Authority
      (FINMA), 120, 220

financial stability, central bank digital
      currencies and, 322–26
Financial Stability Board, 273, 281
financial statements, in initial coin offerings,
      171–72
FinCEN. See Financial Crimes Enforcement
      Network
Finck, M., 48
FINMA. See Financial Market Supervisory
      Authority
Finney, H., 78
FinTech, 27, 272, 279, 292
first-in-first-out (FIFO), 229
foreign exchange (FX) swaps, 203–4
forgers, 3
forging, 230–33
Form 1-A, 182–83
Form A-1, 171
Form C, 179, 181
Form S-1, 171–72, 174–75, 179
fractional reserve banks, 90, 108
Frankenstein (Shelley), 251
French revolution, 102–3
full disclosure model (initial coin
      offerings), 170–78
futures commissions (FCMs), 204, 205
FX swaps. See foreign exchange swaps

gains, disposal, 228–29
gatekeepers, 121
GDPR. See General Data Protection Regulation
Gemini Dollar, 73
Gencer, A. E., 57
General Data Protection Regulation (GDPR),
      148–49, 247–48
Germany, 155, 232
GFC. See Global Financial Crisis
giro banking, 19–20
GitHub, 160–61, 184, 185–86
global financial crisis, 103
Global Financial Crisis (GFC), 89–90
GoFundMe, 288
Goldman Sachs, 99–100
good faith, presumption of, 121
Goodfriend, M., 27–28, 30
goods and services tax (GST), 233
Google, 42–43, 263
governance rights, and valuation of
      cryptoassets, 75–77
Governatori, G., 249
Graski, D., 256
Graziani, A., 93
Great Depression, 108, 170

Greco-Roman Egypt, 17–18
Greece, Ancient, 15–16
GST. *See* goods and services tax

Habermeier, K., 317
Hacker, P, 63–64, 66
hard forks, 56–57, 236–37
hard money, 33–34
Hasan, I., 318
hash function, 32
hashing, 148–49
hashing power attack. *See* 51% attacks
hashrate, 81, 82–83
Hayek, F., 106
He, D., 310
Hedqvist case, 223
Hegel, Georg, 94
Her Majesty's Revenue & Customs (HMRC),
    224, 232
Hinman, Andrew, 39, 40, 43–45, 46
Hinman Token Standard, 46
HMRC. *See* Her Majesty's Revenue & Customs
Hong Kong, 268*t*, 279–80, 283*t*, 299*t*
Hong Kong SAR, 314
Hong Kong Securities and Futures Commission,
    294
Howey test, 44–45, 169–70, 175–76
hybridity problem, and taxation, 220–28
Hyperledger, 274

IBs. *See* introducing brokers
ICOs. *See* initial coin offerings
IDbox, 277
identity persistence with blockchain, 243–59
    and Bitnation, 253–54
    and blockchain technology, 243–45
    and criminal justice records, 256–57
    decentralized identifiers as protection
        against, 257–58
    digital identity, 246–47
    legal identity, 247–50
    and money laundering, 254–55
    narrative identity, 250–52
    use cases of, 252–57
incentivization, investor, 121–22
independence standards (initial coin offerings),
    174
India, 257–58, 271*t*, 283*t*, 299*t*, 314, 317–18
Indonesia, 268*t*, 283*t*, 299*t*
IndyMac Bancorp, 96
initial coin offerings (ICOs), 2, 117–56,
    157–87
    accounting and finance aspects of, 136–38

alternative methods of raising capital vs.,
    125–29, 126*t*
anti-money laundering implications of,
    146–48
in Asia, 289–94
bans on, 130–32
blockchain governance in, 174–75
and blockchain technology, 124
and comprehensive token regulation, 134–35
concept/features of, 118–19
contractual approach to regulating, 129–30
corporate governance issues with, 139–45
and crowdfunding rule, 179–82
and crowdsale/distribution of tokens, 122–23
cryptocurrencies as proceeds of, 123
and cryptocurrency "hype," 133
and data protection, 148–49
demand-side factors in, 164–65
description of token in, 172–74
disclosure models for, 169–84
financial statements in, 171–72
full disclosure model, 170–78
as funding source, 117
and the future, 153–55
Howey test in, 169–70, 175–76
initial public offerings vs., 164
and insolvency, 149–51
international challenges and cooperation
    in, 151–52
investment ICO, 288
management/technology teams for, 175–76
and "plain English" requirements for, 184–85
privacy law implications of, 148–49
private offerings, 183–84
pump-and-dump, 293
and Regulation A+, 182–83
regulatory approaches to, 129–36
risks with, 177–78
scaled disclosure regimes with, 179–84
and secondary trading, 176–77
and security token regulation, 132–34
as "shot-in-the-dark" investments, 159–62
speculative bubbles in, 263
supply-side factors in, 165–66
and third-party validators, 185–87
and token airdrops, 234–35
and token presales, 121–22
token pricing in, 162–66
as token sales, 119–23
typology of, 288–89
and white papers, 124–25
white papers as disclosures in, 167–69
initial public offerings (IPOs), 164

input, transaction output vs., 32–33
interest rate channel, 326
interest rate swaps (IRS), 203–4
intermediated payment systems, 282
Internal Revenue Service (IRS), 224, 281
International Standards Organization (ISO), 295
International Swaps and Derivatives
    Association (ISDA), 210
introducing brokers (IBs), 204, 205
investment(s)
    and distributed ledger technologies, 276–77
    "shot-in-the-dark," 159–62
Investment Advisers Act, 186–87
investment contracts, 169
investor incentivization, 121–22
IPOs. See initial public offerings
Ireland, 219–20, 232
IRS. See interest rate swaps; Internal Revenue
    Service
ISDA. See International Swaps and Derivatives
    Association
ISO. See International Standards Organization
Israel, 76, 283t
Italy, 313b

Jamie, Sarah-Lewis, 48
Japan, 267, 268t, 279–80, 283t, 299t
Jersey, 232
JOBS Act, 179, 182
JPMorgan, 89–90

Kahn, C., 313b
Kazakhstan, 283t
Kearney, R., 251–52
Keen, S., 93
Kenya, 314, 317–18
Keynes, J. M., 92, 105, 106
know-your-customer (KYC) requirements, 94,
    110, 147, 255, 267
Kocherlakota, N., 92
Krugman, P., 93–94
Kublai Khan, 91
KYC requirements. See know-your-customer
    requirements
Kyrgyzstan, 283t

Laeven, L., 325–26
language gap risk, blockchain and, 209–11
Lannquist, A., 72
last-in-first-out (LIFO), 229
legal decisionmaking, and decentralization,
    58–67
legal identity, blockchain and, 247–50

legal tender, currency used as, 223
Lehdonvirta, V., 66
Levy, H., 76
LIBOR. See London Interbank Offered Rate
LIFO. See last-in-first-out
liquidity, 150–51
liquid secondary markets, 145
litigation rules (initial coin offerings), 145
loans, 14
London Interbank Offered Rate (LIBOR), 96
Luria, G., 79–80
Lydia, 12

Macau, 267, 299t
Macknight, J., 258
MakerDai, 104
MakerDAO, 74–75, 84–86, 104
Malaysia, 267, 299t
malleable tokens, 65–67
Malta, 86
management teams (initial coin offerings),
    175–76
man-in-the-middle attacks, 186
marriage, 254
Marshall Islands, 283t, 327–28
Massachusetts Institute of Technology, 106–7
Mastercard, 33
Mesopotamia, Ancient, 15
Metcalfe, Robert, 81
Mexico, 129, 134–35
Middle Ages, 12
middlemen, 95
millennials, 307
miner solvency, 84
mining, 32, 230–33
mining pools, 230
mixing, 109
MKR tokens, 75, 85
ML/TF. See money laundering and terrorist
    financing
mobile money, 26–27
Monero, 241, 244–45
Monetary Authority of Singapore, 146, 293,
    330–31
monetary policy, central bank digital currencies
    and transmission of, 326–27
Monetas, 330
money
    changes in forms of, 307
    commercial-bank, 23
    functions of, 310–11
    hard, 33–34
    history and evolution of, 12–14

history of, 91–93
as legal tender, history of, 20
as means of payment, 312, 317–18
mobile, 26–27
plain sovereign, 29
as social contrivance, 94
social criteria for, 317–21
sovereign, 29
as store of value, 312, 318
as unit of account, 312, 317
users and forms of, 311
money laundering
blockchain and, 254–55
and terrorist financing (ML/TF), 146
See also anti-money laundering (AML)
requirements
money laundering and terrorist financing
(ML/TF), 146
monopolies, payment systems as, 320–21
Moody's, 217
More Stamps Global, 223
Morris, S., 51
M-Pesa, 314, 317–18
Munchee case, 121, 134

Nakamoto, Satoshi, 32, 98–99, 125, 167
narrative identity, blockchain and, 250–52
narrow banks (narrow banking), 28, 90, 107–9,
314
narrow finance solutions, 314
Narula, Neha, 39
Nenova, T., 76
Netherlands, 231, 237, 283t, 313b
networks, cryptoasset value and access to,
71–73
network structure, cryptocurrency, 44
network value to transactions ratio (NVT), 80
New Deal, 158–59, 170, 171, 186
NewLibertyStandard, 82
New York State, 176, 177
New Zealand, 328
NFTs. See non-fungible tokens
Noble Bank, 73–74
nodes, 244
non-fungible tokens (NFTs), 227, 229
non-security tokens, 121
non-sovereign currencies, 69
Norges Bank, 308
NVT. See network value to transactions ratio

obligor thereon, 12
OECD. See Organisation for Economic
Cooperation and Development

Office of Foreign Assets Control, 147
Ohta, K., 93
Oilcoin, 105–6
Okamoto, T., 93
Omni Layer Protocol, 102
Oresme, Nicholas, 89, 92
Organisation for Economic Cooperation and
Development (OECD), 227–28
OTC. See over-the-counter trades
output, transaction input vs., 32–33
Overstock.com, 153, 223
over-the-counter (OTC) trades, 204

Pagnotta, E., 71, 83
paper money, elimination of, 321
Papua New Guinea, 277, 283t
Paxos, 73
pay as you earn (PAYE), 237
pay as you go (PAYG), 237
payment(s)
in Bitcoin, 32–33
changes in forms of, 307
defined, 13
fast, 314
money as means of, 312, 317–18
systems of, as monopolies, 320–21
payments intermediation, historical
perspectives on, 14–23
payment tokens, 120, 220
PayTM, 317–18
pension funds, purchase of tokens by, 136
People's Bank of China, 106, 308, 328–29
permanency risk, blockchain and, 211–12
permanent digital identity, 246–47
permanent establishments (PEs), 231–32
permissioned blockchain systems, 274
permissioned networks, 310
permissionless blockchain systems, 274
decentralization and concentrations of
power in, 52–58
legal complexities of, 60–61
power dynamics in, 65–67
person-to-person transactions, 309
PEs. See permanent establishments
Peticolas, F., 257–58
Petro cryptocurrency, 285–86
Pfeffer, John, 71–72, 80
phishing, 186
Phrygia, 91
"plain English" rule, 184–85
plain sovereign money, 29
PMMMF. See prime money market mutual fund
Polynesia, 91

Potts, J., 71, 75
pre-blockchain biometric identity system,
    257–58
presale, token, 121–22
presumption of good faith, 121
pre-trade credit checks, 206
price-hashrate dynamics, 81–82
prime money market mutual fund (PMMMF),
    109
privacy
    Bitcoin and transaction, 160
    and cash payment, 315
    central bank digital currencies and, 321–22
    and narrow finance solutions, 314
    semi-, 256
    tokens and, 110
privacy coins, 244–45
private e-money, 315
private key, 32–33
private offerings, 183–84
profiling, customer, 311
proof-of-stake systems, 3, 13, 233
proof-of-work systems, 34–35, 81–82, 230–33,
    273–74
proxy advisors, 145
pseudo-anonymous reputation system, 253
pseudonymization, 148–49
pseudonymous data, repersonalization of, 294
Ptolemaic Egypt, 18
public-key cryptography, 207
pump-and-dump ICO schemes, 293

Qtum, 223
Quantity Theory of Money (QTM), 105
quantum mechanical process, 36
Quinn, S., 313b

Rauchs, Michael, 48
real estate, 227
real time gross settlement (RTGS), 37, 272
record-keeping, 286
RedCab, 292
registration information, and digital identity,
    246
Regulation A+, 182–83
Regulation D, 183
regulatory sandbox, 121
Reijers, W., 251
remuneration, taxation of employment, 237–38
Renaissance, 313b
request-for-quote (RFQ), 205–6
Reserve Bank of New Zealand, 329–30
retail tokenholders, 136

Reves v Ernst & Young, 134
Reyes, C., 64
RFQ. See request-for-quote
ring keys, 109
Ripple (XRP), 75, 98–99, 307, 314–15
Roberds, W., 313b
Roberto Giori Company, 330
Rodrigues, Usha, 63
Rome, Ancient, 16–17
RTGS. See real time gross settlement
Ruff, Tim., 257–58
Rule 10b-5 violations, 178
Russia, 131, 249, 255, 283t

SAFT. See Simple Agreement for Future Tokens
Sams, R., 104–5
Samuelson, P., 94
sandbox, regulatory, 121
savings and loan crisis, 108
scaled disclosure regimes (initial coin
    offerings), 179–84
Schmiedel, H., 318
SDRs. See swap data repositories
SDs. See swap dealers
SEC. See Securities and Exchange Commission
secondary markets, liquid, 145
Securities Act of 1933, 45, 157–59, 162–63, 169,
    183, 186
Securities and Exchange Commission (SEC),
    40, 46, 123, 147, 162–63, 176, 177, 293
    and crowdfunding regulation, 179–80
    Form 1-A, 182–83
    Form A-1, 171
    Form C, 179, 181
    Form S-1, 157–58, 171–72, 174–75
    "plain English" rule, 184–85
Securities and Futures Act, 146–47
securities law, 44–45
securities tokens, taxation of, 225–27
security tokenholders, 140–41
security tokens, 120–21
SEC v. W.J. Howey Co., 44–45, 134
SEFs. See swap execution facilities
selfdestruct contract option, 248–49
self-regulatory organizations (SROs), 205–6
semiprivacy, 256
Senegal, 283t, 330
Sheerin, D., 251–52
Sheng, Tony, 39
"shot-in-the-dark" investments, 159–62
SiaFund, 74
Silk Road, 51
Simmel, Georg, 92

Simple Agreement for Future Tokens (SAFT),
   122, 238
Singapore, 129, 133, 146, 219–20, 230–31, 268t,
   272, 283t, 292, 299t
size of transactions, limitations on, 321–22
smart contracts, 248–49, 276
SmartLove, 253
social engineering, 186
South Africa, 230–31, 283t
South Korea, 129, 130–31, 254, 267, 268t, 283t,
   292, 299t
sovereign digital currencies, 281–82
   benefits of, 286
   and cybersecurity, 287
   and financial markets, 287
   and record-keeping, 286
sovereign money, 29
Sovrin, 257–58
Sovrin Foundation, 257–58
spamming, chat channel, 186
spider charts, 315
spoofing, 186
stablecoins, 77, 314–15
staking wallets, 230
standard formula, 12–13
state-issued currency, 11
static digital identity, 243
stock buy-backs, 166
stock market crash (1929), 170
stored-value product (SVP), 24–25
supply, and initial coin offerings, 165–66
Surujnath, R., 207
Suspicious Transaction Reporting Office, 146
Sveriges Riksbank, 308
SVP. See stored-value product
Swan, Melanie, 42–43
swap data repositories (SDRs), 204, 206
swap dealers (SDs), 204, 205
swap execution facilities (SEFs), 205–6, 212–13
swaps, 203–4
Sweden, 223, 283t, 318, 328, 329–30
Sweetcoin, 105–6
Swiss franc, 77–78
Switzerland, 129, 133, 220, 292, 318, 328
Szabo, Nick, 39

T. Rowe Price, 154–55
Taiwan, 249
Taula de Canvi, 313b
taxation of cryptoassets, 219–41
   asset-based tokens, 227–28
   disposal gains, 228–29
   employment remuneration, 237–38

hard forks, 236–37
and hybridity problem, 220–28
and mining/forging, 230–33
securities tokens, 225–27
token airdrops, 234–35
token burning, 239–40
token pre-financing, 238–39
windfalls, 234–35
taxing rights, 231–32
TCP/IP, 91, 100
technology(-ies)
   and changes in forms of payment, 307
   distributed ledger, 1
   and electronic banking, 27
   wrapper, 314
   See also blockchain
technology risk, blockchain and, 211
technology teams, in initial coin offerings,
   175–76
Telegram, 234
Templehof, S., 253
terrorism, financing of, 146, 312
Tether, 73, 77, 101
Tezos, 75
Thailand, 249, 283t, 299t
third-party validators, 185–87
third-party verification, 243–44
Tiberiuscoin, 105–6
TMMMF. See Treasury Money Market Mutual
   Fund
token airdrops, 234–35
token burning, 239–40
tokenholders, 136–38
   and conduct obligations, 144–45
   legal protection of, 143–45
   and litigation rules, 145
   non-security, 144–45
   retail, 136
   security, 140–41, 143–44
tokens (tokenization), 89–111
   asset, 220
   and banking system, 91–96
   burning of, 166
   and central bank digital currencies
      (CBDCs), 309–10
   challenges of, 73
   collateralization of, by fiat, 101–3
   collateralization of, with assets, 105–7
   crowdsale and distribution of, 122–23
   description of, in initial coin offerings,
      172–74
   design of, 100–1
   as digital assets, 119

tokens (tokenization) (*Cont.*)
    and distributed ledgers, 96–100
    distributed ledger technologies and, 292–93
    dynamically stabilized coins as, 104–5
    functional classification of, 120
    hybrid, 227
    and instability of *status quo*, 89–90
    and investor incentivization, 121–22
    and KYC/AML requirements, 110
    legal classifications of, 120–21
    lock-up of, 166
    and mixing/tumbling, 109
    and narrow banks, 107–9
    non-fungible, 227, 229
    overcollateralization of, with cryptocurrency,
        103–4
    payment, 120, 220
    pre-financing of, 238–39
    presale of, 121–22
    pricing of, in initial coin offerings, 162–66
    and privacy, 110
    and problems with current banking system,
        95–96
    registration of, 137*t*
    securities, 225–27
    taxation of asset-backed, 227–28
    taxonomy of, 101–10
    utility, 120
    and value-added tax, 227–28
Tomaino, Nick, 72
transactional identity, 246
transaction history, and digital identity, 246
transactions
    anonymous, 311
    Bitcoin, 98*f*
    limitations on size of, 321–22
transparency
    blockchain and, 212
    with distributed ledger technologies, 294–95
Treasury Money Market Mutual Fund
        (TMMMF), 108–9
TrueUSD (TUSD), 73, 101
trust, blockchain and, 243–44
tumbling, 109
Tunisia, 330
Turner, A., 79–80
Twitter, 234
tZERO, 153

Uniform Commercial Code, 30
Uniform Securities Transactions Act, 30
UniqueID, 257–58
United Kingdom, 283*t*
    Department for International Development,
        317–18
    taxation of cryptoassets in, 219–20
    and VAT, 232
    See also Her Majesty's Revenue & Customs
        (HMRC)
United Nations Security Council, 146
United States
    anti-moneylaundering efforts in, 147
    initial coin offerings in, 129, 133
    narrative identities in, 252
    taxation of cryptoassets in, 230–31
unit of account, money as, 312, 317
Universal Declaration of Human Rights, 311
Uruguay, 318, 330
U.S. Department of the Treasury (USDT), 102
U.S. Dollar (USD), 101, 102, 106
U.S. Supreme Court, 44–45
usage tokens, 72
USD. *See* U.S. Dollar
USDC, 73
utility tokens, 69, 120

Valencia, F., 325–26
Validation Hierarchy, 36
validators, 57, 185–87
valuation, 69–88
    of 0x, 87
    with asset-backed cryptoassets, 73–74
    of Binance Coin, 86–87
    of Bitcoin, 77–84
    and cash flows, 74
    and consumability, 75
    difficulty vs. impossibility of, 69–70
    and governance rights, 75–77
    of Maker tokens, 84–86
    and unique access to network services,
        71–73
    and value drivers, 70–77
value
    of bitcoin, 33
    money as store of, 312, 318
value-added tax (VAT), 221–22, 224–25,
        226–28, 232, 233, 235, 239
VAT. *See* value-added tax
veil of decentralization, 61–65
Venezuela, 254, 282, 283*t*, 285–86
Venezuelan bolivar, 77–78
Venice, banking in, 19–20
Venmo, 314
venture capitalists, 47
Vermont, 64
Vidan, G., 66

Vietnam, 249
virtual commodities, 267
Visa, 33
Vision Hill Advisors, 85
Volcker, P., 102–3

Walch, A., 209
wallet(s)
    anonymity of, 328–29
    Bitcoin, 32–33
    staking, 230
    and taxation, 235
"web of trust" protocols, 257
WePay, 314
Werbach, K., 211–12
white papers, as disclosures in initial coin
        offerings, 167–69
WingCash, 35–36
Winton, Brett, 72
Woo, W., 80
Wood, G., 98–99

Woodford, M., 327
WorldCom, 171
World War I, 246
wrapped real assets, 69
wrapper technology, 314
Wyoming Blockchain Coalition, 155

XRP. See Ripple

Yermack, D., 77
Yeung, K., 63–64

Zamfir, V., 76
Zcash, 109, 241
zealots, crypto, 1
0x, 76, 87
Zerocash, 244–45
Zetzsche, D. A., 63
Zhao Xiaochuan, 106
ZRX. See 0x
Zyskind, G. O., 244–45